Praise for *Fiasco*

"The title of this devastating new book about the American war in Iraq says it all: *Fiasco*. [Thomas E. Ricks] serves up his portrait of that war as a misguided exercise in hubris, incompetence and folly with a wealth of detail and evidence that is both staggeringly vivid and persuasive. . . . *Fiasco* is absolutely essential reading. . . . [T]his volume gives the reader a lucid, tough-minded overview of this tragic enterprise that stands apart from earlier assessments in terms of simple coherence and scope."　　　　　　　　　　—Michiko Kakutani, *The New York Times*

"Thomas E. Ricks's *Fiasco* . . . offers a comprehensive and illuminating portrait of the willful blindness of the Bush administration to Iraqi realities. A veteran Pentagon correspondent for *The Washington Post*, Ricks has done his homework: he has interviewed numerous Bush administration officials, traveled extensively in Iraq and consulted thousands of pages of military documents. . . . Ricks makes a powerful case that, far from being inevitable, the insurgency was the direct product of American bungling."

—Jacob Heilbrunn, *The New York Times Book Review*

"Few, if any, journalists know the U.S. military better than Ricks, its organizational strengths, its flaws, its capacity for battlefield heroism and its tendency to do the wrong thing with the right motive. . . . *Fiasco* is not a screed but a well-researched, strongly written account of the miscues that led from shock-and-awe to rampant sectarian strife."　　　　　　　　　　—*Los Angeles Times*

"In his compelling and well-researched book, Thomas E. Ricks, a Pulitzer Prize–winning reporter for *The Washington Post*, painfully but clearly reveals an important truth about the Iraq debacle: it has a thousand fathers. As the title implies, *Fiasco* pulls no punches. . . . devastating . . . damning . . . [Thomas Ricks's] reporting is impressive indeed. News on Iraq usually comes with blaring headlines, but Ricks's work allows us to fit seemingly disparate events into an overall pattern. Powerful."　　　　　　　　　　—*The Washington Post*

"It is not an exaggeration, or at least not much of one, to say that with his new book, *Fiasco*, Thomas Ricks has changed the debate over Iraq. . . . Ricks is doggedly thorough. . . . convincing . . . it may leave your hand shaking just a bit when you finish and put it down."　　　　　　　　　　—*Slate*

"This is a carefully researched account of the Iraq war by one of America's premier defense correspondents, Thomas Ricks of *The Washington Post*. His findings of pervasive high-level ineptitude, based on hundreds of interviews and thousands of pages of documents, will be much harder for reflexive defenders of the Bush administration to dismiss than the usual farrago of ideologically motivated accusations from political adversaries. . . . Damning . . . an incisive chronicle."
—Max Boot, *The Weekly Standard*

"*Fiasco* is one of the most complete accounts you'll read on how the Bush administration, decision by wrongheaded decision, created a situation that literally blew up in its face."
—*Rocky Mountain News*

"Unsparing . . . Illuminating . . . Like it or hate it, the book is a good read."
—*The Washington Times*

"Ricks builds a devastating case. . . . With the critique offered in *Fiasco*, Ricks makes a solid contribution to our shared understanding."   —*National Review*

"Among all the books on the war in Iraq, the most scathing critique yet comes from Thomas E. Ricks."   —*Pioneer Press* (St. Paul)

"Predictably, critics of [*Fiasco*] contend Ricks is one more biased journalist bashing the Bush administration. But many military officers and conservatives have celebrated the reporter's devastating account of errors in judgment and strategy."
—*The Roanoke Times*

"Remarkable."   —*Marine Corps Gazette*

"[*Fiasco* is] not a political rant nor is it shrill. But in its low-key, extraordinarily well-sourced, highly detailed portrait of the run-up to and conduct of the war it is devastating. . . . *Fiasco* is for those who want a serious, on-the-ground picture of what's actually happened with the war."   —*The Christian Science Monitor*

"As a first draft of military history, Ricks' *Fiasco: The American Military Adventure in Iraq* is devastating. . . . At the heart of Ricks' incisive account is his grasp of strategy, honed over his decades as a chronicler of military affairs. . . . Ricks' rock-solid understanding of counterinsurgency warfare resonates throughout the narrative."   —*Harvard Political Review*

"If enough Americans, especially key decision-makers, read [*Fiasco*] . . . and learn from the many mistakes that have been committed, perhaps we can still emerge from the conflict with some semblance of victory."   —*On Point*

ABOUT THE AUTHOR

Thomas E. Ricks is *The Washington Post*'s senior Pentagon correspondent, where he has covered the U.S. military since 2000. Until the end
of 1999, he held the same beat at *The Wall Street Journal,* where he
was a reporter for seventeen years. A member of two Pulitzer Prize–
winning teams for national reporting, he has covered U.S. military
activities in Somalia, Haiti, Korea, Bosnia, Kosovo, Macedonia, Kuwait,
Turkey, Afghanistan, and Iraq. He is the author of *Making the Corps*
and *A Soldier's Duty.*

FIASCO

THE AMERICAN MILITARY ADVENTURE IN IRAQ

THOMAS E. RICKS

PENGUIN BOOKS

PENGUIN BOOKS
Published by the Penguin Group
Penguin Group (USA) Inc., 375 Hudson Street, New York, New York 10014, U.S.A.
Penguin Group (Canada), 90 Eglinton Avenue East, Suite 700, Toronto,
Ontario, Canada M4P 2Y3 (a division of Pearson Penguin Canada Inc.)
Penguin Books Ltd, 80 Strand, London WC2R 0RL, England
Penguin Ireland, 25 St Stephen's Green, Dublin 2, Ireland (a division of Penguin Books Ltd)
Penguin Group (Australia), 250 Camberwell Road, Camberwell,
Victoria 3124, Australia (a division of Pearson Australia Group Pty Ltd)
Penguin Books India Pvt Ltd, 11 Community Centre, Panchsheel Park, New Delhi – 110 017, India
Penguin Group (NZ), 67 Apollo Drive, Rosedale, North Shore 0745, Auckland,
New Zealand (a division of Pearson New Zealand Ltd)
Penguin Books (South Africa) (Pty) Ltd, 24 Sturdee Avenue,
Rosebank, Johannesburg 2196, South Africa

Penguin Books Ltd, Registered Offices:
80 Strand, London WC2R 0RL, England

First published in the United States of America by The Penguin Press,
a member of Penguin Group (USA) Inc. 2006
This edition with a new postscript published in Penguin Books 2007

1 3 5 7 9 10 8 6 4 2

THE LIBRARY OF CONGRESS HAS CATALOGED THE HARDCOVER EDITION AS FOLLOWS:
Ricks, Thomas E.
Fiasco : the American military adventure in Iraq / Thomas E. Ricks.
p. cm.
ISBN 1-59420-103-X (hc.)
ISBN 978-0-14-303891-7 (pbk.)
1. Iraq war, 2003–   2. United States—History, military—21st century.   I. Title.
DS79.76.R535 2006
956.7044'3—dc22   2006045357

Printed in the United States of America
Designed by Amanda Dewey
Photo insert by Nicole Laroche   Maps by Gene Thorp

For the war dead

Know your enemy, know yourself,
One hundred battles, one hundred victories.

SUN TZU, ancient Chinese military strategist,
as quoted in Jeffrey Race's *War Comes to Long An*

The Sunni "Triangle": *Heart of the Insurgency*

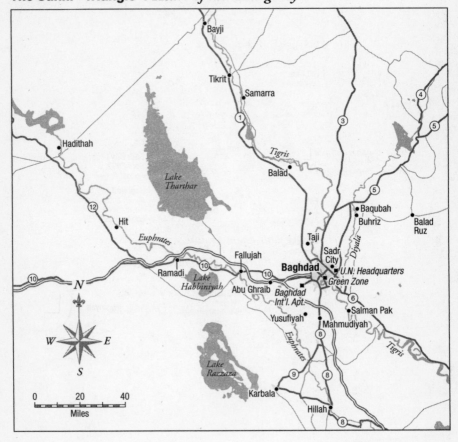

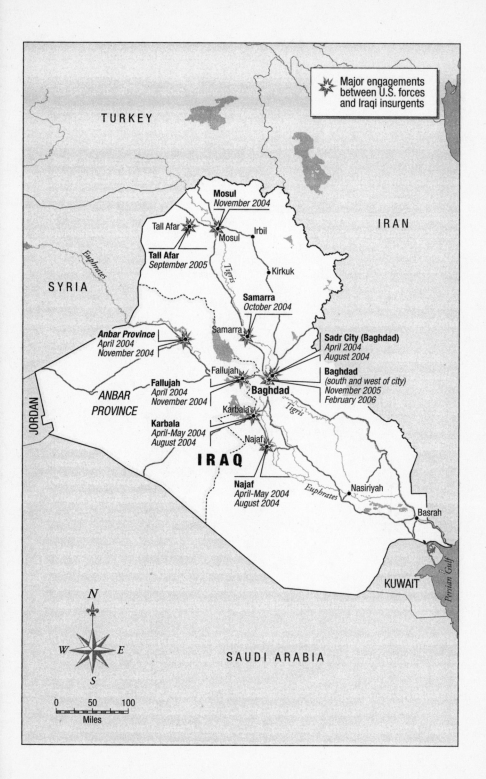

TURKEY

IRAN

SYRIA

Euphrates

Mosul
November 2004

Tall Afar

Mosul

Irbil

Tall Afar
September 2005

Tigris

Kirkuk

Samarra
October 2004

Anbar Province
April 2004
November 2004

Samarra

Sadr City (Baghdad)
April 2004
August 2004

JORDAN

ANBAR
PROVINCE

Fallujah
April 2004
November 2004

Fallujah

Baghdad
(south and west of city)
November 2005
February 2006

Baghdad

Tigris

Karbala
April-May 2004
August 2004

Karbala

I R A Q

Najaf

Nasiriyah

Najaf
April-May 2004
August 2004

Euphrates

Basrah

KUWAIT

Persian Gulf

SAUDI ARABIA

✸ Major engagements
between U.S. forces
and Iraqi insurgents

N

W   E

S

0   50   100
Miles

CONTENTS

CAST OF CHARACTERS

THE BUSH ADMINISTRATION (2002–4)

President George W. Bush
Vice President Richard B. Cheney
I. Lewis "Scooter" Libby, Cheney's chief of staff and national security adviser
National Security Adviser Condoleezza Rice
Secretary of State Colin L. Powell
Deputy Secretary of State Richard Armitage
CIA Director George Tenet

AT THE PENTAGON

Defense Secretary Donald Rumsfeld
Deputy Defense Secretary Paul Wolfowitz
Under Secretary for Policy Douglas Feith
Lawrence Di Rita, chief Pentagon spokesman
Air Force Gen. Richard Myers, chairman of the Joint Chiefs of Staff
Army Lt. Gen. George Casey, director of the Joint Staff;
    later replaced Sanchez in Iraq

Marine Lt. Gen. Gregory Newbold, director of operations, the Joint Staff

Gen. Eric Shinseki, chief of staff of the U.S. Army

Richard Perle, chairman, Defense Policy Board

Ret. Marine Col. Gary Anderson, consultant to Wolfowitz

U.S. CENTRAL COMMAND (2003–4)

Army Gen. Tommy R. Franks, commander; retired mid-2003

Army Lt. Gen. John Abizaid, deputy commander; promoted to replace Franks

Air Force Maj. Gen. Victor Renuart, director of operations

Army Col. John Agoglia, deputy chief of plans

Gregory Hooker, senior intelligence analyst for Iraq

Army Lt. Gen. David McKiernan, commander, Coalition Forces Land Component
    Command (CFLCC), the ground component of the invasion force

Army Col. Kevin Benson, chief planner at CFLCC

IN IRAQ (2003–4)

Ret. Army Lt. Gen. Jay Garner, chief of the Office of Reconstruction and
    Humanitarian Assistance, first senior U.S. civilian official in Iraq

Coalition Provisional Authority

Amb. L. Paul "Jerry" Bremer III, chief, Coalition Provisional Authority;
    replaced Garner

Ret. Army Lt. Gen. Joseph Kellogg, Jr., deputy to Bremer

Army Col. Paul Hughes, strategic adviser

Maj. Gen. Paul Eaton, first chief of training for Iraqi army

Marine Col. T. X. Hammes, staff, Iraqi security forces training program

Keith Mines, CPA representative in al Anbar province

Military

Army Lt. Gen. Ricardo Sanchez, senior U.S. commander

Army Brig. Gen. Barbara Fast, senior intelligence officer for Sanchez

Ret. Army Col. Stuart Herrington, consultant to Fast

Army Maj. Gen. David Petraeus, commander, 101st Airborne Division,
    later returned to oversee the training of Iraqi forces

Col. Joe Anderson, a brigade commander in the 101st Airborne

Maj. Isaiah Wilson, first served as an Army historian,
    later as strategist for Petraeus

Army Maj. Gen. Charles Swannack, Jr., commander, 82nd Airborne Division

Col. Arnold Bray, commander of a brigade of the 82nd Airborne

Army Maj. Gen. Raymond Odierno, commander, 4th Infantry Division

Army Col. David Hogg, a brigade commander in 4th ID

Army Lt. Col. Christopher Holshek, commander of a civil affairs unit
    attached to Hogg's brigade

Army Lt. Col. Steve Russell, commander of an infantry battalion in the 4th ID

Army Lt. Col. Nathan Sassaman, another of Odierno's battalion commanders

Army Lt. Col. Allen West, commander of a 4th ID artillery battalion

Army Lt. Col. David Poirier, commander of MP battalion attached to 4th ID

Army Col. Teddy Spain, commander of U.S. military police forces in Baghdad

Army Capt. Lesley Kipling, communications officer on Spain's staff

Army Brig. Gen. Martin Dempsey, commander, 1st Armored Division

Army Brig. Gen. Janis Karpinski, commander of U.S. military detention
    operations

Army Col. David Teeples, commander, 3rd Armored Cavalry Regiment

Maj. Gen. James Mattis, commander, 1st Marine Division

Army Col. Alan King, civil affairs officer, 3rd Infantry Division; later a tribal
    affairs specialist at CPA

Other

David Kay, head, Iraq Survey Group, U.S. government organization searching
    for weapons of mass destruction

Ahmed Chalabi, leader of the Iraqi National Congress, an exile political group

IN IRAQ (2004 AND LATER)

Civilian

Amb. John Negroponte, replaced Bremer

Amb. Zalmay Khalilzad, replaced Negroponte

Military

Gen. Casey, promoted and replaced Sanchez

Kalev Sepp, adviser to Casey on counterinsurgency

Army Maj. Gen. John Batiste, commander 1st Infantry Division

Army Capt. Oscar Estrada, civil affairs officer attached to 1st ID in Baqubah

Army Col. H. R. McMaster, commander, 3rd Armored Cavalry Regiment

Col. Clarke Lethin, chief of operations, 1st Marine Division

Col. John Toolan, commander, 1st Marine Regiment

Others appearing frequently

Retired Marine Gen. Anthony Zinni, former chief, U.S. Central Command

Rep. Ike Skelton of Missouri, senior Democrat, House Armed Services
Committee

Patrick Clawson, deputy director, Washington Institute for Near East Policy

Judith Miller, national security reporter, *New York Times*

Grand Ayatollah Ali Sistani, Shiite leader and Iraq's most important
political figure

Moqtadr al-Sadr, nationalist Shiite cleric

ACRONYMS & CONTRACTIONS

AAR	After Action Reviews
AC-130	Attack-Cargo-130 (transport aircraft fitted with weapons)
ACLU	American Civil Liberties Union
ACR	Armored Calvary Regiment
AD	Armored Division
AGM	Air-to-Ground Missile
AH	Attack Helicopter
AID	Agency for International Development
AIM	Air Intercept Missile
AMRAAM	Advanced Medium Range Air-to-Air Missile
AO	Area of Operation
AWOL	Absent With-Out Leave
BCT/DIV	Brigade Combat Team / Division
BDE	Brigade (sic) (1,500 to 3,000 soldiers with mixed specialties)
CA	Civil Affairs
CALL	Center for Army Lessons Learned
CAP	Combined Action Platoon
casevac	Casualty Evacuation
Centcom	Central Command
CFLCC	Coalition Force Land Component Command
CG	Commanding General

CIA	Central Intelligence Agency
CID	Criminal Investigation Division
CinC	Commander in Chief
CJTF-7	Combined Joint Task Force - 7
CMOC	Civil Military Operations Center
CNN	Cable News Network
COIN	COunter INsurgency
CPA	Coalition Provisional Authority
CRS	Congressional Research Service
CSIS	Center for Strategic and International Studies
CTC	Combat Training Center
DEPSECDEF	Deputy Secretary of Defense
DIA	Defense Intelligence Agency
DoD	Department of Defense
EPW	Enemy Prisoners of War
FID	Foreign Internal Defense
FIF	Free Iraqi Fighters
FM	Field Manual
FOB	Forward Operating Base
FRE	Former Regime Elements
FSE	Fire Support Element
GAO	Government Accounting Office (old name)
GAO	General Accountability Office (new name)
GOP	Grand Old Party
GWOT	Global War on Terror
H & I	Harassment and Interdiction
HUMINT	Human Intelligence
IBAS	Individual Body Armor System
ICDC	Iraqi Civil Defense Corps
ICE	Interrogation Control Element
ID	Infantry Division
IED	Improvised Explosive Device
IFC	Intelligence Fusion Center
INC	Iraqi National Congress
ISC	Intelligence Systems Command
ISF	Iraqi Security Force
ISG	Iraq Survey Group
ISST	Iraqi Stabilization Study Team
JDAM	Joint Direct Attack Munition
JPOTF	Joint Psychological Operations Task Force

JTF	Joint Task Force
LoC's	Lines of Communication
M-240	Military [rifle] -240 (11 kg. or 24 lbs.)
M-249	Military [rifle] -249 [SAW] (7 kg. or 15 lbs.)
M-4	Military [rifle] -4 (3 kg. or 6½ lbs.)
MEF	Marine Expeditionary Force
MET	Mobile Exploitation Team
MI	Military Intelligence
MNF	Multi-National Force
MP	Military Police
MPRI	Military Professional Resources Incorporated
MRE	Meal, Ready to Eat
MSR	Main Supply Routes
NATO	North Atlantic Treaty Organization
NCO	Non-Commissioned Officer
NIA	New Iraqi Army
NIC	New Iraqi Corps
NIE	National Intelligence Estimate
Noforn	Not to be seen by foreign governments
NSC	National Security Council
NTC	National Training Center
OH	Observation Helicopter
OIF	Operation Iraqi Freedom
ORHA	Office of Reconstruction and Humanitarian Assistance
OSD	Office of the Secretary of Defense
PBXIH-135	Polymer Bonded eXplosive, Insensitive High explosive-135
PE-4	Plastic Explosive -4
PFC	Private First Class
PGM/PGW	Precision Guided Munitions or Precision Guided Weapons
PM	Prime Minister
PSD	Personal Security Details
PUC	Person Under Control
RIP/TOA	Relief In Place / Transfer Of Authority
ROE	Rules Of Engagement
ROTC	Recruit Officers' Training Corps
RPG	Rocket Propelled Grenade
SASO	Security (Stability) And Support Operations
SAW	Squad Automatic Weapon (M-249)
SCIRI	Supreme Council of Islamic Revolution in Iraq
SEAL	SEa, Air Land commandos

SF	Special Forces
SGCC	Strategic Guidance for Combatant Commanders
Signit	Signal Intercept Intelligence
SIPRNET	Secret (formerly Secure) Internet Protocol Router NETwork
sitrep	Situation report
SOF	Special Operations Forces
SOP's	Standard Operating Procedures
SSI	Strategic Studies Institute
SVTC	Secure Video TeleConference
TCP	Traffic Control Point
TF	Task Force
TFIH ICE	Task Force Iron Horse Interrogation Control Element
THI	Tactical Human Intelligence
TOA	Transfer Of Authority
TPFDL	Time-Phased Force Deployment List
TTP	Tactical Techniques and Procedures
UH-60	Utility Helicopter-60, also known as a Black Hawk
UN	United Nations
UPI	United Press International
VFW	Veterans of Foreign Wars
WMD	Weapons of Mass Destruction

Acronym list compiled by Bill Nye, the Science Guy

PART I

CONTAINMENT

1.

A BAD ENDING

SPRING 1991

President George W. Bush's decision to invade Iraq in 2003 ultimately may come to be seen as one of the most profligate actions in the history of American foreign policy. The consequences of his choice won't be clear for decades, but it already is abundantly apparent in mid-2006 that the U.S. government went to war in Iraq with scant solid international support and on the basis of incorrect information—about weapons of mass destruction and a supposed nexus between Saddam Hussein and al Qaeda's terrorism—and then occupied the country negligently. Thousands of U.S. troops and an untold number of Iraqis have died. Hundreds of billions of dollars have been spent, many of them squandered. Democracy may yet come to Iraq and the region, but so too may civil war or a regional conflagration, which in turn could lead to spiraling oil prices and a global economic shock.

This book's subtitle terms the U.S. effort in Iraq an adventure in the critical sense of adventurism—that is, with the view that the U.S.-led invasion was launched recklessly, with a flawed plan for war and a worse approach to occupation. Spooked by its own false conclusions about the threat, the Bush administration hurried its diplomacy, short-circuited its war planning, and assembled an agonizingly incompetent occupation. None of this was inevitable. It was made possible only through the intellectual acrobatics of simultaneously "worst-casing" the threat presented by Iraq while "best-casing" the subsequent cost and difficulty of occupying the country.

How the U.S. government could launch a preemptive war based on false premises is the subject of the first, relatively short part of this book. Blame must lie foremost with President Bush himself, but his incompetence and arrogance are only part of the story. It takes more than one person to make a mess as big as Iraq. That is, Bush could only take such a careless action because of a series of failures in the American system. Major lapses occurred within the national security bureaucracy, from a weak National Security Council (NSC) to an overweening Pentagon and a confused intelligence apparatus. Larger failures of oversight also occurred in the political system, most notably in Congress, and in the inability of the media to find and present alternate sources of information about Iraq and the threat it did or didn't present to the United States. It is a tragedy in which every major player contributed to the errors, but in which the heroes tend to be anonymous and relatively powerless—the front-line American soldier doing his best in a difficult situation, the Iraqi civilian trying to care for a family amid chaos and violence. They are the people who pay every day with blood and tears for the failures of high officials and powerful institutions.

The run-up to the war is particularly significant because it also laid the shaky foundation for the derelict occupation that followed, and that constitutes the major subject of this book. While the Bush administration—and especially Donald Rumsfeld, Paul Wolfowitz, and L. Paul Bremer III—bear much of the responsibility for the mishandling of the occupation in 2003 and early 2004, blame also must rest with the leadership of the U.S. military, who didn't prepare the U.S. Army for the challenge it faced, and then wasted a year by using counterproductive tactics that were employed in unprofessional ignorance of the basic tenets of counterinsurgency warfare.

The undefeated Saddam Hussein of 1991

The 2003 U.S. invasion and occupation of Iraq can't be viewed in isolation. The chain of events began more than a decade earlier with the botched close of the 1991 Gulf War and then it continued in the U.S. effort to contain Saddam Hussein in the years that followed. "I don't think you can understand how OIF"— the abbreviation for Operation Iraqi Freedom, the U.S. military's term for the

2003 invasion and occupation of Iraq—"without understanding the end of the '91 war, especially the distrust of Americans" that resulted, said Army Reserve Maj. Michael Eisenstadt, an intelligence officer who in civilian life is an expert on Middle Eastern security issues.

The seeds of the second president Bush's decision to invade were planted by the unfinished nature of the 1991 war, in which the U.S. military expelled Iraq from Kuwait but ended the fighting prematurely and sloppily, without due consideration by the first president Bush and his advisers of what end state they wished to achieve. In February 1991, President Bush gave speeches that encouraged Iraqis "to take matters into their own hands and force Saddam Hussein the dictator to step aside." U.S. Air Force aircraft dropped leaflets on fielded Iraqi units urging them to rebel. On March 1, Iraqi army units in Basra began to do just that.

But when the Shiites of cities in the south rose up, U.S. forces stood by, their guns silent. It was Saddam Hussein who continued to fight. He didn't feel defeated, and in a sense, really wasn't. Rather, in the face of the U.S. counterattack into Kuwait, Saddam simply had withdrawn from that front to launch fierce internal offensives against the Shiites in the south of Iraq in early March and then, a few weeks later, against the Kurds in the north when they also rose up. An estimated twenty thousand Shiites died in the aborted uprising. Tens of thousands of Kurds fled their homes and crossed into the mountains of Turkey, where they began to die of exposure.

The U.S. government made three key mistakes in handling the end of the 1991 war. It encouraged the Shiites and Kurds to rebel, but didn't support them. Gen. H. Norman Schwarzkopf, in the euphoria of the war's end, approved an exception to the no-fly rule to permit Iraqi helicopter flights—and Iraqi military helicopters were promptly used to shoot up the streets of the southern cities. Army Capt. Brian McNerney commanded an artillery battery during the 1991 war. "When the Iraqi helicopters started coming out, firing on the Iraqis, that's when we knew it was bullshit," he recalled fifteen years later, when he was serving as a lieutenant colonel in Balad, Iraq. "It was very painful. I was thinking, 'Something is really wrong.' We were sitting in a swamp and it began to feel lousy."

Second, the U.S. government assumed that Saddam's regime was so damaged that his fall was inevitable. "We were disappointed that Saddam's defeat did not break his hold on power, as . . . we had come to expect," the first president Bush and his national security adviser, Brent Scowcroft, wrote in their 1998 joint memoir, A World Transformed.

Third, the U.S. military didn't undercut the core of Saddam Hussein's power. Much of his army, especially elite Republican Guard units, were allowed to leave Kuwait relatively untouched. Army Col. Douglas Macgregor, who fought in one of the 1991 conflict's crucial battles, later called the outcome a "hollow" victory. "Despite the overwhelming force President George H. W. Bush provided, Desert Storm's most important objective, the destruction of the Republican Guard corps, was not accomplished," he wrote years later. "Instead, perhaps as many as 80,000 Iraqi Republican Guards, along with hundreds of tanks, armored fighting vehicles, and armed helicopters escaped to mercilessly crush uprisings across Iraq with a ruthlessness not seen since Stalin."

Having incited a rebellion against Saddam Hussein, the U.S. government stood by while the rebels were slaughtered. This failure would haunt the U.S. occupation twelve years later, when U.S. commanders were met not with cordial welcomes in the south but with cold distrust. In retrospect, Macgregor concluded, the 1991 war amounted to a "strategic defeat" for the United States.

Wolfowitz objects

The most senior official in the first Bush administration urging that more be done in the spring of 1991 to help the rebellious Shiites was Paul Wolfowitz, then the under secretary of defense for policy. Defense Secretary Dick Cheney, Joint Chiefs chairman Colin Powell, and National Security Adviser Brent Scowcroft disagreed—and so thousands of Shiites were killed as U.S. troops sat not many miles away. This is one reason that many neoconservatives would later view Powell not as the moral paragon many Americans do but rather as someone willing to sit on his hands as Iraqis (and later, Bosnians) were killed on his watch.

Back then Powell was more often than not an ally of Cheney, who then was an unquestioned member of the hard-nosed realist school of foreign policy. "I was not an enthusiast about getting U.S. forces and going into Iraq," Cheney later said. "We were there in the southern part of Iraq to the extent we needed to be there to defeat his forces and to get him out of Kuwait, but the idea of going into Baghdad, for example, or trying to topple the regime wasn't anything I was enthusiastic about. I felt there was a real danger here that you would get bogged down in a long drawn-out conflict, that this was a dangerous, difficult part of the world." Sounding like a determined foreign policy pragmatist, Cheney said that Americans needed to accept that "Saddam is just one more irritant, but there's a long list of irritants in that part of the world." To actually invade Iraq, he said, "I don't think it would have been worth it."

Likewise, Schwarzkopf would write in his 1992 autobiography, "I am certain that had we taken all of Iraq, we would have been like the dinosaur in the tar pit— we would still be there, and we, not the United Nations, would be bearing the costs of that occupation."

Wolfowitz, for his part, penned an essay on the 1991 war two years later that listed the errors committed in its termination. "With hindsight it does seem like a mistake to have announced, even before the war was over, that we would not go to Baghdad, or to give Saddam the reassurance of the dignified cease-fire cere- mony at Safwan," he wrote in 1993. "Even at the time it seemed unwise to allow Iraq to fly its helicopters, and all the more so to continue allowing them to do so when it became clear that their main objective was to slaughter Kurds in the North and Shia in the South." He pointed the finger at unnamed members of that Bush administration—"some U.S. government officials at the time"—who seemed to believe that a Shia-dominated Iraq would be an unacceptable outcome. And, he added, it was "clearly a mistake" not to have created a demilitarized zone in the south that would have been off-limits to Saddam's forces and maintained steady pressure on him. Finally, he cast some ominous aspersions on the motivations of unnamed senior U.S. military leaders—presumably Powell and Schwarzkopf. The failure to better protect the Kurds and Shiites, he charged, "in no small part re- flected a miscalculation by some of our military commanders that a rapid disen- gagement was essential to preserve the luster of victory, and to avoid getting stuck with postwar objectives that would prevent us from ever disengaging."

Wolfowitz seemed at this point to be determined that if he ever again got the chance to deal with Iraq policy, he would not defer to such military judgments about the perceived need to avoid getting stuck in Iraq. A decade later he would play a crucial role in the second Bush administration's drive to war, and this book will return repeatedly to examine his statements and actions. It is unusual for so much attention to be focused on a second-level official of subcabinet rank, but Wolfowitz was destined to play an unusually central role on Iraq policy. Andrew Bacevich, a Boston University foreign policy expert, is better placed than most to understand Wolfowitz, having first served a full career in the Army, and then taught at Johns Hopkins University's school of international affairs while Wolfowitz was its dean. "More than any of the other dramatis personae in contemporary Wash- ington, Wolfowitz embodies the central convictions to which the United States in the age of Bush subscribes," Bacevich wrote in 2005. He singled out "in particular, an extraordinary certainty in the righteousness of American actions married to an extraordinary confidence in the efficacy of American arms."

Operation Provide Comfort

There was one bright point for Wolfowitz in the muddled outcome of the 1991 war: the U.S.-led relief operation in northern Iraq. As it celebrated its swift triumph, the Bush administration grew increasingly embarrassed at seeing Saddam Hussein's relentless assault on the Kurds drive hordes of refugees into the snowy mountains along the Turkish-Iraqi border. The United States responded with a hastily improvised relief operation that gradually grew into a major effort, bringing tens of thousands of Kurds down from the mountains, and at first feeding and sheltering them, and later bringing them home. Largely conducted out of public view, Operation Provide Comfort was historically significant in several ways. It was the U.S. military's first major humanitarian relief operation after the Cold War, and it brought home the point that with the Soviet rivalry gone, it would be far easier to use U.S. forces overseas, even in sensitive areas on or near former Eastern Bloc territory. It involved moving some Marine Corps forces hundreds of miles inland in the Mideast, far from their traditional coastal areas of operation—a precursor of the way the Marines would be used in Afghanistan a decade later. It employed unmanned aerial vehicles to gather intelligence. In another wave of the future for the U.S. military establishment, it was extremely joint—that is, involving the Army, Marine Corps, Air Force, Navy, Special Operations troops, and allied forces. But most significantly, it was the first major long-term U.S. military operation on Iraqi soil. And in that way it would come to provide Wolfowitz with a notion of how U.S. policy in Iraq might be redeemed after the messy end of the 1991 war. In retrospect, Provide Comfort also becomes striking because it brought together so many American military men who later would play a role in the U.S. occupation of Iraq in 2003.

Provide Comfort began somewhat haphazardly, without clear strategic goals. It was initiated as an effort simply to keep Iraqi Kurds alive in the mountains, and so at first was seen just as a matter of air-dropping supplies for about ten days to stranded refugees. Next came a plan to build tent camps to house those people. But United Nations officials counseled strongly against setting up refugee camps in Turkey for fear they would become like the Palestinian camps in Lebanon that never went away. So U.S. forces first tried to create a space back in Iraq where the refugees could go, and ultimately decided simply to push back the Iraqi military sufficiently to permit the Kurds to return to their homes.

"And we carved out that area in the north," recalled Anthony Zinni, then a Marine brigadier general who was chief of staff of Provide Comfort. Once that last step had been taken, he said, it became clear that "we were saddling ourselves with an open-ended commitment to protect them in that environment."

Wolfowitz meets Zinni

Wolfowitz flew out to northern Iraq to see the operation. "We were pushing the Iraqis real hard," then Army Lt. Gen. Jay Garner, the commander of the operation, would recall. The leading edge of the U.S. push was a light infantry battalion commanded by an unusual Arabic-speaking lieutenant colonel named John Abizaid, who in mid-2003 would become the commander of U.S. military operations in the Mideast. Abizaid was fighting what he would later call a "dynamic 'war' of maneuver." He was operating aggressively but generally without shooting to carve out a safe area for the Kurds by moving around Iraqi army outposts. He also had the advantage of having U.S. Air Force warplanes circling overhead, ready to attack. Wary of having American troops behind them, with routes of retreat cut off by the planes overhead, the Iraqi forces would then fall back and yield control of territory. "We moved our ground and air forces around the Iraqis in such a way that they could fight or leave—and they left," Abizaid said later.

American troops were pushing farther and farther south into Iraq. Alarms went off in Washington when officials at the State Department and National Security Council learned just how far south U.S. forces had thrust. In the words of the Army's official history of Provide Comfort, "They expressed concern that the operation was getting out of hand." In the words of Gen. Garner, looking back, "The State Department went berserk." Orders soon arrived from the Pentagon to pull Abizaid's battalion back to the town of Dahuk.

Zinni recalled that Wolfowitz was interested in seeing how this nervy mission was being conducted. With Garner, the two met briefly at an airfield built for Saddam Hussein at Sirsenk in far northern Iraq. How was the U.S. military operating? Wolfowitz asked. Well, Zinni explained, this Lt. Col. Abizaid is pushing out the Iraqi forces, and we've got more and more space here inside Iraq for the Kurds, and we've kind of created a "security zone," or enclave, of some thirty-six hundred square miles.

"I started giving the brief and he really, really got into it," recalled Zinni. "This was capturing him in some way, this was turning some lights on in his head. He was very interested in it. He was very excited about what we were doing there, in a way that I didn't quite understand." Zinni was puzzled. He had thought of the effort as a humanitarian mission—worth doing but without much political meaning. Wolfowitz saw it differently. "It struck me that he saw more in this than was there," Zinni said. Carving out parts of Iraq for anti-Saddam Iraqis would become a pet idea of Wolfowitz's in the coming years.

That meeting in Sirsenk would be one of the few times that Zinni and Wolfowitz would meet. But over the next fourteen years the two men would become the yin and yang of American policy on Iraq, with one working near the top of the U.S. military establishment while the other would be a sharp critic of the policy the first was implementing. Wolfowitz departed the Pentagon not long after his review of Provide Comfort, when the first Bush administration left office, and returned to academia.

Zinni went fairly quickly from being chief of staff in northern Iraq to deputy commander at Central Command, and then to the top job in that headquarters, overseeing U.S. military operations in Iraq and the surrounding region, from the Horn of Africa to Central Asia. In his command his main task was overseeing the containment of Iraq. In that capacity, he would be "kind of a groundbreaker for Marine four stars," showing that a Marine could handle the job of being a "CinC" (commander in chief), or regional military commander, an Air Force general recalled. Other Marines had held those top slots, but until Zinni none had really distinguished himself in handling strategic issues.

Wolfowitz, by contrast, spent the 1990s in opposition. His path intertwined briefly with Zinni's in the 2000 presidential election campaign, when both endorsed the Bush-Cheney ticket, though for very different reasons. After a year, Zinni would go into opposition against the Bush administration's drive toward war with Iraq, while Wolfowitz would became one of the architects of that war.

They are very different men: Zinni is a Marine's Marine who still speaks in the accents of working-class Philadelphia, while Wolfowitz is a soft-spoken Ivy League political scientist, the son of an Ivy League mathematician. Yet both men are bright and articulate and utterly sincere. Retired Col. Gary Anderson, who knew Zinni in the Marines and later consulted with Wolfowitz on Iraq policy, said it was this very similarity between the two men that so divided them. "They both believe in their bones what they are saying," he observed. "Neither one is in any way disingenuous."

Former deputy secretary of state Richard Armitage, who has worked closely with both and who has been an ideological ally of Wolfowitz but a close friend of Zinni, when asked to compare the two, said, "They have more similarities than differences." Both are smart and tenacious, and both have strong interests in the Muslim world, from the Mideast to Indonesia—the latter a country in which both have done some work. "The main difference," Armitage continued, "is that Tony Zinni has been to war, and he's been to war a lot. So he understands what it is to ask a man to lose a limb for his country."

Wolfowitz later would say that "realists" such as Zinni did not understand that their policies were prodding the Mideast toward terrorism. If you liked 9/11, he would say after that event, just keep up policies such as the containment of Iraq. Zinni, for his part, would come to view Wolfowitz as a dangerous idealist who knew little about Iraq and had spent no real time on the ground there. Zinni would warn that Wolfowitz's advocacy of toppling Saddam Hussein through supporting Iraqi rebels was a dangerous and naive approach whose consequences hadn't been adequately considered. Largely unnoticed by most Americans during the 1990s, these contrasting views amounted to a prototype of the debate that would later occur over the 2003 invasion and occupation of Iraq.

2.

CONTAINMENT AND ITS DISCONTENTS

1992–2001

For over a decade after the 1991 war, it was the policy associated with Gen. Zinni that prevailed, even through the first year of the presidency of George W. Bush. The aim of the U.S. government, generally in its words and certainly in its actions, was containment of Iraq: ringing Saddam Hussein with military forces, building up ground facilities in Kuwait, running intelligence operations in Kurdish areas, flying warplanes over much of his territory, and periodically pummeling Iraqi military and intelligence facilities with missiles and bombs. The Saddam Must Go school associated with Paul Wolfowitz was a dissident minority voice, generally disdained by those holding power in the U.S. government.

The coming of containment

Had all the steps that became part of the containment policy over the course of 1991 and 1992 been taken at once, they might have delivered a culminating blow to Saddam's regime, especially if combined with a few other moves, such as seizing southern Iraq's oil fields and turning them over to rebel forces, or making them part of larger demilitarized zones. Rather, seemingly as a result of inattention at the top of the U.S. government, a series of more limited steps were taken, like slowly heating a warm bath, and Saddam Hussein's regime found ways to live with them. In April 1991 a no-fly zone was created in the north to protect the Kurds through a U.S. declaration that Iraqi aircraft couldn't operate in the area. Some sixteen months later a similar zone was established to aid the battered Shiites of the south, with U.S. warplanes flying out of Saudi Arabia and from carriers in the Persian Gulf. None of the other possible steps was taken.

Looking back, Zinni said, "We were piecemealing things without the coherence of a strategy. I'm not saying that the piecemealing things when it came about weren't necessary or didn't make sense, but they needed to be reviewed, and we needed some sort of strategic context back here to put them all inside of." It was a problem he would try to address when he became chief of Central Command in 1997.

But overall, he thought, the policy worked. "We contained Saddam," he said. "We watched his military shrink to less than half its size from the beginning of the Gulf War until the time I left command, not only shrinking in size, but dealing with obsolete equipment, ill-trained troops, dissatisfaction in the ranks, a lot of absenteeism. We didn't see the Iraqis as a formidable force. We saw them as a decaying force."

The containment life

Operation Northern Watch, the northern no-fly zone, was typical of U.S. military operations in and around Iraq after the 1991 war: It was small-scale, open-ended, and largely ignored by the American people. U.S. aircraft were occasionally bombing a foreign country, but that was hardly mentioned in the 2000 presidential campaign. Iraqis occasionally were killed by U.S. attacks, but not U.S. pilots.

Northern Watch was based at Incirlik Air Base, an old Cold War NATO base in south-central Turkey originally picked for its proximity to the underbelly of the Soviet Union, but now convenient for its nearness to the Middle East. A typical day at the base late in 2000 began with four F-15C fighter jets taking off, each bristling with weaponry: heat-seeking Aim-9 Sidewinder missiles near the wingtips, bigger radar-guided Aim-7 Sparrows on pylons closer in, and four even bigger AMRAAM missiles under each fuselage. Each taxied to the arming area, where their missiles were activated, and screamed down the runway, the engines sounding like giant pieces of paper being ripped.

The fighters were followed by an RC-135 Rivet Joint reconnaissance jet, a Boeing 707 laden with surveillance gear. Next came two Navy EA-6B electronic jammers, then some of the Alabama Air National Guard F-16s carrying missiles to home in on Iraqi radar. A total of eight F-16s were in the twenty-aircraft package. The final plane to take off was a big KC-10 tanker, a flying gas station that joined three others already airborne, as was an AWACS command-and-control aircraft. The package flew east toward northern Iraq, the Syrian border just twenty miles to the right of their cockpits. It took just over an hour for the American planes to travel four hundred miles to the ROZ, the restricted operating zone, over eastern Turkey, where the pilots got an aerial refueling and then turned south into Iraqi airspace.

Most patrols lasted four to eight hours, with the fighters and jammers flying over Iraq and then darting back to the ROZ to refuel two or three times, and the refuelers and command-and-control aircraft flying lazy circles over the brown mountains of southeastern Turkey, where Xenophon's force of Greek mercenaries had retreated under fire from central Iraq in 400 B.C., the epic march that became the core of the classic ancient military memoir, *Anabasis.* Even nowadays some of the villages amid the deep canyons and escarpments carved by the headwaters of the Tigris River are so remote that they have no roads leading to them, just narrow pathways up the ridges.

When the day's mission was over, the pilots gave the planes back to the mechanics, turned in their 9 millimeter pistols, and attended a debriefing. Most aviators preferred operating in the southern no-fly zone, which was three times as large as the cramped northern one. Also, the northern zone was bounded in part by Syria and Iran, unfriendly airspace in which to wander. But the ground crews preferred the northern no-fly operation, where the weather was cooler. In Saudi Arabia, recalled Chief Master Sgt. Dennis Krebs, a veteran of six no-fly tours there, "in the summer the surface temperatures on the aircraft get to 150 degrees, and you have to wear gloves" just to touch an aircraft. Also, in Turkey, unlike in Saudi Arabia, the troops were allowed off base.

By the late 1990s, containment was accepted by the U.S. military as part of the operating environment. "The key thing was how normal it got," remembered one Air Force general. "There were bumps. But it got to be a kind of steady white noise in the background. It really was just background noise. . . . It was almost like our presence in the Cold War, in Germany, in the early days, when we'd fly the Berlin Corridor, and occasionally the Russians would do something to intimidate us, just like Saddam would try to do something."

Out in the Persian Gulf, Cmdr. Jeff Huber, the operations officer aboard the aircraft carrier USS *Theodore Roosevelt,* thought through his doubts about the no-fly mission. "Given that no-fly zones don't make any sense in any traditional airpower context, how can we determine whether one is succeeding?" he asked. It was impossible to tally "Kurds/Shia Moslems not bombed," he noted. He wound up giving the mission a tepid approval. "Many look at the no-fly zone this way: Yeah, it's pretty stupid, but it beats letting international scumbags get away with anything they want and doing nothing about it."

The overall cost of the two no-fly zones was roughly $1 billion a year. Other U.S. military operations, such as exercises in Kuwait, added another $500 million to the bill. That total of $1.5 billion a year was a bit more than what one week of occupying Iraq would cost the U.S. government in 2003-4, when the burn rate was about $60 billion a year, increasing slightly to about $70 billion in 2005.

In retrospect, one of the astonishments of the no-fly zones was that in twelve years not a single piloted U.S. aircraft was lost. Among some reflective military intelligence officers that raises the question of why not. Saddam Hussein clearly had some military capability, they noted, even if it wasn't anywhere near what the second Bush administration later would claim he had. In retrospect, said one senior military specialist in Middle Eastern intelligence issues who is still on active duty, it appears that Saddam Hussein really didn't want to shoot down any American aircraft. Rather, he walked a fine line in his behavior. "To my mind, it was carefully calibrated to show defiance, but not to provoke us," this officer said. "He was doing enough to show his people he was confronting the mighty United States, but not more than that. It was all about internal consumption. If they had wanted to be more serious, even with their weakened military, they could have."

In that sense, Saddam's ambiguous stance on the no-fly zones paralleled what we now know to be his handling of weapons of mass destruction. He got rid of his chemical and biological stocks, but wouldn't let international inspectors prove that he had done so, probably in order to intimidate his neighbors and citizens. Likewise, with the no-fly zones, his words were more threatening than his actions, but the U.S. government didn't pick up that signal.

Wolfowitz out of power

One day in 1996, Paul Wolfowitz toured Gettysburg with a group of specialists in military strategy from Johns Hopkins University's school of international studies, where he became dean after his service under Cheney at the Pentagon.

Late in the afternoon, as the sun dipped toward Seminary Ridge, Wolfowitz stood at the center of the battlefield, near the spot where the soldiers of Pickett's charge had hit the Federal line and were thrown back by point-blank cannon blasts. Pointedly, Eliot Cohen, the Johns Hopkins professor running the tour, had Wolfowitz read aloud to the group the angry telegram that President Lincoln had drafted but never sent to the new commander of the Army of the Potomac, Gen. George Meade. Why, Lincoln wanted to ask his general, do you stop, and not pursue your enemy when you have him on the run?

Wolfowitz came to believe that the policy of containment was profoundly immoral, like standing by and trying to contain Hitler's Germany. It was a comparison to which he would often return. It carried particular weight coming from him, as he had lost most of his Polish extended family in the Holocaust. His line survived because his father had left Poland in 1920.

He talked about the Holocaust more in terms of policy than of personal history, most notably in giving him a profound wariness of policies of containment. He told the *New York Times*'s Eric Schmitt that "that sense of what happened in Europe in World War II has shaped a lot of my views." What if the West had tried to "contain" Hitler? This orientation toward Nazism would prove central to his thinking on Iraq. Again and again, he would describe Saddam Hussein and his security forces as the modern equivalent of the Gestapo—it was almost a verbal tic with him.

Some observers of Wolfowitz speculate that another lesson he took from the Holocaust is that the American people need to be pushed to do the right thing, because by the time the United States entered World War II it had been too late for millions of Jews and other victims of the Nazis. Asked about this in an interview before the war, Wolfowitz agreed, and expanded on the thought—and himself linked it to Iraq: "I think the world in general has a tendency to say, if somebody evil like Saddam is killing his own people, 'That's too bad, but that's really not my business.'" That's dangerous, he continued, because Hussein was "in a class with very few others—Stalin, Hitler, Kim Jong Il. . . . People of that order of evil . . . tend not to keep evil at home, they tend to export it in various ways and eventually it bites us." The analogy to Nazism gave Wolfowitz a tactical advantage in that it instantly put critics on the defensive. If one was convinced that Saddam Hussein was the modern equivalent of Hitler, and his secret police the contemporary version of the Gestapo, then it was easy to see—and portray—anyone opposing his aggressive policies as the moral equivalent of Neville Chamberlain: fools at best, knaves at worst. So for years Wolfowitz prodded the American people toward war with Iraq.

After teaching political science at Yale, Wolfowitz as a diplomat helped bring democracy to South Korea and the Philippines in the 1970s and 1980s. He took away from those experiences a belief that every country is capable of becoming democratic—and that their becoming so aids the American cause. "I think democracy is a universal idea," he would say. "And I think letting people rule themselves happens to be something that serves Americans and America's interests."

Wolfowitz's bookish background also gave him an academic manner that can be disarming. There is in Wolfowitz little of the blustery Princeton frat boy towel-snapping banter on which Defense Secretary Donald Rumsfeld seems to thrive. His soft voice and mild manner frequently surprise those who have braced themselves for the encounter. "I actually was surprised to find, the first time I met him, that he was pretty likeable, which surprised me, because I hate him," said Paul Arcangeli, who served as an Army officer in Iraq before being medically retired. (His loathing, he explained, is a policy matter: "I blame him for all this shit in Iraq. Even more than Rumsfeld, I blame him." His bottom line on Wolfowitz: "Dangerously idealistic. And crack-smoking stupid.")

But Wolfowitz's low-key manner cloaked a tough-minded determination that ran far deeper than is common in compromise-minded Washington. One of the most important lessons of the Cold War, he wrote in the spring of 2000, was "demonstrating that your friends will be protected and taken care of, that your enemies will be punished, and that those who refuse to support you will live to regret having done so."

Saddam must go

In January 1998, the Project for the New American Century, an advocacy group for an interventionist Republican foreign policy, issued a letter urging President Clinton to take "regime change" in Iraq seriously. Among the eighteen signers of the letter were Wolfowitz, Rumsfeld, Armitage, future UN ambassador John Bolton, and several others who would move back into government three years later. "The policy of 'containment' of Saddam Hussein has been steadily eroding over the past several months," they wrote. "Diplomacy is clearly failing . . . [and] removing Saddam Hussein and his regime from power . . . needs to become the aim of American foreign policy." The alternative, they concluded, would be "a course of weakness and drift."

"Containment was a very costly strategy," Wolfowitz said years later. "It cost us billions of dollars—estimates are around $30 billion. It cost us American lives. We lost American lives in Khobar Towers"—a huge 1996 bombing in Saudi Arabia that killed 19 service members and wounded 372 others. But he also saw other costs. "In some ways the real price is much higher than that. The real price was giving Osama bin Laden his principal talking point. If you go back and read his notorious fatwah from 1998, where he called for the first time for killing Americans, his big complaint is that we have American troops on the holy soil of Saudi Arabia and that we're bombing Iraq. That was his big recruiting device, his big claim against us."

Wolfowitz also saw another cost, one that most Americans hadn't noticed much: "Finally, containment did nothing for the Iraqi people." Large parts of the Iraqi population suffered hugely under a contained Saddam, and the Marsh Arabs of southern Iraq were on the route to being wiped out, he noted. "That's what containment did for them. For those people, liberation came barely in time."

Zinni too was growing uncomfortable with the price containment was inflicting on the Iraqi people, but from his perspective, the solution was to refine what was being done, not topple Saddam. He thought that international sanctions could be narrowed to focus more on keeping weapons components and other militarily useful items out of Iraq, while dropping economic sanctions that imposed unnecessary suffering on Iraqis. This was a theme that his old friend Colin Powell would take up a few years later, in 2001, when he became secretary of state under President George W. Bush. But Zinni recalled that he didn't get much of a response in his attempts to interest Clinton administration officials in refining the containment strategy.

As he made the rounds of Middle Eastern capitals, Zinni found himself crossing paths with Dick Cheney, then an ex-defense secretary who was CEO of Halliburton, the oil services and logistics company that did much business in that part of the world. "I'd be traveling around out there and I'd run into him all the time," he said. "At Halliburton he was always going into the tent to see the emir or the king." The two men weren't close, but Zinni felt he had a good enough sense of Cheney to know that he was "a realist in terms of what happens on the ground, how to get things done. Very much someone who wanted to work through the United Nations and through building coalitions, masterful at it."

The Desert Fox strikes

The climax of Zinni's time as commander in the Mideast was the four-day-long Desert Fox bombing campaign. There had been military movements in 1994 and 1996, but the 1998 raids would be the biggest U.S. military strikes in Iraq since the end of the 1991 war. This turned out to be the most intense enforcement of the containment policy that occurred in the entire twelve-year period between the 1991 war and the 2003 invasion.

Launched in reaction to a standoff with Saddam Hussein over weapons inspections, the attacks began on December 16, 1998, with a volley of over 200 cruise missiles from Navy ships and Air Force B-52 bombers. The next day another 100 cruise missiles were fired. On the third night of air strikes, B-1 swing-wing supersonic bombers made their first ever appearance in combat. After a fourth night, the raids ended. A total of 415 cruise missiles had been used, more than the 317 employed during the entire 1991 Gulf War. They and 600 bombs hit a total of 97 sites, the major ones being facilities for the production and storage of chemical weapons and those associated with missiles that could deliver such munitions. In part because U.S. intelligence was able to locate only a limited number of sites associated with weaponry, the strikes also hit government command-and-control facilities, such as intelligence and secret-police headquarters.

Some congressional Republicans were deeply suspicious of President Clinton and suggested that the strikes were simply a ploy to undercut the impending impeachment proceedings against him. As the bombing began, Sen. Trent Lott, then the Senate majority leader, issued a statement declaring, "I cannot support this military action in the Persian Gulf at this time. Both the timing and the policy are subject to question." Rep. Dana Rohrbacher, a California Republican, called the military action "an insult to the American people."

Yet the raids proved surprisingly effective. "Desert Fox actually exceeded expectations," wrote Kenneth Pollack in *The Threatening Storm: The Case for Invading Iraq,* his influential 2002 book. "Saddam panicked during the strikes. Fearing that his control was threatened, he ordered large-scale arrests and executions, which backfired and destabilized his regime for months afterward."

Zinni was amazed when Western intelligence assets in Baghdad reported that Desert Fox nearly knocked off Saddam Hussein's regime. His conclusion: Containment is clearly working, and Saddam Hussein was on the ropes. A U.S. military intelligence official, looking back at Desert Fox years later, confirmed that account. "There were a lot of good reports coming out afterward on how he changed his command and control, very quickly. It was especially clear in areas involving internal control." Interceptions of communications among Iraqi generals indicated "palpable fear that he was going to lose control."

Arab allies of the United States were hearing the same reports, and that led them to go to Gen. Zinni with an urgent question: If you do indeed topple Saddam Hussein, what will come next? "This is what I heard from our Arab friends out there—you almost caused an implosion," Zinni recalled. "And that worried them. An implosion is going to cause chaos. You're going to have to go in after an implosion. The question was, do you guys have a plan?" The Arab leaders especially wanted to know what was going to be done to stem the possibility of a massive exodus of refugees into their countries, along with major economic dislocations. Also, they wanted to know, if Iraq disintegrates, what is going to be the Arab world's bulwark against the age-old threat of Iran? "You tip this guy over, you could create a bigger problem for us than we have now," Arab officials said to Zinni. "So, what are you going to do about it?"

Zinni realized that he didn't have good answers to those questions. So in June 1999 he had Booz Allen, the consulting firm, hold a classified war game on what such an aftermath might look like—what problems it would present, and how the U.S. government might respond. He asked that representatives not just of the military but of the State Department and the Agency for International Development also participate. "It brought out all the problems that have surfaced now," he said later. "It shocked the hell out of me." In the wake of the war game, Zinni ordered Central Command to begin planning in case humanitarian relief operations in Iraq became necessary. But he wasn't able to interest other parts of the government in participating in that preparatory work.

Two conclusions from Desert Fox

Back in the United States, Desert Fox looked different to some. At the time it was fashionable to dismiss the operations as more avoidance by the Clinton administration, as simply throwing cruise missiles at a problem that required more than that. "Desert Fox was a sham," Danielle Pletka, a national security analyst at the American Enterprise Institute, said in a 2004 interview. "They were so casualty averse. They did nothing but bomb empty buildings." The quotable Pletka put it more pungently than many, but this was not an uncommon view.

"The Clinton administration was totally risk averse" on Iraq, Richard Perle, a leading Iraq hawk, would argue later. "They allowed Saddam over eight years to grow in strength. He was far stronger at the end of Clinton's tenure than at the beginning." Perle made those assertions in July 2003, just about the time they were becoming laughable to those who understood the situation on the ground in Iraq.

David Kay, a more sober observer, also was skeptical at the time about the effects of Desert Fox. It was only years later, after his Iraqi Survey Group, the U.S. government's postwar effort to find Iraq's supposed stockpiles of weapons of mass destruction, had interviewed and interrogated two hundred officials from Iraqi weapons programs, that he realized that the four-day campaign had indeed had a devastating effect, far more than had been appreciated back in Washington. His postinvasion survey found to his surprise that after 1998 the Iraqi weapons programs, with the exception of missile building, "withered away, and never got momentum again." In a series of in-depth postwar interrogations, a score of veterans of Iraqi weapons programs told Kay's group that the Desert Fox raids had left Iraqi weaponeers demoralized and despairing. "They realized that they'd never be able to reestablish the type of industrial facility they were aiming at," he said in an interview. "They'd spent years, lots of money, and lots of energy on it, years and years. And they realized that as long as Saddam was in power, they'd never be able to reestablish production." In short, they had given up. The other point that Desert Fox made to Iraqis was that visible elements of weaponry, such as missile programs, which require a large, easily observed infrastructure such as engine test stands, could be hammered at any time.

Kay added that he was taken aback to hear their accounts. "For me, it was a bit of an eye-opener, because I'd always denigrated Desert Fox. What I failed to understand was that it was cumulative, coming on top of eight years of sanctions." More than the physical damage, it was the devastating psychological effect that had really counted, and that was what U.S. intelligence assessments had missed in examining Iraq during the run-up to the war, he decided.

In the spring of 2003, Army Col. Alan King, who was the chief civil affairs officer attached to the invading 3rd Infantry Division, would come to the same conclusion about the powerful effect of the Desert Fox raids. "The chairman of the Iraqi atomic industry surrendered to me, and I found out that our reason for invading pretty much went away in 1998," he recalled. Most of it was destroyed by Saddam Hussein in the two years before then, when he was fearful of the revelations made by his son-in-law, Hussein Kamel, the principal director of the Iraqi weapons programs, who temporarily defected to Jordan in 1995 along with other relatives, only to return to Iraq early the following year. The manufacturing capability remained and was largely finished off by Desert Fox. King also was told in interrogations that when the head of an Iraqi delegation to Russia returned to Baghdad in the late nineties with news that he might be able to obtain a nuclear warhead, Saddam Hussein had him executed for fear that the U.S. government might catch wind of it.

But there also was an unexpected disadvantage to the success of Desert Fox. As Saddam reacted by tightening his internal controls, Iraqis inside the country in contact with U.S. intelligence grew far more wary. The Senate Intelligence Committee, in a 2004 autopsy of the intelligence failures made in handling Iraq, would report that after the raids the U.S. intelligence community "did not have a single HUMINT [human intelligence] source collecting against Iraq's weapons of mass destruction programs."

"That was the big cutoff point in intel," agreed a U.S. military intelligence official specializing in Middle Eastern affairs. After that "there was a real difference in the quality and verifiability of the information." A catastrophic side effect of this new lack of information was that it led to a data vacuum in which the basis for the United States going to war five years later would be created: All sorts of wild claims could be made about Saddam's armaments programs in 2002 that later would be proven wrong but at the time couldn't be refuted.

Zinni's conclusion was that U.S. policy on Iraq succeeded in the late nineties. "Containment worked. Look at Saddam—what did he have?" Zinni asked later. "He didn't threaten anyone in the region. He was contained. It was a pain in the ass, but he was contained. He had a deteriorated military. He wasn't a threat to the region." What's more, he said, it wasn't a particularly costly effort. "We contained, day-to-day, with fewer troops than go to work every day at the Pentagon." It was sometimes messy, and it could have been done better, especially if sanctions had been dropped. But it had worked.

Wolfowitz and his fellow neoconservatives—essentially idealistic interventionists who believed in using American power to spread democracy—drew the opposite conclusion: If the regime is so weak, it would be easy to remove it, perhaps by having the United States arm and train Iraqi rebels. In his writings Wolfowitz began to construct the mirage that ultimately would become the Bush administration's version of Iraq—a land saturated both with weapons of mass destruction and a yearning to be liberated by American troops.

Zinni vs. Wolfowitz

Even before Desert Fox, Wolfowitz and Zinni clashed publicly over the issue of arming Iraqi rebels to try to overthrow Saddam. At a congressional hearing Zinni pointedly dismissed that as a "Bay of Goats" approach destined to fail, as the CIA-sponsored Bay of Pigs attack on Castro had in 1961. "I think a weakened, fragmented, chaotic Iraq, which could happen if this isn't done carefully, is more dangerous in the long run than a contained Saddam is now," he told a group of defense reporters in October 1998. "I don't think these questions have been thought through or answered." He also took direct aim at the Iraqi exiles: "I don't see that there is a viable opposition." Arming them, he said, would likely be a waste of money.

Wolfowitz took a pop at Zinni in his published critique of the Clinton administration's Iraq policy. "Toppling Saddam is the only outcome that can satisfy the vital U.S. interest in a stable and secure Gulf region," he wrote in the *New Republic* magazine in December 1998. "The administration has continued to display paralyzing ambivalence. . . . Marine Gen. Anthony Zinni, commander of U.S. Gulf forces, was even authorized to express the view that a 'weak, fragmented, chaotic Iraq' would be more dangerous than Saddam's continuation in power and to complain that the opposition isn't 'viable.'" Wolfowitz saw such "realism" as both immoral and wrongheaded. In 1999, he wrote that "the United States should be prepared to commit ground forces to protect a sanctuary in southern Iraq where the opposition could safely mobilize."

Zinni made it clear that he believed Wolfowitz and his ally Ahmed Chalabi, the Iraqi exile leader who later would become a Pentagon favorite, were dangerous naifs who knew little about the reality of war. "This is where they jumped on Chalabi's idea—'create an enclave, give me some special forces and air support and I'll go in and topple the guy over,'" Zinni remembered. "And I said, 'This is ridiculous, won't happen. This is going to generate another one of our defeats there where we get a bunch of people slaughtered.'"

As a senior U.S. commander, Zinni also was offended by their presumption. A retired Special Operations general, "Wayne Downing, was up there with Danny Pletka and her husband [Pletka, then an aide to Sen. Jesse Helms, was married to another congressional staffer], scheming. They had this scheme for arming Chalabi. It upset me, 'cause I'm the CinC, these are my forces. I got staffers in Congress and retired generals working war plans!" In addition to the potential for a small anti-Saddam force being massacred, he worried that their plan could wind up dragging the United States into war. "The second issue is, they lead us into a mess, they piecemeal us into a fight," he said. "Okay, it's Special Forces, it's small units, create an enclave, it's air support. But what do they [then] drag us into?"

Wolfowitz's alleged "fantasy"

Perhaps the low point for the Wolfowitz view was a biting article in *Foreign Affairs* magazine that appeared during winter 1998–99. Siding with Zinni, it mocked the idea of having Iraqi exiles seize territory, supported by U.S. airpower. Essentially, the three authors, each from a mainstream national security institution—the Rand Corporation, the National Defense University, and the Council on Foreign Relations—argued that only people who know nothing about military affairs could think that a small force of Iraqi rebels could topple Saddam easily. The article cited a few proponents of what it disparaged as the "Rollback Fantasy," but singled out Wolfowitz, quoting him disapprovingly, and then stated that he was wrong, and that, in fact, "for the United States to try moving from containment to rollback in Iraq would be a terrible mistake that could easily lead to thousands of unnecessary deaths." Given the background of the authors and the venue carrying their words, it was almost as if Wolfowitz were being taken to the woodshed by the foreign policy establishment.

The article deeply angered Wolfowitz. "I thought it misrepresented and caricatured a serious position and even dismissed it as politically motivated," he said later. But the letter he coauthored in response to the article was restrained in tone. Among other points, it stated that the Bay of Pigs analogy was misleading, and that the better parallel was Operation Provide Comfort, in which "the Iraqi army surrendered the northern third of the country to a small U.S. ground force and lightly armed Kurdish guerrillas because they had lost the stomach to fight." It also warned that if or when containment collapsed, "the United States will face a Saddam who has new nuclear, biological and chemical weapons."

The Bush campaign vows military restraint

Neither Iraq nor terrorism were issues in the 2000 presidential campaign, and in fact were hardly mentioned by the candidates of either party. Everything George W. Bush and Dick Cheney said during the campaign indicated that they thought Bill Clinton had used the military too much in his foreign policy, not too little. They outlined a stance of maintaining the policy of containment while being more selective about the use of force. Bush also argued against using the military in noncombat missions, hitting the issue hard in both debates of the presidential candidates. "He believes in nation building," Bush said of Democratic candidate Al Gore at their first debate, on October 3, 2000. "I would be very careful about using our troops as nation builders. I believe the role of the military is to fight and win war and therefore prevent war from happening in the first place." As a result of wanton Clinton administration policies, he added, "I believe we're overextended in too many places."

Bush emphasized this admonition at the next debate. "I don't think our troops ought to be used for what's called nation building," he said on October 11. "I think our troops ought to be used to fight and win war. I think our troops ought to be used to help overthrow a dictator . . . when it's in our best interests."

During the campaign, vice presidential candidate Cheney also defended the decision during the 1991 war to not attack Baghdad. The United States, he said during an interview on NBC's *Meet the Press,* should not act as though "we were an imperialist power, willy-nilly moving into capitals in that part of the world, taking down governments." Cheney appeared to endorse the Clinton administration's containment policy, saying that "we want to maintain our current posture vis-à-vis Iraq."

Cheney: "Help is on the way" for the U.S. military

Instead, the prime national security issue in the campaign was the state of the U.S. military, which Bush and Cheney argued was parlous. The Clinton administration had eroded the armed forces, used them haphazardly, and neglected their health. The Republican candidates vowed to use the military more wisely, not sending it all over the world, and instead would restore military trust in political leaders.

This is how Cheney put it on August 2, 2000, in accepting the Republican vice presidential nomination at the party convention in Philadelphia:

> For eight years, Clinton and Gore have extended our military commitments while depleting our military power. Rarely has so much been demanded of our armed forces and so little given to them in return. George W. Bush and I are going to change that, too. I have seen our military at its finest, with the best equipment, the best training, and the best leadership. I am proud of them. I have had the responsibility for their well-being. And I can promise them now, help is on the way. Soon, our men and women in uniform will once again have a commander in chief they can respect, a commander in chief who understands their mission and restores their morale.

Many in the military quietly reciprocated Bush's support. One Army colonel on active duty boasted that he had helped polish a Bush campaign speech on Republican national security policy. Zinni and dozens of other retired generals endorsed Bush. Zinni was wary of Wolfowitz's presence as a Bush foreign policy adviser but was reassured by the balancing presence of realists such as his old friend Richard Armitage, who also was, and remains, one of Powell's closest friends. Zinni later said he supported Bush because of Powell's role in the campaign, while Wolfowitz appears to have supported Bush somewhat despite it.

Bush vs. Iraq—or Bush vs. China?

After just a month in office, the Bush administration launched air strikes against five sites in the Iraqi antiaircraft network—three big radar systems and two command-and-control facilities. The attacks were neither well managed nor particularly successful. The February 2001 attack was the biggest in more than two years, since Desert Fox. But Bush and his national security adviser, Condoleezza Rice, who were on a short trip to Mexico, were to some extent blindsided by them. Because of poor communications with Rumsfeld's Pentagon, Bush had been led to expect that the strikes would occur after he left Mexico. But at the last minute, they were moved up by six hours. It was the kind of slip that can occur in any new administration, but it wound up overshadowing the first foreign trip of a president with notably little overseas experience.

"A routine mission was conducted to enforce the no-fly zone," Bush said that day in San Cristobal, Mexico. "And it is a mission about which I was informed, and I authorized. But I repeat, it's a routine mission, and we will continue to enforce the no-fly zone until the world is told otherwise."

The U.S. military deemed the strikes essential because the Iraqis were installing a fiber optic communications network in their air defense system that would have greatly increased the threat to U.S. pilots operating in the southern no-fly zone. Antiaircraft batteries in southern Iraq once had used their own radars to track U.S. and British jets, but radar-seeking missiles launched against those systems had proven so lethal that Iraqi troops had turned them off. Instead, the Iraqis were taking the innovative step of using powerful radars near Baghdad—and outside the no-fly zone—to track aircraft, and then planned to transmit the targeting data to the missile batteries in the south. Chinese workers were installing the network that would link up this new system.

The strikes had an unusually delicate setup. The weaponry would reach across the 33rd parallel, the northern limit of the southern no-fly zone, twenty miles south of Baghdad. It was the first time this had been done since Desert Fox, but the aircraft launching those long-range bombs and missiles would turn away before crossing the line. Even more unusual was the timing of the strikes. They were to be executed on a Friday, the Muslim sabbath, in order not to hit the Chinese workers involved in the construction, who presumably would be at rest that day. In the end, the air strikes didn't do much damage, because many of the bombs used—of a relatively new type called the AGM-154A joint standoff weapon, delivered by Navy jets flying from the USS *Harry S. Truman* in the Persian Gulf— veered left of where they were supposed to hit and missed most of their targets.

The raid had the odd and unexpected side effect of focusing the new administration less on Iraq and more on China. "We're concerned about the apparent involvement of the Chinese with fiber optics" in the Iraqi system, Condoleezza Rice said. "Under the sanctions regime, there appears to be a problem." Powell took up the matter with the new Chinese ambassador when he arrived to present his credentials, and Bush vowed in his first White House press conference that "we're going to send a message" to China over its aid to Iraq's military.

Iraq was almost an afterthought at that conference, with Bush saying he would conduct a review of Iraq policy in order "to make the sanctions work." Indeed, that was the task that Powell took on during his first tour of the Mideast as secretary of state. Containment and sanctions, he said, "have worked," and Saddam Hussein wasn't a threat. "He has not developed any significant capability with respect to weapons of mass destruction. He is unable to project conventional power against his neighbors. So, in effect, our policies have strengthened the security of the neighbors of Iraq, and these are the policies that we are going to keep in place." Powell would himself take almost the opposite position two years later at the United Nations. But as he toured the Middle East in February 2001, he found general agreement with his procontainment view. "Everyone I spoke to said, you've got to go down this track" of improving sanctions, Powell told reporters during the trip.

Wolfowitz didn't agree with that policy, but he was in a minority even inside the Bush administration. As Powell traveled, Wolfowitz appeared before the Senate Armed Services Committee, which was weighing his nomination to be Rumsfeld's deputy. Wolfowitz candidly said that he favored toppling Saddam Hussein. "I think there's no question that the whole region would be a safer place, Iraq would be a much more successful country, and the American national interest would benefit greatly if there were a change of regime in Iraq," he testified. "If there's a real option to do that, I would certainly think it's still worthwhile."

There really wasn't a "war party" inside the Bush administration before 9/11, said Patrick Clawson, a Middle East expert who moved in Washington's neoconservative circles. Rather, he said, there really was just Wolfowitz, pleading for more attention to Iraq, and Wolfowitz's former Pentagon aide, I. Lewis "Scooter"

Libby, Cheney's chief of staff in the new administration, listening supportively. Clawson dismissed the allegation made later by former treasury secretary Paul O'Neill and others that the Bush administration came into office determined to invade Iraq. "What O'Neill doesn't notice is that those who wanted to go to war lost, and those who supported 'smart sanctions' won," he said. In the spring of 2001, he added, Rice, the new president's national security adviser, made it "extremely clear" to colleagues that they weren't going to do anything in Iraq.

Wolfowitz and his few allies—mainly Libby and a few others in the office of the new vice president, traditionally not a powerful political base from which to operate—were stymied by Powell, who talked not about regime change but about improving containment by imposing smart sanctions. This was essentially an attempt to breathe new life into containment by paring the list of items being watched, focusing more energy on controls related to weapons of mass destruction, and loosening oversight of food imports and other civilian goods.

In the summer of 2001, it looked like Powell was winning the internal arguments that would shape the foreign policy of the new and inexperienced president. "Powell's influence had been steadily growing," the *New York Times*'s Bill Keller wrote later that year. Powell had negotiated a successful end to the confrontation with the Chinese, smoothed relations with Russia, and gotten the president engaged on Mideast peace negotiations. "In all of this, the president was following the instincts of his secretary of state," Keller wrote.

Powell's deputy, Richard Armitage, agreed with that assessment. "Prior to 9/11 we certainly were prevailing" on the Iraq argument, he said in an interview in 2005.

As William Kristol and Lawrence Kaplan, two Iraq hawks, wrote in a 2003 prowar monograph, "far from transforming containment into rollback, the White House proceeded to water down even the demands that the Clinton team had imposed on Iraq."

The *Washington Post*'s Jim Hoagland, one of the most hawkish columnists on Iraq, captured the unhappiness of those who wanted a more aggressive stance on Iraq. At the end of the 1991 Gulf War, he argued in April, the U.S. government had been headed for victory in Iraq but instead found a way to snatch "stalemate from the jaws of victory." The new administration's open-minded review of Iraq policy, he warned, "risks becoming a way of letting the mistakes of Bush 41 become the mistakes of Bush 43." Hoagland returned to the subject of the Iraq policy review in the summer of 2001, warning, "By September Bush needs to show that he knows where he is going on Iraq and the Middle East, and that he knows how he intends to get there."

3.

THIS CHANGES EVERYTHING: THE AFTERMATH OF 9/11

On the bright blue morning of September 11, 2001, Col. Paul Hughes was in his office in the Pentagon's D Ring, in Army staff space—not the high-rent outer ring, where top civilians and higher ranking generals had their offices, facing the Potomac River or Arlington National Cemetery. Despite its airshaftlike view, the office of the National Security Policy Division, G-3 was a decent place to work, one of the hundreds of such small but vital wheels and cogs within the machinery of national defense.

Hughes and his office workers had gathered to watch CNN's reporting on the two aircraft that had hit the World Trade Center. A civilian contractor turned to Hughes. "What the hell is happening?" the man asked. "I don't understand it."

It was 9:37 A.M. Hughes was beginning to respond when the room exploded. Plaques and a clock shot off the walls, and bookshelves pitched forward. Hughes looked out the window and saw, above the Pentagon's roof, a huge fireball. "I am going to die today," he thought. He looked around and wondered why everyone and everything was silent, not realizing that the explosion of American Airlines Flight 77 hitting underneath his office at 530 miles per hour had temporarily robbed him of much of his hearing.

He and his coworkers made their way through the acrid smoke to the Pentagon's courtyard, a football field of space with a hot dog stand in the middle. Security officers announced that a fourth plane was heading toward Washington, so the crowd moved out to the Pentagon's sprawling south parking lot. After waiting awhile he realized that it would be a long time before he got back into his office. So without briefcase or Army beret, he walked the four miles to his sister's house in Alexandria. As he did, he dwelled on another American defeat. "I thought to myself, This is what a Union officer must have felt like in July of 1861, walking back from Bull Run"—the first big battle of the Civil War, which ended with Federal troops streaming back 25 miles to Washington. His bottom line on the day: "We got our ass kicked." So began a path that two years later would have Col. Hughes working on the strategy of the U.S. occupation in Iraq, and then moving into opposition to U.S. policy there.

The opening

The explosion at the Pentagon of Flight 77 and the day's three other hijack attacks provided the political opening that Paul Wolfowitz, Richard Perle, and others needed. Perle and Wolfowitz quickly began to make the case that 9/11 was precipitated by a myopic and false realism that wrongly had sought accommodation with evil. "The idea that we could live with another 20 years of stagnation in the Middle East that breeds this radicalism and breeds terrorism is, I think, just unacceptable—especially after September 11th," Wolfowitz later told the *Jerusalem Post*. In a talk in New York, he added, "We cannot go back to business as usual. We cannot think that this problem of Islamic extremist-based terrorism is going to leave us alone."

Four days after the attacks, the president and his national security team met at Camp David to discuss the response to 9/11. The briefing materials that Rumsfeld and Wolfowitz brought offered three targets in the war on terrorism: al Qaeda, Afghanistan's Taliban and Iraq. But only Wolfowitz pressed the case that day for attacking Iraq.

Wolfowitz's advocacy of attacking Iraq in response to 9/11 stemmed from the same views that later led him to underestimate the strength of the Iraqi insurgency, said a person who reviewed those Pentagon briefing materials. "In both cases, you have this know-it-all who won't believe the intelligence community, and won't believe that nonstate actors can do this much damage," he observed. Yet this person came away, as many critics do, finding himself oddly sympathetic to Wolfowitz. "There are two types of villains in Washington, hacks and fools," he concluded. "He isn't a hack. He's deeply misguided, he's impervious to evidence—and he's a serious, thoughtful guy."

Wolfowitz's own account of the discussion at Camp David that day softens the differences that were aired and instead depicts them as related to tactics and strategy. "There was a long discussion during the day about what place if any Iraq should have in a counterterrorist strategy," he said later. His account turns somewhat fuzzy: "There seemed to be a kind of agreement that yes it should be, but the disagreement was whether it should be in the immediate response or whether you should concentrate simply on Afghanistan first. There was a sort of undertow in that discussion. I think that was, the real issue was whether Iraq should be part of the strategy at all." He came away thinking, he said, that the president had decided tactically on an Afghanistan first approach but strategically on the objective of ousting governments that supported terrorism. Wolfowitz left still determined, sending follow-up memos to Rumsfeld on September 17 and September 18 that continued to make the case for attacking Iraq.

On September 20, Ahmed Chalabi went to the Pentagon to speak to the Defense Policy Board, an advisory group headed by Richard Perle. The first speaker at the meeting in Rumsfeld's conference room was Bernard Lewis, a historian of the Middle East whose pessimistic writings on Islam and terrorism had grown deeply influential within the Bush administration. The second speaker was Chalabi, an Iraqi exile leader. It was around this time, a senior military intelligence official recalled, that Perle's old subordinate Douglas Feith, who had become the Pentagon policy chief, put out the word to his aides to focus on Iraq.

But the same day, President Bush met with British Prime Minister Tony Blair and delivered a very different message. "When Blair asked about Iraq," the 9/11 Commission reported, quoting from an NSC summary of the two leaders' conversation, "the president replied that Iraq was not the immediate problem. Some members of his administration, he commented, had expressed a different view, but he was the one responsible for making the decisions."

Powell usually was an astute judge of Washington politics, but in the fall of 2001 his judgment seemed off. He no longer had the upper hand, but he didn't seem to recognize it, at least in his public comments. "Iraq isn't going anywhere," he told Bill Keller of the *New York Times* in his trademark, "everybody calm down" mode. "It's in a fairly weakened state. It's doing some things we don't like. We'll continue to contain it."

But the tide already was shifting. By seeming to catch the intelligence community asleep, the 9/11 attacks had created a new opportunity for those arguing that the professional intelligence analysts were underestimating the threat presented by Iraq, and especially the likelihood of its possessing chemical or biological weapons or its willingness to share them with anti-American terrorists. If you missed the warning signs on 9/11, the argument went at the time, what else are you missing now about Iraq?

The new doubts about intelligence, along with the caution of top military officers, combined to deeply frustrate Rumsfeld, recalled one covert operations specialist who worked for the defense secretary during this period. "What I saw from 9/11 forward was Don Rumsfeld's shock and disillusion with intelligence. He had been working for decades with an intelligence community that was focused on one question: the Soviet order of battle. But when the intelligence community had to move down the scale to low-intensity conflict, well . . ." His voice trailed off in the quiet disapproval of the disappointed professional.

"The first shock was on September 25, 2001, when Rumsfeld met with Charlie Holland," the Air Force general who then headed the U.S. Special Operations Command, which had been thrust into the limelight as one of the military commands most needed in response to al Qaeda's attack. "Holland laid out a bunch of targets," including a terrorist training camp in northwest Africa, an arms shipment point on the Somali coast, and a camp in the Philippines. "Rumsfeld's mouth was watering. 'When do we go?' And Holland said, 'Well, we can't because we lack actionable intelligence.'"

Rumsfeld was perturbed by that phrase, and seized on it. "What is 'actionable intelligence'?" the defense secretary began asking. "Is there such a type of intelligence that is 'inactionable'?" In the following weeks, Rumsfeld would take steps to substantially increase the role his office played in gathering and analyzing intelligence.

The Iraq war planning begins

Formal Pentagon consideration of how to attack Iraq began in November 2001, just after the fall of Kabul. By early December, Army Gen. Tommy R. Franks, the career artilleryman who had succeeded Zinni as head of the Central Command, was shuttling between his headquarters, located in Tampa, Florida, and Washington, D.C., reviewing planning for an invasion of Iraq. "There was a sense of urgency to get a conceptual plan in front of the president," recalled Air Force Maj. Gen. Victor Renuart, who held the key job of director of operations for the Central Command, and who accompanied Franks to most of his Washington meetings.

From the outset, there was tension between the uniformed military and the office of the secretary of defense (OSD) over two related issues: whether to attack Iraq, and if so, how many troops to use. Gen. Jack Keane, the Army's number-two officer, told colleagues that he thought that the United States should put aside the Iraq question and keep its eye on the ball. He recommended keeping two Army divisions—perhaps twenty-five thousand troops—on the Afghan-Pakistani border until bin Laden was captured and his organization there destroyed.

Caught between the Army's caution and Rumsfeld's impatience was the Central Command, commanded by Franks. Officials who served in that headquarters offer conflicting accounts of the role it played in the debate over the war plan, but there is general agreement that Franks became the fulcrum in the planning for the war. He could go either way—he was a career Army officer—but with the passage of time he sided with the Rumsfeld view. Franks was a cunning man, but not a deep thinker. He ran an extremely unhappy headquarters. He tended to berate subordinates, frequently shouting and cursing at them. Morale was poor, and people were tired, having worked nonstop since 9/11. "Central Command is two thousand indentured servants whose life is consumed by the whims of Tommy Franks," said one officer who worked closely with him. "Staff officers are conditioned like Pavlovian dogs. You can only resist for so long. It's like a prisoner-of-war camp—after a while, you break."

It wasn't just a matter of low spirits among staffers, this officer added. Franks's abusive style tended to distort the information that flowed upward to him. "I am convinced that much of the information that came out of Central Command is unreliable because he demands it instantly, so people pull it out of their hats. It's all SWAGs [scientific wild-assed guesses]. Also, everything has to be good news stuff. . . . You would find out you can't tell the truth."

All military staffs feel burdened on the eve of war, but Centcom was in the unusual position of planning the invasion of Iraq just a few months after carrying out the invasion of Afghanistan. It wasn't a good way to go into a war, especially under a commander perceived by some as unreceptive to contrary views. The extreme fatigue and low morale at his headquarters may explain in part why Franks and his staff would spend over a year figuring out how to take down a reeling, hollow regime, and give almost no serious thought to how to replace it. They would focus almost all their energies on the easier of the two tasks, with disastrous consequences for the U.S. position in postwar Iraq.

Many senior Army staff officers had worked at Centcom during the 1990s, and so were familiar with the series of war plans refined there during that decade.

Others had rotated through Kuwait. As a group, they were comfortable with the work that Zinni had left behind calling for a big invasion force of about 350,000 troops. But the world had changed, Renuart argued in an interview, so there was no longer a need for an invasion force of that size. "We had many more precision weapons," said the veteran pilot, who had commanded a fighter squadron in the 1991 Gulf War and later led units in both the northern and southern no-fly zones. "We'd been flying over Iraq for twelve years and had substantially degraded their air defenses. We had good ISR [intelligence, surveillance, and reconnaissance], and so good situational awareness of their ground forces."

The conclusions of Desert Crossing, Zinni's post–Desert Fox study, were taken into consideration but weren't a shaping factor, Renuart said. That plan envisioned attacking Iraq with three heavy armored divisions. "It wasn't discarded—it just didn't fit the planning constraints we were given," he said. Among those were to make the force smaller and faster than either the 1991 invasion force or Zinni's Desert Crossing force package. Ultimately, Gen. Franks would employ a plan that used just one heavy division to spearhead the attack, backed by the helicopter-rich 101st Airborne, as well as lighter elements—part of the 82nd Airborne and some Marine and British units.

Zinni said he heard a rather different account of why his plan was discarded late in 2002, which essentially was that Rumsfeld and his aides simply vetoed his work. "When the military guys, the Joint Staff [officers working on the staff of the Joint Chiefs of Staff] brought it up, the civilian leadership said, 'No, its assumptions are too pessimistic,'" he said.

Col. John Agoglia, who was the deputy chief of planning at Central Command, said that the quality of planning done under Zinni may have improved in Zinni's memory with the passage of time. "There wasn't as much as Zinni claimed there was," he said. "Desert Crossing? I don't remember that specific name," he added, in an interview. "But we looked at everything that was on the shelf." This casual dismissal of years of planning overseen by a highly regarded general isn't credible, but it illuminates the intellectually shoddy atmosphere that characterized war planning under Franks.

Indeed, contrary to Agoglia's account, another Centcom official, Gregory Hooker, the command's top intelligence analyst for Iraq, recalled that Zinni's Desert Crossing plan had been refined for years, even after Franks took over from him, and that it eventually was made the peace operations part of 1003-98, the standing Centcom war plan for the invasion of Iraq. Had it been heeded, the U.S. occupation might have had a smoother course.

Meanwhile, other powerful institutions were adding to the pressure to go to war.

Miller's tale

"An Iraqi defector who described himself as a civil engineer said he personally worked on renovations of secret facilities for biological, chemical and nuclear weapons," began a story carried by the *New York Times* under the byline of Judith Miller on December 20, 2001. The article featured the sort of piquant, unexpected details that bolstered its verisimilitude. For example, not only had Adnan Ihsan Saeed al-Haideri "personally visited at least 20 different sites" that he believed were part of Iraq's weapons programs, he also had installed Saddam Hussein's "first whirlpool bath."

It was a blockbuster for Miller, a Pulitzer Prize winner renowned for her sharp journalistic elbows. There was just one major problem with the story: It wasn't true, not one bit of it. As the *Columbia Journalism Review* noted in the summer of 2004, long after the invasion, "None of the weapons sites—which al-Haideri claimed were located beneath hospitals and behind palaces—have ever been located."

No one knew it at the time, but with that story Miller began one of the more dismal chapters in modern American journalism. She had lit the fuse of a running story about the Iraqi arsenal that eventually would blow up in her face, tarnishing not just her own career but also one of the proudest names in American journalism. The *New York Times,* the "paper of record," would carry more than its share of misinformed articles that helped drive the nation toward war in Iraq.

"That was a declaration of war"

Rep. Ike Skelton, the senior Democrat on the House Armed Services Committee, was alarmed as he listened to President Bush point to Iraq, Iran, and North Korea as threatening adversaries in his 2002 State of the Union address. "States like these and their terrorist allies constitute an axis of evil, arming to threaten the peace of the world," Bush warned. "We'll be deliberate; yet time is not on our side. I will not wait on events while dangers gather. I will not stand by as peril draws closer and closer. The United States of America will not permit the world's most dangerous regimes to threaten us with the world's most destructive weapons."

When the speech ended that January night, Skelton walked back across the Hill to his congressional office and glumly told his staff, "That was a declaration of war."

Skelton was a classic conservative Democrat from the heart of the heart of the country, representing a swath of twenty-five rural Missouri counties running from the edge of the Ozark Mountains north to the soybean fields along Interstate 70. His dream of attending West Point died when he was stricken with polio as a teenager, but he never lost his interest in the military, and especially in military education. He is so deeply read in military affairs that he once released a national security book list, a compilation of fifty volumes he considered key to understanding the armed forces. It is a thorough offering, heavy on American and British campaigns, but ranging from biographies of Alexander the Great and Hannibal to Grant's memoirs and strategic thinker Eliot Cohen's *Supreme Command*.

The more Skelton heard the Bush administration talk, the more he worried. The last of the Truman Democrats sensed he was about to be run over by the first of the twenty-first-century Republicans. For George W. Bush was a bit of a revolutionary, having much more in common with the freewheeling 1960s than did Isaac Newton Skelton, a restrained son of the middle border. In the following months Skelton would begin asking questions—including, why did there appear to be no plans for postwar Iraq?—and got few answers. For the next several years his unhappy role would be that of a congressional Cassandra, his foresight accurate but disregarded.

The next month Wolfowitz trekked to Munich for the Wehrkunde meetings, an annual conference on security issues that brought together scores of top European and American defense officials and politicians. There he confronted the contemptuous Germans. "Countries must make a choice," he told them, about whether they would join the United States as it sought to preempt the threats it perceived in Iraq, Iran, and North Korea. He and Joseph Lieberman, the conservative Connecticut Democrat whose mother-in-law had been held in the Dachau concentration camp just a few miles away, received moralistic responses from German and French politicians. Another member of the congressional delegation, Sen. John McCain, the Arizona Republican, stood up at the end of the meeting to voice his support for Lieberman and Wolfowitz. The unified U.S. front seemed to make it clear: The United States had Iraq in its sights.

And it was going to be easy, some added. Rumsfeld's onetime assistant, Ken Adelman, sought to argue away worries about invading Iraq. "I believe demolishing Hussein's military power and liberating Iraq would be a cakewalk," he wrote for the *Washington Post*'s op-ed page in memorably provocative language. "Let me give simple, responsible reasons: 1. it was a cakewalk last time; 2. they've become much weaker; 3. we've become much stronger; and 4. now we're playing for keeps." What's more, he wrote, there was a clear and present danger. "Hussein constitutes the number one threat against American security and civilization. Unlike Osama bin Laden, he has billions in government funds, scores of government research labs working feverishly on weapons of mass destruction—and just as deep a hatred of America and civilized free societies." It was rash, over the top, and characteristic of the debate at the time. And, as subsequent investigation by the U.S. government determined, it was wildly wrong in its feverish assertion about those scores of Iraqi laboratories.

While Wolfowitz was in Munich, Central Command's rough draft of a plan for the invasion of Iraq began circulating quietly in parts of the Pentagon. "The initial timetable was 1 October"—just over half a year away—recalled one planning officer who was handed the document in an office of the Joint Staff one February afternoon. The plan led to a series of war games titled Prominent Hammer that sought, among other things, to judge the regional impact of a war in Iraq, as well as the strain that a war would impose on the U.S. military. Each game—a tabletop exercise in which likely second- and third-order consequences were gauged—took three or four days to play out, and each was followed by an in-depth staff analysis that kept parts of the Joint Staff working days stretching from 6:00 A.M. to 10:00 P.M.

In the first part of May, the conclusions of the first two games were sent across the Potomac to the White House to brief President Bush. Essentially, the briefing concluded that October would be too soon to invade Iraq. There were two major reasons offered. First, the planning officer recalled, "you've got to set the conditions" to lower the political risks of going to war, by conducting an intense round of preparatory diplomacy. Also, there was a shortage of precision-guided weapons: "We'd just dropped a bunch of PGMs in Afghanistan [over the previous six months], and based on the combatant commander's statement, it would take several months to get back up" to the level needed to go to war. In the wake of that briefing the military had a sense that it had won some breathing room in the debate. The sense that an invasion of Iraq was imminent was undercut.

The officers on the Joint Staff also thought they had given Franks the analytical results he needed to persuade Rumsfeld to go with a larger number of troops. "Rumsfeld is a great bureaucratic infighter," recalled the planner. "He's also not as doctrinal as people think." In this officer's account, Rumsfeld put on the table Gen. Downing's plan for invading Iraq with just ten thousand troops as a bargaining move, done in the knowledge that the existing Central Command invasion plan, written under Gen. Zinni, called for an invasion force of at least three hundred thousand. What's more, Rumsfeld almost certainly knew that the invasion force ultimately chosen would be closer in size to Zinni's than to Downing's.

But he was going to make the military fight for every incremental increase in the size of the force. "A lot of folks say the military rolled over" for Rumsfeld, this officer concluded. "We didn't. We did the best we could."

Gen. Franks sometimes makes assertions that are wildly inaccurate, but he offers them with great certitude. One such occasion was May 21, 2002, when he was asked at a press conference about the size of the force that would be required to invade Iraq. At this point planning for the mission had been under way for several months. There already had been two major Commanders' Conferences inside the military to consider the course of action, and the president had already been briefed four times on the plan. At least one of those presidential discussions was quite thorough, recalled Col. Agoglia. Franks could have deflected the question by saying that he didn't respond to hypotheticals, or he could have been blunt and said that he didn't discuss planning for possible future operations. Or he could have evaded it as Bush sometimes did, by saying he didn't have a plan "on his desk." But instead he quibbled. "That's a great question, and one for which I don't have an answer," he said, "because my boss has not yet asked me to put together a plan for that."

Nor did he leave the issue there. Instead, he elaborated on his untruth: "Beyond speculation that I read much about in the press, my bosses have not asked me to put together anything yet, and so they have not asked me for those kinds of numbers. And I guess I would tell you, if there comes a time when my boss asks me that, then I'd rather provide those sorts of assessments to him. But thanks for the question." (In his autobiography, Franks would weakly claim that "it was the truth. In May 2002, we were offering the president options, not a plan.")

The birth of preemption

In June 2002 Bush traveled to West Point to drop the other shoe. There, at the most identifiably Army post in the nation, the U.S. Military Academy, he made preemption the national strategy—an astonishing departure from decades of practice and two centuries of tradition. Henceforth, the United States was prepared to attack before threats became full-fledged. "We must take the battle to the enemy, disrupt his plans, and confront the worst threats before they emerge," Bush told the cadets assembled on West Point's football field. "If we wait for threats to fully materialize, we will have waited too long." Between the State of the Union address and the West Point speech, Bush had shown the political route toward attacking Iraq. The first speech had done the targeting—that is, stated the goal. The West Point speech provided the doctrinal, or intellectual, rationale for doing it.

It was that month that Renuart, sitting in the hot seat of operations director at Central Command, began to believe that the war plan he was working on for Iraq was going to be executed. But his discussions were extremely "close hold," he recalled, really involving just Rumsfeld and Franks, with Bush and Cheney briefed on occasion. "Franks was told to keep a very tight control on decisionmaking, with it [just a matter of] Rumsfeld to Franks, and a lot of decisions pushed up to Franks" that usually would have been handled by lower ranking officials, but who in this case were not included in the planning. One unfortunate side effect of this narrowing seems to have been to limit consideration both of dissenting views and of longer term issues—two problems that Franks already had experienced in his handling of the war in Afghanistan, which insiders said had been extremely messy.

Those who could read the Bush administration best saw that war was coming, even before there had been much public debate. Two very different meetings bring this home—one among top British officials in London, the other among Marine commanders near San Diego. In midsummer, Sir Richard Dearlove, the head of MI6, the British intelligence agency, came to Washington for meetings at the CIA and with other officials. When he returned to London, he met with the top officials in the British national security establishment. "There was a perceptible shift in attitude" in the Bush administration, he told his colleagues on July 23, according to a memo summarizing the talk that subsequently was leaked. "Military action was now seen as inevitable. Bush wanted to remove Saddam, through military action, justified by the conjunction of terrorism and WMD. But the intelligence and facts were being fixed around the policy. . . . There was little discussion in Washington of the aftermath after military action."

A few weeks later, on August 3, 2002, Maj. Gen. James Mattis, one of the more perceptive senior officers in the U.S. military, took over as commander of the 1st Marine Division. That afternoon, at his first staff meeting, he called in his commanders, his senior sergeants, and his top staff officers. "It became immediately obvious that he had gathered them for a single purpose: To give them a warning order for the invasion of Iraq," the draft of the official Marine history of the division reports. Mattis wasn't operating on any secret information, just an understanding of how the world worked, he said later. "The commander's job is to be a sentinel for his unit, and focus it," he explained.

Persistent doubts at the Pentagon

But much of the top brass wasn't persuaded of the wisdom of invading Iraq. Especially in the Army, there were profound doubts both about invading Iraq and about adopting a policy of preemption. Even one of the few military men Rumsfeld listened to, a retired four-star general, said at the time that containment was the way to go: He argued that what the U.S. government wanted was a secular, unified Iraq led by someone kinder and gentler than Saddam—and that was what it was getting closer to every day, as Saddam aged and weakened.

That summer many generals had three major concerns about invading Iraq: the possibility of Saddam's using weapons of mass destruction, the danger of becoming enmeshed in urban warfare, and the worry that a postwar occupation could be costly, especially if the United States had to put in thousands of troops to hold the country together. "I can't tell you how many senior officers said to me, 'What in the hell are we doing?'" recalled Marine Lt. Gen. Gregory Newbold, who had been the J-3, or director of operations on the Joint Staff, since October 2000. In that key job he oversaw the daily employment of U.S. forces around the globe, and so was the link between the Pentagon and senior American commanders in the field. Those top officers and their staffs were coming back to Newbold. "They just didn't understand," he recalled. "'Why Iraq? Why now?'" They were especially worried about undercutting the counteroffensive against al Qaeda: "All of us understood the fight was against the terrorists, and we were willing to do anything in that regard—so, 'Why are we diverting assets and attention?'"

Yet for all those doubts, only one top officer really deeply objected to the entire war plan. That was Newbold, who as the Joint Staff's director of operations was aware of almost everything of significance going on in the U.S. military, and to the classified information it was receiving. "I had virtual access to every bit of intelligence other than the presidential daily briefings," he said in subsequent congressional testimony. "I think I had one hundred percent other than that. And I participated in all the planning . . . of operations for Afghanistan and all the planning for operations for Iraq."

Many other senior officers weren't as opposed as Newbold but still were worried about the particulars of the plan. Despite Franks's determined efforts to keep them from reviewing it, some began to get glimpses. One officer spent a summer weekend studying Annex Bravo, the intelligence section of the war plan. He came away deeply puzzled by a major discrepancy in its treatment of weapons of mass destruction. "The target list didn't match the text," he said. "The text was full of 'we're not sure, we don't know this.'" But then, when he turned to the target list, it offered, as if certain of its information, "about one hundred 'confirmed or positive' weapons of mass destruction sites." Nor did the plan assess the impact on the region: "It was completely stovepiped on Iraq—nothing about terrorism, or the impact on Saudi Arabia." This was just incomplete work, in his view. He sent his comments along, but never received a response.

Also on the Joint Staff was Army Brig. Gen. Mark Hertling, the J-7, or director for operational plans, who also had concerns. "Hertling goes to the director of the Joint Staff, and said he was so worried about the errors," said an administration official involved in defense policy. Hertling's military specialty was war planning, this official noted.

"As the J-7 I was involved in several things concerning the planning of both the conflict and the postconflict operations, and there were some interesting things going on then," Hertling explained in 2004. "And I did approach a few folks concerning what I saw as some shortcomings that later came to fruition." Asked later to elaborate on those inadequacies, Hertling declined, saying, "Because of classification levels, I'm not going to clarify any part of that conversation. Suffice it to say that there were several issues discussed in that meeting, some involved the plan, some involved my thoughts about how it would be executed based on my knowledge of training and capabilities, some explorations of alternative courses of action, and some other things that I believed were not being properly considered by those who were supervising the plan and the sourcing of the plan."

There were two basic points of friction between the military and senior Pentagon civilians over the war planning for Iraq. The first was the role that those civilians would play in formulating the plan. The second was the number of troops that those civilians thought were needed. "They were into precision targeting, use of proxy forces, and minimizing the ground forces," said an officer familiar with the exchanges that went on at that time. In fighting in Afghanistan in 2001 and 2002, Rumsfeld's office achieved that minimization by having Gen. Franks impose a "force cap" that sharply limited the number of troops in the country. This cap caused much angst among commanders, because it required them to leave behind parts of their units, which in turn forced them to violate the U.S. military maxim of fighting as you train, especially fighting alongside those with whom you train. This became controversial at the battle of the Shahikot Valley in March 2002 when the Army, executing Operation Anaconda, lacked artillery pieces to hit al Qaeda forces who had heavy machine guns dug in under overhanging cliffs, cleverly creating positions that couldn't be struck from the air.

Even with that experience, the emphasis on keeping a ceiling on the number of ground forces would become a key aspect of the planning for the invasion of Iraq. "There was always pressure from OSD—could we do it smaller?" recalled Col. Agoglia, the Central Command planner.

The military concerns bubbled under the surface but never rose to the level of confrontation, said a senior officer on the Joint Staff: "All this dissent—the truth of it is, there were lots of concerns, anxieties, and private conversations, but it never went public, or into a formal dissent."

When Rumsfeld was asked about the worries being expressed inside the military—and specifically about a *Washington Post* article that summarized those concerns using mainly unnamed sources—his response was both disingenuous and dismissive. "You know, the Pentagon's a big place—hundreds and hundreds of thousands of military personnel, hundreds of thousands of civilian personnel," he said at a press conference at the headquarters of the Joint Forces Command in Suffolk, Virginia. "Any reporter who wants to can go find one or more that'll have a position on any issue, all the way across the spectrum. Then what they do is, they write stories that seem to fit what they feel might make a good story. And they go around and ask questions until they find people that say those things, and then they print.

"Now, I don't know," he continued. "They don't say who those people are. So I can't go and say, 'Gee, have you got a better idea?' Can't seem to do that. Who they are, no one knows. It's a big mystery, and life's like that."

The officers who were talking to the *Post* and other news outlets, Rumsfeld concluded, were ill informed. The defense secretary said he talked to senior military officers all the time and didn't hear such concerns. "They all have every opportunity in the world to express their views, to discuss things. And they do, and they do it intelligently, and they do it constructively, and they don't do it to the press. Now, if they're not doing it to the press, somebody else is doing it to the press, and it's obviously somebody who knows a heck of a lot less than they do." Thus, in Rumsfeld's formulation, military dissent about Iraq had to be considered the result of ignorance.

To some at Central Command's headquarters in Tampa, the view was less mysterious. Hooker, the command's lead intelligence analyst for Iraq, later would blame Rumsfeld squarely for undermining the formulation of the war plan. From the outset, he said, the disagreements between Rumsfeld's office and the military—about whether to invade Iraq, and if so, how many troops to use—were rooted in conflicting assessments of the threat Iraq presented and the difficulties that would result from invading and occupying the country. But instead of examining and reconciling the differences, Hooker wrote, Rumsfeld and Franks let them fester for months as Rumsfeld pushed for a smaller invasion force. "There was no authoritative, systematic review and consolidation of viewpoints between intelligence producers and senior policymakers," Hooker concluded in a postwar analysis of intelligence problems in the war plan. Rather than determine which point of view was correct, the planners simply split the difference, he wrote.

It appears likely that Rumsfeld's intervention, especially his demand that three successive versions of the invasion plan be produced, didn't improve planning and, in fact, weakened it. "The continual production of new operational concepts had a cost—it contributed to the inadequate development" of the final plan, Hooker wrote. "The iterative approach, with its greater involvement of the OSD in the process of deliberate military planning, injected numerous ideas into the dialogue, many of which were amateurish and unrealistic."

The strains of containment

It was one thing to enforce the containment policy before 9/11, but after it, Afghanistan and other smaller actions were keeping parts of the Air Force—air lift, AWAC command-and-control aircraft, and refuelers—extremely busy. By late 2001, parts of the U.S. military felt badly stretched by enforcing the policy of containment. An average of thirty-four thousand sorties—that is, one mission by one airplane—were flown a year in the no-fly zones, which, as Michael Knights later noted, amounted to the equivalent of flying the 1991 Gulf War every three years.

One of the best places to see the effects of this pace was Prince Sultan Air Base, an isolated facility on the edge of Saudi Arabia's Empty Quarter that was home to the Air Force planes and pilots who patrolled the big southern no-fly zone over Iraq. With swimming pools, tennis courts, and movies, all inside a big chain-link fence with guard towers, it was half prison, half spa. It was a miragelike place that would exist for just six years, having been created in 1997 following the Khobar Towers bombing and then shut down shortly after the U.S. military took Baghdad in 2003.

The hermetically sealed enclave of low buildings, guard towers, and checkpoints stretched across the flat, gravelly wasteland 70 miles southeast of Riyadh, the Saudi capital. On the southern side of the base, there was nothing on the horizon but horizon—maps indicated that for several hundred miles there lay only one road. Air Force Brig. Gen. Dale "Muddy" Waters, commander of the base's 363rd Air Expeditionary Wing, described the outpost as "a tract of 250 square miles, literally in the middle of nowhere."

Capt. Shawn Coco, an F-15 pilot from Baton Rouge, Lousiana, described his typical workday, which revolved around five-hour missions into the Container, as pilots called the no-fly zone over southern Iraq: "Forty-five minutes to Iraq, hit the tanker [for refueling], go into the Container, then go back to the tanker, go back in, and you're done." At night he played sports, watched movies, and studied for his master's degree. Except for missions in the air, he had never been off the base. In fact, U.S. policy was that no one could leave the base to go elsewhere in Saudi Arabia, except on official business, and even then only with approval from headquarters.

When they finished their duties for the day—or for the night, when no-fly-zone missions often were conducted—the four thousand U.S. personnel stationed on PSAB, as they acronymized it, would ride several miles across the red sands to the big rectangular compound where they lived, itself sealed off from the rest of the base by multiple checkpoints and barbed-wire fences.

"It's not too different from a college dorm," Maj. Chuck Anthony, a spokesman for the base, said hopefully.

But officials knew what it looked like, with its two-story, sand-colored living quarters surrounded by a ring of tall guard towers. "The fact of the matter is that people at Prince Sultan are actually living in a prison," Gen. Chuck Wald, a former commander of U.S. air forces in the region, once said at an Air Force gathering.

Inside the fence was an odd little American wonderland that felt as if it were run by a particularly watchful but benevolent correctional authority. On one Sunday in January 2003, lunch at Camel Lot, one of the facility's three whimsically named mess halls (the other two were the Mirage and the Rolling Sands), was beef stroganoff or baked chicken, along with sandwiches, soup, and a salad bar, all served under a large-screen TV playing CNN. Across the way four forgettable but distracting movies were showing under a large rubberized tent—*The Sum of All Fears, Mr. Deeds, Insomnia,* and *The Bourne Identity.* Nearby was a library and a pool, the latter closed during the brief Arabian winter when it was too cool to swim comfortably but a welcome relief when summer temperatures reached 120 degrees. A jogging track encircled the entire facility.

Despite the amenities, troops seemed eager to head home. At Boot Hill, a mock graveyard built in the desert behind an aviation fuel storage area, a picket fence encircled more than two hundred pairs of boots slung over the pretend grave sites. A sign warned that Air Force personnel should not look back after burying their boots or they would be doomed to return for another tour of duty here. For many of the troops there, it was a curse that had come true many times.

Capt. John Rhone, a weapons control officer in AWACs planes, said that in his seven and a half years in the Air Force he had done seven rotations at Prince Sultan. He was growing tired of this life. "I think I'm ready for a break," he said.

Lt. Col. Matt Molloy, an animated young F-15 squadron commander, noted that in 2002 alone his men and women had flown out of nine countries—Saudi Arabia, Turkey, Malaysia, Thailand, Australia, South Korea, Japan, Iceland, and the United States. "We need to put this thing to the north to rest," he said, pointing across the room in the direction of Iraq. "My airframes are cracking. We are doing too much with what we've got."

"We're running back-to-back marathons," added Capt. Scovill Currin, a tanker pilot from Charleston, South Carolina. "The airplanes may not be able to take it, and more importantly, the people may not. At some point you've got to say, I love my country, but I can't stay away from my family for eight years."

4.

THE WAR OF WORDS

AUGUST 2002

In August 2002 the tone of the Bush administration's rhetoric changed sharply. That was the month, said Greg Thielmann, then director of proliferation issues in the State Department's intelligence bureau, when "the administration started speaking about Iraq in much shriller tones." It no longer was just a concern that needed watching; it became "an imminent security threat that has to be dealt with right away."

It also was the time when the administration's public statements about Iraq's weapons grew more distant from the intelligence on which they were supposedly based, said Thielmann, who a month later retired from his job at the State Department, not in protest but privately disturbed by what he later called the administration's "sustained campaign of misrepresenting the intelligence on Iraq."

Scowcroft says no to war

The debate on invading Iraq effectively began with two days of hearings held by the Senate Foreign Relations Committee on July 31 and August 1. These discussions with eighteen experts on national security and the Middle East spurred widespread discussion, most notably by sending Brent Scowcroft into public opposition to Bush administration policy on Iraq.

So-called Republican realists, no fans of the neoconservatives, were alarmed by the shift they saw in the administration's posture. This group, which included many veterans of the first Bush administration, saw Colin Powell as its primary ally inside the government. Scowcroft, national security adviser to the first president Bush, staked out the realist position on CBS's *Face the Nation,* where he warned that a U.S. invasion of Iraq "could turn the whole region into a cauldron, and thus destroy the war on terrorism." A few days later he made a more comprehensive argument on the editorial page of the *Wall Street Journal*—a significant location because the *Journal*'s conservative editorial page sometimes acts like an internal bulletin board for Republican policy making. Scowcroft's article appeared in the newspaper's edition of August 15, 2002, under the headline DON'T ATTACK SADDAM.

"We will all be better off when he is gone," the retired general and Bush family confidant began. But he wanted to know what the case was for doing so at the moment. There was "scant evidence to tie Saddam to terrorist organizations, and even less to the Sept. 11 attacks." What's more, there "is little evidence to indicate that the United States itself is an object of his aggression." So, Scowcroft methodically proceeded, attacking Iraq would undercut the U.S. counteroffensive against terrorism.

Some of his secondary points were prescient, such as his prediction that a "military campaign very likely would have to be followed by a large-scale, long-term military occupation." Others were less so, such as his concern that a cornered Saddam would hit Israel with weapons of mass destruction, possibly provoking a nuclear response. Scowcroft was most worried by the regional effects. His bottom line: "If we reject a comprehensive perspective, however, we put at risk our campaign against terrorism as well as stability and security in a vital region of the world."

That heavy, Latinate, noble-sounding sentence captures the essence of Scowcroft's problem, because it reflects his misreading of the thinking of the Bush administration after 9/11. Wolfowitz and Cheney had split with the wisdom of the first Bush administration that stability was the lodestar of American foreign policy. The first Bush had been shaped by World War II. The second Bush was a product of the 1960s, at times more in sync with the attitudes of sixties radical Jerry Rubin than with those of Winston Churchill. Efforts by the so-called realists such as Scowcroft and James Baker to produce stability had led to decrepit regimes, sallow economies, and growing terrorism, the new president's men said.

If you liked 9/11, they said quietly, just keep it up. "Stability" wasn't their *goal*, it was their *target*. They saw it as synonymous with stagnation. They wanted radical change in the Mideast. They were determined to drain the swamp—that is, to alter the political climate of the region so that it would no longer be so hospitable to the terrorists inhabiting it. A less charitable way of putting it was that they were willing, a bit like Jerry Rubin, to take a chance and then groove on the ensuing rubble.

In the following days, Republican mandarins Henry Kissinger and James Baker issued their own warnings to President Bush. A spate of cautionary articles echoing Scowcroft's concerns also appeared in the following weeks in publications aimed at military professionals. Retired Army Gen. Frederick Kroesen, a former commander of the U.S. Army in Europe, asked in an article in *Army* magazine if the invasion plan rested on incorrect assumptions. Army Special Forces Maj. Roger Carstens argued in *Proceedings*, the professional journal of the Navy, that the Bush administration needed to clearly state its long-term goals for Iraq. In *Army Times*, an independent newspaper, retired Army Lt. Col. Ralf Zimmerman said it was time for the American people to think through the issue. "Maybe we should have an open public debate over war vs. containment as the proper option when dealing with Iraq," he cautioned. The messages reflected concerns among many senior officers: This was not a military straining to go to war.

Like nighttime clouds illuminated by flashes of distant artillery fire, the public discussion reflected dimly the fight inside the Bush administration. Powell—who was not only the secretary of state, but a retired four-star general who maintained ties to the top brass—launched a final effort to stop the run-up to war. Bob Woodward relates in his book *Plan of Attack* how Powell sat down with Bush on the evening of August 5, first over dinner and then in the president's office in his residence. "You are going to be the proud owner of twenty-five million people," Powell said, according to Woodward. "You will own all their hopes, aspirations, and problems. . . . It's going to suck the oxygen out of everything. . . . This will become the first term."

But Condi Rice, who knew Bush better, read the situation differently. Rather than trying to stop the move toward war, she was constructing the bureaucratic machinery to coordinate the execution of the war. On August 14, according to Woodward, she chaired a principals' meeting on a draft of a strategy for Iraq. She also took a major bureaucratic step toward war, taking control of an interagency group then being run by the staff of the Joint Chiefs at the Pentagon and putting one of her own NSC subordinates, Franklin Miller, in charge. Renamed the Executive Steering Group, and including representatives from the State Department, the CIA, the White House, the Joint Chiefs, and the Pentagon's policy operation, this body was charged with coordinating about one hundred government actions leading up to the invasion, such as securing the use of bases in the region, improving them so they could support U.S. military operations, and getting overflight permission from other countries.

Cheney says "no doubt" on Iraqi WMD

Vice President Cheney emphatically shut down the nascent debate on August 26 when he asserted, "There is no doubt" that Iraq possessed weapons of mass destruction, or WMD. In a speech to the national convention of the Veterans of Foreign Wars at the Opryland Hotel in Nashville, Cheney flatly called for war, proclaiming that Iraq was a clear and present danger to the United States. After a few preliminary niceties, the vice president struck his theme: "The president and I never for a moment forget our number-one responsibility: To protect the American people against further attack and to win the war that began last September eleventh." Despite various measures like creating a Department of Homeland Security, he said, "We realize that wars are never won on the defensive. We must take the battle to the enemy."

In retrospect, the speech is even more stunning than it appeared to be then, because it has become clear with the passage of time that it constructed a case that was largely false. Containment may have worked in the Cold War, Cheney said, but is "not possible when dictators obtain weapons of mass destruction and are prepared to share them with terrorists who intend to inflict catastrophic casualties on the United States." It was time to be "candid," he said. "The Iraqi regime has in fact been very busy enhancing its capabilities in the field of chemical and biological agents, and they continue to pursue the nuclear program they began so many years ago. . . . Many of us are convinced that Saddam Hussein will acquire nuclear weapons fairly soon." Nothing the U.S. government had tried in the previous decade had stopped Saddam, Cheney warned—not inspections, not the revelations of defectors, not Desert Fox. "Simply stated, there is no doubt that Saddam Hussein now has weapons of mass destruction," he said, as flatly as possible. "There is no doubt that he is amassing them to use against our friends, against our allies, and against us."

Not only that, but the situation was getting worse. "Time is not on our side," Cheney added. "The risks of inaction are far greater than the risks of action."

Zinni goes into opposition

Anthony Zinni, recently retired from the Marine Corps, sat behind Cheney on the stage that day as the speech was delivered. Zinni was there to receive the VFW's Dwight D. Eisenhower Distinguished Service Award in recognition of his thirty-five years as a Marine. He had been a Bush-Cheney supporter in the 2000 campaign. But as he listened to the vice president in Nashville he nearly fell off his chair. "In my time at Centcom, I watched the intelligence and never—not once—did it say, 'He has WMD.'" Since retiring he had retained all his top-secret clearances, he was still consulting with the CIA on Iraq, he had reviewed all the current intelligence—and he had seen nothing to support Cheney's certitude. "It was never there, never there," he said later. These guys are going to war without the evidence to back them up, he thought to himself that day. His second chilling thought, he recalled, was that they didn't understand what they were getting into.

For his part, he couldn't figure out the change in Cheney. In Zinni's experience, the vice president was a realist, a hardheaded man who demanded the hard facts. From their encounters in Arab capitals in the 1990s, he had said, he had come to think of Cheney as very practical. But that wasn't what he was seeing that August day in Nashville. "When he sort of got tied up and embraced all this, it seemed to be out of character, it really confused me." What he didn't know then was that Cheney had changed—perhaps because he knew the Bush administration hadn't performed well in heeding warnings before 9/11, or perhaps because of his heart ailments, which can alter a person's personality.

Like many Marines, Zinni doesn't shy away from a fight. He is an engaging conversationalist, even an intellectual at times. But he also steps easily into confrontation, verbal or physical. When two men tried once a few years ago to mug him at a rest stop on I-95, he slugged one and, pretending he had a gun, chased the other away. And so he went into opposition. Zinni would feel at times that no one was really listening to him, but his principles made him persist. Just as Wolfowitz's outlook was shaped to a surprising degree by the Holocaust, Zinni's was formed on a cold day in November 1970, when he lay on a monsoon-soaked hillside west of Danang, his lifeblood seeping into the dirt from three North Vietnamese AK-47 rounds in his side and back. In subsequent operations, one third of his back muscle was removed. While recuperating, he vowed that if he ever had a chance to stop a situation like this from happening again to another young soldier, he would.

After watching Cheney in Nashville, Zinni stewed for some time. One day that fall, he went fishing with a close friend, retired Marine Lt. Gen. Paul Van Riper.

"Rip, there are no weapons of mass destruction programs in Iraq," Zinni told Van Riper. "There may be some isolated weapons, though I doubt even that, but no programs as you and I would think of them."

In early October, Zinni went public with his doubts. "I'm not convinced we need to do this now," he told a meeting of the Middle East Institute. Of Saddam, he said, "I believe he is . . . containable at this moment." There were other priorities in U.S. foreign policy. "My personal view is, I think this isn't number one—it's maybe sixth or seventh."

But Zinni's cause was already lost. Inside the Bush administration, Cheney's speech hit like a preemptive strike. Bush himself had been at his ranch in Crawford, Texas, when it was delivered. "My understanding was that the president himself was very surprised at that speech, because it was kind of constraining his options," said a former senior Bush administration official. "It had the effect of somewhat limiting the president's options, in my view."

Cheney's speech had a powerful effect elsewhere in the government. His hardline no debate stance was adopted by others in the administration. "We know they have weapons of mass destruction," Rumsfeld would assert a month later at a Pentagon briefing. "We know they have active programs. There isn't any debate about it."

Cheney's certitude also dampened skepticism in the intelligence community. "When the vice president stood up and said 'We are sure'—well, who are we to argue?" said the senior military intelligence official. "With all the compartmentalization, there's a good chance that a guy that senior has seen stuff you haven't." Some analysts figured Cheney must have been told about a piece of highly classified "crown jewel" information to which lower ranking officials lacked access.

In fact, Cheney played that insider's card himself, dismissively telling Tim Russert in an appearance on *Meet the Press* on September 8, 2002, that those who doubted his assertions about the threat presented by Iraq haven't "seen all the intelligence that we have seen."

Outside the government, Cheney's certainty framed the debate in a way that powerfully helped the administration. He had put the opposition on the defensive, effectively saying, If you think I'm wrong, prove it. After this point the Bush administration's statements about Iraq were not so much part of a debate about whether to go to war, they were part of a campaign to sell it—from Bush's appearance at the United Nations to the congressional vote, and ultimately to Powell's appearance at the UN six months later. Most important, the administration itself fell into line. In the following weeks, first Condoleezza Rice and then Bush himself would adopt the alarmist tone that Cheney had struck that day in Nashville.

A flawed NIE does the trick

In September 2002 the U.S. intelligence community prepared a comprehensive summary, called a National Intelligence Estimate, or NIE, of what it knew about "Iraq's Continuing Programs for Weapons of Mass Destruction"—the title of the ninety-two-page classified version of the report. It was prepared at the request of members of Congress who expected to vote on going to war with Iraq and wanted something on which to base their vote. Written by a group of senior intelligence officers and then approved by the leaders of the U.S. intelligence community, the estimate pulled together in one place the core data of the Bush administration's argument for going to war. It reported that Iraq possessed chemical and biological weapons, was making advances in developing ways to weaponize and deliver biological weapons, and was "reconstituting its nuclear program." The report appeared more certain on all fronts than previous intelligence assessments, but the finding on the nuclear program was especially surprising, because it was a shift from a series of previous conclusions by the intelligence community. In fact, the estimate amounted to a serious misrepresentation of views in the intelligence community, maximizing alarming findings while minimizing internal doubts about them. It effectively presented opinion as fact.

The effect of this NIE can't be underestimated, said one general who talked frequently to Rumsfeld during this time. During the summer of 2002, he said, both Bush and Rumsfeld had been on the fence. "Cheney, Wolfowitz, and Armitage were the hawks," he remembered. Each argued that "we had to get rid of this guy, that time isn't on our side, and that there will be no better time to get rid of him." On the other side of the argument were Colin Powell and some lesser figures in the administration. They "thought it was time to leverage the international community, especially since we'd scared the hell out of everybody."

But then came the NIE, which had been pushed out unusually quickly, in just a few weeks. Bush's view became that CIA director George Tenet says they have WMD, and Cheney says don't get caught napping again like we did on 9/11, this general recalled. "The president became convinced" by that document and by Tenet's interpretation of it, "that [going to war] was the right thing to do."

Over a year later, when the Senate Intelligence Committee reviewed the NIE in light of evidence that became available after the war, it came to the conclusion that the collective wisdom of the U.S. intelligence community, as represented in the estimate, had been stunningly wrong. "Most of the major key judgments [in the NIE] either overstated, or were not supported by, the underlying intelligence reporting," it would find. "A series of failures, particularly in analytic trade craft, led to the mischaracterization of the intelligence." Moreover, the errors and exaggerations weren't random, but all pushed in the same direction, toward making the argument that Iraq presented a growing threat. As a political document that made the case for war the NIE of October 2002 succeeded brilliantly. As a professional intelligence product it was shameful. But it did its job, which wasn't really to assess Iraqi weapons programs but to sell a war. There was only one way to disprove its assertions: invade Iraq, which is what the Bush administration wanted to do. Responsibility for this low point in the history of U.S. intelligence must rest on the shoulders of George Tenet.

Redefining the intelligence

Richard Perle's influence in the events leading up to war likely has been overstated. At the time the chairman of the Defense Policy Board, he also seems to have wielded some influence with the office of Vice President Cheney. Perle's main role, at least in public, seems to have been the one willing to be quoted in the media, saying in public what his more discreet allies in the Bush administration, such as I. Lewis "Scooter" Libby, Cheney's chief of staff, would say to reporters only on background.

Perle resembles Wolfowitz in his approach—bright, incisive, and somewhat academic in tone, with an air of deliberation and precision. Yet while Wolfowitz seeks to persuade, Perle attacks, often seeming eager to pounce on his opponents' capabilities and to cast doubt on their integrity or intelligence. He also has a habit of making doubtful assertions as though they were generally accepted facts—such as his belief, now known to be wildly off base, that Saddam Hussein "was far stronger at the end of Clinton's tenure than at the beginning."

Perle would later explain how, at the Pentagon, analysts working for Feith, his old subordinate who had become under secretary of defense for policy, produced their alarming interpretation of the murky intelligence about Saddam Hussein, WMD, and terrorism. "Within a very short period of time, they began to find links that nobody else had previously understood or recorded in a useful way," he said of those analysts. "They [noticed] things that nobody else had noticed. It was there all along, it simply hadn't been noticed." This key information had been overlooked "because the CIA and DIA [Defense Intelligence Agency] were not looking."

The way he described it, all that was needed was the fresh, unbiased eye of competent analysts—which in his view was provided by Feith's office at the

Pentagon. "The whinging, the complaints from the intelligence establishment who had overlooked this material, [are] really quite pathetic." Perle's argument, ultimately, was that he and his allies simply were better at parsing the data than were their opponents in the intelligence community: "Let me be blunt about this: The level of competence on past performance of the Central Intelligence Agency, in this area, is appalling."

It was at this point that the Bush administration's views diverged from that of the intelligence community. "There wasn't anyone in the intelligence community who was saying what" the Pentagon analysts around Feith were saying, a senior military intelligence official recalled. "There were a few stray analysts who connected some of those dots, but no one in the mainstream." The NIE, and especially its doubt-free summary version, offered only a dim and distorted reflection of their views.

This particular official is more sympathetic than most of his peers to the Bush administration, but still emphatically rejects the administration's ex post facto defense that everybody got it wrong. The core conclusion of the best intelligence analysts was, he said, that "we were looking for evidence, but we weren't finding it." But the failure to stop 9/11 had tarnished the credibility of the intelligence professionals, and lessened the deference that others might give them. On top of that, relative amateurs working for Feith and Cheney felt free to seize on existing bits of data and push them as hard as they could, this official added. "They would take individual factoids, build them into long lists, and then think because of the length of the list, it was credible." When the lists were rejected by intelligence professionals, they would be leaked to friendly journalists.

Yet even with that sort of pressure from Feith's office, he concluded, "There was never a bow wave in the intelligence community for this case." That is, the appearance of consensus that the NIE gave was a false one, especially because it underplayed the lack of solid information about what had happened to Iraq's weapons programs since Desert Fox. Also, there was a long-range worry. Intelligence analysts calculated that if current trends continued, sooner or later, Saddam Hussein definitely again would obtain those munitions of mass death. "In the back of our minds, at the fringes of the discussion, was: If we don't do something now, then he would eventually dupe the UN, get the sanctions lifted, and we lose containment. Then he has money and new power, and he opens up his plants, and he is back in business."

Others lower in the intelligence hierarchy are less forgiving of themselves and of the Bush administration. Basically, said Greg Thielmann, the State Department

proliferation expert, the administration was looking for evidence to support conclusions it already had reached. "They were convinced that Saddam was developing nuclear weapons, that he was reconstituting his program, and I'm afraid that's
where they started," he said. "They were cherry-picking the information that we
provided to use whatever pieces of it that fit their overall interpretation. Worse
than that, they were dropping qualifiers and distorting some of the information
that we provided to make it seem even more alarmist and dangerous than the information that we were giving them." The impulse to push the conclusions was
especially worrisome, he added, because the intelligence community, not wanting
to be caught napping, already tends "to overwarn, rather than underwarn."

"What I saw was that a lot of analysts, of low-level people, had it about right,"
said a senior military intelligence official specializing in Middle Eastern affairs
who is still involved in this area and so couldn't speak on the record without en-
dangering his security clearances. But as the intelligence moved up the chain of
command rather than have its level of certainty diluted, as is generally the case
when information is passed upward, in this case it was treated as more definite.
This was especially true in the National Intelligence Estimate on Iraq. "By the
time you get to the executive summary level, it didn't look a lot like the analysts'
views," he said. "And by the time you get to the unclassified public portion, all the
mushiness and doubts were washed out."

Feith and his subordinates, especially Bill Luti, a former Navy officer who became a factotum for administration hawks, "were essentially an extra-governmental
organization, because many of their sources of information and much of their
work were in the shadows," said Gregory Newbold, the Marine general who was
then the Joint Staff's operations director. "It was also my sense that they cherry-
picked obscure, unconfirmed information to reinforce their own philosophies
and ideologies."

The Times goes nuclear

Also fouling the intelligence process were certain breaking newspaper stories,
especially Judith Miller's in the New York Times. In September she peeled off a string
of articles based on the accounts of defectors. Most notable was one she coauthored
with Michael Gordon, the Times's respected senior military correspondent. U.S.
SAYS HUSSEIN INTENSIFIES QUEST FOR A-BOMB PARTS, it reported on page one of the
edition of Sunday, September 8. "The closer Saddam Hussein gets to a nuclear
weapon, the harder he will be to deal with," it quoted a senior administration

official as warning. It related that hardliners were saying that the first irrefutable evidence "may be a mushroom cloud."

Such stories had an insidious effect on intelligence estimates, said the senior military intelligence officer: "The media has far more effect on intelligence analysis than you probably realize." It would only emerge later—and long after the war began—that the *Times* story had been flat wrong.

The combination of hyped newspaper stories and selective use of intelligence data had a powerful effect, said Rand Beers, who served on the staff of the National Security Council during the run-up to the war. "As they embellished what the intelligence community was prepared to say, and as the press reported that information, it began to acquire its own sense of truth and reality," he said.

Chalabi's distorting effect

Ahmed Chalabi, a clever, secular Shiite who spent the 1990s rallying support for a U.S. effort to depose Saddam Hussein, had two major means by which to influence the deliberations of the U.S. government. The first was indirect, through the media. Discussing his methods later, Chalabi told an interviewer from *Frontline,* the PBS documentary series, about how in 2001 his organization consciously took a source, Adnan Ihsan Saeed al-Haideri, first to the *New York Times,* which published a story in December 2001, and then to the U.S. government. Most notably, al-Haideri told his questioners that three hundred secret weapons facilities had been reactivated since the withdrawal of UN inspectors. Chalabi's organization later provided this information to the *Washington Post,* which carried an account in a July 2002 summary of what was thought to be known about Iraqi WMD programs.

"He told us, we told Judy Miller, she interviewed him, then we give him to the U.S. government," Chalabi said. "The thinking is that if we believed him to be credible, we wanted his story out, because we knew that if the U.S. took him, we would never see him again."

Chalabi also was able to introduce misinformation directly into the system. One senior military intelligence officer recalled being awed by Chalabi's ability to inject himself into the internal deliberations of the U.S. government. "He always got access" during 2002 and 2003. "His views always got where he wanted them to go." At first, senior Defense Intelligence Agency officials working in Middle Eastern affairs tried to prevent that, but it became clear that Douglas Feith and other senior Pentagon officials disliked those efforts. So, this officer recalled, by the spring of 2003 "we stopped complaining about him."

A Defense Intelligence Agency official said Feith and Luti made it clear that "Chalabi was liked." They weren't particularly interested in hearing arguments against him.

Chalabi had powerful allies. On March 17, 2002, Wolfowitz lunched with Christopher Meyer, the British ambassador to the United States. "It was true that Chalabi was not the easiest person to work with," Wolfowitz told Meyer, according to a memorandum the envoy sent the next day to the office of British Prime Minister Tony Blair. "But he had a good record in bringing high-grade defectors out of Iraq."

"The arguments about Chalabi have been without substance," Richard Perle intoned in July 2003. "He is far and away the most effective individual that we could have hoped would emerge in Iraq. . . . In my view, the person most likely to give us reliable advice is Ahmed Chalabi."

The intelligence community, by contrast, had no agents sending reliable reports from inside Iraq. That left a vacuum—and gave Chalabi an opening that he exploited adeptly. He described his allies in the U.S. government as being from the office of "the vice president" and "the office of the secretary of defense," the latter a broad term covering not just Rumsfeld's immediate aides but the offices of Wolfowitz and Feith and hundreds of people working for them.

Views of Chalabi tended to be shaped, pro or con, by where one stood in a divided administration. His reports became just one more issue in a running feud. "CIA and State were against Chalabi," said one intelligence veteran who during this period was working at the Pentagon. "So at DoD, any challenge to Chalabi was seen as just CIA or State attacks. And DoD's attitude was, Don't you call my baby ugly."

Sometimes all these forces would converge, as in an October 2, 2002, article by Judith Miller that quoted Richard Perle criticizing the CIA for not heeding tips from Chalabi's organization, the Iraqi National Congress. "The INC has been without question the single most important source of intelligence about Saddam Hussein," Perle asserted. This was a sad moment in American journalism and governance. The U.S. government during this period was paying Chalabi's organization substantial amounts, totaling more than $36 million from 2000 to 2003.

5.

THE RUN-UP

By the time the public really focused on it, the decision to go to war had been made, though more through drift than through any one meeting. In September 2002 word began to circulate inside the military that an invasion of Iraq was inevitable, and the march to war began.

At the heart of this part of the run-up to the war from the late summer of 2002 is the tale of how two contradictory delusions were pursued and sold by the Bush administration. To make the case for war, administration officials tended to look at the worst-case scenarios for weapons of mass destruction, dismissing contrary evidence, asserting that Saddam Hussein possessed chemical and biological munitions and was on the road to getting nuclear weapons, and emphasizing the frightening possibility of his sharing them with terrorists to use against the United States. On September 7, Bush, speaking at Camp David with Prime Minister Tony Blair at his side, flatly asserted that Saddam Hussein possessed weapons of mass destruction. "The problem here is that there will always be some uncertainty about how quickly he can acquire nuclear weapons," Condoleezza Rice said on CNN on September 8, echoing that morning's *New York Times* story. "But we don't want the smoking gun to be a mushroom cloud."

Yet at the same time, the administration's consideration of postwar issues took a leap of faith in the opposite direction, emphasizing best-case scenarios that assumed that Iraqis generally would greet the U.S. presence warmly and that a successor Iraqi government could be established quickly, permitting the swift homeward movement of most U.S. troops. In order to make this case, more pessimistic views repeatedly had to be rejected and ignored, even if they came from area experts.

Both the pessimism of the threat assessment and the optimism of the postwar assessment helped pave the way to war. By overstating the threat of Iraq, the former made war seem more necessary. By understating the difficulty of remaking Iraq, the latter made it seem easier and less expensive than it would prove to be.

Bush beats the drums of war

On the morning of September 4, 2002, Rep. Ike Skelton and a group of seventeen other congressional leaders met with President Bush at the White House to discuss Iraq. At the meeting's end, Skelton said later, he and Bush had a quick private exchange.

"What are you going to do once you get it?" Skelton asked the president.

"We've been giving some thought to it," Bush responded

So had Skelton, who that afternoon wrote and sent to Bush a letter laying out his questions about the costs and duration of a U.S. occupation of Iraq. In typical Skeltonian fashion, he quoted the Prussian military theorist Karl von Clausewitz, to remind the White House of the requirement in war "not to take the first step without considering the last." He also invoked the other great philosopher of strategy, Sun Tzu, who had observed, "To win victory is easy; to preserve its fruits, difficult."

The official Bush administration line later would become that no one really foresaw the difficulties of postwar Iraq. But Skelton certainly was pointing out the direction, as were a host of experts on the Mideast and some strategic thinkers inside the Army. "I have no doubt that our military would decisively defeat Iraq's forces and remove Saddam," Skelton stated in his letter. "But like the proverbial dog chasing the car down the road, we must consider what we would do after we caught it." He was especially worried, he told Bush, about the "extreme difficulty of occupying Iraq with its history of autocratic rule, its balkanized ethnic tensions, and its isolated economic system." So he asked to see "detailed advanced occupation planning," and to know more about "the form of a replacement regime . . . and the possibility that this regime might be rejected by the Iraqi people, leading to civil unrest and even anarchy." Before invading Iraq, he concluded, the president should tell the American people what they were getting into. "The American people must be clear about the amount of money and the number of soldiers that will have to be devoted to this effort for many years to come." He added: "We need to ensure that in taking out Saddam, we don't win the battle and lose the war."

There was no White House response. But in a meeting a White House congressional liaison official named Daniel Keniry told him, Skelton recalled, "Well, Congressman, we really don't need your vote. We've got the votes." Nor was there much reaction from his congressional colleagues. One of the reasons for this is that Skelton is a bit of an outrider in his own party, well to the right of most of Democratic congressional representatives. But it also was because most of the senators who had led their party on defense issues during the Cold War had moved on and hadn't been replaced, noted Kurt Campbell, a veteran of the Clinton Pentagon. Also, party politics had shifted away from supporting such figures. "The defense intellectuals tended to be centrists, and in the last decade, you've seen a hollowing out of the center," noted Campbell.

The drumbeat steadily intensified. On September 9, Franks briefed the Joint Chiefs of Staff on the state of the war plan. The military was beginning to move, laying the groundwork by expanding the ramp space at airports in the Persian Gulf and upgrading key gear, such as Special Operations helicopters.

Two days later, on the first anniversary of 9/11, more than three dozen senators were invited to the Pentagon for a briefing by Rumsfeld on weapons of mass destruction. One of those attending, Sen. Max Cleland of Georgia, was surprised to find Vice President Cheney and CIA director Tenet also waiting there. "It was pretty clear that Rumsfeld and Cheney are ready to go to war," Cleland wrote later that day in a note to himself. "They have already made the decision to go to war and to them that is the only option." Cleland had lost three limbs as a 1st Cavalry Division soldier in Vietnam in 1968, and was worried about Iraq becoming a similar mess. His note concluded, "Our country is divided at this point and God knows what will happen."

The next day President Bush addressed the UN General Assembly for twenty-six minutes, most of them devoted to a description of Iraq as "a grave and gathering danger." He explained his feeling of urgency: "With every step the Iraqi regime takes toward gaining and deploying the most terrible weapons, our own options to confront that regime will narrow." And if anyone didn't get the point, the administration also issued a document titled "The National Security Strategy of the United States of America" that formalized the preemption doctrine outlined by the president at West Point in June. "We cannot let our enemies strike first," it stated. "The overlap between states that sponsor terror and those that pursue WMD compels us to action. . . . To forestall or prevent such hostile acts by our adversaries, the United States will, if necessary act preemptively."

Culminating the campaign that had begun with Cheney's VFW speech six weeks earlier, Bush traveled to Cincinnati in early October to make his case to the American people: The decades-old policy of containment of Iraq hadn't worked, even when executed aggressively, Bush argued. "The end result is that Saddam Hussein still has chemical and biological weapons and is increasing his capabilities to make more," Bush stated, in the first of a series of assertions in the speech that were presented as fact and are now known to be incorrect. "And he is moving ever closer to developing a nuclear weapon."

Bush didn't quite maintain that Iraq was an imminent threat to the United States, but he came close, saying, "The Iraqi dictator must not be permitted to threaten America and the world with horrible poisons and diseases and gases and atomic weapons." Nor could we afford to wait for more evidence, he warned. "America must not ignore the threat gathering against us. Facing clear evidence of peril, we cannot wait for the final proof, the smoking gun that could come in the form of a mushroom cloud."

Congress goes along

Congress wasn't looking for a fight with the president.

The National Intelligence Estimate, in its full, ninety-two-page classified form, contained a host of doubts, caveats, and disagreements with Bush's assertions. Copies of that long form of the NIE were sent to Capitol Hill, where they sat in two vaults, under armed guard. Yet only a handful of members of Congress ever read more than its five-page executive summary. Delving into the dissent in the intelligence community would only have gotten a politician on the wrong side of the issue with the president. (Many months later, after the U.S. military invaded Iraq, White House officials would disclose that neither Bush nor Rice had read the entire NIE.)

The congressional vote itself, authorizing President Bush to attack Iraq, was anticlimactic. When the House debate began there was just one reporter in the press gallery. At their most intense points, the debates in both the House and the Senate attracted fewer than 10 percent of each body's members. "Usually, when there are few people around, it means that they don't like what's happening but don't feel they can do anything about it," observed one Capitol Hill veteran.

The exchanges on the Senate floor offered little of the memorable commentary seen in the two other most recent congressional debates on whether to go to war, in 1991 and in 1964, regarding the Gulf of Tonkin resolution. "The outcome—lopsided support for Bush's resolution—was preordained," wrote the *Washington Post*'s Dana Milbank. Republicans were going to support the president and their party, and Democrats wanted to move on to other issues that would help them more in the midterm elections that at that point were just three weeks away.

"With Democrats, the longest shadow was cast not by Karl Rove but by Sam Nunn," said Kurt Campbell, now head of the International Security Program at the Center for Strategic and International Studies. A decade earlier, nearly three quarters of the congressional Democrats had balked at attacking Saddam Hussein's troops in Kuwait, led in this opposition by Sen. Sam Nunn, the Georgia Democrat they trusted to protect their flank on military affairs. Nunn, in turn, appeared to have been persuaded to go slow by Colin Powell and other generals with whom he had had private conversations. But Democrats felt abused by that outcome, because after that war was concluded, their party looked less capable of handling national security issues. For the next three presidential election cycles, no Democrat who had been in his party's majority opposing the 1991 war was able to make headway in presidential politics. Those who appeared on the next three Democratic tickets—Bill Clinton, Al Gore, and Joseph Lieberman—had all been Gulf War hawks, in their party's minority.

The Democrats weren't going to make that mistake again. This time they were going to stay well out of the way of President Bush. In fact, said Sen. Robert Byrd, a West Virginia Democrat, the Democratic caucus decided on September 19 to get the vote out of the way as soon as possible, so they didn't have it hanging over them on election day. "Members were intimidated," Byrd said later.

Like an old-time Southern mossback obstructionist confronting the New Deal, Byrd stood astride the train tracks of history, knowing he wasn't going to change the course of events but protesting nonetheless. "The Senate is rushing to vote on whether to declare war on Iraq without pausing to ask why," he said in a Senate speech at the time. "Why is war being dealt with not as a last resort but as a first resort?" But he was seen by many in Congress as a blowhard, given to long-winded talks bristling with allusions to the Bible, ancient history, and the Constitution. He would remind his fellow senators of Croesus's comment to Cyrus the Great, and quote to them from the Roman orator Cicero and from the Roman historian Livy, whom he correctly but pedantically referred to as Titus Livius. At a time when many senators, elected through carefully massaged television commercials, arrive in Washington seemingly unable to speak well spontaneously, the white-maned Byrd was capable of churning out eloquence at great and sometimes numbing length. He had little influence even in his own party, and was mocked by some Republicans, who were fond of remembering that as a young man Byrd had belonged to the Ku Klux Klan, and in fact had been the exalted cyclops of his local chapter in West Virginia.

Ultimately, 77 of 100 senators and 296 of 435 House members voted to authorize the president to "use the armed forces of the United States as he determines to be necessary and appropriate in order to defend the national security of the United States against the continuing threat posed by Iraq." The majority of House Democrats voted against the war, but in the Senate, 29 Democrats backed the Bush administration's stance while 21 voted against it.

One of those voting for it was a successor to Sam Nunn as a Georgia Democrat: Max Cleland, who was in a tight campaign for reelection in which his challenger, Saxby Chambliss, was running commercials that showed images of Osama bin Laden and Saddam Hussein and implied that Cleland wasn't standing up to them. Despite his misgivings, Cleland felt under intense political pressure to go with the administration. "It was obvious that if I voted against the resolution that I would be dead meat in the race, just handing them a victory," he said in 2005. Even so, he now considers his prowar choice "the worst vote I cast."

Waiting to vote, Cleland looked over and saw Byrd, who had been in the Senate for forty-four years. "I knew he had been through the Gulf of Tonkin resolution. I knew he wanted me to show some political courage."

Cleland's name was called. "Aye," he said. He glanced again at Byrd, who, he recalled, "got up and walked away."

Despite his vote for war, the next month Cleland lost his Senate race by a margin of 53 percent to 46 percent, in part because of a statewide controversy over the Confederate battle flag that helped get out the rural white vote. He said he took it harder than being blown up by a hand grenade in Vietnam. "I went down—physically, mentally, emotionally—down into the deepest, darkest hole of my life," he recalled. "I had several moments when I just didn't want to live."

He began attending group therapy sessions every Tuesday afternoon at Walter Reed Army Medical Center in northwest Washington, D.C., where he had been medically retired from the military on Christmas Eve 1968. "I wound up back at Walter Reed! I look down the hall, and it's like Salvador Dali is painting my life. Thirty-seven years later, and I have another president creating a Vietnam. Kids are dying, getting blown up—that's me." Sitting in his office overlooking Farragut Square in downtown Washington long after the start of the war, he propped himself sideways in his armchair, pushing the stump of his right arm into the side of the chair. "I see these young Iraq veterans, missing legs and arms and eyes. They are so brave. They have no idea what is down the road for them."

Lingering doubts

In October, the *Atlantic Monthly*, which would do an exemplary job in posing the right questions about Iraq both before and after the invasion, carried a clarion call by James Fallows titled "The Fifty-first State?" Fallows began by explicitly rejecting the analogy to the 1930s on which Wolfowitz so relied. "Nazi and Holocaust analogies have a trumping power in many arguments, and their effect in Washington was to make doubters seem weak—Neville Chamberlains, versus the Winston Churchills who were ready to face the truth," he wrote. But "I ended up thinking that the Nazi analogy paralyzes the debate about Iraq rather than clarifying it." Yes, Saddam was brutal. But Iraq was hardly a great power. It had few allies, no industrial base, and was split internally by religious and ethnic differences. Also, the U.S. military had been confronting it and containing it successfully for over a decade. So, Fallows said, a more apt parallel was an earlier war. "If we had to choose a single analogy to govern our thinking about Iraq, my candidate would be World War I." This wasn't just because Iraq was created by that conflict, but also because that war is "relevant as a powerful example of the limits of human imagination," especially about the long-term consequences of an action. He then proceeded to analyze the likely problems a U.S. occupation would encounter, from manning an occupation force to standing up an Iraqi government to keeping Iraq in one piece. It was a powerful call to debate, a reminder of the urgent necessity of parsing the issues. What exactly was the job the United States was taking on? How long would it last? What were the chances of success? And what were the likely costs?

Similar questions were being raised in some meetings in Washington. In one particularly revealing exchange at a meeting at the American Enterprise Institute, Michael O'Hanlon, a defense analyst at the Brookings Institution, predicted the course of the American occupation of Iraq. "We have got to go in and win this war quickly, and then be prepared to help stabilize Iraq over an indefinite period, five to ten years, at a minimum, I believe, using a large fraction of American forces. This is a major undertaking," he said, that likely would require a total of 150,000 troops and "could stay above 100,000 for several years, based on the precedents and models that I've seen."

That prediction, which time has proven impressively accurate, was promptly slapped down by Richard Perle. "I don't believe that anything like a long-term commitment of 150,000 Americans would be necessary." There would be no one fighting for Saddam Hussein once he was gone, Perle said, so "it seems to me ironic that Michael envisions 150,000 Americans to police a post-Saddam Iraq."

Two days later, the Washington Institute for Near East Policy held a three-day seminar at a plush conference center in Leesburg, Virginia, on the western edge of the Washington suburbs. Attendees, including officials from the Pentagon policy office, the Defense Intelligence Agency, and the staff of the National Security Council, were told by a panel of experts that there was a gaping discrepancy between the Bush administration's ambitious rhetoric and its limited commitment: Either it should plan to be in Iraq for years, the speakers warned, or it should scale back its goal of transforming Iraq and the Middle East. "It is overly optimistic to think that we can take a country that has emerged from under a totalitarian regime with its institutions of civil society and create a beacon of democracy within five years," cautioned Patrick Clawson, the Washington Institute's deputy director. "We could run into serious trouble if we operate under that notion." He advised against the United States overstaying its welcome: Get in, get out, and don't try to plant a new type of politics. "If we try to transform Iraq into a democracy, we will need more and more troops over time because we will have to quell nationalistic revolts."

"I am not clear that we have a clear idea of where we want to be the morning after an invasion," said Alina Romanowski, a former Pentagon official who at the time of the conference was on the staff of the National Defense University. "The U.S. military will be stepping into a morass. Iraq presents as unpromising a breeding ground for democracy as any in the world. It has never really known democracy or even legitimate, centralized rule for any great duration." Given the ethnic divisions and the "brutally violent" politics of the country, she said, it should be considered that a "small U.S. force sufficient to bring about Saddam's demise might not be sufficient to stop the subsequent bloodletting."

Amatzia Baram, a University of Haifa expert on Iraq and Middle Eastern history, added that he was "a little more pessimistic" than his fellow panelists. A U.S. occupation would need to show that it could improve conditions in Iraq rapidly, or risk alienating the Iraqi population. "You will need to win Baghdadis quickly." Someone should tell the president, he said, that U.S. forces would need to be in Iraq for two to five years, "and they will not have an easy time there."

The meeting amounted to an anti-Wolfowitz gala, a broadside at all the optimistic assumptions that the deputy defense secretary was offering to persuade a doubtful military and a wary Congress. But administration insiders were dismissive, seeing these conferences and reports not as genuine criticisms but more as underhanded ways of opposing the invasion.

A message from the Joint Staff

Rather than refute the skeptics, the Pentagon's leaders followed Cheney's example and simply decided that the time for debate was past. Such an assertion might not affect civilians outside the government, but inside the military establishment it could be issued with the force of an order. The Joint Staff effectively stated that view in the form of a Strategic Guidance for Combatant Commanders. In mid-October a draft of this guidance was sent out to planning officers on the staffs of the senior U.S. military commanders around the world, often called the CinCs. The message was simple: We are preparing to order that a war with Iraq be considered part of the war on terror.

That was an unusual order, and smacked of a politicized military leadership. It provoked a series of swift responses, some of them quite blunt. "How the hell did a war on Iraq become part of the war on terrorism?" was how one officer on the Joint Staff summarized the reaction of four of those commanders' staffers. The draft didn't seem consistent with a Pentagon directive exactly a year earlier that had laid out five clear lines of attack in a global counteroffensive against terrorism, all focused on hitting terrorist groups with global reach, and their state sponsors. "There is no link between Saddam Hussein and 9/11," one of the responses argued. "Don't mix the two. This is going to work hell with the allies. What is going on?"

One of the officers who was caught in the middle of this went to Army Lt. Gen. George Casey, then the J-5—the chief of strategic plans and policy on the staff of the Joint Chiefs—and reported these puzzled, angry comments from the field. Casey, who in 2004 was to become the top U.S. officer in Iraq, laid down the law. The discussion was over. "Look, this is part of the war on terror," this officer remembered Casey instructing him. "Iraq is one of those state supporters, and it is a state that has used weapons of mass destruction." That was the message that went back out to the CinC's staffs near the end of 2002, in the form of a highly classified five-paragraph order. In a bureaucratic maneuver, in order to keep Feith from trying to edit it word by word and comma by comma—an excruciating process that the Joint Staff had come to dread—it was sent out as a change to an existing strategic guidance rather than as a new statement. Its third paragraph said that should it become necessary to conduct combat operations against Iraq, this activity was to be thought of as part of the wider war against terrorism. (Casey said through a spokesman that he didn't remember the conversation or the wording of the strategic guidance, but added, "I did and do believe that operations against Iraq, designated by our government as a state sponsor of terror, were and are part of the war on terror.")

As that message was being finalized, Lt. Gen. Newbold quietly retired from his job on the Joint Staff and left the military. It had been common knowledge on the staff that he opposed the invasion of Iraq, but he managed to keep that from leaking out. His is the only known departure from the senior ranks of the military over the looming Iraq war. Publicly, Newbold was discreet, saying he was leaving because he felt he owed it to his family and to younger officers, so they could move up. At any rate, he said, the job of operations director "is a square hole, and I am a round peg."

In the intelligence community, analysts and their bosses began to shut up in the fall of 2002. No one had to tell them to do so. "The feeling was, our job is to do what we're told, and this thing is going to happen," said the senior military intelligence official. "The feeling was, it wasn't our place to raise a ruckus."

Indeed, by this point the war already was beginning in quiet ways. Officers in the Gulf were told to be ready for war in spring. Army Lt. Gen. David McKiernan, the commander of the ground invasion force, said in an official Army debriefing interview in the summer of 2003 that "I think from last fall we knew it was a question of just when, not if."

Likewise, in September, a senior U.S. intelligence official in Bahrain told colleagues, "You'll see all this diplomatic stuff, but it's clear we're going to war."

Wars don't always commence with a bang. In the Gulf, the information campaign began with the sound of paper rustling, as millions of leaflets were dropped on Iraqi troops. "In September we really began to ratchet that up, because we had more assets to drop leaflets and transmit radio messages," recalled Maj. Gen. Renuart, the operations chief at Central Command, referring to specialized aircraft that were being moved into the Gulf region. Among these were EC-130 Commando Solo planes that could transmit television and radio broadcasts, and EC-130H Compass Call planes that could jam enemy communications. This was, in some ways, a quiet beginning of the war. "The fuse was long and slow burning, and we could cut it off at any point," Renuart said. "The design was to explore if you could topple the regime without having to take action. Maybe as the pressure stepped up, as the UN took action, maybe somebody in Iraq would move against Saddam."

An unhappy Army plans for war

Running through planning of the war was unresolved friction between Rumsfeld and the Army, whose relationship had begun badly and deteriorated further with time. In hindsight, many Army officers would remember the situation simply as being that Gen. Eric Shinseki, the chief of staff of the Army, was right, and OSD—the civilian leadership of the military—as being wrong. But it is a more complex story than that.

The Army that went into Iraq wasn't a happy institution at its top levels. Of all the services, it was the one most at odds with Rumsfeld and other senior Pentagon civilians, distrusting their views, and believing they were interfering on matters in which they were professionally uninformed. The Army also would be the service shouldering most of the burden in Iraq. People around Rumsfeld, in turn, saw the Army as unresponsive, unimaginative, and risk averse. "The secretary is asking the Army to do things it is unable to do—like think innovatively," cracked one of Rumsfeld's aides.

"Rumsfeld doesn't hate the Army," said another civilian Pentagon official, who attended meetings with the secretary about the service. "He is frustrated with tendencies he sees in the Army to be impervious to change."

Tension between senior civilians and Army generals unresponsive to their concerns had been escalating for some time, and predated Rumsfeld's arrival. In June 1999, Deputy Defense Secretary John Hamre, a low-key, soft-spoken sort, had fired a shot across the service's bow. "If the Army only holds onto nostalgic versions of its grand past, it is going to atrophy and die," he had warned in a public speech.

The Army wasn't inclined to spend too much time worrying about such warnings from civilians. On the battlefield it considered itself the best in the world. At home it had intimidated the Clinton administration. Army Lt. Gen. Joseph Kellogg, Jr., recalled advising Shinseki during the 2000 campaign to take seriously the Republican presidential candidate's speech promising to cancel the Army's new mobile artillery system, called the Crusader. "Shinseki said, 'Not gonna happen,'" Kellogg recalled. "There was a kind of arrogance there, like these guys are just temporary help."

Kellogg also remembered running into a three-star Army general after church one Sunday and commiserating about some of Rumsfeld's moves. "Oh, we'll wait these guys out, we always do," this general told him. The military is very good at "slow rolling" initiatives from its civilian overseers. The top brass won't directly disobey an order, but they can be ingenious at finding ways to vitiate and delay implementing it. After all, the military rationale goes, in a few years the civilians will all be gone from this Pentagon—but those in uniform will still be in those uniforms, and perhaps burdened by the poor decisions of long-gone former bosses.

But the new crowd wielded sharper elbows than the Army had experienced since Dick Cheney had stepped down as defense secretary eight years earlier. In August 2001, when the administration had been in office just a few months, Rumsfeld's subordinates were hinting to the Army that it might need to be cut from ten active-duty divisions to eight, recalled retired Lt. Gen. Johnny Riggs. Shinseki came in from summer leave to argue against the move, which was put on hold. Interestingly, Wolfowitz sided with the Army and against Rumsfeld on the issue of cutting the service. The impasse continued until the September 11 attacks, which would result in a flood of funding for all the services. Wolfowitz recalled that after those attacks, he said to Rumsfeld, "Aren't you glad now that we didn't cut Army force structure?"

The Afghanistan campaign that followed those attacks produced additional bad blood, with profound unhappiness in the Army with both Rumsfeld and Franks over the handling of the war there, with some officers reporting that Franks didn't address key strategic questions and instead meddled in tactical issues, where he often disregarded the views of subordinates. Then, in April 2002, Rumsfeld's aides let it be known that he had decided to name Gen. Jack Keane, the Army's vice chief of staff, as its next chief. This was some fifteen months before Shinseki was scheduled to retire. The leak made Shinseki a lame duck and undercut his ambitious transformation agenda to make the Army more agile and deployable, a plan he had set forth in 1999, well before Rumsfeld was defense secretary.

Next, Rumsfeld killed the Army's Crusader artillery program because he saw it as too heavy to deploy to distant battlefields and not "transformational" enough to be relevant in future wars. Army leaders had coveted the Crusader for years as a weapon that would finally make the Army second to none in artillery firepower. They were particularly steamed at how Rumsfeld and Wolfowitz killed the system, keeping the Army in the dark about what was happening until Congress was ready to vote on the fiscal 2003 budget. Wolfowitz, for his part, felt that the Army had been untruthful in producing information about the system.

After this, Shinseki became almost sullen in his dealings with Rumsfeld. "There was a meeting at Fort McNair on transformation," said one general. "The CinCs were there. All the service chiefs were there—but one. Shinseki didn't go. And a wall built up between the Army and OSD." Likewise, when an advisory panel told Rumsfeld that the Army needed to think more about peacekeeping and other postwar stabilization missions, Shinseki strongly objected, recalled a retired four-star general. This was a tragic situation for generals such as Shinseki, who had begun their careers as the lieutenants of the Vietnam era and spent much of their careers rebuilding the Army. Now, at the culmination of decades of service, Shinseki and his peers were facing a quagmirish scenario of the very sort they had vowed for decades to avoid.

In the summer and fall of 2002, a series of warnings were issued inside the military establishment about the right and wrong ways to approach Iraq. Most of these appear to have been ignored, mainly because the Bush administration tended not to listen to people outside a small circle of insiders. On August 26—the same day that Cheney effectively launched the march to war with his "no doubts" speech to the VFW—a group of Army commanders and other top service officials met at the Army War College's bucolic campus on the outskirts of Carlisle, Pennsylvania, to review, among other things, the Central Command's middling performance in the Afghan campaign. The meeting concluded that major errors had been committed in the conduct of that offensive, especially in the handling of the larger, strategic issues. This conclusion was meant to be descriptive of what had happened in the previous year, but it would also prove accurate in predicting what would go wrong in the handling of the Iraq war.

The first major criticism on which the participants agreed was that the Afghan situation had been marred by the excessively short-term approach of top defense leaders. This problem of a "tactical focus that ignores long-term objectives" was especially notable at Central Command, said an internal Army memo that summarized the meeting's conclusions and that has never been released. As Sean Naylor of the *Army Times* later pointed out, Franks failed to grasp in waging the Afghan war that taking the enemy's capital wasn't the same as winning the war, a conceptual error he would repeat in Iraq. But the problem extended beyond that—and thus those meeting at the Army War College laid it at the feet of Rumsfeld and the new chairman of the Joint Chiefs of Staff, Air Force Gen. Richard Myers, who took over just before the Afghan war began. "All participants at the conference from all commands complained about the problems caused by a lack of clear higher direction," the summary emphasized.

A more specific grievance was the insistence of the Pentagon on not using established deployment plans for units, and instead sending them out piecemeal.

"Headquarters have had to utilize scores of individual Requests For Forces (RFF) to build organization in key theaters instead of formal TPFDL," another Army report on the meeting stated. Back then this complaint about messing with the painstakingly developed TPFDL—an awkward acronym that military types pronounce "tip-fiddle" and which stands for Time-Phased Force Deployment List—seemed minor, even obscure, but it would grow into an angry chorus in the Army during the invasion and occupation of Iraq, as it caused endless turmoil and confusion. "The pernicious effect of these grab-bag augmentations is to create headquarters staffs with little experience or cohesion," this second report stated. "One conference participant described the situation as 'playing the Super Bowl with a pick-up team.'" Most ominously, the report warned that by overburdening undertrained staffs, the resulting turmoil especially undercut the military's ability to develop effective long-range plans.

In November, Maj. Gen. James Mattis, the commander of the 1st Marine Division, which would spend much of the next two years in Iraq, invited Gen. Zinni to be the speaker at the division's Marine Corps birthday dinner, the most important day of the year for the Corps. On the afternoon before the dinner, Mattis had Zinni speak to all his senior commanders. "If you guys don't go through the enemy in six weeks, we'll disown you," Zinni said, according to Mattis. "But then the hard work begins. . . . We have lit a fuse, and we don't know what's at the other end—a nuke, a hand grenade, or a dud?"

Zinni's message to the assembled Marine commanders that afternoon was: You are about to get into something that is going to be tougher and more chaotic than you might think. "I was worried that we didn't understand the importance of maintaining order, that we had to come in with sufficient forces to freeze the situation, to understand that when we're ripping the guts out of an authoritarian regime, you've got responsibility for security, services, everything else. You have to be prepared to handle all that."

He also warned the Marines that in such situations the U.S. government tends to look to the military for solutions. "The other caution I gave them was don't count on it when somebody tells you 'Well, the State Department's got that,' or 'OSD's planning for that.' Don't believe them. You're going to get stuck with it. So, have a plan. This is the Desert Crossing philosophy: You're going to end up being the 'stuckee' on this."

A week later seventy national security experts and Mideast scholars met for two days at the National Defense University, one of the military's premier educational institutions, located in Washington, to discuss "Iraq: Looking Beyond Saddam's

Role." They concluded that occupying Iraq "will be the most daunting and complex task the U.S. and the international community will have undertaken since the end of World War II"—a sweeping statement that placed a war with Iraq in the class of the Vietnam War and the containment of the Soviet Union. The group's first finding, both underlined and italicized in its report, was that the primary postinvasion task of the U.S. military "must be on establishing and maintaining a secure environment." It also strongly recommended against a swift, uncoordinated dissolution of the Iraqi military. "There should be a phased downsizing to avoid dumping 1.4 million men into a shattered economy."

Col. Paul Hughes sent a copy of the conference report to Douglas Feith's office in the Pentagon, but "never heard back from him or anyone else" over there, he recalled. "I cannot tell you if it had any impact at all." Both its recommendations quoted here would be effectively ignored in the following months by military planners and by the civilian occupation authority.

On December 10 and 11, the Army staff at the Pentagon convened about two dozen military experts, Middle East area specialists, diplomats, and intelligence officials, at the Army War College to look at the missions that the service likely would face in postwar Iraq. On the morning of the second day of meetings, remembered Conrad Crane, the Army historian running the study, "We were struck by a massive ice storm" that forced the cancellation of many commercial passenger flights in the mid-Atlantic region. It was an unexpected boon in that it delayed some planned departures and permitted the group to dig a bit deeper than expected.

Read now, with the benefit of hindsight, the report the group produced clearly is stunning in its prescience. "The possibility of the United States winning the war and losing the peace is real and serious," they wrote in a lapel-grabbing tone that was an unusual departure for government experts giving their bosses unwelcome advice. "Thinking about the war now and the occupation later is not an acceptable solution." That was what the Army War College group had seen happen with Afghanistan—and some members of that group were hearing from friends at Central Command that the same screwup was happening again.

They also delivered a clear warning about the fragile state of the Iraqi economy—something that Bush administration officials would insist after the invasion had been a rude surprise. Iraq had been strained by decades of misrule, wars, and sanctions, they observed. "If the United States assumes control of Iraq, it will therefore assume control of a badly battered economy." The writers repeatedly emphasized that Iraq was going to be tougher than the administration thought, or at least was admitting publicly. "Successful occupation will not occur unless the special circumstances of this unusual country" are heeded, they warned.

They specifically advised against the two major steps that Ambassador L. Paul Bremer III would pursue in 2003 after being named to run the U.S. occupation. The Iraqi army should be kept intact because it could serve as a unifying force in a country that could fall apart under U.S. control: "In a highly diverse and fragmented society like Iraq, the military . . . is one of the few national institutions that stresses national unity as an important principle. To tear apart the army in the war's aftermath could lead to the destruction of one of the only forces for unity within the society." They likewise were explicit in warning against the sort of top-down "de-Baathification" that Bremer would mandate. Rather, they recommended following the example of the U.S. authorities in post–World War II Germany who used a bottom-up approach by having anti-Nazi Germans in every town review detailed questionnaires filled out by every adult German, and then determining, one by one, who would have their political and economic activities curtailed.

The report received an enthusiastic response from the Army, Crane said later. He believes it also influenced the thinking of some Army generals preparing for the invasion of Iraq. But all that was preaching to the converted. The group heard very little from the office of the secretary of defense or from Central Command. "It was not clear to us until much later how unsuccessful General Shinseki and his staff had been in shaping the final plans," Crane said later. Then, in mid-2003, after the occupation had gotten off to a fumbled start and Franks had left Central Command and retired from the Army, Crane was told that John Abizaid, the new commander, was handing the report to everyone he met and telling them to read it. It was small consolation.

What is remarkable is that again and again during the crucial months before the invasion, such warnings from experts weren't heeded—or even welcomed. Almost no Middle Eastern experts inside the military were consulted on the war plan, in part because the plan was produced on a very close hold basis that involved few people, and even then only parts of it were shown to most of those involved.

Shinseki and his aides were seeing many of the warnings. In the fall of 2002, when Rumsfeld met with the Joint Chiefs to discuss the planning for Iraq, Shinseki brought up his concerns. Centcom's Renuart, who attended the session, recalled the Army chief arguing that "the mission was huge, that you needed a lot of troops to secure all the borders and do all the tasks you needed to do." Franks's response at the time, Renuart added, was that it wasn't known how many Iraqi troops would capitulate and work for the Americans, so it wasn't clear that tens of thousands of additional U.S. soldiers would be required. This essentially was best-case planning, which is as much an error as is planning only for the worst outcome.

Then, as winter approached, Shinseki and the other members of the Joint Chiefs met with the president. Gen. Franks, who joined them, recalled the meeting in an interview as "a very, very positive session." Franks recalled Shinseki as not so much expressing concern about the overall war plan, but rather pointing out that "the lines of communication and supportability were long. . . . I took it, and I think everyone in the room took it, [to mean that] this isn't going to be a cakewalk."

Franks also heard concern from Powell about the war plan. "I've got problems with force size and support of that force, given such long lines of communication," the former chairman of the Joint Chiefs said in a telephone call, according to Franks's autobiography. It was a difficult position for Powell to put Franks in, because Franks had to report to Rumsfeld, not to Powell, and the two secretaries were like old bulls facing each other down. So Franks essentially thanked Powell for his interest and reported the conversation to Rumsfeld.

Ground commanders vs. Franks

Franks also was being squeezed from below. In 1991, Gen. Schwarzkopf had made himself both the overall commander and the commander of land forces for the attack into Kuwait. Some in the Army thought that he had been overwhelmed by both tasks—one reason that the Army wasn't able to adjust its operations when the Marines moved into Kuwait faster than expected, and couldn't close the door on the Iraqi army before it escaped northward. Franks took a different course, creating the Coalition Forces Land Component Command. That was the awkward name for the ground forces—the Army, the Marine Corps, and the British army, along with a handful of Poles and other troops—who would ultimately invade Iraq. The CFLCC (which the military took to pronouncing "sif-lik") was another element of the war plan that amounted to a repudiation of Schwarzkopf's handling of the 1991 war: This time they were going to go to Baghdad and do it right.

Not all was well at CFLCC. Its senior officers had worked for months to get Franks to stand up to Rumsfeld and the Pentagon. Maj. Gen. James Thurman was

CFLCC's director for operations, arguably the second most important post in the organization. Neither he nor his commander, Army Lt. Gen. David McKiernan, was happy with the war plans Franks was bringing back from his meetings with Rumsfeld. The initial plan put on the table had in their view been ridiculous. It called for a tiny force, consisting of one enhanced brigade from the 3rd Infantry Division and a Marine Expeditionary Unit—all in all, fewer than ten thousand combat troops. It was little more than an update of the notions that had been kicked around during the nineties by Iraqi exiles, and that Zinni had nixed as a potential Bay of Goats. Over the course of 2002 the planned size of the force got larger, but hadn't quite reached what McKiernan saw as the minimum.

Rumsfeld had come out of the Afghan war believing that speed could be substituted for mass in military operations. Franks had bought into this, summarizing it in the oft-repeated maxim "Speed kills." McKiernan and Thurman weren't at all sure of that, and disliked the prospect of being Rumsfeld's guinea pigs.

On December 8, 2002, in what Thurman would remember as "a key point in the planning," McKiernan and Thurman flew to Franks's headquarters in Qatar and put their doubts in front of him. McKiernan "laid out to the CinC and showed him that we needed more combat power for the basic stance," Thurman later told an official Army historian. The first troop deployment order had just been issued. The two generals pushed their commander for more, and got some, but never got quite enough, in their view. Even four months later, as the invasion began, Thurman later said, "We wanted more combat power on the ground."

McKiernan had another, smaller but nagging, issue: He couldn't get Franks to issue clear orders that stated explicitly what he wanted done, how he wanted to do it, and why. Rather, Franks passed along PowerPoint briefing slides that he had shown to Rumsfeld. "It's quite frustrating the way this works, but the way we do things nowadays is combatant commanders brief their products in PowerPoint up in Washington to OSD and Secretary of Defense. . . . In lieu of an order, or a frag [fragmentary] order, or plan, you get a set of PowerPoint slides. . . . [T]hat is frustrating, because nobody wants to plan against PowerPoint slides."

That reliance on slides rather than formal written orders seemed to some military professionals to capture the essence of Rumsfeld's amateurish approach to war planning. "Here may be the clearest manifestation of OSD's contempt for the accumulated wisdom of the military profession and of the assumption among forward thinkers that technology—above all information technology—has rendered obsolete the conventions traditionally governing the preparation and conduct of war," commented retired Army Col. Andrew Bacevich, a former commander of an armored cavalry regiment. "To imagine that PowerPoint slides can substitute for such means is really the height of recklessness." It was like telling an automobile mechanic to use a manufacturer's glossy sales brochure to figure out how to repair an engine.

The "black hole" of Feith's policy office

At the Pentagon, the policy shop run by Douglas Feith was the organization that was in many ways the civilian parallel of Franks's Central Command in formulating the American stance on going to war in Iraq. Centcom was responsible for handling the war, while Feith's office was supposed to oversee the policies guiding the war and its aftermath.

Both Franks's headquarters and Feith's policy office had notably low morale, but a major difference was that Feith's office was managed worse. While Franks was at least effective in getting what he wanted from underlings, the owlish Feith was a management disaster who served as a bottleneck on decision making. "He basically was a glorified gofer for Rumsfeld," said Gary Schmitt, who was hardly an ideological foe—he was the executive director of the Project for a New American Century, a small neoconservative advocacy group that pushed hard for the invasion of Iraq. "He can't manage anything, and he doesn't trust anyone else's judgment."

People working for Feith complained that he would spend hours tweaking their memos, carefully mulling minor points of grammar. A Joint Staff officer recalled angrily that at one point troops sat on a runway for hours, waiting to leave the United States on a mission, while he quibbled about commas in the deployment order. "Policy was a black hole," recalled one four-star general about Feith's operation. "It dropped the ball again and again."

In the summer of 2001, Feith had been confronted on his management flaws by top aides at a large meeting. Lisa Bronson, a veteran specialist on weapons proliferation, stood and said, "This is the worst-run policy office I've ever seen." Another Feith aide agreed, saying later that the decision-making process in Feith's office was the most tangled he'd seen in twenty years of government work.

Feith stood his ground, explaining to subordinates that "I don't treat you any differently than Rumsfeld treats me." He said his fussiness over memos reflected the importance he and Rumsfeld placed on precision in thinking and writing.

Feith amounted to a less impressive version of Wolfowitz, filling the post the older man had held during the 1991 Gulf War. A 1975 graduate of Harvard, he was similar to Wolfowitz in his academic approach. To the military way of thinking, which tends to like orderly discussions that march toward clear decisions, he appeared far too woolly. For Feith, as for Wolfowitz, the Holocaust—and the mistakes the West made appeasing Hitler in the 1930s, rather than stopping him—became a keystone in thinking about policy. Like Wolfowitz, Feith came from a family devastated by the Holocaust. His father lost both parents, three brothers, and four sisters to the Nazis. "My family got wiped out by Hitler, and . . . all this stuff about working things out—well, talking to Hitler to resolve the problem didn't make any sense to me," Feith later told Jeffrey Goldberg of the *New Yorker* in discussing how World War II had shaped his views. "The kind of people who put bumper stickers on their car that declare that 'War is not the answer,' are they making a serious comment? What's the answer to Pearl Harbor? What's the answer to the Holocaust?"

"Doug's very smart, almost too smart," said a Bush administration official who has known Feith for decades and generally is sympathetic to his views. "He's a very impressive conceptual thinker, a rapid-fire genius. But. But. Not everyone else is so smart. And once in a while, something very hard comes along, something that requires a lot of deliberate thought." And in such cases, Feith's rapid-fire approach becomes dangerous.

"Doug is a first-generation American, and the son of a Holocaust survivor," a background that has shaped Feith's views and approach. "And the fact that they are minoritarian views, shared by only a few people, makes him believe it all the more. He takes almost as axiomatic some of his views—for example, that weakness invites aggression. Or invoke diplomacy only when you have your adversary cornered."

The personal histories of key players in the Bush administration may have made for an unusual and volatile mix. It was an unusual and powerful combination: The men at the White House were risk takers, while their subordinates and ideological allies at the Pentagon were men counseling that it was unwise to wait to act against evil, no matter what the conventional wisdom was. Add them up, said this unhappy Bush administration official, and you get an unusual mix: "These people are brinksmen."

Rumsfeld, who rarely seems to go out of his way to praise his subordinates, did so with Feith, later defending him as "without question one of the most brilliant individuals in government . . . just a rare talent. And from my standpoint, working with him is always interesting. He's been one of the really intellectual leaders in the administration in defense policy aspects of our work here."

Not everyone was so impressed. Senior military officers especially seemed to be rubbed the wrong way by him. Franks, the Central Command chief, called Feith "the dumbest fucking guy on the planet." Jay Garner, the retired Army lieutenant general who reported to Feith for five months as the Bush administration's first head of the postwar mission in Iraq, came to a similar conclusion. "I think he's incredibly dangerous," Garner said later. "He's a very smart guy whose electrons aren't connected, so he arc lights all the time. He can't organize anything." Remarkably, Feith was the person in charge of day-to-day postwar Iraq policy in Washington—the official that Franks was told would handle the postwar end of things. A man who couldn't run his own office very well, by many accounts, was going to oversee the rebuilding of an occupied nation on the other side of the planet.

Incoherent planning for the aftermath

The U.S. invasion of Iraq, Army Lt. Col. James Scudieri wrote later, "may be the most planned operation since D-Day on 6 June 1944 and Desert Storm in 1991." The irony is that in eighteen months of planning, the key question was left substantially unaddressed: What to do after getting to Baghdad. Franks, Rumsfeld, Wolfowitz, Feith, and other top officials spent well over a year preparing to attack Iraq, but treated almost casually what would come after that. "I think people are overly pessimistic about the aftermath," Wolfowitz flatly stated in an interview in December 2002.

At first, in the summer of 2002, the ball was tossed to the exhausted planning staff at Central Command, which had just finished invading Afghanistan and then written two versions of a plan to invade Iraq. "End of July, we've just finished the second plan, and we get an order from Joint Staff saying, 'You're in charge of the postwar plan,'" recalled Col. John Agoglia. They were flabbergasted. At that point they thought the invasion would be launched in just six months. "We said, 'Oh, shit,' did a mission analysis, and focused on humanitarian issues," such as minimizing the displacement of people, stockpiling food to stave off famine, and protecting the infrastructure of the oil fields, he said.

The decision to place the Defense Department—whether at the Pentagon or at the Central Command headquarters—in charge of postwar Iraq may have doomed the American effort from the start. As a subsequent Rand Corporation study put it, "Overall, this approach worked poorly, because the Defense Department lacked the experience, expertise, funding authority, local knowledge, and established contacts with other potential organizations needed to establish, staff, support and oversee a large multiagency civilian mission."

It wasn't that there was no planning. To the contrary, there was a lot, with at least three groups inside the military and one at the State Department working on postwar issues and producing thousands of pages of documents. But much of the planning was shoddy, there was no one really in charge of it, and there was lit-tle coordination between the various groups. Gen. Franks appeared to believe that planning for the end of the war was someone else's job. The message he sent to Rumsfeld's subordinates, he wrote in his autobiography, was: "You pay atten-tion to the day after and I'll pay to attention to the day of." The result would be that while there was much discussion, and endless PowerPoint briefings, there wouldn't be a real plan for postwar Iraq that could be implemented by com-manders and soldiers on the ground.

To handle the stepped-up load of planning for postwar Iraq, Franks created a new office, Joint Task Force IV, under Brig. Gen. Steve Hawkins, an Army engi-neer. For months Hawkins had scores of staff planners working on Phase IV—that is, the phase that followed Phase III's major combat operations—but failed to produce much. "We were told that JTF-IV would be a standing task force," recalled Agoglia. "We thought that it would be the core of planning for a post-conflict headquarters. Instead, it was Steve Hawkins and fifty-five yahoos with shareware who were clueless."

Despite months of work, "they didn't produce a plan," Army Lt. Gen. Joseph Kellogg said. "They may have war-gamed it, but planned it? Nope." That may seem a harsh verdict, but it is borne out by a look at the classified PowerPoint briefings JTF-IV produced. It is fashionable to criticize the U.S. military's heavy reliance on PowerPoint, but the thirty-two slides in the JTF-IV summary of planning for postwar Iraq are extreme in their incoherence, with unexplained distinctions be-tween "military success" in Phase III and "strategic success" under "civilian lead" in Phase IV. (Interestingly, another briefing, on reconstruction issues, noted in an aside that the Army experience in Bosnia and Kosovo indicated that the postwar situation in Iraq would require around 470,000 troops, more than triple the number that actually would be deployed.)

Maj. Eisenstadt, an intelligence officer in Central Command's headquarters in 2001–2, said that most of Hawkins's work was discarded for reasons that were never clear to him. Another military expert who reviewed the product of the task force said its work was so mediocre that insiders just began ignoring it. "It was a very pedestrian product, and it looked like a war college exercise," he said. "They were not reaching out to real-world people and information."

A V Corps planner agreed with that account. "Centcom set up a cell to do Phase IV planning before the war, but it never produced anything," he said. "It just got tied up in scenarios—like what happens if there are large refugee flows?" It never actually produced a usable blueprint for running postwar Iraq.

But no one appears to have informed other military planners about the flimsiness of Centcom's Phase IV work. A classified prewar briefing by the next lower headquarters, the Coalition Forces Land Component Command (CFLCC), on its own Phase IV plans breezily noted that it was "Working with CJTF-4 to ensure seamless transition."

Calling Gen. Garner

By late December, it was clear both at Central Command and at the Pentagon that the JTF-IV effort to plan for postwar Iraq was faltering. "If there was something that as a planner we didn't do so well, it was that we didn't prepare Franks so well for the reconstruction and stabilization piece," Agoglia said. "We didn't do as good a job as we should of walking him through the postconflict piece." And "in January '03 we realized that JTF-IV wouldn't work. It was broken."

In mid-January, just eight weeks before the invasion, the lead in planning for the postwar situation was taken away from Central Command and moved to the Pentagon. Retired Army Lt. Gen. Jay Garner, who had led the relief effort in northern Iraq in 1991, was eating in a restaurant in New York when he received a call from Feith's office. Rumsfeld wanted him once more to lead postwar operations in Iraq—a task that was expected to be mainly humanitarian work, likely focused on aiding refugees and perhaps the civilian victims of Iraqi chemical or biological weapons. Garner initially refused, but agreed to go see Rumsfeld. "He can be pretty persuasive, and I said I'd do it if my company agreed and if my wife agreed," he recalled.

Garner told Rumsfeld that he would need some retired generals, senior officers who understood the military and the management of a large organization. "Rumsfeld said, 'OK, anybody but Zinni,'" he recalled. Garner interpreted this not as a personal grudge on the part of the defense secretary, but rather an assessment that the White House saw Zinni as an adversary. "It came across to me that we wouldn't be able to sell Zinni, because he already was against the war." Indeed,

Garner soon would run into trouble on several lower profile staff members he proposed, especially from the State Department's own planning project, called the Future of Iraq.

On January 20, the White House issued a classified National Security Presidential Directive that established the Pentagon postwar planning office, the Office of Reconstruction and Humanitarian Assistance. But the creation of this new office hardly cleared the way for more effective postwar planning. "ORHA stands up, and it's a second ad hoc organization," said Agoglia. "We thought they worked for Franks, they said they worked for Sec Def, and that began some pissing contests. . . . They didn't listen to anyone, because they were a bunch of friggin' know-it-alls."

Conrad Crane, the Army historian who later studied the record of the planning for the war, concluded that the establishment of ORHA just two months before the beginning of fighting simply came too late to be helpful. "It created much more confusion than coherence," he said, because it cut off Centcom's work. "Everybody said, 'I'm working with ORHA now.'"

A bad feeling inside the Army

Watching the moves toward war, the Army community fretted, no one more so than Norman Schwarzkopf. Retired generals play a shadowy but important role in the U.S. military establishment, and especially in the Army. They are part Greek chorus and part shadow board of directors, watching and commenting on their successors' work. They tend to be well informed about current operations, because some are hired as consultants and mentors in war games and war college seminars, and others maintain friendships with former subordinates who have risen to the top.

Within the retired community, four-star generals play a particularly weighty role. Within that tiny group, none are more influential than four stars who have commanded combat operations. After Colin Powell—who was necessarily muted in his military commentary because of his struggles with Rumsfeld and Wolfowitz—the retired four-star general with the most public influence during this period likely was Schwarzkopf. As if that weren't enough, he also was allied with the Bush family. He had hunted with the first president Bush and had campaigned for the second, speaking on military issues at the 2000 GOP convention in Philadelphia and later stumping in Florida with Cheney, his secretary of defense during the 1991 war.

In the months before the invasion of Iraq, Schwarzkopf was worried. In January 2003 he made it clear in a lengthy interview that he hadn't seen enough evidence to persuade him that his old comrades from twelve years earlier—Cheney, Powell, and Wolfowitz—were correct in moving toward a new war. He thought UN inspections were still the proper course to follow. He also worried about the cockiness of the U.S. war plan, and even more about the potential human and financial costs of occupying Iraq. "The thought of Saddam Hussein with a sophisticated nuclear capability is a frightening thought, okay?" he said, sitting in his office in Tampa, overlooking a bland skyline of hotels, bank headquarters, and glass-sheathed office buildings. "Now, having said that, I don't know what intelligence the U.S. government has. And before I can just stand up and say, 'Beyond a shadow of a doubt, we need to invade Iraq,' I guess I would like to have better information."

He hadn't seen that evidence yet, and so—in sharp contrast to the Bush administration—he supported letting the UN weapons inspectors drive the timetable: "I think it is very important for us to wait and see what the inspectors come up with, and hopefully they come up with something conclusive." He had a far less Manichaean view of the Middle East than Bush and Cheney had developed after the September 11 attacks. "It's obviously not a black-and-white situation over there. I would just think that whatever path we take, we have to take it with a bit of prudence." Had he seen sufficient prudence in the actions of his old friends in the Bush administration? He didn't want to touch that question. "I don't think I can give you an honest answer on that," he said. He also was unhappy with what he was hearing out of the Army about Rumsfeld. "Candidly, I have gotten somewhat nervous at some of the pronouncements Rumsfeld has made."

Schwarzkopf was a true son of the Army, where he served from 1956 to 1991, and some of his comments reflected the deepening estrangement between that service and the defense secretary. "The Rumsfeld thing . . . that's what comes up," when he calls old Army friends in the Pentagon, he said. "When he makes his comments, it appears that he disregards the Army. He gives the perception when he's on TV that he is the guy driving the train and everybody else better fall in line behind him—or else."

That dismissive posture bothered Schwarzkopf because he thought, like many in the Army, that Rumsfeld, Wolfowitz, Feith, and their subordinates lacked the experience or knowledge to make sound military judgments by themselves and were ignoring the better informed advice of senior generals. He said he preferred the way Cheney had operated during the Gulf War. "He didn't put himself in the position of being the decision maker as far as tactics were concerned, as far as troop deployments, as far as missions were concerned."

Rumsfeld, by contrast, worried him. "It's scary, okay?" he said. "Let's face it: There are guys at the Pentagon who have been involved in operational planning for their entire lives, okay? . . . And for this wisdom, acquired during many operations, wars, schools, for that just to be ignored, and in its place have somebody who doesn't have any of that training, is of concern."

So, said Schwarzkopf, he doubted that an invasion of Iraq would be as fast and simple as some seemed to think. "I have picked up vibes that . . . you're going to have this massive strike with massed weaponry, and basically that's going to be it, and we just clean up the battlefield after that." Like many in the Army, he expressed even more concern about the task the U.S. military might face after a victory. "What is postwar Iraq going to look like, with the Kurds and the Sunnis and the Shiites? That's a huge question, to my mind. It really should be part of the overall campaign plan."

The administration may have been discussing the issue behind closed doors, but he hadn't seen it explained to the world, especially its assessment of the time, people, and money needed. "I would hope that we have in place the adequate resources to become an army of occupation," he warned, "because you're going to walk into chaos."

Col. Spain's prewar gutting

The first time that Col. Teddy Spain got a bad feeling about the Iraq war was two months before it actually started. In late January the military police commander participated in Victory Scrimmage, a big preparatory exercise for the war held at Grafenwoehr, Germany, at the U.S. training base there, in the cold hills near the Czech border. At one point during the exercise, after some notional troops had been "killed," Spain, who would lead an MP brigade into Iraq, turned to some Army chaplains sitting nearby and ordered them to plan a memorial service. They thought he was joking, he recalled. "No, this is serious business," he emphatically responded.

Even as the exercise was held, the size of the U.S.-led invasion force was being whittled down. "First AD and First Cav were there," he said, referring to two of the Army's big armored divisions, the 1st Armored Division and the 1st Cavalry Division. "Then they got knocked out of the plan." He chuckled, years later, at the

memory. "They call themselves 'America's First Team,'" referring to the 1st Cavalry's motto, "and we said, 'Yeah, the first team to go home.'"

But it was less amusing when the planners then turned to Spain and informed
him that his brigade was being kept in the plan, but with a major reduction in its
troop numbers. "They just gutted my assets." Rather than lead twenty companies
into Iraq, he was told, he would begin the war with less than three. It was a decision that Spain, a tall, drawling southerner with a passing resemblance to television
journalist Tom Brokaw, would think back on repeatedly in the coming months
and years, as he dwelled on how he could have done better securing Baghdad in
the spring and summer of 2003. He could have done it, he believed, if only he'd
had those missing companies of MPs.

Others felt the same way. Van Riper, the retired Marine general who was an
old friend of Zinni's, had seen the war plan in October 2002, and noted that it included a division west of the 3rd Infantry Division to control much of Anbar
Province. But in January 2003, he was told, that division was dropped from the
plan. Instead, Anbar would be treated as an "economy of force" area, with a relatively small number of Special Forces sent in, with the mission of preventing Scud
missile launches westward against Israel. This last-minute change was crucial, because it left open the door northwest of Baghdad for Baathists and intelligence officials to flee to the sanctuary of Syria, taking money, weapons, and records with
them with which to establish a safe headquarters for the insurgency that would
emerge that summer. (Some of this movement occurred before the war began,
when, according to retired Air Force Lt. Gen. James Clapper, the head of the U.S.
National Imagery and Mapping Agency, satellite imagery showed a heavy flow of
traffic from Iraq into Syria.) The Army division deleted from the plan "would
have blocked much of the movement to the Syrian border," Van Riper said.

6.

THE SILENCE OF
THE LAMBS

JANUARY–MARCH 2003

I n previous wars, Congress had been populated by hawks and doves. But as war in Iraq loomed it seemed to consist mainly of lambs who hardly made a peep. There were many failures in the American system that led to the war, but the failures in Congress were at once perhaps the most important and the least noticed.

One of the rules of thumb in military operations is that disasters occur not when one or perhaps two things go wrong—which almost any competent leader can handle—but when three or four go wrong at once. Overcoming such a combination of negative events is a true test of command. Similarly, the Iraq fiasco occurred not just because the Bush administration engaged in sustained self-deception over the threat presented by Iraq and the difficulty of occupying the country, but also because of other major lapses in several major American institutions, from the military establishment and the intelligence community to the media. In each arena, the problems generally were sins of commission—bad planning, bad leadership, bad analysis, or in the case of journalism, bad reporting and editing. The role of Congress in this systemic failure was different, because its mistakes were mainly sins of omission. In the months of the run-up to war,

Congress asked very few questions, and didn't offer any challenge to the administration on the lack of postwar planning.

Congress takes no for an answer

The last chance was offered by hearings on Iraq held in February 2003, but
this was not an opportunity that Congress would take. It had made its choice the
previous October when it gave the president a blank check to go to war. As a body
it was willing to ask questions, but that was little more than a pose, because it
didn't object when it didn't get responses that spoke to the issue. It was a Congress
that would take no, or something close to it, for an answer.

Douglas Feith's appearance before the Senate Foreign Relations Committee at
its major prewar hearing on Iraq was a memorable demonstration of testimony
as tap dancing. He couldn't say how many troops might be required, or what
a war might cost, or even what other countries might join the U.S.-led effort.
"Senator, it's hard to answer a lot of these what-ifs because a lot depends on, you
know, future events that we don't know," Feith told Sen. Joseph Biden, the
Delaware Democrat who was the ranking minority member on the panel. "There
are enormous uncertainties." As for the key question of the duration of the occupation, Feith deferred answering. "I don't think I want to venture into the prediction business," he parried.

The senators knew they weren't getting straight answers. "There's a kind of
disconnect between the rhetoric we're hearing and all the rosy scenarios," noted
Sen. Lincoln Chafee of Rhode Island. "Why aren't we hearing some more about a
worse case, and what are we prepared for in that instance?"

Sen. Russell Feingold also expressed puzzlement. "Why do we give the president
a blank check to go ahead with this before we had the answers to these questions?"
he asked.

"You're not giving us much," added Sen. Barbara Boxer, the California Democrat. And that was pretty much it—a hearing with many questions and few
answers.

"The American people have no notion of what we are about to undertake,"
Biden concluded that day. It was an important observation about a democracy
about to launch a war in a distant land, alien culture, and hostile region. But it
was made in a tone of passive resignation.

Zinni, waiting to testify, sat in the room and grew increasingly uneasy as he listened to Feith and other administration officials. "They were nowhere near capa-

ble" of transforming first Iraq and then the Middle East, he thought to himself. They didn't know what they were getting into. They were unprepared. His private conclusion that day, listening to Feith and the other administration witnesses was, "These guys don't have a clue."

When it came his turn to move to the witness chair, Zinni came close to lecturing the Foreign Relations Committee on how they might better have handled the administration's witnesses. First of all, he said, you all need to abandon the idea of an "exit strategy," because there isn't going to be one: "There's things in this part of the world that are too important for us to think that this is a 'go in, do the job as best we can, and pull out.'" Also, you could have pinned them down on their goals. Is it really "a magnificent democracy" they're aiming for? he asked. "I mean, is it truly this transformed Iraq that we've heard about, or are we just going to get rid of Saddam Hussein and hope for the best? . . . What is it that you want?"

Zinni decided that day that the neoconservatives in the administration really were consciously rolling the dice. "I think—and this is just my opinion—that the neocons didn't really give a shit what happened in Iraq and the aftermath," he said much later. "I don't think they thought it would be this bad. But they said: Look, if it works out, let's say we get Chalabi in, he's our boy, great. We don't and maybe there's some half-ass government in there, maybe some strongman emerges, it fractures, and there's basically a loose federation and there's really a Kurdish state. Who cares? There's some bloodshed, and it's messy. Who cares? I mean, we've taken out Saddam. We've asserted our strength in the Middle East. We're changing the dynamic. We're now off the peace process as the centerpiece and we're not putting any pressure on Israel.'"

After the hearings, Zinni asked an old comrade at Centcom what he thought of Desert Crossing, the plans he had drawn up after Desert Fox for dealing with the end of Saddam Hussein's regime. What do you guys think of it, and was it useful, and how have you changed it? This senior officer looked at Zinni blankly: Desert *What?* He had never heard of it. Years of in-depth planning had been discarded.

In the following weeks, as he listened to Wolfowitz and other administration officials talk about Iraq, Zinni became ever more convinced that interventionist neoconservative ideologues were plunging the nation into a war in a part of the world they didn't understand. "The more I saw, the more I thought that this was the product of the neocons who didn't understand the region and were going to create havoc there. These were dilettantes from Washington think tanks who never had an idea that worked on the ground." He dwelled on the fact that U.S. soldiers would wind up paying for the mistakes of Washington policy makers. And that took him back to that bloody day in the sodden Que Son mountains of Vietnam. That war remained painful for him. "I only went to the Wall once, and it was very difficult," he said, talking about his sole visit to the Vietnam Veterans Memorial, the black V-shaped slab that cuts into the Mall in downtown Washington. "I was just walking down past the names of my men. My buddies, my troops—just walking down that Wall was hard, and I couldn't go back."

As one national security official in the Bush administration put it, the passivity of Congress during this period made it far easier to go to war: "Rumsfeld and Wolfowitz are saying, 'We can't tell you how long it will take, or what it will cost, that's unknowable.' Why did Congress accept that?"

Sen. Byrd took to the Senate floor five weeks before the war began and puzzled over why Congress had gone AWOL. "This chamber is, for the most part, silent—ominously, dreadfully silent," he admonished his colleagues. "There is no debate, no discussion, no attempt to lay out for the nation the pros and cons of this particular war. There is nothing. We stand passively mute in the United States Senate, paralyzed by our own uncertainty, seemingly stunned by the sheer turmoil of events." It was just one in a series of speeches Byrd gave on the prospect of war in Iraq, and like the others it had no perceptible effect on his colleagues. "What is happening to this country?" he would ask in a plaintive speech the day before war began. "War appears inevitable."

Congress as a whole became unusually unimportant during this period, especially the Senate and House Armed Services committees, the two panels that oversee the military establishment and so held the keys to airing Pentagon dissent and other concerns about going to war in Iraq. The Republicans didn't want to question the Bush administration. The Democrats couldn't or wouldn't, so Congress didn't produce the witnesses who in hearings would give voice and structure to opposition. Lacking hearings to write about, and the data such sessions would yield, the media didn't delve deeply enough into the issues surrounding the war, most notably whether the administration was correctly assessing the threat presented by Iraq and the cost of occupying and remaking the country.

The House, the Senate, and the executive branch were in Republican hands. Bush was the first Republican president since the 1920s to hold office while both houses of Congress were in the long-term control of his party, and his fellow Republicans weren't inclined to ask many probing questions. The Democrats in 1994 lost control of the House of Representatives for the first time in forty years, and essentially lost control of the Senate in the same year, except for a brief interruption several years later. By 2002–3 they were cowed by the post–9/11 atmosphere, in which almost any measure to fight terror seemed to some to be justified. And they still hadn't learned how to operate effectively in the minority position—and a minority that didn't have an executive branch to lean on and help it with research and responses, as the Republican minority frequently had over the previous four decades. So Democrats generally clammed up, especially when faced by an administration that resolutely stuck by its story. "The Congress didn't do it, because the Republicans weren't going to confront their own president, and the Democrats were enfeebled," said one mournful Democratic veteran of Capitol Hill. "The media didn't stand up because they had no one to quote. So, in combination, the two institutions didn't work."

On top of that, fewer members of Congress had military experience, or, lacking any time in uniform, had spent time studying the military, as Ike Skelton had done. There was little political incentive to do so. "They don't know what questions to ask, and they're afraid to show their ignorance by asking what to ask," said one dismayed congressional staffer.

Nor did Congress have a separate opening with the military—the old back channel that Sam Nunn, when he was chairman of the Senate Armed Services Committee, used to talk to the generals to help him monitor the Pentagon's civilian leadership. Instead, Congress faced an unusually strong secretary of defense and an unusually weak chairman of the Joint Chiefs. Air Force Gen. Richard Myers, the nation's top military officer in 2002, seemed an incurious man, and certainly not one to cross a superior. He had ascended to the chairmanship somewhat by accident, having been selected to be the number-two officer on the Joint Chiefs by people who later said they never envisioned him to go on to the top slot. Myers's term as chairman of the Joint Chiefs was characterized by an extraordinary deference to Rumsfeld. He let himself being overruled on issues such as picking his own staffers for the Joint Staff. Inside the military, he was widely regarded as the best kind of uniformed yes-man—smart, hard-working, but wary of independent thought. The vice chairman, Marine Gen. Peter Pace, was seen as even more pliable, especially by fellow Marines. "The most damaging sort of mistakes that Rumsfeld has made have been on senior officer selection," said one Bush administration official involved in defense issues. "You wind up with smiling Pete Pace and smiling Richard Myers."

Myers is said to have told colleagues that he was doing the best job he could with this secretary of defense. "General Myers believed that in order to have an effect, you had to avoid being confrontational, but get the most you could from the man," said another senior officer on the Joint Staff.

Powell pitches a curveball

The first casualty of the Iraq war may have been the reputation of one of Myers's predecessors, Secretary of State Colin Powell. In February 2003 Powell went to the United Nations and staked his personal credibility on going to war. It was the old general's ultimate sacrifice as a good soldier, throwing his good name behind the administration's campaign and using it to clear out some of the remaining opposition to going to war.

"My colleagues, every statement I make today is backed up by sources, solid sources," Powell said early in the speech, as the CIA's Tenet sat behind him, as if literally backing him up. "These are not assertions. What we are giving you are facts and conclusions based on solid intelligence." Indeed, Powell appeared to lift the veil on highly classified intelligence sources and methods, sharing crown jewel information such as intercepted Iraqi military communications. "We have first-hand descriptions of biological weapons factories on wheels and on rails. Our conservative estimate is that Iraq today has a stockpile of between one hundred and five hundred tons of chemical weapons agent. . . . He remains determined to acquire nuclear weapons. . . . What I want to bring to your attention today is the potentially much more sinister nexus between Iraq and the al Qaeda terrorist network."

Powell didn't know it, but his bravura performance was a huge house of cards. It is now known that almost all of what he said that day wasn't solid, that much of it was deemed doubtful even at the time inside the intelligence community, and that some of it was flatly false. The official, bipartisan conclusion of the Senate Select Committee on Intelligence's review of the prewar handling of intelligence was, "Much of the information provided or cleared by the Central Intelligence Agency for inclusion in Secretary Powell's speech was overstated, misleading, or incorrect." The assertion about chemical weapons would be proven flat wrong. The assertion about the nuclear program was based heavily on the belief that Iraq was seeking aluminum tubes for centrifuge to enrich uranium for a nuclear program. The key question was whether the tubes were of a lower quality alloy suitable for military rockets, or more finely made for nuclear work. "It strikes me as quite odd that these tubes are manufactured to a tolerance that far exceeds U.S. requirements for comparable rockets," Powell said. But the State Department's own intelligence office had contradicted that very assertion two days earlier in its critique of a draft of Powell's speech. It objected to that statement about manufacture. "In fact," it stated in a memorandum, "the most comparable U.S. system is a tactical rocket—the U.S. Mark-66 air-launched 70 mm rocket—that uses the same, high-grade (7075-T6) aluminum, and that has specifications with similar tolerances." Worst of all, the assertion about biological weapons was based largely on the statements of one defector, codenamed Curveball, whose testimony already had been discredited. There was a second source for the statements about biological efforts—and that source had been formally declared a fabricator ten months earlier by the Defense Intelligence Agency, which was handling him, but no one had told Powell about that.

The saga of the informant codenamed Curveball underscores the shoddiness of the case for going to war. Curveball wasn't actually under U.S. control and hadn't been interviewed by any U.S. officials—he was in the hands of German intelligence, which didn't permit U.S. officials to see him before the war. After the war, it was learned that he was the brother of a top aide of Ahmed Chalabi, the *Los Angeles Times* reported. (Chalabi would deny this, without explanation.) Investigators in Iraq also would learn that Curveball hadn't even been in Iraq for some of the time during which he claimed to have witnessed key events. In May 2004 the CIA and DIA would issue a classified report that recanted everything Curveball had asserted—which had been distributed in 101 separate intelligence agency reports.

Some of the doubts about Curveball already were known when Powell headed to New York. David Kay, who would later head the Iraq Survey Group, said that even before the National Intelligence Estimate was published in the fall of 2002, the Germans had warned the CIA that Curveball was a questionable source. The day before Powell delivered the UN speech, a Defense Department employee working at the CIA sent an apprehensive e-mail to the deputy chief of the CIA's Iraq task force. Reviewing a draft of Powell's speech, he was alarmed to see that it leaned heavily on Curveball's assertions. But the deputy chief of the CIA task force was dismissive of such concerns, because, he responded, he saw war with Iraq as inevitable. "Let's keep in mind the fact that this war's going to happen regardless of what Curveball said or didn't say, and that the Powers That Be probably aren't terribly interested in whether Curveball knows what he's talking about," the intelligence officer wrote in the note, which was quoted in the Senate Intelligence Committee report.

When asked by committee investigators why he thought the war was inevitable, the intelligence officer said, "My source of information was the *Washington*

Post"—an indication of the significant role the media played in paving the road to the Iraq war, and especially in influencing the views of intelligence operatives.

Powell believed what he said. Richard Armitage, who had gone out to the CIA's headquarters in Langley, Virginia, to help prepare Powell for the speech, recalled the effort that the secretary of state put into it. "He worked for three days, and parts of all those nights," Armitage recalled. "He called me up and said, 'Can you come with me tomorrow? I need your help.' And I went up there, and was there all day. And he went through each point in the speech, every single one, and looked at everybody in the room, and nobody dissented. Are we sure of the information? Are we sure of the sourcing? Is there anything wrong with the sourcing? And I don't know what more he could have done." George Tenet, the CIA director, was also there as Powell prepared, and kept coming in and out of the room, ordering his station chiefs to go back and check individual bits of information, Armitage recalled. "George would go out of the room, 'Call this country,' he'd say. . . . 'Call that country.'"

"They're in the room, and they're nodding, 'Everything's fine,'" Armitage recalled. "What are you going to do? What is he to do? I don't know." Armitage's conclusion, two years later, was that "the agency let him down big time. . . . The speech clearly didn't turn out to hold water."

In military intelligence circles the speech provoked head shaking at the time. "After Colin Powell's address at the UN, my boss and I looked at each other and said, 'What is going on here?'" recalled a senior military intelligence officer. "There was no doubt in my mind how weak the intel was."

An officer on the Joint Staff, steeped in the war planning, was similarly bothered. As he watched the speech, he thought to himself that the Bush administration, determined to go to war with Iraq, had constructed a trap in which any evidence or lack of it led to the same outcome. "If we find weapons, that means Saddam is cheating and that means we go to war." Conversely, "if we don't find weapons, that means Saddam is cheating, because he is hiding them." Yet this officer's faith in Powell was such that watching the speech persuaded him to put aside such doubts. "If he believes it, I believe it, because I put a lot of stock in what he says," he recalled thinking after the UN speech. "And I figured that people above me had information I didn't have access to."

In fact, the opposite was the case: The people above this officer weren't getting a complete account of the doubts within the intelligence community. As the Senate Intelligence Committee report showed seventeen months later, much of Powell's speech was based on the National Intelligence Estimate of October 2002, and that document had been mistaken in all its major findings.

Powell had done the job. His performance had the desired effect of calming doubts in two camps of notable skeptics—the U.S. military and the pundits of journalism. The Bush administration's approach to selling a war in Iraq was to say, "Trust us," and Powell was one of the nation's most trusted figures, especially among moderates and liberals. So liberal columnists such as Mary McGrory and William Raspberry, who would be highly skeptical of assertions by Cheney and Wolfowitz, were more willing to listen to someone like Powell. What persuaded them more than anything was Powell's personal credibility and the certitude of his style. Indeed, little that Powell said that day in New York was even particularly new. "Almost all of the information in the speech was from intelligence that had previously been in IC [intelligence community] finished intelligence documents, in particular from the 2002 NIE on Iraq's Continuing Programs for Weapons of Mass Destruction," the Senate Intelligence Committee noted. "Several of the IC judgments in the NIE were not substantiated by intelligence source reporting." Nonetheless, "he persuaded me," the *Post's* Mary McGrory wrote immediately after Powell's speech. "Powell took his seat in the United Nations and put his shoulder to the wheel," she wrote. "He was to talk for almost an hour and a half. His voice was strong and unwavering. He made his case without histrionics of any kind, with no verbal embellishments."

From around the country, other editorials were even more glowing. "Impressive," said the *San Francisco Chronicle.* "Masterful," said the *Hartford Courant.* "Overwhelming," added the *Tampa Tribune.* To the Portland *Oregonian* it was "devastating." "Marshal Dillon facing down a gunslinger in Dodge City," gushed the *Denver Post.*

New York Times columnists were more skeptical. While the *Washington Post's* news columns were dubious of war and its editorial page was hawkish, the *Times* was the opposite: Its news coverage had beat the WMD drums for months, especially under the byline of Judith Miller, but those who wrote for its opinion pages generally were not persuaded. To be sure, Bill Keller, not yet the editor of the *Times,* wrote of becoming a member of the "I-Can't-Believe-I'm-a-Hawk Club." But Maureen Dowd was perceptively critical. "The case was less persuasive than the presenter," she discerned. "And it was not clear why the presenter had jumped to the warlike side." (A few weeks later, she was even sharper: "They stretched and obscured the truth. First, they hyped CIA intelligence to fit their contention that

Saddam and Al Qaeda were linked. Then they sent Colin Powell out with hyped evidence about Iraq's weapons of mass destruction.")

Voices presenting other dissenting views—and ones that it is now clear had a better factual basis—were drowned out by Powell's performance. In February, Mohammed ElBaradei, director of the International Atomic Energy Agency, a nuclear watchdog office, reported to the United Nations, "We have found to date no evidence of ongoing prohibited nuclear or nuclear-related activities in Iraq." Three weeks later, he returned and stated even more emphatically that Iraq's weapons capabilities had deteriorated badly since the time of the Desert Fox raid. "During the past four years," he told the security council, "at the majority of Iraqi sites industrial capacity has deteriorated substantially due to the departure of foreign support that often was present in the late eighties, the departure of large numbers of skilled Iraqi personnel in the past decade and the lack of consistent maintenance by Iraq of sophisticated equipment." He was all but ignored.

Rumsfeld says diplomacy is ending

A few days later Rumsfeld flew to the annual Wehrkunde security conference in Munich, where he was even more confrontational than Wolfowitz had been at the previous year's meeting, delivering a bellicose speech and then going head-to-head in an on-stage discussion with German foreign minister Joschka Fischer. His message was that the train was leaving the station, and that the occasion for argument was over, at least among reasonable people. Rumsfeld insisted he had a coalition behind him. "A large number of nations have already said they will be with us in a coalition of the willing—and more are stepping up each day," he told hundreds of European and American defense and foreign policy officials crowded into a hotel ballroom. "Clearly, momentum is building." We are right and you are both wrong and ignorant about the threat presented by Iraq, Rumsfeld asserted. Secretary of State Powell's UN speech, he declared, "presented not opinions, not conjecture, but facts." So, Rumsfeld said, "It is difficult to believe there still could be question in the minds of reasonable people open to the facts before them."

The Bush administration's patience was wearing thin. If the UN didn't back the United States against Iraq, he continued, it would be on "a path of ridicule"— a path, he pointedly noted, that led to the graveyard where the League of Nations had wound up, "discredited." In a lengthy question-and-answer session afterward with the audience, Rumsfeld parried adroitly. Saddam Hussein "wasn't 'in the box.' . . . He has not been contained," and has been able to obtain pretty much whatever weapons he wanted. "Their programs are maturing every day. . . . Diplomacy has been exhausted, almost."

Foreign Minister Fischer, whose impassioned speech immediately followed Rumsfeld's, seemed taken aback by the relentlessness of the U.S. defense secretary's criticism. On the question of attacking Iraq, Fischer asked several times: "Why now? . . . Are we in a situation where we should resort to violence now?" At one point Fischer faced the U.S. delegation to the conference and, switching from German to English, pointedly said, "Excuse me, I am not convinced."

Fischer also warned the United States against biting off more than it could chew in Afghanistan and the Middle East. "You're going to have to occupy Iraq for years and years," he said. "The idea that democracy will suddenly blossom is something that I can't share. . . . Are Americans ready for this?"

Wolfowitz says "salaam"

"Salaam alikum," Paul Wolfowitz said later that month, on a wintry Sunday in Dearborn, Michigan. The Arabic phrase means "peace be with you," but he was attending a war party, meeting with about three hundred Iraqi exiles living in the Detroit area. "Surely God does not change the condition of the people until they change their condition," Wolfowitz said, attributing the quotation to the Koran. The crowd was a rare one, more hawkish than even Wolfowitz, and it greeted him with a standing ovation. Waiting for the speech under a banner that read "Saddam Must Go," Ghazi Shaffo, a native of Baghdad, said, "Every Iraqi wants to change the regime, everyone."

"They should do it soon," added Atheer Karmo, a dentist, also formerly of Baghdad.

Even among this overwhelmingly friendly crowd, there were discordant notes of Shiite distrust. One exile rose to give a passionate summary of recent Iraqi history. Considering that the U.S. government had supported Saddam in the 1980s, he asked, considering that the U.S. had abandoned the Shiites to massacre in 1991, "why should we here, with all due respect, trust or believe" your new promises?

Wolfowitz knew well that the Shiites had been wronged in 1991. "I know there's a lot of history," he said. "This is a time not to look to the past but to the future." And that future, he said, was "one of the most powerful military forces ever assembled" now on the borders of Iraq. "If we commit those forces, we're not going to commit them for anything less than a free and democratic Iraq." The

U.S. government would not settle for removing Saddam Hussein only to put in office someone similar, Wolfowitz reassured his listeners. "It's not going to be handed over to some junior Saddam Hussein. We're not interested in replacing one dictator with another dictator."

The same day, Wolfowitz was interviewed by the *Detroit News*. "Our principal target is the psychological one, to convince the Iraqi people that they no longer have to be afraid of Saddam," he said. "And once that happens I think what you're going to find, and this is very important, you're going to find Iraqis out cheering American troops." He was dismissive of the notion that a U.S. intervention might unleash fighting among Sunnis, Shiites, and Kurds. "I think the ethnic differences in Iraq are there but they're exaggerated," he said.

Shinseki breaks ranks

Gen. Shinseki was less optimistic. Worried by the possibility of "a major influx of Islamic fighters" from elsewhere in the Middle East, former Army secretary Thomas White said later, Shinseki concluded that it would be necessary "to size the postwar force bigger than the wartime force."

The Army chief of staff prepared carefully for the Capitol Hill appearance at which he would unveil that thought and effectively go into public opposition against the war plan being devised under Rumsfeld's supervision. A series of war games over the previous year had strengthened his sense that the U.S. military would need a larger force than Rumsfeld was contemplating. Shinseki had served in Bosnia, and thought the U.S. military would need at least the per capita representation of troops it had deployed there. In Bosnia, said former defense secretary William Perry, the Pentagon had used a formula of one soldier for every fifty Bosnians, which would indicate a force for Iraq of about 300,000, once the relatively peaceful Kurdish area in the north was subtracted. "Shinseki knew there would be a tough Phase IV, and who won that would win the second Gulf War," said Johnny Riggs, who is now retired but at the time was a lieutenant general at the Army's headquarters. "He knew, from his experience, that you need to dominate and control the environment. If you're so thin and small that you're predictable in your movements, then you are just treating the symptoms."

Before heading to Capitol Hill on February 25, 2003, the Army chief asked historians on the Army's staff to research the number of peacekeepers used in Germany and Japan after World War II and after other conflicts. The data came back from the Army's Center of Military History: In Iraq the postwar peacekeeping force should probably number about 260,000, the researchers told him. That was the number in the back of his mind when he went to Capitol Hill and was pinned down on the issue. "Gen. Shinseki, could you give us some idea as to the magnitude of the Army's force requirement for an occupation of Iraq following a successful completion of the war?" asked Sen. Carl Levin, the senior Democrat on the Senate Armed Services Committee.

"In specific numbers, I would have to rely on the combatant commander's exact requirements," Shinseki replied, obeying the military protocol of deferring to the responsible commander—in this case, Gen. Franks. "But I think—"

"How about a range?" Levin interrupted.

"I would say that what's been mobilized to this point, something on the order of several hundred thousand soldiers, are probably, you know, a figure that would be required." His reasoning, he added, was that Iraq was a large country with multiple ethnic tensions, "so it takes significant ground force presence to maintain a safe and secure environment to ensure that people are fed, that water is distributed, all the normal responsibilities that go along with administering a situation like this."

Shinseki didn't know it, but that exchange—virtually the only discussion of Iraq in a hearing that focused more on mundane issues of military force structures and budgets—would be the most remembered public moment of his four years as chief of staff of the U.S. Army. His comments were not greeted warmly by his civilian overseers at the Pentagon. White, the Army secretary, recalled being told by Wolfowitz that Shinseki had been out of line. "He was not happy that we had taken a position that was opposed to what his thinking on the subject was."

Wolfowitz told senior Army officers around this time that he thought that within a few months of the invasion the U.S. troop level in Iraq would be thirty-four thousand, recalled Riggs, the Army general then at Army headquarters. Likewise, another three-star general, still on active duty, remembers being told to plan to have the U.S. occupation force reduced to thirty thousand troops by August 2003. An Army briefing a year later also noted that that number was the goal "by the end of the summer of 2003."

When Wolfowitz was on the Hill two days later he slapped down Shinseki's estimate. "There has been a good deal of comment—some of it quite outlandish—about what our postwar requirements might be in Iraq," he told the House Budget Committee. "Some of the higher end predictions that we have been hearing recently, such as the notion that it will take several hundred thousand U.S. troops to provide stability in post-Saddam Iraq, are wildly off the mark." His reasoning,

he explained, was that "it is hard to conceive that it would take more forces to provide stability in post–Saddam Iraq than it would take to conduct the war itself
and to secure the surrender of Saddam's security forces and his army—hard to
imagine."

In an intellectually snide aside, he also said that "one should at least pay attention to past experience." Bosnia, Wolfowitz maintained, wasn't the proper precedent to study. "There has been none of the record in Iraq of ethnic militias fighting
one another that produced so much bloodshed and permanent scars in Bosnia,"
he said. Rather, one should look to the far more benign environment of Operation Provide Comfort in northern Iraq. At any rate, Wolfowitz said, he had met
with Iraqi Americans in Detroit a week earlier. Based on what he had heard about
Iraq from them, he said, "I am reasonably certain that they will greet us as liberators, and that will help us keep requirements down." So, he concluded, "we don't
know what the requirements will be. But we can say with reasonable confidence
that the notion of hundreds of thousands of American troops is way off the mark."

In keeping with this extraordinarily optimistic assessment, Wolfowitz also
would assert that same day that oil exports likely would pay for much of Iraq's
postwar reconstruction. "It's got already, I believe, on the order of $15 billion to
$20 billion a year in oil exports, which can finally—might finally be—turned to a
good use instead of building Saddam's palaces," he told the House Budget Committee. "There is a lot of money there." He repeated the point a month later to
another congressional committee, saying that Iraq "can really finance its own reconstruction." As for an administration official who had told the Washington Post
that the war and its aftermath could cost as much as $95 billion, Wolfowitz said,
"I don't think he or she knows what he is talking about." (By mid 2006, the cost of
the war, counting the expenditures in Iraq of all parts of the federal government,
would be close to triple that.)

The Army wasn't buying the optimism. Retired Army Maj. Gen. William
Nash, who had led the U.S. peacekeeping forces into Bosnia, forecast that spring
that the occupation would take 200,000 troops—almost exactly the troop total in
much of 2004–5, if to the 150,000 U.S. personnel there are added 20,000 private
security contractors and 30,000 allied soldiers.

The debate was far more than a technical squabble about troop numbers.
Andrew Bacevich observed that Shinseki's comments amounted to a broad attack
on Wolfowitz's entire approach to the Middle East. "Given that the requisite additional troops simply did not exist, Shinseki was implicitly arguing that the U.S.
armed services were inadequate for the enterprise," Bacevich wrote in the *Ameri-*

can Conservative. "Further, he was implying that invasion was likely to produce something other than a crisp, tidy decision. . . . 'Liberation' would leave loose ends. Unexpected and costly complications would abound. In effect, Shinseki was offering a last-ditch defense of the military tradition that Wolfowitz was intent on destroying, a tradition that saw armies as fragile, that sought to husband military power, and that classified force as an option of last resort. The risks of action, Shinseki was suggesting, were far, far greater than the advocates for war had let on."

That subtext about the nature of military force and the wisdom of using it in Iraq may have been one reason the effects of the exchange between Shinseki and Wolfowitz were so far reaching. The message the top brass received in return was that the Bush administration wasn't interested in hearing about their worries about Iraq. "There were concerns both before we crossed the line of departure and after," said one four-star general, looking back much later. "There was a conscious cutting off of advice and concerns, so that the guy who ultimately had to make the decision, the president, didn't get the advice. Well before the troops crossed the line of departure"—that is, invaded Iraq on March 20, 2003—"concern was raised about what would happen in the postwar period, how you would deal with this decapitated country. It was blown off. Concern about a long-term occupation—that was discounted. The people around the president were so, frankly, intellectually arrogant," this general continued. "They *knew* that postwar Iraq would be easy and would be a catalyst for change in the Middle East. They were making simplistic assumptions and refused to put them to the test. It's the vice president, and the secretary of defense, with the knowledge of the chairman of the Joint Chiefs and the vice chairman. They did it because they already had the answer, and they wouldn't subject their hypothesis to examination. These are educated men, they are smart men. But they are not wise men."

This senior general said he had come to believe that this disinclination to listen to the doubters would go on to help create the insurgency. By refusing to consider worst-case scenarios, the Pentagon's civilian leaders didn't develop answers to questions about how to conduct an occupation or what to do with the Iraqi army if it were dissolved. "It's almost as if, unintentionally, we were working with Zarqawi to create the maximum amount of chaos possible," he said, referring to Abu Musab al-Zarqawi, the Jordanian terrorist who operated in Iraq and affiliated himself with al Qaeda.

At the time Pentagon officials publicly played down Shinseki's comments, claiming he had been mousetrapped into making them. But a month later, when the Army chief was again on Capitol Hill, he was asked about them again. Yes, he told the House Defense Appropriations Subcommittee, he stood by his estimate of the occupation force that could be necessary in postwar Iraq. "It could be as high as several hundred thousand," Shinseki said. "We all hope it is something less."

Wolfowitz's slapdown of Shinseki echoed for months across the military, said Sen. Jack Reed, a member of the Senate Armed Services Committee, who as a young man had served in the 82nd Airborne. "Not only was he honest, but he turned out to be right," Reed, a Rhode Island Democrat, noted two years later. "He was treated very poorly. I think it's had a chilling effect, very destructive, corrosive."

Inside the uniformed military, officers kept quiet, at least publicly. But their private unhappiness ran deep. A few weeks before the war began, one civilian deeply involved in Army affairs meditated on this sad situation. "There is so much disdain in the services right now for OSD that it has just been reduced to, 'Fuck you, whatever you want, we don't.' If OSD ordered the Navy to build another carrier, the Navy would say it wanted sail power." It was not a healthy state for a military establishment to be in on the eve of war.

Myers: Iraqis will lead us to the WMD

In early March, not long before the war began, Myers, the chairman of the Joint Chiefs, met with reporters for a breakfast in a plush meeting room in a downtown Washington hotel a few blocks from the White House. Like Cheney, Myers played the secret intelligence card. Some of the inside information about Iraq's WMD had been revealed by Powell in his United Nations speech, Myers said, "but there are things you can't reveal because then your sources and methods are compromised, and in some cases, people get hurt."

No, he conceded in response to a reporter's question, we don't know where the WMD are. But he wasn't worried, he added, because he was confident the Iraqis would lead American troops to the weapons stockpiles soon after the war began. "They're playing a giant shell game right now. That shell game, with forces on the ground, would come to a halt." At that point, "people will come forward and say, 'Here's where this is, here's where that is.' "

That, the nation's top military officer said, was what the war would be all about. "The ultimate objective isn't Saddam Hussein," he explained. "The ultimate objective is to ensure that Iraq doesn't have chemical or biological weapons."

Rumsfeld was similarly emphatic when interviewed by Al Jazeera, the Arabic satellite television news channel. "I would like to put it to you straight away," began Al Jazeera's Jamil Azer. "The issue between you, the Bush administration, and Iraq is not weapons of mass destruction. It is for you, how to get rid of Saddam Hussein and his regime."

The defense secretary could not have been clearer in his response. "Well, wrong," he said. "It is about weapons of mass destruction. It is unquestionably about that."

And on that issue, the Bush administration would go to war with rock-hard certainty. The last word on the issue on the eve of hostilities would be the president's: "Intelligence gathered by this and other governments leaves no doubt that the Iraq regime continues to possess and conceal some of the most lethal weapons ever devised."

The planning for postwar Iraq stumbles

On February 21 and 22, 2003, Garner convened experts from across the U.S. government to discuss postwar Iraq. The session was notable because, according to participants, it was the sole occasion before the war when all the warring factions within the U.S. government met. The official attendance list carries 154 names, but attendees remember many more. "This was the only time the interagency really sat down at the operator level with policy presence and discussed in detail the activities each of the pillar teams had planned," recalled Col. Hughes, now retired but then on active duty. "Folks were seated on windowsills and standing in the aisles."

Among those present, according to the official attendance list, were Bill Luti and Abram Shulsky from Feith's policy office in the Pentagon, Elliot Abrams from the National Security Council, Eric Edelman and others from Cheney's office, and, in the Central Command contingent, Brig. Gen. Steve Hawkins, the chief of Phase IV planning for that headquarters. There also were representatives from the CIA and DIA, the Treasury and Justice departments, and the British and Australian governments. At twenty-five members, the group from State was nearly the equal of the Pentagon delegation, which came from a variety of civilian and military offices.

The problems were clear. The group had been set up "far too late," according to exhaustive notes taken by one official at the meeting. There weren't enough troops in the war plan "for the first step of securing all the major urban areas, let alone for providing an interim police function." Without sufficient troops "we risk letting much of the country descend into civil unrest, chaos whose magnitude may defeat our national strategy of a stable new Iraq, and more immediately, we place our own troops, fully engaged in the forward fight, in greater jeopardy." The meeting concluded that security "is far and away the greatest challenge, and the greatest shortfall. If we do not get it right, we may change the regime, but our national strategy likely will fall apart." This issue of having sufficient troops to meet minimum requirements had been brought to Rumsfeld, "who has yet to be convinced."

What's more, the note taker wrote, "The humanitarian, reconstruction and civil affairs efforts will be tremendously expensive." That conclusion stood in direct contrast to the public statements of the Bush administration.

Of all those speaking those two days, one person in particular caught Garner's attention. Scrambling to catch up with the best thinking, Garner was looking for someone who had assembled the facts and who knew all the players in the U.S. government, the Iraqi exile community, and international organizations, and had considered the second- and third-order consequences of possible actions. While everyone else was fumbling for the facts, this man had a dozen binders, tabbed and indexed, on every aspect of Iraqi society, from how electricity was generated to how the port of Basra operated, recalled another participant.

"They had better stuff in those binders than the 'eyes only' stuff I eventually got from CIA," said a military expert who attended.

"There was this one guy who knew everything, everybody, and he kept on talking," Garner recalled. At lunch, Garner took him aside. Who are you? the old general asked. Tom Warrick, the man answered.

"How come you know all this?" Garner asked.

"I've been working on it for a year," Warrick said. He said he was at the State Department, where he headed a project called the Future of Iraq, a sprawling effort that relied heavily on the expertise of Iraqi exiles.

"Come to work for me on Monday," Garner said. Warrick did.

But it wouldn't be as easy to keep him. Garner, a straightforward old soldier, didn't realize that he had walked into the middle of a running feud between the State Department and the Defense Department. There were multiple points of friction. Powell and Rumsfeld didn't seem to get along, or even be able to address their differences. There were deep disagreements between them over Iraq, and those ran down into their departments. Richard Armitage, the deputy secretary of state, came to believe that one reason Rumsfeld's office wanted to invade Iraq with a relatively small force was "because they wanted to disavow the Powell doctrine" of using overwhelming or decisive force in military operations.

Aides at each department used the media to take potshots at the other. "A country that has its own major agencies at war is not going to fight a war well," said Dov Zakheim, who was a Vulcan—one of Bush's advisers on national security policy during the 2000 presidential campaign—and later the Pentagon's top financial officer. "And State and Defense were at war—don't let anyone tell you different. Within policy circles, it was knee-jerk venom, on both sides. Neither side was prepared to give the other a break. It began in 2001, got exacerbated during the buildup to Iraq, and stayed on." The split began at the top, but extended down to the "working level," Zakheim said, of "people who had to work with, and trust, each other—and they didn't."

So while the task and stakes facing Garner were huge—certainly the future of Iraq, possibly the future of the Mideast, perhaps that of U.S. foreign policy in the region, perhaps the future of the Bush administration—he found himself focused instead on sniping inside the Bush administration, at Warrick and others he was recruiting. Apparently there was some sort of ideological test they had failed, but it was all very mysterious to Garner, even to the extent of exactly who was administering the exam.

A few days later Garner briefed Rumsfeld on the state of his planning. The briefing slide on the Iraqi army stated that it would be "necessary to keep Iraqi army intact for a specified period of time. Serves as ready resource pool for labor-intensive civil works projects." As the meeting was breaking up and aides were leaving, Rumsfeld took Garner aside and said he had an issue he needed to discuss privately. He walked over to his desk and took out some notes, which he reviewed for a moment, Garner recalled. He then looked up and said, according to Garner, "You've got two people working for you—Warrick and [Meghan] O'Sullivan—that you need to get rid of."

"I can't, they are smart, really good, knowledgeable," Garner protested.

Rumsfeld said it was out of his hands. "This comes from such a level that I can't do anything about it," he said, according to Garner. That could mean only one thing: The purge had been ordered by someone at the White House, and not just from some underling on the staff of the National Security Council. Garner felt his group, just getting off the ground, was being hamstrung. Worried and upset, he went to see Stephen Hadley, the low-key deputy to Condoleeza Rice at the NSC. Again he was faced with a senior official telling him it was out of his hands. "I can't do anything about it," Hadley told Garner.

Garner then had one of his staffers call around national security circles in the government to find out what was going on. "He was told the word had come from Cheney," he recalled.

When Powell got word of the ouster of Warrick and O'Sullivan, he called Rumsfeld and asked, "What the hell is going on?" Rumsfeld responded that the work of postwar planning had to be done by people devoted to the task who supported the policy.

The tug-of-war over Garner's personnel picks never really ended. "Anybody that knows anything" was removed, Armitage said later. "They didn't like Warrick and Meghan [O'Sullivan], because they were both inconvenient—you know, wanted the facts to get into the equation. These were not people who stood up for the party line, that we'd be welcomed with garlands. We bitched about it, and all Rumsfeld said was, 'I got the higher authority.' And he didn't say whom. Well, not many higher."

Garner to Feith: "Shut the fuck up or fire me"

On March 11, Garner met the media at the Pentagon for a backgrounder, which meant he spoke under ground rules that allowed reporters to identify him at the time only as a senior defense official. Among the principles he laid down for postwar Iraq was that an obtrusive U.S. role would be short and the Iraqi army would continue to exist. "We intend to immediately start turning some things over, and every day, we'll turn over more things," Garner said. "I believe that's our plan." As for the Iraqi military, "a good portion" would be useful to work in the reconstruction of the country. "We'd continue to pay them. Using army allows us not to demobilize it immediately and put a lot of unemployed people on the street." The overall duration of the U.S. presence, he said, would be short. "I'll probably come back to hate this answer, but I'm talking months."

Each and every one of these statements was destined to be reversed just eight weeks later, when Garner would be succeeded in mid-May by Ambassador L. Paul Bremer. But the comment that got Garner in trouble that day in the Pentagon wasn't any of those. Rather, it was his repeated denial of any intention to give a role to Ahmed Chalabi's Iraqi National Congress. When specifically asked about working with the group the Iraqi exile had formed as the putative core of a new government, Garner was dismissive. "I think you're going to see a lot of people putting forth groups," he said. Nor, he said, was he seeking to hire INC members for his humanitarian operations.

The undersecretary of defense for policy was livid with him afterward for his attitude toward Chalabi, Garner recalled. "Feith loved him." One day during planning sessions, "Feith spent an afternoon extolling the virtues of Ahmed Chalabi. He said, trying to show how good Chalabi was, 'You know, Jay, when you get there, we could just make Chalabi president.'" (Many in the uniformed military had a different view of Chalabi. "I never liked him, and none of my analysts ever trusted him," said a military intelligence official.)

After the briefing Feith summoned Garner and shouted at him over the disrespect shown Chalabi. "You've ruined everything, how could you say this?" Feith said, according to Garner.

"Doug, you've got two choices," Garner remembers responding. "You can shut the fuck up, or you can fire me." Garner thought afterward that Feith had settled for the first of the two options. But he also was told that he wasn't allowed to speak to the media, even on background. One result was that over the next several weeks, relations between his group and a frustrated press corps worsened notably. And then, by mid-May, he would find out that Feith and others at the Pentagon essentially had settled on option two.

The next day Garner took his whole staff out to Fort Meade, a sprawling Army base in the Maryland suburbs of Washington, for training in the use of pistols, maps, and other military basics. Two days later, as the training was ending, Rumsfeld called and asked for a final briefing. It was a Friday, and the Garner group was leaving for Kuwait on Sunday.

Garner went down to the Pentagon on Saturday, March 15. "What are you going to do for de-Baathification?" Rumsfeld asked, according to Garner.

Garner saw two possibilities. Either the locals will have killed the most offensive Baathists, or over time, the locals will point them out. So, Garner said, his plan was to remove just two people in each ministry and major government office—the top Baathist and the chief personnel officer. "Well, that sounds fine with me until we get you a policy," Rumsfeld responded.

Garner also reviewed with the defense secretary his plans for dealing with famines, epidemics, and oil fires—the problems he expected to face upon arrival in Iraq. At the end, Rumsfeld appeared uneasy, Garner recalled. "I'm very uncomfortable with this," the defense secretary told Garner.

Garner was almost speechless. "This is a hell of a time to tell me," he said. "I'm leaving tomorrow."

No, said Rumsfeld, I'm not objecting to your perspective on the likely problems. "It's not the plans, it's the people," he said, according to Garner. There were too many outsiders, too many State Department types. "I think we should have Defense Department people."

Rumsfeld was replicating in microcosm with Garner nit-picking he had done with Franks over the war plan. There the numbers had been tens of thousands, but here the issue was just a few dozen people. Garner said it was simply too late to rejigger the staff. Instead, Rumsfeld exacted a promise that on the long airplane ride to Kuwait, Garner would review his roster and see if any last-minute substitutions could be made.

Even then, Feith and his aides didn't give up. A week later, Garner recalls, one of them, Ryan Henry, called him in Kuwait with a list of Defense Department picks for Garner's staff. "When are they gonna be here?" Garner asked. Henry, an assistant in Feith's policy office, said he didn't know. Well, said Garner, I'm going to be in Baghdad in a couple of weeks.

Three days later, Henry called him again. "There's a little glitch in that list," he said.

"The whole goddamn list is a glitch," snarled Garner.

"Well, the White House wants to put in some of their own people," Henry said, according to Garner. The result, he said, was that some staff members didn't appear in Baghdad until the end of May—an absence that may have helped undercut the U.S. presence during the crucial transitional period.

Meanwhile, he said, the continued squabbling between Defense and State made Garner's staff feel unsupported, even beleaguered, as it prepared for its mission. "That DoD fighting with the State Department—that caused all sorts of despair on the team," Garner said.

One day while Garner and his team were still waiting in Kuwait to head into Iraq, Col. Hughes was told to go out to the airport to pick up Lawrence Di Rita, a brash ex-Navy officer who was one of Rumsfeld's closest aides, and who was being sent out to Iraq more or less as the personal emissary of the defense secretary. For Hughes, who was working on long-term strategy for Garner, it was an opportunity to get the inside skinny from someone familiar with the thinking at the top. So as they were driving on the broad freeway back down into Kuwait City, heading toward the Kuwait Hilton, Hughes brought up the subject. I'm putting together a strategy paper for postwar Iraq, and would welcome your input, he said.

Don't bother, he recalled Di Rita responding. "Within 120 days, we'll win this war and get all U.S. troops out of the country, except 30,000," Di Rita said, Hughes recalled. Di Rita also told him that the office of the secretary of defense "viewed Haiti, Kosovo, Bosnia, and even Afghanistan as failures, and this wasn't going to be their failure."

The next morning they had breakfast together. "Look," Hughes said, "this is the good, the bad, and the ugly." The good was the hard work Garner's group had done. The bad was that there was going to be a war. "But the ugly is the shenanigans that are going on inside the Beltway between State and Defense." Di Rita just stared down into his eggs and didn't respond, Hughes recalled.

"That was the last real conversation I ever had with him," Hughes added.

Di Rita, for his part, remembered the conversations differently. First he flatly denied that the conversation had occurred. "I never said anything approaching what he says I said," he insisted in a telephone interview. "It is false." Later, in a face-to-face interview, he said that before arriving in Kuwait he visited Centcom's headquarters in Qatar, where he had heard much discussion of quick troop reductions. "I may have repeated some of that thinking when I got to Kuwait," he said.

The Unified Mission Plan drawn up by Garner and his staff during that period in Kuwait was surprisingly clear-eyed. It began with the statement, "History will judge the war against Iraq not by the brilliance of its military execution, but by the effectiveness of the post-hostilities activities." Nor did it expect a free ride: "The potential for instability is likely to exist for some time after the war is over. The most probable threat will come from residual pockets of fanatics, secessionist groups, terrorists and those who would seek to exploit ethnic, religious, and tribal fault lines."

Yet at the same time, Garner had a short-term conception of his task that seems to have led him to underestimate it. He seemed to think he faced simply a larger version of Provide Comfort, the 1991 relief operation in the north, said a U.S. government official who was involved both in that earlier effort and in the U.S. occupation in 2003. "That was a big mistake—it was not going to be a big Provide Comfort," this nonmilitary official said. When Garner was told that he needed a large and well-designed information management system, he would respond, "If it's not useful in two weeks, we don't want it; our time is short, and this job's going to be over quick."

Experts' prewar concerns about postwar Iraq

In the messy aftermath of the invasion, the Bush administration tended to dismiss critics as "Monday morning quarterbacks." That phrase conveniently disregarded the fact that many of the critics had expressed their worries before the war even began, in part because of the accounts they were hearing from insiders at the Pentagon and in Garner's organization.

"I don't see a lot of operational risks in the front end," Frank Hoffman, a consultant to the Marine Corps who is steeped in military history, said on March 12.

"I think the larger risks are the length and costs of post-Iraq stability operations and the opportunity costs we will be incurring."

Likewise, retired Col. John Warden, one of the Air Force's brightest strategists since the Vietnam War, wrote the same day in an e-mail, "Biggest risk by far is strategic and is in the post-war period. When the British took over after WWI from the Ottomans, they found themselves being assassinated from almost the first day and saw the whole area in open rebellion within a year. . . . What do we do when small bands of fanatic Muslims start creeping across the border from Iraq, Syria, or Saudi Arabia?" The bottom line, he added, was that the United States faced a "very high risk from the strategic side with years of difficult and very expensive occupation."

"What will be the reaction in this country when/if nothing much is discovered regarding WMD?" asked Daniel Kuehl, a professor at the National Defense University, in an e-mail on March 10. Also, said Kuehl, an airpower expert who had been a planner in the 1991 war, "I think the course of the war itself will be measured in a few weeks, but the Reconstruction (upper case intended, as a comparison to our own 1865–76) will last years. It won't be a physical reconstruction so much as a political one."

Yet where the critics went off course was in predicting that domestic political effect of prolonged fighting in Iraq, the first sustained ground combat involving U.S. forces since the Vietnam War. Most of those who correctly envisaged a difficult occupation also wrongly foresaw that Bush's presidency would be severely hampered by that outcome, rather than sailing to reelection even as the Iraqi insurgents launched a fierce offensive. Nor were Bush's fortunes much damaged by the failure to find stockpiles of chemical or biological weapons. It may be that the Bush administration's misjudgment of the outcome in Iraq was balanced by its more accurate sense of the mood of the post-9/11 American public, which had suffered three thousand dead that day, and in the years that followed would prove more tolerant of military casualties and less sensitive about the reasons for going to war in Iraq than many experts expected.

On March 18, Rep. Ike Skelton sent a second letter to Bush. He still felt that he didn't understand what the president had in mind. Among other things, he was worried about "a ragged ending to a war as we deal with the aftermath." This time the White House sent two National Security Council staffers, Eliott Abrams and Stephen Hadley, to Capitol Hill to reassure Skelton. "They told me, 'It's going to be all right, Ike,'" he recalled, shaking his head slowly.

The Bush administration's official line of empty optimism would reach its nadir a few weeks later when Andrew Natsios, head of the U.S. Agency for International Development, assured Ted Koppel on *Nightline* that the U.S. government's contribution to rebuilding Iraq would be just $1.7 billion. Koppel, incredulous, asked him if he was really suggesting that that number would be the total tab.

"Well, in terms of the American taxpayers' contribution, I do, this is it for the U.S.," Natsios responded. Other countries would chip in. "But the American part of this will be $1.7 billion."

Koppel later returned to this question: It's going to be that number no matter how long it takes? Absolutely, said Natsios. "That is our plan and that is our intention," he said. Then, characteristically of the Bush administration at this time, he attacked those who said it would cost more. "These figures, outlandish figures I've seen, I have to say, there's a little bit of hoopla involved in this." (Oddly, six months later, Rumsfeld said he doubted that Natsios ever had said this: "He is administrator of AID, and he has to know that the total cost, to use your phrase, of reconstruction in Iraq is not 1.7, and I just can't believe he said that," the defense secretary said at a Pentagon press conference.)

Since then, the American taxpayer has paid more than ten times Natsios's predicted figure, with no end in sight, to rebuild in Iraq. And that is before the cost of the continuing war—as of the middle of 2006, a total of about $250 billion, according to the Congressional Research Service, which includes expenditures by both the Pentagon and the State Department.

Heading north without a plan

As war was about to begin, everything was ready except for one thing: a real war plan. The official view at the Pentagon is that solid planning was done. "The idea that the U.S. government had no plan for the aftermath of war is false," Wolfowitz insisted in July 2003. It was just, he said, that "every plan requires adjustment once conflict begins."

But many other participants disagree, as—increasingly—do military historians who have examined the record. Lt. Gen. Kellogg was one of the senior members of the staff of the Joint Chiefs of Staff, overseeing systems for the command and control of forces. "I was there for all the planning, all the execution" of the Iraq war plan, and then later served in Iraq. "I saw it all." But what he never saw was a real plan for Phase IV—that is, what to do after toppling Saddam Hussein's regime. "There was no real plan," Kellogg said. "The thought was, you didn't need it. The assumption was that everything would be fine after the war, that they'd be happy they got rid of Saddam."

Despite the many studies and briefings done, wrote Maj. Isaiah Wilson, who served as an official Army historian during the spring 2003 invasion and later as a strategic planner in Iraq, "there was no Phase IV plan" for occupying Iraq after the combat phase. While various offices had produced studies, he said in a paper later delivered at Cornell University, there was "no single plan as of 1 May 2004 that described an executable approach to achieving the stated strategic endstate for the war."

Marine Col. Nicholas Reynolds, an official Corps historian, agreed that he found nothing worthy of being considered a plan: "Nowhere in Centcom or CFLCC had there been a plan for Phase IV that was like the plan for Phase III, let alone all of the preparations that accompanied it, including the cross talk during its development, the many rehearsals of concept drills, and the exchange of liaison officers."

The reason for this omission, said Army Col. Gregory Gardner, who served on the Joint Staff and then was assigned to the Coalition Provisional Authority (CPA), the U.S. occupation headquarters, as his last post before retiring, was that it was seen as unnecessary. "Politically, we'd made a decision that we'd turn it over to the Iraqis in June" of 2003, recalled Gardner. "So why have a Phase IV plan?"

Eclipse II, as the Army's plan for Phase IV operations was code-named, was founded on three basic assumptions, all of which ultimately would prove false. These were, according to an internal Army War College summary:

- That there would be large numbers of Iraqi security forces willing and able to support the occupation. Or, as the War College's Strategic Studies Institute put it in PowerPointese, "Availability of significant numbers of Iraqi military and police who switched sides."
- That the international community would pick up the slack from the U.S. military—that is, "significant support from other nations, international organization, and nongovernmental organizations." It isn't clear what this assumption was based on, given the widespread and building opposition to the U.S.-led invasion.
- That an Iraqi government would quickly spring into being, permitting a "quick handoff to Iraqi interim administration with UN mandate."

A Rand Corp. study written in 2005 after a review of the classified record noted in a matter-of-fact manner, "Post-conflict stabilization and reconstruction were addressed only very generally, largely because of the prevailing view that the task would not be difficult." It recommended that in future, to remedy such shortsighted thinking, "some process for exposing senior officials to possibilities other than those being assumed in their planning also needs to be introduced."

When assumptions are wrong, everything built on them is undermined. Because the Pentagon assumed that U.S. troops would be greeted as liberators and that an Iraqi government would be stood up quickly, it didn't plan seriously for less rosy scenarios. Because it so underestimated the task at hand, it didn't send a well-trained, coherent team of professionals, but rather an odd collection of youthful Republican campaign workers and other novices. Nor did it send enough people. In part because of the poor quality and sheer lack of CPA personnel, the U.S. occupation authorities would prove unable to adjust their stance quickly when assumptions proved wrong. Because of that incompetence, the CPA would be unable to provide basic services such as electricity, clean water, and security to the Iraqi population, and so in the fall of 2003 it would begin to lose the lukewarm support it had enjoyed.

But on March 19, 2003, that unfortunate chain of consequences still lay hidden in the future. "I hope this thing goes down as fast as everyone thinks," Capt. Lesley Kipling, an Army communications officer on the staff of Col. Teddy Spain, the MP commander, wrote that night to her boyfriend, an Army captain back in Germany. But just in case, the small brown-haired female officer wrote as she sat in her tent near the Iraqi border, please put in the mail a new leg holster to hold her 9 millimeter pistol.

PART II

═══

INTO IRAQ

7.

WINNING A BATTLE

MARCH–APRIL 2003

History will record that America's strategy for fighting terrorism was a good strategy, that the plan for Operation Iraqi Freedom was a good plan—and that the execution of that plan by our young men and women in uniform was unequalled in its excellence by anything in the annals of war," Gen. Franks asserted in his memoir, *American Soldier*.

It now seems more likely that history's judgment will be that the U.S. invasion of Iraq in the spring of 2003 was based on perhaps the worst war plan in American history. It was a campaign plan for a few battles, not a plan to prevail and secure victory. Its incompleteness helped create the conditions for the difficult occupation that followed. The invasion is of interest now mainly for its role in creating those problems.

In the spring of 2003 the U.S. military fought the battle it wanted to fight, mistakenly believing it would be the only battle it faced. This was a failure of thinking, and planning, and the first of several strategic missteps that would place the U.S. occupation of Iraq on a foundation of sand. "I like Rumsfeld," said one Air Force general. "I appreciate him. But he should have said to Franks sometime in 2002 that there was an error of omission" in the failure of the plan to consider how to consolidate the victory. "Looking back on it, it was the absolute wrong thing to do" to go to war with a half-baked plan, he said. "Once they made the decision that there would be a separate plan for the postwar, that was the mistake."

Others blame Franks for devising a plan that didn't link actions on the ground to the ultimate goal of the war. "It was a horrible war plan," said Washington Institute for Near East Policy's Patrick Clawson, "because everybody was saying that you need to fight the war in such a way that you stand up a new authority afterward—and the war plan didn't have a depth of thinking about that." In military terms, there was a disconnect between the stated strategic goal of transforming the politics of Iraq and the Mideast and the plan's focus on the far more limited aim of simply removing Saddam Hussein's regime.

COBRA II, the ground component of the classified U.S. war plan, began by flatly stating the intention of the nation in going to war: "The purpose of this operation is to force the collapse of the Iraqi regime and deny it the use of WMD to threaten its neighbors and U.S. interests in regions." The plan that follows that statement of intent is designed to achieve that relatively narrow goal. "The end-state for this operation is regime change," COBRA II states a few paragraphs later.

But the United States wasn't invading Iraq just to knock off a regime. "If the intent of operations in Iraq in 2003 was merely 'regime destruction,' which it was not, then the short, decisive warfighting operation of March and April 2003 might in itself have constituted success," Maj. Gen. Jonathan Bailey noted shortly after retiring from the British army in 2005. "In all other respects it might have been counterproductive."

A false start

Fittingly, a war justified by false premises began on false information.

Combat commenced on March 20, 2003, in Iraq—it was still the evening of March 19 in Washington, D.C.—with a volley of cruise missiles and bunker-penetrating bombs against Doura Farms, a group of houses sometimes used by Saddam Hussein located in a palm grove on the western bank of the Tigris in the southern outskirts of Baghdad. After the CIA received hot intelligence indicating that Saddam was there, Tenet rushed with the information to the White House, and the decision was made to accelerate the invasion plan. At the time, it was thought the air strike might have killed or wounded Saddam, but in fact he seems to have been nowhere in the area. The activity in the tree line that had excited the CIA that day likely was just the security guards and farmhands from Doura

Farms. Sajad Hassan, a guard at the main gate, said in an interview that everyone knew war was coming and that the U.S. bombing would target Saddam's palaces, so they had moved their families and most valuable possessions into the groves nearly a mile outside the walls of the compound. "We were damned sure the presidential palaces would be bombed," he said.

Richard Perle later concluded that the U.S. government had been fooled. "There is reason to believe that we were sucked into an initial attack aimed at Saddam himself by double agents planted by the regime," he would tell the House Armed Services Committee in April 2005. "This was, I believe, a successful intelligence operation by Saddam Hussein in which we were led to believe that he was in a certain location, and he wasn't there."

What followed on the U.S. side was a very conventional campaign designed as an attack by one state's military on another's, Maj. Isaiah Wilson later concluded. "It was a war focused operationally on the destruction of the Iraqi army—the state's warfighting capability—and destruction of the Hussein state apparatus," he wrote. In this sense, he added, it was effectively "a continuation" of the 1991 war.

The ground attack began at dawn on March 21, when it was still March 20 back in Washington, the reason some accounts differ on the date. The total U.S.-led invasion force consisted of fewer than three Army divisions, plus a big Marine division and a British division. Underscoring the relatively small size of the force, there were just 247 Army tanks in the force driving into Iraq from Kuwait, and about an equal number of Bradley fighting vehicles. The entire ground invasion force amounted to about 145,000 troops, including the British contribution—that is, well under half the size of the force that Gen. Zinni had called for in his Desert Crossing invasion plan. In March 2003 there was just one heavy Army division, the 3rd Infantry Division, plus a helicopter-rich light division, the 101st Airborne, and two infantry brigades (from the 82nd Airborne and a freestanding unit, the 173rd Airborne Brigade) plus some Special Operations units, for a total of about 65,000 troops. The Marine contingent added another 60,000, and the British 1st Armored Division some 20,000. They were attacking a weakened Iraqi military that was one-third the size it had been in 1991, but which still fielded about 400,000 troops and 4,000 tanks and other amored vehicles. More significantly, it would develop, the Iraqis also had in waiting tens of thousands of irregular fighters called fedayeen.

The 3rd Infantry Division—despite its name, it is a unit heavy in tanks and other armored vehicles—sprinted about 90 miles from the Kuwaiti border across the desert to An Nasiriyah, where it seized a key airfield and, even more importantly, some bridges over the Euphrates. After turning those key spans over to the Marines, the division turned left and charged northward along the western bank of the Euphrates, toward Karbala. The Marines secured the southern oil fields, then moved north and began crossing the Euphrates around Nasiriyah and attacking up into the land between the rivers. British armored forces, meanwhile, peeled to the right from Kuwait to besiege Basrah, Iraq's second biggest city. Much smaller numbers of Special Operations troops swarmed into the far west, where their mission was to prevent Scud missile launches against Israel, and into the north, where they linked up with Kurdish fighters.

It didn't take long for the Iraqi side to begin operating unconventionally. The first taste of what lay in store for the Americans in Iraq for the next several years came just over one day into the war, early on March 22, when Sgt. 1st Class Anthony Broadhead, a platoon sergeant in the Crazy Horse troop of the 3rd Infantry Division's cavalry unit, the spearhead of the division, was looking out of a tank heading toward a bridge in As Samawah, a town 60 miles past Nasiriyah on the invasion route. He waved at a group of Iraqis. Instead of waving back, they began attacking with AK-47 rifles, rocket-propelled grenades, and mortars, riding at the American tanks in pickup trucks. "For the first, but not the last time, well-armed paramilitary forces, indistinguishable, except for their weapons, from civilians—attacked," recorded the Army's official history of the invasion. Another taste of the difficult future waiting for the United States in Iraq came several days later, when four U.S. soldiers were killed in Najaf in the first suicide car bombing of the war.

The expectation that Iraqi commanders in the south would surrender and even bring their forces over to the side of the Americans by the thousands proved wrong: not one commander did so. "We were absolutely convinced, in a lot of ways, that this guy was going to capitulate with all these southern forces," Gen. Thurman, the operations director for the ground invasion, said later. "We were told that by the CIA. We were told that by . . . intel reports, in the assessment. And that isn't what happened. We had to fight our way through every town."

Public debate over troop strength

In the following days the long-running debate about whether there were enough troops in the invasion force, which mainly had occurred behind closed doors, burst into the open. It would continue to be argued for years.

The issue was driven into public view by the Jessica Lynch debacle, in which a poorly trained and led support unit got lost in Iraq in part because of a lack of troops to direct convoy traffic at key points. Early on the morning of March 23, Lynch's unit, the 507th Maintenance Company, was at the tail end of a slow-moving six-hundred-vehicle convoy when it missed a turn and drove into Nasiriyah, where it ran into a series of ambushes. Of thirty-three soldiers in the lost section, eleven were killed, nine were wounded, and seven captured. The unit "was not trained to be in the situation they were in, was not equipped to be there, no GPS [Global Positioning System, a satellite-guided navigation system], no radios, no training on crew-served weapons, only one crew-served weapon in there, no night vision" gear, was the harsh but accurate judgment later delivered by Gen. Peter Schoomaker after he became Army chief of staff.

That night brought another ugly surprise, when the 11th Attack Helicopter Regiment was hammered when it carried out an attack deep behind the front lines. Its mission was to destroy the armored vehicles and artillery pieces of the Medina Division northeast of Karbala before they reached the front. But the helicopters never really engaged the enemy unit, and instead turned back after running into a storm of rifle fire. One helicopter was lost and its two crewmen captured. Of thirty-two aircraft that returned to base, thirty-one had been hit by enemy fire. One aircraft alone had twenty-nine bullet holes, according to the Army's history. It was a shock to Army aviators who liked to think of their AH-64 Apaches as flying tanks. The defeat would reverberate through the Army for years. Early in 2006, the Army quietly disclosed that it had concluded that the Apache was so vulnerable to rifle fire that it would no longer have a major role in attacks deep behind enemy lines.

The two setbacks combined to sharpen questions among defense experts about the wisdom of going to war with the force Rumsfeld had dictated to the military. Most notably, Army Gen. Barry McCaffrey, commander of the 24th Infantry Division in the 1991 war, was sharply critical at the time. "In my judgment, there should have been a minimum of two heavy divisions and an armored cavalry regiment on the ground—that's how our doctrine reads," said the hard-bitten soldier, who to the irritation of the Pentagon had become a frequent commentator on television. "They chose to go into battle with a ground combat capability that was inadequate, unless their assumptions proved out."

Another Gulf War commander agreed. "It is my position that we would be much better off if we had another heavy division on the ground, and an armored cavalry regiment to deal with this mission in the rear," said retired Army Lt. Gen. Thomas Rhame, who had led the 1st Infantry Division in 1991.

A third Gulf War veteran, the retired Army Maj. Gen. William Nash, said that he was especially worried that the lack of troops could undercut the postwar occupation. "The stability of the liberated areas is clearly an issue," he said. "The postwar transition has to begin immediately in the wake of the attacking forces, and they seem to be short of forces for those important missions at this time."

The chorus of criticism got under Myers's skin; he was in the difficult position of being a career pilot and Air Force officer responding to the views of men who had been senior commanders in ground combat. He responded with uncharacteristic ferocity in a Pentagon briefing. "My view of those reports—and since I don't know who you're quoting, who the individuals are—is that they're bogus," began the usually bland Myers. "I don't know how they get started, and I don't know how they've been perpetuated, but it's not been by responsible members of the team that put this all together. They either weren't there, or they don't know, or they're working another agenda, and I don't know what that agenda might be."

He then went on to hint that such criticism was unpatriotic, coming during wartime. "It is not helpful to have those kind of comments come out when we've got troops in combat, because first of all, they're false, they're absolutely wrong, they bear no resemblance to the truth, and it's just, it's just harmful to our troops that are out there fighting very bravely, very courageously," Myers said.

Additional troop cuts

One likely reason for the antagonism in Myers's comments was that there were intense discussions under way at the Pentagon of just that issue, of how many more troops to send to Iraq. "That week was bad juju," recalled a planner on the Joint Staff who participated in a series of briefings to Rumsfeld that became a running discussion of whether all the additional troops on the deployment list were really needed. The military overwhelmingly believed that all the troops on the list should be sent. This officer recalled one briefing that came not long after the Jessica Lynch mess in which Abizaid, speaking in a secure video teleconference, said to Army Lt. Gen. Walter "Skip" Sharp, the J-5, or director of plans and strategy, for the Joint Chiefs of Staff, "Hey, Skip, I think we're going to need the whole force package." A few weeks later, when planners at Combined Joint Task Force-7 did a formal troop to task analysis, they concluded that they needed a force of 250,000 to 300,000—almost double what they had on hand at the time.

The war plans called for additional forces to be sent after the fall of Baghdad, noted Conrad Crane. But the two top civilians at the Pentagon remained skeptical. "I don't see why it would take more troops to occupy the country than to take down the regime," Wolfowitz said in one meeting, recalled the officer involved in Pentagon planning. Rumsfeld had similar reservations about whether the 1st Cavalry Division was really needed, the officer said. It and the 1st Armored Division had been in the plan as insurance in case some of the lead forces in the invasion were hit with chemical or biological weapons, said Agoglia. With the passage of time, when it became less likely that the U.S. invasion force was going to be attacked, pressure increased from the Pentagon civilians to stop moving those two follow-on divisions.

At one point, the war planner spoke up to urge that the military "fly in the 2nd ACR now—at least one squadron, and the whole regiment, if you can." The point he remembered making to Rumsfeld was that the invasion force needed to do a better job of protecting its lines of communication, and that the regiment would be ideal for operating independently, securing key intersections, and reconnoitering routes. Even with the 2nd Armored Cavalry Regiment in the pipeline, senior military officials in both Washington and on the ground in Iraq worried as Baghdad was about to fall that the force lacked combat depth. Wolfowitz remained strongly opposed to sending the two heavy divisions, the 1st Armored and the 1st Cavalry.

After one meeting, the senior officers involved in the discussion trudged downstairs to the offices of the Joint Staff. Casey, who by that point had been promoted to the important job of director of the Joint Staff, looked at his two key subordinates—Sharp, the J-5, and Air Force Lt. Gen. Norton Schwartz, the J-3, or head of operations—and said, "I think we just lost the 1st Cav." Casey indicated that he thought the running argument was eroding relations with Rumsfeld and Wolfowitz and so needed to be brought to an end, another Joint Staff officer recalled.

Top officers feared that if the discussions dragged on, Rumsfeld would decide that the 1st Armored Division really wasn't needed either. So they made the argument to Rumsfeld that it was essential to send it, and to keep the 1st Cav on hold, possibly for sending in midsummer. The defense secretary ultimately agreed to that hedge plan. But there was an edge of bitterness to that session: "As we're walking out the door of the office, the secretary is behind his desk and he looks up and says, 'Goddamit, I wonder how long it's going to take *this* to get in the newspaper.'" Years later, this officer remained unhappy with his role in those discussions. "They did not take best military advice," he said. He felt that he had succumbed to a process in which he had compromised his judgment, making bids

and agreeing when Rumsfeld okayed just half of what he believed was truly necessary. "There's a bargaining that goes on," he said. "To this day I feel I let people
down, because we bargained. . . . I failed." More than two years later, he added,
"I have angst every day about that. We didn't get it right, and fifteen hundred
troopers"—the number of U.S. dead in Iraq at the time he was speaking—"have
paid a price for that."

In all these weeks of arguments over troop deployments, the voice that he
thought was missing was that of Gen. Franks. "The military could have gotten it
if the combatant commander had come down on it firmly and said, 'I want the
whole force package.'"

Col. Kevin Benson, the chief planner at CFLCC, the headquarters for the
ground invasion force, would later argue that the decision not to send additional
troops was the tipping point that led to the subsequent insurgency. "You know,
"there was probably a moment"—and now this is Benson's personal opinion—
"there was a moment where some of my Arab friends told me that if we'd have
kept the lid on, we probably wouldn't have had these problems. OK, conjecture.
How do we keep the lid on? Well, we continue the force flow. We don't stop. We
leave everyone in place."

Another, more insidious effect of these endless arguments with Rumsfeld and
Wolfowitz was its opportunity cost, said Agoglia. "Every friggin' request, they
wanted to see the numbers, they wanted to know how many reservists," he recalled. "It delayed every move, and sucked energy out of Centcom staff. It was
ridiculous. There is only so much capacity a staff has, and this was bullshit. It
sucked the energy out of long-term thinking."

If anything, commanders on the ground were even more deeply concerned
than the Joint Staff about their thinness. Gen. Thurman expressed his regret a few
months later to an official Army historian over the small size of the force on hand.
Despite pushing from him and his superior, McKiernan, the ground force commander, the 1st Cavalry Division had been dropped at the last moment. "It's
turning out right now that we need these forces," Thurman said in mid-2003.

McKiernan, in his own official debriefing later that June, sounded almost
wistful. "I think everybody's going to come to the conclusion that we came to
early on": He needed more troops than he had. "While we might not have needed
them to remove the top part of the regime, and to get into Baghdad, we needed
[them] for everything after that." Dropping the 1st Cavalry Division hadn't been
his idea, he noted elsewhere in the interview. "It would have been nice to have another heavy division," he said. "Well, it would have been more than nice—it would

have been very, very effective to have another heavy division fresh going into the fight."

Some feared that lines of communication would be cut. That worry landed square on Col. Teddy Spain, the commander of military police in the operation. In combat operations, one of the major missions of MPs is to make sure those lines are kept open and free from attack. But Spain was sorely missing the troops that had been knocked out of the plan months earlier. Had he retained all twenty companies of troops that he originally had in the war plan, he said later, "I could have guarded those MSRs [main supply routes]. I don't think Jessica Lynch and the 507th Maintenance Company would have happened. I truly believe that had I had those assets, I would have had troops right behind the 3rd ID, securing the route."

Chalabi's worrisome chums

Another disquieting note was that as the U.S. military invaded Iraq, U.S. intelligence picked up indications that Ahmed Chalabi's organization was conveying information about U.S. troop movements to the government of Iran. "I don't want to say what the source was, but there was some evidence that there was an operational relationship" between Chalabi and Tehran, said a senior U.S. military intelligence officer. It was during the first ten days of the war, "about the same time that we saw solid evidence that Iran had a plan—operators in the south, people moving back and forth." The difference between Tommy Franks and Tehran, he said grimly, was that "the Iranians had a good Phase IV plan."

A Central Command official had a less malevolent interpretation of the communications between Chalabi's organization and the Iranian government during the invasion. "It pissed me off that they were talking to the Iranians," he said. But, he continued, it was hardly a shock, in part because the U.S. government also was in touch with Tehran through the British government. The Iranians had signaled, for example, that if a U.S. pilot went down in their territory that they wouldn't fire on U.S. combat search and rescue aircraft sent to fetch him or her. Also, he said, it was important to convey the message to Tehran that the U.S. government wasn't interested in widening the war, and had no plans to take "a right turn" on the way to Baghdad. "So," he concluded, "it wasn't necessarily a bad thing" for Chalabi to tell the Iranian government about U.S. troop locations.

Asked much later about his relations with the Iranian government, Chalabi said, not completely clearly, "I did not pass any information to Iran that compromised any national security information of the United States."

Despite these tremors, Chalabi still looked like the Pentagon's choice to lead postwar Iraq. In early April, the U.S. Air Force flew a few hundred members of Chalabi's militia to southern Iraq. The vice chairman of the Joint Chiefs of Staff, Marine Gen. Peter Pace, envisioned a major role for them. "These are Iraqi citizens who want to fight for a free Iraq who are, who will become basically the core of the new Iraqi army once Iraq is free," said Pace, the nation's number-two military officer. "They are the beginning of the free Iraqi army."

A statement issued by the Iraqi National Congress in Chalabi's name said that the number of fighters "is expected to increase quickly." As it happened, the force actually proved ineffective and did little. The official history produced by the Army Special Operations Command blamed its stallout partly on internal divisions in the U.S. government. "The U.S. Defense Department championed Chalabi and the FIF [Free Iraqi Fighters], and saw them as a transitional force to be used in lieu of the police," it reported. "The State Department, on the other hand, saw the FIF as nothing more than the military arm of the INC." That assessment, while accurate, is incomplete. Another more important division, one within the military establishment, actually crippled this force. Pentagon civilians, most notably Wolfowitz and Feith, supported the training of Iraqi forces, while Central Command dragged its feet. Chalabi later maintained that Abizaid, then one of Franks's two deputies, had told him not to fly to southern Iraq. "I did it anyway, and he was very angry," he said.

It isn't clear why Rumsfeld and his subordinates were unable to make Central Command more responsive to civilian control. In principle, the training of Iraqis was exactly the right course—and ultimately the one that the U.S. military would settle on as the exit strategy for Iraq. But in the spring of 2003 the U.S. military wasn't yet interested. Retired Marine Lt. Gen. Michael DeLong, Franks's other deputy, called the training effort "a waste of time and energy for us." He reported of Chalabi's militia, "While some of them were helpful in small battles, we received many reports of their looting and thievery in Baghdad."

The sandstorm pause

The charge northward from Kuwait to the outskirts of Baghdad generally went swiftly but was sufficiently troubled, with long and vulnerable lines of supply, that just one week into the invasion some U.S. commanders began issuing warnings. "The enemy we're fighting is different from the one we'd war-gamed against,"

Lt. Gen. William S. Wallace, commander of V Corps and a candid man, told reporters. That remark briefly became hugely controversial.

On top of that, a huge sandstorm and rainstorm descended on Iraq on March 24 and lasted for three days, grounding the invasion force's helicopters and miring many troops. "It was like a tornado of mud," Maj. Gen. David Petraeus, commander of the 101st Airborne Division, said a few weeks later.

But even then, the U.S. military was able to use sophisticated radars and other sensors to peer through, with devastating effect. Late one night during the tempest, a Republican Guard missile unit concealed its FROG-7 launcher vehicles deep in a palm grove in the Sabaa Abkar, or Seven Virgins, area on the northern suburbs of Baghdad. They were off the road, cloaked by the trees, by the darkness, and by the dirt-laden winds of the storm. Even so, they were hit by two enormous bombs, and then by a spray of flesh-shredding cluster bomblets.

Omar Khalidi, a Republican Guard captain, said that this aerial attack demoralized his men enormously. "They were hiding and thought nobody could find them," he said. "Some soldiers left their positions and ran away. When the big bombs hit their target, some of the vehicles just melted. And the effect of the cluster bombs was even greater, because they covered a larger area." The only way their concealed vehicles could have been detected, Khalidi wrongly calculated, was by betrayal—a powerfully damaging conclusion for troops under fire to reach. "Most of the commanders were sure it was through spies, because it was impossible to find through satellite or aircraft. Even if you drove by it, you couldn't find it."

Likewise, when Qusay Hussein ordered three elite Republican Guard divisions to move southwest of Baghdad to confront the American offensive, American bombers destroyed them before they could even get near the U.S. forces. "This affected the morale of the troops," an Iraqi general staff officer later told the *Washington Post*'s William Branigin. "The Iraqi will to fight was broken outside Baghdad."

"Thunder runs"

On April 3, the 3rd Infantry Division took Saddam International Airport, on the western fringe of Baghdad. Two days later it launched the first of two "thunder runs"—monstrous charges of tanks and other armored vehicles—into the capital. These probes showed the U.S. Army at its best, taking tactical risks that paid off handsomely. Most notably, they led to an abandonment of the U.S. plan to cordon off the city and move in slowly. Rather, the two thunder runs led to the swift collapse of the regime.

The opposition to these audacious forays was fierce. When the 3rd Infantry Division's 2nd Brigade, commanded by Col. David Perkins, drove into the city for the first time just after dawn on the morning of April 5, it was slammed repeatedly with rocket-propelled grenades (RPG) and rifle fire "at effectively point-blank range along nearly its entire route," according to an Army War College report. "Every single vehicle in the column was hit at least once by Iraqi RPGs, and many took multiple hits."

Lt. Col. Stephen Twitty, one of Perkins's battalion commanders, later described their first run into the city as "eight hours of continuous fighting." At one point, one unit at a key intersection appeared in danger of running out of ammunition and being overrun.

The first attack consisted of an armored column built around twenty-nine tanks that swung up a major highway, Route 8, that cut into the southwestern part of Baghdad, a mix of industrial areas and square, two-story, adobe-style houses, and then veered out to catch the arrow-straight four-lane expressway to the sprawling international airport west of the city. In these battles, Franks's maxim that "speed kills" did indeed apply. Perkins observed that the Iraqi defenders were only prepared to fight in one direction, so a fast move through their lines tended to disorient their response. "If I could push through, and get in behind them, and then reattack out from the center, what I was doing was reattacking from a direction that they weren't used to defending from, and it was very hard for them to turn around and redefend," he recalled later.

The tanks and Bradley fighting vehicles arriving at the airport at the end of the first run appeared to be in flames because the intense shooting had set fire to the backpacks and other gear that U.S. armored soldiers carry on the outside of their vehicles. The 3rd Infantry Division estimated that it killed two thousand enemy fighters during this mission. Its official history offers no figure for the number of civilians killed, but Iraqis said there were many. "I was emotionally spent," said Lt. Col. Eric Schwartz, who commanded an armored battalion in the first attack. "One of my tank commanders had been killed. I had a soldier shot in the eye, shot in the forehead, shot in the shoulder, shot in the back, shot in the face. . . . I just needed time for myself. One of the other battalion commanders from 1st Brigade came over and . . . asked me, 'Are you okay?' And I said, 'I don't know.'"

On April 7, the second foray cut through to Saddam's palace complex in the center of Baghdad, on the left bank of the Tigris, and decided to stay. The American military believed it had taken Baghdad.

Franks flunks strategy

To understand that mistaken conclusion, it is necessary to step back and examine Gen. Tommy Franks, the senior U.S. commander in the war, and particularly his misunderstanding of strategy. That is a grand-sounding word, and it is frequently misused by laymen as a synonym for tactics. In fact, strategy has a very different and quite simple meaning that flows from just one short set of questions: Who are we, and what are we ultimately trying to do here? How will we do it, and what resources and means will we employ in doing it? The four answers give rise to one's strategy. Ideally, one's tactics will then follow from them—that is, this is who we are, this is the outcome we wish to achieve, this is how we aim to do it, and this is what we will use to do it. But addressing the questions well can be surprisingly difficult, and if the answers are incorrect or incomplete, or the goals listed not reachable, then the consequences can be disastrous.

Why would the United States invade Iraq without a genuine strategy in hand? Part of the answer lies in the personality and character of Gen. Franks. The inside word in the U.S. military long had been that Franks didn't think strategically. For example, when the general held an off-the-record session with officers studying at the Naval War College in Newport, Rhode Island, in the spring of 2002, not long after the biggest battle of the Afghan war, Operation Anaconda, one student posed the classic Clausewitzian question: What is the nature of the war you are fighting in Afghanistan? "That's a great question for historians," Franks sidestepped, recalled another officer who was there. "Let me tell you what we are doing." Franks proceeded to discuss how U.S. troops cleared cave complexes in Afghanistan. It was the most tactical answer possible, quite remote from what the officer had asked. It would have been a fine reply for a sergeant to offer, but not a senior general. "He really was comfortable at the tactical level," this officer recalled with dismay.

Franks's plan for making war in Iraq was built around U.S. technological and mechanical advantages. "Speed kills," the general insisted to his subordinates as they wrote and rewrote the massive plan. It sounded good—like a tough-minded way of slicing through all the bureaucratic nonsense. But it reflected the larger misconception of the war at hand. Speed didn't kill the enemy—it bypassed him.

It won the campaign, but it didn't win the war, because the war plan was built on the mistaken strategic goal of capturing Baghdad, and it confused removing Iraq's regime with the far more difficult task of changing the entire country. The result was that the U.S. effort resembled a banana republic coup d'état more than a full-scale war plan that reflected the ambition of a great power to alter the politics of a crucial region of the world.

So where Franks's plan should have been grounded in a wide-ranging strategy, it instead was built on a series of operational assumptions, many of which proved incorrect. Probably the single most startling passage in his memoir is his description of "nine slices representing Iraqi centers of gravity in Iraq," which is an abuse of Clausewitz's definition of the key target in war. He relates how in December 2001 he sketched a "working matrix" of targets in Iraq—leadership, internal security, and so on—along with the tools he intended to use against them—"operational fires," "operational maneuver," "SOF operations," and so on. This was, as the names of those tools indicate, a relentlessly operational approach, a collection of tactics—nothing more, nothing less, and certainly not a strategic formulation for what he wanted Iraq ultimately to look like and how he planned to achieve that end. When he showed this chart to Gen. Renuart, he said proudly, "This is what you call your basic grand strategy." It was an amazingly wrong assertion. The chart had little of strategy in it. In the way Franks used the term, there were so many centers that they added up to nothing, no one real center of gravity. In describing these numerous centers of gravity, Franks inadvertently underscored his lack of strategic understanding.

Col. Agoglia, the Central Command planner, argued that Franks is more thoughtful than the general's own account makes him seem. In his view, Franks had come to the unhappy realization that his civilian bosses—Rumsfeld, Wolfowitz, Feith, and others in OSD—simply lacked the capability to discuss Iraq usefully in military terms. "There was no use discussing 'centers of gravity' with people in OSD who didn't understand centers of gravity. Franks knew what a center of gravity is. OSD didn't." The centers of gravity matrix, Agoglia insisted, was "looked upon as a way of explaining to OSD what we were thinking." Franks didn't trust his civilian overseers at the Pentagon. "He had an ability to translate to the folks at OSD, who weren't very brilliant, the intent of the plan. But Franks also had to play close hold with them, because they were always pushing him for less." This was especially true of Wolfowitz, Agoglia said, who suffered from a "complete and total lack of understanding" of what was needed to invade Iraq. For example, "We *knew* we needed more troops to consolidate than to get there"—a position

Wolfowitz would repeatedly reject in the spring of 2003, before, during, and even after the invasion.

There is no doubt that Franks executed the mission given him. As a military professional, he should have done more to question that mission and point out its incomplete nature. Ultimately, however, the fault for the lapse in the planning must lie with Rumsfeld, the man in charge. In either case, it is difficult to overstate what a key misstep this lack of strategic direction was—probably the single most significant miscalculation of the entire effort. In war, strategy is the searchlight that illuminates the way ahead. In its absence, the U.S military would fight hard and well but blindly, and the noble sacrifices of soldiers would be undercut by the lack of thoughtful leadership at the top that soberly assessed the realities of the situation and constructed a response.

From Saigon to Baghdad

Franks was a product of his Army, and his faults reflected those of that institution. The Army went into Iraq with a considerable amount of hubris, a circumstance notably different from that of the first Gulf War, whose leaders had been the junior officers of the Vietnam War and had gone to the Mideast determined not to go down in defeat again. Gen. McCaffrey recalled that his assistant commander, then Brig. Gen. Terry Scott, said as that war began, "I hope we don't fuck this up like we did Vietnam—I'd rather die than go through twenty years of that again." In contrast to McCaffrey and Scott, the commanders of the 2003 war had known mainly success—in Panama in 1989, in Kuwait in 1991, in Haiti in 1994, in Bosnia in 1996, in Kosovo in 1999, in Afghanistan in 2001. The one exception was Somalia, which they tended to count as a tactical success that then was undermined by the missteps of the Clinton administration.

Franks's war plan combined aspects of many of those post-Vietnam operations: the armored fist of the tank-heavy thrust into Kuwait, the speed of the overnight takedown of Panama, the precision bombing of the campaign in Afghanistan. The Army would go into Iraq harboring few doubts about its abilities. "Information dominance" and "information superiority" were popular phrases in the military. "I think these guys were overconfident," going into Iraq, said Danielle Pletka, the former foreign policy adviser to Sen. Jesse Helms and longtime Iraq hawk. "We entrusted far too much political responsibility in Iraq to our military commanders. I don't think they knew anything about the politics of the region."

An invasion plan that focused too much on the fall of Baghdad to the exclusion of other tasks necessary to securing the victory had some of its intellectual roots in the fall of another Asian city nearly thirty years earlier: Saigon.

Every military strength contains the seeds of its own weakness. Make a weapons system too strong and it will be slow or will consume so much energy in moving that it requires a burdensome supply chain to keep it fueled. Make it too light and fast and it will be dangerously vulnerable when it breaks down, which is inevitable. Make it too successful and commanders will stick with it too long, until its weaknesses are revealed by the enemy. Likewise, the flaws of the 2003 plan for the U.S. invasion of Iraq arguably had their roots in one of the great success stories of the U.S. military, its impressive recovery—physical, spiritual, and intellectual—in the fifteen years after the end of the Vietnam War. Open the memoirs of any modern Army general, from Schwarzkopf to Franks, and there is likely to be a major section devoted to the Vietnam War and the galvanizing effect it had had on the writer.

The modern U.S. Army was born in the ashes of that war. A new generation of weaponry—the Apache attack helicopter, the Bradley fighting vehicle, the M-1 Abrams tank—was introduced. Army training was revamped at the National Training Center (NTC), out in the high Mojave Desert near the California-Nevada border. Rampant drug abuse and pervasive indiscipline were dealt with effectively. Also, those who stayed tended to be persistent, tough, determined, and devoted to the Army. Like Gen. Shinseki or Colin Powell, they could be stubborn, even dogged and single-minded, in defending the institution they had spent their lives rebuilding.

But the most significant post-Vietnam fix may have been doctrinal—that is, in how the Army thinks about how it fights. Arguably, the rebuilding began on the Golan Heights in 1973, as the Army's leaders, trying to figure out the path beyond Vietnam, watched the Arab-Israeli Ramadan War, or Yom Kippur War, with astonishment. Shocked by surprise attacks from Syria and Egypt, the Israelis quickly rallied and launched a counteroffensive, losing only 250 tanks and 772 troops as they destroyed 1,150 tanks and killed 3,500 of the enemy. Among those tracking this was Gen. William DePuy, the first chief of the U.S. Army's new Training and Doctrine Command, which was created in July 1973. DePuy, who in Vietnam had held the key position of operations officer for Gen. William Westmoreland, and also had commanded the 1st Infantry Division, developed "an intense interest in the reform of tactics and training, in line with tactical lessons drawn from the 1973 Arab-Israeli War," wrote John Romjue in an official history of the evolution of modern Army doctrine. Three years later the Army revised for the first time since 1968 its core statement on how to fight, titled "Operations," but in those days more commonly referred to as Field Manual 100-5 (FM 100-5).

The 1976 version of this capstone doctrinal statement warned that the Army must aim to "win the first battle of the next war." That ultimately led the Army's thinkers to focus too much only on that first fight. During World War II, tanks had opened fire at an average range of 750 yards, but in the 1973 Yom Kippur War, Israeli tanks engaged at two thousand yards and more. This changed the shape of the battlefield and meant fighting in-depth, rather than just on a front, observed retired Army Maj. Gen. Robert Scales, a former commandant of the Army War College and later coauthor of an account of the spring 2003 invasion. "It doesn't matter how much you put on the front line, because the lethality of weaponry is such that you can't just fight on the front line, you have to fight all echelons at once, in depth," Scales said.

Ultimately, that long view across the battlefield meant focusing on the operational level of war—that is, looking beyond tactics to the entire area in which fighting is occurring. When the Army next revised FM 100-5, in 1982, it made that concept official doctrine. "Between tactics and strategy, the manual inserts the intermediate level traditionally recognized by the German and other armies as the operational level of large units," Romjue wrote. This operational level was defined as going after the enemy's center of gravity, whatever it was that made the foe most able to keep on fighting.

This new emphasis also was meant to address what the Army had decided was a major failing during the Vietnam War. Retired Army Col. Harry Summers, Jr., began *On Strategy: A Critical Analysis of the Vietnam War,* perhaps the most influential book to come out of that conflict, by recounting an exchange he had had in Hanoi on April 25, 1975, with a North Vietnamese colonel.

"You know, you never defeated us on the battlefield," Summers said.

The North Vietnamese officer considered this assertion for a moment, and then responded, "That may be so, but it is also irrelevant." Hanoi's center of gravity had not been on the battlefield.

The new focus on the operational level of war was meant to fix this disconnect, in which tactical success had failed to lead to an overall strategic victory.

The Army learned the lesson well—perhaps too well, Scales said. The new doctrine, the new weaponry, and the new attitude of the Army all came together at the National Training Center. During the 1980s, the Army radically improved its combat abilities by providing tough realistic training there. It also used after-action reviews—a kind of U.S. military version of Maoist self-criticism, enforced by carefully collected data—to make commanders address their weaknesses and mistakes. The lessons learned during mock battles at NTC were credited with paving the way for the swift victory the U.S. military achieved in Kuwait in 1991, just sixteen years after the fall of Saigon. The 1991 war had the unfortunate side effect, though, of reinforcing the changes the Army had made—which made it an unchallenged force for short, blitzkrieg-style warfare against other states, but badly positioned for protracted ground combat, especially of an irregular or unconventional nature.

So for all the good it did, the NTC also planted some of the seeds of the flawed plan of 2003. In making performance at the NTC the measure of an officer, the Army tended to fall into thinking, mistakenly, that what makes a good battalion commander is what makes a good general. But the trainers at the NTC taught commanders how to win battles, not how to win wars. What came after the battle became someone else's business. By that point, the Army commander was focused on packing up his force and redeploying home, which is fine for a battalion commander but not for the top commander.

In learning how to be more operational, Scales said, the Army may have lost its hold on both the higher, strategic lessons of generals such as Eisenhower, as well as on the lower, tactical lessons of counterinsurgency that it had learned in Southeast Asia. Rather, it devoted its attention and effort to that midlevel of war—the operational art, as it came to be called. The NTC's scope covered only the fighting—defeating the enemy force, not figuring out what would follow. The plan for the spring 2003 invasion of Iraq reflected that view of war, emphasizing what it would take to get to Baghdad with little regard for what would follow. It was an operational plan, strategically deficient.

In an essay examining this issue, Army Lt. Col. Antulio Echevarria II concluded that Franks and other U.S. military commanders in 2003 had confused winning the battle of Baghdad with winning the war for Iraq. Today's commanders tend to see battles as an end in themselves, rather than properly as a means to a political outcome, he wrote. Echevarria was not just any Army officer but the director of national security affairs at the Army War College's Strategic Studies Institute. This issue was at the core of his specialty. The result, he warned, was a military built and trained for the wrong job. "Its underlying concepts—a polyglot of information-centric theories such as network-centric warfare, rapid decisive operations, and shock and awe—center on 'taking down' an opponent quickly, rather than finding ways to apply military force in the pursuit of broader political aims," he concluded. "The characteristics of the U.S. style of warfare—speed, jointness, knowledge, and precision—are better suited for strike operations than for translating such operations into strategic successes."

That conceptual flaw, that lack of understanding of how to complete the job, may be the reason that after both the 1991 war and the 2003 invasion the U.S. military seemed to fall asleep at the wheel. After the end of the 1991 war, noted Rick Atkinson in *Crusade,* his history of that conflict, there was a "postwar American passivity, a policy of drift and inaction." A similar period of American drift would follow the fall of Baghdad in 2003.

The doctrinal revamping of the Army in the mid-1970s had another long-term effect on the Army. After it came home from Vietnam, the Army threw away virtually everything it had learned there, slowly and painfully, about how to wage a counterinsurgency campaign. Under Gen. DePuy, noted Army Lt. Col. John Nagl, who in the 1990s wrote a study of the Army and counterinsurgency and then a few years later fought an insurgency in western Iraq, "the post-Vietnam army intentionally turned away from the painful memories of its Vietnam experience." In his study *Learning to Eat Soup with a Knife: Counterinsurgency Lessons from Malaya and Vietnam,* Nagl pointedly noted that the 1976 edition of FM 100-5, the Army's core document, "did not mention counterinsurgency."

So the Army that went to war in Iraq in March 2003 was well aware of its strengths, but like Franks, seemed blind to many of the conceptual weaknesses it was bringing to the fight.

Regime removal

Two images marked the fall of Saddam Hussein's government.

One was the Iraqi information minister, Mohammed Saeed Sahhaf, insisting at loony press conferences that U.S. forces were being hurled back into the desert where early graves awaited them—even as the U.S. Army was setting up camp a few miles to the west at the Baghdad airport and the Marine Corps was approaching from the southeast. "There is not any American presence or troops in the heart of the capital, at all," Sahhaf said at a press conference at the Palestine Hotel on April 7. "The soldiers of Saddam Hussein gave them a great lesson that history will not forget." The next day he told reporters that U.S. soldiers approaching the city center "are going to surrender or be burned in their tanks." It was a bravura performance, his last before being taken into captivity for questioning by U.S. military authorities.

One little noted oddity of this is that U.S. intelligence concluded that Sahhaf, or Baghdad Bob, as soldiers dubbed him, actually thought that what he was saying was the truth. At the time, the Iraqi military was claiming that it had counterattacked the U.S. invasion force and destroyed about eighty tanks and other vehicles, killed four hundred U.S. soldiers, and taken two hundred prisoners. He said later that his information came "from authentic sources, many authentic sources."

"We believe he believed what he was reporting," Army Col. Steve Boltz, the deputy chief of intelligence for V Corps, later said. Saddam Hussein's Iraq ran on fear, and bearers of bad news tended to suffer for what they delivered. "No one would want to tell him the truth, so they lied to him." Iraqi officers so feared the consequences of conveying negative news up the chain of command that they "fell into telling the high command they were all okay," Boltz concluded. One result of this systemic self-deception within the Iraqi hierarchy was that when a 3rd Infantry Division unit entering the capital captured an Iraqi general, the surprised officer said in an interrogation that "he had no idea that U.S. troops were so close to Baghdad," according to the division's official history.

The invasion's second memorable image was the fall of the statue of Saddam Hussein in a square in downtown Baghdad on April 9. The few days that followed were "as good as it got, the high-water mark of the invasion," observed Rick Atkinson, the military historian who embedded with the 101st Airborne Division during the 2003 invasion.

This moment also brought one of the highest points in George W. Bush's popularity as president. The first big jump in his polls numbers came after 9/11, when his approval level shot from 55 percent to a stratospheric 92 percent. That slowly settled back down into the high 50s, but spiked back up to 77 percent with the fall of Baghdad.

Yet even as the enemy capital fell, there was a quiet chorus of concern, especially from seasoned Army officers. "The hard part is yet to come," retired Col. Johnny Brooks, an old infantryman, warned on the day Baghdad fell. "We can easily win the fight but lose the peace." The United States needed to move quickly to restore electricity and other basic services. "If we do not give the people positive signals, and soon, that Iraq is getting better rapidly, and that they have hope, then the gunmen will start appearing and taking shots at U.S. military. Then the suicide bombers will appear."

Retired Army Col. Robert Killebrew, another infantryman, was even more specific about how things might go wrong. "We should not lose sight of the fact that, from the opposing point of view, the war isn't over," he told a group of defense-minded friends on April 18. "I suspect that serious people somewhere—probably hiding out in Syria—are planning the counterattack, which I suspect will take the shape of popular demonstrations against U.S. occupation, feyadeen attacks on coalition troops and Iraqis who cooperate with efforts to establish a new government, and general operations to destabilize and deny U.S. efforts to move to a secure and reformed Iraq." That would prove to be an extraordinarily accurate summary of the enemy concept of operations that would emerge in the following months.

Intelligence officials also were sending up rockets of warning. "It is premature to be doing victory laps," a senior military intelligence expert on the Middle East said at the time. "The hard part is going to be occupation. The Israelis won in six days—but have been fighting ever since—for thirty years."

Jeffrey White, a former analyst of Middle Eastern affairs at the Defense Intelligence Agency, added, "My worry is that we could see the beginning of some kind of resistance based on regime diehards, nationalists, disaffected tribal elements, etc."

But in the view of Franks and other military commanders, the assigned job had been completed. "We designed success in negative terms—getting rid of the regime, instead of establishing a democratic regime," said Army Reserve Maj. Michael Eisenstadt, an intelligence officer and specialist in Middle Eastern security issues who worked in Central Command during the run-up to the war. "When President Bush landed on that carrier with the 'Mission Accomplished' banner, it was right: The mission, as defined for the military as getting rid of the regime, had indeed been accomplished."

Rumsfeld dismisses the looting

As U.S. forces triumphed, Iraqis rose up and expressed their hatred for Saddam Hussein's regime in an extraordinary wave of vandalism. Mobs attacked government buildings across the country, carting off not just valuables but everything that could be pried off walls and floors. During this period it wasn't uncommon to see a pickup truck carrying doors, window frames, and piping from government offices.

"Stuff happens!" Defense Secretary Rumsfeld exclaimed at a Pentagon briefing on April 11, 2003, when asked about the looting. "But in terms of what's going on in that country, it is a fundamental misunderstanding to see those images
over, and over, and over again of some boy walking out with a vase and say, 'Oh,
my goodness, you didn't have a plan.' That's nonsense. They know what they're
doing, and they're doing a terrific job. And it's untidy, and freedom's untidy, and
free people are free to make mistakes and commit crimes and do bad things.
They're also free to live their lives and do wonderful things, and that's what's
going to happen here."

But that's not the way the looting felt to many of those on the ground in Iraq.
During this period, the U.S. military was perceptibly losing its recent gains; it gave
the sense that it really didn't know what to do next and was waiting to pass the
mission to someone else. "A finite supply of goodwill toward the Americans evap-
orated with the passing of each anarchic day," Lt. Nathaniel Fick, an elite force re-
con Marine officer, wrote of being in Baghdad during this time.

"There wasn't any plan," recalled a Special Operations officer who was in
Baghdad at the time. "Everyone was just kind of waiting around. Everybody
thought they'd be going home soon." Looking back on the period, he recalled it as
a slow loss of momentum. "It wasn't like all hell broke loose. It was more like the
situation eroded."

Rumsfeld's fundamental misunderstanding of the looting of Iraq, and the casual manner in which he expressed it, not only set back U.S. forces tactically, but
also damaged the strategic standing of the United States, commented Fred Ikle,
who had been the Pentagon's policy chief during the Reagan administration.
"Some senior officials in Washington chuckled about a 'new spirit of freedom'
that had suddenly sprouted . . . among 'grateful,' liberated Iraqis," he wrote. "America lost most of its prestige and respect in that episode. To pacify a conquered
country, the victor's prestige and dignity is absolutely critical." This criticism was
leveled by a man who not only had impeccable credentials in conservative national security circles, but actually had brought Wolfowitz to Washington from
Yale during the Nixon administration.

The message sent to Iraqis was far more troubling than Americans understood. It was that the U.S. government didn't care—or, even more troubling for
the future security of Iraq, that it did care but was incapable of acting effectively.
In either event, the U.S. government response to the looting undercut the beginning of the U.S. occupation.

Watching the situation unfolding from his perch as a defense consultant in

Washington, Gary Anderson was beginning to get worried. He had war-gamed this scenario, and he knew just how vulnerable the U.S. position was if it faced an intelligent and adaptive enemy. Anderson is a retired Marine officer, of whom there sometimes seem to be two main types: big guys who resemble offensive linemen in football, and more compact, wiry sorts who look more like knife fighters. Small, bandy-legged, and gravelly voiced, Anderson fit well in the second category. A life spent figuring out how to take down foes bigger than himself prepared the retired colonel well for his post-Marine specialty: acting the role of the enemy in military exercises, in what the Pentagon calls red teaming. In the sprawling U.S. defense establishment, there is a small but steady market for such faux foes, and it became nearly a full-time job for Anderson.

He had spent much of early 2003 figuring out how to best combat U.S. forces operating in urban environments. Where were the American military's vulnerabilities? What were the seams in the U.S. approach? How could such a high-tech force, wielding an overwhelming arsenal, operating freely on the ground, in the air, and far overhead in space, be countered by an enemy lacking secure communications and possessing just explosives and light infantry weapons, such as AK-47s and rocket-propelled grenades? Those were the questions Anderson was paid to address.

As he watched the U.S. advance into Baghdad early in April, he began to worry. He had played a very similar scenario just eight weeks earlier. "We're fucked," he had said to his "enemy" staff as he contemplated a U.S. attack on his conventional forces. "We can slow them down, but they're coming to Baghdad." What he meant in that barracks shorthand was that it was clear that there was no way a regular military force could stand up to the U.S. onslaught. So, he said, the first step was to slow the advance and make as much trouble for the Americans as possible. Second, his career officers and intelligence officials would take off their uniforms and disappear into the neighborhoods, stay in contact with some key subordinates, and "tell our people to keep their weapons oiled."

In late March he began to fear that Saddam Hussein's Baathist functionaries were following just that course. "Phase I assumes eventual defeat in a conventional war," he wrote in a prescient opinion article published in the *Washington Post*. "The second phase would be a protracted guerrilla war against the 'occupation.'" Anderson suggested that the U.S. military needed to "be prepared to react to an enemy game plan that may be different from our own." It was an oddly pessimistic article to write as U.S. forces moved toward triumph. But it caught the attention of senior officials at the Pentagon. A few weeks later, a secretary in

Wolfowitz's office called Anderson. Would he be willing, she asked, to come in for a chat with the deputy defense secretary?

Though only a few inside observers like Anderson suspected it, the victory was already beginning to unravel. Publicly, at least, as late as April 28, Wolfowitz continued to minimize the need for U.S. troops. "We're not going to need as many people to do peacekeeping as we needed to fight the war," he told the *Washington Times* that day, when there were 135,000 U.S. troops in Iraq. Even as Wolfowitz spoke, Iraq was heating up.

A fuse is lit in Fallujah

In late April U.S. commanders were growing concerned about activity in Fallujah and Ramadi, two conservative Sunni towns an hour to the west of Baghdad, on the western fringe of the land between the rivers. The area generally had been neglected in the war planning, which had focused on Baghdad. The only attention paid to al Anbar province was an effort to stop Scud launches against Israel from the remote western part of the province. The rest of it—far closer to Baghdad and able to influence events in the capital—seems to have been ignored. This is inexplicable, even for a war plan built around the narrow aim of knocking off Saddam Hussein's regime, because Fallujah was home to an estimated forty thousand former Baathist Party operatives, intelligence officials, and Iraqi army officers who should have been expected to defend their interests vigorously.

Central Command's planning for the postwar period, never good, was particularly inaccurate in predicting the likely state of the Sunni heartland north and northwest of Baghdad. "Continued armed opposition to coalition forces unlikely once Saddam flees or is captured/killed," stated a classified Central Command briefing on Phase IV issues. The briefing notes attached in the PowerPoint are even more optimistic: "Reporting indicates a growing sense of fatalism, and accepting their fate, among Sunnis. There may be a small group of diehard supporters that is willing to rally in the regime's heartland near Tikrit—but they won't last long without support."

"This part of the Sunni Triangle was never assessed properly in the plan," Maj. Gen. Charles Swannack, Jr., the commander of the 82nd Airborne Division, recalled later in an e-mail.

Writing about operating in this part of Iraq during World War II, Field Marshal Sir William Slim, one of the greatest British generals of his time, remarked that Iraq is "a cruel, hard, desolate land." The Americans were about to find out why. On April 27 in Ramadi, Swannack recalled, a hand grenade was thrown from a crowd at 82nd Airborne soldiers, severely wounding two.

The next day there was an incident in which a number of Iraqis—between six and seventeen—were shot dead by U.S. troops. The event did much to poison relations in the town, ultimately leading the following year to two major battles there in which thousands of fighters died and well over a hundred thousand civilians were displaced. The facts of the April 28 incident are in dispute, as is often the case with such situations. Army officers from three different units offered different accounts, and an investigation by Human Rights Watch found discrepancies not only among the U.S. military accounts but also among the versions offered by different Iraqis. The most likely explanation of what happened is that Iraqi provocateurs took advantage of the demonstrations to shoot at U.S. troops and trick them into firing into the crowds.

As Swannack recalled it, on April 28, part of the division was based in a school in downtown Fallujah. The 82nd had been operating in Fallujah for five days. The Americans thought their presence was reassuring. "We came in to show presence just so the average citizen would feel safe," Col. Arnold Bray, commander of the 82nd brigade in the area, told Human Rights Watch. But the people of the city—known for their cultural conservativism and a xenophobia considered intense even by other Iraqis—found the patrols unsettling and an insult to their personal dignity, perhaps the core value of Iraqi culture. April 28 also was the birthday of Saddam Hussein, and so a natural day for his loyalists to reassert themselves.

"Several Iraqis instigated a crowd and approached this school," Swannack wrote. He continued:

5–6 instigators from within the crowd and on the roof of an adjacent building fired AK-47s at our soldiers within the school grounds. Our troopers returned very accurate and precise fires killing/wounding these 5–6 instigators. The crowd withdrew with the killed and wounded—AK-47 shell casings were found on the adjacent rooftop and from within the area where the crowd stood. A check of hospitals and morgue produced only these 6 killed as I remember.

The leader of the platoon of Charlie Company that was responsible for security in the school when the demonstration began, 2nd Lt. Wesley Davidson, said, "The bullets started coming at us, shooting over our heads, breaking windows. It was coming from the street, the guys behind the taxicab and some in the street."

Some Iraqi demonstrators told Human Rights Watch that people not near the school were firing rifles in the air, and they claimed that the demonstrators had no weapons. "They suddenly started shooting at us," said Falah Nawaar Dhahir, whose brother was killed.

Others said that there was no firing at all until the American soldiers opened up. "There was no shooting and they suddenly started shooting at us," said Mutaz Fahd al-Dulaimi.

The Americans said that six Iraqis died that day. The director of Fallujah's hospital, Dr. Ahmad Ghanim al-Ali, told Human Rights Watch that thirteen people were killed at the scene and seventy-five were wounded, with four of those dying in the following days. As with many such incidents, the differing accounts remain irreconcilable.

Round two in Fallujah

The 82nd, said Lt. Col. David Poirier, had "the itchy trigger finger." Poirier was about to lead an MP battalion into Fallujah a few days later, in early May, when he was taken aside by Col. David Teeples, the commander of the 3rd Armored Cavalry Regiment, to whom he temporarily reported. "Let me just pass on to you what happened when we did a RIP [relief in place] with 2nd Brigade, 82nd Airborne," Teeples began, Poirier later recalled.

Teeples had been in Fallujah because the 3rd ACR was temporarily taking control of the city from Col. Bray's brigade. He said he was standing alongside Bray on the roof of a building in downtown Fallujah on April 30, watching a convoy of Bray's troops begin moving west to east on Highway 10, the main road, when the convoy encountered about one hundred demonstrators in front of a government building.

"The lead vehicle fires a warning shot to get them out of the way," Teeples later recounted to Poirier. "A gunner in one of the rear vehicles puts his head down and opens up with a fifty cal, just opens up, and lays down seven people." (A .50 caliber is a heavy machine gun, its rounds capable of penetrating many armored vehicles. When those big rounds hit the human body they can sever limbs and explode skulls. More than one American soldier described the fire as coming from a .50 caliber; Bray later said emphatically that it was a lighter M-240.) Teeples was very clear, Poirier said in an interview, that "it was unaimed fire," and "some innocent people died."

Teeples declined to be interviewed for this book. But Lt. Col. Tobin Green, a

3rd ACR officer who was standing next to him atop the Baath Party headquarters building, said the convoy was attacked by the demonstrators. "I witnessed soldiers from the 82nd come under attack from Iraqis throwing rocks and bricks at exposed men with complete force at distances of no less than three feet. The column came under fire from enemy riflemen on the edge of the crowd," he said by e-mail.

Another 3rd ACR officer who was an eyewitness that day came down between Swannack's and Poirier's accounts.

> The demonstration was approximately 200 persons. . . . [S]ome shots were fired from AK-47 assault rifles from the rear of the demonstration. Generally, these shots were not aimed, sometimes they were. The Humvee gunner from their D Co. (Anti-Tank Company), did fire a burst of .50 cal. The Iraqi who was killed I remember the most was an elderly man who took a .50 cal round to the head at short range. Given that I was not in that soldier's position, I cannot say he made a bad call.

The Fallujah hospital director told Human Rights Watch that three people were killed that day, and sixteen wounded.

Bray argued credibly that his unit behaved well and honorably in both incidents. He noted that both before and after Fallujah, it handled difficult situations well. His one regret, he said, is that some soldiers used automatic weapons to return fire when it would have been better to respond with single shots. But at the same time, he recalled the *Black Hawk Down* incident in Mogadishu, Somalia, in October 1993, in which eighteen American soldiers had died. "I didn't want my soldiers cut off and isolated," and so didn't want them to second-guess themselves about responding when threatened.

The key to the events in Fallujah, Bray said, isn't the behavior of his soldiers but the malignant character of some people in the town. By April 25, the sole policeman there who had been helping U.S. troops operate a checkpoint was shot in front of his house, and the word "Traitor" was written on his forehead. "There was something evil in that town," Bray recalled. In his view, Human Rights Watch overestimated the casualties in the first incident because it collected statistics that reflected violence all the way from Ramadi to Baghdad for a three-day period. As for the criticism by fellow American soldiers, he said it came from units fresh to Iraq and unfamiliar with the situation. "Dave [Teeples] doesn't quite understand what is happening" that day in Fallujah. "This is the first fight for him and his guys. I tell them, 'The war's not over.'" Earlier that day he had seen a 3rd ACR soldier standing on a balcony in Fallujah without any body armor on. "I told him, 'Son, you don't know where you are.'"

The incidents of April 28 and 30 became a cause célèbre for the people of Fallujah, who would raise them repeatedly in negotiations with U.S. forces over the next year. "It continually comes up," said a U.S. military intelligence official who sometimes dealt directly with insurgents there.

Added Col. John Toolan, commander of the Marines who would fight a battle in Fallujah a year later, "They used it against us all the time."

Francis "Bing" West, the embedded defense analyst and author who has spent more time studying U.S. military operations in al Anbar province than any other unofficial observer, concluded that the Sunnis—and especially the people of Fallujah and the rest of al Anbar province—had never been defeated in the spring invasion. In that sense, the April incidents may have been not so much a cause of later troubles as a reflection of an existing problem: The Sunnis still wanted to slug it out.

At any rate, Fallujah would continue to be the victim of U.S. military absent-mindedness, with its problems underestimated and a variety of different Army units deployed to it in stopgap moves. "In Fallujah, they didn't trust us," recalled Capt. Lesley Kipling, the MP officer. "Units were constantly rotating through there. I think that is one of the biggest reasons that place never calmed down." Over the course of a few months, the city was patrolled by parts of 82nd Airborne, then by Poirier's MP-led task force, then by the 3rd Armored Cavalry Regiment, then by part of the 3rd Infantry Division, and then by the 82nd Airborne when it returned later in 2003. Finally it would be turned over to the Marines, with a battle following soon after. "Fallujah had five different units handling it between April '03 and April '04," said one Army intelligence officer who served in al Anbar province. "This is exactly the wrong way to prosecute a counterinsurgency fight."

The 4th Infantry Division vs. the Marine Corps

At the northern end of the Sunni Triangle, another Army division made a similarly belligerent entrance. In mid-April the Marines briefly occupied Saddam Hussein's hometown of Tikrit, and were preparing to turn it over to the Army's 4th Infantry Division. Unusual for an officially produced document, the official history produced by the 1st Division of the Marine Corps is disapproving, even contemptuous, of what it calls the 4th Infantry Division's "very aggressive" posture as that unit came into Iraq. "The lead elements of this division began to arrive in Tikrit on the 19th [of April], and were given a thorough orientation to the peaceful situation in town, and the continuing exercise in self-governance being worked with local leaders," stated the draft of the 1st Marine Division history of its time in Iraq in 2003. Despite that, it continued,

> [t]he arriving staff of the 4th Infantry Division had a sterner perspective on the situation. They characterized their recent road march to Tikrit from Kuwait as an "attack," and remained convinced that the situation in Tikrit required a very aggressive military enforcement posture. The dichotomy between the two peace-keeping strategies was unsettling for the Marines, and many winced when Army Apache attack helicopters swooped into the division battlespace without coordination and began to strafe abandoned enemy equipment indiscriminately, often in close proximity to Marine forces or innocent civilians.

Strikingly, the draft of the Marine history became even more pointed when it was revised. The final version noted that the Marines threw a farewell dinner to cement relationships with local tribal leaders. "The design was to use this opportunity to pass down relationships based on trust and mutual respect," the history stated. "The meeting was successfully concluded, with plans for future contact with the northern tribes established." Then, it goes on to say, somewhat ominously, "the meeting might have been even more productive had senior officers from 4th Infantry Division been willing to attend."

The history dryly notes that the Marines, "despite some misgivings," turned over the area to the 4th Infantry Division and departed on April 21. "Stores that had re-opened quickly closed back up as the people once again evacuated the streets, adjusting to the new security tactics," the final draft of the history reported. "A budding cooperative environment between the citizens and American forces was quickly snuffed out. The new adversarial relationship would become a major source of trouble in the coming months."

The Army perspective was quite different. Lt. Col. Gian Gentile, who was executive officer of the Army brigade relieving the Marines in Tikrit, later argued, "The Marines' velvet glove covered some dangerous problems that we were soon to face." When the Army sent out a night patrol, which he said the Marines hadn't done, it encountered looters carrying off rocket-propelled grenades and mortar rounds.

Maj. Gen. Raymond Odierno, the 4th ID commander, later said that he was "very confused" by the Marines' criticism. "It was such a short period of time" that the two services overlapped in Tikrit, he said. At any rate, he knew of only one instance of an Army Apache helicopter firing without needed clearance from the Marines.

But it wasn't just Marines who were taken aback by the 4th ID's aggressive stance. Unlike most Army divisions, it hadn't been deployed for decades, missing out on Panama, the 1991 Gulf War, Somalia, Bosnia, Kosovo, and Afghanistan. At its home base of Fort Hood, Texas, it sometimes was mocked as the second team, taking a backseat to its neighbor, the 1st Cavalry Division. Then it was assigned the role of invading Iraq from the north in the spring 2003 attack, only to be prevented from executing that mission when the Turkish government declined to permit the movement of U.S. troops through its territory.

It is remarkable how consistently other soldiers were put off by the 4th Division's stance during its early days in Iraq. "We slowly drove past 4th Infantry guys looking mean and ugly," recalled Sgt. Kayla Williams, then a military intelligence specialist in the 101st Airborne. "They stood on top of their trucks, their weapons pointed directly at civilians. . . . What could these locals possibly have done? Why was this intimidation necessary? No one explained anything, but it looked weird and felt wrong." Her gut sense would be borne out in the coming months, as the 4th ID would commit more than its share of abuses of Iraqis.

On April 19, as Pentagon officials continued to insist that there were enough troops to do the job and that commanders on the ground agreed with them, Maj. Gen. Mattis, one of the senior U.S. military commanders in Iraq, noted in an internal message that the incoming Army occupation force lacked sufficient numbers of troops. "The lack of Army dismounts [regular infantry] is creating a void in personal contact and public perception of our civil-military ops," Mattis wrote.

At month's end, despite the concerns about the lack of troops, the Marines were told to execute previously existing plans to pull out and head home. "Most of us were flabbergasted to be told to leave Baghdad at the end of April," recalled Marine Col. John Toolan. "I turned over my sector, which was east Baghdad, to 2nd ACR [Armored Cavalry Regiment], which had about one-fifth the capability of my regiment."

Even before he left Iraq, Toolan recalled, Mattis, his commander, took him aside and said he thought that the situation was deteriorating and that the Marines would be pulled back into Iraq eventually. "Don't lose sight of what you've learned," he recalled Mattis telling him, "because you're going to need to get your guys ready to come back." Off the top of his head, Mattis picked November 10—an easily remembered date because it is the Marine Corps's birthday—as the target date by which he wanted his troops to be ready to head back to Iraq. In fact, the deployment order would arrive on November 7.

"Mission accomplished"

Publicly, at least, all was going well.

One of the roles of a president is to provide strategic context—to explain how the public, and especially how subordinate officials, should think about a situation. On May 1, 2003, President Bush ostentatiously flew in a Navy combat aircraft to the USS *Abraham Lincoln,* an aircraft carrier steaming off the coast of southern California. The day is remembered, somewhat unfairly, as the occasion of Bush's Mission Accomplished speech. Bush never used that phrase, which was hanging prominently on a huge banner displayed on the ship's island—the tower where the captain and the flight controllers operate—so that television cameras focused on the president would pick it up. But his comments were in line with that theme. "Major combat operations in Iraq have ended," he began, standing on the ship's flight deck. "In the battle of Iraq, the United States and our allies have prevailed."

He did nod toward the operations that remained, which he seemed to characterize as a mop-up job. "We have difficult work to do in Iraq. We're bringing order to parts of that country that remain dangerous. We're pursuing and finding leaders of the old regime, who will be held to account for their crimes. We've begun the search for hidden chemical and biological weapons and already know of hundreds of sites that will be investigated." Doing all this, and establishing democracy, "will take time, but it is worth every effort." And, as he often would do in discussing Iraq in public, he circled back to the 9/11 attacks, clearly his starting point on the road to Baghdad. "The battle of Iraq is one victory in a war on terror that began on September the eleventh, 2001," he said.

In both image and word that day, what Bush did was tear down the goalposts at halftime in the game. But even as he spoke it was becoming clear on the ground that contrary to official expectation the stockpiles of WMD weren't going to be found. The poor intelligence on WMD would continue to haunt troops in the field—and, arguably, helped arm and protect the insurgency that would emerge in the following months. In bunkers across Iraq there were tens of thousands of tons of conventional weaponry—mortar shells, RPGs, rifle ammunition, explosives, and so on. One estimate, cited by Christopher Hileman, a U.S. intelligence analyst for Mideast matters, was "more than a million metric tons." Yet U.S. commanders rolling into Iraq refrained from detonating those bunkers for fear that they also contained stockpiles of poison gas or other weaponry that might be blown into the air and kill U.S. soldiers or Iraqi civilians. The COBRA II invasion plan unambiguously stated, "The

Iraqi Ministry of Defense will use WMD early but not often. The probability for their use of WMD increases exponentially as Saddam Hussein senses the imminent collapse of his regime."

Such certitude made American commanders wary of destroying weapons bunkers. "You never knew which one was WMD, okay?" said one regretful Marine battalion commander. So the bunkers often were bypassed and left undisturbed by an invasion force that already was stretched thin—and the insurgents were able to arm themselves at leisure.

The U.S. focus on WMD also provided a kind of smokescreen that unintentionally protected the insurgents during the spring of 2004. One senior military intelligence officer recalled arguing that a good roadmap of the nascent opposition in Fallujah could be developed simply by translating the roster of residents of that city—that the U.S. military possessed—who had volunteered for suicide missions against Israel. Then, he recommended, map their houses and visit each one—as soon as possible. But he couldn't "get it translated—all the assets were focused on WMD." Thousands of weapons experts, translators, and other specialists, along with all their support personnel, were working to find unconventional weapons that didn't exist, and soon were being attacked with conventional weapons that did but that had been ignored by U.S. officials.

The United States loses the initiative

When top Pentagon officials refused to acknowledge the realities of Iraq, the opportunity to take hold of the situation slipped between the fingers of the Americans. In military terms, in April and May, the U.S. military lost the initiative—that is, it stopped being the side in the conflict that was driving events, acting at the time and place of its choosing. "When the statue came down, that moment, we could have done some great things," Zinni said, looking back. "The problem is, we had insufficient forces to secure and freeze the situation and capitalize on that moment."

A year later, a formal Pentagon review, led by two former secretaries of defense, James Schlesinger and Harold Brown, came to a similar conclusion about the lack of mental agility at the Pentagon. "In Iraq, there was not only a failure to plan for a major insurgency, but also to quickly and adequately adapt to the insurgency that followed after major combat operations," they wrote, along with two other members of the panel appointed to review the military establishment's handling of Iraq during the summer and fall of 2003. "The October 2002 Centcom war plan presupposed that relatively benign stability and security operations would precede a handover to Iraq's authorities."

When those rosy assumptions weren't borne out, the Pentagon's leadership failed to adjust, most notably by sending more troops. Keith Mines, a State Department diplomat assigned by the CPA to al Anbar province in 2003, later wrote an analysis of how what he called "the minimalist force structure" undercut the occupation in the summer of 2003. He was uniquely placed to do so: A former Special Forces officer, he had a solid understanding of both military and political tactics and a feeling especially for how they interact. "First," he wrote, "a larger force could have stopped the looting," which tainted the occupation and destroyed necessary infrastructure. For lack of troops, the border was left largely open, a particular problem in western Iraq, where he operated, and where jihadists could move freely across from Syria. In addition, there weren't enough soldiers to train Iraqis, and so contractors were used, but their "timeline stretched into 2006 before the new force would begin to deploy." But the worst effect may have been the lack of adequate troops to manage detainees—a problem top commanders in Iraq wouldn't recognize until 2004, after it had led to a scandal that damaged the American image globally. The oddity, Mines concluded, was that there were two known models for successful counterinsurgency operations, and the U.S. had managed to avoid both. One was El Salvador in the 1980s, where a tiny group of just fifty-five U.S. military advisers had worked with local military units. The other was postwar Germany, where a large and overwhelming force was garrisoned. But in Iraq "we have worked the middle ground, with just enough forces to elicit a strong response from Iraqi nationalists but inadequate forces to make the transition work."

Maj. Gen. John Batiste, who would command the 1st Infantry Division in Iraq for a year, said that the initial U.S. approach helped create the mess that followed. "We set ourselves up for what happened when we violated two principles that are absolutely fundamental for success. One is unity of command. The other is mass." In other words, he argued, the U.S. approach failed to heed two of the most basic rules of military operations: First, have everybody working toward the same goal, with one person in charge. Second, have enough people and machines to get the job done. Together these flaws "led directly to Abu Ghraib," because inadequate leaders and overstrapped units were given tasks far beyond their limited abilities and resources.

Col. Teddy Spain, from his front-row seat as chief of U.S. military police forces in Baghdad, came to agree with that assessment. In April, Spain made his first foray into Baghdad, conducting a reconnaissance mission before moving his headquarters north to the capital. He was surprised by what he saw. "The first time I went into Baghdad, they were breaking into ministries and burning buildings, but I didn't have the assets—all my people were down south guarding supply routes and EPWs," or enemy prisoners of war.

With those troops, he said later, he might have been able to bring security to Baghdad. If he had had those MP units that had been dropped from the invasion plan months earlier, "I think we could have taken control of the streets much better. I think Baghdad would have been different. I just didn't have the assets." He would prove not to be alone in these bitter regrets.

8.

HOW TO CREATE AN INSURGENCY (I)

SPRING AND SUMMER 2003

My soldiers are starting to lose their positive attitudes and are constantly asking when we will go home," Capt. Lesley Kipling, the MP officer, wrote to her boyfriend on May 9.

The feeling of postwar impatience was the same at the Pentagon, recalled an officer who was on the Joint Staff at that time: "There was a mind-set by the first part of May: Major combat operations are over, let's think about drawing down the force."

From late spring to midsummer 2003 was a time of meandering and drift for the U.S. occupation of Iraq. It took months for incorrect assumptions to begin to be discarded and for commanders to recognize that large numbers of U.S. troops were going to be in Iraq for some time. "In the two to three months of ambiguous transition, U.S. forces slowly lost the momentum and the initiative they had gained over an off-balance enemy," Maj. Isaiah Wilson later wrote. "During this calm before the next storm, the U.S. Army has its eyes turned toward the ports, while Former Regime Loyalists (FRL) and budding insurgents had their eyes turned toward the people. The United States, its Army, and its coalition of the willing have been playing catch-up ever since."

As the situation turned violent, some U.S. soldiers began to question why they were in Iraq. "Motivation was not a problem during the initial stages, however once we transitioned into SASO [stability and support operations, the U.S. military term for peacekeeping] it became a problem," one Army lieutenant observed that summer on an Internet discussion board for young officers. "It didn't take much time before I realized that they were lacking any sense of purpose. . . . They didn't know why they weren't going home, why they couldn't see their first child born, and why we were helping an ungrateful and hostile populace."

Added an intelligence officer who was attached to a Navy SEAL unit at the time, "The air went out of the tires almost overnight."

Watching sofas go by

Baghdad was falling apart in front of the eyes of the U.S. military, with buildings being looted and parents afraid to let their children outside, but no one had orders to do anything about it. Looking back several years later, Col. Alan King, the head of civil affairs for the 3rd Infantry Division, spoke of April 2003 with a slow, chilled tone of horror in his voice. "I got to Baghdad and was told, 'You've got twenty-four hours to come up with a Phase IV plan. . . . On the night of April 8, Col. [John] Sterling, the chief of staff of the 3rd ID, came to me and said, 'I just got off the phone with the corps chief of staff, and I asked him for the reconstruction plan, and he said there isn't one. So you've got twenty-four hours to come up with one.'" King was stunned. He had been asking for months for just such a plan, and had been told that when the time came, he would be given it.

Lacking clear orders about what to do once in Baghdad, the 3rd ID more or less stayed in place in the capital. "You didn't find many dismounted patrols with the 3rd ID," recalled Jay Garner, a retired Army general and not one to lightly criticize his old peers. "They kind of stayed with their platforms"—that is, their tanks and Bradley fighting vehicles.

On April 6, Lt. Douglas Hoyt, a platoon leader with the 3rd ID, saw looters for the first time. "I remembered looking through the sights on my tank at people and trying to determine if they were hostile or not," he recalled later. He didn't stop them. "It was not our mission at the time."

The division's official after-action review states that it had no orders to do anything else: "3RD ID transitioned into Phase IV SASO with no plan from higher headquarters," it reported. "There was no guidance for restoring order in Baghdad, creating an interim government, hiring government and essential services employees, and ensuring that the judicial system was operational." The result was "a power/authority vacuum created by our failure to immediately replace key government institutions." In a surprising criticism for an Army division to make—especially one that had led the way in toppling an enemy government—the 3rd ID report laid the blame for all of this at the feet of its chain of command, leading to Franks to Rumsfeld and Bush: "The president announced that our national goal was 'regime change.' Yet there was no timely plan prepared for the obvious consequences of a regime change."

The report also faulted the political thinking that led American forces to be declared liberators rather than occupiers, because that led military commanders to operate in a hands-off way that allowed the chaos to increase in Baghdad. "As a matter of law and fact, the United States is an occupying power in Iraq, even if we characterize ourselves as liberators," stated the staff judge advocate's section of the division report. "Because of the refusal to acknowledge occupier status, commanders did not initially take measures available to occupying powers, such as imposing curfews, directing civilians to return to work, and controlling the local governments and populace. The failure to act after we displaced the regime created a power vacuum, which others immediately tried to fill."

"No one had talked about what would happen when we got there," said Capt. David Chasteen, a 3rd ID officer. "There was no plan for that. They literally told us once we got there they'd pull us back out, take us home. Once we got there it was a clusterfuck, just trying to figure out what to do." Normally the division's officer for coordinating defenses against nuclear, biological, and chemical attacks, Chasteen was assigned in Baghdad to work at the city's international airport, which had become a giant U.S. military base. "I was customs, immigration, looking at people's passports, I had no idea what I was doing. Such a nicely planned operation that went so well, why didn't anyone think about what the next step would be?"

It wasn't just a lack of planning or guidance from civilians that led to the U.S. inertia, it also was a lack of understanding or interest among senior military commanders. "The civilian leadership did not foresee the need for extensive Phase IV operations, and thus did little planning beyond near-term relief," said one Pentagon official who was involved in war-gaming the invasion plan, and who later quietly analyzed its failures. "This was fine with the military, which had traditionally focused on Phase III operations, did not want to do Phase IV operations, and figured that someone else would step in."

Brig. Gen. David Fastabend told the story of reading an article in which a fellow Army general was quoted as saying that Army doctrine hadn't prepared him for what he faced in Iraq during the late spring of 2003. When he met this officer, Fastabend, who was involved in developing doctrine—that is, how to think about how to fight and operate—questioned him about that statement. "I don't understand why you said that," Fastabend said. "Look, in 1993 we introduced 'military operations other than war,' and then we introduced the idea of 'full-spectrum operations.' From '97 to 2001 we introduced the idea that operations are a seamless combination of offense, defense, stability, and support. How could you say that your doctrine didn't prepare you for what you experienced in Baghdad?"

"Yeah, Dave, I know," this officer responded. "I read all that stuff. Read it many times, and thought about it. But I can remember quite clearly, I was on a street corner in Baghdad, smoking a cigar, watching some guys carry a sofa by—and it never occurred to me that I was going to be the guy to go get that sofa back."

The pacification of Ar Rutbah

One of the notable exceptions to this sense of drift was in areas where Army Special Forces operated, in far northern and western Iraq. Those soldiers were much more accustomed to living and working with foreign populations.

The experience of Army Maj. Jim Gavrilis showed the road that unfortunately was not taken by the overwhelming majority of the U.S. military in Iraq. At six o'clock on the morning of April 9, the career Special Forces officer drove into Ar Rutbah, the only town of any size in far western Iraq. His troops had come under intense fire from this town of about twenty-five thousand people, but he didn't enter it in a hostile fashion. "I understood that this was a war of liberation and therefore the people were ultimately the center of gravity," he later wrote, in a simple sentence of great insight. "As a result, it was natural for us to focus on the people and build positive relationships with them."

He drank tea with Bedouins in the desert, smoked cigarettes with farmers near the towns, and broke bread with police chiefs, and even with Iraqi army officers. He listened. He ate with his fingers, as they did. He emphasized that it was their country and that he was a guest who hoped to help. "Our behavior sent the clearest message," he later wrote. "We showed we cared more about the people of Ar Rutbah than did the Saddam Fedayeen." This was a classic counterinsurgency move, implemented at the most opportune time—before there was an insurgency.

Along the same lines, Gavrilis moved quickly to empower the locals. By the time the calls rang out from the minarets for noon prayers on the day he arrived, he had named an interim mayor. He also took steps to integrate the local police into his checkpoints. "This allowed the Iraqis to do their part and increased their comfort with us," he recalled. And, "in practical terms, the police knew who was from the city and who had legitimate business."

He co-opted the existing power structure. When some sheikhs came to complain about looting, he knew some of them were behind those acts, he said. So he put those very sheikhs in charge of a neighborhood-watch program—and held them accountable for any continued looting, with U.S. troops monitoring the situation in random patrols. "The stealing dropped to almost nothing." He also gave relief food supplies to the sheikhs and imams, because he realized that they knew who really needed it. To help the rest of the population obtain food, he lent his satellite phone to local merchants so they could contact business partners in Jordan. "In a day, the market had fresh fruit and vegetables, and fresh fish and meat for the first time in months."

One hallmark of his approach was a humility about his role and his limited ability to alter a culture whose roots reached back to the days of Abraham and Ezekiel. "The laws and values of their society and culture were just fine," he wrote. "All we needed to do was enforce them." Emphasizing this attitude of restraint, he lived simply, not moving into any palaces, as conventional U.S. forces were doing elsewhere in Iraq.

He also took a gentle approach to de-Baathification. First he offered to turn the Baath Party headquarters—"the nicest building in the city"—into a hospital. He also developed a renunciation form in which people who were becoming part of the interim government repudiated the party and pledged to serve and protect the people of the new Iraq. Signing the form wasn't done punitively. "It was more of a commencement where we congratulated each person for their courage in turning this new leaf," he wrote. Those who wanted to sign the form in private were allowed to do so. "Simply put, de-Baathifcation meant political change, not political purge."

At any rate, he preferred a functioning city administered in part by some former Baathists to a stricken one stripped of them. "By quickly establishing an effective Iraqi alternative to the regime and not alienating anyone, we made resistance irrelevant," he said.

The one area in which Gavrilis took a hard line was on violence. No one but U.S. forces were permitted to carry a weapon. "I made it very clear . . . that I retained the monopoly on the use of force."

In sum, he treated Iraqis as partners. Rather than seek to break the structure of an ancient society, he sought to use it to achieve his ends. But he was careful in establishing those goals and realistic in seeking to achieve them, acting with both humility and common sense. In other words, he took almost the opposite course that the U.S. occupation authorities based in Baghdad would dictate in the following months. He left Ar Rutbah on April 23. By midsummer, the atmosphere in those towns in the province, from Ar Rutbah east to Fallujah, would be far more hostile.

Garner's troubled tenure

In Baghdad, meanwhile, Garner was off to an uneven start. His initial moves were making Ahmed Chalabi uneasy—and the Iraqi exile had better contacts in the U.S. government and in the media than the retired general did. Garner found that he had a particularly difficult relationship with Chalabi as well. "Very tense," he said. "He didn't like me." The reason for the mutual unease, Garner believed, was that Chalabi thought that control of Iraq would be turned over to him. "I think he'd been led to believe that by Perle and Feith," Garner said later. And Garner didn't like that idea. "I thought he was a thug, very sleazy." When he heard a year later that Chalabi allegedly had been passing intelligence to the Iranian government, "I thought, 'No shit.'"

Chalabi, for his part, was doing his best during this period to undercut Garner. "The problem with Garner was that he was employing Baathists in senior positions, and the U.S. press got hold of that," Chalabi later said. "They went ahead and put in the *New York Times* that Baathists were being made to run the university, Ministry of Health. . . . That created a big fuss with the United States, because the U.S. policy was de-Baathification." Chalabi acknowledged that he was pushing this view "very hard" at the time.

Also, even as it occupied Baghdad, the U.S. government was still undecided on the basics of what it planned to do there. Most notably, officials went back and forth on the issue of whether to maintain the Iraqi military. The U.S. military generally advocated keeping the Iraqi forces relatively intact. "We'd been briefing, 'Keep the Iraqi army,'" said a military intelligence officer. "It is solid, it has structure and discipline, and credibility inside Iraq."

In mid-April, Abizaid "strongly recommended" to the Pentagon that a substantial Iraqi army be established immediately, according to an internal summary of a secure video teleconference. This interim force would have three divisions—the U.S. Army at the time had just ten, for the entire world—and would "take over internal security functions as quickly as possible," the document stated. A subsequent memo noted that there was an "urgent need to maintain order, suppress various militias, put an Iraqi face on security and relieve burden on Coalition military." Wolfowitz, who participated in the video teleconference, expressed concern about having the Iraqi army perform internal security missions. But he and Abizaid concluded by agreeing to start up a force and worry later about its mission.

By month's end, Central Command staffers were hard at work on this New Iraqi Corps, which they inevitably acronymized as the NIC—not knowing that that sound was Arabic slang for "fuck." When, several weeks later, this was pointed out to U.S. officials, the planned organization was renamed the New Iraqi Army. Garner's team began to work toward the goal of assembling Iraqi army units—talking to former officers and getting their advice about how to go about it.

At the same time, there was growing unease back in Washington with Garner's performance. Rice was told that "Garner just isn't pulling things together," recalled Franklin Miller, the National Security Council's staff director for defense issues.

On the night of April 24, Garner was standing in the looted mess of Saddam Hussein's main palace downtown, broken glass under his shoes, when Rumsfeld called to tell him that a retired diplomat named L. Paul Bremer III would be coming in as a presidential envoy. "He asked me to stay on under Bremer, but I said that wouldn't work. He asked me to stay on for a transition, and I said I would."

American leadership goes MIA

One of the unexplained oddities of this time was the absence of much of the nation's top military leadership: Just as the situation in Iraq was deteriorating, there was a series of retirements and replacements among the top commanders handling it. The changes would occur just as Garner was succeeded by Bremer, with ill effect.

At the top of the chain of command for operations in Iraq, Gen. Franks seemed quickly to have detached from Iraq issues. Some of those who worked with him found him remote and even out of touch in the weeks after the fall of Baghdad. Franks was getting ready to retire, while Abizaid was not yet confirmed by Congress to succeed him as the top U.S. military commander for Iraq and the rest of the Mideast. A Pentagon official said that top officials got wind at one point that Franks planned to fly from the Mideast to Tampa, pick up his wife, and take a long weekend, maybe in the Bahamas. Franks ultimately was ordered not to. He "put his pack down early," said a former senior administration official. "He couldn't even be found a lot of the times."

"Franks was strangely absent" in May and June of 2003, agreed Army Col. Gregory Gardner, who was serving at the CPA. "He blew into Baghdad once, signed the freedom order, and left. It was like, 'I've done it, I did the offensive operations.' I really felt he was disengaged."

Franks, who declined to be interviewed for this book, wrote in his own that "Phase IV was actually going about as I had expected"—which, if it were indeed true, would make his decision to retire from the battlefield all the more inexplicable. Even more bizarrely, Gen. Franks later would blame journalists for the lack of an adequate U.S. military response to the situation. "I remember a time long about the 9th, 10th, 11th of April of last year where there was a lot of media coverage of the fact that Saddam's statue came down in Baghdad," he said in Washington late in 2004. "And then pretty soon there was created—and I would not take credit as the guy who created an expectation, I will just say that all of the reporting, and none of it was evil—but the reporting we all saw kind of created an expectation, 'Well probably peace is going to break out very, very quickly.'" This attempt by a top commander to shift responsibility to the media for poor military leadership and a flawed understanding of the strategic situation is unbecoming—especially because it was uttered not in the heat of the moment but almost eighteen months after the fact.

Gen. Shinseki, the chief of the U.S. Army, left the stage at about the same time. Neither Defense Secretary Rumsfeld nor Deputy Defense Secretary Wolfowitz attended the scorned general's retirement ceremony. Wolfowitz asked to come but Shinseki declined to invite him. It was an extraordinary situation: While the nation was at war and American soldiers were dying, the Pentagon's top civilians were estranged from the Army's leadership. What's more, it was the second bitter departure of an Army four-star general under Rumsfeld: Gen. Henry "Hugh" Shelton, the chairman of the Joint Chiefs of Staff, had retired in 2001, just weeks after 9/11, disgusted with Rumsfeld and feeling he had recklessly disregarded sound military advice.

Shinseki struck two dissonant themes in his farewell address that warm June day. First, there was a difference between being a boss and being a leader. "Mistrust and arrogance are antithetical to inspired and inspiring leadership," he said in reference to the contumely of his civilian leaders. (This was "a subtle rebuke to Secretary Rumsfeld," according to a biographical pamphlet by veteran journalist Richard Halloran that was written with Shinseki's cooperation and published by the Hawaii Army Museum Society.) His second theme was even more sensitive. Looking at Iraq as his Army career ended, Shinseki said, he was reminded of the war where his career had begun, Vietnam, where he had been wounded three times, the last time losing half his right foot to a land mine. It was striking that the chief of the Army was the first major public figure to draw this analogy, only two months into the occupation. "The current war brings me full circle to where I began my journey as a soldier," he said. "The lessons I learned in Vietnam are always with me." One of his warnings was that the Army needed to be big enough for the missions assigned it. "Beware the twelve-division strategy for a ten-division Army," he cautioned. Then he retired and all but disappeared from public view, a samurai ashamed of the behavior of his shogun. Over the next couple of years he would surface only a few times in low-profile speeches far from Washington—in Georgia, California, and Hawaii.

After Gen. Keane declined the job of succeeding Shinseki, Rumsfeld, in an unusual move, passed over all the Army's active-duty three- and four-star generals—normally the ones who would be considered—to appoint as chief a retired general named Peter Schoomaker. When Rumsfeld's aides first contacted Schoomaker, they reached him on his cell phone in his pickup truck near rural Hico, Texas, a bit north of Fort Hood. The retired general thought he might be getting a prank call from the rancher he'd just left. Furthering the Army's isolation, Schoomaker was an outsider. He had spent most of his career in Special Operations, which often acts—and is treated—as if it were a separate service from the Army.

On the ground in Iraq, the structure of U.S. forces also was in flux. After being told for two weeks that both the 1st Cavalry Division and 1st Armored Division would be deploying, Col. Agoglia was told on April 30 that the 1st Cav wouldn't be coming after all—and that the 3rd ID would be leaving after the 1st AD arrived. "So we have a net gain of zero," he calculated to himself. "You're kiddin' me!"

In addition, instead of having Iraq run by Gen. McKiernan and his staff at CFLCC, the headquarters for the ground invasion force, the staff of V Corps, a smaller group, was going to be put in charge. This meant that an experienced team that had worked for months on Iraq issues was being replaced by a smaller, less capable, and less seasoned staff. McKiernan's headquarters was especially attuned to the tribal structure of Iraqi society, an intelligence officer recalled: "They were sent home, and that expertise and capability went with them. We spent from May '03 to December '03 trying to rebuild that capability."

What's more, a general named Ricardo Sanchez was going to take over V Corps at the same time. "So now you have the most junior headquarters in theater, with the most junior commander in theater, taking over," Agoglia recalled. "You've got the entire military chain of command changing." Agoglia also moved, rewarded for his two years of nonstop work in the frying pan of planning wars for Gen. Franks by being thrown into the fire as the military liaison between the CPA and Central Command.

Bremer's opening blunders

Bremer headed for Iraq in early May, determined to show that there was a new sheriff in town. In a memo to the Pentagon's general counsel written just before his departure, he noted his desire "that my arrival in Iraq be marked by clear, public and decisive steps" to "reassure Iraqis that we are determined to eradicate Saddamism." One of those steps, he decided, would be the total dissolution of the Iraqi army. He attached the draft of an order to that end that, he said, "Walt Slocombe has suggested that I issue . . . immediately after my arrival." (Slocombe was a former Pentagon official who had agreed to be Bremer's adviser on defense issues.)

On May 12, 2003, Bremer arrived in Baghdad aboard a Special Operations MC-130 Combat Talon aircraft. He and Garner overlapped for just a few weeks. Garner had told Rumsfeld he would stay as late as early July, but soon found that his views weren't particularly welcome. "Bremer didn't want my advice. . . . He's a hardworking guy, twenty hours a day. But he cut me out the first day, didn't have me to any of his meetings. So on the third day he was there, I said, 'Jerry, I'm going home.' We just didn't get along."

For his own part, Bremer, a veteran diplomat who had gone on to work as a consultant, was taken aback by the situation on the ground. "I found a city that was on fire, not from the war, but from the looting," he later said. "I found a city where there was virtually no traffic except for American military vehicles or coalition tanks and Humvees, a city where there was a lot of gunfire still going on."

In mid-May, Bremer quickly made three moves that radically altered the American approach to Iraq and went a long way toward creating support for an anti-American insurgency. Oddly, these early moves contradicted the decisions made by President Bush on March 10 and 12 at briefings on postwar Iraq, according to an administration official who participated in both. "They were not the decisions that the administration had reached," Richard Armitage confirmed in an interview.

One of the first things Bremer did after arriving in Iraq was show Garner the order he intended to issue to rid Iraq of Baathist leadership. "Senior Party Members," it stated, "are hereby removed from their positions and banned from future employment in the public sector." In addition, anyone holding a position in the top three management layers of any ministry, government-run corporation, university, or hospital and who was a party member—even of a junior rank—would be deemed to be a senior Baathist and so would be fired. What's more, those suspected of crimes would be investigated and, if deemed a flight risk, would be detained or placed under house arrest.

Garner was appalled. This went far beyond what he had planned for months and, in fact, had briefed for Rumsfeld and President Bush. The message Garner had given his subordinates, recalled his strategy chief, Col. Paul Hughes, was, "Let them sort out their own de-Baathification—either kill them or force them to leave."

If issued as written, the order Bremer was carrying would lead to disaster, Garner thought. He went to see the CIA station chief, whom Garner had seen work well with the military. "This is too hard," Garner told the CIA officer, who read it and agreed. The two allies went back to Bremer.

"Give us an hour or so to redo this," Garner asked.

"Absolutely not," Bremer responded. "I have my instructions, and I am going to issue this."

The CIA station chief urged Bremer to reconsider. These are the people who know where the levers of the infrastructure are, from electricity to water to transportation, he said. Take them out of the equation and you undercut the operation of this country, he warned.

No, said Bremer.

Okay, the veteran CIA man responded. Do this, he said, but understand one thing: "By nightfall, you'll have driven 30,000 to 50,000 Baathists underground. And in six months, you'll really regret this." (The U.S. intelligence estimate was that the party had a total membership of 600,000 to 700,000, of which between 15,000 and 40,000 were senior members, depending on how one counted.)

Bremer looked at the two. "I have my instructions," he repeated, according to Garner, though it isn't clear that he really did, as the policy he was implementing wasn't what had been briefed to the president. A few months later, the veteran CIA man would leave Baghdad, replaced by a far more junior officer. In the fall of 2005 he would resign from government service.

The next day, Bremer met in his conference room—the only big room in the palace with working air conditioners—with his senior CPA staff members. He showed them the de-Baathification order. "They went nuts and said, 'You can't do this,'" recalled Gardner, the Army colonel assigned to CPA. "It just cleaned out the ministries. The guys said, 'We can't run our ministries now.'"

"I was extremely vocal with the people who were coming in that that was a huge mistake, that it really did not reflect the experience of these kinds of situations for the past twenty years," agreed David Nummy, a former assistant treasury secretary who is an expert on the financial systems of transitioning and developing countries. He called on his knowledge of Ukraine, Bosnia, and Kosovo to argue that Iraq "was not the first totalitarian system we had engaged with, not the first one-party state that we had worked with, and that there was absolutely no experience in any country that said that being a member of the dominant political party meant you were a bad guy."

Bremer again refused to budge. His response, said Gardner, was that he wasn't bringing up the issue for discussion but rather just to inform them of what was going to happen. It appears that with this move, Chalabi, operating behind the scenes, had won a major victory. Army Lt. Gen. Joseph Kellogg, Jr., then on the staff of the Joint Chiefs of Staff, recalled that Chalabi had been a strong backer of the radical de-Baathification plan Bremer brought with him. "He was calling for total de-Baathification, which was extreme."

"I think the world of Jerry Bremer," said Kellogg, who sat across from Bremer on the Special Operations C-130 aircraft that took them into Iraq. "He is personally courageous, and a good guy." But his management style didn't work well. "If you went up to him and said, 'You gotta do this, because your way is wrong,' he'd blow you off. So you'd have to work the sides. We'd kind of work around him."

On May 16, De-Baathification of Iraq Society was issued over Bremer's signature as Coalition Provisional Authority Order Number 1. It purged tens of thousands of members of the Baath Party—perhaps as many as eighty-five thousand. Ultimately, nine thousand would seek and be granted exemptions permitting them to go back to work. "I did that because I thought it was absolutely essential to make it clear that the Baathist ideology, which had been responsible for so many of the human-rights abuses and mistreatment of the people in the country over the last forty years, had to be extirpated finally and completely from society, much as the American government decided to completely extirpate Nazism from Germany at the end of the Second World War," Bremer said later.

Ultimately, the U.S. military in Iraq came to have a mixed view of the purge. Maj. Gen. Swannack spoke for many when he later said, "I was not very happy from day one with the de-Baathification program."

A 101st Airborne Division summary of issues for a meeting at the CPA later that year listed the "Big Five" concerns of the division commander, Maj. Gen. David Petraeus: "Arbitrary de-Baathification" was at the top of the list. One of

Petraeus's brigade commanders, Col. Joe Anderson, later summarized the effect of Bremer's order: "All of a sudden you say, 'These guys are not part of society.' . . . These were guys and gals in the doctor arena, in the professor arena, that you can't do without" in running a society.

But not everyone agreed. Brig. Gen. Martin Dempsey, who commanded the 1st Armored Division in Baghdad—and so had more top Baathists in his area of operations—said that in retrospect, Bremer's radical de-Baathification was the right move to make for changing Iraq, albeit a somewhat difficult one. If it hadn't been done, he said, "it would have gone easier for us in the near term, but less well for the Iraqi population in the long term."

Bremer dissolves the Iraqi armed forces

Next came the dissolution of the Iraqi army and national police force.

"We didn't disband the army," Walter Slocombe would later contend. "The army disbanded itself."

That's not the way many others remember what happened. "We were working with the army when we were told to disband them," recalled Marine Maj. Gen. Mattis.

Col. Hughes discussed the moment he learned about this order with the same passion that he recounted the events of 9/11, when his side of the Pentagon was hit by a fuel-laden jet. He was on leave in the United States, staying at a hotel in Boston for his daughter's graduation from Emerson College. One day just before leaving town, he idly turned on the hotel room's television to check the news. "They were saying on Channel Four that the Iraq army was being abolished." Incredulous, Hughes spoke to the television. "*What?*" The report made no sense to him. At Garner's behest he had spent the previous several weeks working on the future of the Iraqi military. Before going on leave he had been meeting every day with a group of Iraqi generals, and with them had developed a list of 125,000 former Iraqi soldiers.

This decision was another significant departure from what Garner had discussed with Rumsfeld and others before leaving Washington for Iraq. "One of our goals is to take a good portion of the Iraqi regular army" and put them to work in reconstruction, Garner had told reporters at the Pentagon in March. "The regular army has the skill sets to match the work that needs to be done." On February 19, Garner had briefed Rice, the national security adviser, on his plans for the Iraqi army. "Cannot immediately demobilize . . . 300K–400K unemployed," his briefing slide stated. "Take advantage of ready labor force . . . Reconstruction is labor-intensive." According to notes he prepared for that meeting, he told her of his preparations for "Iraq Regular Army: Plan for Rapid Reorganization." His plan was to use $1.2 billion in frozen assets to pay the military, police, and key civil servants for a few months. Garner had been so determined to stand up the Iraqi military quickly that he had demanded that the job of retraining not be given to the U.S. Army, which he had felt would move too slowly, but to contractors. In response, MPRI, a military consulting firm, had drawn up a detailed plan to use up to one hundred thousand Iraqi troops as the low-tech end of reconstruction projects. "Start with short, simple tasks (clear garbage, remove debris, improve drainage), then longer and more complex tasks," the company's plan stated.

"We planned to bring it back," Garner said in an interview. "I'd briefed the president on it." Having an operating Iraqi army was a key element of U.S. military planning. "Abizaid was all for it, Tommy Franks, McKiernan," the three top U.S. Army commanders in the region. Lt. Gen. David McKiernan, in particular, Garner said, "beat me up every day, saying, 'When are you going to get the army back?'" In addition, Prince Bandar bin Sultan, the Saudi Arabian ambassador to the United States, had strongly suggested to the U.S. government that it find a way to keep together some remnant of the Iraqi military, recalled Maj. Gen. Renuart, the operations director for Central Command.

As late as May 15, a CPA Web site stated that thirty thousand former members of the Iraqi army had registered for emergency payments, of which nine thousand were sergeants and enlisted men. The Web site said that the CPA goal was to bring them back to active duty.

But on May 23, Bremer issued CPA Order Number 2, Dissolution of Iraqi Entities, formally doing away with several groups: the Iraqi armed forces, which accounted for 385,000 people; the staff of the Ministry of the Interior, which amounted to a surprisingly high 285,000 people, because it included police and domestic security forces; and the presidential security units, a force of some 50,000. "Abruptly terminating the livelihoods of these men created a vast pool of humiliated, antagonized, and politicized men," noted Faleh Jabar, an expert on the Baathist Party who was a senior fellow at the U.S Institute of Peace. Many of these men were armed.

In addition, Bremer's order clarified his de-Baathification standard, saying that "any person holding the rank under the former regime of Col. or above, or its equivalent, will be deemed a Senior Party Member"—and so would not be eligible for any pension payments. This cut off tens of thousands of influential Iraqis, some of them wrongly, because it mistakenly assumed that one couldn't be a senior officer without being a party member. Only later did the CPA learn that even some top Iraqi generals were not in the party, a former CPA official recalled.

Central Command was taken aback by the announcement. "We were surprised at the dissolution of the army," said Maj. Gen. Renuart, adding mildly, "so that gave us a challenge." It is a verbal tic of the U.S. military that officers tend to say challenge when they mean problem. Agoglia, working as the military liaison to Bremer, told his boss, "You guys just blindsided Centcom." That was the day, he recalled, "that we snatched defeat from the jaws of victory and created an insurgency."

Likewise, another planner, Col. Kevin Benson, said that Bremer's move undercut the entire postwar plan: "We expected to be able to recall the Iraqi army. Once CPA took the decision to disband the Iraqi army and start again, our assumptions for the plan became invalid."

Rumsfeld was surprised by Bremer's move, said a general who spoke frequently with the defense secretary at this time. The Joint Staff was informed simply by a written note, said Col. Hughes. There was also some concern inside Feith's office. Abram Shulsky, an intelligence expert and former classmate of Wolfowitz at Cornell University and the University of Chicago, weighed in, writing a note to the Pentagon's general counsel raising concerns about the plan. "I'm not certain I like this," he wrote. "It seems to me we could accomplish the same effect if we said that the regular army . . . weren't dissolved, but would be thoroughly vetted and reformed."

Together, Bremer's two orders threw out of work more than half a million people and alienated many more dependent on those lost incomes. Just as important, in a country riven by sectarian and ethnic fault lines—Sunni versus Shiite versus Kurd—and possessing few unifying national institutions, Bremer had done away with two of the most important ones. Moreover, the moves undercut the fragile remnants of the police structure. "The CPA decision to cleanse the political system of Hussein sympathizers—notably, the 'de-Baathification' effort—effectively decapitated the IPS," or Iraqi police services, a joint study by the inspectors general of the Pentagon and State Department would find two years later.

Zinni believed Chalabi had maneuvered Bremer and his subordinates into the moves. "I think the de-Baathification and the dissolution of the army was at Chalabi's insistence," he said. "Because Chalabi wanted to replace the Baathists at every level with his people. Iraqis told me this, Iraqis from inside during the war said that Chalabi was pushing Bremer to get rid of all of the Baathists because he wanted to put his people in those positions, he could control them. And I think, obviously, he saw the army as a threat to him. If the army stayed intact, he wouldn't have control of the security forces."

The move also resulted from Bremer's lack of experience in the region, Zinni speculated. "Bremer comes in, he doesn't know the planning. We had spent a decade psyopsing the Iraqi army, telling them we would take care of those who didn't fight. And he disbands it."

The move also worried some soldiers on the ground. When Maj. Jeffrey Madison, a finance officer working for the 1st Armored Division, heard about it, he wrote that night to his wife, "This is going to be a problem. This is going to come back and haunt us."

Col. King saw and heard the reaction close-up on the hot streets of Baghdad. "When Bremer did that, the insurgency went crazy. May was the turning point" for the U.S. occupation, he said later. "When they disbanded the military, and announced we were occupiers—that was it. Every moderate, every person that had leaned toward us, was furious. One Iraqi who had saved my life in an ambush said to me, 'I can't be your friend anymore.'"

At the end of May and in early June, dismissed ministry workers and former Iraqi army soldiers held a series of demonstrations. Some vowed they would violently oppose the U.S. decisions. "All of us will become suicide bombers," former officer Khairi Jassim told Reuters. The wire service article was distributed at the CPA with that quotation highlighted.

"The only thing left for me is to blow myself up in the face of tyrants," another officer told Al Jazeera.

Bremer insisted he wouldn't be moved. "We are not going to be blackmailed into producing programs because of threats of terrorism," he said at a press conference in early June.

The protests continued. On June 18 an estimated two thousand Iraqi soldiers gathered outside the Green Zone to denounce the dissolution decision. Some carried signs that said, PLEASE KEEP YOUR PROMISES. Others threw rocks. "We will take up arms," Tahseen Ali Hussein vowed in a speech to the demonstrators, according to an account by Agence France Presse. "We are all very well-trained soldiers and we are armed. We will start ambushes, bombings and even suicide bombings. We will not let the Americans rule us in such a humiliating way." U.S. soldiers fired into the crowd, killing two.

In the weeks after that, U.S. commanders grew increasingly concerned by the unrest the order caused. At about this time, Gen. Sanchez was formally promoted from commander of the 1st Armored Division to commander of V Corps, the headquarters for all U.S. military operations in Iraq. At the reception after the change-of-command ceremony, Maj. Gen. Petraeus confronted Walt Slocombe. The failure to pay ex-officers was getting U.S. troops hurt, he warned Slocombe. And the longer the demobilized Iraqi soldiers were left hanging, the more dangerous they would become. "They are really tinder out there just waiting for a spark," Petraeus told him, who then promised to press the issue. A few days later Rumsfeld approved the payment, and the officers' protests ended.

In early July, after those demonstrations stopped, the J-2—the top U.S. military intelligence staff in the country—discontinued its reporting on the former Iraqi army officers, citing the end of the protests, according to an officer who received an order related to that decision.

Perhaps just as significant as those two controversial moves of Bremer's was his third major decision: There wouldn't be an Iraqi government anytime soon, despite Garner's plan to set one up. "It simply was not possible," he later said.

He also soon began pursuing a program aimed at moving Iraq toward a free-market economy, beginning by shutting down unprofitable state-run industries. This had the political effect of further alienating the middle class, which already had been hit by de-Baathification, and which was full of managers from those inefficient industries.

The combination of all these moves—a prolonged foreign occupation that was built on de-Baathification, dissolution of the military, and economic upheaval—radically undercut social stability and built opposition to the American presence. "What we have done over the last six months in al Anbar has been a recipe for instability," Keith Mines would write in a November memo. "Through aggressive de-Baathification, the demobilization of the army, and the closing of factories the coalition has left tens of thousands of individuals outside the economic and political life of the country."

Taken together, Bremer's approach had for many Iraqis a punitive feel, a result that was a key misstep, Wolfowitz's old mentor Fred Ikle would later observe. "Democracies that have achieved a military victory ought to refrain from seeking revenge," Ikle wrote.

Taking revenge is a Neanderthal strategy. Instead of giving priority to a policy that can transform the defeated enemy into an ally, the revenger helps the hawks on the enemy's side to recruit angry fighters who will undermine the peace settlement. During the critical weeks following the collapse of Saddam Hussein's rule in Baghdad, the emphasis on punishment and revenge clearly harmed America's long-term objectives. . . . Obsessed with a desire to punish and revenge, the U.S. managers of Iraq's occupation delayed this [taking a conciliatory] approach for more than a year, at which time the United States was confronted by an organized, hostile insurgency.

The occupation takes hold

It didn't take long for Iraqi resentment to become palpable. Maj. Christopher Varhola, a reservist trained as an anthropologist, recalled being at a meeting in the Green Zone in late May 2003 between Ambassador Hume Horan, a senior CPA official, and a group of about 270 tribal leaders. The general mood was one of impatience with the American effort and a suspicion that it was intentionally slow, Varhola recalled. Sheikh Munthr Abood of Amara began by thanking Horan for the removal of Saddam Hussein. But, he continued, he needed to know if the United States believed itself to be an occupier or a liberator. Horan, an honest man, replied that he believed the U.S. was somewhere "in between" those two approaches.

If America was a liberator, then Americans were welcome as guests, the sheikh responded, according to notes of the meeting. "He stated however that if we were occupiers, then he and his descendants would 'die resisting us.' This met with energetic applause from the audience." Then about one quarter of those present— about sixty-five of the Iraqis at the meeting—stood and walked out.

Late in the spring of 2003 an Army officer filling an intelligence position in Baghdad began using some of the Iraqi exiles assigned to him to conduct a quiet survey of what was being said in mosques on Fridays. He was worried that there was little unbiased, systematic reporting of Iraqi public sentiment, which he thought needed tracking. In addition, he thought it was important to get a handle on the structure of the clergy and of the alliances between them. Wanting to share his results, he went over one day and mentioned his reporting system to the communications people at CPA. They weren't interested, and told him, "That's tactical, take it to the Army." So he sought out an Army colonel, who read the reports eagerly and focused on anti-American comments made in one sermon. The colonel told the officer that the offending cleric must be arrested. The officer protested—all the religious leaders were anti-American, at least in their rhetoric. "You can't survive as a cleric if you don't denounce the Americans," the officer explained. The key, he thought, was to distinguish between those clerics who settled for using only words and those who advocated violence. Worried that additional reporting could provoke more arrest orders, as well as endanger the Iraqis gathering the information, the intelligence officer shut down his collection network.

Garner heads home

In early June Garner made his exit, driving across southern Iraq to Kuwait and then flying home on a one-way ticket. The journey could hardly have been more of a comedown. In Baghdad he had been treated by Iraqis as the virtual ruler of the country. Now, as an anonymous air traveler leaving the Mideast for the U.S. on a one-way ticket, which made him an instant subject of suspicion in the post-9/11 world, he was subjected to searches at every stop along the way, from Kuwait to Dubai to Paris to Washington's Dulles airport.

Before heading home to Florida, Garner went to the White House and the Pentagon. "I told the president, you made a good choice on Jerry Bremer—he's a good, hardworking guy," said the old, white-haired general, ever the loyal team player.

Bush responded, "Hell, I didn't choose him, Rumsfeld chose him, just like he chose you."

Garner then crossed the Potomac to visit the defense secretary. "I sat down with Rumsfeld and said what I thought had gone wrong," he later said. He listed three errors. "The first was, de-Baathification went too deep. The second was: not bringing along the Iraqi army fast enough." Third was Bremer's capricious dismissal of a group of Iraqi political leaders that Garner had assembled.

Rumsfeld wasn't interested in his critique. The defense secretary said, Garner recalled, "Well, we are where we are, there's no need to discuss it." It was classic Rumsfeld, brisk but seemingly unable to deal with mistakes made on his watch.

A Pentagon official who met frequently with Rumsfeld and Feith at this time recalled it almost as a time of stagnation. For weeks during May and June 2003, the same outstanding issues on the agenda for their morning meeting never seemed to change, this official said.

"Feith ought to be drawn, quartered, and hung," said a Bush administration official who worked with him frequently. "He's a sonofabitch who agitated for war in Iraq, but once the decision is made to do it, he disengages. It was clear there were problems across the board—with electricity, with de-Baathification, with translators, with training the Iraqi police—and he just had nothing to do with it. I'm furious about it, still."

Later, as the extent of the chaos in Iraq would become evident, Bush administration officials would begin blaming each other. Feith, for his part, pointed at Franks and Bremer. He told the *New Yorker* in the spring of 2005 that he had sent a memo to Franks at Central Command before the war, warning him about "major law-and-order problems after the war." As for postwar planning, he said, "what people don't understand is that we had all kinds of plans. But when Bremer went over there, he was given autonomy over all kinds of plans that he didn't implement."

Back in Baghdad, Chalabi commented, "Jay Garner was a nice man." It wasn't clear that he meant that as praise.

Rumsfeld vs. reality

The root cause of the occupation's paralysis may have been the cloud of cognitive dissonance that seems to have fogged in Rumsfeld and other senior Pentagon officials at this time. They were not finding what they had expected: namely, strong evidence of intensive efforts to develop and stockpile chemical and biological weapons, and even some work to develop nuclear bombs. Meanwhile, they were finding what they had not expected: violent and widespread opposition to the U.S. military presence. There were no big battles, just a string of bombings and snipings that were killing U.S. troops in ones and twos, and also intimidating the Iraqi population.

But U.S. officials continued to speak about Iraq with unwarranted certainty, both in terms of WMD and the situation on the ground there. "There is absolutely no doubt in my mind that we will find the weapons of mass destruction," Marine Gen. Peter Pace, the vice chairman of the Joint Chiefs of Staff, said as Baghdad fell.

For weeks in the late spring and early summer, Rumsfeld and other officials declined to say that they were facing a continuing war in Iraq. His exchanges with reporters during this period underscored what one defense expert termed the "institutional resistance to thinking seriously" about the situation. Rumsfeld's refusal to say he was facing war sent a signal downward across the military establishment, that most hierarchical of institutions, built to act on the words and views of those at the top.

More than at any other time in the painful history of the U.S. intervention in Iraq, even more than during the formulation of the war plan, that late spring was the point at which Rumsfeld might have made a decisive difference. Some in the military saw Rumsfeld as a strong leader, while others disparaged him as a bully. In either case, it was at this point that his strong personality could have been useful in forcing the U.S. military to understand that it was caught in a counterinsurgency campaign and would need to make wrenching adjustments to win, just as other conventional militaries had in similar situations.

Instead, Rumsfeld's self-confident stubbornness made him a big part of the problem. The defense secretary's vulnerability wasn't that he made errors, it was that he seemed unable to recognize them and make adjustments. Andrew Rathmell, a British defense expert who served as a strategic planner at the CPA, later wrote:

> The fact that pre-war planning assumptions proved to be badly flawed is not a sign of a systemic problem in itself—mistakes happen and the weakness of the Iraqi state surprised many observers. The systemic problem was that these assumptions could not be effectively challenged in the coalition political-military planning process. This unwillingness to challenge assumptions and question established plans persisted during the course of the occupation, giving rise to the ironic refrain among disgruntled coalition planners that "optimism is not a plan." This failure was compounded by a persistent tendency in both the military and civilian chains to avoid reporting bad news and not to plan for worst case, or other case, contingencies.

As Baghdad was looted, the defense secretary seemed to freeze. Rumsfeld was having difficulty recognizing the reality of what was happening in Iraq, and instead was arguing powerfully for his mistaken point of view. "Donald Rumsfeld is a remarkably complex study, with huge reservoirs of talent and intelligence, marred by towering hubris," retired Army Col. Lloyd Matthews, a former editor of *Parameters,* the Army's premier journal, commented that summer. "He's up, he's down, and he'll continue in this sine wave pattern throughout his public career, and very likely be down at the end, because he fails to realize that despite his gifts, he is in a business where defeats are inevitable, where all victories are fleeting, and where one's best defense is the homely quality of grace and humility which he so sorely lacks."

On June 19, Rumsfeld appeared at the Pentagon briefing room, Garner standing by his side. He wouldn't call the situation in Iraq a war: "There's no question but that in those regions where pockets of dead-enders are trying to reconstitute,

General Franks and his team are rooting them out." He also engaged in a verbal sleight of hand about the forty-two U.S. soldiers who had died in Iraq in the previous six weeks, since Bush's declaration that the war was over. "Look, you've got to remember that if Washington, D.C., were the size of Baghdad, we would be having something like 215 murders a month," he said. "There's going to be violence in a big city. It's five and a half million people." In fact, there probably were many more murders than that in the chaos of Baghdad. It wasn't unusual at that time to see cars swerving around a dead body lying in morning traffic. What Rumsfeld was looking at were the statistics on the deaths of U.S. troops—that is, the people trying to bring security to the area. So the equivalent would not be the murder rate in the general population but among law enforcement personnel. If 215 police officers were being killed monthly in Washington, D.C., it would be regarded as a major crisis—as indeed was the case in Baghdad at the time, despite Rumsfeld's anodyne insistence that "the coalition is making good progress."

On the same day, Wolfowitz, testifying on Capitol Hill, portrayed the nascent insurgency as "remnants of the old regime." He told the House Armed Services Committee, "I think these people are the last remnants of a dying cause."

At the time, Wolfowitz also was arguing that the situation in Iraq didn't qualify to be considered a war. "I think it is worth emphasizing that these guys lack the two classical ingredients in a so-called guerrilla war, if that's what you want to say they are conducting," he said. "They lack the sympathy of the population, and they lack any serious source of external support." In retrospect, it appears that Wolfowitz was wrong on both counts: Iraqi sympathy for anti-American forces was growing, and external support was coalescing, because many top Iraqi Baathists had taken refuge in Syria, from where they were able to send in money and fighters, and also to where they could begin receiving aid from supporters in Saudi Arabia, the Gulf states, and elsewhere in the Arab world.

To be fair, Rumsfeld and Wolfowitz were reflecting what they were hearing from some subordinate commanders. On June 18, Maj. Gen. Raymond Odierno, commander of the 4th Infantry Division, which had taken over in Tikrit, emphatically rejected the idea that he was facing an insurrectionary movement. "This is not guerrilla warfare," he told reporters. "It is not close to guerrilla warfare because it's not coordinated, it's not organized, and it's not led. The soldiers that are conducting these operations don't even have the willpower. We find that a majority of the time they'll fire a shot, and they'll drop the weapon, and they'll give up right away. They do not have the will. And, in most cases, I'm not sure they really believe in what they're doing."

Odierno launched a series of operations—Peninsula Strike, Desert Scorpion, Sidewinder, and Ivy Serpent—that were portrayed as efforts to mop up bits and pieces of the Iraqi military and the Baathist Party leadership. Looking back on that time over a year later, he said, "I didn't believe it was an insurgency until about July. What we really thought was, remnant." After the first and second operations, "I thought that would be the end of it." But while Odierno's mistaken assessment may explain why Rumsfeld and Wolfowitz spoke as they did, it doesn't excuse them. One of the most important responsibilities of senior leaders is to assess a given situation and set the strategic response.

By month's end, the media was baiting Bush administration officials, asking them at every opportunity whether they were willing to admit they were in a war in Iraq. Isn't it accurate to call it a guerrilla war? a reporter asked Rumsfeld as the defense secretary emerged from a closed meeting with senators on Capitol Hill. "I don't know that I would use the word," Rumsfeld said. Rather, he said there was "no question" that criminals and "leftover remnants of the Saddam Hussein regime" were being unhelpful.

Three days later, Rumsfeld was pressed on the issue once again by reporters at a Pentagon briefing. "Can you remind us again why this isn't a quagmire?" asked CNN's Jamie McIntyre, a veteran of over a decade on the Pentagon beat. "And can you tell us why you're so reluctant to say that what's going on in Iraq now is a guerrilla war?"

"I guess the reason I don't use the phrase 'guerrilla war' is because there isn't one, and it would be a misunderstanding and a miscommunication to you and to the people of the country and the world," Rumsfeld responded.

McIntyre's easygoing persona often obscures the toughness of his reporting. He persisted, reading aloud to Rumsfeld the official Defense Department definition of guerrilla war: "military and paramilitary operations conducted in enemy-held or hostile territory by irregular ground indigenous forces."

"This seems to fit a lot of what's going on in Iraq," McIntyre noted.

Rumsfeld brushed aside his assertion. "It really doesn't," he said.

The chairman of the Joint Chiefs, who always seemed to make his top priority staying in step with Rumsfeld, also insisted that the situation was better than it looked—or than the media was reporting. "There's been a lot of work done," Gen. Myers said in early July. "A lot of the country is relatively stable." Over the next year, Myers would make similar comments, repeatedly insisting that the situation was better than it looked, even as Iraq descended into guerrilla war and hundreds of U.S. troops died. This pattern of fatuity raises the question of whether Myers provided in private the blunt advice that Rumsfeld and other senior officials needed to hear.

Behind closed doors, some were telling Rumsfeld and Myers to think again. Gen. Jack Keane, the Army's number-two officer, who had taken over many functions of the top job as Shinseki's term waned, including many contacts with Rumsfeld, insisted in a meeting of the Joint Chiefs that it was essential to understand the nature of the war in Iraq. It was, he said, according to an officer who was there, "a low-level insurgency that has the potential to grow." Keane warned that it was time to come to grips with that fact.

President Bush's response to the growing violence in Iraq was even more painfully wrong than Rumsfeld's. The defense secretary was mistaken in understanding the situation, but the president's comments may have actually exacerbated it. On July 2, Bush took the unusual step of taunting Iraqis and others violently opposed to the U.S. presence in Iraq. "There are some who feel that the conditions are such that they can attack us there," he said. "My answer is: Bring 'em on. We've got the force necessary to deal with the security situation." The president's words were reported and remembered in Iraq and across the Middle East. A year later, the Islamic Jihad Army would issue a communiqué that pointedly inquired, "Have you another challenge?"

Lt. Gen. Ricardo Sanchez

In mid-May the 1st Armored Division moved into Iraq, and at month's end it took over as the leading edge of the occupation in the capital. Its commander was Army Maj. Gen. Ricardo Sanchez, who soon would be promoted and given command of the U.S. ground effort in Iraq. If there is any tragic figure at the top of the American effort in Iraq, it is Sanchez. He was by all accounts a good man, somewhat gruff, but hardworking, dedicated, and doing what he was trained to do. But there are few people who contend that he was the man for the job, or that he succeeded in Iraq.

Sanchez was an American success story, a dirt-poor Mexican American kid from the Rio Grande Valley who became the first in his family to go to college and then rose to become a senior commander in the U.S. Army. He joined the Army, he said in an interview at the Baghdad airport on the day the 1st Armored Division took responsibility for the capital, because "I saw that as a means of escaping poverty."

Invasion opponents: Marine Gen. Anthony Zinni (*above*) oversaw the 1998 Desert Fox raids on Iraq, which were far more effective in terminating Iraq's weapons programs than was understood at the time. Four years later he would go into opposition against invading Iraq. Marine Lt. Gen. Gregory Newbold (*below*) would join him, resigning his position under the Joint Chiefs of Staff over his worries.

ABOVE: The Washington Post/*Frank Johnston*   BELOW: © *Reuters/Corbis*

Invasion supporters: Vice President Dick Cheney (*above*) effectively declares war, stating on August 26, 2002, that there was "no doubt" that Iraq possessed weapons of mass destruction. Another leading hawk, Richard Perle (*right*), was chairman of the Defense Policy Board and a backer of Iraqi exile leader Ahmed Chalabi.

ABOVE & RIGHT: *AP Images*

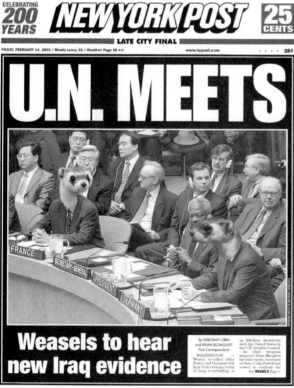

Colin Powell's defining moment as secretary of state was his presentation (*above*) on Iraqi weaponry to the United Nations on February 5, 2003. It is now known that much of his speech was based on false information. CIA director George Tenet (*left*) and U.S. ambassador to the UN, John Negroponte (*right*), sit behind him. The media also tended to play down contrary information: The *New York Post* (*left*) graphically depicted foreign skeptics as weasels.

ABOVE: *AP Images*

LEFT: *Reprinted with permission of the* New York Post, *2006,* © *NYP Holdings, Inc.*

Divisions within the Bush administration deepened during the run-up to war: Here Powell (*left*) argued with Defense Secretary Donald Rumsfeld (*right*) outside the White House as Condoleezza Rice, then national security adviser, watched.

Operation Iraqi Freedom

Rumsfeld (*above, left*), with Air Force Gen. Richard Myers, chairman of the Joint Chiefs of Staff, presented an image of steely certitude in his briefings on the invasion of Iraq. But behind the scenes, planning for the occupation was chaotic. Below is a confused slide from an official Central Command briefing depicting how the United States intended to progress from "military victory" to "strategic success."

ABOVE: The Washington Post/*Larry Morris*   BELOW: *U.S. Central Command, Department of Defense*

Achieving Representation

President Bush (*above*) flew to the USS *Abraham Lincoln*, an aircraft carrier, on May 1, 2003, and under a banner asserting MISSION ACCOMPLISHED declared the war in Iraq all but finished. In fact, the war had hardly begun. Jay Garner (*below*), the first chief of the U.S. occupation in Iraq, quickly ran into trouble as U.S. civilian and military leaders failed to grasp that the country was on the edge of chaos.

ABOVE: *AP Images*

BELOW: © *Reuters/Corbis*

Above, L. Paul Bremer (*left*), who succeeded Garner as head of the occupation; Army Gen. John Abizaid (*middle*), who as chief of Central Command oversaw U.S. military operations in the Middle East; and Deputy Defense Secretary Paul Wolfowitz (*right*), a leading hawk, appear before the House Armed Services Committee. Below, Maj. Gen. Raymond Odierno, whose 4th Infantry Division, operating in the heart of the Sunni Triangle, was criticized by other commanders for its harsh tactics and several instances of detainee abuse.

ABOVE: The Washington Post/*Ray Lustig*   BELOW: *AP Images*

An early high point: Above, Army Lt. Gen. Ricardo Sanchez (*left*), the top U.S. commander on the ground in Iraq in 2003–4, and Paul Bremer announce the capture of Saddam Hussein in December 2003. At the time, some officials thought the apprehension would be a turning point in putting down the insurgency, but heavy-handed U.S. tactics already were beginning to prove counterproductive and attacks on U.S. troops were escalating, especially with road-side bombs (*below*).

ABOVE: *AP Images*   BELOW: © *Bruno Stevens/AURORA*

Some of those hooded by U.S. troops were insurgents, as appears to be the case (*above*) with this man caught with a cache of rocket-propelled grenades in Fallujah. But the majority of detainees were deemed to be not guilty and were released. The use of dogs to terrorize prisoners at Abu Ghraib (*below*), plus other abuses, tainted the occupation and helped the insurgency gather support.

ABOVE: © *Staff Sgt. Charles B. Johnson/USAF/Handout/Reuters/Corbis*　BELOW: The Washington Post

RIGHT: *The survivor:* Iraqi exile leader Ahmed Chalabi stands behind First Lady Laura Bush at the 2004 State of the Union Address. Ten months earlier, U.S. intelligence officers say, his organization had provided information on U.S. troop movements to the Iranian government. Five months later, U.S. and Iraqi forces would raid his Baghdad offices seeking data on the insurgency.

The Washington Post/*Jonathan Newton*

BELOW: A savage attack on four U.S. security contractors in Fallujah on March 31, 2004, changed the tone of the war. Here two of their charred bodies hang from a bridge over the Euphrates River at the west end of town as townspeople celebrate.

AP Images

Two insightful generals who saw better ways than most to operate in Iraq: Marine Maj. Gen. James Mattis (*above*) and Army Maj. Gen. David Petraeus (*below*). After serving in Iraq, the two would take charge of their services' professional educational systems.

ABOVE: *Department of Defense*

BELOW: The Washington Post/*Rick Atkinson*

The 82nd Airborne Division, commanded by Maj. Gen. Charles Swannack (*top*), shot into a crowd in Fallujah in April 2003, spurring opposition to the U.S. presence. Brig. Gen. Janis Karpinski (*above*) was blamed by Lt. Gen. Ricardo Sanchez and others for the Abu Ghraib detainee abuse scandal. Col. Teddy Spain (*right*) never thought he had enough troops to secure Baghdad or enough support from Lt. Gen. Sanchez, his commander.

ABOVE: President Bush bestows the Presidential Medal of Freedom on Gen. Tommy Franks, who retired as head of Central Command shortly after the invasion of Iraq. Other recipients that day were George Tenet and Paul Bremer. The ceremony brought together four of those officials most responsible for the fiasco in Iraq.

AP Images

LEFT: Shiite cleric Moqtadr al-Sadr began as a fierce opponent of the U.S. occupation, launching waves of attacks on U.S. forces in the spring and summer of 2004, but ultimately may be one of the major beneficiaries of the invasion as he gathers much of the power the U.S. transferred from Iraq's Sunni population.

AP Images

Rep. Ike Skelton, shown above on his back porch in Lexington, Missouri, as he discusses that morning's news of more U.S. casualties in Iraq. Skelton, a conservative Democrat, issued a series of warnings before the invasion about the difficulty of occupying Iraq but was ignored. Below, a chart of enemy attacks in Iraq shows that despite persistent official optimism from Bush administration officials, the insurgency remained robust into 2007.

ABOVE: *Craig Sands for* The Washington Post

Number of Attacks

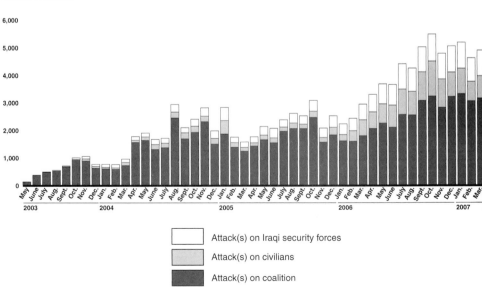

Attack(s) on Iraqi security forces

Attack(s) on civilians

Attack(s) on coalition

Source: Multi-National Force-Iraq, Apr. 2007.

Col. H. R. McMaster (*above, left, by children*), commander of the 3rd Armored Cavalry Regiment, seen here with Iraqi officials in downtown Tall Afar, led one of the most successful U.S. units in Iraq in 2005–6. Even so, worries about the country's disintegrating into civil war or chaos mounted, as reflected in the "Get Your War On" cartoon below.

ABOVE: © *Thomas E. Ricks*   BELOW: *"Get Your War On" © 2004 by David Rees, used with permission.*

American soldiers were among those who paid for the mistakes of top officials. Most troops tried to do their best under difficult circumstances, coming to Iraq untrained to wage a counterinsurgency campaign and under uncertain strategic leadership. And every summer brought the stunning heat, like a humid Death Valley, as here with a 3rd Infantry Division soldier resting against a wall in Taji.

He explained: "We lived on welfare, in a single-parent home. When you grow up like that, the military looks pretty darn good." In the Army he had studied systems analysis, had led a battalion under Gen. McCaffrey in the 1991 Gulf War, had been director of operations at Southern Command (the U.S. military headquarters for operations in South America), and commanded the peacekeeping force in Kosovo.

"Rick Sanchez is a great guy given a really, really hard job," said Maj. Gen. Renuart, who worked closely with him. "I think he's a smart thinker, intuitive. . . . I'm not sure *anyone* could have been totally successful in that environment."

There was, and is, much to respect about Sanchez, even if one thinks that he failed as a commander in Iraq. "I think there are some really admirable qualities," said Maj. Gen. Petraeus, who reported to him for a year. "A degree of patience, stoicism, indefatigability, capacity to deal with enormous pressure and demands, requests from above and below, impatience from above and below, probably a lack of understanding from above and below. An appreciation of the complexity of the issues with which he was dealing, and yet he essentially maintained his cool through all of this, which is really something quite extraordinary."

Even so, the methodical Sanchez often appeared overwhelmed by the situation, with little grasp of the strategic problems he faced. The opinion of many of his peers was that he was a fine battalion commander who never should have commanded a division, let alone a corps or a nationwide occupation mission. "He was in over his head," said Lt. Col. Christopher Holshek, who served in Iraq in 2003. "He was a fulfillment of the Peter Principle," which holds that people working in hierarchies such as the U.S. Army are promoted until they reach their level of incompetence, at which point they tend to fail spectacularly.

"It was my view after seeing him that Rick Sanchez was exactly in the wrong place," said Richard Armitage, the former number-two official at the State Department, who is blunter when speaking on the record than most Washington officials are when speaking on a background, not for quotation basis. "He was much too secretive. He and Bremer, if they didn't hate each other, they could barely tolerate each other, let's put it that way. And when you look in retrospect, a lot has improved since Rick went out. . . . I came away from my first meeting with him saying that this guy didn't get it."

Sanchez's most visible failing was his relentless focus on minutiae. He was aware that subordinates criticized him for that. "I am very comfortable with a macro look at things—unless I see we have issues," he said one day in his headquarters at the Baghdad airport. When he saw a troubled area, he said, he was determined to dive into it. "When I see we are not paying attention to detail, I get into that," he said. "It is the deep, penetrating questions that embarrass people. I can be pretty rough and penetrating, and sometimes that can get embarrassing if you don't know what you're talking about."

But what Sanchez saw as incisive leadership, some around him saw as trivially minded distraction. "All trees, no forest," said one State Department official. "A great logistician, but what's he doing commanding American forces in that part of the world? Not a strategic or political thought."

On top of that, Sanchez was placed in the middle of an extraordinarily difficult and tangled command situation. In other U.S. occupations, the commander had been a four-star general, such as Douglas MacArthur in postwar Japan and Lucius Clay at the same time in Germany. Sanchez was a three-star—that is, a lieutenant general—and in fact the most junior one in the U.S. Army. He jumped from commanding a division of fewer than 20,000 troops to leading a combined U.S. and allied force of about 180,000 men and women. And in doing so he was woefully undersupported—the Pentagon calculated that he needed a headquarters staff of 1,400 but during 2003 he was given a fraction of that, at one point hitting a low of just 495.

"The whole staffing of CJTF-7 [the new name for Sanchez's command, the top U.S. military headquarters in Iraq] at the time was completely inadequate," said an Army colonel who worked with it in Iraq and later, while at the Army War College, studied its troubles. "Putting a division commander in charge of a corps [a group of divisions, support units, and staffs], then giving him responsibility for a whole country in the throes of insurgency, multinational forces, an army corps, a MEF [Marine Expeditionary Force, similar to reinforced Army division], et cetera, with the staff for a single corps was too broad a mandate. No commander with Sanchez's experience level and resources should have been saddled with this responsibility."

That understaffing was symptomatic of a far larger problem: Sanchez was working for a chain of command that was laboring under a series of false assumptions about postwar Iraq, and that didn't understand the situation it was facing, and so it was consistently underestimating the difficulties it faced and the resources it would need to devote to the problem. On top of that, he was burdened by a jerry-rigged command structure, in which there was no one American official, civilian or military, on the ground in Iraq in charge of the overall American effort. Rather, both Sanchez and Bremer reported up to Secretary Rumsfeld, who was at the Pentagon, some seven thousand miles away. "Unity of command is a universal principle" in military operations, noted Army Reserve Maj. Michael Eisenstadt, who served as an intelligence officer on the staff of Central Command; it is especially important in putting down an insurgency, he said, because "you need to integrate your political, economic, and military activities."

Even within the military effort, confusion reigned, especially in the ambiguous but crucial area where military operations supported the functions of the civilian occupation authority. Most crucially, the detention of prisoners was supposed to be an Iraqi function—but because there was no Iraqi government, it became the task of CPA. And because the CPA lacked the personnel, resources, or inclination to handle that job, it had the military do it, even though military commanders didn't report to the CPA. This was one reason the situation at the Abu Ghraib prison would get out of hand in the following months: No one was really in charge of overseeing it.

So it was natural that Sanchez would struggle in the following months. Subordinates report that he tried to focus on achieving victory through quantifying progress, rather than by looking at hazier but perhaps better indicators, such as the quality of the Iraqi police or the polls about what concerned the average Iraqi. "I don't think he ever understood the people aspect, that he had to win the will of the Iraqi people," said one subordinate who speaks Arabic and so paid more attention to Iraqi life than most officers.

In personal interactions he also could be difficult. He tended to strike other officers as remote. Lt. Gen. Thomas Metz, his fellow lieutenant general in Iraq, later described him in a legal statement that grew out of the Abu Ghraib situation as "pretty introverted."

People who worked directly for him are less forgiving. "He would rip generals apart on the tacsat"—the military's tactical, satellite-based communications network—"with everybody in the country listening," said one officer who served under Sanchez on the V Corps staff. This was a violation of a fundamental rule of good U.S. military commanders: praise in public, chastise in private.

The result, said Capt. Kipling, was that "Sanchez was not a popular commander." She, too, had heard tales from friends in his headquarters, located not far from hers, that "he liked to tear people down in public."

Nor were Iraqis spared his temper. "I didn't like the way he talked to the Iraqi Governing Council," said one of Sanchez's subordinates. "I mean, these guys are on our side—show a little respect!" It struck this officer that Sanchez, unlike some other Americans, always went into their chambers in the Green Zone armed.

"There is no reason he had to. We were surrounded by his bodyguards, their bodyguards, and a contracted company of Gurkhas and a platoon of tanks. . . . It was like he didn't trust them. It was clear to them."

With groups perceived by U.S. officials as potential rivals for control, Sanchez was even rougher. "He was never conciliatory," this officer recalled. During the summer of 2003, he remembered, U.S. forces raided an office of SCIRI—the Supreme Council for the Islamic Revolution in Iraq, the main Shiite group that had opposed Saddam Hussein, but that also had close ties to the Iranian government. The soldiers took cash, weapons, and printing presses. SCIRI officials protested, saying that the office was a newspaper and that both the presses and weaponry were legal. The SCIRI officials also stated that they had provided the location of the office to the U.S. Army. Upon investigation, that claim was verified—it turned out that they had told a Special Forces captain who hadn't passed on the information. "They had been within their rights to have printing materials and some AK-47s, but Sanchez wouldn't apologize," the officer recalled. SCIRI never got back its machines, weapons, or money.

In midsummer the insurgency began to erupt, with a series of bombings in Baghdad and widespread small-arms attacks on U.S. patrols. Sanchez responded by descending into minutiae. "The more he got snowed under, the more he focused on what he could do, instead of what he should do," the same officer remembered.

He tended to pepper his staff and subordinate commanders with questions about logistics and "metrics"—how to measure progress—rather than strategy. "His style was hard edged and prosecutorial," recalled another Army officer who worked with him. That approach didn't serve him well, because it discouraged the delivery of bad news. "He didn't realize he wasn't getting good, strong advice, because people would just roll over."

The occupation at the tipping point

During this time in mid-2003 it was possible, moving around Baghdad, to sense the occupation teetering on the edge. A walk with an Army patrol through a middle-class neighborhood in western Baghdad brought home the deepening misunderstanding that characterized this period. At about 10:20 A.M., it was 98 degrees when the patrol moved out through the concertina wire that protected their outpost and past two Bradley fighting vehicles parked out front. The patrol was configured so that one fire team of four soldiers was in front, and another in the back. In the middle, leading the patrol, was Staff Sgt. Nathaniel Haumschild, of Stillwater, Minnesota, accompanied by a medic. Haumschild's evaluation was that "maybe ten percent are hostile. About fifty percent friendly. About forty percent are indifferent."

"Everybody likes us," Spec. Stephen Harris, a twenty-one-year-old from Lafayette, Louisiana, said, as the patrol moved through streets drenched in sun. He thought the people wanted the U.S. troops to stay. "Oh, yeah," he said, taking a slug from his canteen. His assessment of the neighborhood: "I'd say ninety-five percent friendly."

Residents gave different estimates—at best, 50-50, and at worst, a significant majority holding hostile views. Sentiments often broke down along the religious cleavages that mark the country. Shiite residents hailed the Americans for ending Hussein's rule, which was particularly brutal toward their sect. "An American dog is better than Saddam and his gangs," said Alaa Rudeini, as he chatted with a friend on the sidewalk. Awatif Faraj Salih, whose eight-year-old daughter Rasul was among the children at the nearby Nablus Elementary School, feared what would happen if they departed. "If the Americans left," she said, a white scarf draped over her head, "massacres would happen in Iraq—between the tribes, between the parties, and between the Sunnis and Shiites, of course."

To Mohammed Abdullah, standing on the sidewalk as the ten-man patrol passed his gated house, their presence was "despicable." In a white *dishdasha,* a long Arab robe, the thirty-four-year-old winced as the soldiers moved along his street, automatic weapons slung across their chests. "We're against the occupation, we refuse the occupation—not one hundred percent, but one thousand percent," he said. "They're walking over my heart. I feel like they're crushing my heart."

To the Americans, this was Sector 37 North, frequently marked as hostile on U.S. military maps of Baghdad, in part because it was a stronghold of Baath Party loyalists. The airport highway that ran along the southern side of the neighborhood was fast becoming one of the most dangerous roads in the world, with daily mine and RPG attacks on U.S. convoys. But soldiers on the patrol said they did not feel particularly threatened. "Basically, people are pretty friendly," said Lt. Paul Clark, a Bravo Company officer from Baltimore.

To residents this was Yarmuk, a western Baghdad neighborhood of proud professionals living in two-story, adobe-style houses that would fit nicely into a wealthier corner of Albuquerque or Santa Fe, New Mexico, the walls enlivened by palm trees and red bougainvillea.

At 11:03 and 100 degrees, Pfc. Kasey Keeling, of Denton, Texas, was walking second in the patrol, carrying the big M-249 squad automatic weapon, a machine gun. Behind his sunglasses he looked back and forth, up and down. "I scan the windows, rooftops, heavy brush, looking for anything out of the ordinary," he said. The most alarming indicator of danger? An absence of children. "There are always kids around," he said. "No kids, you start to wonder."

There were no children on Yarmuk's Fourth Street, a Sunni area where sentiments were distinctly uneasy. Mohammed Abdullah, standing with his neighbors, insisted he would fight the Americans. "They said they came to liberate us. Liberate us from what? They came and said they would free us. Free us from what?" he asked. "We have traditions, morals, and customs. We are Arabs. We're different from the West." As he watched Keeling and the others pass, he called Baghdad a fallen city, a hint of humiliation in his words. It was akin, he said, to the invasion in 1258 of Hulagu, the grandson of Genghis Khan, whose destruction of Baghdad ended its centuries of glory. The Americans, he said, let the National Library burn and permitted looters to ransack the National Museum of Antiquities. "Baghdad is the mother of Arab culture," he said, "and they want to wipe out our culture, absolutely."

At 11:30, it was 103 degrees as the patrol arrived at the Rami Institute for Autistic and Slow Learners, a house on a side street with a big lime tree shading its walled front yard. They left their weapons outside, under a guard. In the small school, they knelt and talked gently with the children, encouraging them to respond. Sgt. Michael Callan, of Dumfries, Virginia, put his helmet on one child's head. He visited all five classrooms. The soldiers lingered for more than half an hour. When they emerged they looked pleased with themselves. They liked helping the school. They admired its teachers, and their hearts went out to the children.

But outside, neighbors took a very different view of the troops' visit to the women who run the school. Saif Din and his friend, Mohammed Ahmed, said they suspected the American soldiers were having sex with the female teachers inside. "Only God knows," Ahmed said. "I haven't seen it with my own eyes. But I've heard about things."

"We don't like it," said Din, wagging his finger. "We don't like it."

At 12:40 the patrol passed the two green Bradleys and stepped through the Army base's concertina wire. A soldier greeted them with cold cans of strawberry and cola soda. They stripped off their helmets, flak jackets, and the uniform jackets called blouses and set down their weapons. "They love us," concluded Spec. Seneca Ratledge, the medic, a soldier of Cherokee heritage from Riceville, Tennessee.

A tangled chain of command

One day in the summer of 2003, Col. Teddy Spain, the MP commander in Baghdad, turned to the general to whom he reported, the 1st Armored Division's Martin Dempsey, and said, "Sir, who the hell is in charge?" Dempsey was too disciplined to say it—instead he just urged Spain to hang in there, Spain recalled later—but the real answer was: no one. Or at least, not anyone who understood the situation on the ground.

Confusion about the U.S. chain of command in Iraq began on the ground in Iraq and extended all the way back to Washington, D.C. The first question was the ambiguous nature of the CPA itself. Was it a federal agency, part of the U.S. government, most likely the Defense Department? On the one hand, Bremer reported to Rumsfeld, and was himself paid by the U.S. Army, according to a subsequent study by the Congressional Research Service. Yet the CPA's Web sites ended in .com, not the .gov used by the U.S. government. And when a Turkish mobile telephone company protested the award of a CPA contract, the report noted, the U.S. Army Legal Services Agency flatly stated, "The CPA is not a federal agency."

The congressional report concluded, "No explicit, unambiguous and authoritative statement has been provided that declares how CPA was established, under what authority, and by whom, and that clarifies the seeming inconsistencies among alternative explanations for how CPA was created."

On top of that, the relationship between the civilian and military wings of the occupation—the CPA and Sanchez's headquarters—was murky. Officially, Bremer and Sanchez had the same ultimate boss: Sanchez reported to Abizaid, who reported to Rumsfeld at the Pentagon, while Bremer reported directly to Rumsfeld. Bremer refused to talk to Feith and often wouldn't respond to Wolfowitz. "He ignored my suggestions," Wolfowitz said later. "He ignored Rumsfeld's instructions." But Rumsfeld was seven thousand miles away and frequently busy with overseeing other aspects of the U.S. military establishment. "The postcombat phase was pretty fuzzy on who was in control, what the command relationships would be," said a general who was involved in some of that planning at the Pentagon. "It was not well thought out." At any rate, Bremer left subordinates with the impression that he really believed he reported to the president.

Again, the effect was that the U.S. occupation in its very nature violated the fundamental military principle of unity of command—that is, having one person in charge of the effort, so that all hands have a common goal and work together toward it. The need for such unity is especially pronounced in a counterinsurgency campaign, which is more difficult to oversee than conventional operations, and in which military actions must always be judged by their political effects. "Chain of command—of all the problems in Iraq, this was the biggest problem," said one former senior CPA official. "You've got to hold one guy responsible. Otherwise, a guy looks at a problem and he can say, 'That's not mine.'"

Another general, a specialist returning from a visit to Iraq, was similarly puzzled. "If you held a gun to my head and told me, 'Tell me what the chain of command is for your people in Baghdad!'—well, I'd just be babbling," he said.

Even at the time, people in the CPA were aware that the system setup wasn't working. On October 1, 2003, Keith Mines, the CPA representative in al Anbar province, wrote in his weekly memo to Bremer, "It would be beneficial to all if there were an integrated national plan that took account of the divergent efforts by CJTF-7 and CPA and attempted to blend a functional [Iraqi security] force from them." Instead, he continued, what he saw was a "refusal by these two parties to join in a common effort."

Sometimes difficult command situations can be resolved through what Gen. Zinni during 1991's Operation Provide Comfort called handcon—that is, cooperation ensured through goodwill and symbolized by a handshake. But no such generosity of spirit seemed to exist between Sanchez and Bremer. "When I attended Sanchez's morning meetings, it was clear to me that they didn't connect," said Army Col. Lloyd Sammons, a Special Forces reservist who served in the CPA in 2003–4. "I felt there was more than just a division of their professional positions. They didn't communicate."

Every month Bremer and his top officials met in the Green Zone with the senior military commanders—Gen. Sanchez, the division commanders, and the commanders of the separate brigades—at what the Army called the monthly commanders' meeting. At the meeting on November 4, 2003, three CPA officials and a general who was there recalled, senior Army officers lashed out at the CPA's free market and de-Baathification policies for throwing people out of work and alienating a large part of the population. They also were openly unhappy with the lack of consultation between the CPA and commanders in the field. "It was quite a spat," recalled one of the CPA officials.

Maj. Gen. Petraeus said he was "astonished" that the CPA's plans had been developed without discussion with affected U.S. commanders, according to the verbatim notes taken at the meeting by a CPA official. "We have huge staffs that can participate," the 101st Division commander added. "It is a mistake to have planning isolated in Baghdad."

Maj. Gen. Odierno supported this protest. "Yes, the campaign plan has to be worked out at all levels," he said. "Frankly my sense is you want to cut us out. Every day we're getting less resources. We've lost momentum in the last forty-five to sixty days."

Some CPA officials maintained that it was the military's fault that the generals had been kept in the dark. They had told Sanchez's military headquarters in Baghdad about their plans, and the word simply wasn't passed along from there. Yet not even everyone in the CPA thought that Bremer's radical privatization was the right course. "Employment is key issue," Keith Mines wrote two weeks later to CPA headquarters. What his province needed was more "Maslow" (a reference to the famed psychologist's hierarchy of human needs) and less "Friedman" (a reference to the influential free-market economist). He argued for a reversal of CPA economic policy, which should instead be built around "a large-scale public sector jobs program" akin to President Franklin Roosevelt's Depression-era efforts.

The friction between the CPA and the military extended even to lower levels. "As a tactical commander, I never understood his [Bremer's] role, his relationship with Sanchez, what the role of the State Department was versus the Defense Department," said Col. Spain. "None of us understood it." That confusion was particularly difficult for Spain, who effectively was serving as the police chief of Baghdad for most of 2003, and so spanned both worlds. "Sometimes I'd be told that CPA wants the Iraqi police to do A, and then I'd be told that CJTF-7 wants the Iraqi police to do B."

Wolfowitz, asked several months later about the chain of command, blithely insisted that if anything, the problem was the opposite case. "Most of the complaints on that are that there is too much unity of command, with both Bremer and Abizaid reporting to the same guy"—that is, Rumsfeld—he said in an interview.

But even at the top of the reporting pyramid there appears to have been confusion. In a meeting in the White House situation room one day, there was a lot of "grousing" about Bremer, a senior administration official who was there recalled. As the meeting was breaking up, Rice, the national security adviser, reminded Rumsfeld that Bremer reported to him. "He works for you, Don," Rice said, according to this official.

"No, he doesn't," Rumsfeld responded—incorrectly—this official recalled. "He's been talking to the NSC, he works for the NSC."

Bremer relates a similar anecdote in his memoir, saying that Rumsfeld told him later in 2003 that he was "bowing out of the political process," which apparently meant he was detaching from dealing with Iraq—a breathtaking step for the defense secretary to take after years of elbowing aside the State Department and staffers on the National Security Council.

Col. Spain vs. the Baghdad police

On a hot May day in downtown Baghdad, Col. Spain met with the senior police officers of Baghdad. They had the look of hard men. Just two months earlier they had been the sworn enemies of the American officers now summoning them to meetings.

He sat at a round table with them in a meeting room at the National Police Academy as flies buzzed in and out the open windows. It was 96 degrees. Spain talked about fuel, cars, pistols, radios, and patrols—the mundane issues that make policing work and bring security to a community. The police officials, some of them longtime Baathists, every one wearing the Saddam-like facial hair of a full black moustache and a shaved chin, seemed instead to be sizing him up. They said there was good reason the police weren't on the streets: They lacked weapons and were afraid of being attacked by both Iraqis and U.S. forces. "One of the traffic policemen was on his motorcycle this morning and was shot," said Maj. Gen. Kais Mohammed Naief, the head of traffic police. "This is the reason they don't feel safe."

Another official chimed in, "If he had a pistol, maybe they wouldn't have shot him!"

"Let's move on," Spain said. "I accept that there are cultural differences between the Iraqi police and the U.S. police. But I also think there are certain basic principles. One of them is that you must be out walking the streets, riding the streets."

An Iraqi looked back at him across the table, coldly. "But that is in normal times," he said.

After the meeting Spain strolled along the sidewalk of a middle-class western Baghdad neighborhood, trailed by a couple of MPs. A year later, that would be a risky act, but in May 2003, Spain was able to stop and chat with shopowners, who said they wanted more security and more electricity. "America is so powerful, why can't it bring back the electricity?" asked Nahrawan Mahdi, a doctor at a women's clinic.

"Things are going to get better," Spain promised a furniture storekeeper.

Spain oversaw a big brigade—all told, including staff and support units, some 7,100 soldiers, as big as many German divisions in World War II. But he would say much later, after a tough year in Iraq, that he never really had the troops he needed. He ultimately received about twenty companies of MPs—but by then his mission required about fifty. He shrugged. "You can just sit around and wring your hands, or you can do the best you can with what you got." Over the next year Teddy Spain's MPs would be attacked 395 times and lose a total of 13 soldiers.

Abizaid calls it a war

In July, Gen. Abizaid took over Central Command from Franks and instantly injected a note of realism, telling members of Congress and reporters alike that America was going to be dealing with Iraq for a long time.

As he took over, Abizaid was the Great Arab American Hope of the Army, widely seen as one of its smartest commanders, and also able to bring an in-depth knowledge of the Mideast. In their 1973 yearbook his West Point classmates described the Lebanese American cadet, who was raised in rural California, as "an Arabian Vince Lombardi. . . . He just couldn't accept second place." Later in the 1970s he studied in Jordan, and when the university was shut down by a student strike, he trained with Jordanian Special Forces. He also earned a master's degree in Middle Eastern studies at Harvard.

He also was known as a good troop leader. As a Ranger company commander during the 1983 invasion of Grenada, he needed to attack a Cuban-manned bunker, so he ordered one of his sergeants to drive a bulldozer toward it, and then had his men advance behind its cover. That improvised moment was memorialized in the climax of Clint Eastwood's 1986 movie *Heartbreak Ridge*—although Eastwood changed it to a Marine action because the Corps was more cooperative in helping him film. In Provide Comfort in 1991, Abizaid maneuvered his battalion aggressively yet deftly in northern Iraq.

As a general Abizaid quickly earned a reputation as a bright thinker and a competent, low-key manager. At the Pentagon in the early 2000s, he was one of the few in the military who seemed to be able to handle Rumsfeld. As director of Joint Staff, a key inside slot, he was one of two senior officers who led the way in easing the tense relationship between Rumsfeld's office and the uniformed military. The question after he took over Central Command was whether he would live up to the high expectations people had of him.

Abizaid faced some formidable tasks: Fight a war in Iraq; prosecute an offensive against terror in Saudi Arabia, Pakistan, Yemen, Afghanistan, and the rest of the region; and also help bridge the gap between the Rumsfeld/Wolfowitz civilian leadership of the Pentagon and the estranged Army.

At the Pentagon in July, he used his first press conference as chief of Central Command to make a major course correction. Yes, he announced, we are indeed in a war in Iraq. "What is the situation in Iraq?" Abizaid said, addressing reporters at the Pentagon after meeting with Rumsfeld. Opponents of the U.S. presence, he said, speaking with precision, "are conducting what I would describe as a classical guerrilla-type campaign against us." He then went on to use the word the Bush administration had been dancing around for weeks: "It's war, however you describe it." This went a long way toward clearing up the strategic confusion about what the U.S. military was doing in Iraq, and how it was doing it.

Asked to explain why he was calling it a war after weeks of hesitancy by Bush administration officials to do so, Abizaid said bluntly, "Well, I think that, you know, all of us have to be very clear in what we're seeing." In that seemingly off-hand comment, Abizaid was making an essential point about strategy and military operations. Abizaid knew that it matters very much whether the nation thinks it is at war, especially to the soldiers on the ground and their commanders. "The first, the supreme, the most far-reaching act of judgment that the statesman and commander have to make is to establish . . . the kind of war on which they are embarking; neither mistaking it for, nor trying to turn it into, something that is alien to its nature," Clausewitz famously wrote. "This is the first of all strategic questions and the most comprehensive."

Strategy, correctly formulated, shapes tactics. But tactics uninformed by strategy, or misinformed by an incorrect strategy, are like a car without a steering wheel: It may get somewhere, but probably not where its driver wants it to go. "In Iraq, we fought the war we wanted to fight, not the war that was," said Bruce Hoffman, a Rand Corp. terrorism expert who consulted with the CPA. "We belatedly recognized it as a large insurgency, after dismissing it as 'dead-enders.'" This lapse gave the enemy breathing space in which to organize and look for vulnerabilities in the U.S. military.

After Abizaid spoke, Pentagon spokesman Lawrence Di Rita, standing at his side in the Pentagon briefing room, jumped in to attempt to undercut the crucial point the general had just made. "The discussion about what type of conflict this is, is—like so many other discussions we're having within the context of Iraq—is almost beside the point," the spokesman told the reporters. The issue to remember, he insisted, was that the fighters wanted to restore Saddam Hussein's regime. "So it's worth remembering that as we kind of have this almost kind of, you know, academic discussion, is it this or is it that." Di Rita appeared to be brushing aside the considered opinion of one of the Army's top generals, the senior commander for Iraq and the rest of the Mideast—who knew more about the area and about war than Di Rita did.

It was a moment that captured in a nutshell the weakness at the core of the Bush administration's national security team: Strategy was seen as something vague and intellectual, at best a secondary issue, when in fact it was the core of the task they faced. It was the same sort of limited thinking that had led the Bush team first to focus in 2002 and early 2003 almost exclusively on its plan of attack for Iraq, rather than on the more difficult but crucial consolidation of that victory, and that also led it to make wildly unrealistic assumptions about postinvasion Iraq, and then to fail to develop operational plans as a fallback if its assumptions proved incorrect.

By failing to adequately consider strategic questions, Rumsfeld, Franks, and other top leaders arguably crippled the beginning of the U.S. mission to transform Iraq. An "overly simplistic conception of the war led to a cascading undercutting of the war effort: too few troops, too little coordination with civilian and governmental/non-governmental agencies (U.S. State Department, as one example) and too little allotted time to achieve success," concluded Maj. Isaiah Wilson.

A lieutenant killed by confusion

A confused strategy can be every bit as lethal as a bullet. If a soldier fighting in Iraq is told that he isn't at war, that he is just conducting a peacekeeping operation, then his every thought and action will be different—his mind-set as he goes out the front gate, as he conducts a patrol, as he apprehends an Iraqi. On the evening of July 30, Army Lt. Leif Nott, a member of Alpha Troop of the 1st Squadron of the 10th Cavalry Regiment in the 4th Infantry Division, was killed in the eastern town of Balad Ruz at least in part by a lack of understanding of the situation in Iraq.

The action began ominously. Sgt. Brian Beem, in one patrol, saw an animal moving toward him out of the darkness. "The dog got louder and started coming forward, so I shot it," he told an Army investigator. "It was hurt and running in circles. I could not leave it like that so I shot it again. The dog died. We kept moving."

The patrol heard a mortar shell impact, then small-arms fire. Beem saw some people, apparently armed, walking toward his patrol. "I was concerned that they were suicide bombers," he wrote. "Why did they line up like they were and walk toward a U.S. building?" He fired a warning shot and yelled at the people to get down. It occurred to him only in retrospect that they couldn't hear his shout over the jet-engine-like roar of the engines of two nearby Bradley fighting vehicles.

In fact, he was shouting at another group of four American soldiers, led by Nott, bringing three Iraqis into an Army outpost for questioning. But Beem's patrol didn't know that. In a posture that seemed more like a cop's than a soldier's, "Nott was walking down the middle of Balad Ruz's main street with the Iraqi prisoners," the *Washington Post*'s Jefferson Morley later wrote in detailing the incident. Adding to the confusion, Sgt. Mickey Anderson, a member of Nott's group, was carrying a AK-47, making him look like an Iraqi attacker to the soldiers in the Bradleys.

"Nobody indicated any friendly personnel were on the ground," Lt. Chris Amaguer told the Army investigator. "There were shadows and silhouettes with an AK-47 identified."

"The senior scout told me to 'get those dismounts,'" Sgt. Christopher Creech stated, using Army jargon for a dismounted soldier, or infantryman. "There was not a question that these dismounts were enemy."

A machine gun on one of the Bradleys opened up on the approaching group. Several other soldiers followed suit with their rifles, as did a .50-caliber gunner aboard a tank. "Then I heard 'Oh God' from a person on the ground," Beem wrote. "In English. 'Oh my God.' English again, and this time I knew the voice. It was Sergeant Anderson. He's been my best friend for four and half years. I walked over to see him lying there with wounds on his legs and his left ankle was wrong." Nott was dead, shot in the chest.

The official conclusion of Maj. David Chase, the investigating officer, was that the fratricidal death of Capt. Nott was "primarily the result of inadequate situational awareness."

Arguably, Nott was a victim of strategic confusion in miniature. He had acted as if he were operating in near peacetime conditions, dealing with a few dead-enders—just as the secretary of defense had said. Also, if senior officials had understood that U.S. forces were indeed at war, they might have acted with more alacrity to provide soldiers such as Nott with body armor. "There was also a significant shortage of Individual Body Armored Systems (IBAS) available to the Troop," Maj. Chase wrote in his report. In fact, at the time, he wrote, there were just 9 sets of body armor to go around for 134 soldiers in Alpha Troop. "This deficiency was corrected shortly after the incident."

"This is not Vietnam!"

When Gary Anderson, the retired Marine colonel, went to see Wolfowitz about his op-ed piece in the *Post* warning that the United States might be facing a guerrilla war in Iraq, he found the deputy secretary more worried than his public comments indicated. "The way things are going, it looks like your diagnosis of the situation is correct," Wolfowitz said to him, he recalled later. "Having identified the problem, what do you recommend we do about it?"

"We're in the early stages of an insurgency," Anderson replied. "We have to nip it in the bud." The danger, he said, was that Baathists not soon countered would begin to intimidate the Iraqi population. The problem was the sort of force needed to confront them, he said. U.S. troops aren't trained to wage counterinsurgency campaigns, while the Iraqi army wasn't going to be positioned to do it, and the task was well beyond the capabilities of the Iraqi police, he said. "So," Anderson said, "you need a native constabulary force, something like what the U.S. did in the Philippines and Haiti" in campaigns in those countries early in the twentieth century.

Wolfowitz liked the idea. "I think he tried to sell it to General Franks, but Franks didn't seem to think it was needed," Anderson recalled. A few weeks later, Wolfowitz asked Anderson if he would go out to Baghdad and pitch the idea to Bremer.

Anderson's employer, a defense consultant, wasn't wildly enthusiastic, but permitted him to become an unpaid adviser in Iraq. Anderson's own worry was that if he were killed there his family wouldn't get an insurance payment. "If you get yourself greased, your family is in bad shape," he warned himself.

The meeting with Bremer, in early July, didn't go well. "Bremer's a talker, not a listener," Anderson soon noticed. A flurry of questions from the career diplomat threw Anderson off his train of thought. It became clear that Bremer hadn't thought much about the issue of having a counterinsurgency militia, or that he thought this interloper from Washington had much to offer. "It was obvious that Bremer saw me as a creature of Wolfowitz," Anderson recalled. "Bremer and Wolfowitz didn't have the greatest relationship, even then."

"Mr. Ambassador, here are some programs that worked in Vietnam," Anderson said, trying to redirect the conversation. He had in mind the popular forces that had been used successfully as village militias in South Vietnam.

It was the wrong word to put in front of Bremer. "Vietnam?" Bremer exploded. "*Vietnam!* I don't want to talk about Vietnam. This is not Vietnam. This is Iraq!"

"That was pretty much the end of the meeting," Anderson recalled

He came away thinking that the top U.S. officials in Iraq really didn't fathom the nature of the conflict they faced. "I don't think he—or Sanchez— ever fully grasped the danger of it." The U.S. occupation stood at the edge of a precipice its leaders didn't see.

9.

HOW TO CREATE
AN INSURGENCY (II)

SUMMER AND FALL 2003

British Lt. Gen. Aylmer Haldane concluded his memoir of his suppression of the Iraqi uprising of 1920 by noting somberly that the fight had been a near-run thing. "From the beginning of July until well into October, ... we lived on the edge of a precipice where the least slip might have led to a catastrophe," the commander of the British counterinsurgency campaign wrote in *The Insurrection in Mesopotamia, 1920.* By luck, pluck, and courage—and the timely arrival of reinforcements—he said, the British force avoided sliding over the cliff into a long and agonizing guerrilla war.

In the spring of 2003, U.S. commanders had fought the war they wanted to fight—lightning fast, relatively bloodless, and generally predictable. But in the summer and fall of 2003, from the beginning of July into October, they slipped over the precipice Haldane had avoided and fell into the war their Iraqi enemies sought. The vulnerabilities that had plagued Haldane returned to haunt this new occupation force—most notably, insufficient troops and supply lines that were dangerously long and exposed to attack. Haldane also had faced insurgents who appeared to be led by former Iraqi officers, and he too had watched his Iraqi police officers desert as fighting intensified. In a comment that foreshadows the haphazard nature of the U.S. occupation authority, the British in 1920, Haldane wrote, were hampered by having a "scratch and somewhat incongruous team" of administrators, with the majority possessing "little exact knowledge of the people they were called upon to govern."

But unlike Haldane, the United States wasn't able to put down the insurgency quickly. In the summer of 2003, the enemy brought it on, as President Bush had taunted them to do, and the U.S. military found itself enmeshed in a guerrilla war for the first time since the Vietnam War. In early summer it was still safe for an American to jog along the east bank of the Tigris in the morning, to lunch on chicken cordon bleu at a nice restaurant in western Baghdad's heavily Baathist Mansur district, and even to walk out at night to visit nearby friends. By late fall of 2003 such actions would still be possible but a bit foolhardy. Two years after that they would be absolutely suicidal, an invitation to being kidnapped or shot on the spot.

Arming, financing, and recruiting the insurgents

It isn't clear that a large and persistent insurgency was inevitable. There is some evidence that Saddam Hussein's government knew it couldn't prevail conventionally, and some captured documents indicate that it may have intended some sort of subversion campaign against occupation. The distribution of arms caches, the revolutionary roots of the Baathist Party, and the movement of money and people to Syria either before or during the war all argue for some advance planning for an insurgency. "I believe Saddam Hussein always intended to fight an insurgency should Iraq fall," Maj. Gen. Swannack, Jr., said in November 2003. "That's why you see so many of these arms caches out there in significant numbers all over the country." But the U.S. approach, both in occupation policy and military tactics, helped spur the insurgency and made it broader than it might have been.

Every insurgency faces three basic challenges as it begins: arming, financing, and recruiting. A peculiarity of the war in Iraq is that the Iraqi insurgency appears to have had little difficulty in any of these areas, in part because of U.S. policy blunders. The missteps made in 2003 appear to be a major reason that the anti-U.S. forces burgeoned despite their narrow appeal, both geographically and ideologically.

In the first area, arms, the unusual situation in Iraq favored the enemy. It was a land awash in weaponry and explosives, both in small collections distributed by Saddam Hussein's government before the U.S. invasion, and in huge dumps, some of them the size of small cities. In this area, policy decisions made at the Pentagon aided the nascent insurgency, because U.S. forces lacked the manpower to monitor the big dumps, let alone unearth the far-flung caches. Had the Iraqi military not been disbanded, it might have been used to cordon off those large caches. There certainly would have been some leakage, but less than occurred with no guards whatsoever in most places.

Finance is a murkier area, but here too U.S. decisions appear to have unwittingly aided the enemy. Before and during the U.S. invasion, intelligence surveillance observed convoys of trucks and cars heading from Baghdad to Syria. At the time there was some speculation that these were carrying weapons of mass destruction or manuals and other technical knowledge related to their manufacture. In retrospect, it appears that many of those convoys actually were carrying top Baathists and their families, and their cash, gold, and other valuables, some of which later would be used to support the insurgency from outside the country. Yet about a year would pass before the U.S. military would launch a serious effort to gain control of Iraq's borders—a step that is a prerequisite to mounting an effective counterinsurgency campaign.

But it was in the third area, recruiting, that the U.S. effort inadvertently gave the insurgency its biggest boost. Finding new members is usually the most difficult of tasks for the insurgent cause, especially in its first growth, because it requires its members to expose themselves somewhat to the public and to the police. U.S. policies—both military and civilian—helped solve that problem. The de-Baathification order created a class of disenfranchised, threatened leaders. (Also, the Baath Party likely was more comfortable with its fugitive status than many a deposed ruling party would have been. "The Baathist Party was born in an insurgency and continued to operate like one," even when in power, noted one Special Forces officer who served in Iraq. "You joined a cell, and reported to the cell leader.") But those leaders still needed rank-and-file members. The dissolution of the army gave them a manpower pool of tens of thousands of angry, unemployed soldiers. "When we disbanded the Iraqi army, we created a significant part of the Iraqi insurgency," said Col. Paul Hughes, who worked for Bremer on strategy issues. On top of that, the lack of U.S. drive and the sense of drift at the CPA gave the Baathists a much needed breather.

A professionally unprepared army

The U.S. Army in Iraq—incorrect in its assumptions, lacking a workable concept of operations, and bereft of an overarching strategy—completed the job of creating the insurgency. Based on its experience in Bosnia and Kosovo, the Army thought it could prevail through "presence"—that is, soldiers demonstrating to the local population that they are in the area, mainly by patrolling. "We've got that habit that carries over from the Balkans," said one Army general. Back then, patrols were conducted so frequently that some officers called the mission there DABing, for Driving Around Bosnia.

The flaw in this approach, wrote Lt. Col. Christopher Holshek, a civil affairs officer, was that after the public opinion began to turn against the Americans and see them as occupiers, "then the presence of troops . . . becomes counterproductive."

The U.S. military jargon for this was boots on the ground, or, more officially, the presence mission. There was no formal doctrinal basis for this in the Army manuals and training that prepare the military for its operations, but the notion crept into the vocabularies of senior officers. For example, in May 2003, as the 1st Armored Division prepared to move from Kuwait to Baghdad, Col. Jackson Flake, the division chief of staff, said its task there would be to provide a safe and secure environment. To achieve that, he explained, "We've got to conduct patrols to give these citizens a sense of security," and also to work with civilian authorities to get the infrastructure up and running. A briefing by the division's engineering brigade stated that one of its major missions would be "presence patrols."

"Flood your zone, get out there, and figure it out," Sanchez ordered one of his brigade commanders at a meeting in a dusty command tent outside a palace in the Green Zone later that May. And he wanted the troops to get out there on foot, he added: "Mounted patrols tell me we are zipping through neighborhoods. I want American soldiers on the ground talking to people. . . . Your business is to ensure that the presence of the American soldier is felt, and it's not just Americans zipping by."

But what if this approach creates problems rather than solves them? In the spring and summer of 2003, few U.S. soldiers seemed to understand the centrality of Iraqi pride, and the humiliation Iraqi men felt to be occupied by this Western army. Foot patrols in Baghdad were greeted during this time with solemn waves from old men and cheers from children, but with baleful stares from many young Iraqi men.

The push for intelligence

U.S. commanders tended to blame their troubles, at least in public, on their lack of good intelligence about their foe. Who was the enemy? How many were there? What were their motivations? How did they operate? Where did their financing come from? Who controlled them? Were they independent cells or did they have a central control? What were their links to Saddam Hussein's regime? What was the relationship between former regime members and their old enemies in the fundamentalist Islamic groups? There were surprisingly few good answers to those questions, then or now.

More than most large organizations, the U.S. Army generally tries to confront and remedy its shortcomings. Newspapers, for example, rarely pause after covering major crises to figure out what they did right, what they did wrong, and what they should remember the next time they face a similar incident. The Army, to its credit, routinely tries to learn from such encounters, in part because of the lethality of mistakes in its line of work. It calls this the lessons learned process, and incorporates the efforts in its major training maneuvers. For example, after each major step in operations at the National Training Center, the Army's premier large unit training facility, commanders pause to critique their own moves. "Observer-controllers" stand by to provide factual data and so ensure that the critique is more than just a barroom quarrel about who did their job best. This process even has its own office, the Center for Army Lessons Learned, or CALL, based at Fort Leavenworth, Kansas, an old cavalry post perched on a bluff overlooking the Missouri River, on the eastern edge of the Great Plains.

In the summer of 2003 CALL sent a team to Iraq to review intelligence-gathering efforts in Iraq. The team found a series of wide-ranging problems in using technology and in training and managing intelligence specialists. Younger officers and enlisted soldiers were unprepared for their assignments, "did not understand the targeting process," and possessed "very little to no analytical skills," the CALL team found. It said that there were 69 "tactical human intelligence" (HUMINT) teams working in Iraq, and that they should have been producing at least 120 reports a day, but instead were delivering a total average of 30. Overall, it said, the teams lacked "guidance and focus." They also were overwhelmed, and at least 15 more teams were needed. Nor did combat leaders understand how to use their intelligence specialists. "HUMINT teams and MI [military intelligence] commanders who were frustrated at the misuse of HUMINT assets by maneuver commanders . . . believed that combat arms officers did not understand the management and capabilities of HUMINT assets," the report said. Also, operations across Iraq were impeded by the lack of competent interpreters; those they had were "working to the point of burnout," and also were being misused. "We can no longer afford to send interpreters in 'support' of units to buy chickens and soft drinks."

Other insiders noticed additional problems. The U.S. military intelligence apparatus tended to overfocus on the role of foreign fighters, a senior Army official later noted, because those fighters tended to use telephones, e-mail, and the Internet—and thus could be monitored by signals interception. So long sessions with top commanders would focus on the movements of four Saudi Arabian citizens while entire tribes in the Sunni Triangle were emerging unnoticed as centers of the insurgency. "The real guys weren't using phones or the Internet," he said. "They were based on human relationships," and so operated below the radar screen of U.S. military intelligence.

In the late summer and early fall of 2003 top commanders launched an extraordinary push to improve the performance of the lackluster military intelligence operation in Iraq. "Actionable intelligence is the key to countering the insurgency," Gen. Abizaid said later, looking back at this time. "All of us were looking for actionable intelligence that would lead us to unlock the leadership of the insurgency." He was especially frustrated that good information gathered at the battalion and brigade levels wasn't making it up the chain of command to the division and corps intelligence operations, where it could be "brought into an overarching theater understanding of the problem." What was the enemy? How was it organized, peopled, trained, and indoctrinated? What did it want, if anything, besides expelling the U.S. forces?

Militaries, like all big organizations, tend to do what they know how to do, rather than what they might need to do differently to address the situation they face. As French counterinsurgency expert Bernard Fall said in a 1964 speech to a U.S. military audience about flaws in the U.S. approach in Vietnam, "Everybody likes to fight the war that he knows best; this is very obvious. But in Vietnam we fight a war that we don't 'know best.' The sooner this is realized the better it is going to be."

It took many years for the Army to adjust in Vietnam, and it would take time—though less than in Vietnam—to do so in Iraq as well. "When it is this huge, this heavy a conventional presence, you're going to get the institutional response," said one general, himself an unconventional thinker from the conventional side of the Army. "They're going to do what they're trained to do."

That unimaginative reaction is hardly a new phenomenon. Field Marshal Saxe, an innovative eighteenth-century French general, complained that "very few men occupy themselves with the higher problems of war," so that "when they arrive at the command of armies they are totally ignorant, and, in default of knowing what should be done, they do what they know." The U.S. mission in Iraq was overwhelmingly made up of regular combat units, rather than smaller, lower profile, Special Forces troops, and in 2003 most conventional commanders did what they knew how to do: send out large numbers of troops and vehicles on conventional combat missions.

"You had to do operations to drive intelligence," said a senior military intelligence official who was in the middle of this drive. In retrospect, he said, "We were not sophisticated or calibrated in our approach. You know the old saying, 'If all you have is a hammer, everything looks like a nail'?"

In the late summer of 2003, senior U.S. commanders tried to counter the insurgency with indiscriminate cordon-and-sweep operations that involved detaining thousands of Iraqis. This involved "grabbing whole villages, because combat soldiers [were] unable to figure out who was of value and who was not," according to a subsequent investigation of the 4th Infantry Division's operations by the Army inspector general's office. On top of that, Army commanders failed to ensure they had a system to process thousands of people. At first, prisoners were held on U.S. bases, but by late summer they were shipped to Abu Ghraib prison to be held by a small unit of demoralized MPs there. By the fall of 2003 this approach would swamp the system and undercut the aim of improving intelligence, because there weren't enough interrogators on hand to detect the genuine adversaries among the thousands of innocent or neutral Iraqis caught up in the sweeps.

It is important to bear in mind the lack of a coherent counterinsurgency strategy at the top. Had there been one, commanders likely wouldn't have used such self-defeating tactics. "When you're facing a counterinsurgency war, if you get the strategy right, you can get the tactics wrong, and eventually you'll get the tactics right," said retired Army Col. Robert Killebrew, a veteran of Special Forces in the Vietnam War. "If you get the strategy wrong and the tactics right at the start, you can refine the tactics forever but you still lose the war. That's basically what we did in Vietnam." For the first twenty months or more of the American occupation in Iraq, it was what the U.S. military would do there as well.

Iraq in midsummer 2003

Paul Wolfowitz was worried about Iraq. Bremer didn't tell him much, so he worked the military channels relentlessly, with a Churchillian drive for information. "There is no limit to the level of detail the DEPSECDEF requests," an official at Central Command griped in an e-mail to a military lawyer on July 7, 2003. Wolfowitz traveled to Iraq that month to rally support. Privately, he may have been worried that Gary Anderson was right about a growing insurgency, but publicly he would argue that steady progress was being made. At lunch one day at the al Rasheed Hotel, which was inside the checkpoints of the Green Zone and had been turned into a CPA dormitory, the deputy defense secretary was relentlessly upbeat. He had with him a handpicked group of reporters and columnists, journalists whose articles had displayed a sympathy to his views, among them the *Washington Post*'s Jim Hoagland, the *Wall Street Journal*'s Paul Gigot, and *Vanity Fair*'s Christopher Hitchens. "The judicial system is functioning at a rudimentary level," he began that hot July day. "Neighborhood councils are stood up. The police force is at sixty percent of requirements." He saw similarly good trends in education and medicine. "It is pretty amazing," he insisted as waiters brought more seltzer water. He was dismissive of the Middle Eastern–area experts who were warning that Iraq was in a dangerous position, and that security was deteriorating. "The great majority seem astonishingly pessimistic," he said.

Abizaid, also at the lunch table, loyally supported his boss's views. "The impatience of the press is always of some interest to me," he said. "The progress here is quite remarkable, actually." Looking over the white tablecloth set with candelabras to the buffet of lamb, rice, and vegetables at the end of the room, swaddled in the tight security of the Green Zone, it was almost possible for a moment to believe they were correct.

To a degree, Wolfowitz was reflecting what he was hearing from top commanders. Even in the Sunni Triangle, U.S. officers were surprisingly optimistic at the time. They weren't over the hump, but they were close, some said. After lunch Abizaid headed up the Tigris Valley in a swift Black Hawk helicopter, flying low and escorted by two Apache attack helicopters. Palm groves, vineyards, and gardens of eggplants, peppers, and tomatoes flashed by underneath his aircraft. At a meeting that afternoon in Tikrit, one brigade commander in the 4th Infantry Division reassured him, "My read, sir, is we're on the tail end of this."

"Our analysis says attacks are going down," added another 4th ID commander.

"Sir, he's getting weaker," said a third officer. "We're breaking his back."

"The gloves are coming off"

The insurgency didn't begin with an announcement or a major event. Rather, it was like a change in the weather. "In three towns that summer—Hit, Fallujah and Khaldiya—I would hear an Iraqi proverb repeated over and over as the occupation lurched on, violence of all kinds escalated, and more Iraqis were killed," Anthony Shadid later wrote. "'The mud is getting wetter,' people said. Things are getting worse, it meant."

As the Iraqi mud moistened, the American gloves were removed. The U.S. military escalation occurred consciously. On August 4, 2003, U.S. authorities reopened the prison west of Baghdad called Abu Ghraib, which was notorious since it had been used to punish the enemies of Saddam Hussein. And at around two o'clock on the morning on August 14, Capt. William Ponce, an officer in the Human Intelligence Effects Coordination Cell at Sanchez's headquarters, sent out a memo to subordinate commands. "The gloves are coming off regarding these detainees," he told them. His e-mail, and the responses it provoked from members of the Army intelligence community across Iraq, are sadly illuminating about the mind-set of the U.S. military during this period. They suggest that the U.S. military was moving in the direction of institutionalized abuse.

Capt. Ponce stated that Col. Steve Boltz, the second highest ranking military intelligence officer in Iraq, "has made it clear that we want these individuals broken"—intelligence jargon for getting someone to abandon his cover and relate the truth as he knows it. Ponce then went on to wave the bloody shirt, a move that would raise eyebrows among some of his e-mail's recipients. "Casualties are mounting and we need to start gathering info to help protect our fellow soldiers from any further attacks," he wrote. So, Ponce ordered them, "Provide interrogation techniques 'wish list' by 17 AUG 03."

Some of the responses to his solicitation were enthusiastic. "I spent several months in Afghanistan interrogating the Taliban and al Qaeda," a soldier attached to the 3rd Armored Cavalry Regiment, operating in western Iraq, responded just fourteen hours later, according to the time stamp on his e-mail. "I firmly agree that the gloves need to come off." With clinical precision, he recommended permitting "open-handed facial slaps from a distance of no more than about two feet and back-handed blows to the midsection from a distance of about 18 inches. . . . I also believe that this should be a minimum baseline." He also reported that "fear of dogs and snakes appear to work nicely."

The 4th Infantry Division's intelligence operation responded three days later with suggestions that captives be hit with closed fists and also subjected to "low-voltage electrocution."

But not everyone was so sanguine as those two units' operations. "We need to take a deep breath and remember who we are," cautioned a major with the 501st Military Intelligence Battalion, which supported the operations of the 1st Armored Division in Iraq. (The officer's name was deleted in official documents released by the Army, as were those of other writers in this e-mail exchange.) "It comes down to standards of right and wrong—something we cannot just put aside when we find it inconvenient, any more than we can declare that we will 'take no prisoners' and therefore shoot those who surrender to us simply because we find prisoners inconvenient." This officer also took issue with the reference to rising U.S. casualties. "We have taken casualties in every war we have ever fought—that is part of the very nature of war. . . . That in no way justifies letting go of our standards. . . . Casualties are part of war—if you cannot take casualties then you cannot engage in war. Period." The "BOTTOM LINE," he wrote emphatically in conclusion, was, "We are American soldiers, heirs of a long tradition of staying on the high ground. We need to stay there." His signature block ended with a reference to "Psalm 24: 3–8," which begins with the admonition, "Who shall ascend into the hill of the Lord? Or who shall stand in his holy place? He that hath clean hands, and a pure heart." But this lucid and passionate response was a voice in the wilderness. The major was arguing against embarking on a course that the Army had already chosen to take.

Brig. Gen. Janis Karpinski, the commander of all prisons in Iraq, was growing concerned about conditions at Abu Ghraib, she said later in a sworn statement. On August 16, insurgents mortared the prison, killing six Iraqi prisoners and wounding at least forty-seven others. At that point the prison held Iraqis brought in under the old regime or as criminals, but not suspected insurgents caught by U.S. raids. In the wake of that incident Karpinski went to see Maj. Gen. Walter Wojdakowski, Sanchez's deputy commander, to ask for help.

"They're prisoners, Janis," Wojdakowski dismissively said to her, she later recounted. "Did you lose any soldiers?"

"I could have," she recalled telling him.

"They didn't care," she said, according to her statement, in which she also said that "Sanchez didn't care until two MI soldiers were killed" a month later.

In the following weeks and months, she added, "the divisions kept giving us more prisoners. 'Well, increase capacity.' Where would you like me to increase capacity?" The answer, she said, was "'Cram some more tents into the compound.'"

About ten days later, the first suspected insurgents captured by the United States arrived at Abu Ghraib, Karpinski later recalled. It was the middle of the night when helicopters arrived carrying thirty-five of them. "My battalion commander is calling me frantically, saying, 'Do you know anything about this? Why are we getting these people?'"

On August 31, Maj. Gen. Geoffrey Miller, commander of the detainee operation at Guantánamo Bay, Cuba, where 660 suspected al Qaeda and Taliban members were held and interrogated, arrived in Iraq to help U.S. commanders improve their intelligence operation, or as his subsequent report put it, "to rapidly exploit internees for actionable intelligence." His team of seventeen experts didn't always get a warm reception. "There was a great deal of animosity on the part of the Abu Ghraib personnel," a subsequent investigation by Army Maj. Gen. George Fay found.

One of the core conclusions Gen. Miller reached during his ten-day visit was that Abu Ghraib should be operated more like the prison he had run on Guantánamo, most notably by using the conditions of detention to soften up prisoners for questioning. "[T]he detention operations function must act as an enabler for interrogation," Miller stated in his own report, which bore the classification "secret/noforn," meaning that it wasn't to be shared with foreign allies.

His recommendation failed to take into account the vast difference between the U.S. base on Cuba's eastern end—a secure and remote area, completely under U.S. military control—and the chaos that surrounded Abu Ghraib, perched in the no-man's-land between Baghdad and Fallujah, a combat zone profoundly hostile to the foreign military presence in its midst. What's more, the ratio of guards to prisoners at peaceful Guantánamo was about 1.4 to 1, while at Abu Ghraib, which was regularly being mortared, the guards were heavily outnumbered, with a ratio of about 1 for every 10 prisoners. As more detainees flooded in, the ratio worsened to 1 to 20, according to Karpinski.

Over the next several months, hundreds of raids were conducted and over ten thousand Iraqis were detained, many of them hauled away from their families in the middle of the night and held without any notification to those families for weeks. All told, in the first eighteen months of the occupation, some thirty thousand to forty thousand Iraqis would pass through U.S. detention facilities, according to a legal statement given by Gen. Sanchez.

By the end of September, Abu Ghraib held more than 3,500 prisoners. A month later that number had almost doubled—but there were still only 360 MPs to guard them, Karpinski said. The huge effort in the late summer and fall of 2003 led directly to the widespread abuses of prisoners that came to be known, far too narrowly, as "the Abu Ghraib scandal." Those thousands of prisoners eventually would overwhelm the undermanned, undertrained, underequipped, undersupervised, and incompetent Army Reserve unit running the prison. And the tactics used in the push for intelligence aided the insurgency it was aiming to crush by alienating large segments of the Iraqi population.

The old prison was growing so crowded that the original purpose of detaining insurgents was being undercut by the sheer number being held. Col. Teeples, who commanded the 3rd Armored Cavalry Regiment, which is smaller than a division and lacked its own seasoned interrogators, said later in sworn testimony, "Several times when we had detainees, . . . they were really bad guys, and we'd try to get them moved to Abu Ghraib, [but] there was no room."

During this crucial period, the U.S. military seemed more concerned about its own well-being than about Iraqis, said Lt. Col. Holshek, who during the summer of 2003 was based at Tallil air base in southern Iraq. "We had all this hardware, all these riches at hand, yet we didn't do anything to help," he said of that time. An extraordinary part of the U.S. military effort was devoted to providing for itself, with a huge push to build showers, mess halls, and coffee bars, and to install amenities such as satellite television and Internet cafés. "At Tallil there were eleven thousand people, hundreds of millions of dollars being spent, and not a goddamn thing being done for the people downtown. so we looked like an occupation power. And we were—we behaved like one. The message we were sending was, we didn't care much about the Iraqis, because we didn't do what we needed to do on things like electricity. And we also looked incompetent."

War comes calling

Lt. Brendan O'Hern, a platoon leader in the 82nd Airborne Division, found out he was at war in a very hard way, in a short action on a scorching hot summer day in Baghdad when his unit was guarding a weapons amnesty collection point. "It was 120 degrees out and there was no relief from the sun," he wrote in a memoir posted on companycommand.com, a semiofficial Web site for younger Army leaders.

At about 3:00 P.M., a volley of rocket-propelled grenades flew at his unit from a nearby house, leaving their signature trail of blue-gray smoke. Several soldiers were blown into the air. One of the rockets, still burning, lodged in a leg of Cpl. Hilario Bermanis, and another soldier pulled it out with his bare hands. Another hit Spec. Gavin Neighbor, a twenty-year-old from Somerset, Ohio, who having finished his guard turn was resting in a nearby bus.

Back at their base, "[e]veryone was in complete shock as we had no injuries prior to all this, over almost three months of combat ops, including some pretty heavy stuff in the early days of the war," O'Hern wrote. It turned worse when his company commander told him a few hours later that Spec. Neighbor was dead. "I was blown away," he recalled. He gathered his men and told them the news. "We just stood there together for a long time, with guys crying or in shock. Neighbor was honestly one of the best soldiers in the platoon, if not the best. He really meant a lot to everyone, and guys took it pretty hard."

O'Hern told the soldiers to make sure to talk to work through their grief, rather than to try to ignore it. Over the next couple of days he found that conversing with them when they were alone worked best. "We'd talk about whatever felt right, whether it was joking about the two guys or talking about what people did during and after the attack, or just something to distract the guy," he wrote.

But O'Hern neglected himself. "I tried to be hard and be the rock the guys could lean on." But he later decided that that was the wrong approach, because he wound up feeling "a tremendous amount of guilt," and he plunged into a severe depression. "I did not really eat or sleep for six or seven days, but just lay around blaming myself in private and focusing on the platoon, outwardly," he wrote. "Eventually I hit a very low point and realized I'd better get some help or I would be in trouble." A talk with Neighbor's squad leader helped, especially because it developed that the other man was having a similarly difficult time.

O'Hern learned from the grim experience. "Up until that day, what we did was little more than a live-action video game," he concluded. After it, "[e]very move I make, every plan that I put together, is now scrutinized from every angle. I have realized that I must be prepared at all times, and that the attack will come when I least expect it. There is a voice inside that senses when something's not right, and I am steadily training myself to always listen to it."

Later that summer, Lt. Col. Poirier, the MP battalion commander who had been in Fallujah and then moved to Tikrit, had his own wake-up call from the insurgency. It came at about eleven o'clock at night, when he was convoying back up to Tikrit—about a three-hour Humvee drive from Baghdad—after a "useless" meeting at Camp Victory, near the Baghdad airport, on police issues. He had been noticing flares arcing in the sky to the west of the highway, and was beginning to suspect that someone was tracking his convoy's movement. A bit south of Samarra, he was out of radio range from his headquarters, so the issue was up to him, as the commander.

"I was trying to figure out a plan—go west?—when all hell broke loose—mortars, machine guns, RPGs," he recalled. One deadly RPG cut diagonally through the cab of his Humvee, passing before his face and behind his driver's head. Two thoughts immediately passed through his mind. First was, "Oh, shit, we got caught flat-footed. The next thought was, If I survive this, I will hunt down every guy doing this."

The convoy sped up and escaped without losing anyone. The next morning, Poirier woke up in Tikrit determined to do better. He began putting his troops through rehearsals for better responses to ambushes, most of them based on using armored vehicles to flank and kill the enemy. "This was a turning point for me," he recalled. A few weeks later another unit was hit in the same spot by a bomb and RPGs, killing Command Sgt. Maj. James Blankenbecler, a forty-year-old senior NCO from Alexandria, Virginia, who had recently arrived in Iraq on assignment as the new top enlisted soldier in the 1st Battalion, 44th Air Defense Artillery Regiment, based at Fort Hood, Texas.

When Bremer flew home to Washington for quick consultations at the end of July 2003, his message was that the situation was far better than it appeared in news coverage. "When I got to Washington this was confirmed—that the people in the United States were not getting an accurate picture of the progress we had made here, the really very substantial progress we have made here," he said later that summer in Baghdad. "They were distracted, understandably, by the trickle of casualties coming in almost every day from Iraq, and not getting the stories, the other two hundred good news stories, about schools reopening, hospitals opening, health clinics opening, the lowest cholera rate in a decade this year in the south, in Basra. . . . Those stories were not getting through." In fact, the U.S. occupation was about to be confronted by a full-blown insurgency. But as the United States entered its first sustained ground combat in three decades, this was his story, and he and the entire Bush administration stuck to it.

10.

THE CPA: "*CAN'T PRODUCE ANYTHING*"

I went to ORHA today to meet with their commo people," Capt. Kipling wrote to her boyfriend in early June, referring to the Coalition Provisional Authority by the acronym of its original name, the Office of Reconstruction and Humanitarian Assistance. "They were not very helpful."

She was far from alone in that conclusion. The U.S. civilian occupation organization was a house built on sand and inhabited by the wrong sort of people, according to many who worked there. "No clear strategy, very little detailed planning, poor communications, high personnel turnover, lots of young and inexperienced political appointees, no well-established business processes," concluded retired Army Col. Ralph Hallenbeck, who worked at the CPA as a civilian contractor dealing with the Iraqi communications infrastructure. Personnel was an especially nettlesome issue. Hallenbeck said that in addition to being young and inexperienced, most of the young CPA people he met during his work as a contractor were ideologically minded Republicans whose only professional experience was working on election campaigns back in the United States. It was, as Zinni later commented, "a pickup team." Scott Erwin, a former intern for Vice President Cheney who worked on the budget for security forces, reported that his favorite job before that was "my time as an ice cream truck driver."

"The tour length for most civilians was initially a mere three months," the British diplomat Hilary Synnott later recalled. "This was far too brief to be effective." Capt. Kipling also noticed this personnel problem on her forays into the Green Zone. "Their turnover rate was too high to be effective," she said. "They'd get good people in, they'd get motivated, and then there would be a big bomb, and they'd all leave."

It was more serious for Brig. Gen. Karpinski. She was regaling her superior with a list of all the problems she was having one day when, she recalled, "he threw his pen down on the desk, and he said, 'We're running a prison system for an entire country by the seat of our pants. What's CPA doing?'"

She responded: "There's two experts there, and they're leaving in about thirty days."

The view from inside the zone was that of a small and beleaguered band, understaffed and underresourced. "We all worked seventeen hours a day, seven days a week, for a year," recalled Sherri Kraham, who was deputy director of the CPA budget office. To some it felt like trying to build and furnish a house while parts of it were on fire—and all the time getting advice and orders from officials thousands of miles away in Washington and London.

"The CPA was always a work in progress," observed Andrew Rathmell, the British defense intellectual who served as a strategist for Bremer and later wrote a clear-eyed assessment of his time there. "Badly flawed pre-war assumptions, which were not effectively challenged, left the coalition unprepared and under-resourced for the task it faced. . . . The CPA ended up creating nation-building institutions on the run, governing Iraq at all levels, supporting a counter-insurgency campaign, reconstructing and reforming Iraqi state institutions and implementing democratic and economic transformation."

Yet it was far from clear what all that hard work was leading to. "One of the things that struck me in the summer of 2003 was how hard people were working, but how little effect it was having," said Gary Anderson.

By mid-August, when she left the CPA, recalled Ambassador Robin Raphel, a career foreign service officer, "it was very obvious to me that we couldn't do this, we could not run a country that we did not understand. . . . It was very much amateur hour to me, with all respect."

In another end-of-tour report, one colonel assigned to the CPA summarized his office's work: "pasting feathers together, hoping for a duck."

It didn't take long to see what poor shape the organization was in, said Col. Sammons, the Special Forces officer attached to the CPA. "I soon knew what CPA meant—Can't Produce Anything." That became a standard gag among military officers dealing with the occupation authority.

By the time the CPA was done away with a year later, the U.S. effort in Iraq had suffered a severe and perhaps crippling setback.

CPA administrator L. Paul Bremer III

Presiding over this mess was Bremer, by all accounts a smart and diligent man, but not the right person for the job—that is, someone who could provide strategic leadership to inspire a diverse collection of people suddenly brought together to handle an ill-defined, difficult, and expanding mission. Hallenbeck said it was his impression that Bremer was "reclusive" and wasn't comfortable with anyone. He recalled that on July 4, 2003, there was a pool party to celebrate the American independence day. Looking for lunch, he walked out to the party and saw people clustering at one end of the pool around a visiting Army general, who was asking about their work on morale. Bremer appeared a half hour later. "He looked totally alone—like he didn't recognize anybody. Alone." Eventually, Bremer's spokesman, Dan Senor, took Bremer around to introduce him to people. "That was Bremer's style," Hallenbeck said.

Nor did Bremer lead his people in such a way as to help them confront the organization's flaws. His morning meetings in the summer and fall of 2003, as Iraq descended into guerrilla war, "were bizarre," recalled Gardner, one of the Army colonels at the CPA. "You'd go around the table. He'd say, 'Anybody got anything?' Most of the time it was 'nope,' 'nope,' 'got nothing.'"

His own work style also tied their hands. "He chose to micromanage," said Dov Zakheim. "Nothing could be done without his okay." This was the biggest single problem in the financial pipeline from Washington, D.C., to Iraq, he said. "Bremer wanted to control the expenditure of money in the field, but he didn't have the people in the field to expend it."

The very structure of the CPA also hurt Bremer, giving him great responsibility without commensurate power. Bremer was understaffed and underbudgeted. He was in the frustrating position of having authority over every aspect of the occupation except for security—the one essential element that was arguably the prerequisite for everything else. "We had a proconsul model, but we didn't give Bremer the power to go with it," said one State Department official, referring to the wide authority that the ancient Roman system gave to the governors of its provinces.

Life in the zone

The CPA existed in a never-never land in Saddam's old palace complex behind high walls in downtown Baghdad. There was a sharp disconnect between its cool, quiet Green Zone and the real world beyond the miles of tall concrete Jersey security barriers that ringed the zone. Some in the U.S. military called the CPA's slice of central Baghdad Oz. To many within the CPA, the rest of Iraq was the Red Zone.

At first, life in the newly created American sector was rough. "We were working 120-hour weeks in Baghdad," recalled Hallenbeck. "It wasn't like we could go home on the weekends." Lacking rooms, he and his colleagues were sleeping on the palace lawn and living on MREs—the military's subsistence-level packaged rations. In the middle of all this, Pentagon auditors appeared and asked to see his company's timecards. But within a few weeks, the quality of life improved notably in the zone—in sharp contrast to the rest of Iraq, where conditions generally were deteriorating. It was a four-square-mile area that felt very different from the rest of Iraq, a novel mix of palm trees and third-rate Iraqi palaces interspersed with Bradley fighting vehicles and a few bombed-out buildings. It was isolated from the city's giant traffic jams and shaded by many more trees than grew elsewhere in Baghdad. It also was attuned to different realities than prevailed beyond its blast walls. Inside the zone, the telephones had a 914 area code, from New York's Westchester County, where the phone system was based. On one visit to the CPA's Office of Strategic Communications, all the televisions but one were tuned to Fox News. "It's almost like being at Walt Disney's version of *Arabian Nights*," said Army Reserve Maj. Jay Bachar, who spent a year working on civil affairs issues in the zone. "I lived in a villa that was originally owned by a Republican Guard colonel." It featured six bedrooms, a hot tub on a balcony, and three Iraqi maids. "We lived very large."

The zone was at the center of one of the most important cities in the Arab world, but inside CPA headquarters the food resembled that of an American high school. Busy staffers would line up at lunchtime for paper plates of hot dogs and baked beans, and would wash them down with cold cans of Coca-Cola. Oddly for being in a Muslim country, "it seemed like seventy-five percent of the entrées were pork, or pork based—pork rings, pork chops, fish-shaped pork, I guess. Pork in our salads, pork stew," said Alex Dehgan, who worked on a special nonproliferation project aimed at gainfully employing Iraqi weapons scientists. "I think Halliburton must have gotten a great deal on pork somewhere."

Nighttime offered just a few choices—more work, exercise, or drinking. "Time off for me was going to the gym," recalled Larry Diamond, who worked for the CPA a few months later, when it was better established. The gym, he wrote, was "a state-of-the-art facility with dozens of weight machines, free weights, floor mats, running machines, bikes, and elliptical trainers, packed almost constantly with sweating civilians and trim, muscular soldiers."

Another evening pursuit was television. "Television in the Green Zone had some of the strangest TV channels," said Dehgan. Out of just fifteen channels, two were dedicated to fashion, and another after 11:00 at night showed only Germans playing video games.

Then there was alcohol. Eventually the zone boasted seven bars, including one for security contractors and another, more exclusive one operated by the CIA called the Babylon. The biggest one was the disco at the al Rasheed Hotel, which was, Dehgan said, "mainly staffed with intoxicated security contractors. . . . There were maybe four hundred intoxicated men and three women in the middle of it."

Soldiers arriving from austere, dusty bases elsewhere in Iraq sometimes were shocked by what they saw in the zone, recalled one officer. Thursday and Friday nights in the zone's bars, he said, had a wide-open feel to them. "Everyone was drunk, and the mission was to hook up. Military guys would walk in there, and their eyes would get big."

Nor were some of the zone's inhabitants much connected to the country they were ostensibly remaking. "There was just a level of ignorance" that was surprising, Hallenbeck said. "There were maybe seven thousand people in the Green Zone, and very few spoke Arabic or ever got out." Even if they had wanted to get outside the confines of their protected area, CPA rules made it difficult: "If you had to go outside the Green Zone, you'd have to have two military vehicles and four armed guys. You'd go in and apply for that, and get your name on the list for escort support. You'd go in at eleven at night and make sure you were good to go, and come back in the morning and find you had been superseded by a higher priority project."

The isolation deepened as the security situation worsened in the summer and fall of 2003. "A lot of people in the Green Zone, in the bubble, never got out to speak with Iraqis," recalled Peter Khalil, an Australian who worked at the CPA on national security policy. "It was easier at first, but then a fortress mentality developed." This was the political effect of the rise of the insurgency: It was driving a wedge between the occupation authority and the Iraqi people.

The result was that all some CPA officials knew of Iraq was what they saw on TV or heard in the mess hall. As a State Department official put it, "You had this odd situation where the journalists knew more about the situation than the briefers did, because the journalists moved around and the briefers generally didn't get out of the Green Zone much."

Richard Armitage said that the State Department grew increasingly worried by the tone of life inside the zone. "I defined it as the bar scene from *Star Wars*," he said in 2005. "The people running to and fro, young people in very heady positions, they didn't have a clue what they were doing." State was so alarmed that one of the orders given to John Negroponte and his aides when they were sent out to replace Bremer in 2004 was, "Clean up that goddamn Green Zone." Armitage's instructions to Ambassador James Jeffrey, the number-two American diplomat in Iraq, were, "I don't want to see people running around with arms out there drinking beer; I don't want to see people I don't know who they are carrying weapons; clean up this freaking place; send people home."

The CPA vs. the media

Relations between the occupation authority and the foreign press corps rapidly deteriorated. By the summer of 2003, Pamela Hess, a veteran defense reporter for the UPI wire service, recalled, "The media operation at CPA was abominable. The mechanics of it were ridiculous." Requests for interviews were filed on slips of paper to a military office, which would then deliver them to the CPA. Arriving in Baghdad for a one-month reporting tour, Hess submitted a series of requests in writing on her first day in the city. "Four weeks later, when I left Baghdad, my requests had never even been formally acknowledged—although a CPA spokesman confirmed they had been received—and none were ever acted upon."

The CPA press office seemed to see itself more as a monitor of the media than as a provider of information. One opportunity the CPA offered up was covering the new garbage collection service in Baghdad. For lack of any other story one August day, Carol Williams of the *Los Angeles Times* dutifully decided to do it. As frequently happens in journalism, she found more than she'd expected: Many of the trash crews were small children who were being shaken down by their bosses for a third of their wages, which amounted to three dollars a day. Iraqis she interviewed were upset by the situation and eager to discuss it, in part because the legal minimum age for such work was supposed to be fifteen.

CPA officials weren't pleased by her coverage. The next time Williams was at a press briefing, she checked in with a press officer about another article she was pursuing on the provision of clean water—there was a local angle for her paper because some of the engineers were from California. She was informed that interviews she had been promised might not occur because of her handling of the trash story. In fact, she recalled, "I never did get access to the water engineers."

In Hess's view, the CPA's relationship with the press soured fundamentally because of the insistence by officials that all was going well, and the consequent determination of reporters to disprove that contention. "Had they been more willing to admit that things were bad instead of putting lipstick on the pig, I think reporters would have been kinder," she said. "I think we felt compelled to rub their noses in it, to try to make them admit it, and maybe do something about it."

Meanwhile, the CPA ceded the playing field in other, more important ways. Charles Krohn, a veteran of Army public affairs, was surprised when he served in Baghdad to see that the CPA early on lifted the ban on TV satellite receivers, but failed to begin satellite broadcasting until months later, in January 2004, leaving a gap in which Iraqis got all their news from Arab stations essentially hostile to the U.S. presence. "What this means is that for the first nine months, we essentially forfeited the contest for hearts and minds to the competition," he wrote later.

The CPA vs. the U.S. military

Underneath the poor image was a poor reality: The CPA was ineptly organized and frequently incompetent, working badly not only with Iraqis and the media, but even with the U.S. military, its partner in the occupation. There are different points of view on almost any issue in Iraq, but there is surprising unanimity, from both sides of the fence, that the relationship between the CPA and the military began badly and deteriorated further with time.

Sherri Kraham said the CPA-military relationship was "very poor." She explained, "I don't think we spoke the same language."

"The CPA—what a dysfunctional arrangement that was!" exclaimed Maj. Gen. John Batiste, who commanded the 1st Infantry Division in Iraq in 2004–5. "It was nuts!"

"We would have been better off if CPA hadn't shown up," said Col. Clarke Lethin, the chief of operations for the 1st Marine Division, which fought in Iraq first in the 2003 invasion and then in the 2004 occupation. "We just built friction into the system."

A general who served in Iraq went even further, saying that the occupation authority "was the single greatest asset the enemy had."

Fundamentally, the CPA and the military had different conceptions of what the United States was doing in Iraq. The civilians, more in line with Bush administration thinking about transforming Iraq and the region, implemented policies that set out to change the politics, economy, and even the culture of Iraq. The military, less culturally sympathetic to the administration's revolutionary goals, thought of its mission as almost the opposite, calling it "stability and security operations." "The military was there to win the conflict, find Saddam and then keep the peace," retired Rear Adm. David Oliver, a veteran submarine officer and an astute analyst of the politics of defense, wrote later in a short memoir of his time devising the CPA's budget. After the war, the military sought to keep the population quiet, while the CPA "focused on change," which meant that it was bound to provoke vocal and violent reactions from some Iraqis opposed to those changes. For example, Oliver noted, as the CPA was seeking to normalize commerce by opening banks, which would reassure merchants that they could conduct business without fear of being robbed of the cash they had to keep on hand, some U.S. commanders were walking into banks and demanding piles of cash from government payrolls to pay for local cleanup projects.

CPA officials were aware of the military's pervasive unhappiness with them. "The 101st and 4th ID are beginning to get frustrated by the lack of progress in key reconstruction work," stated the occupation authority's internal situation report of June 18, 2003. "Recent negative developments in Mosul indicate growing frustrations over perceived inaction by CPA over re-employment of former military officers."

Outfitting Iraqi police was another of those points of friction that emerged in the following weeks. "They were useless," Lt. Col. Poirier, who was trying to set up police forces in Tikrit and Samarra, recalled. "The guidance from them changed daily—'Get the police white uniforms,' then, 'No, get blue uniforms.'"

In al Anbar province, Gen. Swannack was growing increasingly frustrated as he tried to get local police outfitted. In August he put in a requisition request for flak vests, communications equipment, and vehicles for the Iraq security forces working with his troops. There was a clear and pressing requirement, he said: "You need the comms so they can call you when they got in trouble. You need vehicles to get to the battle. You need flak vests so you can fight." First he was told the gear would be delivered by November 1. Then he was told it would be delayed until December. When that month came and went, he called on January 1 to inquire again, only to be told that the CPA official in charge of that contract had gone home on Christmas vacation and had decided not to return. In February he finally went public with his frustration, mentioning it at a press conference—and then the equipment began to arrive.

The CPA and the military also diverged on the PR campaign. In October 2003, as the White House was launching a public relations campaign to emphasize how well things were going in Iraq, Sanchez began to go out of his way in briefings to warn that there would be more insurgent attacks that could inflict many casualties on U.S. forces. For example, on October 2, Rumsfeld and Myers used a Pentagon news conference to chastise the media for not covering all the good news out of Iraq. "Today is D plus 198 in Operation Iraqi Freedom, and while there is no question we have faced some challenges and we've got some ahead of us, we have really achieved numerous successes and expect the situation to continue to improve," said Myers, always one to accentuate the positive.

Rumsfeld even hinted at troop drawdowns, saying that his message to Congress at this time was that he needed supplemental funds to "finish the job in Iraq and Afghanistan, so that we're able to bring the U.S. forces back."

A few days later, President Bush offered a similarly upbeat assessment. "Listen, we're making good progress in Iraq. Sometimes it's hard to tell it when you listen to the filter," he said at a news conference. "The situation is improving on a daily basis inside Iraq. People are freer, the security situation is getting better."

During this same period, Sanchez's public statements were decidedly darker than those of Bush, Rumsfeld, and Myers. "The enemy has evolved," he said at his own October 2 press conference. "It is a little bit more lethal, little bit more complex, little bit more sophisticated, and, in some cases, a little bit more tenacious." And, he added, "as long as we are here, the coalition needs to be prepared to take casualties." He also said that it would be "a few years" before the security situation in Iraq stabilized sufficiently to permit a major drawdown of U.S. troops.

Such statements reflected a fundamental disagreement over communications strategy. "The military guys said that their key audience was Iraq, and emanating out from there," said a public affairs officer at the CPA. "The CPA view was that the center of gravity was the U.S. public."

The CPA public affairs operation also underwhelmed some colleagues. At one meeting, "I was awestruck by the superficiality of the insights that they brought to the table, absolutely awestruck," recalled Larry Crandall, a CPA official involved in reconstruction financing.

The military's discord with the CPA even reached down to the small unit level. "My relationship with the CPA as an infantry commander has been tenuous at best," one company commander in the 101st Airborne wrote in his response to an official Army survey. "First, their guidance has been contradictory at times with the military and definitely not well coordinated." Also, he said, the civilian administrators violated the basic principle of unity of effort. "CPA officials arrived in our AO [area of operations] and conducted meetings in conferences, made promises to local officials that were contradictory to past military-to–local official meetings and/or agreements."

With the passage of time, the CPA and the U.S. military acted less like partners and more like adversaries. "Soldiers . . . blamed civilians for not rebuilding the country quickly enough to pacify the country, while civilians . . . blamed the military for not providing enough security to enable the rebuilding," the *Washington Post*'s Rajiv Chandrasekaran would later write in summarizing this unhappy relationship.

Much later, a study issued in May 2004 by the Center for Army Lessons Learned analyzed the problem. It amounted to an obituary for the failure of the U.S. occupation effort in Iraq—albeit from a distinctly military point of view.

> The common perception throughout the theater is that a roadmap for the rebuilding of Iraq does not exist. There is not a plan that outlines priorities with short, medium and long-term objectives. If such a national plan exists with the CPA, it has not been communicated adequately to Coalition forces. Task force staffs at all levels of command have reiterated that there is no clear guidance coming from Baghdad. The inability to develop or articulate a plan contributes to a lack of unity of effort between the Coalition and CPA. . . . Coalition commanders and staff view the CPA as understaffed, sluggish, hesitant to make a decision, and often detached from the true situation on the ground. With CPA officials on 90-day rotations, much time is required for replacements to become knowledgeable with the specific issues and players they are facing. Nine months after the declared end to major military action, CPA staffs in the center portions of the country are estimated at 20% strength. Whether rooted in the lack of staffing or to security concerns, there appears to be an inability of CPA Headquarters (Baghdad) to get the needed "eyes on" what is happening. Subsequently, CPA directives appear to be out of synch with the current situation.

A growing gap between Iraqis and Americans

The backdrop to that tension in Iraq was a larger, strategic disconnect that was even more troubling. The Bush administration had extraordinary ambitions for Iraq, and indeed for the entire Mideast, but it declined for months to provide the resources needed to fulfill that vision—partly because Wolfowitz and others had said that Iraqi reconstruction would be largely self-financing. By the end of the summer, it was clear that the reconstruction effort was stalling and that restarting it would take far more money than had been contemplated by the U.S. government. On Bremer's desk was a sign that nobly stated, SUCCESS HAS A THOUSAND FATHERS. Sir Jeremy Greenstock, the veteran diplomat who was Bremer's top British aide, later commented that he should have replaced it with the message, "SECURITY AND JOBS, STUPID." The Bush administration would come to agree with that sentiment in private, and asked Congress for a huge supplemental spending bill—$87 billion—to get the effort going. But even then, the wheels of the CPA bureaucracy turned so slowly that it took months to get basic equipment such as flak jackets to Iraqi security forces being trained by the U.S. government.

The cumulative result of this incompetence was that by the late fall of 2003, the U.S. occupation of Iraq began to lose its claim on the lukewarm middle of Iraqi public opinion. In a poll of 1,167 Iraqis conducted for the CPA in five cities in November and December 2003, 62 percent said that security was the most urgent issue facing them. "U.S. has Credibility Problem" reported one slide on the survey, because 59 percent of those polled said the United States would leave Iraq "only when forced to." The United States hadn't yet lost Iraq, but the trends were heading that way.

11.

GETTING TOUGH

SUMMER AND FALL 2003

Across the board, U.S. tactics toughened in the fall of 2003. This was natural, even reasonable, coming in response to the increased attacks on U.S. forces and a series of suicide bombing attacks. But it also appears to have undercut the long-term strategy of the U.S. government. "What you are seeing here is an unconventional war fought conventionally," a Special Forces lieutenant colonel remarked gloomily one day in Baghdad as the violence intensified. Asked later what he meant by that, this officer said that having the U.S. military out in patrols—that is, the presence mission—wasn't in and of itself necessarily stabilizing the situation. And the tactics that the regular troops used, he added, sometimes subverted American strategy.

In other words, U.S. forces were fighting hard, and might even be able eventually to claw their way to victory, but they were working far harder and less productively than necessary. They were following their training, performing according to doctrine, and busting their hearts to do the right thing—and frequently were sweating and bleeding in ways that didn't help them move toward their strategic goal. They were pounding the square peg of the U.S. Army into the round hole of Iraq, a difficult situation that was hardly their fault. Civilian leaders and top military commanders had failed to define what kind of war was being fought, and publicly had insisted that it was something other than what it was. Seen in this light, the abuses that occurred later in 2003 at the Abu Ghraib prison weren't an anomalous incident but rather the logical and predictable outcome of a series of panicky decisions made by senior commanders, which in turn had resulted from the divided, troop-poor approach devised months earlier by Secretary Rumsfeld and Gen. Franks.

The insurgency erupts

After months of maneuvering, the real war in Iraq—the one to determine the future of the country—began on August 7, 2003, when a car bomb exploded outside the Jordanian embassy, killing eleven and wounding more than fifty. The next day, with remarkable timing, the CPA released a public relations document that touted one hundred indicators of how well things were going in Iraq. "Most of Iraq is calm and progress on the road to democracy and freedom not experienced in decades continues," the document, posted on the White House's Web site, blithely asserted in a section titled "10 Signs of Better Security." "Only in isolated areas are there still attacks." In fact, the insurgency was emerging into deadly bloom. While U.S. civilian and military leaders had dithered, letting their policy and posture drift, the enemy had been busy.

The initial focus of insurgent attacks wasn't the U.S. military but allies of the U.S. effort, such as other members of the coalition and international organizations, that were perceived as legitimizing the occupation. Beginning in midsummer, Gen. Sanchez found himself fighting a very different war from that waged by the U.S. military in the invasion months earlier. "As time went on, it became very clear by the fall, by the November timeframe . . . that they had, as best we could tell, a strategy of attacking the different elements of cohesiveness within the coalition," Sanchez said in a subsequent statement in a legal proceeding. He saw four major thrusts of enemy attacks: "They were doing direct action against us. They were attacking the Iraqi security forces as they existed at the time. They were attacking politicians. They were attacking the international community, which was a strike on the Italians, the United Nations, and they were looking to split the coalition." In other words, the insurgents were systematically hitting allies of the U.S.-led effort, turning away from difficult U.S. military targets in favor of softer foreign targets, and in doing so, seeking to peel off support and isolate the U.S. occupation.

On August 19, a cement truck laden with artillery shells and other explosives crashed into the outer wall of the headquarters of the United Nations in Iraq, on the Canal Road in eastern Baghdad. The blast was so powerful that windows in the camp of the 2nd Armored Cavalry Regiment, about half a mile way, were blown in. It destroyed a corner of the three-story UN building, killing twenty-two people and wounding another seventy. One of the dead was Brazilian diplomat Sergio Vieira de Mello, the chief of the UN mission, who survived the blast but was trapped inside the rubble and died before he could be freed.

The effect on the United Nations was devastating. In the attack's wake, the UN began to cut its presence, from eight hundred international staffers to fifteen. This was significant, because the UN had served as a bridge for the Americans to important Shiite leaders, such as Grand Ayatollah Ali Sistani, who wouldn't meet directly with U.S. occupation officials. The act was successful in that it "convinced the organization that continuing to operate in Iraq would be too costly," Col. T. X. Hammes, the Marine expert on counterinsurgency who worked for the CPA on the training of Iraqis in the winter of 2003–4, later wrote in assessing the insurgents' strategy. Other international organizations, such as the World Bank, the International Monetary Fund, and the British relief agency Oxfam, began to pull out in the following weeks. After the UN was hit again, with a smaller bomb a month later, more staffers and other agencies, such as Save the Children (UK), left Iraq. "That was a brilliant campaign," said Hammes. "They hit the UN, the Red Cross, the Jordanian embassy, and the Iraqi police. And we were calling them 'dead-enders'? Who do you think is disorganized at that point?"

Out in Anbar province, Keith Mines also felt the increasing heat. "The level of animosity toward the coalition appears to be rising in al Anbar province, as both quantitatively there is an increasing rage on the streets, and qualitatively the attacks are growing more sophisticated and bolder," he wrote in his weekly report of September 24. "Only a small minority of al Anbarians are taking up arms against the coalition, but the vast middle ground does nothing to stop them and to date does not see it in their interest to help us corner them. And the trends are moving in the wrong direction." Mines also wrote to his family that he was worried about the volatile combination he saw brewing in his province: "hordes of mad young men with too much time on their hands and too many weapons readily available." Some of them were learning how to make and deliver bombs. The enemy may not have had a public face but he certainly was developing a distinctive mode of attack.

The war of the roadside bomb

Each war produces its own artifacts—its distinctive phrases, garments, or technological innovations. The memorable piece of clothing from World War I was the trench coat, which captures a key aspect of that mired conflict. The classic abbreviation of World War II was "snafu"—situation normal, all fucked up.

More than anything else, war is about destruction, and so it is weaponry that most often captures the feel of a given conflict. The cold soul of the limited 1991 Gulf War was the precision-guided "smart bomb," which distilled to one lethal device the technological leap the U.S. military had taken since the end of the Vietnam War just sixteen years earlier.

The emblematic weapon of the new Iraq war was quite the opposite: the inexpensive, low-tech roadside bomb. The U.S. military called it the IED, for improvised explosive device. In unhappy contrast to the earlier U.S. war with Iraq, this weapon was used not by but against U.S. forces. It quickly became the single greatest threat to them: About one third of U.S. troops killed in the first year of the insurgency were victims of these bombs, as were about two thirds of those wounded severely enough to require medical evacuation out of Iraq. Support troops, such as mechanics and supply specialists, were most vulnerable, accounting for three quarters of those killed by the bombs in the summer of 2003.

Even these fairly primitive devices had their own evolution. At first, during the summer of 2003, almost all were hardwired—that is, attached by the lines used to detonate them. U.S. forces learned to look for the wire and kill the person waiting at the other end. By the following winter, about half the bombs were remote-controlled, frequently set off using cellular telephones, car alarm transmitters, or toy car controllers. For charges, insurgents usually used 155 millimeter artillery shells and a variety of mortar rounds, and occasionally TNT or a plastic explosive.

The bombs at first were concealed under rocks or piles of trash, which were everywhere along Baghdad streets, as social services failed to resume after the war. Others were hidden in the carcasses of dead dogs, which in the humid summer heat of Iraq produced a putrid smell that would deter all but the most dedicated soldier from probing for bombs.

Early on, one favored tactic was to block the road with a truck or bus that would appear to be stalled or broken down—and then plant a series of bombs behind the vehicle in the area along the road where the U.S. convoy would be forced to stop. U.S. troops responded by driving up on the sidewalk or in the incoming lane of traffic, which got them out of the trap but inadvertently served the insurgents' secondary purpose, of angering and alienating Iraqis who had to scramble out of the way of the careening convoy.

As the insurgency was heating up in the Sunni Triangle, Lt. Col. Steve Russell, based in its northern part in the town of Tikrit, was dealing with a wave of attacks in which bombers were using the transmitters from radio-controlled toy cars. They would take the electronic guts of the cars, wrap them in C-4 plastic explosive, and attach a blasting cap, then detonate them by remote control. So Russell, who commanded an infantry battalion, mounted one of the toy-car controllers on the dashboard of his Humvee and taped down the levers. Because all the toy cars operated on the same frequency, this would detonate any similar bomb about one hundred yards before his Humvee got to the spot. This "poor man's anti-explosive device [was] risky perhaps," Russell wrote in a fifty-eight-page summary of his unit's time in Iraq, but better than the alternative of leaving the detonation to the bombers.

The most effective counterbomb tactic turned out to be the low-tech sniper. U.S. troops learned to hide and spy on spots, such as traffic circles, where bombs were likely to be emplaced. "Anyone who comes out in the middle of the night to plant an IED dies," a senior Central Command official reported.

As U.S. troops became more sophisticated in countering the devices, the insurgents invented new tactics. Enemy fighters observed that American troops were being trained to stop about two hundred meters short when they spotted a bomb. They adapted by planting a bomb in the open in a highly visible location, and then hiding several more two hundred meters farther up the road, next to where the troops would halt.

The typical IED cell, American intelligence analysts concluded, usually consisted of six to eight people. It was led by a planner/financier. Next came the bomb maker, who handled the construction of the device but not its delivery. The third specialist was the emplacer, who would plant the bomb by pretending to fix a flat tire or, in some customized vehicles, would drop the bomb through a hole cut in the floor of a car. In addition, the cell had a triggerman, who would detonate the bomb, and perhaps a spotter or two to provide security for the rest of the team. Many cells had someone in an additional role: cameraman. According to U.S. intelligence, the majority of bomb attacks were videotaped by the bomb cell, in part as a learning device to improve attacks, in part for propaganda and recruiting purposes. This reliance on video cameras was one reason that U.S. troops became so antagonistic toward television news cameramen, especially those of

Arab ethnicity, who the troops tended to assume were in league with the insurgents. "There is an element—and I am not saying this applies everywhere—but some of the local hires of some of the local media organizations do their agencies a disservice, because they've got links to insurgents and terrorist organizations," said Army Gen. George Casey, who took over command in mid-2004. "We have not found that rampantly, but we know it's true in a few cases."

Most of the U.S. responses to the bomb attacks were reactive. About half the attacks during the summer of 2003 were against soft-skinned Humvees, which were lacking any armor. During the fall and winter of 2003–4, the Army emphasized adding armor to vehicles. But partly because it kept underestimating the depth and breadth of the insurgency, it struggled for over a year to get its people into better protected vehicles. It also studied the frequencies on which car alarm transmitters and other devices operated, and began to jam them with mobile electronic gear.

Despite these steps, the toll from the bombs increased with the passage of time. During 2003 there was only one month—November, when the insurgency took off with a Ramadan offensive—in which more than twenty U.S. personnel were lost to roadside bombs and similar land mines, according to a mortality analysis by the office of the Armed Forces Medical Examiner. But from January through November 2004, more than twenty troops were killed that way in every month but two. November 2004 was the worst of all, with more than forty soldiers lost to the bombs. What those numbers disguise is that the toll would have been higher were it not for the improvements in armor defenses, because the number of bomb attacks increased steadily in 2004. "IEDs are my number one threat," Gen. Abizaid stated in a memorandum sent in June of that year to the chairman of the Joint Chiefs of Staff.

But they were hardly ubiquitous. Most of the bombings occurred along major routes in a surprisingly small area—along about a total of 250 miles of roadway in Baghdad and leading from the capital city to the west, north, and northeast. Every day, hundreds of U.S. convoys traveled these main supply routes, becoming targets that were hit with surprising frequency.

For every military tactic there is a countermeasure. As one Army general noted, military operations are a giant, lethal version of the children's game of rock/paper/scissors. Adding armor to U.S. military vehicles inevitably led to new moves by the bombers. In the winter of 2004–5, they began concealing IEDs among overhanging branches and leaves—Iraq between the Euphrates and Tigris rivers is quite lush—or hanging them from light poles. The purpose of this, said one Army engineer studying the problem in Baghdad, appeared to be to move the bomb blast above the armored doors, so that the effect shattered the windshields and side windows inward, and also to hit the soldiers manning the guns mounted atop many vehicles.

Vehicle-borne IEDs, or car bombs, also became popular in the fall and winter of 2003. Troops soon were taught to be on the lookout for a new set of telltale signs, such as the jalopy so overladen that it sat low on its springs. Another was fresh tires on an old car: "This is a one-way trip, driver wants no flats," a 2004 briefing explained.

Bomb explosions frequently were experienced as overwhelming waves of light. "It just happened in a flash," recalled Sgt. 1st Class Erick Macher, in a typical comment. "You hear it. The blast smashes everything in the vehicle."

Spec. James King, a combat lifesaver—an infantryman trained also as a kind of part-time medic—recalled being in a convoy bombed near Baghdad in late 2004. He went to the Humvee behind his, the one that was hit. "A guy is lying on the seat, feet on the other seat, head hanging low out the door. I don't recognize him."

The soldier's head was hugely swollen, his eyes clouded. King was struck: "I realize I know this guy." He took off the soldier's helmet, but there was something coming with it—the top of the soldier's head. "I see his brain."

Another soldier stepped out of the Humvee and fell to the ground. King continued to work on the first one. "He gurgles in air and blood—he exhales blood. He gets still again. I yell his name. He gurgles in air and blood—he exhales blood. Again and again."

At one point someone suggested an intravenous injection to replace lost blood. King reached for his IV. A full-time medic who had arrived looked at King. "No," the medic ordered. "He's dead."

King picked up his machine gun and his medical kit, then walked back to his own Humvee. "No anger. No remorse. Just sudden clarity and emptiness," he wrote.

"Are you OK to drive?" someone asked him.

"I'm fine," he responded. It was not true, he noted later.

As they treated bomb injuries Army doctors began to notice a new pattern of problems in soldiers that resulted from brains being rattled around in the skull by the blasts. In 2003 and 2004, hundreds of soldiers were diagnosed as suffering some form of damage from such incidents. Even seasoned surgeons were surprised by the extent of it. Army Reserve Maj. Donald Robinson was a trauma specialist in inner-city Camden, New Jersey, before deploying to Iraq, but he was surprised by what he found in the war. "When I got there I was taken aback," he said. "This was penetrating trauma to the nth degree. It was massive. The tissue destruction was like nothing I'd ever seen before. . . . Imagine shards of metal going everywhere. . . . Add the percussion from the blast. Then put someone inside a Bradley fighting vehicle and add fire to it and burning flesh. A person inhales and [suffers] inhalation injury."

But in an insurgency, it is the political result that is always paramount. Though devastating physically, the most significant effect of roadside bombs was that they made U.S. troops wary of operating among the people. The fact that insurgents were able to place so many bombs, often repeatedly along the same stretches of road, also made a political statement, because it meant that the locals weren't reporting on them. "Coalition forces are forced to interact with the Iraqi populace from a defensive posture, effectively driving a psychological wedge between the people and their protectors," Maj. Gen. Peter Chiarelli, who commanded the 1st Cavalry Division in Iraq in 2004, observed. That sort of insight, built on an understanding of the nature of conducting a counterinsurgency campaign, had been rare among Army commanders in Iraq during the summer of 2003.

The U.S. Army cracks down

The Army's original plan was to conduct a force withdrawal beginning in midsummer 2003, bringing its presence down to about 30,000 troops by late summer. Instead, late summer was when the situation in Iraq really began to feel like a war for many of the 130,000 American soldiers in the country.

August 29 brought the third major car bombing of the month, as insurgents hit another ally of the U.S. effort, Shiite political leader Ayatollah Mohammed Bakir Hakim. The leader of SCIRI—the Supreme Council for the Islamic Revolution in Iraq—Hakim had been one of the most important political figures in Iraq, and the most influential religious figure to have openly supported the U.S. occupation. The car bomb that killed him soon after Friday prayers in the holy city of Najaf also murdered more than ninety others. The message was that the United States, for all its firepower, couldn't protect its Iraqi allies.

During late July and August, Generals Abizaid and Sanchez discussed with their division commanders and other top officers three possible responses to the insurgency, recalled Maj. Gen. Renuart. One was tactical withdrawal from trouble spots. "Take a city like Ramadi or Fallujah, and tell them to police it and run it themselves," he said. "The second was, use small elements, like SF [Special Forces] teams, to do raids in a surgical application of power. The third was, you are present in cities, and you are intimidating enough to create security by presence." Ultimately, "we decided all three had a place." One reason for that was that Abizaid didn't want to limit the choices available to the division commanders. "If you need to use a scalpel, here's a scalpel," was the thinking, Renuart said. "If you need to use a mallet, I don't want to take that away from you."

But there were many more sledgehammers than scalpels in the U.S. Army inventory, both physically and mentally. The war in Iraq isn't the Vietnam War. There are more differences than similarities between the two. Yet in one respect, the initial response of the Army, they were eerily alike. Lt. Col. John Nagl's account of how the Army approached Vietnam was echoed in Iraq.

> The American Army's involvement in the Second Indochina War from 1950 to 1972 demonstrates the triumph of the institutional culture of an organization over attempts at doctrinal innovation and the diminution of the effectiveness of the organization at accomplishing national objectives. The United States Army had become reliant on firepower and technological superiority in its history of annihilating enemy forces. . . . The concept that success in counterinsurgency consisted of separating the insurgents from popular support never took hold. The U.S. Army proceeded with its historical role of destroying the enemy army—even if it had a hard time finding it. The United States Army entered the Vietnam War with a doctrine well suited to fighting conventional war in Europe, but worse than useless for the counterinsurgency it was about to combat.

Even the short-term successes of the U.S. Army in Iraq seem to have long-term costs that went unrecognized at the time. The story of how intelligence operations were revamped in the fall of 2003 illustrates this sad pattern. All summer long, commanders had fretted about the poor quality of their intelligence. Several months into the war, they had no idea who the enemy really was. Nor did they know much about what Iraqis thought of them—especially the views of those beyond the narrow world of Iraqis, such as interpreters, who were on the U.S. payroll.

Such ignorance was neither inevitable nor helpful. "American forces are operating in a relative vacuum of Iraqi sentiments," a study by the Center for Army Lessons Learned reported several months later. "This contrasts with the British, who have developed a 20-question survey that is continually administered throughout their area of operations."

Recognizing their profound lack of understanding, American commanders launched a major effort in the fall of 2003 to improve U.S. intelligence gathering and analysis. On October 1, Abizaid issued an order to reorganize intelligence operations in Iraq, so that all the data gathered would pour into one new Intelligence Fusion Center. In this new organization, analysts would work side by side with interrogators and the CIA would cooperate with military intelligence. Until the fall, the CIA, the Special Operations units, and the divisions all had separate databases. Now a new database would be created to try to ensure, for example, that someone detained and released in Ramadi would trigger an alert when he was caught a week later in Mosul with traces of explosives on his hands. Most important, networks would be delineated, so that the U.S. effort would go after not just the front-line deliverymen of roadside bombs, but also some of the commanders running the bomb factories, the keepers of safe houses in villages on the outskirts of Baghdad, the financiers sending in new funds and supplies, and the recruiters training people and sending them in across the Syrian border. In the fall, Centcom spent $11 million to create an intelligence architecture for this, a senior official in that headquarters said.

These steps were seen inside the Army as a major success story, and they were portrayed as such to journalists. Yet it was not so, even though it felt that way to many officers, probably to the majority of those involved. "In insurgencies, lots of things are counterintuitive," one expert who consulted with U.S. military intelligence in Iraq said later. That is, the move that seems reasonable may not actually be the wise one. For example, getting better intelligence was a laudable tactical goal, but launching an all-out offensive that used combat methods against the population to obtain it wasn't, because it undercut the larger strategic goal.

Sanchez later recalled in a legal statement growing out of the Abu Ghraib case, "I was having multiple intel updates, understanding that . . . our effectiveness against the insurgency was going to come from our ability to harvest human intelligence." This was a comment typical of commanders in Iraq, reflecting the view that U.S. forces were adept at executing strategy and tactics, and only needed better intelligence to act upon. "The only way you're going to get yourself inside of their decision cycle and their operating system is by getting individuals to talk," Sanchez said.

The problem was that the U.S. military, having assumed it would be operating in a relatively benign environment, wasn't set up for a massive effort that called on it to apprehend, detain, and interrogate Iraqis, to analyze the information gleaned, and then to act on it. "As commanders at all levels sought operational intelligence, it became apparent that the intelligence structure was undermanned, under-equipped and inappropriately organized for counter-insurgency operations," Lt. Gen. Anthony Jones wrote in an official Army report a year later.

One person in particular was squeezed between the heavy demands and the unprepared military: Brig. Gen. Barbara Fast, the top Army intelligence officer in Iraq. She was under huge pressure to revamp and improve her operation. In effect, she was being told that *she* was the weakest link. We are in a war, the feeling grew among commanders, and while our troops and tactics are doing a great job, and our commanders are great guys, still we are in trouble—so it must be because we have lousy intelligence.

The Army's recent history with female generals also complicated Fast's position. In 1997, Lt. Gen. Claudia Kennedy had been named chief of Army intelligence in what was seen by some subordinates as a gender promotion—that is, a marginally competent officer given her high position because the Army, in a political act, wanted to catch up with other services, which at that point were giving female officers three-star positions for the first time. Kennedy's major mark on the Army was made in 2000, when she became the first general ever to accuse another of sexually harassing her. In retirement she became politically active, and she toyed for a time with running for senator from Virginia, eventually deciding against it. She endorsed John Kerry in 2004 and appeared at the Democratic convention in Boston, along with some other retired generals. Fast, by contrast, was seen by peers as a smart operator who had earned her position. "She's one of the few people who was there under Sanchez who understood what was going on," said an intelligence officer who served under her, and who also found that she was willing to back up subordinates who took unpopular positions or delivered unwelcome news. "She clearly is better than anyone else in [the intelligence branch in] the general officer ranks of the Army."

The key to actionable intelligence was seen by many U.S. commanders as conducting huge sweeps to detain and question Iraqis. Sometimes units acted on tips, but sometimes they just detained all able-bodied males of combat age in areas known to be anti-American. The 4th Infantry Division, operating in the northern and northeastern parts of the Sunni Triangle, soon attracted attention among other commanders for its eager embrace of such tactics. Other commanders were more discriminating. The 82nd Airborne's Swannack said his division detained thirty-eight hundred people between August 2003 and March 2004, but screened them, and ultimately shipped only seven hundred of them to Abu

Ghraib. His staff was wary of the operation at the prison, he recalled: "They saw all these folks going into there, and it was hell to get them out of there. I had to personally intervene to get people out of there—they'd just get scarfed up."

Divided conquerors: the major U.S. unit commanders

Paradoxically, after focusing too much on the operational level in its invasion plan, the Army focused too little on it during its subsequent occupation, said retired Maj. Gen. Robert Scales, one of the Army's most insightful senior officers. Its battlefield orientation didn't prepare it to discern what the operational level was in a counterinsurgency. "The operational level of war in Iraq was dealing with Iraqis, with nongovernmental organizations, with the media, with the rest of the world," he said. "The center of gravity was the will of the people."

Again and again, the jobs that the Army failed to handle in Iraq in the summer and fall of 2003 would be in that crucial but neglected operational area of counterinsurgency, which simply means that no one was connecting all the dots. Supply convoys raced across the countryside to stock big U.S. bases, undercutting the larger effort, as drivers—worried U.S. troops or Third World contractors—shot at Iraqi civilians to make them keep their distance. Personal security details for CPA officials rocketed through Baghdad, forcing Iraqi cars onto sidewalks, needlessly alienating the capital's population. Frustrated combat troops used force first, violating a lesson of every successful modern counterinsurgency campaign: Violence is the tool of last resort, especially for troops foreign to the local population. Civil affairs officers, whose job it is to work with local populations, clashed frequently with the commanders of units they were supposed to support because of the different imperatives they faced, with little direction from higher levels of command.

All of these disparate areas were strands that should have been pulled together and coordinated by Gen. Sanchez, the commander with oversight of operations across Iraq. But he failed to do that. U.S. Army divisions operated like fingers without an operational hand or a strategic arm to guide them. Sanchez took a distant stance that gave each division commander leeway to handle the situation in his own area. Normally such decentralization would be welcome, but it works only if guided by a larger strategy that coordinates each unit's actions. In military shorthand, that direction is called the commander's intent. Sanchez didn't provide it. "I'm not sure that General Sanchez had any impact at all," said Hammes, who served with the CPA, one of his last posts before retiring. "I never got a clear commander's intent" statement from the commanding general.

Indeed, Sanchez's headquarters spent weeks debating a draft campaign plan but never issued one during his time there. One Army intelligence officer who served in Iraq in 2004 was even more emphatic. "For the first year of the war . . . there was no campaign plan issued to military personnel by CJTF-7 to deal with reconstruction of Iraq and to deal with the growing insurgency," he recalled. "Various units subordinate to CJTF-7 essentially did what they thought was the right thing to do, but their efforts were not coordinated by any clear, overarching campaign plan." The result, he said, was that "the divisions were kind of left out there to dry," by themselves.

Andrew Rathmell came to a similar conclusion. "The military leadership . . . did not do a good job of conceptualizing the campaign as an integrated political-military effort; sometimes failing to put tactical 'kinetic' operations in the broader political context." This meant that tactical successes never added up and reinforced each other, but rather tended to peter out by themselves.

In addition, the Army, having forgotten almost everything it had learned in the Vietnam War about counterinsurgency, hadn't taught its commanders in such a way that they would arrive at similar and reinforcing answers to the tactical problems they faced. When Maj. Gregory Peterson studied the issue a few months later at Fort Leavenworth's School of Advanced Military Studies, an elite course that trains military planners and strategists, he found the American experience in Iraq in 2003–4 remarkably similar to the French war in Algeria in the 1950s. Both involved Western powers exercising sovereignty in Arab states, both powers were opposed by insurgencies contesting that sovereignty, and both wars were controversial back home. Most significant for Peterson's analysis, he found both the French and U.S. militaries woefully unprepared for the task at hand. "Currently, the U.S. military does not have a viable counterinsurgency doctrine, understood by all soldiers, or taught at service schools," he concluded.

The result was that each sector felt like a separate war, with different approaches and rules, showing a lack of coordination that runs against the repeated findings of theorists and practitioners of counterinsurgency. French Col. Roger Trinquier's 1961 commentary on the lessons of Algeria is frequently disturbing, especially in its unabashed endorsement of torture in interrogation and its general embrace of terrorist methods to fight terrorism. But the veteran paratroop commander is more persuasive when he echoes other experts in his discussion of the absolute necessity of strategic coordination in putting down an insurgency.

The struggle against the guerrilla is not, as one might suppose, a war of lieutenants and captains. The number of troops that must be put into action, the vast areas over which they will be led to do battle, the necessity of coordinating diverse actions over these vast areas, the politico-military measures to be taken regarding the populace, the necessarily close cooperation with various branches of the civil administration—all this requires that operations against the guerrilla be conducted according to a plan, established at a very high command level. [Trinquier adds in a footnote: In principle, that of the commander of the theater of operations.]

It was common for observers of U.S. military operations in 2003–4 to note that each division's area of operations felt like a different war. In the north, Petraeus's 101st Airborne conducted what was generally seen as a thorough and effective operation, balancing war fighting and nation building. Just to the south, in the Sunni Triangle, there was an increasingly tough little war, especially in the area to the north and west of Baghdad where the 4th Infantry Division was based. The 82nd Airborne and the 3rd Armored Cavalry Regiment, operating to the west of Baghdad, posted a mixed record, with some successes and fewer mass detentions, but also with Fallujah, Ramadi, and the upper Euphrates Valley turning into increasingly tough problems. At the country's center, Baghdad became an area for a series of terrorist bombings.

"The good side of Rick Sanchez is, because all the division areas were different, he . . . kind of left us to figure out what he needed to do, and how to do it," said Swannack, who commanded the 82nd Airborne Division in Iraq twice—first in the invasion in the spring of 2003, and then in the fall and winter of 2003–4. Sanchez didn't offer much strategic guidance, he said. "It was pretty much, 'You do what you need to do, and I'll give you the resources.'" He would try to raise tough issues with Sanchez by e-mail, but sometimes never received a response. "I don't know why. Responsiveness to division commanders' issues was weak."

"I never got a visit from anyone from CJTF-7 staff," concurred Maj. Gen. Odierno, who commanded the 4th Infantry Division in the northern Sunni Triangle. "Sanchez visited me once," he added, holding up a lone index finger.

Arguably, that hands-off approach made some sense, because conditions differed so radically in the north and south, and compared to the Sunni belt across the center of the country. But it also led to a kind of incoherence in the effort, and worse still, to the use of tactics that undercut long-term goals. "Failing to define at the strategic levels the kind of war we were actually fighting—and in various locales, battles civilian and military forces were actually winning—unintentionally

left many of those local efforts without a higher, guiding, and legitimizing purpose," Maj. Isaiah Wilson later commented.

Petraeus jumps through a window of opportunity

Mosul, the biggest city in northern Iraq, could have erupted at any moment in
2003. As a U.S. military intelligence analysis warned at the outset of the invasion,
Mosul came with a ready-made civil war, hosting some 110,000 former Iraqi army
soldiers and 20,000 Kurdish militiamen happy to fight them. It also was the home
base of the Iraqi Islamic Party, which had survived Saddam's efforts to crush it.
The city overflowed with potential enemies of the U.S. occupation, so much so
that Saddam Hussein's sons, Uday and Qusay, chose it as their hiding place.

Despite that troublesome lineup, of all the divisions occupying Iraq in
2003–4, it was the 101st Airborne, commanded by Maj. Gen. David Petraeus and
headquartered in Mosul, that was most successful in launching an effective counterinsurgency campaign. "The 101st under Maj. Gen. Petraeus is considered most
successful in terms of jump-starting the economy and the political process,"
concluded a 2004 Army War College study.

Mosul and northern Iraq under Petraeus in 2003 offer a glimpse of how the
occupation of Iraq might have been conducted more effectively, and in such a
way that the hopes of bringing home most U.S. troops relatively soon might have
been realized. There was no postinvasion pause in the north. Because the pace of
U.S. operations never sagged, there was no breather in which the adversary could
gain the initiative. "The eerie silence and absence of U.S. military operational activity that defined the immediate weeks and months of transition . . . [were] not
present in the northern provinces. There was no hiatus (no 'cease fire') in the
north," commented Wilson, who served in Iraq first as an Army historian and
then as a strategist for Petraeus.

Petraeus had more education about counterinsurgency operations than any
other division commander in Iraq. During the 1980s he had earned a Ph.D. in
international relations at Princeton, where his dissertation subject had been the
effect of the Vietnam War on U.S. military thinking about the use of force. In the
course of his research he had read deeply into the French experience in Indo-
china. While the French didn't win there or in Algeria, the vanquished often learn
more from a war than do the victors. "Counterinsurgency operations, in particular, require close civil-military cooperation," Petraeus wrote in his study. He
warned against U.S. military attitudes that impeded "the crucial integration of

political and military strategies." Also, he noted that the use of force may be necessary, but by itself "it is seldom sufficient."

Petraeus also took quiet steps to ensure unity of command in his area—a fundamental military principle, to be sure, but something that the U.S. effort overall didn't enjoy. Unity was particularly important in the intelligence arena, where he had his chief of staff, Col. James Laufenburg, pull together several divergent intelligence elements by creating a joint interagency task force for counterterrorism—an effort made easier because the CIA officer in Mosul was a former subordinate of Petraeus's with whom he had kept in touch. To ensure that all worked together, Petraeus also fired a warning shot across the bow of the "black" Special Operators in the 101st's area. "We're delighted to have you with us," he told them, "but if you conduct operations without first getting our approval, I'll request your removal from our area of operations." He took pride in conducting targeted raids with a minimum of violence. In one, 101st troops and a Special Operations unit went after thirty-five suspects simultaneously in Mosul at 2:00 A.M. and caught twenty-three of those they were after, with only a single shot fired.

Petraeus said that his role was "a combination of being the president and the pope." Others saw his role as somewhat less elevated. "Petraeus, up north, was like a politician—he bought everyone off," said Kellogg, the retired Army general who served as a senior CPA official.

"Plainly stated, the 101st Airborne waged a different war in the north than was waged in other parts of the country," Maj. Wilson wrote. "Winning the hearts and minds of the Iraqi people was the guiding purpose of all civil-military actions in the north." While other divisions conducted "*anti*-insurgency" operations, aimed at killing the enemy, he concluded, the 101st waged a "*counter*-insurgency" campaign, meant to undercut support for the enemy.

Petraeus's campaign began pretty much as did those of other division commanders. "When we arrived in Mosul, it was chaotic," he said. "I mean, there was no order. There was no police on the street, they were looting, they were looting everything they could put their hands on. The province governate building was completely sacked. We went into Mosul with real force, huge, sixteen hundred soldiers in a single lift, I think the longest air assault in history, [and] established really overwhelming force in the city." The first week saw a spate of small firefights. But by the end of that time the 101st "had established a position of real dominance." He was determined to capitalize on that position. "We had, in a sense, almost a degree of omnipotence, and you had to exploit that—the window of opportunity is there, you had to jump through it."

He and his planners knew that they were in "a race against time. We were very conscious that any army of liberation has a half-life connected to it, where it turns into an army of occupation. And what we wanted to do, of course, was to extend that half-life as long as we possibly could, by good deeds and by getting the word out on those good deeds."

The story that Petraeus tells with some pride about this period involves not a firefight or a raid but how he ensured that government employees were paid. The 101st had picked up a rumor that the manager of a major bank in Mosul had saved a huge amount of Iraqi government money from being looted. The cash was in an underground vault that had been purposely flooded to protect it, with the stacks of currency sealed in plastic. Petraeus had the manager brought to him and sat across a table from him. "I understand you were able to safeguard some money," he began.

The Iraqi leaned forward and said softly, "Yes, I did."

"I understand you have enough to pay the salaries of the government workers," Petraeus said.

"Yes, we do," the banker confirmed.

Great, thought the general. "Let's go ahead and do it," he said, "let's pay the workers."

The banker shrugged. "I'd love to, but I don't have the authority," he replied.

"Who has the authority?" Petraeus asked.

"Baghdad, the minister of finance," the Iraqi said.

"Well, sorry to inform you, I was just down in Baghdad, and there really is no ministry of finance functioning at this point," Petraeus said.

"Yes, that's too bad," the banker sadly agreed.

"Well, what are we going to do?" Petraeus politely asked. It was an insightful question to pose. Had he had wanted to, Petraeus simply could have ordered his combat engineers to blow the door off the safe and take the money. But, thinking strategically, he was searching for Iraqi solutions to the problems he encountered.

"Well, you have the authority," the banker finally said.

"You're right," Petraeus agreed. He had learned what the banker needed. So Petraeus pulled out a sheet of his stationery, which stated on its letterhead that he was "Commanding General, 101st Airborne Division (Air Assault)," and wrote out an order telling the banker to meet the government payroll.

The banker read over the order, then looked up, a mite skeptical. "What, no seal?" he asked. The Americans hadn't known that Iraqi officials always applied official seals to documents. The next day Petraeus sent an aide to find an Iraqi shop to make an official seal of the Commanding General, 101st Airborne, replete with the two stars of a major general.

Petraeus and his subordinate commanders and staff devised a strategy based on three principles. First, "this is a race against time." Second, "the real goal is to create as many Iraqis as possible who feel they have a stake in the new Iraq," which created a yardstick by which to measure any proposed move: Will it give Iraqis a stake? The third principle governed the division's tactics: "Will this operation produce more bad guys than it takes off the street by the way it's conducted?" Understanding this, one of the 101st's company commanders, Capt. Daniel Morgan, recalled that he decided to handle detainees differently than they were treated elsewhere. "My company did not blindfold our detainees. We did upon arrival into Mosul, but we realized within a month—June 2003—that this was of no significance, and hurt us."

Petraeus also decided that cordon and sweep operations, in which every military-age male in a given area was rousted, were pointless. He thought most Iraqi men, even insurgents, so valued their household privacy that they would surrender peacefully rather than subject their families to intrusive nighttime searches. So he had the 101st conduct cordon and knock searches, in which suspects were surrounded and then invited to turn themselves in. In addition, he said, there were so many phony tips passed by Iraqis feuding with each other that this softer approach helped sort out those tips without unnecessarily insulting Iraqi dignity.

During the summer of 2003, a common rumor among Iraqis was that the night-vision goggles used by American troops could enable them to peer through the clothes of women. When a brigade commander in the 101st, Col. Ben Hodges, heard this from sheikhs in his area, rather than just tell them it was false, he decided to show them by putting on an exhibition where a variety of U.S. military observation and imaging devices would be laid out for them to examine and use. The 101st staff laughingly referred to this as the First Annual Tigris River Valley Sheikhfest—and then was pleasantly surprised to see the meeting repeated and evolve into a formal Tigris River Valley Commission in which regional issues could be discussed every month.

A summary written by the staff of the 101st Airborne noted that by January of 2004, the north of Iraq appeared in remarkably good shape. There was an average of just five "hostile contacts"—bombs, ambushes, drive-by shootings—a day in the division's operating area. That figure included attacks not just on U.S. troops but also on Iraqi security forces. By contrast, there were about twenty-five meetings a day between commanders in the division and local Iraqi leaders or managers of key facilities.

But the city would encounter far more trouble after the 101st went home in the spring of 2004 and was replaced by a far smaller, less effective unit. Not all officers thought that Petraeus was blameless for that. "He had eighteen thousand soldiers up there, and the enemy was just biding its time and building capacity, waiting him out," argued one skeptical military intelligence officer. That view seems unfair: Mosul was quiet while Petraeus was there, and likely would have remained so had his successor had as many troops as he had—and as much understanding of counterinsurgency techniques. Also, it is notable that the population-oriented approach Petraeus took in Mosul in 2003 would be the one the entire U.S. Army in Iraq was trying to adopt in 2006.

Divisions go their own way

To the west of Baghdad, Maj. Gen. Charles Swannack got mixed reviews for being aggressive but "very selective," recalled Keith Mines. "They didn't just go bouncing around." But, he told his family at the time in an e-mail, "their answer to everything is more firepower, while my answer to most everything is to get them back in their barracks and send me out with a suitcase of money."

In the capital itself, the 1st Armored Division was led by Brig. Gen. Martin Dempsey, who generally was seen as handling a difficult job well, under the global spotlight of Baghdad.

North of Baghdad, Odierno's 4th Infantry Division operated in the northern part of the Sunni Triangle. His unit proved to be almost the opposite of Petraeus's 101st Airborne. As the Marines had suspected when turning over the area north of Baghdad, Odierno and his division would take a combative posture in Iraq. "Odierno, he hammered everyone," said Kellogg, the retired Army general who was at CPA. Odierno's brigades and battalions earned a reputation for being overly aggressive. Again and again, internal Army reports and commanders in interviews said that this unit—a heavy armored division, despite its name—used ham-fisted approaches that may have appeared to pacify its area in the short term, but in the process alienated large parts of the population.

"The 4th ID was bad," said one Army intelligence officer who worked with them. "These guys are looking for a fight," he remembered thinking. "I saw so many instances of abuses of civilians, intimidating civilians, our jaws dropped."

"Fourth ID fueled the insurgency," added an Army psychological operations of-

ficer. He said that it frequently was manipulated by the insurgents into firing at innocent civilians. "Guys would come up from Fallujah, set up next to a farmhouse, set
off a mortar, and leave. And the 4th ID would respond with counterbattery fire. The
4th ID's CG [commanding general] fostered that attitude. They were cowboys."

"They are going through neighborhoods, knocking on doors at two in the
morning without actionable intelligence," said a senior officer. "That's how you
create new insurgents."

A general who served in Iraq, speaking on background, said flatly, "The 4th
ID—what they did was a crime."

But on most days there were relatively few outside observers watching the 4th
ID. It was operating in the dank palm groves and the hot, dusty towns of the
Tigris River Valley north of Baghdad, an area that was never welcoming for reporters and that grew increasingly difficult for civilian or military travel in the fall
of 2003 and after. In one of his letters home, Lt. Col. Steve Russell, a battalion
commander in the 4th ID, offered his rationale for the strong-arm tactics he
sometimes employed. "We would not win the people of Tikrit over," he said.
"They generally hate us. We are kind and compassionate to those that work with
us but most detest us as a general rule. But they do respect power. Some have
questioned our forcefulness but we will not win them over by handing out
lollipops—not in Tikrit. Too many of my bloodied men bear witness to this.
They are the 'Beer Hall' crowd of Munich in 1945."

Lt. Col. David Poirier, who commanded an MP battalion attached to the 4th
Infantry Division and was based in Tikrit from June 2003 to March 2004, said
that the division's approach was indiscriminate. "With the brigade and battalion
commanders, it became a philosophy: 'Round up all the military-age males, because we don't know who's good or bad.'" He recalled that one brigade commander
in the 4th ID "blew up a house a guy was building" and called it a "demonstration
of force." Poirier was upset in part because the owner of the house had been helping him with operations in the nearby town of Samarra. "They didn't seem to
care," he recalled.

Col. Alan King, who had moved from the 3rd ID to the CPA, had a similar impression of the 4th ID's approach. "Every male from sixteen to sixty" that the
4th ID could catch was detained, he said. "And when they got out, they were supporters of the insurgency."

"It is not black and white," Odierno said at a meeting of the Association of the
U.S. Army. Being too gentle also carried risks, he implied. "We'd go in, do a raid on
a house, and we wouldn't search any of the families, and as we were leaving, they

would hand weapons from under their dresses to their men, who would shoot at us." So, he said, "yeah, initially, we probably made some mistakes." But, he continued, "we adapted quickly." One of the problems, he added, was that only one side in the fighting—his—was required to play by rules. "They were not constrained." He elaborated on his views in an article in the Army's *Field Artillery* magazine. He made the point, worth noting, that his troops faced a population more hostile than in the rest of Iraq: "From June 2003 to January 2004, we had three times more than the combined number of attacks in the rest of the Iraqi theater."

He wrote that he often responded with heavy firepower. "We used our Paladins [155 millimeter self-propelled howitzer systems] the entire time we were there," he said. "Most nights we fired H&I fires [harassment and interdiction, meant to stop the enemy from being able to operate freely], what I call 'proactive' counter-fire." His conclusion was that "artillery plays a significant role in counterinsurgency operations." That assertion is at odds with the great body of successful counterinsurgency practice, which holds that firepower should be as restrained as possible, which is difficult to do with the long-range, indirect fire of artillery.

The decentralization under Lt. Gen. Sanchez sometimes extended even further down, to the levels of brigades and battalions. In the 4th Infantry Division in particular, noticed an Army intelligence officer, there were two brigade commanders whose sectors were side by side in the Sunni Triangle yet used vastly different approaches. On the west bank of the river, around Samarra and Balad, was Col. Frederick Rudesheim. "Rudesheim said, 'I really want to support civil affairs.' He gave them augmentation [additional troops], security. He said that civil affairs was his bread and butter." Meanwhile, on the east side of the Tigris River, around Baqubah, Col. David Hogg was operating on a war footing that focused much more on action against the insurgents and intimidation of others. Targeting insurgent mortar positions, he said, "Hogg was firing H&I every night, and he didn't have a lot of time for civil affairs." (Hogg confirmed that during July 2003, he had fired some 160 rounds of 155 millimeter high-explosive artillery shells and 40 heavy 120 millimeter mortar rounds, but didn't respond to requests for a follow-up interview.)

Hogg said that his forces were there to "kill the enemy, not to win their hearts or minds," recalled Maj. Christopher Varhola, an Army Reserve specialist in civil affairs who worked in a large swath of Iraq.

Bombs vs. sweeps in the Sunni Triangle

The insurgency remained all but invisible except during its attacks. It issued no statements. Unlike other insurgencies, such as in Algeria in the 1950s, it had no visible leaders or spokesmen, no diplomatic offices operating in friendly Arab capitals. All that was really known of it was its location and tactics. Most of the insurgency was in the Sunni Triangle, the area dominated by Sunni Muslims—who were a minority in Iraq but had ruled the country for decades—that extended west of Baghdad to Ramadi and then up the Euphrates River, north from the capital along the Tigris to Samarra and Bayji, and northeast to Baqubah. Tactically, the insurgency was generally low tech.

The U.S. wasn't a colonial power in Iraq, seeking to hold on to a restive province, but it sometimes acted like one. "This is the way an administration caught with its plans down habitually reacts under such circumstances," Alistair Horne wrote in *A Savage War of Peace*, the classic history of the French war in Algeria in the 1950s. "Whether it be the British in Palestine, Cyprus or Northern Ireland, the Portuguese in Mozambique, or the French in Indo-China. First comes the mass indiscriminate round-up of suspects, most of them innocent but converted into ardent militants by the fact of their imprisonment."

Compare Horne's words to those of the International Committee of the Red Cross in describing the way U.S. troops conducted cordon and sweep operations in Iraq.

Arresting authorities entered houses usually after dark, breaking down doors, waking up residents roughly, yelling orders, forcing family members into one room under military guard while searching the rest of the house and further breaking doors, cabinets and other property. They arrested suspects, tying their hands in the back with flexicuffs, hooding them, and taking them away. Sometimes they arrested all adult males present in a house, including elderly, handicapped and sick people. Treatment often included pushing people around, insulting, taking aim with rifles, punching and kicking and striking with rifles. Individuals were often led away in whatever they happened to be wearing at the time of arrest—sometimes in pyjamas [*sic*] or underwear—and were denied the opportunity to gather a few essential belongings, such as clothing, hygiene items, medicine or eyeglasses.

Through their lack of discrimination, such tactics tend to have powerful unintended negative political effects on the population. Not only do they alienate those affected, they also show that the military force conducting the operation is ignorant, because supportive and neutral natives are caught up with hostile ones. "This does two things," concluded a 2005 study by Hicks & Associates, a small but influential Pentagon consulting firm. "For potential government collaborators, it makes them less sure that the government will protect them from harm. For potential insurgents, it makes them less worried that they will be caught if they join the insurgents."

Family members were sometimes taken into captivity to force suspects to turn themselves in. "The families know what's going on," Col. Hogg said one day in late July 2003, standing in the ankle-deep khaki-colored dust at the front gate of his base and wearing his full battle gear of body armor, helmet, and pistol. "So we picked up the family of a Republican Guard lieutenant general last night," he said, puffing on a Dominican cigar. "He wasn't there. We brought in his wife and daughter, and left him a note: 'We know where you are. We know what car you drive. If you want your family released, turn yourself in.'" This really wasn't hostage taking, he contended. "It's an intelligence operation with detainees"—pointing toward a difference that wasn't immediately apparent. "These people have information. The wife denied her husband was in the military until we showed her his general's uniform."

Hogg oversaw a typical sweep one day in late July, on a hunt for Taha Yasin Ramadan, a relatively low-ranking member of the U.S. government's most-wanted list. On the deck of cards designed to familiarize U.S. troops with those fugitive leaders, Ramadan, who had provided security for higher ranking members of the regime, was designated the ten of diamonds. He owned a walled compound of about sixteen one- and two-story buildings in a sprawling palm plantation on the hot, humid lowlands on the east bank of the Tigris, just west of the small town of al Jadidah. The temperature was 108°F, and the settlement felt like a village lost in the jungle. The raid began with two buglike OH-58 Kiowa helicopters darting over the complex, on the lookout for fleeing men or counterattackers. There was a short burst of AK-47 fire in the distance—probably a prearranged warning signal, Hogg guessed. About 125 U.S. soldiers rolled into the compound. "We're not afraid, we didn't do anything," protested an elderly Iraqi man. The wives and children sat and watched while about two dozen men were rounded up, handcuffed with plastic flexicuffs, and placed under the branches of some apple trees.

The residences inside the compound were searched. The soldiers entered a rough one-story structure with unfinished walls of dark cement. A middle-aged woman dressed in black and holding a baby met the soldiers in the living room with shouts. "Saddam is under my feet!" she wailed, looking at once terri-fied and angry. "Saddam is a dog!" She wiped a tear from her cheek with the heel of her hand.

A soldier turned to an interpreter. "Tell her," he ordered, "that if her brother didn't do anything, he is coming back." Two other women stood in a corner, watching, and wept silently. A boy sat near them, wide-eyed.

First Sgt. Andre Harris, a twenty-two-year-veteran of the Army from Miami, stopped to shake his head in deep frustration at the difficulty of commu-nication. Regaining his equanimity, he said, "At the very minimum, we're making a statement."

Hogg poked his head into the room and encouraged the soldiers: "Remember, if you ain't fishing, you ain't catching."

Hogg's major complaint at the time was about the media's coverage of U.S. mili-tary operations, which he saw as negative. "I don't think they're fully reporting the success we're having," he said, genially. "We've put a lot of bad guys away, either through detaining or killing them. That is having a positive side effect with Iraqis, who are coming to us more, telling us more, working with us more." Like many commanders, Hogg thought the media just didn't understand how much progress had been made by the U.S. military. "I think we're fixing to turn the corner," he said that hot day in July 2003. "I think the operations over the next couple of weeks will get us there."

At the time, dozens of roundup operations like this were being conducted every day by U.S. forces. "The reality, at least in this company, is we've been doing raids and cordon searches nearly every day," said Capt. Brian Healey, who com-manded an infantry company in Hogg's brigade. "The past six weeks, our patrols have gotten more aggressive, more frequent. Instead of doing [that is, searching] just one house, for example, we'll do a whole street." That way, he noted, they could unearth weapons that an insurgent had asked or forced a neighbor to hide for him.

But there also was unease being expressed about this heavy-handed approach, both inside the U.S. military and among Iraqis talking to U.S. officers. "Hogg was an excellent brigade commander," recalled Lt. Col. Christopher Holshek, com-mander of the 402nd Civil Affairs Battalion, which moved to Baqubah that fall to work for Hogg. But Holshek thought that in the summer and fall of 2003, Hogg's tactics were unnecessarily aggressive, and even counterproductive. He said he tried a few times, unsuccessfully, to figure out how to make that case. "In places like Fallujah and Baqubah, tactical commanders began to learn when conducting raids and sweeps that, in the process of kicking down doors in the middle of the night to find 'bad guys' (and often kicking down the wrong doors), entering the private space of the house where the women and children were, then tying up and interrogating (i.e., humiliating) the man in the house in front of his family, the premier cultural value of family honor was violated," Holshek later wrote.

Hallenbeck remembered being taken aside by a sheikh in Mosul. The Iraqi leader emphasized that he considered it essential for the Americans to succeed. "If you leave," he told Hallenbeck, "my Mercedes will be right behind the last truck in your convoy." He knew he wouldn't survive without them. "But damn it," the sheikh continued, "you have got to stop these middle-of-the-night knock-on-the-door searches, throwing people on the ground, making them see red."

"Many of the arrests were done with a boot on the head, in front of his woman," said Hammes. "You've created a blood debt when you do that."

A year later, an official Pentagon investigation would come to much the same conclusion. "Line units conducting raids found themselves seizing specifically targeted persons, so designated by military intelligence," the Pentagon's Schlesinger report found. "But lacking interrogators and interpreters to make precise distinctions in an alien culture and hostile neighborhoods, they reverted to rounding up any and all suspicious-looking persons—all too often including women and children. The flood of incoming detainees contrasted sharply with the trickle of released individuals." This indiscriminate approach actually hindered the American goal of improving intelligence, the report noted: "Processing was overwhelmed. Some detainees at Abu Ghraib had been held 90 days before being interrogated the first time."

The results of U.S. tactics

The U.S. military was badly prepared for handling a flood of prisoners. By late autumn, Abu Ghraib contained some ten thousand prisoners. U.S. military intelligence officials later estimated that most of those detained were more or less innocent, and that the vast majority—perhaps 90 percent—had no intelligence value. The detention facilities available were so limited, Sanchez said in a legal statement, "that you had to put them all in there, and it was this challenge of having, at any given time, ten to twelve [thousand], 13,000 of these people that had to be segregated and isolated and prioritized and interrogated in order for us to be able to identify the way these cells were working."

What wasn't widely understood at the time, or even now outside the military, is that the overcrowding at the prison, and some of the resulting lapses in supervision, resulted directly from tactical decisions made by Sanchez and his division commanders, most notably the 4th ID's Gen. Odierno. In the fall of 2003 they were stuffing Abu Ghraib with thousands of detainees, the majority of them bystanders caught up in the sweeps.

When Fast, the top Army intelligence officer in Iraq, questioned the 4th ID's indiscriminate approach, she was told by its intelligence officer that Odierno didn't care, according to a subsequent Army report. "The division commander did not concur with the release of detainees for fear that a bad one may be released along with the good ones," Maj. Gen. George Fay wrote.

Fast said in a statement to investigators that Odierno's attitude was "We wouldn't have detained them if we wanted them released." (Odierno said in an interview that he remembers saying that the intelligence people in Baghdad needed to develop a system so that before they released people, they checked with the division, because his division had caught at least ten suspected insurgents who had been sent to Baghdad and then released. "What I said was, 'When we sent them to Baghdad we thought they were bad guys, so if you want to release them, please ask us.'")

Brig. Gen. Karpinski, the reserve MP officer overseeing detentions across Iraq, drew a distinction between the operations run by Swannack and Odierno. "Mobile interrogators" attached to each division were supposed to interview and screen detained Iraqis, shipping to the Abu Ghraib prison only those who offered the prospect of having some intelligence value. "The 82nd's interrogators did it right," she said in 2005. "They'd interview twenty-five and send three to me. Odierno's guys would grab twenty-five, and send twenty-five, or fifty, by including a bunch from his holding pen. The 82nd was the best. Petraeus was pretty good. But the 1st AD would send a lot, and the 4th ID was the worst." (During its first, yearlong tour in Iraq, the 4th ID would detain about ten thousand Iraqis, of whom Gen. Odierno estimated it sent between one thousand to two thousand to Abu Ghraib, which seems low, given the total prisoner numbers cited by Sanchez.)

Sanchez, frustrated by his puzzling enemy, on September 14 approved twenty-nine interrogation techniques to be used at the prison and elsewhere. It was the first time that an interrogation policy had been set in Iraq by the U.S. military, another reflection of the lack of expectation of an insurgency. His memorandum listed a dozen interrogation techniques not in standard usage by the Army, five more even than were being used at Guantánamo Bay. Even in approving them, his memorandum noted that other countries believed that the detainees were prisoners of war, and that some of the methods being discussed were inconsistent with the Geneva Conventions governing their treatment. Centcom reviewed his decision, and a month later scaled it back, telling him it was "unacceptably aggressive," according to a subsequent Pentagon inquiry. He was told to drop ten of the twenty-nine interrogation procedures he had approved. His superseding memo incorporating that order was issued on October 12.

Friendly fire worsens Fallujah's woes

As the war intensified in the summer, it brought with it a series of incidents in which newly wary U.S. troops fired on civilians, such as carloads of families hurrying to get home before curfew. A Reuters cameraman was killed because a soldier thought the device on his shoulder, seen from a distance, looked like a launcher for a rocket-propelled grenade. In the most consequential of these incidents, on September 12, a platoon from the 82nd Airborne mistakenly became embroiled in a night firefight with Iraqi police near Fallujah. Eight Iraqi police officers died in the clash, which was caused by a lack of coordination with the police and their shortage of proper equipment. A BMW had shot up a police station. Iraqi police gave chase in a truck and passed American troops; then, giving up, they turned around. When the truck, which had a heavy machine gun mounted on it, made its U turn, the platoon thought it was coming under attack. Eventually, Jordanian police working at a nearby hospital also got involved.

Iraqi police interviewed later by reporters said they had tried desperately to get the Americans to stop. Thousands of rounds of ammunition, many of them heavy caliber, were fired, according to *Stars & Stripes,* the U.S. military newspaper. "They shot at us for about an hour," Sgt. Assem Mohammed, one of the police officers, said later, while recovering from a gunshot wound at Fallujah General Hospital. "They kept firing, and we kept shouting at them, 'We are police! We are police!'" In the course of the three-way firefight—which involved U.S., Iraqi, and Jordanian police, who were all ostensibly allies—a good part of the nascent Fallujah police force was killed.

"It was the deadliest friendly-fire incident in the six-month-old occupation, and it left tremendous bitterness on both sides," wrote Bing West, the defense analyst who spent months observing U.S. operations in Anbar province.

In the weeks after that, Kipling, the MP officer, recalled, the Iraqi police frequently were wary of U.S. troops. "More than once the Iraqi police would say something along the lines of 'You and your soldiers are okay, but those others are dangerous,'" she said.

In the wake of the incident, Keith Mines tried to get the attention of his superiors. He had arrived in the province in midsummer, somewhat concerned about the direction of the occupation, but still believing that it could be put right. The diplomat, a former Special Forces officer, knew that in counterinsurgencies, the solutions tended not to be military. "Police, [electric] power and political process," he wrote to his family in August. "That is what will fix this place, and if we give them those three we can get the heck out of here." But that wasn't the path the occupation would take. By September Mines began to turn pessimistic. "The president has received some profoundly bad advice on this, and unfortunately the same people who gave him bad advice to begin with are the ones trying to help dig him out," he wrote in a depressed letter to a State Department colleague. "Things are as bad as the press reports and quite frankly I don't see how with our current strategy it is going to work."

In the Iraqi view, the incident outside Fallujah was just the latest U.S. military blow to Iraqi dignity, Mines noted in a subsequent memo to the CPA and the staff of the 82nd Airborne. "Al Anbar's sheikhs are expressing increasing resentment over what they perceive as lack of respect for them by the coalition," he wrote on September 18. "Between detentions, arbitrary and often destructive house searches, and the recent killing of coalition-sanctioned police officers by coalition forces, the Anbar sheikhs say they are tired of not receiving the respect that their traditional position should convey."

A hardening of views

Back in the United States the split in the views of the situation in Iraq also was deepening. In the fall of 2003, Anthony Zinni began speaking out again, bitterly denouncing Rumsfeld, criticizing the Iraq occupation, and saying it lacked a coherent strategy, a serious plan, and sufficient resources. "There is no strategy or mechanism for putting the pieces together," he told a gathering of the U.S. Naval Institute and the Marine Corps Association in Crystal City, Virginia, within walking distance of the Pentagon. "We're in danger of failing." The situation was worse than the newspapers had been portraying it, he told his audience. He mocked the premature celebration of victory against a weak Iraqi military: "Ohio State beat

Slippery Rock sixty-two to nothing. No shit." Yet now, he said, the jihadis were flocking to Iraq from around the Mideast. "We need to seal the borders"—a view that the Pentagon would come to endorse more than a year later.

The U.S. military was unbeatable at fighting but not much good at the larger task, Zinni said. "We are great at the tactical problems—the killing and the breaking. We are lousy at the strategic part." Nor should the Pentagon be overseeing the occupation. "Why the hell would the Department of Defense be the organization in our government that deals with the reconstruction of Iraq?" he asked. "Doesn't make sense."

Underscoring how much his views had changed since he had endorsed the Bush-Cheney ticket in 2000, Zinni implied that the Bush administration was damaging the U.S. military in the way that Bush and Cheney, during the 2000 election campaign, had charged the Clinton administration with doing. "We can't go on breaking our military and doing things like we're doing now," he said. "It kills me when I hear of the casualties and the sacrifice that's being made," especially because the casualties are being suffered because "some policy wonk back here had a brain fart of an idea of a strategy."

Invoking the most emotional of comparisons for U.S. military officers of his generation, he ended by warning that Iraq was beginning to feel to him like the Vietnam War. "My contemporaries, our feelings and sensitivities were forged on the battlefields of Vietnam, where we heard the garbage and the lies, and we saw the sacrifice," said Zinni. "We swore never again would we allow that to happen. I ask you, Is it happening again?" There were hundreds of Marine and Navy officers present, and many of those present rose to give his denunciation of their civilian leaders a standing ovation.

From the perspective of top U.S. officials, things were going far better than Zinni suggested. At about the same time that he was speaking in Washington, Rumsfeld flew out to Iraq, where his tour turned into a concentrated attack on the media's coverage of events there. At the end of a long day, Rumsfeld, Bremer, and Sanchez met with reporters at Camp Victory, one of Saddam's palaces near the Baghdad airport.

Rumsfeld: There's so much reporting about Baghdad and so little about what's taking place in the rest of the country. . . . I feel that the progress in four or five months is breathtaking.

Bremer: Mr. Secretary, I would just add a little more on the point you made about the good news. Every day in this country there are dozens of success stories.

Schools were being built, he said, hospitals reopened, and local governments stood up.

> *Bremer:* Democracy is on the march in this country.
>
> *Rumsfeld:* And if you think about it, it happened in four or five months. Four or five months. Not four or five years. Four or five months. If one looks back at Germany, at Japan, at Bosnia or Kosovo, and measures the progress that's taken place in this country in four or five months, it dwarfs any other experience that I'm aware of.

At this point, Sanchez got with the spirit of the session.

> *Sanchez:* Mr. Secretary, ladies and gentlemen. It is very disturbing for me when I sit here every day and watch the news back home that focuses on the bad things that are occurring in Iraq, and I see my soldiers that have suffered either wounds or have gotten killed, and we're not paying the right credit to their sacrifices.

So, the general admonished the group of reporters,

> We need to capture the great news out there and make sure that America knows what her sons and daughters are doing and what the rest of the international community is doing here in Iraq.

A few days later, Wolfowitz struck a similar theme in a round of congressional testimony in support of an $87 billion budget supplement for spending on Iraq. He seemed to be saying that talking a good game was essential. "You know, confidence is part of winning," he told the Senate Armed Services Committee. "We need to project confidence. And we have every reason to project confidence, because we've done a fantastic job. We've liberated a country from a horrible dictator. We are cleaning up the remnants of that regime. We have the people with us."

Gen. Sanchez vs. Col. Spain

When Col. Teddy Spain thinks back on his year in Iraq, the one day that stands out, painfully, is October 17, 2003. What he dwells on isn't so much the nasty firefight with Iraqi militiamen—he was actually more than 60 miles away when that broke out the day before—but the confrontation afterward with Gen. Sanchez that helped him decide that he would leave the Army at the end of his tour.

The killings occurred in Karbala, one of the two cities in Iraq holy to Shiite Muslims. Lt. Col. Kim Orlando, commander of the 716th Military Police Battalion from Fort Campbell, Kentucky, was attached to the multinational division operating in southern Iraq and led by Poland; it had been put in that area because it was presumed to be quiet. Col. Spain, the military police commander in Baghdad, had worried that the battalion, which normally would come under his command, should be reporting to him. But he was told by Sanchez's staff that he didn't have tactical or operational control of the unit.

Recalling "that dicked-up frago," or fragmentary order, he said later, "I said, 'Bottom line, can I tell them what to do?' They said, 'No.' I said, 'Okay, got it, they don't belong to me.'" So he turned his attention to the units he actually still did command.

The south generally was quiet. But in early October there was a shootout between militias of two factions—one of them from the dominant Shiite group, led by Grand Ayatollah Ali Sistani, the single most powerful political figure in Iraq, and the other made up of followers of the upstart Shiite cleric Moqtadr al-Sadr. Lt. Col. Orlando was dispatched to investigate and ensure that curfews and other rules intended to curb violence were being followed. He was in a small patrol of three Humvees in the city near the compound of Mahmoud Hassani, a minor Shiite cleric, when he saw a large group of fighters lounging outside, their AK-47 assault rifles in hand. This was a violation of an understanding in the region about the amount of weaponry permitted to be displayed in public, Spain recalled—clerics were permitted bodyguards, but only in limited numbers.

Orlando got out of his Humvee and walked toward the fighters. "Look, you've been told, you can only have two AK-47s out front," he began saying, according to a subsequent Army inquiry.

One of the militiamen waved a hand at Orlando, signaling him and the two soldiers with him to lay down their weapons before coming closer. The Iraqi who was motioning swung his AK-47 upward, as if to fire. At that point, American soldiers said later, one of the Iraqis shot Orlando. One of Orlando's soldiers then shot that Iraqi. "Then all hell broke loose," 1st Sgt. Troy Wallen later said. Wallen had been standing next to Orlando. What felt to him like a planned ambush then unfolded, as Iraqi fighters on rooftops and in alleys and storefronts opened fire on the three Humvees.

A nearby Army convoy responded to the soldiers' call for help and opened fire, an unusual action in that it involved at least four female Army soldiers. They were members of an MP unit and so not officially front-line ground combat troops, as are infantry, armor, and artillery units. Pvt. Teresa Broadwell, a twenty-year-old Texan who wanted to be a modern dancer, opened up with an M-249 Squad Automatic Weapon, a light machine gun, from her turret atop an Army truck. Pvt. Tracie Sanchez, a thirty-year-old mother of four, began to follow suit but was hit in the helmet by a bullet and then knocked out of her turret by a grenade. Her face was peppered with shrapnel. Sgt. Misty Frazier, a twenty-five-year-old combat medic, ran from one wounded soldier to the next. It was the first time she'd heard hostile fire close up. Spec. Corrie Jones, twenty-seven, arrived as the shooting ended.

Three soldiers were down at the end of the short, sharp fight, either wounded or dead: Orlando and two members of his battalion, Staff Sgt. Joseph Bellavia and Cpl. Sean Grilley. Seven Iraqis were dead.

Spain was asleep in his headquarters near the Baghdad airport when he heard a knocking at his door at 12:30 in the morning. "Sir, I need you to wake up," his executive officer shouted from the hallway. She knew that he slept in his underwear and with a loaded weapon near his hand. "I need you to put down your pistol and put on your pants." In the hallway she gave him the sketchy information they had: There had been a firefight, Orlando had been injured but was talking in the Humvee on the way to be medevaced, and was going to make it. At two she woke him again: Orlando and the two others were dead. All three.

Spain felt sure that report was wrong, and stayed up the rest of the night in his headquarters trying to figure out where the miscommunication had occurred. When instead the report was confirmed, he called the battalion's executive officer and told him he was temporarily in command of the unit. He called back to the commandant of the MP school at Fort Leonard Wood, Missouri, and arranged for a new battalion commander to be shipped out as soon as possible. He felt that he was in unknown territory. "You train for a lot, but no one trains you to lose a battalion commander," he said later.

At 8:30 in the morning, Gen. Sanchez called. The general, three ranks higher than Spain, cut immediately to the point. "What intel did you have about Karbala?" Sanchez demanded, according to Spain.

"Sir, I don't know what you mean," Spain responded, a bit perplexed. "That's not an area in my control."

"Don't say that," Sanchez said. "What intel did you have?"

"I don't know," Spain said, growing alarmed at Sanchez's angry persistence. What did the general mean with this line of questioning?

"You come here in two hours and brief me on what intel you had," Sanchez ordered.

At precisely ten-thirty Spain arrived at the Green Zone, walked past the Marine standing guard outside Sanchez's office, and stood before the general. Sanchez thrust a sheaf of papers into Spain's hands. Spain looked down, but as he began to read about the warning of violence in Karbala, Sanchez yanked them back. "Did you know this?" Sanchez demanded.

Spain hadn't been able to read far enough to know precisely what was meant by "this." "Sir, as far as I can tell, from what I could read, no, I didn't," he said.

"That was your battalion," Sanchez said. "Why didn't you?"

Spain now began to understand where the general was going: He was going to blame Spain for the death of Orlando. "Sir," Spain said, "your staff told me that that battalion was not under my control."

"This was your battalion," Sanchez repeated.

Spain was close to losing his temper with the senior U.S. commander in Iraq. "Sir, if you are trying to make me feel any worse about losing a battalion commander, you can't," he said. The colonel and the general glared at each other. It felt like several minutes, Spain said later, but probably was just thirty seconds. He felt that Sanchez was waiting for him to speak, but worried that if he tried to argue further he would overstep the boundaries of military courtesy, especially with a superior officer. "I was smart enough to know that anything I could say would be wrong" in Sanchez's judgment, so he kept his mouth shut and stared into the general's eyes.

"Do you have anything to say?" Sanchez finally said.

"No, sir," Spain said.

"Get out of my office and go visit your battalion," Sanchez ordered.

It was the last one-on-one conversation Spain had with Sanchez in Iraq. He almost shuddered as he recounted the experience over a year later, in his southern Virginia home, having retired from the Army after leaving Iraq. "Lieutenant General Sanchez never did tell me what I should have known about what was going on in Karbala," he said. "To me, it was my worst experience in Iraq. That was, without a doubt, the worst day."

The Ramadan offensive

Unjustified optimism would prove to be one of the enduring characteristics of the U.S. management of the war. As late as mid-October 2003, as violence was spiking, top U.S. commanders were sketching plans for a troop drawdown in the summer of 2004, cutting from 130,000 to perhaps 100,000 in the summer of

2004, and half that by the following year. (In fact, in December 2005, the level would instead be substantially higher, at 159,000.) At the same time, they hoped, Iraqi security forces would be taking responsibility for patrolling the cities while U.S. forces moved offstage, where they would play a less obtrusive role as a quick reaction force to rescue Iraqi units that got into trouble. This phased series of troop reductions was in "the advanced stages of planning, but not yet approved" by Secretary Rumsfeld, a senior official said on October 17.

To others, that talk of troop cuts was unrealistic. "There was this big emphasis on troop reductions," said a civilian U.S. official who frequently interacted with the military at Green Zone meetings. "They should have been doing a risk assessment. Instead, in that October period, CJTF-7 was focused on planning the troop rotation and the reductions that would follow. To me, it was pretty clear that security had not been achieved. They hadn't done an adequate mission analysis—they should have gone back upstairs and said, 'The insurgency is strong, and growing stronger, and the need to train Iraqi security forces is huge, and we need to beef up our forces to give them the space to develop capacity.'"

On October 26, the night that the Muslim holy month of Ramadan began, PFC Rachel Bosveld, a nineteen-year-old MP from Wisconsin in Spain's unit, was at the Abu Ghraib police station, in the town near the prison, west of Baghdad. "A mortar came in, killed her, and blew the leg off another soldier," Spain recalled. Her death was significant for two reasons. First, it was barely noted: In a departure from past wars, the loss of forty-eight female soldiers from 2003 through 2005 hardly caused a ripple in American society.

But in terms of the history of the Iraq war, Bosveld's death is significant because it—along with a rocket attack a few hours later on the hotel inside the Green Zone where Wolfowitz was staying—marked the beginning of the insurgency's Ramadan offensive. This was the first time since the invasion that the foe turned fully on U.S. forces, bringing the highest rate of American fatalities since the spring. At 6:10 on the morning of Sunday, October 26, at least six rockets struck the al Rasheed Hotel, the CPA lodging inside the Green Zone. Wolfowitz, who was staying there during a quick visit, was uninjured, but an Army officer on the floor below him was killed. The rocket barrage likely was intended to get Wolfowitz, as was the downing of a Black Hawk helicopter near Tikrit the day before, just after his visit there. The attacks were militarily insignificant but politically meaningful: The insurgents had been able to reach into the heavily protected Green Zone and threaten the life of a senior U.S. official who had been instrumental in the drive to war.

In another action the same day with political significance, one of Baghdad's three deputy mayors, Faris Abdul Razzaq Assam, was assassinated by gunmen, who shot him in a café. The next morning, four police stations were bombed nearly simultaneously in Baghdad, some of them with trucks painted to look like police vehicles, each carrying one thousand pounds of plastic explosives. At a fifth station a bomb failed to detonate because the wire attaching it to the car battery had accidentally disconnected. The offices of the International Committee of the Red Cross also were hit, by a truck disguised as an ambulance. Altogether, more than thirty-five people were killed and hundreds wounded. "It was a horrible day, with a lot of children dying," said a former Special Forces soldier working on security issues in Iraq. "I felt like the whole city was blowing up, and I was thinking about Mogadishu."

Within a few days, another sad milestone had been passed: More U.S. troops had died in combat since May 1, when President Bush had declared major combat operations finished, than during the spring invasion. In an odd echo of his "Bring 'em on" comment in July, Bush—who was meeting with Bremer in the Oval Office—interpreted the insurgency's escalation as a sign of progress. "The more successful we are on the ground, the more these killers will react," Bush said, Bremer at his side. "The more progress we make on the ground, the more free the Iraqis become, the more electricity is available, the more jobs are available, the more kids that are going to school, the more desperate these killers become, because they can't stand the thought of a free society." (This prompted an officer to send off a reporter heading to Iraq with the warning, "Be careful, or you might become another sign of progress.")

"There are a lot of wonderful things that have happened since July," Bremer added. Sure, he said, there had been some "rough days." But "the good days outnumber the bad days. And that's the thing we need to keep in perspective."

Insurgent attacks grew both more numerous and more sophisticated during Ramadan 2003. In the summer there had been about ten to fifteen attacks on U.S. soldiers a day. By mid-October, that had doubled to twenty to thirty-five a day. By mid-November, as the Ramadan offensive was in full swing, they were peaking at forty-five a day. Also, for the first time, the insurgents began having success attacking aircraft. In late October, in an apparent attempt to target Wolfowitz while he was visiting, a UH-60 Black Hawk was brought down by insurgent fire; no one was killed. In early November a CH-47 Chinook was downed west of Baghdad, killing sixteen soldiers. A few days later another Black Hawk was hit near Tikrit, killing six. Later in the month two Black Hawks collided over Mosul as one tried to evade ground fire, killing seventeen soldiers from the 101st Airborne Division.

Also, attempts to down less vulnerable fixed-wing aircraft were stepped up, with missile and rocket launches at flights at the Baghdad airport. None was successful, but one came extraordinarily close, with a surface-to-air missile's destroying an engine on the left wing of a big DHL Airbus 300 cargo jet as it took off on November 21. Attacks in Baghdad also continued, with a series of rockets launched from donkey-pulled carts at the Oil Ministry and at the Sheraton and Palestine hotels, which were full of American contractors and reporters.

Publicly, U.S. commanders kept a "steady as she goes" attitude. "We think the insurgency is waning," Brig. Gen. Mark Hertling, who now was an assistant commander of the 1st Armored Division, told reporters in Baghdad on November 7. "The ones who continue to fight are losing their support." Hertling had been skeptical about some aspects of the invasion a year earlier, when he was on the staff of the Joint Chiefs of Staff. But now he was in combat, losing soldiers, and was determined to make their sacrifices worthwhile. "The majority of soldiers feel we are making progress every day, and we are beyond the hardest part," he said, speaking at Freedom Rest, his division's rest-and-recreation outpost in a former Iraqi officers' club in the Green Zone, where soldiers were sent for a few days of sleeping on hotel-quality sheets, sitting by the swimming pool, and generally pretending they weren't in Iraq.

But behind the scenes there was concern among commanders. In just two weeks, some sixty American soldiers had died. As the Ramadan offensive intensified, worry grew that the enemy would attempt to stage a spectacular series of attacks on Eid, the holiday that ends the holy month. "We believed there would be an Eid al-Fitr culmination, so it was a ramp-up to stop that," Swannack said later. In Anbar province, "we got their attention."

There was a new edge of toughness to the public comments of American officials at this time. On November 11, Rumsfeld, defining the situation quite differently than he had in June, told a television interviewer, "We're in a low-intensity war that needs to be won, and we intend to win it."

The same day, Sanchez told reporters in Baghdad, "We're going to get pretty tough. And that's what's necessary to defeat this enemy. And we're definitely not shy about doing that when it's required, and we will do that in a precise, intel-driven mode."

The next day both sides made major moves. A car bomb hit the Italian military headquarters in southern Iraq, killing eighteen Italians and eight Iraqis. It was the deadliest attack on a coalition partner of the U.S.-led occupation. It was also the greatest loss of life suffered by the Italian military since World War II.

On the U.S. side, the 1st Armored Division launched an operation in Baghdad called Iron Hammer that involved twenty-six artillery and mortar attacks and twenty-seven missions by strike aircraft. AC-130 gunships, which carry machine guns and a 105 millimeter cannon, began flying nightly missions over Baghdad. To curb the IED attacks, soldiers were ordered to shoot to kill anyone seen digging holes alongside roads at night. In Baqubah, Lt. Col. Mark Young, commander of a battalion in the 4th Infantry Division, said that more tonnage of munitions was used by his unit than ever before in Iraq. "This is to demonstrate one more time that we have significant firepower and can use it at our discretion," he said. To any American familiar with one of the most basic concepts of counterinsurgency campaigns—that they succeed when a minimum of firepower is employed—that was a troubling statement.

Holshek vs. Hogg in Baqubah

Lt. Col. Holshek, the civil affairs officer in Baqubah, was growing increasingly frustrated with attitudes like that, especially when he saw them displayed by his commander, the aggressive Col. Hogg. One day during a briefing in November, Holshek took the unusual step of challenging Hogg with a question. "Sir, what is the battlespace?" he asked.

For a tough combat commander like Hogg, the answer was self-evident: In conventional war, it usually is wherever you are fighting the enemy. "His answer was, basically, 'the bad guys,'" Holshek recalled.

"Sir, wrong answer," said Holshek, who with his shaved head looks a bit like a young Telly Savalas. Holshek was in a pushy New York mood that day, prodding Hogg to recognize that this wasn't a conventional war, it was something else altogether, and it needed to be fought as such. "In counterinsurgency," Holshek remembered telling the colonel, "the battlespace isn't physical, it's psychological. The battle is for the people."

Killing people really wasn't the point, he continued. "Bottom line is, you can kill every bad guy, and there will be two more tomorrow—until you start focusing on their support, active or passive, in the resident population." Holshek was saying that the Iraqi people were the prize in this fight, not the playing field. Here he was introducing Hogg to classic counterinsurgency doctrine, which holds that the objective is first to gain control of the population, and then win their support. What's more, he said, moving out onto even thinner ice with his boss, "your actions are having second- and third-order effects that will kill your soldiers down the road. I'm not selling Girl Scout cookies" (in other words, this isn't just so we can be nicer; this is so we can win). "I am here to keep your soldiers from getting killed." Hogg's tactics could wind up doing just that. He asked his commander to imagine himself the head of a household in an Iraqi village. "Two o'clock in the morning, your door bursts open. A bunch of infantry guys burst into the private space of the house—in a society where family honor is the most important thing—and you lay the man down, and put the plastic cuffs on? And then we say, 'Oops, wrong home?' In this society, the guy has no other choice but to seek restitution. He will do that by placing a roadside bomb for one hundred dollars, because his family honor has been compromised, to put it mildly." Simply to restore his own self-respect, the Iraqi would then have to go out and take a shot at American forces.

Another tactic Holshek argued against was the use of 155 millimeter high-explosive artillery fire to respond to mortar attacks on the base. "Sir, I'm not a maneuver guy," he recalled saying, "but the best way to respond to mortar fire is with boots on the ground—presence patrolling, work with the Iraqi cops, get the intel. Find out where it is, lie in ambush on the guy's two or three known firing points, and get the guy."

Hogg didn't say much during this lecture from a subordinate, or after it, but Holshek believed he absorbed it. Then, two weeks later, Hogg convened his operations officer, his information operations officer (actually an artillery officer detailed to handle that task), and Holshek, and said, "You guys need to fix this."

In the following weeks, the brigade's operations began to change. "He started to evolve," Holshek recalled. "He started to shift operations, started using my CA [civil affairs] teams more effectively." Hogg began to understand that when you make a mistake, you apologize, explain how it occurred, and give the householder one hundred dollars. "We had much better integration of CA with the maneuver units. We had CA on raids."

The wrong doors continued to be smashed on occasion, but when they were, Holshek would issue a letter that stated, "We are sorry for the intrusion, we are trying to help here, and it is a difficult business, and we sometimes make mistakes. If you have information that would help us, we would be grateful." The cash equivalent in dinars of one hundred dollars would accompany the note. Those gestures of regret didn't really win over Iraqis, Holshek recalled later, but he said he thought they did tend to tamp down anger, and so curtail acts of revenge.

Maj. Wilson, the historian and 101st planner, later concluded that much of the firing on U.S. troops in the summer and fall of 2003 consisted of honor shots, intended not so much to kill Americans as to restore Iraqi honor. "Honor and pride lie at the center of tribal society," he wrote. In a society where honor equals power, and power ensures survival, the restoration of damaged honor can be a matter of urgency. But that didn't mean that Iraqis insulted by American troops necessarily felt they had to respond lethally, Wilson reflected. "Honor that is lost or taken must be returned by the offender, through ritualistic truce sessions, else it will be taken back through force of arms." In Iraq this sometimes was expressed in ways similar to the American Indian practice of counting coup, in which damaging the enemy wasn't as important as demonstrating that one could. So, Wilson observed, an Iraqi would take a wild shot with a rocket-propelled grenade, or fire randomly into the air as a U.S. patrol passed. "Often the act of taking a stand against the 'subject of dishonor' is enough to restore the honor to the family or tribe," whether or not the attack actually injured someone, he wrote. "Some of the attacks that we originally saw as 'poor marksmanship' likely were intentional misses by attackers pro-progress and pro-U.S., but honor-bound to avenge a perceived wrong that U.S. forces at the time did not know how to appropriately resolve." But U.S. troops assumed simply that the Iraqis were bad shots.

Tactics: force vs. effectiveness

Counterproductive tactics, like the ones Holshek confronted Hogg about, were all too common in the U.S. military in 2003, and well into 2004. "Heard a horror story this afternoon," Marine Col. T. X. Hammes wrote in his diary one evening.

They had been taking sniper fire from a building for six nights. So that day, they send a civic action team to the high-rise building it came from and they ordered everyone to evacuate because the building was going to be destroyed. That night, two AC-130s pumped rounds into it until it was reduced to rubble. Made lots of friends that way. Suggestion that perhaps they should set an ambush and either kill or capture the sniper since he is being so predictable but that idea was rejected. We had to demonstrate our firepower to these people.

It wasn't the big headline-grabbing mistakes that undercut the U.S. effort as much as the daily, routine operations of U.S. troops not trained for counterinsurgency. A study by the Center for Army Lessons Learned warned especially against the practice of taking hostages.

> Tactics such as detaining the family members of anti-Coalition forces, destroying the houses of captured suspects, destroying the houses of captured suspects without judicial due process, and shooting at Iraqi vehicles that attempt to pass Coalition vehicles on major highways may bestow short-term tactical advantages. However, these advantages should be weighed against Iraqi sentiments and the long-term disadvantages associated with the image this creates. It is a practice in some U.S. units to detain family members of anti-Coalition suspects in an effort to induce the suspects to turn themselves in, in exchange for the release of their family members.

These tactics led in the wrong direction. T. E. Lawrence, the British adviser to Arab guerrillas during World War I, once defined tactics as "the means toward the strategic goal, the steps of its staircase." The tactics that many U.S. commanders used in Iraq in 2003 led away from the strategic goal of winning the political support of the Iraqi people.

Ultimately, eighty-two U.S. troops died in November 2003, making it the worst month of the war up to that point. The Ramadan offensive wore on Teddy Spain. On November 9, a convoy of his MPs came under small arms attack in Baghdad. Sgt. Nicholas Tomko, a twenty-four-year-old reserve MP from Pittsburgh, was killed. The loss was on Spain's mind when he watched Fox News that evening. "It talked about Michael Jackson, and about Martha Stewart, and so on," he recalled, "and about fifteen minutes into it, they said, 'Oh, and yeah, we lost a soldier in Baghdad today.'" He also was upset by fellow commanders who "talked about losing soldiers like they'd talk about losing a weapon."

No, Spain thought. "This is forever." He walked over to his computer and began to write, trying to translate his pain into words. "These heroes left wives, husbands, children and other loved ones behind," he wrote. "They all had great plans for the future, but none of them had planned on dying in combat. These soldiers will never see their children graduate from high school, will never attend their weddings, will never coach their Little League baseball teams." In the following weeks, as warplanes droned overhead at night, Spain returned to this document, adding to it during his quiet times before sleep. He would put it aside sometimes, then remember it on other bad days and open it again, and hone it. He was determined to tell the world about these losses, make them felt, have them remembered.

The Bush administration moves to plan B

Privately that fall, Bush administration officials were more worried than they let on in public. Officials at the White House, Pentagon, and State Department began the week of September 8 puzzling over an op-ed piece by Bremer that had appeared in the *Washington Post* that Monday morning. According to some accounts the article blindsided Bush administration officials back in Washington. In it Bremer laid out a plan for a lengthy, seven-step roadmap to end the U.S. occupation. It actually boiled down to three major goals, in order: First, a constitution would be written and ratified by Iraqis. Next would come a national election. Only after that would the U.S. occupation authority be dissolved.

"It was very clear to us from Bremer's leadership that he thought it would take the Iraqis a *long* time before they were going to be able to take over," said a CPA strategist.

Bremer's plan had one huge flaw: It lacked essential support both in the United States and in Iraq. "Bremer hadn't cleared the piece with his higher-ups in the Pentagon or the White House, and here he was describing a drawn-out American occupation," columnist David Brooks reported ten months later in the *New York Times*. "Iraqis would take their time writing a constitution, and would eventually have elections and take control of their country. For some Bush officials, this was the lowest period of the entire Iraq project. They knew they couldn't sustain an occupation for that long, yet they had no other realistic plan for transferring power to Iraqis."

There was another even bigger problem looming: Ayatollah Sistani, the most important political figure in Iraq, "declared it unacceptable to have a constitution prepared by unelected actors," recalled Sir Jeremy Greenstock, the British aide to Bremer.

The same month, Robert Blackwill, a former U.S. ambassador to India who also taught at Harvard, was brought in to the National Security Council to revamp Iraq policy. Blackwill was known throughout national security circles for riding roughshod over underlings and bureaucratic competitors. "His M.O. is to spook people—'the world is falling apart,'" and then to cover himself in glory by proposing the solution, said a former senior administration official who admires Blackwill's political skills but not his character. "And he spooked Condi, for about a month, in the fall of '03." Rice was receptive to Blackwill's pitch. At that time, "it was clear that things were going badly, [yet] we were getting no reporting" from CPA about its actions and their effects.

Rice had been growing profoundly frustrated with Bremer, this official said. She had been receiving so little information from him that summer that, in order to assess the real state of events at the CPA and in Iraq, she began reading the diplomatic reports that the British embassy in Washington passed to her staff. "Hadley and Rice were avid consumers" of the inside information coming from British diplomats in Baghdad, he said. Among other things, Blackwill convinced Rice that Bremer needed to heed Sistani, and that the long-term occupation the administrator contemplated wasn't viable. Rice in turn took those thoughts to President Bush.

In a series of meetings with Rumsfeld, and then with Rice and Bush at the White House, Bremer and the Bush administration reconsidered the mission of the CPA, and ultimately decided to abandon the idea of having the United States formally occupy Iraq for several years. The seven-step plan was dropped. On November 15, Bremer unveiled a new, swifter plan that abandoned the goal of having a constitution and general elections before the U.S. government relinquished sovereignty. Instead, the United States would officially hand over power less than eight months later, at the end of June 2004.

The move was startling to almost everyone involved in the occupation. "The decision on 15 November . . . came as a complete surprise to CPA administrators," remembered Hilary Synnott, the British diplomat who was the CPA regional coordinator for southern Iraq at the time.

It was indeed a major reversal: Instead of a long-term occupation, the U.S. government would seek to depart as soon as humanly possible. "It was clear that Plan A wasn't going to work," said Patrick Clawson, an Iraq hawk who long had argued for limited goals—basically, remove Saddam Hussein and leave. After more than a year of pursuing sweeping aspirations, such as transforming the politics of the Middle East, he said, "it was the first time we pulled back dramatically from objectives. I read that as the first time we said we weren't going to achieve everything we said we wanted to do."

After the November 15 agreement, Bremer's handling of the CPA felt much more constrained, recalled Charles Costello, who worked as a contractor on local governance issues. "I think from November on, he was just an administrator," he said. "They were calling the shots in Washington."

Convoys through hell

The structure of U.S. forces in Iraq may have undermined the goal of winning; its big bases required a huge support system. These forward operating bases

featured many of the comforts of home, from Internet cafés to mess halls offering a surprising variety of good food. They also separated the troops from the
population and so violated a key tenet of counterinsurgency campaigning. The
classic way to conduct such a campaign would have been to have only support
troops, such as mechanics and logisticians, on the big facilities, with combat
forces operating out of small patrol bases and other outposts located among the
people.

In particular, keeping those big bases supplied with everything from gasoline to ice cream required a constant stream of convoys. Every day roughly eight
hundred trucks headed north from Kuwait to supply the U.S. military effort.
Hundreds more ran ancillary convoys inside the country. "Every single thing
that we provided to our soldiers had to be brought in through Kuwait," Sanchez
noted later.

Protecting the convoys was a major effort, taking up many military resources.
The Polish-led multinational division operating in the south estimated that it
spent about one quarter of its time and energy keeping open the two major U.S.
supply lines, dubbed Route Tampa and Route Sue. Largely unseen and unnoticed
by reporters and other observers of the war, these convoys were a major cause of
friction with Iraqis as they traversed Iraq. "I told Colonel Rudesheim about some
abuse of civilians that occurred that day in his sector," recalled an Army civil affairs officer. Soldiers from another unit, when convoying through his area, were
shooting at passing cars without provocation, the officer reported. Rudesheim
responded, "Oh, shit, those guys come into my sector and do it, and their own
leaders don't stop them."

Official reports described a lack of fire discipline in the conduct of convoys.
"The British sector . . . is relatively free of anti-Coalition attacks, yet American
convoys moving north from Kuwait from the British sector have fired at British
contractors who drove near the American vehicles on a major highway," noted the
Center for Army Lessons Learned.

The Marine Corps, also operating in southern and central Iraq in the summer
of 2003, found that some convoys also were run sloppily, especially those from
support units such as mechanics and clerks. The Marines called those Army convoys manatees, after the big, slow-moving, and defenseless herbivorous sea mam-
mals that are frequently run over by speedboats in the waterways of Florida. "The
Army drivers typically wore CD headphones, assistant drivers were most often
asleep, and few wore helmets or flak jackets as the convoys made their way along
routes Tampa and Sue," reported the 1st Marine Division's official history. "There

were few crew-served weapons mounts on the vehicles, and these were often un-manned as they were uncomfortably hot in the blazing Iraqi sun." The Marines also were critical of the fact that when the Army trucks were fired on, they simply would speed up rather than stop and attempt to kill their attackers. One nervy Marine response was to put Trojan horse trucks on the convoy routes. These bait vehicles carried around the outside of their truckbeds stacks of MRE ration boxes filled with sand. Inside the ring of boxes would wait Marines, ready to return fire or chase their attackers on foot. The tactic worked for a few days before the am-bushers moved away from the roads.

But not all the trucks were driven by U.S. military personnel, or even by American citizens. Many had at the wheel Indians or other third-country nation-als with no vested interest in helping the U.S. cause. These people simply wanted to survive the year and take home their pay to capitalize a small business or build a house. In 2003, there was talk in Iraq that some of them broke the rules pro-hibiting them from carrying weapons, which they would shoot at any Iraqi who they felt came too close to them on the road.

Partly through Darwinian forces, U.S. military convoy operations radically im-proved in the fall of 2003 and the spring of 2004. Rather than drift along wearing earphones playing pop music, gunners wore two-way radio headsets and riot-style face shields that were deemed capable of stopping rifle fire. And trucks were carrying double sets of radios so they could communicate with both their parent unit and the unit whose area they were traveling through.

The number of bomb attacks on logistics convoys increased steadily, with an average of about thirty a week in 2005, according to Brig. Gen. Yves Fontaine, head of the Army's 1st Corps Support Command. That was double the number a year earlier, he said. But he added that because of the increase in the armoring of vehicles, the number of casualties declined. Even so, U.S. troops operating the convoys were deeply affected by the experience. When Army researchers surveyed more than two thousand U.S. troops serving in Iraq in 2004, they found that about 19 percent of those in transportation and support units suffered from acute stress or post-traumatic stress disorder. The comparative figure for combat units was 11 percent, and for other units, just 7 percent.

Despite the improvements, trigger-happy convoys would continue to under-cut U.S. efforts to win over the populace. The number of Iraqis who died in this way is unknown. Lt. Col. Todd Wood, a battalion commander in the 3rd Infantry

Division, complained to a reporter from the *San Francisco Chronicle* about troops passing through his area of operations on Iraq's Highway 1. "Seems like I pick up a lot of people's pieces around here," he said. "These . . . patrols that drive around and shoot people have been a thorn in everybody's side all year."

His senior NCO, Sgt. Maj. Samuel Coston, added, "I hate the fact that American soldiers ride around killing civilians. All you got to say is, 'I felt threatened, the car was driving aggressively,' and you shoot. They have no remorse. They just keep on driving."

Col. Herrington sends a warning

In the fall of 2003, knowing she faced trouble, Brig. Gen. Fast, the top U.S. military intelligence officer in the country, asked one of the "wise men" of the Army intelligence community to fly over to review her operations. The report that would result appears to have been the first major internal recognition that the U.S. effort in Iraq had run off the tracks.

Retired Army Col. Stuart Herrington was a veteran of Army counterinsurgency operations in the Vietnam War, where he was a particularly effective part of the Phoenix Program, a controversial covert effort to capture or kill Vietcong leaders in rural areas. William Colby, the CIA operative who oversaw the program and later became head of the agency, claimed that it eliminated sixty thousand Vietcong agents. That estimate had been greeted with skepticism, but after the war, observed historian Stanley Karnow, top Communist figures reported that Phoenix had done enormous damage. Madame Nguyen Thi Dinh, a Vietcong leader, told Karnow that she considered the program "very dangerous." She recalled that "we never feared a division of troops, but the infiltration of a couple of guys into our ranks created tremendous difficulties for us."

Herrington was one of the last Americans out of Saigon, lifting off the roof of the U.S. embassy at five-thirty on the morning of April 30, 1975. A few years later he wrote a well-received book about the Phoenix operation, titled *Silence Was a Weapon: The Vietnam War in the Villages.* He went on to run intelligence operations for the Army in Panama and during the 1991 Gulf War, and later taught at the Army War College when Fast was a student there. She likely remembered that, unusual for an officer, he was an expert in interrogation, something that military intelligence officials tend to think of as "sergeants' work."

Herrington arrived in early December and was stunned by what he found. The main prison, Abu Ghraib, was stuffed with six thousand prisoners. "The problem of overpopulation at Abu Ghraib is serious, and must be resolved urgently," he warned in a thirteen-page report to Fast submitted on December 12, 2003. "The facility is a pressure cooker where it is only a matter of time before prisoners stage an uprising." But that was the least of the problems, he concluded, because it was easily solved.

A larger concern was how detainees were being treated, and not just by a handful of demoralized Army Reservists at Abu Ghraib. He was shocked by the behavior of Task Force 121, an elite interagency team of about one thousand CIA paramilitaries and black Special Operations forces devoted to finding Saddam Hussein and his top allies. Iraqis "who had been captured by Task Force 121 showed signs of having been mistreated (beaten) by their captors," he wrote, with some having injuries noted by medical personnel. Herrington was no innocent—the Phoenix Program killed thousands—but he was disappointed, he wrote, with the actions of the task force, and especially the sense that it was routine and acceptable to beat prisoners. One officer told him that he knew about the beatings. "I asked the officer if he had reported this problem. He replied that, 'Everyone knows about it.' I advised the officer that this [response] was inadequate." (The Red Cross likewise reported that high-value detainees were being brought in severely burned, apparently from being made to lie across the hoods of vehicles as they were transported, tied down like slain deer.) Herrington, by contrast, had made a point of treating his prisoners generously—feeding a hungry Vietcong captain in a restaurant, and putting up a captured North Vietnamese sergeant in his villa, and at one point, a week into the latter's captivity, handing him a loaded M-16 rifle as a sign of trust.

Broadly interpreting his mandate, Herrington went on to critique the entire U.S. military campaign. He repeatedly singled out the big sweeps that were resulting in the imprisonment of thousands of Iraqis that fall and winter. "Conducting sweep operations in which many persons are detained who probably should not be detained, and who then wind up incarcerated for three to six months, is counterproductive to the Coalition's efforts to win the cooperation of the Iraqi citizenry," he advised Fast.

In some instances, it appeared that U.S. commanders, in seeking to shut down the insurgency in their areas of operations, were using tactics that effectively made them recruiting sergeants for it. Herrington was especially bothered by the actions of Gen. Odierno's 4th Infantry Division, which was headquartered in Saddam Hussein's hometown of Tikrit, near the northern apex of the Sunni Triangle. "Principally due to sweep operations by some line units—the 4th ID was

consistently singled out as the major offender—the number of detainees" was rising steadily, he wrote. He emphasized that point five pages later: "Some divisions
are conducting operations with rigorous detention criteria, while some—the 4th
ID is the negative example—are sweeping up large numbers of people and
dumping them at the door of Abu Ghraib."

He also told Fast to look into the practice of taking family members of suspects into custody. "Recommend that you check to see if, as we were told, some
detainees arrive at Abu Ghraib who were detained because the correct target of a
raid was not home, so a family member was taken in his place . . . who would
then be released when the target turns himself in. This practice, if it is being done,
has a 'hostage' feel to it."

Army combat units were part of the problem, Herrington suggested. Looking
at them reminded him of his time in Vietnam when he saw such units alienate local populations. "They were often heavy-handed, reliant on massive firepower,
and could undo in a few hours what we had striven to accomplish with the people for months." A radically different, far more sophisticated approach was
needed, Herrington suggested. Set up an amnesty program and induce insurgent
leaders to turn themselves in. There were three good ways to put an insurgent out
of business: The preferable way was to foster desertion; the second best was to
capture and interrogate them. "Last resort is to target and kill them." Yet that last
thinking was at the heart of the approach that Sanchez and many of his division
commanders were taking—especially in the Sunni Triangle.

Overall, Herrington concluded, the Army should change its way of thinking
about what it was doing in Iraq. "Keep the U.S. profile as low as possible going
forward," he wrote. Effectively, the veteran interrogator had turned the Sanchez
critique on its head: It's not intelligence that is the problem here, it is your
troops and tactics. Alter your tactics and your intelligence will improve, just as
night follows day. In the following months that criticism would become the
conventional wisdom among Special Forces officers, civil affairs specialists, and
even some regular Army unit commanders. But at the time it was a novel, even
radical, view.

Only two copies of the report were made, with Herrington keeping one and
leaving the other with Fast. There is no indication that Gen. Sanchez, the most
conventional of commanders, was interested in overhauling his approach in such
a revolutionary way. Four months later, orders issued to his subordinate commanders still routinely called for "killing or capturing" the insurgents.

Yet over a year later, after the Abu Ghraib scandal shook the Army, a cascade of reports and investigations vindicated Herrington's views. It is worth quoting at length the conclusions of one investigator, Maj. Gen. George Fay, because in retrospect they read like an obituary for the strategy and tactics employed by the U.S. military in Iraq to respond to the insurgency in 2003.

"There was a general consensus," Fay wrote, from interviews with, among others, Sanchez and then Brig. Gen. Barbara Fast,

> that as the pace of operations picked up in late November–early December 2003, it became a common practice for maneuver elements to round up large quantities of Iraqi personnel in the general vicinity of a specified target as a cordon and capture technique. Some operations were conducted at night resulting in some detainees being delivered to collection points only wearing night clothes or under clothes. Sgt. Jose Garcia, assigned to the Abu Ghraib Detainee Assessment Board, estimated that 85%–90% of the detainees were of no intelligence value based upon board interviews and debriefings of detainees. The Deputy C2x, CJTF-7, CIVILIAN-12 [that is, the number-two military intelligence official and a U.S. official operating in Iraq whose name wasn't being released] confirmed these numbers.

The effect of those numbers of innocents was unintentionally to provide cover to the insurgents also detained, Fay concluded.

> Large quantities of detainees with little or no intelligence value swelled Abu Ghraib's population and led to a variety of overcrowding difficulties. Already scarce interrogator and analyst resources were pulled from interrogation operations to identify and screen increasing numbers of personnel whose capture documentation was incomplete or missing. Complicated and unresponsive release procedures ensured that these detainees stayed at Abu Ghraib—even though most had no value.

The U.S. military response to the rise of the insurgency was fundamentally misguided. An effort to squeeze out more intelligence, involving thousands of American troops and profoundly disrupting the lives of tens of thousands of Iraqis, swamped the intelligence system. The American offensive was undone by a combination of overwhelmed soldiers and indiscriminate generals—especially the 4th ID's Odierno, who sent too many detainees south, and his immediate superior, Sanchez, who should have seen this and stopped it.

The capture of Saddam Hussein

Yet what Gen. Odierno and the 4th ID are remembered for is something very different—in fact, for what may be the high point of the U.S. occupation.

"We got him!" Bremer exclaimed to reporters on December 14. After thirty-eight weeks of searching, Operation Red Dawn, involving six hundred conventional and Special Operations troops, had caught Saddam Hussein hiding in a hole on a farmstead near the village of Dawr, 10 miles southeast of Tikrit and not far from his birthplace of Auja. An informant had said that an important person was there, amid the palm groves and orange orchards. One soldier noticed a prayer rug over a dirt spot that looked swept recently. The rug was removed, and a Styrofoam lid was found underneath it. After it was lifted—carefully, in case it was booby-trapped—it revealed a square-cut hole resembling a mineshaft.

Under standard procedures, said Col. James Hickey, the smart, sad-eyed commander of the operation, soldiers would have dropped a grenade or fired into the "spider hole." But before they could, two hands appeared in surrender. Saddam was taken into custody by a combination of Special Operations troops and members of the 4th Infantry Division.

At last, some commanders thought, the corner had been turned. Not only had Saddam been caught, he hadn't even put up a fight—a circumstance that appeared to undercut the heroic image he had tried to construct. Bremer presented the moment to Iraqis as a potential turning point in the life of their nation. "This is a great day in your history," he said. "With the arrest of Saddam Hussein, there is a new opportunity for members of the former regime, whether military or civilian, to end their bitter opposition. Let them come forward now in a spirit of reconciliation and hope, lay down their arms, and join you, their fellow citizens, in the task of building the new Iraq."

Some U.S. commanders, caught up in the euphoria of the moment, said at the time that they believed it the beginning of the end of the insurgency. "The Wicked Witch is dead," rejoiced Lt. Col. Henry Arnold, a battalion commander in the 101st Airborne, based near the Syrian border. "The capture of Saddam Hussein will have a tremendous negative impact on the Baathist insurgency, and it is all good news for us and the future of Iraq." He predicted that most of the former regime elements, or FRE, active in the insurgency now would be demoralized. "I believe that the majority of the FRE will melt away and begin to reintegrate into normal society."

"I think this puts a nail in the coffin of hopes that the Baath Party could ever regain control of Iraq," an Army general said. "There is no longer any central figure around whom such a movement could coalesce."

Indeed, in the next few weeks the U.S. military obtained the best information it had seen in months. "The peak was in the December timeframe after we took down Saddam and captured him," Gen. Sanchez said in a legal statement given later. On Christmas Eve, Fadhil Mohammed Ahmed, who was believed to be commanding former members of the regime in launching attacks in Baghdad, turned himself in. (He actually had to go to four U.S. checkpoints before finding a soldier willing to take him into custody, said an Army officer.)

January and February 2004 were good times for U.S. military intelligence, recalled one senior officer. "We were rolling up the Baathists," he said. "We had them on their heels in Diyala and al Anbar"—the provinces flanking Baghdad on the east and west. At one point some five hundred insurgent fighters petitioned for amnesty, he said, and ringleaders were putting out feelers for surrender.

This might have been the moment for a political opening to the Sunnis, capitalizing on the stunning capture by reaching out to wavering enemies, said an Army intelligence officer who was based in Anbar at the time. "I think we missed an incredible opportunity to bring the Sunnis into the fold during that December-January time frame," he said. "A lot of infrastructure spending and a push to reach out to religious and tribal leaders could potentially have changed the course of the war."

But neither the CPA nor the Bush administration was inclined to offer reprieves, recalled the first officer. "That was the great missed opportunity," he said with palpable regret.

At the time Sanchez was hearing reassuring reports from subordinate commanders. The number of attacks appeared to be dwindling. The 4th ID's Maj. Gen. Odierno contended that the back of the insurgency was broken. "The former regime elements we have been combating have been brought to their knees," he told reporters. "Capturing Saddam was a major operational and psychological defeat for the enemy." He described the insurgency as "a fractured, sporadic threat, with the leadership destabilized, finances interdicted, and no hope of the Baathists' return to power." There were just a "handful of cells" left fighting in his area, the northern and eastern parts of the Sunni Triangle, he said. In terms of reconstruction, he added, "we see constant improvement. And so it is getting better. . . . [W]e are making significant progress." He even offered a time

line: "I believe within six months you're going to see some normalcy. I really believe that."

In al Anbar province, the 82nd Airborne's Swannack was almost as optimistic.
"We have turned the corner, and now we can accelerate down the straightaway,"
he told reporters on January 6.

But even at the time of the capture, there were indications that the ultimate
payoff wouldn't be as good as commanders hoped. "That was a very unpopular
event in al Anbar province," recalled Keith Mines. "They didn't like to see the
whole thing of checking his teeth on TV. They thought he should be handled with
dignity." He emphasized this in his weekly update to Bremer, recording that he
was seeing "outrage at how Iraq's former leader has been publicly humiliated."

Nor did the display of Saddam play well in other parts of the Arab world.
"No Arab and no Muslim will ever forget these images. They touched something
very, very deep," a Moroccan journalist named Khalid Jamai told Reuters, the
news service. "It was disgraceful to publish those pictures. It goes against human
dignity, to present him like a gorilla that has come out of the forest, with someone checking his head for lice."

Ultimately, the capture of Saddam would prove to be the prelude to a new,
more determined phase of the war. It is possible that removing Saddam from the
equation made it easier for some of the Iraqis who hated Saddam but also disliked the Americans to support the insurgency. "We are not fighting for Saddam,"
Ahmed Jassim, a religious student in Fallujah, said around this time. "We are fighting for our country, for our honor, for Islam. We are not doing this for Saddam."

The U.S. Army vs. the principles of counterinsurgency

In improvising a response to the insurgency, the U.S. Army had worked hard,
and had found some tactical successes. There is no question that the vast majority
of the soldiers in the field had poured their hearts and souls into the effort. Yet they
frequently were led poorly by commanders who had been sent to do a mission for
which they were unprepared by an institution that took away from the Vietnam
War only the lesson that it shouldn't get involved in messy counterinsurgencies.

It is striking how much of the U.S. counterinsurgency campaign in the late
summer and fall of 2003 violated the basic tenets of such efforts. One of the
essential texts on counterinsurgency is *Counterinsurgency Warfare: Theory and
Practice,* written by retired French army Lt. Col. David Galula, who was born in
Tunisia, raised in Morocco, and entered the French army in 1938. For the next

two decades he received an advanced education in modern warfare. He served in World War II, studied Mao Zedong's guerrilla campaign in China in the late 1940s—and briefly was taken captive by the communists—and then spent eighteen months in Greece just as the civil war there ended. Finally, he fought the Algerian rebels in the late fifties. He wrote his book at Harvard University in 1963, and died four years later. In *Street Without Joy,* a study of the French war in Indochina, military analyst Bernard Fall called Galula's book "the best of them all."

"*Counterinsurgency Warfare* is the primer and at the same time the bible" on the subject, agreed Terry Daly, a veteran of U.S. intelligence who worked with provincial reconnaissance units in Vietnam from 1965 to 1967. "It describes what an insurgency is, how it differs from conventional war, and the steps to take to defeat an insurgency on the ground."

Yet in 2003–4 the book was almost unknown within the U.S. military, which is one reason it is possible to open Galula's text almost at random and find principles of counterinsurgency that the American effort in Iraq failed to heed—especially in 2003–4. Take, for example, the divided structure of command, with both military and civilian chiefs of the occupation. "Clearly, more than any other kind of warfare, counterinsurgency must respect the principle of single direction," Galula admonished in his clear, simple style. "A single boss must direct the operations from beginning to end." What's more, he noted, that overseer must be a civilian, because military actions must always be subordinate to political goals. In Iraq, the U.S. presence was controlled by no one person, and the civilian and military efforts frequently were at odds. For a counterinsurgency military, Galula prescribed a radically different approach than the one taken by the Army in Iraq. He warned specifically against the kind of large-scale conventional operations the United States repeatedly launched with brigades and battalions, even if they hold out the allure of short-term gains in intelligence. "True, systematic large-scale operations, because of their very size, alleviate somewhat the intelligence and mobility deficiency of the counterinsurgent," he wrote. "Nevertheless, conventional operations by themselves have at best no more effect than a fly swatter."

Galula did see one part of a country where a heavy military emphasis was required—its frontiers. "The border areas are a permanent source of weakness for the counterinsurgent," he cautioned. Yet the U.S. military neglected Iraq's frontiers for over a year, even though two neighboring nations—Iran and Syria—clearly were hostile to U.S. ambitions in the country and the region.

Galula also insisted that firepower must be viewed very differently than in regular war. "A soldier fired upon in conventional war who does not fire back with every available weapon would be guilty of a dereliction of his duty; the reverse would be the case in counterinsurgency warfare, where the rule is to apply the minimum of fire." The U.S. military took a different approach in Iraq. It wasn't indiscriminate in its use of firepower, but it tended to look upon it as a good, especially during the big counteroffensive in the fall of 2003, and again in the battles in Fallujah.

One reason for that different tactical approach, of course, was the muddled strategic approach of U.S. commanders in Iraq. As civil affairs officers found to their dismay, Army leaders tended to see the Iraqi people as the playing field on which a contest was played against insurgents. Rather, Galula admonished, the people are the prize. "The population . . . becomes the objective for the counterinsurgent as it was for his enemy," he wrote.

From that observation flows an entirely different way of dealing with the people. "Since antagonizing the population will not help, it is imperative that hardships for it and rash actions on the part of the forces be kept to a minimum," Galula mandated. "The units participating in the operations should be thoroughly indoctrinated to that effect, the misdeeds punished severely and even publicly if this can serve to impress the population." Even prisoners should be treated well, he added. He recommended this not on the grounds of morality but of military effectiveness: "Demoralization of the enemy's forces is an important task. The most effective way to achieve it is by employing a policy of leniency toward the prisoners." Fortunately for the U.S. effort, the insurgents frequently were even clumsier, abusing their own prisoners and alienating much of the international media.

Every indication is that the majority of U.S. troops did act well toward Iraqis most of the time. But the emphasis on the use of force, on powerful retaliation, and on protecting U.S. troops at all costs tended to push them toward harsh treatment, especially of detainees. Hundreds of small instances of abuse at bases across Iraq combined into a torrent that became the Abu Ghraib scandal.

Galula was hardly an outrider in counterinsurgency theory. Rather, his work amounts to an updating and refinement of methods British officers had developed during many decades of operations in India, Africa, China, and the Middle East. Sir Charles Gwynn, a British military educator, distilled those lessons in a 1939 textbook titled *Imperial Policing*, which prescribed four basic principles to govern the official response to an insurrection: Civil power must be in charge, civilian and military authorities must cooperate relentlessly, action must be firm and timely, but when force is required it should be used minimally. The U.S. effort in Iraq violated at least three of these rules for at least the first year of the occupation.

Cumulatively, the American ignorance of long-held precepts of counterinsurgency warfare impeded the U.S. military during 2003 and part of 2004. Combined with a personnel policy that pulled out all the seasoned forces early in 2004 and replaced them with green troops, it isn't surprising that the U.S. effort often resembled that of Sisyphus, the king in Greek legend who was condemned to perpetually roll a boulder up a hill, only to have it roll back down as he neared the top. And so, again and again, in 2003, 2004, 2005, and 2006, U.S. forces launched major new operations to assert and reassert control in Fallujah, in Samarra, in Mosul.

It isn't clear why U.S. commanders seemed so flatly ignorant of how other counterinsurgencies had been conducted successfully. The main reason seems to be a repugnance, after the fall of Saigon, for dwelling on unconventional operations. But the cost of such willful ignorance was high. "Scholars are virtually unanimous in their judgment that conventional forces often lose unconventional wars because they lack a conceptual understanding of the war they are fighting," Lt. Col. Matthew Moten, chief of military history at West Point, would comment a year later.

Bremer vs. the world

Back in Washington, frustration with Bremer was growing. "He ignored my suggestions," recalled Wolfowitz. "He ignored Rumsfeld's instructions."

One day late in 2003, while sailing in the Mediterranean, Larry Ellison, founder and chief executive of Oracle, the big software company, received a phone call from the Pentagon: Can we borrow General Kellogg, who had retired from the Joint Staff and gone to work for the software giant? Sure, Ellison replied.

The CPA was limping, staffed at 54 percent of its estimated requirement. And, Kellogg remembered, many of those were "young, inexperienced, and didn't speak the language." He went out to try to fix things, and especially to repair a relationship with the U.S. military that had turned "adversarial."

Early on, Kellogg set up a back channel to Rice's office in the White House, in part because Rice had asked him to provide "ground truth," he said, and partly because he soon came to believe that Bremer was misleading Washington on how much progress he was making. "For example, Bremer would tell congressional delegations that there were one hundred thousand Iraqi security forces trained. I sent a back channel message to Wolfowitz and Rice saying, 'You're setting yourself up, this number isn't right, I am overseeing the training, and there are just ten thousand.' I also told them that electricity was much worse than they thought."

Rumsfeld's response was to send out survey teams that could determine the facts on the ground. Bremer objected to the first team, and its trip was cancelled, Kellogg recalled. The second team was led by Maj. Gen. Karl Eikenberry, an Army general fresh from working on training issues in Afghanistan. He reviewed the training of Iraqi police and military units and concluded that things weren't going well. U.S. commanders told members of the assessment team that "the insurgency was growing much faster than the Iraqi security forces," Bing West, a member of the team, noted in his account of U.S. military operations in Anbar province. The CPA was overseeing the training of the Iraqis while the U.S. military was trying to use those forces. To fix the program, Eikenberry decided, all training and employment of Iraqi forces should be consolidated under the U.S. military.

"You can't have disunity of command in the middle of a war," said the briefing Eikenberry's team prepared for Bremer, according to West, who helped write it. "We have split authority from responsibility."

When Eikenberry apprised Bremer of his plan to recommend the shift, Kellogg recalled, "Bremer just unloaded on him: 'It's not gonna happen, it's wrong, I'll go to the president on this, I'll go to Rumsfeld.'"

West had a more succinct summary: "Bremer went bat shit."

But what Bremer didn't know was that Eikenberry held his own trump card. And he played it, taking the recommendation to Abizaid, the top U.S. commander in the region—and his close friend since the two were roommates in the West Point class of 1973. They had remained close ever since, a fairly unusual duo in Army culture, quirky intellectuals in a peer group that is, as one former officer once noted, more inclined to read *Bass Fishing* magazine than serious military history. Both hold advanced degrees from Harvard and speak non-Western languages—Abizaid, Arabic, and Eikenberry, Chinese. A few months later Eikenberry's consolidation recommendation was implemented, with Petraeus sent back to Iraq to oversee all training of Iraqi security forces, from the army and the national guard to border patrol, interior security, and police.

Another member of Eikenberry's assessment team was Gary Anderson, the retired Marine colonel who had butted heads with Bremer in the summer of 2003 when he mentioned Vietnam. Anderson, anxious to see what was happening on the ground, had been sneaking out of the Green Zone to go on patrol with Iraqi security forces. On the foggy morning of January 18, 2004, he headed across the Tigris River to patrol Sadr City with a platoon of Iraqis. He heard a blast from across the city. A pickup truck loaded with half a ton of PE-4 plastic explosives topped with a cluster of 155 millimeter artillery shells had exploded at a checkpoint at the main gate of the Green Zone, killing twenty and wounding sixty others. When Anderson got back to the zone, he learned that he had been presumed to be one of the victims. "Everyone thought I was dead," he said later.

Holshek loses PFC Bush

Every soldier who served in Iraq seems to have one day—even one moment—that stands foremost in their memory. For Lt. Col. Holshek, it was December 19 at 9:45 in the morning, during the last month of his tour, a few weeks after he had persuaded Col. Hogg to modify the 4th Infantry Division's tactics in Baqubah.

PFC Charles Bush, Jr., was an older private, a thirty-four-year-old from Buffalo, New York, who was a cook but had been retrained to man the Squad Automatic Weapon, a light machine gun, atop a Humvee. He was doing just that on a supply run to the big U.S. base at Balad, about 40 miles to the northwest. As is so often the case in violent incidents, what happened next isn't clear. The small, fast-moving, three-vehicle convoy was west of the Tigris and nearing Balad when the driver of the Humvee thought he heard AK-47s firing. The Humvees were armored, which meant that the soldiers were largely protected from small-arms fire. But it also meant that they were nine hundred pounds heavier than the Humvees the drivers were accustomed to, with a higher center of gravity.

When the driver thought he heard shots, he began to drive evasively, accelerating and swinging the wheel in order to present a more difficult target to hit. Just as he did, a front wheel caught a deep pothole, and the combination of speed and momentum flipped the vehicle forward, over its front end. Bush, manning the hatch gun, was crushed.

The incident hit Holshek hard just as the end of his unit's tour was in sight. "I was at the point of psychological exhaustion," he said, looking back from a year later. "All I wanted to do was get across the finish line, get my people home. I was beginning to doubt the mission, whether or not we were going to succeed. I was beginning to think about all the things we had done to work against ourselves—we had met the enemy, and he was us."

A month later, his tour of duty over and command of the unit transferred to his successor in a quick, middle-of-the-night ceremony at an airport in Kuwait, Holshek flew back to the United States. His first stop, even before seeing his own family, was Buffalo, where he visited PFC Bush's father—and delivered a case of Molson's beer to pay off a Super Bowl bet he had lost with Bush. It was his final act as a battalion commander. "I know what the cost is when you don't do this right," he said.

12.

THE DESCENT INTO ABUSE

SUMMER TO WINTER 2003

Col. Joe Anderson, the energetic commander of the brigade of the 101st Airborne that was headquartered in Mosul, was told one evening late in 2003 by his intelligence officer that soldiers at their detention center had reported that one of their Iraqi prisoners had a broken jaw. As such incidents go, it was routine, similar to dozens of others that occurred across Iraq during the first phase of the American occupation. Yet a warning bell went off in Anderson's head. "I was suspicious," he said later. When people fall down, they sustain a broken nose or a cut chin, but jawbones are broken by a blow. "They said he fell."

What's more, news of the incident came just after the 101st had suffered its worst month ever of casualties while in Iraq, losing twenty-five soldiers in November, and Anderson knew his soldiers wanted payback. "Guys get pissed when they see their buddies blown away," he said. He understood the emotion but felt strongly that it shouldn't be expressed through illegal or immoral acts. He ordered an informal inquiry, which soon turned into a formal investigation. On December 19, the investigation board concluded that the injury was caused either by the Iraqi's being struck or caused to fall. In either case, the harm was "the result of intentional acts by coalition forces."

The soldier directly involved was issued a letter of reprimand, but that was the least of the consequences. The investigation had uncovered a host of other problems. "The detainees were being systematically and intentionally mistreated," one investigator wrote.

"I saw the chief throw them down, put his knee in his neck and back, and grind them into the floor," one witness stated. "He would use a bullhorn and yell at them in Arabic and play heavy metal music extremely loud; they got so scared they would urinate on themselves. He was very aggressive and rough with detainees." Prisoners also were made to exercise until they couldn't stand, and then were doused in cold water. Some were made to wear sandbags on their heads on which were written "IED," signifying to soldiers—incorrectly in most cases, it appears—that their wearer had been caught trying to bomb U.S. troops.

Most important, investigators reported, the brigade detention center was being run by a military intelligence battalion untrained for the job. They knew how to interrogate prisoners, not how to guard and house them. Anderson and his commander, Petraeus, reacted with alacrity. Control of the detention facility was transferred "almost instantly" from the military intelligence battalion to a military police unit that knew how to manage prisoners, Anderson said. Latrines were moved closer to the holding area, to minimize the chances that prisoners would "trip" while being escorted. Fences were erected so detainees could move outside the building while still being controlled. Floodlights were installed. Also, the word went out across the division that abuse wouldn't be tolerated. "Tone is very important," Petraeus said much later. "People say this is a squad leaders' war. But what generals can do is set tone." In addition, to ensure a layer of oversight, Petraeus reached out to the Red Cross and to local religious, political, and civic leaders, inviting them to inspect the 101st's detention facilities often, to talk to prisoners, and to bring any problems to his attention.

In the next two months there was only one case of possible abuse detected, Anderson noted, and that was an ambiguous situation. In his view, the quick reaction to the broken jaw incident was characteristic of the division's style. "We were constantly assessing our operations—were we doing it right, going after the right people, having the effects we wanted to have?" Anderson said. "Dealing with detainees was just part of this."

Communicating with violence

In historical terms, the 101st's broken jaw incident was minor, hardly worth remembering but for the swift and effective response of its leaders. Other divisions posted far different records of abuse than the 101st. It wasn't that soldiers were ordered to be cruel, it is that acts of cruelty were tolerated in some units, to the point that one officer in the 82nd Airborne, Capt. Ian Fishback, would later charge that it was systematic.

The atmosphere of official lawlessness in some Army units is significant for several reasons. It demeaned all those involved. It usually was militarily ineffective and counterproductive. And it tarnished the image of the United States and its military. When a policeman abuses or tortures a suspect, it inevitably diminishes the officer's humanity, wrote French army Capt. Pierre-Henri Simon, who was a prisoner of the Germans during World War II and, a decade later, a critic of his country's behavior during the Algerian revolution. But when a soldier uses abuse or torture, Simon argued, it is worse, because "it is here that the honor of the nation becomes engaged."

Much of the initial mistreatment of Iraqis by American troops seemed to be the result of soldiers' not being trained or mentally prepared for the mission. Faced with looting and unable to speak the language of the people they were trying to police, many soldiers flailed, using force ineffectively or brutally. "It is not uncommon to hear American soldiers explain that the only thing the Iraqis understand is 'force,'" Army Reserve Maj. Christopher Varhola, an anthropologist who traveled widely in Iraq, later noted. "For the most part, however, the people saying this do not speak Arabic and have had little or no interaction with Iraqis."

"Take them out back and beat the fuck out of them"

An incident involving the 2nd Armored Cavalry Regiment captures the Army's predicament during the summer of 2003. It was the finest fighting force in the world for conventional combat, but it was ill-prepared for the irregular war in which it found itself. In this sense, abusive soldiers sometimes were victims of the Army's lack of preparation. One officer in the 2nd ACR, which was assigned to eastern Baghdad in the summer of 2003, recalled to an Army investigator that when he brought looters back to his base, a commander there "told my sergeant that he didn't want them here. Then he told my platoon sergeant to 'take them out back and beat the fuck out of them'"—an account supported by other soldiers.

(The battery commander, whose name was redacted from documents released to the American Civil Liberties Union [ACLU] under the Freedom of Information Act, responded to investigators, "I have never seriously told anyone to do that. . . . Even if I had said that, the NCO should never have thought I meant it.")

Shocked, the sergeant went back outside and told his soldiers what the senior officer had said. "I told my squad leaders what Bulldog 6 told me to do with all the looters," the sergeant continued in a written statement. "I told them we are NOT going to do that." American soldiers were better than that, in his view. But, still wanting to make a point to the looters, he ordered that they be taken to the base's front gate, stripped naked, and set loose. He was trying to do the right thing, but he had violated the rules governing the treatment of detainees—an offense for which he was later charged.

The lack of preparation was also reflected in an incident involving soldiers in the 1st Armored Division. On the fly, they had devised a method of discriminating among the Iraqis they detained for looting: Those who when captured stared back at their captors were considered likely to loot again, but those who cried in fear were deemed to be deterred. On June 20, 2003, a lieutenant told soldiers to move a looter out of a truck. The officer was going to make him cry. "I was standing at the front of our truck when I saw [the name deleted] put the guy on his knees and put a gun to the back of his head," a soldier said in a sworn statement. "Then he bent down and said something to the guy. I did not hear because I was too far away. Then I saw him stand up . . . and shoot. The barrel of the weapon was just high enough to miss the guy." The officer claimed in a statement that he fired his weapon to scare away a feral dog, but six soldiers testified that they hadn't seen any such animal.

Two nights later, a sergeant in the same platoon followed suit. This second incident occurred when an Iraqi man and his two teenage sons were detained for looting. The sergeant radioed his lieutenant, who asked, "Are they crying yet?" The sergeant then told the father he was going to shoot one of the boys, according to an Army investigator's report. Which one will it be, he asked?

"No, please shoot me, don't shoot my sons," the man responded, as would most fathers. The sergeant repeated the question twice, according to another soldier's affidavit. Then he walked one of the boys around to the far side of a truck, where they couldn't be seen, and fired his pistol by the boy's head. The three were then let go.

Many soldiers were troubled by such behavior. In this case, a soldier from another unit stated, "I reported the incident to my platoon sergeant and told him that I didn't want to work with these guys again."

The strategic confusion about why the United States was in Iraq, such as the Bush administration's insistence that the war was part of the counterattack against al Qaeda–style terrorism and so was somehow a response to the 9/11 attacks, may have led some American soldiers to treat ordinary Iraqis as if they were terrorists. Some indeed were. But many—certainly the majority of those raided and detained—were just average Iraqis, not necessarily sympathetic to the U.S. presence but not actually taking up arms against it, at least before they were humiliated or incarcerated.

The 3rd ACR in western Iraq

Asia Times ran an extraordinary account of the 3rd Armored Cavalry Regiment's war, which was off the beaten track in western Iraq, far from most reporters, who tended to focus their work nearer Baghdad, especially as traveling the roads of central Iraq grew increasingly hazardous.

Lt. Col. Gregory Reilly, the commander of the regiment's 1st squadron, seemed to understand the nature of the war he was fighting. "I have to be very careful because what I do can have the opposite reaction from the intention," he told the magazine's Nir Rosen. But the 3rd ACR troops observed by Rosen during his two weeks with the unit in late September and early October 2003 didn't seem to him to translate that understanding into action. One raid began with a tank breaking down the stone wall of a house. Teams charged over the rubble and through the hole in the wall, breaking down a door with a sledgehammer and taking prisoners. None of the men detained in the first house was on the target list, but they were held anyway, Rosen reported. "House after house meets the same fate," he wrote. "Some homes only have women in them; they, too, are ransacked, closets broken, mattresses overturned, clothes thrown out of drawers." He continued:

> Prisoners with duct tape on their eyes and their hands cuffed behind them with plastic "zip ties" sit in the back of the truck for hours without water. . . . By daylight the whole town can see a large truck full of prisoners. Two men walking to work with their breakfast in a basket are stopped at gunpoint, ordered to "shut the fuck up" as their basket's contents are tossed out and they are questioned about the location of a suspect. The soldier guarding them speaks of the importance of intimidating Iraqis and instilling fear in them. "If they got something to tell us I'd rather they be scared," he explains. An Iraqi policeman drives by in a white sport

utility vehicle clearly marked "Police." He, too, is stopped at gunpoint and ordered not to move or talk until the last raid is complete. From a list of 34 names, Apache [the troop, the cavalry branch's equivalent of a company] brings in about 16 positively identified men, along with another 54 men who were neighbors, relatives or just happened to be around. By 0830, Apache is done, and starts driving back to base. As the main element departs, the psychological-operations vehicle blasts AC/DC rock music through the neighborhood streets. "It's good for morale after such a long mission," Captain Brown [Justin Brown, Apache's commander] says.

Rosen, an Arabic speaker who had spent time in Egypt, Qatar, and Jordan, was stunned at how little the American soldiers understood of their environment. On another raid he witnessed, soldiers burst into a house, shot a man named Ayoub in the hand with nonlethal pellets, and arrested him. They seized two compact discs with images of Saddam Hussein on them—not knowing that the titles on the discs, in Arabic, were *The Crimes of Saddam.* "The soldiers saw only the picture of Saddam and assumed they were proof of guilt," Rosen wrote. Several hours later intelligence operatives intercepted a telephone call by another man. "Oh shit," said Army Capt. Bill Ray, an intelligence officer; the man they had detained "was the wrong Ayoub."

The Army was understandably dismayed by Rosen's reporting. "I am devastated by the content of your article regarding my squadron," Lt. Col. Reilly wrote to the young reporter after the article appeared. The message conveyed, he said, was that "this unit has no respect for the Iraqi people and we are nothing but a bunch of hoodlums. . . . It is really too bad, we are trying hard to do the right things here and make a difference and now the reputation of my squadron is completely destroyed." Looking back on the article nearly two years later, during his second tour, Reilly said that the unit didn't dwell much on it.

Sgt. 1st Class Gary Qualls, a public affairs soldier, also wrote to Rosen. "I'm sure what you wrote was true, but I think you should tone it down, Nir," he began. "We came across as thugs in the article . . . and I don't think that is an accurate portrayal. Yes, our soldiers were fired up, but if people were trying to kill you every day, you'd probably be fired up too."

In the following months, the Army itself would conclude that some other 3rd ACR soldiers had indeed acted like criminals. Nine soldiers from a howitzer platoon in the 3rd ACR's 2nd squadron, who were assigned to checkpoint duty in western Iraq, allegedly stole thousands of dollars from Iraqis, but they weren't prosecuted because investigators couldn't locate the alleged victims, according to an internal Army document obtained by the ACLU. One private confessed that "the robberies occurred on nearly every TCP [traffic control point] he participated in," Army investigators reported. Another soldier said the criminal acts were common knowledge in the platoon.

Capt. Shawn Martin was the commander of the regiment's Lightning Troop, which was assigned to occupy the isolated town of Ar Rutbah in far western Iraq, where Maj. Gavrilis's Special Forces company had operated so successfully—and so modestly—that spring. Martin took a different approach. "He thought Ar Rutbah was his private domain," Lt. David Minor later testified.

The captain ordered soldiers to fire a weapon over a prisoner's head and hit people with a baseball bat that was called his Iraqi beater, according to subsequent testimony. One detainee held by Martin was bagged over the head, driven deep into the desert, and ordered to dig the hole that, he was told, would be his grave. Another was told, through an interpreter, to "kiss your family goodbye because I am about to bury you in the desert."

After a roadside bomb exploded and Iraqis in the area were detained and handcuffed, Martin "casually walked over to one of the detained Iraqi civilians and kicked him in his back, saying, 'Motherfucker, did you have something to do with this?' and proceeded to kick him in his ribs at least an additional three times," a soldier in his company wrote in a statement. Martin "put his foot on the Iraqi civilian's neck and [said], 'Don't you know I'll kill you, motherfucker?'" The assaulted Iraqi was released a few hours later. Martin also threatened one of his own soldiers with a pistol for declining to fire a weapon near a detainee.

"I traveled everywhere" with Martin from mid-May to mid-June 2003, an Arabic-speaking Army lieutenant who was attached to the company as an interpreter said in a heartfelt statement given to investigators. "On many occasions I saw him treat Iraqis in a very disrespectful manner, to include leaders of Rutbah, such as the police chief. He would yell at them, cuss them out, belittle them in front of their subordinates, put his finger in their face, etc. On numerous occasions I saw him draw his pistol and wave it around in people's faces as he yelled at them. They had presented no threat to us and were involved in no illegal activity. I have heard him say on numerous occasions how all Iraqis are crooks and thieves and his actions toward them would indicate that he truly believes this. I have often apologized to Iraqis for his treatment of them."

Ar Rutbah, which had once seemed so tranquil and promising for U.S. forces, shifted into the loss column. By November 2004, insurgents were active in the town and attacking the police. In early June 2005 a Marine was killed by a roadside bomb in the town, and later in the month a soldier from the Army's 10th Mountain Division suffered the same fate. Later that summer another soldier was killed, and three more were wounded, by another bomb east of the city. Two Marines were shot to death there in October 2005, and another was blown up near the town a month later. On the first day of 2006, an Air Force F-15 conducted an air strike near it. In March 2006, an Army sergeant was killed there by another roadside bomb.

Col. Teeples, who commanded the 3rd ACR during its tour in western Iraq from April 2003 to March 2004, addressed Martin's wrongdoing with a written reprimand. But after a new commander took over, a review of the unit's operations in Iraq was conducted, and charges were brought in some cases. Capt. Martin was charged with ten counts of assault, obstructing justice, and conduct unbecoming an officer. He ultimately was found guilty of three counts of assault and sentenced to forty-five days of imprisonment and fined $12,000.

In another case, on November 26, 2003, four soldiers from the 3rd ACR put an Iraqi general, Abed Hamed Mowhoush, into a sleeping bag, sat on him, and rolled him around the floor. That abuse followed two weeks of brutal interrogations of Mowhoush by Iraqis working under U.S. supervision, who began with slaps and punches, then used a hose, and finally turned the interrogation into a melee in which "the room collapsed" on Mowhoush, according to testimony by Curtis Ryan, an Army criminal investigator. Redacted documents obscure whether the Iraqis who did this were supervised by the U.S. military or by CIA personnel, but reporting by the *Washington Post's* Josh White found that they were members of the Scorpions, a group of Iraqis recruited before the war by the CIA to carry out small-scale subversion, and then employed afterward for help in interpreting and interrogations. The Scorpions had a technique of holding someone's tongue, then using a rubber band to wrap a rag around it, according to a senior U.S. intelligence official with direct access to that information. "It just swells up inside your mouth like a giant Tampax," making the victim painfully thirsty, he said.

Mowhoush was a former head of Iraqi air defenses who had walked into Forward Operating Base Tiger in Qaim two weeks earlier, seeking the release of his sons from custody. (At the time the U.S. military incorrectly stated that he had been captured in a raid.) He told interrogators at the outset that he was commander of al Quds Division, an organization supplying the insurgency with mortars, RPGs, and small arms. He died of smothering and chest compression, a subsequent Army report found. "He had what's referred to as 'facial suffusion,' which is blood basically being congested in the face," Maj. Michael Smith, a military forensic pathologist, later testified. "He also had numerous bruises on his chest, abdomen, arms, legs, one bruise on the head, and he also had several rib fractures"—five, in fact. After a lengthy investigation three of the soldiers were charged with murder, while the fourth was given immunity so he could testify against the others.

Teeples said that he didn't have enough troops to do a better job. "The year that we were there, we were in an 'economy of force' organization, and that means that we are put into a position to perform a very large mission with a small force," he told investigators. Nor did he have some of the right sort of troops, he added: "In the realm of detainees and interrogation, we did not have official interrogators."

This isn't to conclude that the 3rd ACR did terribly in its first tour in Iraq. Rather, what is significant is that despite the killing of a detainee, the abuse of others, and the taint of criminality in one unit, it was in the middle of the pack— not as effective as the 101st Airborne, but not as wanton as the 4th Infantry Division. Like the 82nd Airborne, it began badly, but unlike the paratroopers, it had a strong learning curve, and did better with the passage of time.

"PUC fucking" in the 82nd Airborne

"Shit started to go bad right away," an infantry fire team leader in the 82nd Airborne later told Human Rights Watch, looking back at September 2003. Beating prisoners until they passed out or collapsed quickly became routine at his outpost near Fallujah, Forward Operating Base Mercury, he said. "To 'fuck a PUC' [for person under control, and pronounced "puck"] means to beat him up," he recalled. "We would give them blows to the head, chest, legs, and stomach, pull them down, kick dirt on them. This happened every day."

These attacks weren't inflicted to collect intelligence but simply to blow off steam. "Everyone in camp knew if you wanted to work out your frustration you show up at the PUC tent. In a way it was sport." One day in the fall of 2003, a cook came by, ordered a prisoner to hold a metal pole, and "broke the guy's leg with a mini Louisville Slugger that was a metal bat." Broken bones from beatings occurred "maybe every other week," the sergeant added. "I think the officers knew about it but didn't want to hear about it."

Another sergeant told the organization that he saw "hard hitting" and heard other things, but didn't pay much attention because "I was busy leading my men." He faulted the Army for putting soldiers in the position of watching over groups of prisoners that included men who had attacked them.

Gen. Swannack said in 2005 that all abuse allegations were investigated, but that he never received "any prisoner abuse allegations from Camp Mercury."

Trouble in the 4th Infantry Division

Of all the major conventional combat units operating in Iraq in 2003, the one that most consistently raised eyebrows was Gen. Odierno's 4th Infantry Division. The warning signals, first picked up by the Marines who temporarily occupied Tikrit in April 2003, grew steadily louder. In July, a member of a psychological operations team attached to the 4th's artillery brigade, which was known as Task Force Iron Gunner, filed a formal complaint about how its soldiers treated Iraqis. (Artillery units seem to have been particularly prone to abuse in Iraq, perhaps because their core mission involves indirect fire, which may make them less comfortable with face-to-face confrontation.)

Psyops and civil affairs are parts of the Special Operations Command, but in Iraq they were frequently placed under the command of regular combat units, such as infantry, armor, or artillery, where they often were unhappy with what they saw. In this case, the psyops specialist said his team was especially concerned that the brigade's commander was employing ineffective tactics. "Few of the raids and detentions executed by Task Force Iron Gunner have resulted in the capture of any anti-coalition members or the seizure of illegal weapons," he wrote. He placed the blame squarely with the artillery unit's commander, Col. Kevin Stramara. "This team has witnessed the colonel initiate these events." He charged that detention practices were capricious, sometimes based on the whim of the commander or because more than one hundred dollars in Iraqi dinars had been found in someone's possession.

One day in June, the psyops soldier said, a Bradley fighting vehicle had opened fire on a house, causing it to burst into flames. In a separate incident, a father of a twelve-year-old boy who had been accidentally killed by U.S. forces and then buried was made to dig up the body himself. In a subsequent sworn statement, this member of the team, whose name was blacked out in the documents released by the Army, conceded that some of his charges were based on hearsay, but he stood by his bottom line: "My overall feeling of the treatment of the civilian population is negative. I go out to the civilian community about three times a week to communicate with the Iraqi population to get an overall assessment of how the people see us. Through interpretation the Iraqi people ask us why we are so unfair to them."

One of the sworn statements filed by a civilian employee of the Defense Department working at the brigade's jail—apparently as an interpreter, although he
didn't say so—seemed to back up that conclusion. "I think 80 percent of the people we bring in are 'at the wrong place at the wrong time' [and] have no intelligence value," he said.

The Army's investigation found credible explanations for most of the specific
charges. The house was fired on, the investigation concluded, because it had a
bunker on its roof that was found to contain mortars and artillery rounds. The
dead boy was buried because there was no place to keep his body, and unearthed
without U.S. help because the family had asked that there be no U.S. participation. But the fundamental question of whether the brigade's tactics were misguided wasn't addressed by the investigation.

Lt. Col. West joins an interrogation

There was one unexpected bit of fallout from this inquiry: Investigators learned
that Lt. Col. Allen West, commander of an artillery battalion in Stramara's
brigade, had threatened one night in August to kill an Iraqi prisoner, fired his pistol next to the man's head, and been present while the man, a policeman, was
beaten. Trying to obtain information about an alleged assassination plot against
him in the town of Saba al Boor, West had personally questioned the policeman,
who had been taken prisoner as a suspected member of the conspiracy. "We're
here for one reason, and that's to find out who's trying to kill me," West said as he
entered the detainee's cell, according to the young soldier who served as the gunner on West's Humvee.

Everyone questioned by investigators agreed that West then removed his
9 millimeter pistol from its holster and "told the detainee he would be shot if he
did not provide information."

First the female interpreter kicked the man. Then the gunner grabbed him
and shouted, "Who the fuck is trying to kill him?" Then, according to several accounts, everyone in the room but West beat the man for some time—"about an
hour or so," according to one private.

During this assault, the Iraqi "kept contradicting himself, and he would say,
'I love you' to Lieutenant Colonel West, cry and scream," a staff sergeant told
investigators.

West then took the man outside. "Either you answer the questions, or die
tonight," West said, according to his gunner. He then had two soldiers hold the

man's head inside a clearing barrel—a sand-filled oil barrel that is tipped side-ways, and which soldiers use when returning to a base to ensure that there isn't a live round in a weapon's firing chamber. "If you don't start giving answers, I will kill you," West said, according to one of the soldiers who held the man. West then fired one or two shots past the prisoner's ear into the barrel. "As Lieutenant Colonel West pulled the trigger, the individual went stiff," this soldier added.

At that point, the senior sergeant present decided he had seen enough. "Sir, I don't think he knows," he said to West. ("It was something I had never experienced before and don't care to again," the sergeant first class added in his statement.)

"Put him back in the cell," West responded.

West then reported his actions to his commander, but nothing happened un-til the officers conducting the general investigation of the climate of command in the brigade stumbled across the incident. "I accept full responsibility for my ac-tions and accept punishment," West wrote in a sworn statement a month later. "I acted in the best interest for my soldiers and yes myself." He ultimately was charged with aggravated assault, fined five thousand dollars, removed from his position as a commander, and then retired from the military.

"I was and am proud to say that I never lost a troop in a combat engagement in my time as a battalion commander," West, who went on to teach high school in Florida, said a year later. "We were tough, and it kept my men alive and Iraqis in my area secure. . . . We also let the local people know that we would not tolerate attacks and that our response would be quick and equitable, not wanton violence. . . . Rules and regulations are necessary and proper, but I have never seen one cry at a funeral or accept an American flag after it had been taken off a casket of one of my fallen comrades."

That view represents the logical outcome of making force protection a top priority in U.S. military operations. Every commander wants to take care of his or her troops, and few of West's peers would fault him for his concern. Yet the relent-less pursuit of that goal can undercut what should be a higher priority for a com-mander: winning. After all, if keeping soldiers alive is the top goal, that could be achieved simply by staying at home.

A shot in the stomach

A subsequent instance of abuse in the 4th ID carried no such moral ambigu-ity. On September 11, a soldier shot a handcuffed Iraqi detainee named Obeed Radad in an isolation cell in a detention center in Camp Packhorse near Tikrit, supposedly when the Iraqi attempted to cross a barbed-wire fence. Radad had turned himself in nine days earlier, after learning that U.S. forces were looking for him. The bullet passed straight through his forearm and lodged in his stomach. Eighteen hours later an Army investigator began to look into the incident, according to an internal Army summary of the case. Maj. Frank Rangel, Jr., the executive officer of a military police battalion attached to the 4th ID, was assigned to investigate. He didn't believe the soldier's account that Radad was trying to escape. "I thought the suspect might have committed negligent homicide" and lesser offenses, Rangel said later. Lt. Col. David Poirier, Rangel's boss as commander of that MP battalion, which was based in Tikrit from June 2003 to March 2004, thought the shooter should be court-martialed. "This soldier had committed murder," Poirier said.

But the division commander, Maj. Gen. Odierno, overruled that recommendation, and ultimately the soldier was simply discharged from the Army for the good of the service. "I made the decision to dishonorably discharge him because of mitigating circumstances," Odierno said. "He was a cook, he didn't get proper training, and this detainee was very aggressive, a bad guy."

"They are terrorists and will be treated as such"

A few months later another 4th ID soldier, the staff sergeant overseeing the interrogation section at the division's main detainee holding pen in Tikrit, was reprimanded after an Iraqi was beaten with a baton while being questioned. "These acts could . . . bring extreme discredit upon the U.S. Army," Lt. Col. Conrad Christman, the commander of the 104th Military Intelligence Battalion, warned him in writing on November 6. The incidents of abuse of the detainee, his letter added, "show a lack of supervisory judgment on your part."

Surprisingly, the sergeant hurled those very conclusions straight back at his chain of command. His detailed and eloquent response amounted to a powerful critique of the U.S. Army's entire approach to Iraq. What previous cases of abuse had implied, he now stated explicitly: The Army wasn't prepared for this mission, so soldiers were being trained, equipped, and led poorly. "With the exception of myself, all interrogators at the TF IH ICE [Task Force Iron Horse Interrogation Control Element] were, and most remain, inexperienced at actual interrogation," wrote the sergeant. The division's intelligence efforts generally were "cursory," he added, because of "insufficient personnel, time and resources." Nor had the Army prepared the sergeant and his soldiers for the job they'd been assigned. "Our unit has never trained for detention facility operations because our unit is neither designed nor intended for this mission. . . . [My soldiers] are assigned a mission for which they have not trained, are not manned, are not equipped, are not supplied and . . . cannot effectively accomplish."

What's more, he wrote, the institutional Army hadn't even taken the proper steps to prepare for this kind of war. "To my knowledge, no FM [field manual] covers counterinsurgency interrogation operations."

But most striking from this NCO was a lengthy denunciation of the strategic confusion of those leading the Army in Iraq. This was, after all, not a stately war college symposium or a retired colonel pondering the past in the quiet of his study, but a staff sergeant writing in the field under near combat conditions responding to a formal admonition issued three days earlier. He laid the mess squarely at the feet of Gen. Odierno and other top officers in the 4th ID. "I firmly believe that [name of subordinate soldier redacted in document] took the actions he did, partially, due to his perception of the command climate of the division as a whole. Comments made by senior leaders regarding detainees such as, 'They are not EPWs [Enemy Prisoners of War]. They are terrorists and will be treated as such' have caused a great deal of confusion as to the status of detainees." (Odierno said that he had made that comment not about detainees but in discussing combat operations. "In some cases, because of their acts, I would call them terrorists," he said. "And we would treat them as such, not in detention, but in operations." But that does not appear to have been the universal practice in his division's detention centers.)

As was occurring elsewhere in Iraq, the NCO also reported signs of U.S. forces practicing a form of hostage taking, detaining family members of suspected insurgents in order to compel those suspects to surrender. "Personnel at the ICE regularly see detainees who are, in essence, hostages," he charged. "They are normally arrested by coalition forces because they are family of individuals who have been targeted by a brigade based on accusations that may or may not be true, to be released, supposedly, when and if the targeted individual surrenders to coalition forces." In fact, the U.S. tended not to keep its end of the bargain because the detention system was so badly operated: "In reality, these detainees are transferred to Abu Ghraib prison and become lost in the coalition detention system regardless of whether the targeted individual surrenders himself." This coercive taking of such prisoners had at least the "tacit approval" of senior leaders in the division, he said, because it had been discussed in front of them at briefings.

The military intelligence commander, Christman, impressed by the staff sergeant's arguments, came to think that it would be wrong to fault him for lack of supervision, and so decided against making the written reprimand part of the staff sergeant's permanent record. "It became apparent to me that since we were dealing with far too many detainees for the small number of personnel and the limited facilities we had available, a close supervisory relationship was not feasible," he later explained.

On September 21, 2003, Odierno issued a memorandum on the treatment of detainees to everyone in his division. "Soldiers will treat all detainees with dignity and respect, and, at the very least, will meet the standards for humane treatment as articulated in international law," he ordered. "While detainees in U.S. custody may be interrogated for intelligence purposes, the use of physical or mental torture, or coercion to compel individuals to provide information, is strictly prohibited. . . . Neither the stresses of combat, nor deep provocation, will justify inhumane treatment."

That sounded good, but it isn't clear how much effect it had. A subsequent review by the Army inspector general said interrogators reported "detainees arriving at the cage badly beaten. Many beatings occurred after the detainees were zip-tied by some units in 4ID. Some units wouldn't take THTs [Tactical Human-Intelligence Teams] on raids because they didn't want oversight of activities that might cross the line during capture." An investigation by Human Rights Watch found that soldiers in Iraq sometimes would lie about injuries inflicted in interrogations, having learned that there would be no questions asked if they told medical assistants that the damage had been done during the capture.

Sassaman's battalion reacts to a loss

The most striking instance of abuse in the 4th ID occurred shortly after January 2, 2004, when Capt. Eric Paliwoda, an engineering company commander in the division's 3rd Brigade, was killed by a mortar attack while in his command post. Most losses hit comrades hard, but Paliwoda's death was a particularly cruel blow. Like Lt. Col. Nathan Sassaman, the commander of the battalion of which his company was part, Paliwoda, who stood out at six foot seven inches, had been an athlete at West Point. He was well liked. Sassaman held the dying officer before putting him aboard a medical evacuation helicopter. Paliwoda "basically died in Nate's arms," said Col. Frederick Rudesheim, commander of the brigade that included Sassaman's battalion.

"When Captain Paliwoda died, it pretty much ruined the war for me," Sassaman said later in sworn testimony. "It ruined my experience in Iraq. Not that the previous deaths didn't, but he had been a friend of mine. I kind of leaned on him."

At West Point twenty years earlier, Sassaman had quarterbacked the Army football team, taking it to its first bowl game, the 1984 Cherry Bowl, where Army beat Michigan State University, 10-6. He had made headlines back then for playing much of the season with three cracked ribs. He would take a similarly tough approach in Iraq.

Sassaman and his men in the 1st Battalion of the 8th Infantry Regiment were already deeply unhappy with the situation around them when Paliwoda was killed. "I was angry because the previous battalion could not get the job done," Sassaman would later say. "I mean, I actually went over there and tried to win. I tried to win the peace, and I actually really did try to help the Iraqi people." He pointedly added: "I can't say that for every other unit that was over there." He singled out another 4th ID unit, the 1st Battalion of the 66th Armored Regiment, which was operating just to the north of him in the unruly Tigris River city of Samarra. "They lost control," he said; "1/66 Armor failed in their mission. They failed in their mission to secure the city and to set it up for civil infrastructure projects."

Sassaman had spent months trying to pacify the town of Balad, and thought he had done so, when he was ordered in mid-December to move most of his men about 30 miles north to Samarra, in an operation the Army dubbed Ivy Blizzard. "We went in hard," he recounted. "There is a reason why 1/8 Infantry was sent up there, and it wasn't to go up there and babysit. So we used explosive breaches on the target we went into. . . . No one really told us to win the hearts and minds, but they did tell us to bring the peace, to stop the insurgency, stop the fighting, so that we could make the life better and build projects."

While there he was quoted by the *New York Times* as saying, "With a heavy dose of fear and violence, and a lot of money for projects, I think we can convince these people that we are here to help them." At that time, there was an incident, not known outside the unit, in which some of his troops forced an Iraqi to jump from a bridge into the Tigris near Balad. The man survived, complained, and later sought compensation.

While Sassaman was fighting in Samarra there was trouble back in Balad, he testified at the court-martial of one of his subordinates, Lt. Jack Saville. "While I'm in Samarra, seven of my Iraqi police that we had trained, that Lieutenant

Saville had trained, were killed in an IED blast. Four ICDC [Iraqi Civil Defense Corps soldiers], which are now considered Iraqi National Guardsmen, were killed, and we lost two Americans, Captain Paliwoda and then another engineer soldier up on the ad Diwanijah bridge." Then, at the end of the three weeks, he was told to head back to Balad and clean up the mess that had erupted there in his unit's absence.

He and his men were feeling put upon: "I mean, I just felt like, 'Does anybody want to help us here with the fight, besides 1/8?'"

The death of Paliwoda had left the unit in the mood for revenge—and it knew how to exact it. When the sun went down that chilly January night, soldiers from 1/8 set out to kill some specific Iraqis. At about nine-thirty a patrol from Sassaman's Alpha Company was stopping drivers outside of Samarra who were violating the curfew. The patrol was led by Lt. Saville. The first car his men stopped had a family returning from a hospital, where the mother had just given birth. They were told to go home. The second was a city council member, who also was given leave to go. The third vehicle was a white pickup truck. Its two occupants were handcuffed, driven to the Tigris, and forced from the ledge of a pump house into the river, a drop of about six feet. One of the men, Zaidoun Fadel Hassoun, age nineteen, drowned, according to the other, Marwan Fadel Hassoun, twenty-three, his cousin.

When 1/66 Armor learned of the incident and passed the word to Gen. Odierno, he tried to check it out but was lied to by his subordinates, he said. "I went to 1/8, and they said, 'Didn't happen,'" he recalled in an interview. "The bottom line on the Sassaman case is . . . he directed a cover-up of an incident, and didn't come clean until he realized the CID had figured it out."

Sassaman's soldiers at first insisted that they had released the men—without mentioning that they had "released" them into the river. Pressed, they subsequently said they'd seen both men swim to shore and emerge. That was a lie, Saville later testified. In fact, he had gone out that night with an order from his company commander, Capt. Matthew Cunningham. "I understood he was directing me and my subordinates to kill certain Iraqis we were seeking that night who were suspected of killing the company commander in our unit," he testified, referring to the death of Paliwoda. "I understood that the order meant that if they were captured, regardless of the circumstances of their capture, they were not to return alive." That order was given twice that night, he added. Saville also testified that his company commander had given him a list of five Iraqis who "were not to come back alive" if captured during the patrol.

A few hours later, sometime after midnight, at the end of a series of raids on suspected insurgents in Balad, another soldier in the same company, Staff Sgt. Shane Werst, led an Iraqi into his home, allegedly struck him about ten times, then shot him at least six times with his M-4 carbine.

"I can't help but feeling like I was part of an execution," PFC Nathan Stewart, the other soldier who was there, later testified. The facts of the matter aren't in dispute. Werst then pulled out a handgun, fired it into a wall, and told Stewart to smear the dead man's fingerprints on it. Charged months later with murder, Werst testified that he acted in self-defense, saying that the Iraqi had lunged for a weapon. Werst said he had planted the handgun on the dead man because "I was second-guessing myself." He was acquitted by a military jury.

In another raid at about this time, Sgt. 1st Class Tracy Perkins, the platoon sergeant for Alpha Company's 1st platoon, had a murky encounter with an Iraqi identified by Army intelligence as one of ten suspects in recent mortar and IED attacks in Balad. He told investigators that the man—"Target No. 1," according to a statement by Perkins—had a pistol in his hand. "I fired a controlled pair [of shots] and the man still continued to raise the weapon," Perkins wrote. "Then I fired a third shot into the man's head and killed him."

Cunningham, the company commander, stated that multiple informants had said the man was a former Baath Party official who was head of an insurgent cell responsible for four bombings.

An Army inquiry found the facts of the matter somewhat less clear, largely because of conflicting and incomplete statements. "After interviewing the majority of individuals present that night," the investigator reported, "it is apparent that all individuals are quite confused in determining the exact facts." It recommended that no action be taken against Perkins.

But Perkins and others were later brought up on a variety of charges related to the bridge incident. Perkins was convicted early in 2005, just after the first anniversary of the event, on two counts of aggravated assault, obstruction of justice, and assault consummated by battery. A few months later, Saville pleaded guilty to charges of obstruction of justice, dereliction of duty, and aggravated assault and battery, and under his plea agreement was sentenced to a total of forty-five days in jail. (Prosecutors had a relatively weak case because they were unable to produce a body that was clearly that of the victim.) The young officer said he was pleased by the outcome because it allowed him to remain in the Army.

An Army lawyer recommended that Cunningham be charged with solicitation of murder, involuntary manslaughter, and other offenses. But after Werst's acquittal the Army decided against prosecuting him, and he left the Army in June 2005.

Saville said that he had had discussions with Sassaman about how to mislead Army investigators. Despite that, Sassaman received only a written admonishment. "On 7 January 2004, you were briefed . . . that soldiers of the 1st platoon pushed two Iraqi men into the Tigris River causing one of them to drown," Odierno wrote. "You ordered them to deny that the men were pushed into the river and to say that they were dropped off at the side of the road. Your conduct was wrongful, criminal and will not be tolerated."

Sassaman remained in command of the battalion for months, an outcome that shocked Poirier, his fellow battalion commander. "When you have a battalion commander who leads his staff in rehearsing a story about a murder—and he's still in command?" Poirier said in April 2005, shortly after he retired from the Army. "That's not right."

Sassaman left the Army at about the same time that Poirier did. He made his departure defiantly, taking a swipe on his way out at Maj. Gen. Odierno, whose division was headquartered in one of Saddam Hussein's former palaces in Tikrit. "If I were to do it all over again, I would do the exact same thing, and I've thought about this long and hard," he testified. "I was taught in the Army to win, and I was trying to win all the way, and I just disagreed—deeply disagreed— with my superior commanders on the actions that they thought should be taken with these individuals [charged in the Tigris bridge case]. And you have to understand, the legal community, my senior commanders, were not fighting in the streets of Samarra. They were living in a palace in Tikrit. So they lacked some of the situational awareness that I had and that the soldiers had on the ground." His bitter bottom line: "Big Army should be ashamed of itself in a lot of ways. . . . Mistakes were made at every single level. Let me just leave it at that."

Poirier said he remained generally much impressed by Odierno—but not in this instance. "My experience with 4 ID was a good one," he said. "You make mistakes. And we didn't have a lot of experience in operating in a Muslim state that had been run by a crazy man." His conclusion on the bridge case, he said, was "I love Odierno, but he granted immunity to the battalion commander and company commander, and gave them letters of reprimand." Generally, he said, "there were some people in 4 ID who were out of control. But I think Odierno's leadership was very sound. His failures, if that's what you want to call them, came from trusting his subordinates."

A senior U.S. intelligence official was less charitable. He thought Odierno intentionally turned a blind eye to certain brutalities: "He's a good guy. But he would say to his colonels, 'I don't want to hear the bad shit.'"

Maj. Gen. Odierno, who by 2005 had been promoted to be the military assistant to the chairman of the Joint Chiefs of Staff, at first agreed to be interviewed for this book, but later cancelled the interview. Then, when a copy of this section of the book was sent to him, along with an invitation for comment, he wrote back, "That is clearly not even close to a complete picture of what happened nor my intent throughout nor with an understanding of the overall strategy of the division. . . . This is unfair to the soldiers and leaders of the division."

In a subsequent interview, Odierno mounted a strenuous defense of his division's performance. He said the preceding description of the 4th Infantry Division makes it appear that "all we did was kill people wantonly and abuse prisoners. In my opinion, that's totally false." Odierno said that he had made detainee operations a major focus of his command after it became clear in the summer of 2003 that the division would have to hold prisoners. He had held a "summit" with his commanders on detainee operations late that summer, and during the division's year in Iraq issued seventeen separate orders relating to detainees. "That's what bothers me about this" discussion of the 4th ID. "I spent so much time on this. It was important to me that we did this right." He also said that no one had ever asked him for comment for the various Army reports that singled out the 4th ID for the abuse of Iraqi captives.

He said that while his division "came in very hard across the AO [area of operations]" in the fall of 2003, he thought those raids were targeted precisely and helped develop the intelligence that had led to the capture of Saddam Hussein. Most notable was the fact that after his division spent a year in the northern part of the Sunni Triangle that area remained largely quiet, even as Mosul and Anbar province exploded. And, he added, despite being attacked more than other divisions, fewer soldiers in his were lost.

Odierno's self-defense shouldn't be dismissed lightly, especially in the collection of intelligence, which clearly worked in the apprehension of Saddam. Yet there is little evidence that his division's unusually aggressive stance was particularly successful. Samarra especially continued to be a trouble spot for the U.S.

effort, and the insurgency remained robust and active in much of the rest of the area where the 4th ID operated.

But perhaps the best way to judge the 4th ID was that the division succeeding his chose a sharply different course of operations. Maj. Gen. John Batiste, who commanded the 1st Infantry Division (which took over from the 4th ID in the spring of 2004), declined to discuss the operations of the 4th ID but emphasized that in his own unit "from day one" that it was essential "to treat people with dignity," even captured insurgents. As Petraeus had done in the north, Batiste established a detailed set of procedures for his jails and brought in sheikhs and imams to inspect his facilities. "I told commanders they would be responsible for everything that happened in them," Batiste said. "They all conformed to the Geneva Conventions, to the rule of law, and to my sense of what was right from the way I was brought up." And like Petraeus, he had only one notable instance of abuse, and that happened not in a detention facility but when a sergeant appears to have had a nervous breakdown during field operations.

Inside Abu Ghraib

One day in the spring of 2004, Maj. Gen. James Mattis was walking out of a mess hall in al Asad, in western Iraq, when he saw a knot of his troops intently hunched over a television, watching a cable news show. Marines weren't usually so attentive to current events. "What's going on?" Mattis asked. It was, he learned, the revelations about Abu Ghraib, along with sickening photos of cruelty and humiliation.

A nineteen-year-old lance corporal glanced up from the television and told the general, "Some assholes have just lost the war for us."

The detainee abuses that would resonate most took place not out in the divisions operating in the provinces, but on the outskirts of the capital, in the Abu Ghraib prison. All of the Army's problems in Iraq in 2003—poor planning, clumsy leadership, strategic confusion, counterproductive tactics, undermanning, being overly reactive—came together in the treatment of prisoners, a wide-ranging scandal that eventually was summarized in the phrase "Abu Ghraib," after the big prison west of Baghdad where many prisoners wound up, and where some were tortured.

There was never supposed to be a problem with detainees, because there weren't supposed to be any, at least in U.S. hands. The war plan had called for the Iraqi population to cheerfully greet the American liberators, quickly establish a new government, and wave farewell to the departing American troops. It was not to be. "As the need for actionable intelligence arose, the realization dawned [among U.S. commanders] that pre-war planning had not included planning for detainee operations," a subsequent Army report noted. And so a series of steps were taken that ultimately would lead to a scandal that would shake the Army and tarnish the U.S. effort in Iraq. As Gen. Mattis put it a year later, "When you lose the moral high ground, you lose it all."

The mess at Abu Ghraib arguably began on October 1, 2003, when Staff Sgt. Ivan "Chip" Frederick II and Spec. Charles Graner, Jr., arrived there as part of the advance party for the 372nd Military Police Company, an Army Reserve unit from rural Cresaptown, Maryland, in the Appalachian foothills. They were part of a larger, troubled unit that until September had been based in southern Iraq. Many had deployed to the country that spring to handle the flood of enemy POWs that war planners had expected but that had never materialized. Their mission completed, they had expected—like many other soldiers in Iraq that spring—to go home sooner rather than later. Instead, the reservists were assigned a new mission. Someone had to run the Iraqi prison system, and in the absence of an Iraqi government, they were handed the job. Their morale plummeted, an official Army inquiry later found. Some began exaggerating medical complaints, such as back pains, to get evacuated out of the country, their brigade commander, Brig. Gen. Karpinski, later complained. In mid-October the 372nd took responsibility, from a Nevada-based MP unit, for Tiers 1A and 1B, the permanent, concrete-walled part of the prison. Called One Alpha, or the hard site, by the soldiers, this was the cell block where interrogations took place and where detainees believed to possess useful information were kept. Other prisoners, deemed to be of less intelligence value, lived in tents in an open area.

Just how poorly prisoners had been treated during the summer, before the 372nd MPs arrived, is a matter of dispute. Some had been kept naked and handcuffed to bars, and others were made to wear women's underwear on their heads, according to Frederick's statement. What is not in question is that once Graner and Frederick took control of the night shift on Tier 1A, they wasted little time in going on a rampage of abuse. "I took it to another level," Frederick said in a sworn statement given much later to Army investigators.

The torture of detainees was first recorded photographically on October 17, according to the time stamp from one of the digital cameras the MPs used. "Graner was a picture person, he loved taking pictures," Frederick said in his confessional declaration. "Graner took pictures all the time." (Indeed, according to

Frederick's sworn statement, Graner went so far as to have Frederick photograph him while he was being fellated in a prison supply room by PFC Lynndie England, another member of the unit, who had become Graner's girlfriend. In one photo, England is giving the thumbs-up she would later use in photos of detainee abuse.) The October 17 photo showed a man stripped naked and handcuffed to his cell door. The next day an Iraqi man was photographed handcuffed to a cot with women's underwear draped over his head. About a week later—official accounts differ on the precise date—PFC England posed holding a dog's leash that had at the other end a naked detainee, nicknamed Gus by the MPs. On October 25, naked Iraqi men with their hands cuffed and legs shackled were piled on their backs like cordwood. Adel Nakhla, a civilian working as a translator on contract, said in a statement later that "they handcuffed their hands together and their legs with shackles and started to stack them on top of each other by ensuring that the bottom guy's penis will touch the guy on top's butt."

In the following nights, detainees were kept naked, with some forced to masturbate in front of female soldiers. On November 4 a detainee was hooded and placed on a box, and had wires attached to him that he was told would electrocute him if he stepped off the box. On the same night a CIA detainee died in custody on Tier 1B, having been beaten by the Navy SEALs who had captured him. One detainee later described to Army investigators being made to "bark like a dog, being forced to crawl on his stomach while MPs spit and urinated on him, and being struck causing unconsciousness." He also said he had been sodomized with a stick. Investigators found it "highly probable" that his allegations were accurate.

Many if not all of these acts were violations of the Geneva Conventions governing the treatment of prisoners of war and of civilian noncombatants. Most notably, Article 3 of the 1949 convention stated that people being detained shall be treated humanely, without "outrages on personal dignity, in particular humiliating and degrading treatment." The abuses occurred not only because of the failings of those who committed them, but because of the lack of supervision and leadership by their superiors. One reason for this was that everyone was overworked, taking twelve-hour shifts in a hostile environment, frequently for seven days a week. Yet good officers know their soldiers, and part of that is knowing who to keep an eye on. They also enforce discipline, so other soldiers understand that the unit has standards all its members are responsible for. Yet here leaders didn't supervise or lead, and other soldiers lacked the discipline to stop the sadistic acts, or at least to report them.

Abu Ghraib was falling apart. Even in a nation sinking into chaos, the prison stood out as particularly troubled. It was regularly being shelled by mortars. Prisoners were routinely escaping—no one knows exactly how many, but at least three dozen. On November 5, during the night shift's watch, several fled Tier 1A. Two days later another detainee went missing. The next day five or six left. "Note: No power. No water. Prison in state of lockdown," a soldier wrote in the One Alpha log on November 17, 2003.

Army teams with working dogs arrived at the prison on November 20, and were used to abuse prisoners four days later, the day an MP was shot with a smuggled pistol. Using dogs to scare prisoners was called the doggie dance, according to Frederick.

On November 24 the prisoners rioted, resulting in the shooting deaths of nine and injuries to nine U.S. troops. A subsequent Army report concluded:

> Contributing factors were lack of comprehensive training of guards, poor or non-existent SOPs [standard operating procedures], no formal guard-mount conducted prior to shift, no rehearsals or ongoing training, the mix of less than lethal rounds with lethal rounds in weapons, no AARs [after-action reviews] being conducted after incidents, ROE [rules of engagement] not posted and not understood, overcrowding, uniforms not standardized, and poor communications between the command and soldiers.

But to Karpinski, the female MP general overseeing detention operations in Iraq, that catalog of missteps merely reflected the lack of support she was getting from her superiors. A few months later she would be blamed by the Army as the seniormost officer to have made grave mistakes in handling Abu Ghraib. She would argue in her own defense that she had worked to call attention to her problems and had sought help from the top commanders in Iraq, generally in vain.

In November, as the Ramadan offensive surged, the 82nd Airborne's commanding general, Swannack, came to see Karpinski. The eastern boundary of his division's area of operations ran up against Abu Ghraib, and he wanted to know about her security arrangements. "What platforms do you have?" he asked her. He was asking a basic commander's question: Do you have Humvees? Armored Humvees? Bradley fighting vehicles? How do your soldiers investigate enemy movement, or respond to attacks?

"None, sir," Karpinski responded.

"What weapons do you have?" Swannack asked.

"Just M-16s, SAWs," she said, referring to the Army's basic rifle and the light machine gun known as a squad automatic weapon. These were the most basic arms a unit could have, but nothing that any platoon leader would want as his only tools available for combat. Such light weaponry was useless, for example, against mortar attacks, which could be fired from miles away, and which needed mortars or artillery pieces for an adequate response, as well as a sophisticated counterbattery radar system to detect the point of origin of the enemy fire. His own troops worked constantly to hone their response time on mortar fire, eventually getting it down to one hundred seconds. One night they were able to hit back in just that amount of time, and the next day a patrol found a 60 millimeter mortar tube on the far bank of the Euphrates, and three dead men at a nearby hospital.

Swannack appeared almost incredulous at the inability of Karpinski's troops to respond in a similar fashion, she recalled in an interview. "What do you have for force protection?" he asked.

"An armored division that doesn't want to help me," she said, referring to the 1st AD, which operated just to her east, in and around Baghdad. He also was stunned that her sentries did not respond to hostile fire from the villages adjacent to the prison. Nor did they conduct patrols through those areas. That amounted to an invitation to the insurgents to launch attacks.

Swannack looked at Karpinski. She remembered him slapping her on the back and saying, "Well, Sanchez really fucked you." (Asked about that, Swannack recalled commenting in a slightly less charged way. He believed he said "something like 'CJTF-7 was screwing you by not giving you sufficient assets to do this job.'") He got into his Black Hawk and flew off. But that night he made sure that a mortar platoon from the 82nd was on her western flank, and two days later he assigned an infantry company to patrol in that area to keep insurgents away from the prison.

In December, at the next monthly meeting of commanding generals in Iraq, Karpinski recalled, she confronted Odierno. "Look, sir, your mobile interrogation teams need to do a better job," and not keep dumping thousands of unscreened Iraqis on her facility.

"I don't have the fucking time to do it," Odierno responded dismissively. "Tell Wojdakowski to get you more facilities," referring to Sanchez's deputy, Maj. Gen. Walter Wojdakowski, who handled a lot of dull but important issues such as logistics and other support functions. Odierno's riposte was a classic combat commander's response, and captures the unequal nature of the exchange. He was an active-duty two-star general, the commander of an armored division, one of the Army's premier units. He was the youngest division commander in the Army. And he was physically imposing, six foot five inches tall and weighing 250 pounds, with a bulletlike shaved head. Everyone around him knew he was destined for three or four stars, and might be chief of staff of the Army one day. She was smaller, a woman, a reservist one-star general, the commander of support troops. In Army terms, that meant her job was to solve his problems, not add to them.

But Karpinski stuck to her guns, according to her account. In a previous confrontation, she'd found that if she weathered his initial blustery response, she could get through to him. She told him that the torrent of detainees, many of them shipped by his outfit, was swamping her operation at Abu Ghraib.

Odierno relented a bit. "Tell me more," he said. "What kind of numbers would you like?"

She said she needed more discrimination in who was shipped to her. "He said he would look into it, and he did," she said in 2005, "but they [Odierno's 4th ID] were still worst offenders." (Asked about this account, Odierno insisted it never happened. "That's bullshit," he said. "I never talked to her about detainees," except for one instance of dealing with an anti-Iranian militia.)

On Christmas Day she went out to Abu Ghraib to check on the state of the operation. The staff there told her, a bit chagrined, that they were over capacity, and just the night before had turned away a shipment of seven prisoners sent down from northern Iraq by Petraeus's 101st Airborne Division. They actually had told the incoming flight to put the Iraqis back on the helicopter and take them away. That worried Karpinski. "I knew Petraeus wouldn't be happy," she recalled. So instead of waiting to be hauled in to explain what was going on, she went to see Wojdakowski. Standing six foot four inches tall, Wojdakowski had played basketball at West Point under Bob Knight, and had gone on to a career in which he specialized in infantry training.

He told her not to worry about all the detainees coming in, she recounted. He got angry. He put down his pen and looked her straight in the eye. "I don't care if we're holding fifteen thousand innocent Iraqis, we're winning the war," he told her, she later said in a sworn statement to Army investigators.

"No, sir, you are not," she responded. "Not inside my wire, you are not winning, you are making enemies. You're making enemies out of every one of those people you're holding without a reason. . . . This isn't a fair carriage of justice. This isn't dignity and respect. This isn't the road ahead you are allegedly preaching all the time. This is smoke and mirrors, a facade of security in Baghdad. There is no such thing."

Wojdakowski didn't respond to requests for an interview.

The Army turns over a rock at Abu Ghraib

On January 12, Karpinski was on a mission near the Iranian border, sent there by Gen. Sanchez, when she checked her e-mail on the military's SIPRNET, its secure internal Internet system. She saw one from the head of the Army's Criminal Investigation Division—its internal FBI. Curious, she opened it first, and read two short sentences notifying her that her unit was being investigated for prisoner abuse. It isn't clear what had sparked that inquiry.

The next day, Spec. Joseph Darby put photographs of the abuse occurring in cell block One Alpha into a plain envelope and slipped them under the door of the CID investigators. They looked at them, then accelerated their inquiry into hyperdrive. Just after midnight on January 14, Capt. Donald Reese, the thirty-nine-year-old commander of one of Karpinski's subordinate units, the 372nd Military Police Company, was awakened and told that his battalion commander wanted to see him. After he had dressed and arrived at the unit headquarters, he was greeted by Chief Warrant Officer 2 Paul Arthur, an official from the Army's CID. "We have to do an investigation on your soldiers," he was told, according to a statement he gave later. "We believe they're involved in some alleged abuse."

Two hours later, Reese, who in civilian life was a salesman from New Stanton, Pennsylvania, knocked on the door of Frederick, the sergeant who was chief of the night shift on One Alpha. "Freddy, CID is here, and they want to talk to you," Reese said. Arthur and other CID agents seized Frederick's weapons and computer and interrogated him until 4:00 A.M. Frederick claimed in a statement that he had questioned some of the practices in the prison, but that "the answer I got was this is how Military Intelligence wants it."

A few days later Karpinski met with Sanchez in his office at Camp Victory, the ornate set of palaces Saddam had built in a series of artificial lakes just east of Baghdad airport. It was their second one-on-one meeting during her time in Iraq. It was a curt meeting, held at nine at night—extremely late for officers whose days begin at dawn. "He was insulted by my presence—that's what he communicated to me," she recalled later, after consulting her daily journal.

"Do you know what this is going to do to my Army?" Sanchez said, she recalled. He issued a formal letter of admonishment to her. This established for the official Army record that her performance was markedly below expectation.

Karpinski wanted to offer some suggestions on how to handle the situation. It was a bad misreading of Sanchez's mood. "Sir, I've been in the Middle East for years, and I have a good relationship with the press here," she began. She offered to have a statement issued in Arabic that would "put this all on my shoulders."

She had even thought about how to release some of the digital images of torture. Her notion was to get out ahead of this mess. "We can choose a couple of photographs, and at least—"

Sanchez cut her off, she recalled. "Absolutely not," he told her. The Army wasn't going to let those photos out. "There's not going to be any contact between you and the press," he added, according to notes she made in her journal that night.

A series of official investigations ultimately would hang the criminal blame for Abu Ghraib on a group of low-ranking soldiers, and the military responsibility on Brig. Gen. Karpinski. The military establishment was unsympathetic. "She felt herself a victim, and she propagated a negativity that permeated throughout the BDE," or brigade, Air Force Col. Henry Nelson, a psychiatrist involved in the investigation, concluded.

It was a tragic moment for a military with a long and proud heritage of treating its prisoners better than most—especially one that had come to Iraq thinking of itself as a liberation force, again solidly in the American tradition. During the Revolutionary War, the historian David Hackett Fischer noted, Gen. George Washington had "often reminded his men that they were an army of liberty and freedom, and that the rights of humanity for which they were fighting should extend even to their enemies." This compassion toward prisoners was extended by Washington expressly in the face of the cruel British handling of American captives. Washington ordered Lt. Col. Samuel Blachley Webb, in a passage quoted by Fischer, "Treat them with humanity, and Let them have no reason to Complain of our Copying the brutal example of the British army in their Treatment of our unfortunate brethren." The United States Army was a long way from home in Iraq.

PART III

THE LONG TERM

13.

"THE ARMY OF THE EUPHRATES" TAKES STOCK

WINTER 2003–4

In Iraq the U.S. Army encountered two of its recent nightmares. The tactical opposition that developed was what it had feared it would find seven years earlier in Bosnia: heavily armed factional fighters using AK-47s, rocket-propelled grenades, and land mines to attack U.S. troops, and then blending in with the population, frequently in urban environments. Meanwhile, its strategic position painfully resembled that of the Soviet Union in Afghanistan in the early 1980s, when the Red Army, after quickly taking the country, found itself mired and suffering increasing casualties. Ironically, when the U.S. military invaded Afghanistan twenty-two years after the Red Army, it was extremely conscious of the quagmire the Soviets had found there and took great pains to avoid replicating it. Instead of going in big and heavy and conventional, it went into Afghanistan fast, small, and innovative, combining soldiers on horses with B-52s in the air, using satellite signals from space to guide smart bombs to their unwitting targets. It was in Iraq that the Americans unconsciously repeated some of the Soviet errors in Afghanistan. They went in big, with lots of conventional forces and a tendency to rely on armored vehicles when possible. They confused swift entry with victory. They built big bases and reacted clumsily to insurgent attacks, using tactics that sometimes alienated the population. An Army built to execute swift, crushing operations designed around heavy armor instead found itself enmeshed in a slow-moving, close-up war of small arms.

It was a situation that defeated many of the technological advantages wielded by the U.S. military. After years of talking about its information superiority, the Army suddenly was in an inferior position. It didn't speak the language, it didn't understand the culture, it didn't know much about its enemy, and it seemed all too often to be the last one to know what was going on. One of the warning signs of attack, for example, was when a crowd of Iraqi civilians suddenly vanished. U.S. military bases and movements were easy to observe, while those of its enemy were largely unknown. The American military lacked a sufficient number of interpreters, but knew that some of those it did employ were in league with the enemy. "It would be better if our working assumption was more modestly one of our own information inferiority," observed British Maj. Gen. Bailey.

As defense analyst Andrew Krepinevich put it, a world-class sprinter was being forced to run a marathon.

Lessons learned "the hard way"

By the end of 2003, the Army was recognizing that it was locked in its first protracted ground combat since the Vietnam War. As they prepared that winter to leave Iraq and turn over the mission to other units, in what would be one of the biggest troop rotations in the history of the U.S. military, the seasoned soldiers who had served there for a year sought to pass on their hard-won knowledge to their successors, in e-mails, in essays, in PowerPoint presentations, and in rambling memoirs posted on Web sites or sent to rear detachments. It was an account far more personal than those offered by the media and generally grimmer than the official statements that painted a picture of steady progress. Taken together, these gritty documents told a story of an unexpectedly hard small war punctuated by casualties that haunted the writers. At the same time, they showed how a well-trained, professional force adjusted to complex ground combat in a harsh climate and alien culture, relearning some timeless lessons of warfare and discovering a few new ones.

"We had to learn the hard way," Capt. Daniel Morgan, an infantry company commander in the 101st Airborne Division, wrote in an essay that rocketed around military e-mail circles. Morgan's essay was popular for two reasons: It was unusually well written, and it was relentlessly specific. One of the most striking lessons the 1992 graduate of Georgetown University passed on: Every soldier in the unit should carry a tourniquet of sufficient length to cut off the gush of blood from major leg wounds. "Trust me," he wrote, "it saved four of my soldiers' lives." Morgan also emphasized to incoming soldiers that they needed to be ready to kill quickly yet precisely. "If an enemy opens fire with an AK-47 aimlessly, which most of these people do, you should be able to calmly place the red dot reticule of your M-68 optic device on his chest and kill him with one shot," he admonished. "If you do this, the rest will run and probably not come back." And while patrolling, if you see an Iraqi notice you and then make a cellular phone call, change your planned route, and especially avoid the next major intersection, where an ambush may be assembling.

Like Morgan's, many of the commentaries that were composed around this time had a tone of no-nonsense urgency. This was no longer a discreet, peacetime military that liked to pretend it could achieve "zero defects." "There was too much crap I saw over there that guys just don't understand, and it meant soldiers' lives," Capt. John Wrann, a 4th Infantry Division engineer, wrote in an essay that was posted on www.CompanyCommand.com, which began as a private Web site by and for junior Army officers, but became sponsored by the Army and received an unusual kind of semiofficial status. Much of what his soldiers were called upon to do were actions for which they hadn't been trained, Wrann said. "They will have to write a new book for this when it's all over."

As a whole the soldiers' commentaries tended to portray a harsh picture of Iraq and its people. Capt. Ken Braeger, a company commander in the 4th Infantry Division, headquartered in Tikrit, deep in the Sunni Triangle, stated that newcomers should "understand . . . that most of the people here want us dead, they hate us and everything we stand for, and will take any opportunity to cause us harm."

Officers in Iraq said the documents tended to be useful, especially because they were more attuned to current conditions there than official publications. One officer based at Balad noted that after reading Morgan's essay he made adjustments in a convoy he was planning at that moment for an operation in the Sunni Triangle. "Our troops are in down and dirty fights in the streets of the Fallujahs of this country, and mostly the Army still trains for the Big Fight," he said in an interview. "So we definitely need these informal debriefs."

Five subjects dominated the new veterans' discussions: the innovative nature of the foe, the need to update tactics and equipment, ways to keep troops alert and, again and again, how to run a safe convoy. And then, less as a lesson than as a warning, there was the impact of casualties.

The writers also repeatedly expressed a growing respect for their adversaries. "The enemy is getting smarter," Braeger wrote in his November 2003 essay. "He watches us and makes adjustments accordingly." This new respect also surfaced in an official Marine summary that said, "The enemy is clever and should not be underestimated. Commanders that [sic] are ignoring or wishing away enemy capabilities and lethality are sustaining casualties."

To a surprising degree, the lessons learned summaries focused on how to operate a military convoy safely. In 2003 highway overpasses became the Iraqi equivalent of ambush points on jungle trails during the Vietnam War. The developing wisdom was always to move toward them with caution, and then swerve from lane to lane at the last minute. Some studies also recommended that a gun truck—that is, a big vehicle with a mounted .50 caliber heavy machine gun—speed ahead of the convoy and train that gun on the bridge while the convoy passed under it.

Capt. Robert McCormick of the 2nd Armored Cavalry Regiment found that in eastern Baghdad "the vehicles that seemed to come under attack were that of soft skin and did not have any weapons noticeable or present." A more official military study warned that to be defensible, convoys should consist of at least five vehicles. The most vulnerable convoys were small ones of three or four vehicles, especially those in which rifles were not held visible and at the ready. "Smaller convoys cannot produce enough firepower to fend off attacks or deal with casualties," it said.

"When possible, travel in large convoys," cautioned Maj. Eric Estep, who was based at the big supply depot at Balad, the destination of dozens of convoys every day. His PowerPoint presentation of a study of insurgent tactics against convoys also noted that they tended to attack the last vehicle. To counter this, he and others recommended putting heavy firepower there. The need for this aggressive posture was repeated often. "It is true that the 'meaner' and more prepared you look that you can return immediate fire, the more likely they'll think twice about attacking," wrote Wrann.

By contrast, Braeger reported, some National Guard troops were so slovenly that they invited attack: "We've noticed the convoys that get hit more often are ones with soldiers out of uniform—the Guard guys usually travel in flak vest and t-shirt—and do not pull security when they stop."

A Marine summary of Army lessons noted that in the lead truck in a convoy, the driver and gunner tended to be too busy with their tasks to adequately scan the ground for roadside bombs. It recommended that a third soldier, equipped with binoculars and night-vision goggles, be posted in that vehicle—and be trained and ready to take over the machine gun should the gunner be hit. In another extraordinarily specific convoy lesson, Morgan trained his driver to take wide right turns in major intersections because, he explained, "[o]n turns, most IEDs, if not all, are placed on the inside turn."

But several commanders warned in their reports that one thing worried them even more than roadside bombings or convoy attacks: complacency among their troops. "Complacency is the no. 1 killer of soldiers," reported Lt. Jessica Murphy, an MP officer. "This is the one that bites most units." She said that even units being shot at can start treating missions as routine. To keep an edge, Capt. Paul Evangelista, commander of an engineer company in the 10th Mountain Division, sought to make sure that all soldiers went on missions outside the base—that is, beyond "the wire." (Support troops, such as mechanics, cooks, and clerks, tended not to leave their bases, with some hardly going outside them during a one-year tour.)

The inevitability of casualties and the need to train for them was a recurring theme. Wrann said that the image that would remain with him was watching a burly platoon sergeant cup the head of his wounded medic and quietly tell him that his left arm was gone. His grim message to the incoming troops: "It's real, and the cost is real. Guys get hurt and guys die."

"Though nobody likes to think about it, you have to train to take casualties," admonished Maj. James Williams, the executive officer of an MP battalion. "You have to practice things like evacuating people from a disabled vehicle, establishing security, treating the wounded, and calling for medevac." In addition, he advised, units should drill for their leaders being wounded, forcing others to take on the jobs of commanding, navigating, and communicating with headquarters.

Capt. Rich Smith, commander of an infantry company in the 101st Airborne, cautioned fellow officers in his posting to be ready for moments such as one that stayed with him, of covering the body of Cpl. Evan Ashcraft, whom he had known for years and who was in a patrol that was ambushed in the desert about 185 miles north of Baghdad on July 24, 2003. Two other soldiers were also killed in the attack. "I never knew how hard command could be until I lost those guys," Smith wrote.

The Army in America: support, regret, and dissent

Back home, Army families also were finding it a very different war. Technology gave it an extraordinary immediacy, with cable TV and e-mail bringing the front lines nearer the kitchen table. One survey by a professor at West Point found that 95 percent of Army soldiers in Iraq used e-mail, and two thirds said they used it three times a week. The speed of communication sometimes was vexing: At Fort Campbell, Kentucky, home of the 101st Airborne Division, almost every wife seemed to have gotten a predawn call from a friend telling her to turn on the television because the crawl on the bottom of the cable news screen was reporting that a soldier had been killed in the region of Iraq where her husband was posted.

To squelch rumors sparked by such reports, the Army had each unit's Family Readiness Group, an unpaid support organization of spouses, quickly transmit information on events in Iraq. "When something happens, the phone tree lights up, so you're not sitting there watching TV trying to figure out if your husband is hurt," said Kristin Jackson, whose husband was a mechanic in the 101st Airborne. Support groups like the one to which she belonged were created in response to problems encountered during the 1991 Gulf War, when the Army—going to war with a heavily married force, in contrast to the Vietnam War—was caught flat-footed by the need to look out for soldiers' families. In response, the Army built a robust network of family supports, ranging from day care to counseling to legal help to instruction in Army life, household finance, and coping with stress.

Despite such aids, most of the basics of war remained unchanged. There was still a chilling fear when the phone rang in the middle of the night. Mothers saw the stress in their children. At Ringgold Elementary School, the school closest to the front gates of Fort Campbell, Amanda Hicks, a teacher whose husband was a pilot in the 160th Special Operations Aviation Regiment, said she and her colleagues had found their students notably fragile while their parents—mainly fathers—were deployed to Iraq and Afghanistan. "I have got the teariest class this year," said Debbie Sanders, a kindergarten teacher. "They just cry all the time."

It was also a war being fought by a professional, volunteer military, and so affecting a relatively small percentage of the American population. Even though they felt somewhat supported by their nonmilitary countrymen, the spouses did not feel particularly well understood by them, even by their own extended families. Many wives said that their own parents and siblings back home didn't "get it." "I would talk to my parents" back home in Texas, said Marisela Martinez, wife of a 4th Infantry Division sergeant who was deployed to the Sunni Triangle in 2003–4. "But they don't know what we're going through. I try to explain to my dad what I'm going through, and he'd say, 'Well, you signed up for this.'"

With the community of wives living on and around Army bases offering an attractive alternative, this generation broke with the long-established pattern of the wife's returning home to her parents for the duration of a husband's deployment. "We have become a sorority of separation," said Anne Torza, wife of an Apache attack-helicopter pilot in the 3rd Armored Cavalry Regiment, "and I wouldn't give up my sisters for anything. You know that 'band of brothers'? We're a band of sisters."

When Col. Spain came home to the United States in the winter of 2004, he realized that many Americans, including some of his colleagues in uniform, had no idea what the troops in Iraq were going through. He read over the letter he had been writing since the death of Sgt. Tomko. He decided to share it with about forty fellow soldiers, most of them officers in the MP corps. "As part of my personal healing process, I felt the need to put down some thoughts on command in combat, having just returned from a year in Iraq," he wrote in an introductory note he sent by e-mail on the morning of February 11.

THOSE OF YOU THAT ARE EITHER CURRENT OR RETIRED SOLDIERS AND HAVE LOST SOLDIERS IN COMBAT WILL UNDERSTAND. THOSE OF YOU THAT ARE CURRENTLY SOLDIERS AND HAVE NOT EXPERIENCED THIS I PRAY YOU WILL NOT EVER HAVE TO. THOSE OF YOU THAT HAVE NEVER SERVED IN COMBAT NEED TO UNDERSTAND THAT THIS IS WHAT IT IS REALLY ALL ABOUT. IT IS NOT GLORIOUS. WAR IS UGLY AND FOREVER CHANGES YOU. FEEL FREE TO FORWARD THIS TO ANYONE YOU WISH. IF IT ENLIGHTENS ONE PERSON ON THE HORRORS OF WAR IT WILL HAVE SERVED ITS PURPOSE.

He felt he had done his duty in his year of command in Iraq, Spain wrote, and accomplished all missions given him. But he wanted the costs—physical and spiritual—to be understood. "I failed to bring every soldier back home alive," he wrote. "I accept full responsibility for that and will have to live with this fact the rest of my life." He then listed the thirteen soldiers he had lost, beginning with Spec. Narson Sullivan, who had killed himself in April 2003, to Lt. Col. Kim Orlando and PFC Rachel Bosveld and Sgt. Nicholas Tomko, and finally to Spec. Todd Bates, a twenty-year-old from Bellaire, Ohio, who drowned in December 2003 while trying to rescue another soldier who had fallen into the Tigris River. But Spain had not turned against the war. He emphatically wrote, "We must continue the fight so the heroes listed above will not have died in vain."

Institutionally, the Army was seeking to understand and adjust to its new and unexpected circumstances. It was trying to become more expeditionary, or

quickly deployable. It was changing the structure of its combat units, emphasizing brigade combat teams over larger, less flexible divisions. It also reversed
decades of practice and decided to try having soldiers stationed at one base for
much of their careers, to ease the stress on families and increase cohesion in units.
Even so, Iraq was placing huge strains on the Army. "Deeply concerned with all
that I'm hearing," one retired Army general wrote after meeting with Army generals home from tours of duty. In private conversations, he said, the returning
commanders were "full of angst" and telling him, "Phase IV was a disaster and
soldiers are paying the price for some of the most egregious miscalculations and
mistakes perpetuated there." Among the problems were "lack of leadership, an inability to understand Arab culture at the most fundamental level, squandering resources, an inability to break through the bureaucracy to get money and effort
dispersed, amateurs playing at reconstruction rather than understanding that the
will of the people is the true center of gravity in this campaign."

Notably, this list of complaints found little fault with the front-line soldier but
much with top officers and the civilian officials leading them. In this respect, the
U.S. military in Iraq looked a bit like the British army in World War I, a force so
poorly led that German generals mocked it as "lions led by donkeys." Looking
back at the winter of 2003–4, one active-duty general said, "Tactically, we were
fine. Operationally, usually we were okay. Strategically—we were a basket case."

In some quiet but significant ways, the Army was moving into intellectual opposition to the Bush administration. The Army War College, the service's premier
educational institution, became a leading center of dissent during the occupation
period, with its analysts issuing scathing reviews. Containment of Iraq had
worked, while the Bush administration's approach hadn't, argued a study written
by Jeffrey Record and published by the War College's Strategic Studies Institute.
He argued that a war of choice had been launched that had distracted the U.S.
military and government from a war of necessity in Afghanistan and elsewhere
that already was under way. "Of particular concern has been the conflation of al
Qaeda and Saddam Hussein's Iraq as a single, undifferentiated terrorist threat,"
Record wrote.

> This was a strategic error of the first order because it ignored crucial differences
> between the two in character, threat level, and susceptibility to U.S. deterrence and
> military action. The result has been an unnecessary preventive war of choice
> against a deterred Iraq that has created a new front in the Middle East for Islamic
> terrorism and diverted attention and resources away from securing the American

homeland against further assault by an undeterrable al Qaeda. The war against Iraq was not integral to the GWOT [Global War on Terrorism] but rather a detour from it.

The unexpectedly difficult occupation, Record added, had "stressed the U.S. Army to the breaking point." This was not some politician or pundit offering that assessment but an official publication of the U.S. Army.

The uneven morale of U.S. troops

There were indeed worrisome signs of trouble in the U.S. military in Iraq in the fall and winter of 2003–4. During the fall the Bush administration launched an antimedia campaign that argued that the situation was better than journalists were portraying it. Troop morale was good, President Bush said in early October, and life in Iraq is "a lot better than you probably think. Just ask people who have been there."

A few days later *Stars & Stripes*, the military's own newspaper, did just that. The Pentagon-managed publication displayed unusual journalistic courage by coming back at the commander in chief with the results of its survey of U.S. troops then in Iraq. Using its embedded reporters to distribute questionnaires to 1,935 troops at several dozen U.S. bases in Iraq, *Stars & Stripes* found that 49 percent of those responding described their unit's morale as low. Many soldiers also described their training as insufficient.

A subsequent, more scientific survey by the Army's own experts from Walter Reed hospital confirmed those findings. There was widespread unhappiness among soldiers in Iraq, especially in the National Guard and Reserve units. In the Walter Reed survey, taken in the late summer and early fall of 2003, 72 percent of soldiers—both active duty and Guard and Reserve—reported that morale in their unit was low. Like *Stars & Stripes*, the Army showed true professionalism in having the intellectual honesty to release the data to the public—even if some of its most startling findings were tucked away deep in thick annexes to a report. The survey also found a surprising degree of unhappiness with battalion commanders, with nearly 75 percent of soldiers saying that leadership at that level was poor. This finding was a shock, because the Army doesn't give command of a battalion to inferior officers, especially in combat. A third survey, of twelve hundred deployed soldiers from the Illinois Army National Guard, found that "the majority of soldiers feel they are poorly informed, inadequately cared for, and that training in their units is boring and unorganized," according to a summary by Brig. Gen. Charles Fleming, the deputy commander of the Illinois Guard.

Holshek was one battalion commander who experienced the disgruntlement with leaders firsthand. In September, not long after his battalion was told that its time in Iraq would be extended by several months, he reported to the chief of civil affairs that the unit was in trouble. "Mission/endstate uncertainty has seriously eroded morale—news of extension has exacerbated this," he wrote in a Power-Point briefing for his superiors. "Ability to maintain mission focus deteriorating." He reported that there had been six major disciplinary charges brought in the previous month.

Holshek said later that he came to believe that the cause of the turmoil among the troops wasn't the quality of commanders, but rather the disconnect between what the Army was designed to do and what it actually found itself doing. "I would say that the U.S. Army, ninety percent, was not structured for success," he said later. "We've got a military designed to fight big wars, and it's constantly fighting small wars." So, he said, he found himself seen by subordinates as the representative of an institution that had failed its members: "Where are our squad automatic weapons? Where is our body armor? How long are we going to be here?"

For months, he added, he had been unable to find out how much longer his unit would serve there. "All we knew was that everyone was being extended, re-gardless. Nor could I get a straight answer from my chain on when we would leave Iraq—until about less than one month before we left." (Indeed, Army morale im-proved sharply when soldiers began to receive clearer signals on the likely dura-tion of their tours of duty. When Army researchers returned a year later to conduct a similar survey, they found that 54 percent of the 2,064 soldiers sur-veyed reported poor morale. That still wasn't good, but was an 18 percentage point improvement on the 2003 figure.)

The Army wasn't broken—yet—but it was being stressed and strained in un-expected ways. No matter what ultimately happened in Iraq, it became clear that it was going to emerge from the war there a very different institution.

14.

THE MARINE CORPS
FILES A DISSENT

WINTER 2003-4

In the winter of 2003-4 the Marine Corps was ordered to head back to Iraq to lend a hand. Its units would replace the Army in one of the toughest parts of the country: al Anbar province in the western desert, a region dominated by the hostile towns of Fallujah and Ramadi.

The Marines were determined to operate differently than the Army in the province. The Corps has long had a different outlook and culture. The smaller, infantry-oriented Corps tends to see war as a matter of the spirit; in other words, it believes less in technology and machinery and more in the human factors—blood, sweat, love, hate, and faith—as the decisive factors in combat. This embrace of the elemental nature of war runs from bottom to top: Marine boot camp indoctrinates recruits into a culture comfortable with killing the enemy, and Marine generals don't shy away from using the word "kill" in interviews about their line of work.

Through much of late 2003 the Marine Corps had watched Army operations in Iraq with growing discomfort. With its experience in occupying Haiti and fighting banana wars in Central America, the Corps quietly thought it had a better feel for how to conduct a counterinsurgency campaign. Some officers said privately that they thought the Army had been unnecessarily heavy-handed in Iraq, firing artillery shells from big bases and taking hostages when it should have been living among the people. Most of this discussion occurred far from public view, but it occasionally surfaced, as when Lt. Col. Carl E. Mundy III, who had commanded a Marine battalion in Iraq in the summer of 2003, wrote an op-ed piece for the *New York Times* later that year that scornfully contrasted the Marine success in pacifying south-central Iraq with the war the Army found itself waging farther north in the Sunni Triangle. When the Marines returned, Mundy promised, they would follow a counterinsurgency approach that "will stand in contrast to the new, get-tough strategy adopted by American forces in the Sunni Triangle."

Unusually for a lieutenant colonel, Mundy, himself the son of a Marine commandant, was specifically critical of a general: in this case, the Army's Gen. Odierno, and the tactics he had employed with the 4th Infantry Division around Tikrit. "We need to abandon techniques like surrounding villages with barbed wire and rounding up relatives of guerrillas," he wrote. Mundy was referring to Lt. Col. Steve Russell, a battalion commander in the 4th ID, who had encircled the village of Auja, home of many of Saddam's relatives, with concertina wire, and made military-age males who wanted to come or go show an identity card. "The insurgents should not be allowed to swim among the population as a whole," Russell had told reporters. "What we elected to do was make Auja a fishbowl so we could see who was swimming inside." Like the toy car controller Russell had used to detonate roadside bombs, the fencing of Auja showed that Russell was a battlefield innovator, seeking new solutions to the problems he encountered. In one of his letters home, he said he was influenced in part by French tactics in Algeria. He apparently didn't subscribe to the judgment of historians that such tactics had won some battles for the French at the cost of losing the war.

Kicking in doors, knocking down buildings, burning orchards, and firing artillery into civilian neighborhoods was bound to be counterproductive in the long run, Mundy warned: "The continued use of such hard-nosed tactics only risks further erosion of trust." He simply was making public what more senior Marines long had been saying behind closed doors. In December, Lt. Gen. James Conway, who would be the senior Marine going back into Iraq, told the *New York Times* that he didn't plan to use air strikes or artillery attacks against insurgents. "That will not be our method of operation," he said.

The Marines thought they could use in the Sunni Triangle the tactics they had employed effectively in the south. "Our expectations were pretty high that we would be successful using our stability operations that we had trained toward," said Col. Toolan, commander of the 1st Marine Regiment. "We had just come out of the southern region, south of Baghdad—Hillah, Diwaniyah, Karbala, and Najaf—and we had had tremendous success. Governments were blossoming, money was being spent in reconstruction efforts. So the perception that we had was, this works, we can actually get there. We can work with the locals. . . . [A]ll of these things led us to believe that our techniques and our procedures were pretty effective, and we could use them in al Anbar."

Marine Maj. Gen. James Mattis

"Be polite, be professional, but have a plan to kill everybody you meet" was one of the rules to live by that Maj. Gen. James Mattis gave his Marines. Mattis, the commander of the 1st Marine Division, began in the winter of 2003–4 to train his troops to operate differently from the Army when they returned to Iraq. Mattis is unusual in many ways, most notably in being one of the more intense intellectuals in the U.S. military. "He is one of the most urbane and polished men I have known," said retired Army Maj. Gen. Robert Scales, himself a Ph.D. in history. "He can quote Homer as well as Sun Tzu." (Once possessed of a huge personal library, Mattis gave away many thousands of books to Marine and local libraries, and in late 2005 estimated that he had reduced his load to about one thousand volumes.) When he deploys Mattis always packs the *Meditations* of Marcus Aurelius, the Roman who was both a Stoic philosopher and an emperor. "It allows me to distance myself from the here and now," and to discern the connection to the eternal verities of warfare, he explained. Mattis also objected to the Rumsfeld Pentagon's emphasis on "net-centric" warfare built around the movement of data. "Computers by their nature are isolating. They build walls. The nature of war is immutable: You need trust and connection." He dismissed the net-centric emphasis as "a Marxian view—it ignores the spiritual."

With his troops he tended to be earthier. "The first time you blow someone away is not an insignificant event," he told two hundred Marines at one session in al Asad. "That said, there are some assholes in the world that just need to be shot. There are hunters and there are victims. By your discipline, cunning, obedience, and alertness you will decide if you are a hunter or a victim. . . . It's really a hell of a lot of fun. You're gonna have a blast out here!" He finished in Pattonesque fashion: "I feel sorry for every son of a bitch that doesn't get to serve with you."

Small, slight, and bespectacled, Mattis didn't fit the Hollywood image of the fire-breathing Marine commander. But retired Marine Col. Gary Anderson, himself a widely respected officer, commented, "I think he's the finest combat leader we've produced since Korea." Mattis genuinely seemed to thrive on the noise and confusion of battle. He adopted Chaos as his radio call sign when he took the Marines into southern Afghanistan in the fall of 2001, and kept it when he led the Marine part of the invasion force for Iraq in the spring of 2003. After the invasion he sent home his tanks and artillery pieces and went to Iraqi military leaders in each area his troops were in. "I come in peace," Mattis recalled telling them. "I didn't bring artillery. But I'm pleading with you, with tears in my eyes: If you fuck with me, I'll kill you all."

Just before Christmas 2003 in California, preparing to take his troops back into Iraq where they would relieve the 82nd Airborne in al Anbar province, he held a two-day meeting of his staff and commanders at Camp Pendleton to plan a different approach. Mattis's Marines would be culturally sensitive, the group decided. They wouldn't wear sunglasses when interacting with Iraqis, so there wouldn't be a barrier between them and the locals. They would learn a smattering of Arabic. They would even grow mustaches so they would look more like the locals. Marine intelligence analysts wouldn't overreact to clerics' Friday sermons blasting the occupiers. "Religious leaders are normally going to be critical publicly of the coalition," said a summary of the meeting's major points. "Otherwise they will be seen as weak by their followers." Also, Marine commanders were warned to brace for Fridays, when Iraqis left the mosques "fired up."

To the degree possible, Marine operations would be comprehensible to Iraqis. Col. Toolan of the 1st Marines recalled: "Transparency was the name of the game. We knew we didn't know who to trust. So go in with the mentality that we care, and we'll work with you." In a tactic that reached back to Marine Combined Action Platoon operations decades earlier in Vietnam, the plan called for small units of Marines to live among the people in many Sunni towns and villages to facilitate the training of the Iraqi police and civil defense forces.

Don't get upset when a family lies to you about one of its members' committing a crime, those at the Marine meeting advised, in an admonition unusual for an institution that places great value on truth telling: "This is not an attempt to cover up, it is an attempt to save the honor of the family. They know he did it. They just don't want to lose face. This is fine, you know the truth, let the family keep its honor intact." In an even more extraordinary conclusion, the Marine meeting called for an almost deferential approach to searching Iraqi houses. "If you knock at the door for a 'cordon and knock,' try not to look directly into the house when the door opens. If searching, be careful. Do not destroy possessions

and furniture," and ask the leader of the household to open rooms and cup-
boards. Nor should that man be dishonored before his family. "If something is
found, do not throw the leader of the house to the ground in front of his family,"
the meeting advised. "Give him some honor. Tell them he needs to explain to his
wife and children that he is coming with you."

Most controversial, at least inside the U.S. military, were the steps the Marines
chose to underscore to Iraqis that they weren't the U.S. Army. To emphasize to
Iraqis that the Marines arriving in Fallujah and other centers of resistance were a
new and different organization, the Marines planned to wear green camouflage
uniforms and black Marine boots for their initial forty-five days of patrolling, instead of the tan desert uniform worn by Army soldiers in Iraq. "The green uniforms will be one very visible difference and symbolically represent that break
between the old and the new," said one Marine officer who attended the Pendleton discussion. It was important to do so, he continued, because of the counterproductive approach some Army divisions had taken in 2003. "I'm appalled at the
current heavy-handed use of air and artillery in Iraq. I don't believe there is any
viable use for artillery or JDAMs [joint direct attack munitions, precision-guided
bombs weighing one thousand or two thousand pounds] in the current environment." This officer, like many Marines, had concluded that "success in a counterinsurgency environment is based on winning popular support, not on blowing
up people's houses."

That view probably represented the most basic difference in the approach the
Marines aimed to take when they returned to Iraq early in 2004. "At the end of the
day it all boils down to whether you are fighting the insurgents or the insurgency,"
said one veteran Marine officer. "The Army, writ large—I exempt the 101st—has
chosen to fight the insurgents, and the Corps, the insurgency." This is, he added,
"the same argument we had in Vietnam." Mattis concluded the December meeting
by saying that "both the insurgency and the military force are competing for the
same thing: the support of the people." At the same time, you have to kill the insurgents when you are confronted. "There is only one 'retirement plan' for terrorists."

This generally softer, more culturally sensitive approach, combined with a
hard-nosed willingness to mix it up when necessary, got good reviews from some
others. "The Marines are on to something here," said a Defense Intelligence
Agency analyst with experience in Iraq.

"I like the Marine approach, and I think it'll succeed," said Lt. Col. David
Poirier, the MP commander in Tikrit who had been appalled by some of the actions of Army soldiers, especially the 82nd Airborne, when he operated in Fallujah.

"I believe that some of the insurgency is due to families acting out against American forces for deaths occurring as a result of collateral damage."

An Army major serving on the CPA staff who had studied Iraqi tribal issues also thought it was wise to try a new approach. "I think this is a sound strategy and a good start to begin the reconciliation process," he said. His view was that the U.S. military had gotten off to an ugly start in that region on April 28, 2003, when the 82nd Airborne had fired into a crowd. "I am of the opinion that much of our trouble in the triangle is the result of the April incident in which thirteen locals were killed by U.S. forces. The tribal code demanded a restitution and reconciliation ritual, and lacking this ritual required vendetta. . . . I believe that the Marines may be able to break this cycle of violence with a fresh start."

But the express intention of the Marines to distinguish themselves from the Army drew angry responses from many others. Retired Army Col. Lloyd Matthews said he found this aspect of the Marine discussions distasteful. "It is hardly advisable in joint operations to denigrate the tactics of the sister service that preceded you in the trenches, and to suggest that you are going to do a lot better," he said. "If one is going to do better than his predecessor, it is wiser to wait and let his success speak for itself rather than trumpeting it in advance." He was especially unhappy with the intention to wear a different uniform. "The green cammy phase is for no other purpose than to differentiate the lovable Marines now in town from those detestable Army ruffians who just left."

Matthews, a former editor of *Parameters,* the Army's premier professional journal, was also skeptical about whether the Marine Combined Action Platoon program would be viable in the hostile atmosphere of the Sunni Triangle. "First, CAPs work only when they operate in a broadly secure environment," he said. "They can't go up against a significant encroaching force. Second, they fragment your own force and consume manpower. Third, CAPs presuppose the availability of a reliable, loyal, ample local militia. That may become so. It is not so now." In fact, as Matthews suspected, that lack of dependable local forces was to become a major problem for the Marines in the spring of 2004.

Others warned that the Marines were in for a rude surprise. Lt. Col. Gian Gentile, who served with the 4th Infantry Division in the area around Tikrit, commented at the same time, "Unfortunately, the Sunni Triangle is nothing like southern Iraq or the part of northern Iraq around Mosul. . . . I hope the Marines' velvet glove works, that it saves the lives of Marines and Iraqis, and leads to a stable and secure region. But I also fear that this approach, by dismissing the cultural and tactical differences in the Sunni Triangle, will ignore the hard-won gains of Army units over the past eight months."

An Army general who was experienced in Iraq privately applauded the Marines' intentions but quietly cautioned, "I don't think it will prove as easy as it briefs. . . . Some of this reflects a degree of intellectual smugness that might be warranted after, say, six successful months on the ground." He would prove clairvoyant.

The meditations of Gen. Mattis

To prepare his officers mentally to go back, Mattis had them read over one thousand pages of material culled from seventy-two commentaries and news articles on insurgencies, sent out in three mass e-mails during the winter of 2003–4. "Ultimately, a real understanding of history means that we face nothing new under the sun," he wrote to a colleague on November 20, 2003.

> FOR ALL THE "4TH GENERATION OF WAR" INTELLECTUALS RUNNING AROUND TODAY SAYING THAT THE NATURE OF WAR HAS FUNDAMENTALLY CHANGED, THE TACTICS ARE WHOLLY NEW, ETC., I MUST RESPECTFULLY SAY, "NOT REALLY": ALEXANDER THE GREAT WOULD NOT BE IN THE LEAST BIT PERPLEXED BY THE ENEMY THAT WE FACE RIGHT NOW IN IRAQ, AND OUR LEADERS GOING INTO THIS FIGHT DO THEIR TROOPS A DISSERVICE BY NOT STUDYING—STUDYING, *VICE* JUST READING—THE MEN WHO HAVE GONE BEFORE US. WE HAVE BEEN FIGHTING ON THIS PLANET FOR 5,000 YEARS AND WE SHOULD TAKE ADVANTAGE OF THEIR EXPERIENCE. "WINGING IT" AND FILLING BODY BAGS AS WE SORT OUT WHAT WORKS REMINDS US OF THE MORAL DICTATES AND THE COST OF INCOMPETENCE IN OUR PROFESSION.

Each selection in Mattis's reading list carried his explanation of what he considered noteworthy in it. Battalion commanders were required to certify in writing that their subordinates had read and understood the material. "While learning from experience is good, learning from others' experiences is even better," Mattis wrote in his introductory comment. Again and again the theme of the readings was that Iraq could be frustrating, difficult, and complex, and that leaders needed to prepare their troops for that environment. The articles called for maintaining discipline, honing skills, and having faith in each other—and warned of what can go wrong when soldiers lose hold of those fundamentals.

The first of the seventy-two selections was a magazine article titled, "The Tipping Point: How Military Occupations Go Sour," about mistakes the Israelis had committed in Lebanon. The second was a news story about the mistaken shooting by a U.S. soldier of the head of the U.S.-appointed municipal council in Sadr City. The third was about a similar incident involving the 82nd Airborne. On an article about the Army bringing charges against Lt. Col. West, the battalion commander in the 4th ID who fired a weapon next to a detainee's ear, Mattis wrote, "this shows a commander who has lost his moral balance or has watched too many Hollywood movies. By our every act and statement, Marine leaders must set a legal, moral and ethical model that maintains traditional Marine Corps levels of discipline."

For another article, about the assassination of two Shiite politicians, he wrote, "Recall Beirut, my fine young men, and the absolute need for Iraqis to see the American military as impartial. We will be compassionate to all the innocent and deadly only to those who insist on violence, taking no 'sides' other than to destroy the enemy. We must act as a windbreak, behind which a struggling Iraq can get its act together."

He also sent out to his officers T. E. Lawrence's "27 Articles," a distillation of everything that eccentric but insightful British officer had learned about leading and advising Arabs in combat. Article 15 in particular would resonate: "Do not try to do too much with your own hands. Better the Arabs do it tolerably than you do it perfectly. It is their war, and you are to help them, not to win it for them. Actually, also, under the very odd conditions of Arabia, your practical work will not be as good, perhaps, as you think it is." Also, Lawrence warned in Article 22, keep in mind that these people may actually know more about certain types of fighting than you do: "Unnumbered generations of tribal raids have taught them more about some parts of the business than we will ever know." Mattis's introduction to the Lawrence piece wisely emphasized what some Marines had been neglecting: In returning to Iraq, the Marines would be operating in a Sunni area, an environment very different from the Shiite south.

Mattis hammered home the message in a series of face-to-face meetings with his troops. "The general talked to every Marine in the division at least three times, usually in battalion size," recalled Col. Clarke Lethin, Mattis's chief of operations. "He wanted to talk them through, and image them through, the issues they would face. He wanted to talk about morality on the battlefield, how to go through an ambush one day and have your buddy blown up, and then face Iraqis the next day." The message: Iraqis aren't your enemy, don't let the insurgents make you think that. *The people are the prize.*

The Marines vs. al Anbar

When Mattis arrived in Iraq, Maj. Gen. Swannack, the 82nd Airborne's commander, told him he had three pressing concerns about the Marines' contemplated approach. First, he said, you guys need artillery. "After seeing how we got mortared and rocketed in the evenings, they decided to bring it," Swannack recalled. Second, he advised them to think twice about trying to institute the Marine Combined Action Platoon program. "I told them that the CAP program wouldn't work, that al Anbar province wasn't ready for it then, and maybe never, because they didn't want us downtown." Third, he vigorously objected to the Marine plan to wear green uniforms and black boots. "I told him that was a personal affront to me, and that a relief should be seamless," Swannack said.

Mattis deferred to Swannack on the uniform issue, not wanting to cause a breach. "What I was trying to do was break the cycle of violence. He took it personally. I appreciated his candor."

Mattis also maintained that he wasn't replicating the Vietnam-era CAP program, but adapting it—successfully, in his view—to local cultural conditions. Each battalion would have one platoon that was given a thirty-day course in Arab customs and language, and that unit in turn could help teach its company, and then the company could affect the entire battalion.

Swannack thought he had done well in Fallujah. "I think Fallujah was being managed appropriately, with surgical operations based on precise intelligence," he said.

Yet elsewhere in the U.S. military there was a growing belief that the 82nd Airborne had lost control of the city. Abizaid and Sanchez had been pressuring Swannack to do more about Fallujah, said an Army officer familiar with those exchanges.

Mattis had a plan to handle the city. "I knew Fallujah would be tough," he recalled. But he thought he could prevail through combining high-profile infrastructure projects, especially on electricity and water, with low-profile raids against specific individuals. "We were going to use the softer forms, focus on lights and water, and go in with small teams to kill the bad guys at night." But as it turned out, he would never get the chance to implement this approach. Instead, Fallujah went off the tracks almost immediately. In the view of some Marine officers, what would follow was a tragedy, beginning with a mistake and followed by death and retribution. Mattis's plan for Fallujah would become for the Corps's commanders a great lost opportunity, yet another of the many roads not taken.

Marine commanders found that their broader plan for the pacification of Anbar province would be undercut by the chronic lack of troops. Col. Toolan, commander of the 1st Marines, recalled that he had four basic missions: control
major supply routes (MSR), develop Iraqi security forces (ISF), eliminate insurgent sanctuaries, and create jobs. "The challenge was, when we controlled the
MSR and developed the ISF, there was no one left to eliminate sanctuaries or create jobs. So it was like whack-a-mole." And so, within weeks of arriving, the Marine Corps, which had wanted to go back to show how to work better with the
people, would wind up instead involved in some of the most savage fighting U.S.
troops had experienced in decades.

15.

THE SURPRISE

SPRING 2004

By the late winter of 2003–4, it was clear that the U.S. effort, both in pacification and reconstruction, was faltering. But it wouldn't be until spring that it would become clear just how troubled it was. The key change in the disposition of forces was a major rotation that withdrew the units that had been there a year and replaced them with a new set of divisions. Notably, this rotation cut the U.S. troop presence in the north, replacing the 101st Airborne, which along with its attached units had fielded twenty thousand troops, with a patched-together outfit called Task Force Olympia that had less than half that number, and also far less mobility than the helicopter-rich 101st.

One reason such a reduction was still thought possible was that midwinter had gone by quietly, perhaps lulling commanders, especially those who thought that the capture of Saddam Hussein in mid-December would quell the enthusiasm of the insurgents. And February 2004 brought the lowest death toll so far of any month during the U.S. military presence in Iraq, just twenty—and a relatively peaceful fraction of the number in every subsequent month of that year. It was also the low point in terms of total U.S. troop presence in the country in 2003–5, dipping briefly to about 110,000. For the next twenty-two months the number of

U.S. troops would creep upward, until finally, by the end of 2005, it hit 159,000, the highest level since the occupation began.

The troop rotation itself may also have contributed to the misplaced sense of calm, as many experienced U.S. units began disengaging, doing less patrolling and more packing up. So in retrospect, this period of quiet wasn't necessarily as reassuring as it was interpreted to be at the time. The insurgency was quiet in order to lay the groundwork for a spring offensive, a security expert who worked in the Green Zone said later. "I think enemy forces were planning, solidifying their support base, getting ready to hit us in the spring. I was talking to Iraqis, and they were saying things were going to get bad. We got intelligence that they were going to hit the Spanish and Italians, drive them out. That was the model: Isolate the U.S., then drive us out and embarrass us."

Seasoned insurgents vs. newcomer troops

U.S. forces learned but then went home, while the enemy learned and, if he survived, fought better the next time. In 2003, one ill-conceived drive-by shooting was conducted from a horse-pulled cart, remembered Col. Spain. The Iraqi police who had come under attack simply shot the trotting horse and then finished off the stranded attackers. "The insurgents grew more proficient" with the passage of time, noted Ahmed Hashim, a professor of strategic studies at the U.S. Naval War College, who as a reservist would later serve with the 3rd Armored Cavalry Regiment. "American forces had killed most of the incompetent ones; the tactics, techniques, and procedures of the surviving insurgents became more lethal as a result of experience."

This change became apparent early in 2004, when the insurgents began to contend with fresh U.S. troops. Some disruption had been expected from the troop rotation, but commanders thought they could ensure that knowledge would be passed on. Yet the change seems to have given the insurgency a major opening. "We didn't expect the level of violence that we ran into," Sgt. 1st Class Erick Macher, who operated in Bayji and Tikrit, recalled much later. "You're coming in for OIF II [the second rotation of Operation Iraqi Freedom]; they captured Saddam Hussein before we got there. We thought that would change things."

The new troops had two strikes against them. In a culture where social life turns not on official positions but on personal relationships, they were blank slates. And with a fast and constantly moving insurgency, where the enemy was quickly adapting, as well as operating on his own turf, anything that can be distilled into written knowledge is already likely to be a bit too old, a bit stale. The cutting edge of operations against an insurgency is the gut instinct that tells a squad leader that a street scene that appears safe really isn't, or the backlog of experience that allows a battalion commander to discern a new twist in what a sheikh is telling him. Much of that was lost when new troops rotated in. They were enthusiastic and hardworking but alien in the situation, while the other side had just gone through months of hard fighting.

Nor had many commanders really grasped the nature of the war in which they were engaged. "I don't think we came in with leaders fully prepared to fight counterinsurgency," Lt. Col. Jim Chevallier, commander of the 1st Squadron of the 4th Cavalry Regiment in the 1st Infantry Division, told *Army* magazine much later, after his 2004–5 tour of duty was concluded. "I don't think we understood what the enemy's basic scheme of maneuver was." So, he said, "until you understand counterinsurgency, it's difficult to tell what success is. If I had to do it all over again, I'd train my leaders more on counterinsurgency operations."

Also, overoptimistic planners and commanders, encouraged by the midwinter lull, thought the U.S. military posture could be altered and that the new troops could take a more distant stance from the fledgling Iraqi security forces. Unlike the unit of Capt. Kipling, the MP officer, the MPs who replaced her brigade were told not to operate from the police stations. "It had taken us months to develop a rapport, and we were in the stations," sometimes as much as nine hours a day, she said later. "I didn't see how they could develop a rapport, not being in the stations."

As Kipling and more than one hundred thousand other troops departed, there was a worrisome falloff in the quality of the intelligence gathered. "The actionable intelligence improved in the late summer, early fall, into the winter," Gen. Sanchez said in a legal statement. "And then in the spring, it went into a significant, very noticeable decrease." He blamed the decline squarely on the big troop rotation. "We changed out every single unit in that country, so you had the natural dip in situational awareness."

Oddly, the Army recognized the problem but persistently failed to respond adequately, said one Army officer, after watching two more major rotations. "During every RIP/TOA [relief in place/transfer of authority] all the intelligence gets flushed down the drain," this officer said. "It's like, 'If our unit didn't develop the intelligence, we don't trust it.'"

An Army War College study later arrived at a similar conclusion. "Rotating nearly the entire force at once degraded capability, [and that] may have contributed to

loss of control over several cities in the Sunni Triangle," wrote the Iraq Stabilization Study Team, a group at the college's Strategic Studies Institute that has produced some of the military establishment's most insightful work on the Iraq war.
This wasn't just a theoretical problem about the loss of abstract data, but rather
an urgent issue that involved the deaths of U.S. troops and Iraqi allies.

On top of that, the radical reduction in U.S. troops in Mosul and elsewhere in
the north began to have a corrosive effect on Iraqi security forces. The replacement
units were less engaged with local security forces than the 101st had been, according to people who observed its operations. Police officials who had been visited
daily were now seen only weekly or monthly. "When you only have contact with
him once a week, once every two weeks," a police chief begins to feel isolated and
more likely to cut a deal with the insurgents, noted the 101st's Col. Joe Anderson.
The cutback in the U.S. presence in the north was even more severe in smaller towns
there: As the troop contingent in Tall Afar was reduced from three thousand to
about five hundred, friction between Sunnis and Shiites there increased.

But the inaccurate U.S. assessment of the situation wasn't attributable solely to
the rotation. The 82nd Airborne had been operating in al Anbar province for over
six months when its commander incorrectly declared the insurgency all but dead
there. The enemy was "in disarray," Swannack told reporters on March 10, just
weeks before the province erupted. "When we first got here, I felt very, very strongly
about fighting the insurgency, and there was a very sophisticated insurgency here."
Since then, he said, the Army had successfully deprived it of its leadership, financing, and support structure. "And so that's why I'm discounting a very serious insurgency ongoing here right now, because of those factors." In fact, Iraq was on the
verge of some of the worst fighting it would see during the entire U.S. occupation.

A sour feeling

But the CPA and the U.S. military were too busy fighting each other to notice
the gathering storm. There was general agreement on both the civilian and military sides that their leaders in Iraq, Bremer and Sanchez, were profoundly unhappy with each other. "It was very clear that they hated each other," recalled a
senior administration official who visited them in March. "They lived in the same
palace and didn't talk to each other."

Many in the military also saw Sanchez as a failure. "We always wondered why
there wasn't relief"—that is, why Sanchez wasn't simply replaced—remembered
an intelligence expert who worked on Sanchez's staff that winter.

In the spring of 2004, Gen. Kellogg finished up his effort to shore up the administration of the CPA. When he got back from Iraq, he went to the chairman of the Joint Chiefs of Staff and recommended that Sanchez be removed. "I said to General Myers, you need to get Rick Sanchez out of there, because he's tired," Kellogg said in an interview. "At our morning meeting, Sanchez's body language was telling. He was sitting with his arms crossed, every morning. . . . My point to him was, I believe, Rick Sanchez was tired and that there was an uneven working relationship with Bremer."

An active-duty officer said, with an edge of disgust in his voice, "In Vietnam we left Westy in. In Iraq we left Sanchez in." Neither Gen. William Westmoreland nor Sanchez understood the war he was fighting, this officer said.

Nor was the White House nearly as enthusiastic about Bremer as it had been a year earlier. "By early '04, the president was quite aware of Bremer's flaws," said a former administration official. "But he couldn't let him go in an election year. He knows that Bremer is a control freak, that he won't release information, that he wouldn't listen to anyone's suggestions or direction." Most important, the star-crossed American effort wasn't producing results. It was during this period, the official noted, that Condi Rice began calling Bremer nearly every day in an effort to get Iraq policy on track.

Gary Anderson, on his two assessment trips for Wolfowitz, in July 2003 and January 2004, noticed the frustrating lack of progress. "In the summer of '03 I was impressed with how hard they were working. I had no way to gauge how successful they were being," he said later. "It wasn't until January, when I returned, that it struck me how little effect they were having outside the Green Zone, and that was a result of my interaction with the troops in the field."

Hallenbeck, the retired Army colonel working on Iraqi media infrastructure for the CPA, had the same experience a month later. After spending much of 2003 in Iraq, he went back to the United States and then returned in February 2004. The occupation felt different to him—no longer flailing but failing, and moving toward being moribund. In Baghdad, he said, "I had the feeling driving around downtown that there was no longer any sense that we were part of their solution. We clearly weren't getting it. They didn't want Americans to go away. They just wanted us to stop trying to run things, because we couldn't."

"Over time Iraqis became disappointed," said David Dunford, a retired foreign service officer who helped set up the new Iraqi ministry of foreign affairs. "Each Iraqi owed it to himself and his family to decide whether it made more sense to cooperate with us or to cooperate with somebody else, the insurgents.

Unfortunately, because of our incompetence, more and more Iraqis have made the decision that their interests don't lie with us."

"Nobody was waving"

Iraqis never had been particularly welcoming of the U.S. presence. But in the spring of 2004, some Americans were noticing a subtle shift in the reception they received. "The real way that you could tell the frustration was growing was when you drove around the city [and saw] how people would respond to the Humvees," recalled Lt. A. Heather Coyne, an Arabic-speaking Army reservist who—unusually—joined the Army Reserve while working on terrorism issues in the White House's budget office. She served in the Army in Iraq for over a year, from the beginning of the occupation until the end of the CPA in June 2004: "After a while they would wave a little tentatively. After that, they would watch the Humvees with suspicion or concern, but they still waved back when I waved to them. Right toward the end, nobody was waving."

The numbers in the CPA's own polls bore out Coyne's sense of decline. Late in 2003 the U.S. effort still had the benefit of the doubt of the broad Iraqi middle— the group that U.S. commanders would come to call "the fence-sitters." But the support dwindled steadily as the occupation wore on without producing either the security or the services it promised. In November 2003, according to a survey conducted for the CPA, nearly half of Iraqis polled—some 47 percent—expressed confidence in the CPA. By March 2004, it was down to just 14 percent.

"There was no security" for Iraqis under the occupation, and that antagonized them, said Hallenbeck. "People would read about every U.S. troop who dies. But we never heard about all the kidnappings, robbings, rapes of Iraqis. The average house- wife was just terrified, and we didn't get that." There has been much subsequent hand- wringing about the CPA's lack of strategic communication with the Iraqi people, Hallenbeck said. But, he countered, the CPA communicated some points all too well, if unconsciously. The Green Zone had security, it had services, it had the things that Iraqis wanted. "A lot of people had no electricity but could look across the river and see the CPA all lit up at night. And that was the way we really communicated." In the fall and winter of 2003–4 he witnessed Iraqis beginning to turn against the occupation. "I remember watching that turn—Iraqis were saying, 'Not only do I not like these guys, they can't do anything for me, and they step on my dignity.'"

"Bremer and his most trusted CPA advisers simply did not grasp the depth of Iraqi disaffection, suspicion, and frustration, even among many of our partners and philosophical allies within the Iraqi political class," remembered Larry Diamond, an expert on democratization processes at Stanford University's Hoover Institution who, at the invitation of his old Stanford colleague Condoleezza Rice, went to work at the CPA in the winter of 2003–4.

The U.S. military fared no better in terms of winning hearts and minds: In November, only 11 percent of respondents had said they would feel safer if the U.S. forces left Iraq immediately. By January 2004, that figure had more than doubled, to 28 percent. By April 2004, it would be 55 percent. As the pollsters put it, in analyzing what they termed this "substantial deterioration of image," Iraqis had come to see the U.S. military as part of the problem, a "liability whose presence makes things more dangerous."

"We were like the Wizard of Oz," said Col. Alan King, who served in Iraq from March 2003 to July 2004, a tour longer than that of most soldiers. "They expected magic from us, in terms of living standards. They really thought we could do it— they'd seen it happen in Kuwait," with the swift rebuilding there after the 1991 war.

By early 2004, "we begin to smell like losers" in Iraq, said analyst Patrick Clawson, "because we can't deliver on personal security for Iraqis. There were robberies, kidnappings, carjackings. At that point, the military brass and the CPA were still pretty clueless."

One day that spring, Col. Lloyd Sammons, a Special Forces reservist who had been working at the CPA, just packed it in and went home, taking advantage of a backlog of leave he had accumulated. "When I left, I didn't tell anybody. I was there one day, one day I wasn't, and that was it. I cleaned out my desk drawer." He had had enough of the CPA, which he considered misguided and ineffective. "You can sort of smell when you're losing," he said. "You can sort of figure it out. It was Pollyanna all day long. I mean, they were living in La-la Land, acting like they were doing great things, but I couldn't see it." He was especially disgusted with Bremer. "When Bremer would walk in every once in a while—he had to pass my desk on the way to the john—I'd just look at him like he was a piece of shit, and that's how I felt about him."

The failure to train Iraqis

In February 2004, Keith Mines also left Iraq to return to his life in the State Department. In a summary of his seven months as the CPA representative in al Anbar province, Mines used his background both as a diplomat and a Special Forces officer to puzzle through some of the problems in the American effort.

"The economy is gradually improving," he wrote. Eventually, oil production and U.S. government spending would reduce unemployment and raise living standards. But he was worried by the other two thrusts of the U.S. occupation: creating a new political process and putting together a new security structure. "The Iraqis know they are looking over the edge of a cliff and into the abyss. This one is still ours to lose."

The problems began at the top of the U.S. operation in Iraq, he had decided. "Most lacking is simple leadership," he wrote to his family. "There is no substitute in this business for experience, or for surrounding oneself with those with experience. Bremer for some reason was not able to do so."

He especially was worried by the sluggish pace of outfitting and training Iraqi police and soldiers, which lay at the core of the U.S. strategy. "The development of the security forces . . . is a failure that is difficult to comprehend. Ten months into the operation there is not a single properly trained and equipped Iraqi security officer in the entire al Anbar province. There are over 10,000 police and civil defense officers on the rolls, but none have received anything more than ad hoc training and rudimentary equipment."

The training program had been handled in a way that, like so many other early policy decisions in Iraq, ignored the lessons of history. Special Forces units specialize as much as anything else in training foreign militaries. This isn't just a matter of military knowledge, or even primarily of it. Rather, at its core it requires cultural understanding, the skill of being able to operate at the interface of the U.S. military and a foreign culture, and to somehow produce foreign soldiers in cohesive units that are not only militarily trained but willing to obey commands.

Having reversed course on so many other of Jay Garner's initiatives, Bremer and his subordinates decided to stay with one: to have the Iraqi security forces trained not by Special Forces experts, but rather by defense contractors and some regular soldiers, including some from the National Guard and the Army Reserves. "The feeling was manpower—why waste precious Special Forces manpower when you can get pretty much the same thing with Vinnell and MPRI?" said Col. Gregory Gardner, who was a senior adviser on Ministry of Defense issues, referring to two companies that ran training programs. Rumsfeld agreed with that view, he added. In a meeting at the Pentagon in June, "the Sec Def told us, 'These precious Special Forces guys have been busy in Afghanistan and Iraq and didn't need to be wasting their time training Iraqis—they should be out on the cutting edge, not sitting on an Iraqi base somewhere.'" It was a decision that would come back to haunt Bremer and the U.S. effort nearly a year later, when it became clear that Iraqi forces lacked leaders, either Iraqi or American, whom they were willing to follow into battle.

By early December 2003 it was clear that training of the new Iraqi army was going badly. More than half the recruits in the first battalion to be trained deserted while on leave. When officers from the headquarters set up to oversee the training of Iraqis observed National Guard soldiers instructing Iraqis, they judged them "almost wholly substandard, as a function of the limited training and experience of the National Guard soldiers themselves," said Kalev Sepp, a retired Special Forces officer with much advisory experience and a frequent consultant in Iraq, in congressional testimony. He also testified that on Christmas Eve 2003, the U.S. trainers of one Iraqi unit so distrusted their students that they carried loaded pistols at a graduation ceremony in case of a mutiny.

At the CPA, officials began to write off the entire program. "It took us about six months to see that these processes weren't really working," said Gardner. "The first battalion of the Iraqi army was shit, and we knew it. It started in July, and by August and September we kept hearing them complaining about their pay, and going on leave and not coming back."

Looking back, Marine Col. T. X. Hammes, who was involved in training the Iraqi army, called it "a bad plan, poorly executed, and underfunded." The numbers being released by the Bush administration, he wrote in his diary that winter, were a "fantasy."

Lt. Fox's year

The spring of 2004 brought a steady increase in the average number of daily bomb, mortar, and grenade attacks on U.S. troops, from about twenty-five a day during January to about twice that by June. "It's been a long year," Lt. Jay Fox, a young platoon leader from Warner Robins, Georgia, said one day in northern Baghdad. His dominant memory of the time was an incident on March 2 when he watched Baghdadis celebrate the bombing death of one of his soldiers, Spec. Michael Woodliff, a young Floridian. It happened on the Canal Road, just south of Sadr City. "The Humvee was burning, and the soldier was still in it. We couldn't tell if he was alive. And I looked over, across the canal, and people were dancing and singing—people we'd tried to help." Lt. Fox was most proud, he said, of his soldiers' reactions. There were fighters hiding inside the crowd, trying to provoke the Americans into firing on the people, just as had happened almost a year earlier in Fallujah. Undisciplined troops might have succumbed to the temptation.

But Fox recalled that his platoon "didn't open up on them, even when somebody fired an RPG at them."

The first battle of Fallujah

Then Fallujah blew.

It was a bad time. Maj. Gen. Paul Eaton, who oversaw the training of Iraqi forces at that time, recalled, "This thing evolved in front of us. And each day it got incrementally worse, until it exploded" in late March.

The outburst of attacks caught the U.S. military off guard, in part because of persistent friction between Army headquarters and Marines operating near Fallujah and in the rest of western Iraq. One Marine officer remembered walking into the Army's big operations center at Camp Victory that spring and being appalled. He surveyed the ascending rows of desks, as in a modern movie theater, each with multiple laptops, each with an unencumbered view of several screens displaying troop locations or showing live video from Predator drone aircraft surveilling convoy routes. It was all enough to give a staff officer the illusion that he knew what was going on out there. It was the opposite of the Marine Corps practice of having a small headquarters as close to the front as possible. "Oh, my God," this officer thought to himself, "this is a bunch of people writing e-mails home." Some in the Army, by contrast, resented the Marine Corps's attitude that it had a better handle on how to deal with an insurgency and was returning to Iraq to show the Army how to operate in Anbar province.

On Wednesday, March 24, the Army's 82nd Airborne turned over responsibility for Fallujah to the Marine Corps. Under the 82nd, Fallujah had been relatively quiet, in part because the 82nd had trod lightly in the city, not conducting intrusive patrols. "John Abizaid had said to me in November 2003 that we didn't want Fallujah to become a flashpoint," recalled Gen. Swannack. Under the Marines, he pointedly noted, "it did."

The Marine view is different. "Fallujah *looked* good," said Toolan, who commanded the 1st Marines, based just outside the city. "It had a mayor, a police chief, all the trimmings. But it had termites. You always tread lightly, talking about the guys before you. But they [the 82nd Airborne] weren't out enough to do the termite inspections." He also was shocked during the turnover of command when the Army convoy he was in just pushed through an ambush outside the mayor's office rather than launch a determined counterattack. "If my guys did that, I'd have their ass."

By Friday, just three days into Marine control, the city erupted. A group from Task Force 626, a successor to earlier elite organizations dedicated to killing or capturing high-level officials from the old regime, was hit by a bomb. Marine patrols into the city then engaged in a thirty-six-hour-long series of firefights that left at least fifteen Iraqis dead. The Marines were looking to engage both the people and the enemy—the first with friendship, the second with guns. "You want the fuckers to have a safe haven?" asked Lethin, the 1st Marine Division's operations officer. "Or do you want to stir them up and get them out in the open?"

But the Marine plan for Fallujah was thrown off track, irretrievably, by what happened next. Marine patrols into Fallujah were familiarizing themselves with the city, and in the process purposely stirring up the situation. Inside the city, insurgents were preparing to respond—warning shops to close, and setting up roadblocks and ambushes with parked cars. One week into this new, more volatile situation, two SUVs carrying security contractors from a company called Blackwater bypassed a Marine checkpoint and drove into the hornet's nest, not understanding that the American approach to the city had changed and that it was in turmoil over the recent shootings.

Just why the contractors were heading into the unsettled city is unclear. Some say it was just a mistake. "CJTF-7 had very poor movement controls," said Lethin. "That route was closed, but they went in. Because they went in there, we had to change our campaign plan." There was some talk that the Blackwater men were on CIA business, but insiders dismiss that, saying that they were checking out the route that contractor Kellogg Brown & Root's logistics convoy would take the next day, and had been lured into Fallujah by members of Iraqi security forces. "Very vanilla," or routine, said Dave Scholl, a former Special Forces soldier who speaks Arabic, was friendly with some of the Blackwater people, and was working for another security contractor in Iraq at the time.

There is little question about what happened next: The Blackwater vehicles ran into a well-prepared ambush that had been set up the day before. There had been a leak out of the Green Zone about their movements, said a senior U.S. intelligence official with direct access to that information. That morning nearby shops were warned to close, and roadblocks were set up to prevent the contractors from escaping, according to a Marine briefing that summarized the events of this period. Cans of gas were stashed and standing ready in a nearby alley. The four American contractors were attacked near the center of town, hit by fire from AK-47s and RPGs. They were dragged from their car, beaten, and dismembered. Two of their torsos were dragged westward and hung from the girders of a bridge over the Euphrates on the edge of the town, then taken down and tossed on a pile of tires to burn while crowds cheered and crowed.

At the Marine headquarters outside Fallujah, senior commanders learned about the Blackwater situation from CNN. Mattis saw the attack as a ploy designed to provoke a massive retaliation. He devised a methodical plan to respond to the atrocity. "If the Marines took it step by step, the ringleaders would be arrested or killed over the course of the next month," Francis "Bing" West, the author and former Pentagon official who was embedded with Marine commanders, wrote in *No True Glory,* his lively history of Marine operations in al Anbar in 2004.

But the televised atrocity in Fallujah provoked a powerful response down the chain of command, starting from Washington, where the images of Muslim mobs burning Americans evoked memories of October 1993 in Mogadishu, Somalia. The civilian leadership of the U.S. government didn't want to wait for a careful, quiet counterattack. Robert Blackwill, who had been brought into the NSC staff to advise on Iraq policy, began pushing for a swift and tough retaliatory raid, according to officials who worked with him. That would knock the Marines off the course they'd planned, and top military commanders in Iraq, including Lt. Gen. Sanchez, advised against it, said several people involved in the exchanges. Bremer was somewhere in the middle, said a former Bush administration official. "Bremer asked for time to try to deal with the situation," he said. But the word came back from the White House: If there was no political movement, the president wanted action within a few days.

Bremer talked to Sanchez about launching a vigorous attack, and soon the Marines got a call from Sanchez's headquarters. "Go in and clobber people" was the way one officer remembered it. Conway, the senior Marine in Iraq, wanted to hear the order from Abizaid, who told him the order had come from high up—that is, either Rumsfeld or the White House. "This is what the enemy wants," Mattis protested. He had been preparing to take Fallujah for months, but didn't want to do it this way—hastily, clumsily, acting in anger rather than with cool detachment. He was ordered nonetheless to get into Fallujah within seventy-two hours. He requested to see that order in writing, but didn't get it.

"Mattis wanted to do a police operation: 'Let's find out who did this, and get them; this is a city of three hundred thousand in which a few hundred people did something,'" said another Marine general. "The answer was: 'No, go in there with the power of a Marine division.' He argued against this. What would be the consequences of doing this? Mattis knew that the consequence of sending in a big conventional unit inevitably would be large amounts of damage."

Nor was a sudden movement a militarily effective way to operate. As a summary by retired Marine Lt. Col. Frank Hoffman put it, the Marines were ordered to attack "without time to insert human intelligence assets or sensors, conduct formal reconnaissance, add reinforcements, or shape the battle space."

Conway, the senior Marine commander, later publicly said that he objected to how the attack on Fallujah was ordered. "We felt like we had a method that we wanted to apply to Fallujah: that we ought to probably let the situation settle before we appeared to be attacking out of revenge," he said as he prepared to leave Iraq a few months later. "Would our system have been better? Would we have been able to bring over the people of Fallujah with our methods? You'll never know that for sure, but at the time we certainly thought so." He wouldn't tell reporters where the attack order originated, only that he received it from Sanchez. "We follow our orders," Conway said.

So on April 5 the Marines launched Operation Vigilant Resolve. Almost exactly a year after the fall of Baghdad, the U.S. military was again engaged in a major offensive. First, small teams of special operators went in to try to capture "high-value targets," according to the Marine summary. Next came a full-scale assault carried out by about twenty-five hundred Marines from three battalions backed up by some tanks and other armored vehicles. It quickly became a grinding, toe-to-toe fight. The enemy was better prepared than the Marines had been told to expect. "Insurgents surprise U.S. with coordination of their attacks: coordinated, combined, volley-fire RPGs, effective use of indirect fire," the Marine summary states. "Enemy maneuvered effectively and stood and fought."

Over the course of several weeks, the intense fighting was occasionally interrupted by either ceasefires or agreements that broke down, and was followed by a new round of air strikes and the use of AC-130 gunships and Cobra gunship helicopters. In order to seal off the estimated twelve hundred fighters inside Fallujah, Mattis asked for more troops—the Army's theater operational reserve—and was turned down, Lethin recalled. So, he said, Mattis stripped out troops from elsewhere in Anbar: "We thinned out our forces in the west, and turned over part of our southeastern sector [to the Army] to concentrate our forces on Fallujah." One of the results, said Toolan, was that the Iraqi National Guard commander in the town of Mahmudiyah, on the main highway south of both Fallujah and Baghdad, "went over to the dark side" and wouldn't train his people anymore. Mattis also requested that he be given another regiment of several thousand Marines, plus a tank unit, according to a Marine officer. It isn't clear where that request died in the chain of command, but the fact that he asked and didn't get them casts doubt on the Bush administration's repeated insistence that senior commanders would get more troops any time they asked for them.

The fighting environment was unlike anything Marines had trained for, a group of Marine scout/snipers wrote in an after-action review. "The layout of the city is random," they reported. "Zones distinguishing between residential, business, and industrial are nonexistent."

The roadside bomb was the everyday weapon of choice for the Iraqi insurgency, but in battles such as First Fallujah it favored the RPG. Gunnery Sgt. Nick Popaditch, a tank commander, would recall facing this weapon in the April battle for Fallujah. "The first enemy RPG was a good one, taken from very close. It was so close that I felt the heat of its rocket propulsion in my face."

Later that day, attacking into the center of Fallujah, Popaditch was in an alleyway so narrow that he couldn't traverse the turret of his tank, but he was able to keep fighting with two machine guns. Standing in the hatch of his tank, he saw one fighter shoot at him with an RPG, but not the second shooter. "I heard a hiss about a split second before it hit me," exploding inside the hatch. "I saw a bright flash of light and then nothing but blackness. I had been blinded [temporarily] in both eyes. It felt as though I had been hit in the head with a sledgehammer so I stood back up. I couldn't hear anything except a dull static-like humming in my ears. I knew at the time that it was an RPG that had hit me. I couldn't see anything so I reached up and felt my face. It was a wet and gooey feeling. My first concern was to get the tank moving out of what was obviously a bad place for it to be."

Popaditch's crew members drove the tank back to the Marines' defensive line. He focused on staying awake. Once inside Fox Company's perimeter, he climbed to the top of the turret. "When they started treating me, I knew I was safe, and I knew my family would never see a picture of me hanging from a train trestle somewhere," he said later.

As medics worked on Popaditch, mortar rounds began to hit nearby. "The corpsmen who were treating me took off their own body armor and piled it on top of me to protect my wounded body." He awoke later in darkness, sedated after his right eye had been removed. "Where am I?" he asked.

"You're on a plane to Germany, dude," came an answer out of the dark.

Popaditch also was on his way to a new life: He would receive the Silver Star for his actions, be medically retired from the Corps, and then enroll in college with the ambition of becoming a high school teacher.

A two-front war

As Fallujah ground on in early April 2004, and the fighting spread to nearby Ramadi, the broad middle of Iraq, from Mosul in the north to Baghdad to Najaf in the south-central area, began to spin out of control.

On April 9, 2004, Bruce Hoffman, a Rand Corporation terrorism expert who had been consulting at the CPA, was leaving the country at the end of a four-week visit. "We had three incidents on the way to Baghdad's airport, and then heard a huge explosion while we were there—it was the attack on the convoy that got Thomas Hammill." Hammill was a truck driver taken captive in one of the worst incidents involving contractors of the entire war. A twenty-six-vehicle convoy bringing an emergency shipment of jet fuel from the big U.S. base at Balad to the Baghdad airport was ambushed five miles short of its destination. PFC Jeremy Church, a National Guardsman who was a Wal-Mart security guard in civilian life, was driving for the convoy commander, Lt. Matt Brown, when he noticed that all the Iraqi cars and trucks on the highway had disappeared, leaving the Americans alone after what had been heavy traffic. A moment later a fusillade of small arms fire hit the convoy, including a bullet that knocked Brown's helmet from his head. Brown's left eye popped out of its socket and his brain began to bleed and swell. A bomb blew out a tire in the truck, but Church drove on the bare rim until he came to a base operated by a unit of the 1st Cavalry Division. He then helped organize a relief column to head back into the kill zone to rescue the survivors of the ambushed convoy, an act for which he received the Silver Star. Six drivers had been killed—some by rocket-propelled grenades, others by small arms fire, and others apparently by flames. Huge plumes of black smoke were visible for miles. Two Army soldiers on escort duty also were killed, and one was taken captive.

Around this time, Dan Senor, Bremer's spokesman, vowed at a Green Zone press conference, "We will not allow this country to head down the path toward destabilization." But even as he said it, it seemed like that was precisely the course Iraq was on. It was an unusual press conference, conducted in a big, formal meeting room, upholstered with an orange carpet, and featuring a soldier in battle fatigues and body armor carrying an automatic weapon and surveying the assembled reporters.

In addition to Fallujah and Ramadi, the U.S.-led coalition lost any semblance of authority in several other south-central cities, most notably in Najaf and Kut. The ability of armed U.S. forces to operate routinely in much of the rest of central Iraq diminished. The major difference from the previous nine months or so of fighting was that for the first time, even as the Sunnis were fighting in Fallujah and Ramadi, a Shiite militia was attacking across a broad area. The forces of Moqtadr al-Sadr, the rabble-rousing radical Shiite cleric who strongly opposed the U.S. presence, would take a different approach than the Sunnis, who had been doing the bulk of the fighting for many months. Just thirty years old, Sadr was the son of Grand Ayatollah Mohammed Sadiq Sadr, who had been assassinated along with two of his sons in Najaf in 1999, presumably on the order of Saddam Hussein. Sadr puzzled U.S. officials, who judged him an awkward, unintelligent young man who, they calculated, could be neglected into obscurity. That view tended to underestimate the power that Sadr's populist strain of Shiism derived from nationalist sentiments. Unusually for a Shiite, Sadr's posters tended to feature the Iraqi flag, which also was flown by his followers at demonstrations.

U.S. authorities repeatedly planned to confront Sadr in 2003, leading to one of the many arguments between U.S. civilian and military leaders in Iraq. "We had a couple of operations laid down in the fall of '03 to take him out, and they got called off by CPA very shortly before execution" of the plans, said a U.S. military intelligence officer. This is just one of the many murky areas in the history of the U.S. occupation, where the buck is passed with surprising frequency. Bremer states in his memoir of his time in Iraq that he wanted to arrest Sadr but was held back by Rumsfeld and the CIA.

"We were prepared to act," said a senior Army officer in Iraq. "We were almost there. Then we were throttled back. Due to pol-mil issues, we were told to hold off—'timing's not right.'" Instead, the U.S. military monitored the state of Sadr's militia and conducted what it called shaping operations—basically, broadcasts and leaflets—to try to diminish Sadr's influence. The militia was purchasing lots of AK-47s but not the larger caliber weapons that were thought to be necessary for anyone planning to take on the U.S. military, a senior Army officer in Iraq said a few weeks later. In addition, the militia appeared to be under strict orders to avoid confrontations with U.S. forces. Sanchez was said to be skeptical of the need to confront Sadr directly.

Sadr's weekly newspaper, *al-Hawza*, kept up its attacks on the U.S. occupation during the fall and winter. BREMER FOLLOWS IN THE FOOTSTEPS OF SADDAM, one of its headlines charged in late February. As best as can be determined, Bremer was appalled by a rampage conducted by Sadr's militia against Gypsies living in southern Iraq and, impatient with Sanchez, took the nonmilitary steps available to him. In late March he used his civil authority to shut down Sadr's newspaper. A few days later he ordered the arrest of Sadr's top deputy, Mustafa Yaqoubi, who was believed by U.S. intelligence to be the brains behind the thirty-year-old cleric. U.S. Special Operations troops apprehended Yaqoubi in Najaf before dawn on April 3—again, it isn't clear who gave them the order—and turned him over to Iraqi police. The next day a warrant was issued for Sadr's arrest.

U.S. intelligence analysts in Baghdad calculated that Sadr, cut off from his best adviser, likely would respond with riots and a few attacks but nothing that would last long. "You think it will spike, emotionally, for forty-eight to seventy-two hours," the senior Army officer said a few weeks later, alluding to an intelligence forecast of three to four days of angry demonstrations. "We did not anticipate it would go to the level it did." During most of the U.S. occupation there had been around 200 incidents a week aimed at U.S. and allied forces. That had increased to 300 just once, during the Ramadan offensive in early November 2003. But the occupation forces had never seen a spike like the one in the spring of 2004— about 280 incidents in the last week of March, then about 370 in the first week of April, then 600 in the second week.

The U.S. intelligence analysis soon was proven dramatically off base. "I and my followers of the believers have come under attack from the occupiers, imperialism, and the appointees," Sadr said in a Friday sermon in Kufa, a town just outside the holy city of Najaf. "Be on the utmost readiness, and strike them where you meet them." What followed that battle cry grew into the most widespread fighting U.S. forces had seen since the invasion a year earlier, as Shiite fighters engaged the occupation forces for the first time. That night gunmen killed Kufa's police chief, Col. Saeed Tiryak. Four Salvadoran soldiers were caught by a mob, and one was murdered when rioters placed a grenade in his mouth and pulled the pin. The next day the police chief for Mahmudiyah, a small town just south of Baghdad, was shot to death along with his driver while passing through a traffic tunnel in the capital. Witnesses said those attackers were dressed in police uniforms. Meanwhile, in Mahmudiyah itself, six other gunmen killed another police officer.

Eastern Baghdad erupts

In Sadr City, the Bronx-sized slum that forms Baghdad's eastern third, a reconnaissance patrol of soldiers from the 1st Cavalry Division, which was just rotating into Iraq, ran into groups of armed fighters from Moqtadr al-Sadr's Mahdi army and was pinned down and isolated overnight. At the same time, Sadr's fighters took over all seven police stations in the sector. Eight U.S. soldiers were killed and fifty-one wounded in heavy fighting before they were rescued the next morning. Several hundred Iraqi fighters were believed killed in the encounter.

"We have had full-scale combat ops for two weeks, and the days are running together," the commander of the 1st Brigade of the 1st Cavalry, Col. Robert "Abe" Abrams, said later in the month, as he reviewed his operations. "This is not what anyone thought was going to happen." Those first few days were the most intense, he said, listing the different sorts of actions: "Defense in sector, attack in zone, movement to contact, some raids, some cordon and search. It's more intense than any CTC [Combat Training Center] rotation I've ever had." That was a striking comment, because in those maneuvers, Army trainers aimed to concentrate the experience of combat, condensing weeks of incidents into just a few days. Mortar shells pounded Col. Abrams's main base, with a record of seventy-five rounds landing on May 9, 2004, recalled Dennis Steele, a reporter for *Army* magazine who was embedded there. "Back then, there was a fifty-fifty chance of a patrol making enemy contact within two hundred meters of the front gate, and the chances increased the farther it went into Sadr City," he later wrote.

Like the Marines in Fallujah, Army soldiers began to develop a new respect for their foe. "The Mahdi army fought very courageously and demonstrated good tactical patience, waiting to engage until we were within effective range of their weapons systems," Capt. John Moore wrote later in describing the fighting in Sadr City. "Once battle is joined, Mahdi army elements demonstrated incredible commitment to recover their casualties and equipment."

Next to erupt were Karbala, Basra, and Nasiriyah, three of the most important cities in the south, with attacks on police stations and government offices. This was followed by a wave of kidnappings of foreigners perceived by Iraqis to be working with the occupation—not only Americans, but also Israelis, South Koreans, Russians, Chinese, and others. Sadr focused the firepower of his Mahdi army not on U.S. troops but on their local allies in the police and fledgling Iraqi military.

The Iraqi army refuses to fight

Monday, April 5, also brought the second big surprise of this time: Not only were the enemy fighters better than U.S. military intelligence had thought, the

Iraqi allies were worse. As the Sunni and Shiite revolts threatened to merge, American leaders decided to put the new Iraqi army to the test. As the assault on Fallujah began, commanders ordered an Iraqi battalion to go help the Marines there. It was the first time the U.S. military had sought to involve the newly formed postwar Iraqi army in its major combat operations, and it led to major disappointment. To the chagrin of U.S. commanders, the 620-man 2nd Battalion of the Iraqi Armed Forces refused to join the battle.

The trouble began when the unit was in a convoy to Fallujah—a Sunni stronghold—and to its surprise found itself under fire in a Shiite neighborhood in northwest Baghdad. Six members of the unit were wounded, two seriously. An American soldier from a patrol that came to the aid of the convoy was killed. A crowd of Shiites gathered and surged at the convoy, which then retreated to its post on a former Republican Guard base in Taji, a town north of the capital. American advisers then hoped to have the unit helicoptered to Fallujah, but so many of the Iraqi soldiers refused to go that the plan was abandoned almost as soon as it was hatched. Of a total of 695 soldiers on the rolls, 106 had deserted and another 104 refused. All the Iraqi interpreters attached to the unit—more than a dozen—also quit, one of the Iraqi battalion's Marine advisers said in an interview.

"We did not sign up to fight Iraqis," the troops said, according to Army Maj. Gen. Paul Eaton. When the 2nd Battalion had graduated from training camp on January 6, Rumsfeld had hailed it as a major part of the future of Iraq. Gen. Sanchez had attended the graduation ceremony and said, "We are now into the accelerated period of providing Iraqi security forces, and these soldiers look very proud, very dedicated. I have high expectations that in fact they would help us bring security and stability back to the country."

In an interview in his office in a palace in the Green Zone one steamy April afternoon a few days later, Eaton, a former chief of infantry training for the U.S. Army, said his review of the situation had found a series of problems. One was that the Iraqi troops were not informed about their actual role; they were to be given the relatively benign assignment of operating checkpoints, but they assumed they were being hurled into the middle of a bloody fight, battling on the side of Americans against fellow Arabs. In intense discussions back at their base, Eaton added, "We could not move them off that mark."

Complicating communications, he said, was that the battalion had ten new U.S. advisers who had rotated into their jobs April 1, just four days before the incident, replacing the advisers who had trained the unit for months. This was a violation of the longtime principle that when training a foreign force, the advisers accompanying it into battle should be familiar and trusted. "The point is training and advising and assisting in combat," said a veteran Special Forces officer. "It takes a lot of rapport building to gain the trust of the Iraqis to work alongside our forces."

Instead, the new advisers were Marines who treated the Iraqis as if they were raw recruits at boot camp. This was not the best course in a culture that places an extraordinary premium on personal dignity, especially in interacting with distrusted foreigners. "We treated them like recruits, green as June grass," Staff Sgt. Andrew Garcia told Bing West. "We rolled them out at zero five hundred [5:00 A.M.] for physical training, then spent the day drilling in infantry basics. We got in their faces, we screamed, the usual routine, gave them back their self-respect a little at a time." Garcia had come to Iraq directly from being a drill instructor at the Marine boot camp on Parris Island, South Carolina.

The near mutiny was a setback for the Marines' plans for Fallujah. "The demonstrated unreliability of Iraqi security forces has precluded us from putting an Iraqi face on our operations in Fallujah," the Marine battle summary later noted. "The desertion of the 2nd NIA [New Iraqi Army] battalion, reported as the best in the NIA, has significantly reduced our flexibility and diminished the possibility that we can do so."

Even more troubling, it also was a strategic failure for the entire U.S. approach in Iraq, which hinged on developing a new Iraqi security force that could take over from U.S. troops. "That was stunning," recalled a veteran Army planner who had served in Iraq for most of 2003 and into early 2004. "It was the first real attempt to use Iraqi forces, and it just flopped." There was a worrisome political dimension to the situation, as well: When push came to shove, Iraqis had found it difficult to stand alongside their occupiers. "The lines are blurring for a lot of Iraqis right now, and we're having problems with a lot of security functions right now," Gen. Eaton said.

The refusal also revealed major flaws in the U.S. training effort. Some Iraqi police and soldiers felt let down by the U.S. effort to train and equip them. A subsequent report by the General Accountability Office (GAO), the congressional watchdog agency, found that in March 2004, the provisioning of the Iraqi Civil Defense Corps was "months behind schedule," with the result that "no Iraqi Civil Defense Corps units possessed body armor, and many were using Saddam-era helmets for protection." In addition, as of late April, many units were still awaiting the delivery of the most basic equipment—uniforms, helmets, vehicles, radios, rifles, ammunition, and night-vision gear. "A multinational force assessment noted that Iraqis within the Iraqi Civil Defense Corps felt the multinational force never took them seriously, as exhibited by what they perceived as the broken promises and the lack of trust of the multinational force," the GAO report stated.

For all these reasons—the blurring of loyalties, American failure to properly outfit their would-be allies, and Sadr's concerted attacks on police in Shiite areas—Iraqi security forces collapsed in several cities. Almost three thousand police officers left the rolls in just one short period, the week of April 17. At about the same time, twelve thousand troops deserted the Iraqi Civil Defense Corps, according to the GAO. In western Iraq, about 82 percent left; in Baghdad, about 50 percent; farther to the north and south, about 30 percent quit.

"No single mission is more important than security, and no Iraqi popular desire is clearer than that this mission be done by Iraqis," wrote Anthony Cordesman, a respected defense analyst at the Center for Strategic and International Studies, an independent Washington think tank, in assessing the training of Iraqi security forces. His verdict: "The U.S. has been guilty of a gross military, administrative and moral failure."

Less often spoken was the distrust that many U.S. officers developed of the Iraqi security forces. U.S. officers believed that many officers were in league with the insurgency, or at the very least were so fearful of it that they cooperated with it. As one Marine put it to a friend, "Any Iraqi officer who hasn't been assassinated or targeted for assassination is giving information or support to the insurgents. Any Iraqi officer who isn't in bed with the insurgents is likely already dead."

CSIS's Cordesman concluded in a spring 2005 assessment of the Iraqi insurgency, "Dual loyalty and HUMINT penetration of Iraqi security and military forces may be the rule, rather than the exception."

Through all these mistakes, said retired Gen. John Keane, the former number-two officer in the Army, "we lost about a year, to be frank about it," in training the Iraqi military. It had been a very expensive lesson, in both blood and money.

"Take fucking Vienna!"

The fighting in Fallujah was fierce, and surprisingly widespread, involving not just the city but the roads leading to it. That created quiet concern about supplies: Insurgent attacks had reduced the Marines to just two days' worth of some critical goods.

On April 7, a Marine supply convoy run by a twenty-five-man platoon was south of Fallujah when it was surprised by a sophisticated, half-mile-long ambush that began with a volley of RPG fire followed by mortar shells. Then approximately ten machine guns opened up from bunkered positions, according to Marine documents. The Marines, following their training, attacked into the ambush, killing twenty-six enemy fighters out of an estimated total of forty to sixty. One Marine was killed and six others were wounded, four severely. Marines involved in the action were awarded five of the nation's highest medals—one Navy Cross and four Silver Stars.

"We'll get Fallujah under control," Abizaid vowed in an interview on April 8. But the next day the order came down to stop. It isn't really clear where the order came from. Some Marines believed it had come from the White House. One former State Department official said on background that he thought it was ordered by Bremer, who, despite his lack of authority over military operations, was worried that the Fallujah battle was destroying support for the occupation within Iraq.

So on April 9, the first anniversary of the fall of Baghdad, the Marines found themselves implementing a unilateral ceasefire. "We were relatively close to seizing the final objectives," Col. Toolan remembered.

Mattis was furious. Thirty-nine Marines and U.S. soldiers had died—for what? "If you're going to take Vienna, take fucking Vienna!" he snarled to Gen. Abizaid, updating a famous comment made by Napoleon Bonaparte. Abizaid only nodded, Mattis recalled.

Mattis believed he had the enemy on the ropes and was within a few days of finishing them off. The insurgents lacked bunkers and ammunition. They weren't able to get additional supplies through the cordon the Marines had thrown up around the city. He went out to see Toolan, operating from a command post in Jolan, a neighborhood in northwest Fallujah. "He was very frustrated," recalled Toolan. "It was hard for him to tell me. He didn't understand why we were told to stop."

"It was like going in half-assed and then running away," said another Marine general. "They hadn't thought about the consequences. It was the same as the way they went to war, and the same way that Bremer operated."

For another two weeks, the Marines stood by, expecting to go back into the city. But then, after a series of quiet conversations among the U.S. government and its allies, word trickled down to the Marines that the White House thought that resuming the attack could shatter the coalition. Bremer told Abizaid that the Fallujah attack was threatening to fracture Iraqi support for the American presence.

"If you're not confused," Mattis told Bing West on April 26, "then you don't know how complex the situation is."

But the Marines had no uncertainty about their unhappiness with the outcome. As Lethin, the division operations officer, noted, "Our job was not to be emotional. Our job was to put lipstick on that pig as best we could."

Fallujah in enemy hands

The end of the first battle of Fallujah was one of the lowest points of the entire U.S. military effort in Iraq. "Most of Fallujah is returning to normal," President Bush asserted on April 28, after a series of aerial bombardments. It was a stunningly inaccurate statement. Not one of the objectives of the Marine attack had been achieved. The attack order, as stated in a Marine briefing, was to "capture/kill the murderers of the coalition contractors while conducting offensive operations . . . to restore law and order and build long-term stability." The desired end state, as stated in that briefing, was to make it impossible for terrorists to destabilize the city again. When the fight ended, the murderers had not been apprehended and law and order had not been restored. What's worse, in the following weeks it would become painfully clear that it was the murderers of the contractors who enjoyed free rein in the city, not the Marines. "We turned the city over to the Fallujah Brigade—which was made up of people we'd been fighting against," said Toolan.

It was a moment that would have been comic were it not so tragic. The Fallujah Brigade was created as a fig leaf for the U.S. withdrawal. When told that the city would be controlled by this new Iraqi organization, Abizaid is said to have called Bremer and asked, "'Why did you create the Fallujah Brigade?" In his memoir Bremer reports that his own reaction to the creation of the brigade was "What the hell is going on?" In fact, the brigade had been cooked up between the CIA and the Marines as a way of ending the political standoff over the city. "The MEF [Marine Expeditionary Force, the senior Marine headquarters in Iraq] came up with the idea, and floated it to CJTF, and they approved it," Lethin later said with evident regret. "My opinion, that was hiring the inmates to run the asylum."

It soon became clear that the members of the Fallujah Brigade had far more in common with the insurgents than they ever would with the Marines. The Iraqi officer chosen to lead the brigade, Jassim Mohammed Saleh, a former commander of a brigade of the old Republican Guard, entered Fallujah wearing the green uniform and red beret he had worn as a major general in Saddam Hussein's army. When authorities learned more about his background—Bremer's spokes-man, Dan Senor, said much later that "Saleh oversaw the slaughtering of five thousand" Shiites in Karbala in 1991—they removed him from the position. But that was just a face-saving move. The fact was that the U.S. military had stopped fighting, withdrawn from the city, and left it to the other side.

Gen. Myers, the chairman of the Joint Chiefs of Staff, attempted to put a good face on this strange outcome. "I'm going to try to set the record straight," he pro-claimed during a Sunday morning interview on Fox News. "The reporting to date has been, let me just say, very, very inaccurate. Here are the facts." The situation was being controlled by commanders on the ground—"primarily them, not us here in Washington"—he said, somewhat surprisingly, given the reports from senior Marine commanders that they were ordered from the highest levels first to attack and then to unilaterally cease fire. More brazenly, he portrayed the creation of the Fallujah Brigade as just one more step in the "Iraqification" of security. "You know, we want Iraqis to do this work, and that's—this is a microcosm of what we want to happen all over Iraq." The members of the brigade were "Iraqis that have shown up that want to be helpful. If they can be helpful, fine."

But as was often the case in his public explanations and discussions of this war, the chairman's comments had only a loose relationship with the realities of Iraq, where there was little dispute that the outcome in Fallujah represented a set-back for the U.S. cause, and most certainly wasn't something commanders wanted to replicate elsewhere. The arrangement was a "stunning victory" for the insur-gency, charged a memo written by Nathaniel Jensen, a State Department diplo-mat attached to the CPA. As for the Fallujah Brigade, he added, "I strongly doubt it will work."

"I looked Iraqis in the eye, and they were thinking, 'We can get rid of these guys,'" recalled a Special Forces veteran who was working on security issues. "That was the day we lost the initiative. The Iraqis realized that they could kick our ass—that they had the option to bring the fight to us."

"This turn of events represented a political victory for the insurgents," wrote Ahmed Hashim, the expert on the Iraqi insurgency at the U.S. Naval War College. "The United States had backed down, and, more important, had negotiated with the enemy. It also was a military victory: the insurgents had fought the Americans to a standstill."

"We won," agreed an Iraqi insurgent in Fallujah.

It wasn't long before the Fallujah Brigade became indistinguishable from the insurgency. Wearing their old Iraqi army uniforms, some of its members, far from being "helpful," began shooting at Marines based on the eastern edge of the city. The U.S. military said it considered the brigade to be disbanded. The eight hundred AK-47s issued to the brigade wound up in the hands of insurgents, as did some heavy machine guns and rocket-propelled grenade launchers, U.S. officers said.

Fallujah, which the Marines had hoped to make a showcase for how to fight smarter and better in Iraq, instead had become an international rallying point for anti-American fighters. "In June, after we had turned everything over to the Fallujah Brigade, Fallujah was like a siren, calling to the insurgents," said Toolan, commander of the 7th Marines. "It was like the bar in *Star Wars*." All summer long, he said, foreign fighters poured into the city.

The fighting in the area wore on quietly for months. It reverted to the previous pattern of U.S. raids and occasional air strikes on the one hand, and insurgent car bombs, sniper firings, and mortar attacks on the other. Both sides knew that another big battle was looming. The insurgents dug 306 fighting positions in Fallujah, many of them well-constructed bunkers rigged with explosive booby traps. "There were constant probing actions, attacks, attempts to move weapons caches," Toolan recalled. By late summer, when it became clear that it would take a major battle to pacify the city, the Marines pulled back and waited for the U.S. presidential election campaign to conclude. They were determined not to fight half a battle again, and some in the military thought the next round would be so ugly that it shouldn't be waged until after the election was past. The experiment of the Fallujah Brigade was also pronounced dead, with the Iraqi unit officially disbanded in early September.

Fallujah was emblematic of what would be a Sisyphean year for U.S. troops. There would be two battles for Fallujah, two for Najaf, a running battle in eastern Baghdad for much of the year, and finally an effort to retake Samarra, which was thought to have been pacified in 2003 by the 4th Infantry Division, but had again grown unruly. Also at this time, the fighting in Baghdad involved both Sunni insurgents, who were fighting in the western part of the city, and Shiite fighters, mainly in Sadr City. At one point, the 1st Armored Division had troops engaged near Abu Ghraib, on the western outskirts of Baghdad, for seventy-two straight hours. "I've got to tell you, we've killed a lot of people carrying weapons and RPGs this week," Brig. Gen. Hertling, a deputy commander of the division, told the Associated Press. "And when I say a lot, I am talking in the hundreds."

Myers, as usual, managed to portray the spring explosion as positive. At a Baghdad press conference on April 15 he called it "a symptom of the success that we're having here in Iraq." With Lt. Gen. Sanchez at his side, he said, "I think it's that success which is driving the current situation, because there are those extremists that don't want that success."

Less than forty-eight hours later, the U.S. military closed long sections of two of the major highways running into Baghdad, saying the step was a necessary response to a series of attacks and bombings. Privately, U.S. commanders expressed concern about their supply lines. At one point, according to Bremer, a military officer at the CPA ordered that the Green Zone go on food rationing. "The guys in Baghdad were really concerned, and thought they'd have to evacuate Baghdad," recalled one general.

The incredible shrinking coalition

The U.S.-led effort in Iraq stood on three legs: U.S. forces, Iraqi forces, and international forces. As a result of the wave of violence, the second leg and then the third began to crumble.

"We've got a huge coalition," President Bush had insisted in March 2003. "As a matter of fact, the coalition that we've assembled today is larger than the one assembled in 1991, in terms of the number of nations participating." But the son's wasn't a solid alliance, based on common interests, as the father's had been, but rather a jerry-rigged series of deals that couldn't survive much pressure. Countries sent soldiers to Iraq as a political favor to the U.S. government, and except for the British contingent, that good turn didn't extend to getting them into combat. One CPA official recalled sitting at a meeting in March 2004 at which first Bremer and then Sanchez chewed out the Spanish commander, who was preparing to pull out, and who was making the case for cooperating with the militias. "Bremer dressed him down, and said, 'We don't talk to militias, they're illegal,'" this official recalled. (A few months later, after Bremer's departure, the U.S. military began not only talking to militias, but aiding and equipping some of them.)

"Except for the Brits, they weren't there to fight," this CPA official recalled. "The Dutch did good patrols, on foot. The Italians only patrolled by vehicle. . . . The Japanese didn't patrol at all." In fact, he said, under their rules of engagement, which provided only for self-defense, the Japanese weren't permitted to secure their own perimeter and had to rely on the Dutch to do it. Nor did their rules allow them to come to the aid of others under attack. The Thai battalion's rules didn't even allow them to leave their camp near Karbala, said Army Col. Peter

Mansoor, because they were in Iraq for humanitarian work that under current conditions couldn't be done.

Indeed, some coalition partners felt that they had been brought into the country under false pretenses—that is, signed up for a peacekeeping mission that partly through American bungling had deteriorated into combat. "We came for Phase IV—security and stabilization operations," said Lt. Gen. Mieczyslaw Bieniek, the Polish paratrooper who commanded the multinational division operating in south-central Iraq. That was how his mission statement was framed to him. But, he added, "it has never happened. . . . All of a sudden, against our will, we find ourselves in the combat zone." That caught him in a bind: His parliament had forbidden him to conduct offensive operations, yet when he said that to U.S. officers, they treated him as if he were shirking his duty.

Polish Prime Minister Marek Belka was later scathing about the U.S.-led effort in Iraq. "It failed totally," he said at an international forum on nation building held in Sweden. "Many mistakes, major mistakes, have been committed."

This set of political circumstances made the coalition strategically vulnerable. Many troops in Iraq were deployed on the diplomatic understanding that they would not really be in harm's way—a condition that proved easy for the foe to challenge. When so attacked, the multinational units "lacked the cohesion needed to respond quickly to the uprising," Michael Knights, a defense analyst at the Washington Institute for Near East Policy, noted.

In May 2004, Spain withdrew its contingent of thirteen hundred troops, which had made up a big part of Bieniek's multinational division. Honduras, the Dominican Republic, and Nicaragua also pulled out their small contingents, totaling about nine hundred people. During that summer, the Philippines left after a Filipino contractor in Iraq was taken hostage. Hungary left at the end of the year, and the Netherlands and Ukraine withdrew in 2005. Poland, Bulgaria, and Italy, probably the three strongest European supporters of U.S. policy in Iraq, also in 2005 announced plans to leave eventually.

To a surprising degree, the rump coalition consisted of veterans of the Warsaw Pact. Of the thirty-one countries that would remain as troop-contributing nations by the fall of 2004, more than half were former communist states, and more than one third hadn't existed as sovereign nations when the United States fought the first Gulf War. (Those eleven recently born states were: Azerbaijan, the Czech Republic, Estonia, Georgia, Kazakhstan, Latvia, Lithuania, Macedonia, Moldova, Slovakia, and Ukraine.) Some of the other, older nations were trivial

players on the global stage—among those listed on the State Department's official internal list of coalition partners were Albania, El Salvador, and Tonga.
Altogether, the troop contribution of the thirty-one coalition partners amounted
to less than twenty-four thousand. The real "coalition of the willing" that was in
Iraq was the one of international jihadists flocking to Iraq to fight the Americans,
tartly commented Marine Col. Hammes. "These are people willing to fight."

The thin green line

Because of the pervasive hostility of the population in much of central Iraq
from Mosul to Najaf, U.S. troop levels felt thin. The official line was that there
were adequate numbers, but privately many commanders said they lacked enough
soldiers for the mission, and that they had to move units around and leave gaps
that were soon filled by insurgents. One of the hard-earned lessons of 2003 and
the spring of 2004 was that the most dangerous form of presence was being inter-
mittent. Moving a unit in, spending a few weeks, and then moving it elsewhere
tended to identify allies—a town's mayor, its police chief, local interpreters—and
then leave them vulnerable to attack. When those allies were left exposed and
then killed, or intimidated into supporting the insurgency as they often were, the
net of the entire U.S. military movement was a loss. Yet U.S. commanders tended
not to see the killings of Iraqi allies as tactical setbacks, and still would boast that
they had never lost an engagement in Iraq.

"We need to send significantly more troops and equipment," Larry Diamond
wrote in a memorandum to national security adviser Rice on April 26, 2004,
shortly after the conclusion of his tour at the CPA. "In my weeks in Iraq, I did not
meet a single military officer who felt, privately, that we had enough troops. Many
felt we needed (and need) tens of thousands more soldiers, and at this point
(within the limits of the possible) at least another division or two"—that is, at
least an additional fifteen thousand to thirty thousand troops.

U.S. forces in Baqubah, a dusty town that is a forty-five-minute drive northeast of Baghdad, were fighting pitched battles in April 2004 with Shiite militiamen but lacked sufficient forces to see whether some of those fighters were
driving up the highway from Baghdad's Sadr City slum, forty-five minutes to the
south. "We've had reports of busloads of armed guys coming up from Baghdad,
but we didn't have the combat power to check it out," said Maj. Kreg Schnell, the
chief intelligence officer for the Army brigade based outside Baqubah.

As a stopgap, in mid-April thousands of troops from the 1st Armored Division and other units that had been in Iraq for twelve months had their time in the country extended. Some were just hours from leaving Iraq when they were told they'd be staying for another few months. But they took the news with surprising equanimity. Many soldiers in one battalion credited their commander, Lt. Col. John Kem, for handling the situation in a reasonable way. When he got the word on April 9, he immediately called all the soldiers in the unit into formation and spoke to them. "There were a few hysterics, a few tears," recalled Kem. He told them to take a day to wallow in their unhappiness and then to put it behind them. This approach helped the unit avoid the morale problems that plagued the 3rd Infantry Division in June 2003, when its postwar tour in Baghdad was unexpectedly extended. Back then, the grumbling was so bad, with soldiers denouncing President Bush and Defense Secretary Rumsfeld, that orders were issued to shut up.

Also, a year on the ground in Iraq had brought a new realism to the troops' assessments of the situation. Few expected overnight solutions anymore, as many troops had in Iraq during the spring of 2003. "It's going to have to be a permanent presence here," Lt. David Dake of Savannah, Georgia, said one morning over a breakfast tray of scrambled eggs, bacon, fried potatoes, pancakes, and cake, all prepared and delivered by the contractor Kellogg Brown & Root. "We're going to be here a long, long time." As Dake's hearty morning meal indicated, the soldiers were also enjoying a considerably better quality of life than the 3rd Infantry had the previous year, when its stay in the rubble of Baghdad was extended.

The battalion's base on an island in the Tigris also felt surprisingly safe, with a moatlike lake on one side and the broad river on the other. Located just above the northernmost of the thirteen bridges spanning the river in Baghdad, the base was hit by a mortar shell or two on most nights, but no one had ever been killed by those attacks, which were minor compared to those at many U.S. bases. The troops also had hot showers and big television sets showing a variety of American news, sports, and entertainment programs. For hunger pangs between meals, a snack bar served kabobs and cheeseburgers. Each of the Internet cafés boasted fifteen to twenty terminals, which during the evenings were full and had waiting lines. One popular subject being researched: the cars the troops planned to buy with all the money they were saving while serving in Iraq. Capt. Michael Baim, of Corpus Christi, Texas, commander of the battalion's Bravo Company, said many of his soldiers had saved ten thousand to twenty thousand dollars over the previous year—and now would get one thousand dollars a month bonus pay for each of the three months of their extended duty. On a bulletin board at the battalion head-quarters a sign read DILBERT OF THE DAY: THE KEY TO HAPPINESS IS SELF-DELUSION.

The unit made it look easy, but it wasn't. Turning the 1st Armored Division around and throwing it back into the fight required extraordinary feats of leader-ship and logistics management. When the order came down to stay in Iraq for an additional ninety days, after it already had been there for one year, the division was well into its redeployment. More than seven thousand of its soldiers already had left the country, and about half of its major pieces of equipment were in Kuwait. Even more significant, in preparation for leaving, the division had drawn down its supplies of ammunition and other consumable commodities. "By April 8, almost all stockpiles were gone," Maj. Martha Granger, an officer in the divi-sion's support command, later wrote.

The most profound cost to the 1st Armored Division was that during the additional three months it would spend in Iraq it would lose more than forty soldiers.

A small hard war

The feel of the war changed in the spring of 2004, both politically and tacti-cally. In May, for the first time, a majority of Americans polled—51 percent—said the war wasn't going well, according to a survey by the Pew Research Center. That was double the percentage in January. At the same time 53 percent of those polled favored keeping U.S. troops in Iraq until it had a stable government. In the spring of 2004 it also became common to see U.S. troops having their blood types inked into the cloth of their helmet covers.

In early April the insurgency offensive hit Baqubah, just northeast of Bagh-dad. "You knew it was coming," recalled Capt. Oscar Estrada, a member of the 415th Civil Affairs Battalion, who was working at the CPA office in downtown Baqubah. "The tension was in the air." An intelligence analyst had said to expect an attack at 1:00 P.M.—that is, 1300 on the twenty-four-hour military clock. As a cautionary step, he recalled, all Iraqi workers were asked to leave the CPA office, and Iraqi National Guard soldiers still there were disarmed. "They weren't too happy about it." Sure enough, at precisely 1300, a "crump"-like boom of a mortar shell impacted. Then several more hit. For once, Estrada thought with perverse satisfaction, the intelligence had been good.

Iraq felt different after that April offensive, he recalled. He brought an unusual background to his Army position as a civil affairs officer—he specialized in working with local government and with relief groups to coordinate humanitarian operations and other services. Born in Nicaragua, he had studied international relations at the University of California at Berkeley, where he also had joined ROTC. "I always thought that military service was part of being a man and a good citizen," he said later. He then spent eight years in the Foreign Service before leaving to attend the University of Michigan's law school, which he had almost completed before being called to active duty and sent to Iraq. It was his second major deployment, having served in Kosovo earlier. He was a thirty-six-year-old reservist captain with a decidedly independent point of view.

He arrived in Iraq in February 2004. "Back in February, you'd get IEDs, but there weren't that many direct attacks. In February, there were areas you could go to that after April you wouldn't go in without a company"—that is, perhaps 120 infantrymen. When the insurgency launched its offensive in April "it was just a shock. It was like a movie, with constant indirect fire—mortars, bombs, artillery, even a helicopter went down. The April attacks just changed everything. I think it changed the attitudes of soldiers. And it emboldened the enemy. For the units that arrived in the spring, it put them into a warrior mentality. It was a full-out war. Everything was allowed. I remember a company commander saying on the net that he didn't have room to maneuver an Abrams tank. The battalion commander said, 'Park it in the house, just park it in the house.' It was like World War II."

As a civil affairs officer who focused on the local population, Estrada thought that harsh tactics like that were profoundly unproductive. "I felt like we were falling into a trap—getting suckered into going out and provoking people into joining the insurgency." His views crystallized one day in early May on a mission to nearby Buhriz to assess the state of that city's water treatment plant. He took down all the information about the town's daily requirements for potable water, and its need for a working pump and high-capacity filters. Then he asked about security. "The treatment plant manager tells me that his biggest threat is coalition soldiers, who shoot up the compound whenever the nearby MP station and government building are attacked. He shows me the bullet holes and asks, 'Why?'" The plant caretaker then tugged on Estrada's sleeve and took him to his father, who described being beaten by American soldiers when he was detained. Estrada felt a "wave of shame" as he left the caretaker's hut.

That night he stayed up late in his office in Baqubah and wrote a summary of his views as an assessment that could be included in his commander's daily "sitrep," or situation report, for higher authorities. Three months of confusion and frustration poured out. He thought about an incident a few weeks earlier on a road east of Baqubah the soldiers called RPG Alley. The groves of date palms along the road provided insurgents with hiding places from which to fire their rocket-propelled grenades. When a unit ahead of them in a convoy reported taking fire from one such grove, he recalled, everyone began firing—automatic weapons, grenades, and .50 caliber heavy machine guns.

"What the hell are we shooting at?" he had screamed at a buddy as he fired his M-16.

"I'm not sure," the soldier had responded. "By that shack. You?"

"I'm just shooting where everybody else is shooting," Estrada had said, continuing to squeeze off rounds.

When the firing ended, he heard the commander on the radio. "Dagger, this is Bravo 6. Do you have anything, over?"

"Roger. . . . We have a guy here who's pretty upset. I think we killed his cow, over."

"Upset how, over?"

"He can't talk. I think he's in shock. He looks scared, over."

"He should be scared. He's the enemy."

"Uhm, ahh, roger, 6. . . . He's not armed and looks like a farmer or something."

"He was in the grove that we took fire from. He's a fucking bad guy."

"Roger."

Estrada wondered what was gained from that minor incident, and what was lost. "Did his family depend on that cow for its survival? Had he seen his world fall apart? Had we lost both his heart and his mind?" Fundamentally, Estrada was asking himself whether the U.S. Army should be in Iraq, and if so, whether it was approaching the occupation of Iraq in the right way. "I was beginning to come to terms with serious doubts about our cause," he later said, "and whether even if I accepted that our cause was just, our day-to-day actions did anything to champion it."

The insurgents get smarter . . .

One of the most striking aspects of the fighting in the spring of 2004 was the increasing sophistication of insurgent tactics. "We started to lose visibility of the enemy in the March, April, May time frame," Sanchez said later, in a statement given in legal proceedings related to the Abu Ghraib scandal. "In the March,

April, May time frame when the fighting was heaviest, we were having a hell of a time figuring out what his organizational structures were, how he was conducting operations and how the heck it was that he was managing to do the things he did to us in April, where it was some very coordinated, synchronized operations." He added: "What happened to us in April was a major effort on the part of the Saddam loyalists. . . . They cut our LoCs [lines of communication] by coordinated attacks on bridges. . . . So in the April time frame, the enemy significantly stepped up their activity to the point where we experienced the higher number of attacks in the last 18 months."

The new tactics of the enemy were notably on display when the 1st Infantry Division moved south to Najaf, into what had been the area covered by the faltering multinational division led by the Poles, to confront Sadr's militia. It was the single biggest operation conducted by the U.S. military since the invasion of Iraq a year earlier.

At midnight one warm April night, one of the big convoys prepared to leave Baqubah—where fighting was still going on—for Najaf. Sgt. James Amyett, a scout from Searcy, Arkansas, sat on the hood of a Humvee and faced a cluster of soldiers who stood around him in the dark. "We're going south," said Amyett, whose intensity made him appear older than his twenty-three years. "We go out from the front gate and straight through RPG Alley. There's going to be shooting. I guarantee it. There's a ninety-nine percent chance we're going to get hit. If they shoot, kill them. Shoot them in the fucking face." He looked at the two soldiers who would man the .50 caliber machine guns atop the two Humvees. "Gunners, controlled bursts," he ordered, meaning that they should not fire indiscriminately, and should conserve ammunition. "If a gunner gets hit, roll out of the way so a guy can jump up and keep it rocking. No hero bullshit." In a firefight, he said, "keep it simple. Just squeeze the trigger and kill the fuckers."

At 2:19 A.M. on a Monday morning, the forty-four-vehicle convoy rolled out through the maze of bomb barriers at the front gate of the base near Baqubah. The parade comprised not just tanks, Humvees, and Bradley fighting vehicles, but many of the more exotic parts of the U.S. Army inventory, such as the new Stryker armored vehicle, huge portable bridges, and special trucks for carrying M-1 Abrams tanks. The convoy was scheduled to take six hours, but the cautious Amyett warned his men that it could take twice that long.

Sgt. Maj. John Fourhman, a forty-six-year-old grandfather of seven from Columbus, Georgia, pointed at a cluster of palm trees along the side of the road. "This is the gauntlet," he said, a frequent launching pad for rocket-propelled grenades.

A few miles to the south, at 4:30 A.M., Capt. John Combs, the convoy commander, radioed back, "This is a known ambush point." It was a message he repeated frequently on the first part of the journey. Near dawn, Combs radioed back with another worrisome message: The bridge ahead had been hit with explosives. "We'll have to find another route, maybe through Baghdad," Combs said with a sigh. An hour later he called to report that the convoy had adopted Plan C: "The bridge at the secondary route is untenable, so we're going with a new route."

Asked later about this enemy tactic, Col. Dana Pittard, the commander of the brigade that had replaced Col. Hogg's in Baqubah, said the attacks on the bridges had impressed him. "The dropping of the bridges was very interesting, because it showed a regional or even a national level of organization." The insurgents appeared to be sending information southward, communicating about routes being taken by U.S. forces, and then getting sufficient amounts of explosives to key bridges ahead of the convoys. One of Pittard's combat engineers noted that several hundred pounds of explosive material and a fair degree of expertise were required to destroy a span on the solidly built expressway bridges, which could support tank traffic.

The vehicles paused for two hours while alternatives were explored back at brigade headquarters. Finally, they proceeded into the Shiite Muslim heartland south of Baghdad, along the Tigris and Euphrates rivers. The land was flat and hot, with farmers' fields dotted by palm groves. Above mud houses flew the black and green banners denoting Shiite Iraq. At 11:37, as the day grew sweltering, the convoy finally arrived at the Tigris. The bridge ahead was still standing. Over the radio came Combs's latest and most ominous message: "When we get to the far side, I've got absolutely no clue where we are going."

One mishap led to another. A Humvee driver, fatigued by the long haul and lulled by the warm weather, dozed off and rear-ended a truck, smashing his headlights and puncturing his radiator. Trucks sitting and waiting for accidents to be resolved and bridges to be checked for explosives began to run low on fuel, necessitating a six-hour stop at the Skania Convoy Support Center, a kind of Fort Apache with gas pumps not far from the site of ancient Babylon. Hundreds of big civilian trucks supplying the U.S. military were lined up at the center, their Third World contractor drivers dozing in the shade. While the 1st Infantry Division troops waited to refuel, some watched a thunderstorm to the north that sent flashes of lightning across the entire Mesopotamian horizon. Others talked smack about how much they hated their ex-girlfriends.

At 11:00 P.M. on Monday night, nearly twenty-four hours into the operation, the convoy arrived at a small town on the east bank of the Euphrates River. Groups of Iraqi men stood along the street, silently watching the vehicles pass, many of them with their arms crossed on their chests, their eyes glaring with hatred or wounded pride. "No one waved, they just stood there looking at us," commented PFC Steve Ratcliffe, a nineteen-year-old who worked at a grocery store in Sacramento until he enlisted in the Army, and now stood manning the big .50 caliber machine gun atop the sergeant major's Humvee.

As the last vehicles in the convoy crossed the river, a parachute flare shot up across the moonless night sky, then descended slowly, a white ball high to the right of the convoy. Fourhman tensed. Flares often were used by Iraqi fighters to signal comrades lying in wait for the approach of U.S. troops. A minute later, another one shot up. Then two orange flares arced up and slowly descended. Four minutes after the last flare, a flash of light and a huge noise hit the middle of the convoy. "IEDs, IEDs," Fourhman calmly but quickly said over the radio, reporting the improvised explosive devices. Red dots began zinging at the convoy from a dark grove on the left. Then there were other flashes and colors. "RPG, RPG," Fourhman radioed as rocket-propelled grenades flew in from the grove. He looked up at the .50 caliber and said, "Ratcliffe, aim for the base of fire." Ratcliffe and the driver—Spec. Sean Yebba, a twenty-two-year-old from near Boston—reacted calmly, doing their jobs. No one spoke unnecessarily. Ratcliffe swung the machine gun, searching for a target, his face illuminated only by the green glow of the night-vision scope atop his big weapon.

The convoy kept moving. "I have one wounded," came a soft, anonymous voice over the radio. About a mile farther down the road, the convoy halted to tend three wounded soldiers and repair a fuel truck hit by the bomb.

At 12:06, a call came over the radio to Fourhman. "Duke 7, birds five mikes out," meaning that the medical evacuation helicopter and the Apache gunship escorting it would arrive in five minutes. "Duke 7," Capt. Combs called again. "As soon as the bird lifts off, I want to get the hell out of here." The UH-60 Black Hawk medevac helicopter arrived with its lights out, nearby but detectable only by the sounds of its rotors and engine. A wounded soldier was lifted out; he later died.

Before getting back on the road, the soldiers conducted a head count. A driver, a civilian employed by Kellogg Brown & Root, was missing. The convoy couldn't leave without him. The soldiers stood and waited, stretching their legs on the north side of the Humvees, away from the side where the shooting in the ambush had originated. Worried by the delay in resuming movement, Fourhman radioed Combs to advise looking for the missing Brown & Root driver aboard the medevac helicopter. The aviation unit reported back that it had taken no uninvited passengers. Two hours later, when the aviators were again asked to check the helicopter, they found the man still hiding in it, cowering. "Let's get out of here," the sergeant major said with a sigh. "I don't like this neighborhood."

Four hours later, out in the desert west of the Euphrates, some of the big trucks in the convoy became mired in fresh mud, the result of the storms the troops had watched while gassing up. It was 2:00 P.M. Tuesday when the exhausted convoy finally arrived at Forward Operating Base Duke, about 12 miles to the northwest of Najaf, out in the empty desert. A primitive Army camp with few amenities, it looked and felt like home to the exhausted men in the convoy.

Over the next several days, Iraqi fighters repeatedly brought home the message that the nature of the war had changed. In another ambush near Najaf, a group of fighters suspected to be part of Sadr's militia let a group of six U.S. armored vehicles pass their position, then placed obstacles across the highway behind them, cutting off their line of retreat. The armored vehicles were forced to move forward across a bridge. While they were on it and approaching a police checkpoint, Iraqi fighters, some of them wearing police uniforms, began firing on them.

In Baghdad, meanwhile, insurgents began dynamiting highway overpasses. Though they did not destroy the spans, they succeeded in slowing traffic, depriving U.S. supply convoys of their best defense against ambushes—speed. It is far easier to use roadside bombs and rocket-propelled grenades against a truck mired in traffic than it is to hit one moving at 60 mph.

Some insurgents also developed shockingly good methods of infiltration. When one group of fighters was captured at about this time, its members possessed identification cards that allowed them full access to U.S. military bases, recalled Kalev Sepp, the retired Special Forces officer who was an adviser on U.S. strategy in Iraq. They "even had a photograph of themselves posing with a U.S. brigade commander," he noted.

. . . and U.S. troops learn as well

Before deploying to Iraq, Capt. Timothy Powledge thought that the best way to counter roadside bombs would be to aggressively pursue the person who triggered the blast. But after serving in Iraq for five months as commander of a company in the 3rd Battalion of the 7th Marine Regiment, he concluded that "hunting down the triggerman after the detonation is nearly impossible." His battalion, operating in western Iraq, was the target of 137 bomb attacks from March to July 2004, and didn't catch one bomber after the fact. What worked, he said, was awareness—having the same unit operate in the same area repeatedly, so it recognized anything out of place. To a far lesser degree, lying in wait at likely spots for bombs to be planted also worked. His unit conducted four hundred such "counter IED ambushes" and killed, captured, or disrupted likely bombers six times.

Commanders also were learning. Brig. Gen. Martin Dempsey, Sanchez's successor as the commander of the 1st Armored Division, later said that his unit had reacted far differently to Sadr's uprising than it might have a year earlier. "We had a different understanding of the things that make you successful. A year earlier we might have been too imprecise and heavy-handed."

But some units continued to use heavy-handed tactics. In May, two DIA interrogators filed complaints against the Special Operations team with which they were working. One said that he saw prisoners arriving at a detention facility in Baghdad with burn marks on their backs. (A June 2004 memo from Vice Adm. Lowell Jacoby, the director of the DIA, that summarized the charges doesn't indicate how those burns were suffered, but most likely they resulted from the practice of tying prisoners across the hot hoods of Humvees.) The other stated that on May 9, 2004, he had witnessed U.S. personnel taking hostage the wife of a suspected Iraqi terrorist in Tarmiya in order to compel the husband to turn himself in. "During my initial screening of the occupants of the target house, I determined that the wife could provide no actionable intelligence leading to the arrest of her husband," he wrote in a secret memorandum to his superiors. "Despite my protest, the raid team leader detained her anyway." The woman was released two days later.

On May 24, the CPA filed a memorandum to the State Department on a recent meeting in Samarra, where the 4th Infantry Division had been busy. "Sheik Nahid Faraj told the council that while no one wanted to admit it, the situation in Samarra was a direct result of Coalition Forces excesses over the past year," the cable stated. The CPA's interpretation of this critique was that the sheikhs were warning that U.S. military actions were eroding their authority, and that if the military's overly aggressive tactics continued, the sheikhs would lose control of their people.

On June 2, 2004, the CPA reported to State that "the security situation in Baghdad is a serious concern." It said that insurgents were operating in the western part of the city, that Sadr's militias were moving in the east, and that criminals were active across the city.

The spring battles end inconclusively

Both the Shiite uprising and the first battle of Fallujah ended indeterminately. With Sadr, the U.S. military arrived at a negotiated solution in which he stopped his militia's attacks and U.S. forces stopped trying to "kill or capture" him, and a murder charge against him was ignored.

Col. Alan King was asked by his boss at CPA to write out talking points for a meeting with Sadr's deputies to arrange a cease-fire. King listed several issues for discussion, but the main one was an offer that U.S. forces would pull back from the streets of Sadr City and stay mainly on their bases near the area. "That was the crux—climb down from a military confrontation," said King. His thinking was that after a stand-down, the U.S. authorities would instead try to use the tribal leaders to confront Sadr. But King was taken by surprise. Without his knowledge, his boss passed his paper to Bremer, who in turn gave it to Sanchez, who then turned it over to the commander of the 1st Armored Division, Martin Dempsey.

The next day King's phone rang. "Alan?" said a voice, which King quickly recognized as that of Dempsey, under whom he had served for a period after the 3rd ID left Iraq.

"Yes, sir," said King.

"You motherfucker!" Dempsey said, his voice intense with anger, King recalled. "If you ever tell me what to do with my division again, I will cut your fucking nuts off." Then he hung up. After that, King avoided Dempsey. But under a deal reached on May 27, both Sadr and the Americans withdrew their forces from Najaf and the nearby town of Kufa. Despite weeks of insistence by U.S. officials that his militias give up their weapons, "Sadr was not required to surrender or disarm, though the CPA would not admit this publicly," noted Larry Diamond, the former CPA official. U.S. forces later that summer would go back into Najaf and clean out the Sadr militia there, but Sadr's forces would remain in Sadr City and launch an average of more than one hundred attacks a week in August and September. They also began establishing a major presence in Basra and some other southern cities. Sadr also established an alliance of sorts with former Pentagon favorite Ahmed Chalabi. Of the six major deputies to Sadr who had been arrested, four eventually were released.

Meanwhile, in Fallujah, with the Marines withdrawn and the Fallujah Brigade fallen apart, the Sunni insurgents and their foreign allies were digging in. They spent months building dirt berms, sniper positions, fighting bunkers, and roadblocks. Fallujah effectively became a huge, city-sized, anti-American fortress.

"It was a closed city," said Capt. Stephen Winslow, a Marine historian who spent much of 2004 in or around Fallujah. "They owned it."

That outcome deepened the ill will between some Army and Marine officers. When the 82nd was in Fallujah and eastern al Anbar in 2003–4, said Gen. Swannack, its commander, it operated with precision, attacking small groups. But after that, he said, "Fallujah became a quagmire," because the large-scale operation conducted by the Marines had worked to "alienate the population." But that assessment seems unfair—after all, Mattis had gone in with a plan to engage the population, only to be overruled and ordered to launch an aggressive attack.

Journalism under siege

Life for reporters in Iraq became even more constrained in the spring of 2004. It was journalism under siege, with hotels being mortared and every trip out of them risky, made in armored SUVs and wearing body armor. Reporting trips became dashes to the Green Zone or to the front gates of U.S. military bases, where bombings were always a threat. One American newspaper had to move its reporters after men in their neighborhood were heard saying, "We are looking for the Jewish journalists." An Australian journalist was kidnapped from the steps of his hotel, but released after he persuaded his captors that his coverage was anti-occupation, which they confirmed by Googling him. At night reporters traded tales of "shark attacks"—ambushes by gunmen driving fast BMW sedans on the highways.

The world of reporters narrowed steadily in late 2003 and early 2004, recalled Rajiv Chandrasekaran, the *Washington Post*'s Baghdad bureau chief. He kept a map in his hotel room in which he crossed off roads as "no-go zones." First to go off-limits were the roads south of Baghdad, with Highway 8, the road to Hillah, becoming known as "the highway of death." One afternoon he passed several cars there that had been shot up. The next day he learned that seventeen people had been killed along that stretch just before he came through it. Then a CNN crew was shot up on that road. Next to be lost was the road west to Fallujah, then the road north to Tikrit and Mosul. Finally even the airport road—the path to escape from Iraq—became a kind of gauntlet. By late March, parts of the city of Baghdad itself began to be crossed off as too dangerous. Security became so bad that even the short drive across the city to the Green Zone carried risks that made reporters wonder whether it was worth it just to listen to officials—some of whom themselves rarely ventured out of the zone—talk in press conferences about the steady progress being made. "The whole world of foreign correspondence changed in Iraq," Chandrasekaran said. "We started out like other reporters—go out, report, do a day trip, come back, write the story. By the end, I wasn't going anywhere much. Sometimes press conferences in the Green Zone. And also bringing Iraqis to the hotel. And an awful lot of reporting by remote control, sending out Iraqis to report on a bombing, and giving them questions to ask."

In April 2004, John Burns, a veteran foreign correspondent for the *New York Times,* was kidnapped south of Baghdad along with his photographer. "We were taken hostage for twelve hours and driven out into the desert, blindfolded, and put at some risk," he said in a television interview. He also was shown the knife that he was told would be used to kill him.

A few months later, Farnaz Fassihi, a *Wall Street Journal* reporter based in Baghdad, sent out her usual periodical update to family and friends. It had been a rough time for Western journalists in Iraq, the thirty-one-year-old Iranian-born, American-educated reporter wrote in her e-mail. "Being a foreign correspondent in Baghdad these days is like being under virtual house arrest," her two-and-a-half-page missive began. "I can't go grocery shopping any more, can't eat in restaurants, can't strike a conversation with strangers, can't look for stories, can't drive in anything but a full armored car, can't go to scenes of breaking news stories, can't be stuck in traffic, can't speak English outside, can't take a road trip, can't say I'm an American, can't linger at checkpoints, can't be curious about what people are saying, doing, feeling. And can't and can't."

But she wasn't simply frustrated; she was growing angry with the official American portrayal of the situation. "Despite President Bush's rosy assessments, Iraq remains a disaster," she wrote, ". . . a foreign policy failure bound to haunt the United States for decades to come." It was a "raging barbaric guerrilla war." Moreover, journalists recently had been subjected to special targeting for abduction. She came away from a U.S. embassy cautionary briefing even more alarmed. "We were somberly told our fate would largely depend on where we were in the kidnapping chain once it was determined we were missing," she reported. "Here is how it goes: criminal gangs grab you and sell you up to Baathists in Fallujah, who will in turn sell you to al Qaeda."

More than the daily reports of car bombings, which had a sameness to them, Fassihi's letter captured the feeling of being a Westerner in Baghdad at the time. Reporters who received it forwarded it to each other, and soon it was being posted on Web sites. Some in the military pointed to the letter as evidence of a media bias, especially because of its criticism of President Bush, but that was tempered somewhat by the fact that Fassihi wrote for the *Wall Street Journal*, the most conservative major American newspaper. Lt. Jonathan Morgenstein, an unusually liberal Marine specializing in civil affairs, recommended to friends back home that they read her account, calling it "a laser-sharp portrayal of the reality of Iraq today."

The U.S. military itself also presented somewhat of a threat to reporters. Approaching a checkpoint was always worrisome, with rifles and machine guns pointed at approaching cars by troops not inclined to take the chance of letting a suicide bomber get too close. Nor was checkpoint duty pleasant for soldiers: They were given three seconds in which to act against a suspicious vehicle, with the first shot fired into the pavement in front of the car, the second into the grille, and the third at the driver. "We told them, you don't have the right not to shoot," recalled Lt. Gen. John Sattler, a commander of the Marines in western Iraq. "It's not about you. You are being trusted by everybody behind you. You are the single point of failure."

But it was even harder for those on the other end of the rifle barrel. Not only were reporters handled with great suspicion, they were sometimes singled out as especially threatening to the security of U.S. troops. For example, U.S. government officials were taught in an official 2004 CPA briefing on bomb threats that the "presence of news crews may be an indicator" of an imminent bomb attack. "Bomber does not want his picture taken, but he loves to have his dirty work on film," the briefing explained.

The odd result of the deterioration in security was that the harder it became to collect information, the easier it was for the Bush administration to assert that steady progress was made in Iraq but that cowed reporters simply weren't seeing it.

Winning tactically, losing strategically?

"Boss, we're losing," a young major told Lt. Gen. Thomas Metz, one of the top U.S. generals in Iraq, after the rough month of April. Others were arriving at similar conclusions. When Col. Paul Hughes returned home from Iraq that spring to serve out his time until retirement in a post at the National Defense University, he decided to take a public stand on the conduct of the war. "Unless we ensure that we have coherency in our policy, we will lose strategically," he told the *Washington Post*, knowing that these types of on-the-record remarks from an active-duty officer who had served in Baghdad would appear prominently in the newspaper. "I lost my brother in Vietnam," he said, in explaining his decision to go public. "I promised myself when I came on active duty that I would do everything in my power to prevent that [sort of strategic loss] from happening again.

Here I am, 30 years later, thinking we will win every fight and lose the war, because we don't understand the war we're in."

One Army general predicted the Army would start falling apart in the spring of 2005, while another one said flatly it was time for Rumsfeld and Wolfowitz to go. "I do not believe we had a clearly defined war strategy, end state and exit strategy before we commenced our invasion," he said. "Had someone like Colin Powell been the chairman [of the Joint Chiefs of Staff], he would not have agreed to send troops without a clear exit strategy. The current OSD refused to listen or adhere to military advice."

Was the United States in fact losing in Iraq? That was the question posed in May 2004 to Chuck Swannack, who had spent much of the previous year in western Iraq. "I think, strategically, we are," he said. "I think, operationally, maybe we are. But tactically, we are not."

In the spring of 2004, Swannack recounted in a later interview, "three things went wrong in Iraq." First, he said, was the Abu Ghraib scandal, "a tactical miscue by seven or eight people that had strategic consequences." Hard on its heels was the Marine Corps's siege of Fallujah, a move he argued broadly alienated the Sunni population. Third, the confrontation with Moqtadr al-Sadr similarly estranged much of the Shiite population. The United States had indeed dug itself a deep hole, and it wasn't clear that it knew how to climb out of it.

When Army mine expert Paul Arcangeli returned to Iraq late in 2004, having been away since the previous summer, "it bore no resemblance to the country I was in" a year earlier, he said. In the summer of 2003 he had freedom to leave the Green Zone as he pleased. "The difference between now and then is incredible," he said at the end of 2004. "They're driving 60 miles an hour through the Green Zone, combat style. It feels like they are no longer masters of their domain. They really do not rule the country."

There was no good military solution, he said. "I don't want to say we've lost, but everything we do helps us lose. More patrols—bad. Less patrols—bad. How do we get out of it? I don't know." The American people also were beginning to worry. In late May 2004, the majority of people surveyed by the *Washington Post*/ABC poll said the war in Iraq was not worth fighting. It was the first time that the majority of respondents in that poll felt that way.

Gen. Zinni came to a similar conclusion. "I have seen this movie," he said in April 2004. "It was called Vietnam."

16.

THE PRICE PAID

A t the end of its first twelve months in Iraq the Army began to confront the fact that it had suffered its first significant setback since the Vietnam War: The security situation had worsened, essential services were still not restored, and Iraqi faith in the American occupiers was dwindling. Some three hundred thousand U.S. troops had served there. The invasion force, and then the first rotation of the occupation, had gone home—the 101st Airborne, the 4th Infantry Division, the 1st Armored Division, and the 3rd Armored Cavalry Regiment. They had been replaced by the 1st Infantry Division, the 1st Cavalry Division, the Marines, and a grab bag of National Guard and Reserve units, all thrown into missions for which those backup forces hadn't been designed. And it was increasingly clear that the units that had gone back to the United States would be coming back for a second tour. The Army had little to show for its time in Iraq since the fall of Baghdad but eight hundred dead and five thousand wounded. It was a shaken institution, losing good people and provoking others to question it as it hadn't been in decades.

The death of a "star man"

"I'm extremely proud of the soldiers in my platoon," 2nd Lt. Leonard Cowherd, a twenty-two-year-old tank platoon commander in the 1st Armored Division, wrote to his hometown newspaper, the *Culpeper* (Virginia) *Star-Exponent*, in March 2004. "They have endured countless hardships here in Iraq as well as the overall hardship of being away from one's home and family." Two months later, on May 16, Cowherd was shot and killed by a sniper in Karbala. He was just short of a year of the first anniversary of his graduation from West Point. His death was a painful reminder of how much the Army—and the country—was losing.

When a memorial service was held a week later, four hundred mourners arrived at St. Stephen's Episcopal Church, a small building in Culpeper that had been used as a Civil War hospital. There were so many people in attendance that some watched the proceedings on video in a tent outside. The day was warm, and attendants served bottles of chilled water. "A beautiful kid," retired Army Gen. Barry McCaffrey, who had taught Cowherd at West Point, and who delivered one of the eulogies, noted afterward in clipped military fashion. "Star man . . . enormous maturity . . . great athlete . . . historian . . . very strong spiritual character. Went armor. Married his childhood sweetheart. His wife is an Army brat and daughter of a West Pointer." The two had announced their engagement at McCaffrey's apartment at West Point.

Cowherd's widow, Sarah, a schoolteacher whom he had married eleven months earlier, said, "He was my everything, and he was ever since the day I met him. My heart, my soul, my friend, and my husband."

Family, friends, and many of the dozens of young officers who attended the funeral met at a Culpeper pub that night for a wake. Cowherd's father-in-law, retired Army Lt. Col. Anthony Cerri, described the evening for those who weren't there: "Amidst the open beams, the cigarette smell, and the dim lighting, two guys with electrified acoustic guitars played songs like 'Tennessee Waltz' and 'Take Me Home to West Virginia' and 'Whiskey for My Men and Beer for My Horses.' We drank, and talked, and laughed, and yes—even danced a little. . . . We were there to tell Leonard stories and family stories and military stories. And we cried and held each other when the need arose."

May 26 brought the burial in Arlington National Cemetery. "The day was early-summer, Southern gem," wrote Cerri. "Hot but not stifling. Blue sky with wispy white." Then the hearse's doors were opened. "I placed my hands upon my daughter's shoulders . . . and I felt her shudder." The young officer was laid to rest in Site 7983 of Section 60 of the cemetery. The ceremony was conducted with grace and precision. A bagpiper played "Amazing Grace" and walked into the distance, "til the strains faded in the cicada whine." Then the 3rd Infantry Regiment, the Old Guard that serves at the cemetery, fired a rifle salute. "The 21 guns were three, crisp firings of seven," Cerri wrote. "The Old Guard does not make mistakes." "Taps" was played, and the U.S. flag that had adorned the casket was folded and presented to the lieutenant's young widow. "Leonard's wife . . . my Kiddo. Leonard was her everything."

The Army loses another officer

As Lt. Cowherd was being buried, Capt. Estrada was finishing the essay he had begun in his green notebook that argued that the Army's entire approach to Iraq was wrongheaded. In early June he went public with those concerns. What happened to him next was very different from the death of Lt. Cowherd, but it is still a tale of loss. The reserve civil affairs officer showed his essay to Maj. Peter Davis, his company commander, and then to some other civil affairs officers. He didn't encounter a lot of disagreement, he said later. His sense was that his peers agreed that the actions of the U.S. Army were alienating the Iraqi people. "I think it generally reflected the frustration that many of us were experiencing," he said later. Estrada decided to send the essay to the *Washington Post,* which in years of working at the State Department he had come to consider his hometown newspaper. He casually mentioned the submission to a military lawyer with whom he sometimes worked. "He told me, as long as I didn't reveal classified information or attack the president, I was within my rights."

On June 6, 2004, the *Post*'s Sunday Outlook section carried Estrada's lengthy opinion piece questioning what the Army was doing in Iraq and how it was doing it. Estrada related the question he had heard at the Buhriz water treatment plant—*Why?*—and the puzzlement he felt after the thoughtless killing of the farmer's cow.

> I think of . . . the children who burst into tears when we point our weapons into their cars (just in case), and the countless numbers of people whose vehicles we sideswipe as we try to use speed to survive the IEDs that await us each morning. I think of my fellow soldiers and the reality of being attacked and feeling threatened, and it all makes sense—the need to smash their cars and shoot their cows and point our weapons at them and detain them without concern for notifying their families. But how would I feel in their shoes? Would I be able to offer my own heart and mind?

Clearly, the U.S. effort was losing the faith of Capt. Estrada. After the article appeared, his commander called him in and ordered him to proceed to Forward Operating Base Warhorse to see Col. Dana Pittard, the commander of U.S. forces in the sprawling region from the eastern suburbs of Baghdad to the Iranian border. At that first meeting, Estrada recalled, "Colonel Pittard asked why I wrote it, expressed his view that it was too negative, said he was disappointed, and asked if I could continue to do my job or if I wanted to leave." Estrada said he wanted to stay with his unit. "He said that was fine, and I left."

The next day Estrada was summoned again by the colonel. "I went in, and he told me he'd lost confidence in me and wanted me out of his AO"—area of operations. Pittard also told Estrada that the article was inaccurate, because the caretaker's father at the Buhriz water plant had been visited by a battalion commander and had signed a paper saying he hadn't been mistreated. Estrada thought to himself that if he were an Iraqi and an American lieutenant colonel showed up with a well-armed security entourage, he also would sign whatever was put before him.

Among many civil affairs and other Special Forces soldiers, there was a good deal of sympathy for Estrada's comments. In their view, there was no governing strategy, and because of that lack, battalion and brigade commanders were each fighting their private wars, often employing tactics that alienated Iraqis. But not all civil affairs officers sided with him. Capt. Trampes Crow, who was operating about 85 miles to the north, said his experiences were "nearly polar opposite." In an e-mail to friends, he accused Estrada of wallowing in pessimism and spending too much energy dissecting problems and not enough in devising solutions.

Most of the soldiers at Baqubah were regular Army, and they tended to dismiss Estrada's critique as the disenchanted whining of someone who didn't understand that there was a war on, and that harsh methods sometimes were required. Among some active-duty troops there also was a feeling that this sort of defeatist attitude was a problem among undertrained, half-civilian reservists. (Almost all Army civil affairs units are from the reserves.) Capt. Thomas Johnson, commander of F Troop, 4th Cavalry, who was the Bravo 6 officer referred to in the story of the killing of the cow, accosted Estrada in the cavernous mess hall at Warhorse. "He kept asking me if I knew that the man whose cow had been killed had been compensated," Estrada later said. "I said yes, and tried to explain that it didn't matter. But he wasn't buying my argument, and kept getting in my face." Finally, Maj. Davis, Estrada's company commander, who was also at the table, told Johnson to back off.

That night Estrada would be sleeping at the Warhorse base, and Maj. Davis noted that the room he was assigned didn't have a lock on its door. "I think he feared for my safety that night," Estrada said, thinking the concern was justified. "I did halfway expect those guys to look for me and try to do something, given the level of anger they exhibited." After that day, whenever Estrada was visiting Warhorse, he would pick up his food at the mess hall and take it elsewhere. Next Estrada found that his two-week leave, during which he had planned to fly back to the United States to be married, had been canceled. In mid-June Estrada was transferred to a job near the Iranian border, far to the east, where he served out the rest of his tour.

Special Forces vs. the Army

Special Forces troops like Estrada were leading indicators of the problem the U.S. military faced. Better educated than most soldiers and trained to be culturally sensitive, SF soldiers were among the first to speak out and criticize the approach the military was taking. Estrada was typical of Army Special Forces officers in believing that the U.S. military still could prevail in Iraq, but only if it radically altered its approach. "I think we need to pull back," Estrada said. "Not pull out, but find a way to stop feeding the insurgency. Our presence there is feeding the fire." Like many others in Special Forces, he recommended revising the U.S. military presence to make it look more like the one in Afghanistan, where conventional troops are largely kept out of sight, and where the U.S. bases around the country are small facilities manned mainly by Special Forces troops.

By June 2004, most Iraqis endorsed that view. In a poll conducted for the CPA in the country's biggest cities, two thirds said they opposed the U.S. presence. But an even larger portion said the foreign troops should minimize their presence. On the question of whether the U.S. bases should be moved away from cities, 82 percent agreed. And Iraqis were almost unanimous in their view that U.S. troops should stop conducting street patrols, with 94 percent supporting such a change.

It became increasingly common for Special Forces soldiers to say that the regular Army was not fighting the insurgency effectively, and perhaps was not capable of doing so. Special operators also began to argue that they were not being employed well or even being allowed to do their jobs correctly. Lt. Col. Rich Young, a Special Forces officer who served in Baghdad from March to August of

2004, said much later that the first patrol he went on was with engineers from the 1st Cavalry Division. "I asked, 'What is this patrol about?' They said, 'It's a presence patrol.'" That made little sense to Young, especially as so many patrols were being bombed in the spring and summer of 2004, resulting in casualties to U.S. troops and doing little to reassure Iraqi bystanders. "We've been through a couple of years now, and IEDs are blowing off, and the people are tired of it."

The training of Iraqis as it was structured in 2003 and early 2004 also was heavily criticized in Special Forces circles. Foreign internal defense (FID) is a classic Special Forces mission, but in Iraq it was carried out mainly by contractors and members of the conventional side of the military. "One of the biggest failures of OIF will be the improper use of SF," said one Special Forces officer. He argued that SF should have

> been involved from the beginning in training security forces, . . . living, working, eating, and fighting with these forces to build strong bonds—because in Iraq, like [in] most countries we deal with, relationships are everything. If we had done this instead of allowing contractors and conventional forces and reserves to conduct basic training like committee training we might be much farther along.

Another Special Forces officer criticized the emphasis on raids and other direct action missions, which he felt came at the expense of the training mission, and also were counterproductive. "We have become locked on kill or capture as a mission statement. . . . The kill or capture charter has led to chasing bad guys (and subsequently making more)." Indeed, in the fall of 2003, the commander of 5th Special Forces Group, the unit specializing in Middle Eastern operations that was full of Arabic speakers, withdrew his A Teams from the Iraq countryside and consolidated them in Baghdad, where they focused almost exclusively on those direct action missions, according to an intelligence expert who disapproved of the move. "This move surrendered influence in the countryside and failed to secure Baghdad," commented Kalev Sepp, the counterinsurgency expert who later was brought in by top commanders to review their operations.

The Army's base structure, with a string of big establishments around the country that were ringed by high dirt walls, barbed wire, and watchtowers, also bothered Special Forces officers, who knew that classic counterinsurgency doctrine calls for living and moving among the people. "We have the wrong force structure to fight the insurgents," one SF veteran wrote to a friend in 2004. He continued:

> The big Army is like a mammoth elephant trying to squish the mouse. It is slow, bureaucratic and fearful of loss. The enemy have freedom of action, decentralized operations and care little about the political or environmental impacts of the actions as long as it gets on CNN or CBS. The more we go to bunker mentality and pull away from the people, the harder it will be. We are making this war longer than it has to be. Every day the big Army tries to get more operational control over the only force trained and ready for the FID mission needed here—SF. They want us to stay in the wire and coordinate to the BCT/DIV [brigade combat team/division] level for every action.

The perceived misuse of Special Forces had an especially pernicious effect, because dangling in front of demoralized SF troops were thousands of private-sector security contractor jobs, a clear alternative in which they could still work in a combat environment with trusted comrades but operate as they liked, and in the process receive far better compensation. "Because it is not being employed correctly, we are suffering from a growing attrition problem," said one senior Special Forces officer in the spring of 2004. "SF troopers are getting out to take lucrative jobs—the difference being they can go do important work with more autonomy, and as a side benefit make some more money." While the leaders of the special operations community thought the exodus was driven simply by the salaries, this officer disagreed: "I have been talking to a lot of senior NCOs, warrant officers, and junior officers who just want do their job the way they have been trained."

The Special Forces critique of the U.S. military approach was supported by many contractors—who as noted often were former SF themselves, and were more outspoken about what they saw. Dave Scholl, an Arabic-speaking veteran of the 5th Special Forces Group, became pessimistic about the prospects for the U.S. effort as he knocked around Iraq working on security for reconstruction projects. "We are the hated occupier," he wrote in a 2004 essay that circulated by e-mail among occupation insiders. "How many Iraqis have seen an American who wasn't pointing a gun at them?" His radical recommendation: Draw down the U.S. military and aid presence, freeze all reconstruction, and only venture out to build something when asked to do so by a delegation of Iraqis.

In Vietnam, the professional critique offered by Special Forces counterinsurgency experts was never accepted by conventional commanders. "The Special Forces were the only soldiers who had the knowledge and experience to point out the answer, but the Regular Army absolutely wouldn't listen to them," Robert Wright, the official historian of the 25th Infantry Division, told Lt. Col. Nagl, author of a study of the Army's failure to adapt during the Vietnam War. "They'd have listened to the French before they listened to their own Special Forces."

In Iraq, the views of Special Forces officers ultimately would find a warmer reception. At first theirs was clearly a minority view, disparaged as barely patriotic. But by the end of 2004, as the war dragged on, their views would gain a new respect. And by the end of 2005 they would become almost the conventional wisdom—not dominant among all commanders, but understood by many, and embraced by most planners and strategists studying how to alter the U.S. military's approach. By then, even President Bush would promise in a speech at Annapolis, "We will increasingly move out of Iraqi cities, reduce the number of bases from which we operate, and conduct fewer patrols and convoys." That was what officers such as Capt. Estrada had been talking about for a long time. But by the time the president made his speech, all that Estrada wanted to do with the U.S. military was leave it.

Corporate mercenaries

There was a flip side to the heavy reliance on all those security contractors: They amounted to a small private army that existed outside the U.S. chain of command and wasn't subject to U.S. military discipline or even U.S. law. One day in February 2004, Marine Col. T. X. Hammes, who was serving at CPA's headquarters, was driving in the city just across the Tigris from the Green Zone. He was in his Marine battle fatigues, but somewhat disguised by a windbreaker and a civilian cap. At the first traffic circle east of the river, his beat-up Toyota Land Cruiser was forced to the side of the road by a carload of gun-toting private security guards who were escorting a CPA official. Hammes looked closely at the rifle pointed nearest him. "I was trying to see if his finger was on the trigger guard, because then you're four pounds of pressure from being gone," he said. He understood what they were doing, and why. "They did it because their single mission was to get their guy through," without regard to the effect they had on the population of the capital. But they didn't understand that "just by getting their guy around, they were out making enemies."

He understood why they were necessary. "We didn't have enough troops," he said. "But they scared the hell out of me. These shooters, you'd see them in the gym. Steroids, tension, and guns are not a good mix." Nor were all of sterling character: One company, ArmorGroup, employed a former British Royal Marine named Derek Adgey who in 1995 had been jailed for four years on ten counts of soliciting murder by passing information to Johnny "Mad Dog" Adair's Ulster Freedom Fighters, a Loyalist gang in Northern Ireland.

Fundamentally, the bodyguards' mission differed from that of the U.S. military, noted Hammes. "The contractor was hired to protect the principal. He had no stake in pacifying the country. Therefore, they often ran Iraqis off the roads, reconned by fire, and generally treated locals as expendable." Yet Iraqis saw them as acting under American authority. "You have loosed an unaccountable, deadly force into their society, and they have no recourse."

One of the aspects of the Iraq war that historians are likely to remember is the heavy reliance on these corporate mercenaries, or private security contractors, as they were called. In 2003–4 alone, some $750 million was spent on them, according to the U.S. Government Accountability Office; by early 2006, the total expenditure had amounted to over $1 billion. When the U.S. troop level was about 150,000, and the allied troop contributions totaled 25,000, there were about 60,000 additional civilian contractors supporting the effort. Of those, perhaps 15,000 to 20,000 were shooters—that is, people hired as bodyguards or for other security roles, rather than as truck drivers, cooks, and other support personnel. Most of those hired to perform security functions were Iraqi, but many— at least 6,000, and perhaps many more—were Americans, South Africans, Fijians, and other nationalities. To put this in perspective, private security firms were fielding about as many combat forces as the total non-U.S. contingent in the coalition.

The armed contractors, or "trigger pullers," comprised the rough equivalent of at least one Army division, but they had a higher casualty rate than the military units. During 2003 and 2004 private contractors suffered at least 275 deaths and 900 wounded, which was, the Brookings Institution's Peter Singer observed, "more than any single U.S. Army division and more than the rest of the coalition combined." Others said that the number of casualties might be far higher, because the numbers made public included only U.S. citizens that by law had to be disclosed to the U.S. Labor Department. So, for example, the loss of a Nepali guard bombed at a checkpoint or of an Indian truck driver in an ambush of a convoy might not show up in that data.

The contractors had two high-profile tasks in 2003–4, and their efforts at both provoked much unhappiness. The first was training Iraqi forces. The near mutiny of an Iraqi army battalion in the spring of 2004 underscored how badly that had gone. Subsequent reviews by Army experts found that the training effort had been a numbers game, placing too much emphasis on the quantity of trained Iraqis and too little on their quality. It especially had faltered in developing a chain of command—that is, leaders trusted both by Iraqi foot soldiers and the American advisers. The company doing much of the initial training work was Vinnell, which had a one-year contract valued at $24 million to train nine battalions of one thousand men each. "American observers from U.S. Central Command headquarters assessed the military basic training conducted under contract by the Vinnell Corporation to be unsatisfactory, and the contract was terminated," Sepp, the retired Special Forces expert in counterinsurgency, told a congressional committee.

The security work of contractors was even more controversial. Col. Hammes's experience on the road that February day was all too common in Baghdad in 2003 and 2004. Scholl concluded that these personal security details had done much political damage to the U.S. effort, especially where they were most active—in the capital: "If there are one hundred PSDs a day in Iraq (there are) and they each anger one hundred people in a day (they do), that is ten thousand Iraqis a day getting extremely agitated at us over the past year."

Nor was there a system of accountability for such excesses. "Even when contractors do military jobs, they remain private businesses and thus fall outside the military chain of command and justice systems," Peter Singer observed in a *Foreign Affairs* article.

Tensions between troops and contractors arose frequently. In May 2005 the Marine Corps accused a security detail from Zapata Engineering, a company with a contract to dispose of explosives, of shooting wildly at Iraqis and U.S. troops while driving west from Baghdad toward Fallujah. The nineteen contractors, sixteen of them Americans and the other three Iraqi translators, were treated like regular security detainees. They were disarmed and made to wear blackout goggles while being moved to a detention facility, where they were held for three days before being shipped out of the country. Some of them later said they had been handled roughly and jeered by Marines as rich contractors, but the Marines insisted in a statement that the Zapata men were given the standard treatment and handled "humanely and respectfully."

Contractors, for their part, complained to GAO investigators that they were more often on the receiving end of fire. "Private security providers have told us that they are fired upon by U.S. forces so frequently that incident reports are not always filed," the GAO reported. It noted two instances of passing military convoys shooting at private security vehicles, and a third of a checkpoint opening fire, allegedly without warning, on another such vehicle. A total of twenty incidents were reported in the first five months of 2005, but the actual number likely was higher, the GAO concluded.

The Army at ebb tide

By mid-2004 more and more officers in the Army were growing vocal in their unhappiness with their leaders, not just with the civilians around Rumsfeld but also with their own superiors in uniform. Some expressed the feeling that a generation of conformist generals was the problem. "They are organization men," one Army colonel said dismissively. "They are extremely careful."

Others found themselves in an unsettling round of soul searching about the institution to which they had given their adult lives. "You're starting to get the undercurrent in the Army, a feeling of breaking faith, that 'people aren't being truthful with me,'" said another Army colonel, a longtime true believer. "You've got guys who want to get out, their terms are up, and instead they're being sent back to Iraq for a second tour. The things that we are doing to get the job done now, for a third Iraq rotation out there, may be really hurting us in the long term." Recruiters and trainers were being pulled from their assigned tasks and sent to Iraq—a classic way of solving today's problems while worsening tomorrow's. Then this colonel used a word that was coming up all too often in discussions of the Army in Iraq: "What we are doing is 'counterproductive.'"

17.

THE CORRECTIONS

SPRING 2004

One day early in 2004, Col. Alan King, the civil affairs and tribal specialist at the CPA, held an unhappy meeting at a Baghdad mosque with Sheikh Harith al-Dari, the chairman of the Association of Muslim Scholars, a hard-line group with links to the Sunni insurgency. The encounter had been arranged to discuss the security situation, but the sheikh was clearly bothered by another issue. He changed the subject and began to speak in a matter-of-fact manner about what he had been hearing of cruel, even sadistic, handling of prisoners by U.S. soldiers at the Abu Ghraib prison west of the capital.

King was having none of it. "I got really pissed," King later recalled. He was personally affronted by such allegations. "I said, 'I'm an American soldier, we don't act that way.'" So, King concluded, confrontationally, "If you've got pictures, documents, you show me." And if you don't, he added, don't insult me with these false allegations.

Four months later, after the Abu Ghraib scandal broke and the images of torture and cruelty had gone around the world, King would receive a tart message from the sheikh: *Have you seen enough pictures now?*

The Bush administration offered three basic rationales for the U.S. intervention in Iraq: the threat it believed was posed by Saddam's WMD; the supposed nexus it saw between Saddam Hussein's government and transnational terrorism; and the need to liberate an oppressed people. In the spring of 2004, the first two arguments were undercut by official findings by the same government that had invaded Iraq, and the third was tarred by the revelation of the Abu Ghraib scandal.

The arguments evaporate

In January 2004, David Kay, as he stepped down from his post as head of the Iraq Survey Group, the U.S. government intelligence organization created to hunt for Saddam's weapons of mass destruction, announced that he concluded that Saddam Hussein had destroyed his weapons stockpiles in the 1990s, but had tried to bluff about still having them in order to maintain an image of power. "Everyone was wrong," Kay said.

President Bush was asked about this by Tim Russert on *Meet the Press* on February 8, 2004. Though difficult at spots to follow, the exchange is worth reproducing at length, because it captures Bush at his most exposed on the issue, facing a tough questioner who has time and is permitted to follow up at length:

> *Russert:* The night you took the country to war, March seventeenth, you said this: "Intelligence gathered by this and other governments leaves no doubt that the Iraqi regime continues to possess and conceal some of the most lethal weapons ever devised."
>
> *President Bush:* Right.
>
> *Russert:* That apparently is not the case.
>
> *Bush:* Correct.
>
> *Russert:* How do you respond to critics who say that you brought the nation to war under false pretenses?
>
> *Bush:* Yes. First of all, I expected to find the weapons. Sitting behind this desk making a very difficult decision of war and peace, and I based my decision on the best intelligence possible, intelligence that had been gathered over the years, intelligence that not only our analysts thought was valid but analysts from other countries thought were valid. And I made a decision based upon that intelligence in the context of the war against terror. In other words, we were attacked, and therefore every threat had to be reanalyzed. Every threat had to be looked at. Every potential harm to America had to be judged in the context of this war on terror. And I made

the decision, obviously, to take our case to the international community in the hopes that we could do this—achieve a disarmament of Saddam Hussein peacefully. In other words, we looked at the intelligence. And we remembered the fact that he had used weapons, which meant he had had weapons. We knew the fact that he was paying for suicide bombers. We knew the fact he was funding terrorist groups. In other words, he was a dangerous man. And that was the intelligence I was using prior to the run-up to this war. Now, let me—which is—this is a vital question—

Russert: Nothing more important.

Bush: Vital question. And so we—I expected there to be stockpiles of weapons. But David Kay has found the capacity to produce weapons. Now, when David Kay goes in and says we haven't found stockpiles yet, and there's theories as to where the weapons went. They could have been destroyed during the war. Saddam and his henchmen could have destroyed them as we entered into Iraq. They could be hidden. They could have been transported to another country, and we'll find out. That's what the Iraq Survey Group—let me—let me finish here. But David Kay did report to the American people that Saddam had the capacity to make weapons. Saddam Hussein was dangerous with weapons. Saddam Hussein was dangerous with the ability to make weapons. He was a dangerous man in the dangerous part of the world. And I made the decision to go to the United Nations. By the way, quoting a lot of their data—in other words, this is unaccounted for stockpiles that you thought he had because I don't think America can stand by and hope for the best from a madman, and I believe it is essential—I believe it is essential—that when we see a threat, we deal with those threats before they become imminent. It's too late if they become imminent. It's too late in this new kind of war, and so that's why I made the decision I made.

Despite Bush's theories that the case for WMD might still be made, the negative returns would continue to pour in. In October 2004, Charles Duelfer, who suceeded Kay as head of the ISG, produced the group's final findings. There was no such arsenal, the weapons inspector concluded in a one-thousand-page report. Saddam had indeed eliminated his weapons in the early 1990s, but had tried to preserve the intellectual and physical ability to restart the weapons programs at some point. Duelfer also said that he had found no evidence of an effort to buy uranium from other countries. And he testified to the Senate that, as some analysts had suspected, the aluminum tubes Iraq was buying, which the Bush administration had made central to the argument that Iraq was developing a nuclear capability, were indeed for conventional military rockets.

"In front of the whole world, the United States government asserted that Saddam Hussein had reconstituted his nuclear weapons program, had biological weapons and mobile biological weapon production facilities and was producing chemical weapons," the Robb-Silberman commission noted six months later. "And not one bit of it could be confirmed when the war was over."

Also in 2005, the CIA issued an internal report that amounted to a major correction of its previous conclusions on chemical weapons. Titled "Iraq: No Large-Scale Chemical Warfare Efforts Since Early 1990s," the report concluded that "Iraq probably did not pursue chemical warfare efforts after 1991."

Usually the aftermath of intelligence errors is somewhat ambiguous, Richard Kerr, a former senior CIA official who was hired by the agency to review its prewar analyses, told the *Los Angeles Times*, which was consistently solid in its coverage of intelligence issues. "But the situation is rather unique," he said, because of the ability of the U.S. government to scour occupied Iraq for WMD. "Ordinarily, you're never proven wrong in a clean, neat way."

As the rationale for war crumbled, dissent began to appear again in military publications. Lt. Cdr. Richard Riggs, who had served as the tactical action officer aboard a Navy ship that fired Tomahawk cruise missiles in the opening salvo of the war, said that the WMD situation was forcing him to reexamine his role. "A year has passed since those heady days, and I am forced to look at the role I played in Iraqi Freedom in a different light." Lacking the evidence that Iraq had possessed WMD, he said in an article in *Proceedings*, the professional magazine for Navy officers, "I have begun to question our motivations. . . . I am asking, not only as a subordinate to a superior seeking justification for our course of action, but as a U.S. citizen holding my elected officials responsible for my country's leadership: Where are the weapons of mass destruction?"

Meanwhile, no solid evidence of a nexus between Iraq and Islamic extremist terrorists, such as al Qaeda, surfaced either. In June 2004, the bipartisan 9/11 Commission—formally known as the National Commission on Terrorist Attacks upon the United States—released its report, which concluded, unanimously, that while there had been contacts between al Qaeda and Saddam Hussein's Iraq, it had seen no evidence of "a collaborative operational relationship." Instead, by the end of 2004, the U.S. intelligence community would conclude that the invasion had turned Iraq into a new breeding ground for a fresh generation of tougher, more professional Islamic extremist terrorists.

Abu Ghraib breaks

With the invasion rationales of WMD and terrorism collapsing under the weight of authoritative postwar inquiries, the Bush administration began to lean more on the third leg of the rationale—liberation. Wolfowitz especially stepped up to this, in part because he always had believed it. But just as that became an emphasis, the abuses at the Abu Ghraib prison broke into public view, damaging that argument. On the evening of April 28, 2004, *60 Minutes II,* a CBS television show, revealed the extent of the abuse at Abu Ghraib and broadcast some of the memorable photographs taken of brutalities committed in the prison. Two days later, the *New Yorker* magazine posted on its Web site an extraordinarily thorough account of abuse at Abu Ghraib by Seymour Hersh, a veteran investigative journalist. Hersh had more photos, he had transcripts of some testimony from military legal proceedings, and most important of all, he had the Army's own stunning report. "Between October and December 2003, at the Abu Ghraib Confinement Facility, numerous incidents of sadistic, blatant and wanton criminal abuses were inflicted on several detainees," wrote the Army report's author, Maj. Gen. Antonio Taguba, his disgust evident throughout. But it was the images that made people— even in Congress—pay attention. It was a painful moment for anyone who wore the nation's uniform or who wanted to be proud of the U.S. military.

Rumsfeld later disclosed that twice during this period he had offered to step down as defense secretary. But both he and Myers, his top military adviser, appeared to have learned little from the scandal, if their public comments are any indication. In its wake, over a dozen official inquiries were conducted. One of the best of those, a review of the role played by Pentagon officials, was led by former Defense Secretary James Schlesinger. It concluded that there had been a failure not only to plan for an insurgency, but also to react to the insurgency once it erupted. It specifically faulted the assumptions that shaped the war plan. Asked about that criticism, Rumsfeld insisted in September 2004 that it was "an excellent war plan . . . a highly successful war plan."

"In retrospect you can be supercritical about anything you want to be critical about," said Myers, speaking at the same Pentagon press conference. "And so with perfect hindsight, you'd say, 'Well, gee, maybe we should have anticipated this, maybe we should have anticipated that.'" It was a response to a serious and important criticism brought by an officially appointed inquiry and was unworthy of his position as the nation's top military officer.

Seeming to ooze resentment, Myers also rejected Schlesinger's finding that the general and his staff had been slow to react to events in Iraq. "We've been very good at adjusting," he insisted. "Could we have been faster, sharper, quicker? Sure, we could have been, in probably many areas it goes without saying, particularly if we have the benefit of looking backwards and not looking forward. And that's the way I would address that." Myers essentially refused to conduct the cold, hard review of the errors of the U.S. effort, from assumptions to strategy to tactics, that was so desperately needed, especially as the reasons for going to war fell apart.

To a surprising degree, those punished for the crimes committed at Abu Ghraib would be the lowest of the low—England, Graner, and the like, which is to say, a low-ranking female reservist enlisted soldier and her ex-lover. The Army repeatedly insisted that its top commanders were not at fault, and seemed to refuse to consider the possibility that that stance was wrong. Even former Defense Secretary Melvin Laird—such a longtime friend of the defense secretary that he had helped in Rumsfeld's first campaign for Congress—found that outcome unacceptable. "To stop abuses and mistakes by the rank and file, whether in the prisons or the streets, heads must roll at much higher levels than they have thus far," he wrote over a year later. "The best way to keep foot soldiers honest is to make sure their commanders know that they themselves will be held responsible for any breach of honor." But that was not the message the Pentagon or the Army chose to send.

Over the next year, additional information about abuses would continue to surface. There were many more Pentagon reviews but no independent ones, and because most of the internal reviews seemed to blame the privates while excusing the generals, a lingering air of unfairness hangs over the entire affair. Also, because the top brass seemed unwilling to confront what really happened and continued to insist that each instance was an isolated case, each additional disclosure of abuse would be cited by journalists and others to challenge the theory that a few low-ranking bad apples were entirely to blame. To anyone who knew the military, that just didn't sound right. "As former soldiers, we knew that you don't have this kind of pervasive attitude out there unless you've condoned it," said retired Army Col. Larry Wilkerson, who had been Colin Powell's chief of staff at the State Department. "And whether you did it explicitly or not is irrelevant."

An unfortunate side effect of that continued suspicion was that it shadowed the courage shown by thousands of other U.S. soldiers. "We now spend ninety per-cent of our time talking about the Abu Ghraib stuff, and one percent talking about the valor of the troops," said Bing West, the chronicler of the Marines in Iraq.

The op-ed pages try reverse gear

In the wake of the unraveling of the Bush administration's rationales for inva-sion, and the tarring of the U.S. military presence, expert opinion in the United States began to catch up with the facts on the ground. The op-ed pages of the *New York Times,* the *Washington Post,* and the *Los Angeles Times* in May 2004 looked almost like the reverse of the 2002 and 2003 stampedes that culminated in the gushing reviews of Powell's presentation to the UN.

The *New York Times'* Thomas Friedman, probably the most influential writer on foreign affairs in the United States, and one of the more prominent journalis-tic supporters of going to war in Iraq, sounded the alarm in early May. "This ad-ministration needs to undertake a total overhaul of its Iraq policy," he wrote. "Otherwise, it is courting a total disaster for us all."

A week later, his *Times* colleague David Brooks, who had been even more hawkish back in 2002, when he argued that "Bush has such an incredibly strong case to go in there," sounded even more chagrined. "This has been a crushingly depressing period, especially for people who support the war in Iraq," Brooks wrote. "The predictions people on my side made about the postwar world have not yet come true. The warnings others made about the fractious state of post-Saddam society have." In retrospect, he added, the plan to simply remove Sad-dam, establish democracy, and depart the country "seems like a childish fantasy."

Fouad Ajami, a Johns Hopkins University expert on the Mideast who had been a strong supporter of invading, was almost confessional in his new tone. "A year or so ago, it was our war, and we claimed it proudly," he wrote later in May. "But gone is the hubris. Let's face it: Iraq is not going to be America's show-case in the Arab-Muslim world."

Newsweek columnist Fareed Zakaria, another thoughtful writer who had been an Iraq hawk, wrote in the magazine's May 17, 2004, issue that George W. Bush's "strange combination of arrogance and incompetence" had proven "poisonous" for American foreign policy. "On almost every issue involving postwar Iraq—troop strength, international support, the credibility of exiles, de-Baathification, handling Ayatollah Ali Sistani—Washington's assumptions and policies have been wrong," he charged.

The crowd of proinvasion columnists perched on the *Washington Post*'s op-ed page also were having emotional second thoughts. "All but the most blindly devoted Bush supporters can see that Bush Administration officials have no clue about what to do in Iraq tomorrow, much less a month from now," wrote Robert Kagan, a prominent neoconservative intellectual. "It's not even clear that he [Bush] understands how bad the situation in Iraq is or how close he is to losing public support for the war."

The Abu Ghraib scandal drove the *Washington Post* editorial page into vocal opposition—not to the war itself, but to the Bush administration's handling of postinvasion Iraq. The *Post*'s editorialists long had been bothered by the administration's approach, and especially by Rumsfeld's. "We believe that there has been more progress in Iraq than critics acknowledge, but also that the administration has made serious mistakes," the *Post* had said in an October 2003 editorial. During the month of May 2004, the *Post* carried thirteen editorials on the subject, most of them lengthy. The first struck a theme to which the newspaper would return repeatedly: "The rule of law matters." The second one struck the counterpoint, hanging the blame around the neck of Defense Secretary Rumsfeld: "The foundation for the crimes at Abu Ghraib was laid more than two years ago, when Mr. Rumsfeld instituted a system of holding detainees from Afghanistan not only incommunicado, without charge, and without legal process, but without any meaningful oversight mechanism at all."

The Pentagon's response to the *Post* editorial page's campaign was to accuse it of being as bad as the torturers. Pentagon spokesman Lawrence Di Rita wrote in a letter to the editor, "The *Post*'s continued editorializing on narrow definitions of international laws and whether our soldiers understand them puts the *Post* in the same company as those involved in this despicable behavior in terms of apparent disregard for basic human dignity." It was a remarkable way for the Pentagon to treat an editorial page that had been a political ally in the Iraq war.

Yet it would prove to be an oddity of the Iraq war that, despite the loss of such supporters, President Bush would win reelection six months later, as his opponent, John Kerry, seemed unable to articulate a clear stance on the war.

The New York Times *asks some questions*

The newspaper that would be most affected by postinvasion reconsiderations was the *New York Times,* which for a year had resisted looking under the rock of Judith Miller's coverage. It is an old saying in the public relations business that bad news is like dead fish: It doesn't improve with age, it only begins to stink more. That axiom proved doubly true for the *Times,* whose resistance to review was becoming embarrassing by the spring of 2004.

On the heels of her reckless prewar coverage of Iraqi WMD, Miller had traveled to Iraq and cut a wide swath. Embedding with an Army unit searching for weapons of mass destruction, she filed a series of articles in the spring of 2003 that suggested that large amounts of stockpiles were about to be uncovered. Like the Bush administration, Miller seemed to believe what she was saying about WMD. It was almost as if she were operating in a parallel universe. On April 21, she reported that members of a search team had been told by an Iraqi scientist that "Iraq [had] destroyed chemical weapons and biological warfare equipment only days before the war began." Two days later, the lead on her story was that American forces "have occupied a vast warehouse complex in Baghdad filled with chemicals where Iraqi scientists are suspected of having tested unconventional agents on dogs within the past year." On May 4, she reported that experts had "found sources of radioactive material." Later that week they concluded that they had found "a mobile biological weapons laboratory." Then, she reported, they found another radiation source.

When Mission Exploitation Team Alpha, the unit to which she was attached, was reassigned, she even sent a note to the Army protesting the move. "I intend to write about this decision in the NY Times to send a successful team back home just as progress on WMD is being made," she wrote in an e-mail.

More than a half-dozen military officers said that Miller had played an extremely unusual role as an embedded reporter, effectively operating as a middleman between Chalabi's organization and the Army unit, MET Alpha. Through the Chalabi connection, she also got MET Alpha involved in interrogating deposed Iraqi officials, a U.S. military officer said. Zaab Sethna, an INC adviser, would later dispute that account, but U.S. military officers said that Miller had played an unusually obtrusive role for a journalist. "This woman came in with a plan," one officer said. "She ended up almost hijacking the mission."

A staff officer on the 75th Exploitation Task Force, of which MET Alpha was a part, said, "It's impossible to exaggerate the impact she had on the mission of this unit, and not for the better."

The *New York Times'* official reaction to stories about Miller's antics was a Nixonian stonewall. "She didn't bring MET Alpha anywhere. . . . It's a baseless accusation," the newspaper's assistant managing editor for news, Andrew Rosenthal, said. "Singling out one reporter for this kind of examination is a little bizarre."

Even more embarrassing for the *Times,* Miller also asserted in an angry e-mail intended only for internal consumption that her main source for stories on Iraqi weapons of mass destruction was Ahmed Chalabi. "I've been covering Chalabi for about 10 years, and have done most of the stories about him for our paper, including the long takeout we recently did on him," she wrote to John Burns, the *Times*'s Baghdad bureau chief. "He has provided most of the front-page exclusives on WMD to our paper." (Miller later backed down from that assertion, telling the *Post*'s Sally Quinn that she had been using a kind of journalistic shorthand in that note: "In my reporting experience, it is not accurate to say that he provided most of the WMD material to the *Times* or to the U.S. government." But both she and Chalabi had made statements that undercut that revised account.)

Miller's troubles were only beginning. When she returned to the United States that summer she would have several talks with I. Lewis "Scooter" Libby, the former Wolfowitz aide who had become Cheney's chief of staff at the White House. Those meetings ultimately would carry major legal consequences.

Jack Shafer, the media critic for *Slate,* the on-line magazine, became a powerful critic of Miller's stories, observing that she seemed to have agreed to a series of unusual coverage rules, that her sourcing was awkward at best, and—worst of all—that her stories weren't standing up. Where, he asked, were the editors, and when was the *Times* going to address the issue? "Miller was one of the more eager consumers of defector baloney," he wrote in April 2004, "but the newspaper of record has yet to untangle the lies from the Iraqi defectors and exiles that Miller dutifully published."

First, in May 2004, more than a year after the invasion of Iraq, the *Times* responded with an official once over lightly. It declined to name the people it was writing about, though they were reporters whose names were readily available at the top of each article examined. Though the review didn't say so, five of the six articles it called into question had been written or cowritten by Miller. Seemingly more solicitous of the sensibilities of the *Times*'s staffers than of its readers, the article backed into the point, beginning by saying that in checking its work, "we found an enormous amount of journalism that we are proud of." This was rather like an airline beginning a press release about a crash by listing all the flights that had landed successfully. But, it continued, "we have found a number of instances of coverage that was not as rigorous as it should have been." This review ran on page ten of the newspaper, though it was clearly going to be the most noticed *Times* story of the day.

A few days later, Daniel Okrent, the *Times*'s new public editor, or ombudsman, lowered the boom. He named Judith Miller and Patrick Tyler as authors of the bad stories and faulted editors for a variety of errors, such as never telling the newspaper's readers that Ahmed Chalabi's niece had been employed by the *Times*'s Kuwait bureau in 2003. The ombudsman's own reporting led him to conclude that the paper had a "dysfunctional system" of managing certain reporters. The next installment in the saga came in September, when the *Times* exorcised one of its demons with a huge review of the Bush administration's handling of intelligence about Iraq's supposed nuclear program. The story, which ran nearly ten thousand words, was among other things effectively a correction of the *Times* story on the same subject that had run in September 2002.

In the *New York Review of Books*, Michael Massing's verdict was that many major newspapers had erred, but that the *New York Times* stood out in particular. "Compared to other major papers, the *Times* placed more credence in defectors, expressed less confidence in inspectors, and paid less attention to dissenters." Shortly after leaving his post at the *Times*, Okrent would summarize its coverage of the WMD issue as "really very bad journalism."

But Miller wasn't giving up. Speaking at the University of California at Berkeley in 2005, Miller would defend her coverage, saying that she "wrote the best assessment that I could based on the information that I had."

"Do you have any misgivings?" she was asked.

No, Miller said. "I think I did the best possible job I could do," she said. "So no, I really don't."

Iraq ultimately would prove lethal to Miller's career at the *New York Times*. The last act began with others' articles in her own newspaper and in the *Washington Post*: On July 6, 2003, the *Times*'s op-ed page carried an article by former ambassador Joseph C. Wilson IV alleging that President Bush, in his State of the Union address seven months earlier, had exaggerated intelligence about Iraqi efforts to buy uranium in Niger for its nuclear weapons program. He related how he had traveled to Africa for the CIA to look into those intelligence reports, and had found that Niger's uranium mines were a small industry with "too much oversight" to permit such leakage. Eight days later, conservative pundit Robert Novak wrote a column in the *Washington Post* that, in the course of responding to Wilson, disclosed that "two senior Bush administration officials" had told him that Wilson's wife was a CIA operative named Valerie Plame, who specialized in WMD issues, and that she had helped arrange his trip to Niger.

For a federal official to leak the name of a covert intelligence operative may have been a crime. The subsequent investigation led Justice Department lawyers to want to talk to reporters who had had contact with Bush administration officials. One of them was Miller. She declined to cooperate, so in 2004, a federal court held her in contempt. Ultimately, she was jailed for refusing to testify. After eighty-five days behind bars in the federal facility in Alexandria, Virginia, Miller changed her mind, announcing that Libby had told her she could name him, and appeared before the grand jury. On September 30, 2005, she testified that her source had been Libby, Cheney's aide. She wouldn't share her notes with *Times* reporters writing about the situation. Jill Abramson, the newspaper's tough managing editor, all but called Miller a liar in print, following a dispute over what the two had said to each other. Within a few weeks Miller's career at the *Times* ended.

Congress stirs

In the spring of 2004, Congress briefly embraced a more significant role in overseeing the management of the Iraq war. Congress was awakened by the Abu Ghraib prison torture scandal, and by the realization, forced by mounting casualties and persistent widespread violence, that the administration line wasn't playing out. At an unusually contentious hearing of the Senate Armed Services Committee, Sen. Hillary Clinton issued a virtual indictment of Wolfowitz: Given your track record, the New York Democrat asked, why should we believe your assurances now? "You come before this committee . . . having seriously undermined your credibility over a number of years now. When it comes to making estimates or predictions about what will occur in Iraq, and what will be the costs in lives and money, . . . you have made numerous predictions, time and time again, that have turned out to be untrue and were based on faulty assumptions." As Wolfowitz sat before her at the witness table, she quoted his previous testimony from the run-up to the war in which he had asserted that the Iraqi people would see the United States as their liberator, that Iraq could finance its own reconstruction, and that Gen. Shinseki's estimate that it would take several hundred thousand troops to occupy Iraq was "outlandish." Wolfowitz ignored most of Clinton's comments in his response, but told her that in disputing Shinseki's estimate he had been siding with Gen. Franks, who was closer to the action in Iraq.

Wolfowitz took on a somewhat haunted look during this period. In private meetings he sometimes seemed profoundly fatigued. He could be disjointed when defending his views, in striking contrast to his challenging stance of the previous summer and fall. One friend said that Wolfowitz had begun to worry that he would be scapegoated for Iraq.

Wolfowitz took another pounding when he appeared before the House Armed Services Committee in June 2004. Rep. Skelton looked at Wolfowitz and said he had no doubt that the administration intended to stay the course. But, he added, "There's a difference between resolve, on the one hand, and competence, on the other." That comment, unusually pointed from the soft-spoken Skelton, set the tone of the hearing. "I see two Iraqs," he continued. "One is the optimistic Iraq that you describe, and we thank you for your testimony. And the other Iraq is the one that I see every morning, with the violence, the deaths of soldiers and Marines." Watching CNN with his breakfast each day and hearing announced the small towns that had been the homes of soldiers killed in Iraq, Skelton was beginning to suspect that rural America was suffering disproportionately in this war. The previous day, five soldiers had died—from Glade Spring, Virginia; Cleburne, Arkansas; Hardin, Kentucky; Whitfield, Georgia; and Harris, Texas. "I must tell you, it breaks my heart a little more every day."

"You said I presented an optimistic picture," Wolfowitz responded. "Maybe it's optimistic compared to the total gloom and doom that one otherwise hears, but I in no way mean to minimize the security problem." It is important to remember, Wolfowitz added, that Saddam hadn't acted alone in his evil acts. As he did so frequently when his back was to the wall on Iraq, Wolfowitz played the Nazi card. "He had some thousands of people in his so-called Mukhabarat, the so-called intelligence service, which is probably best described as the modern-day equivalent of the Nazi Gestapo. He had other even more horrendous killers in something called the Fedayeen Saddam, which I guess is like the Hitler Youth, or like the SS perhaps." Later in the hearing he even went so far as to say some Iraqis might have been worse than the Nazis: "We are dealing with several thousand people who are as bad or worse than the Nazi Gestapo."

What the hearing would be most remembered for was Wolfowitz's own attack—on the American press corps in Baghdad. There was lots of good news to report, he insisted, but the reporters somehow were too cowardly to get out there and cover it. "Frankly, part of our problem is [that] a lot of the press are afraid to travel very much, so they sit in Baghdad and they publish rumors," he said. "And rumors are plentiful." It wasn't a particularly logical statement, and Wolfowitz would back down from it two days later, issuing a letter of apology.

Gen. Myers, the chairman of the Joint Chiefs of Staff, insisted that "great progress" was being made on all fronts in Iraq. "I think we're on the brink of success," he told the House Armed Services Committee.

Ultimately, that was enough for Congress, which again backed away from the subject of Iraq. There was little follow-up investigation or oversight. There were, for example, no hearings with returning division commanders. In retrospect, the hearings of May and June 2004 were a spasm before the election season. They made it appear that Congress was paying attention, but they did little to affect the course of events on the ground or to produce more information for the American people. "I know a bunch of folks on the Armed Services committees," said a former Bush administration official who was deeply involved in defense issues, and especially in the handling of Iraq. "If any of those folks had called me and asked me to speak to them candidly about Iraq, I would have. But no one ever did."

At Fort Bragg, North Carolina, Capt. Ian Fishback, who had served with the 82nd Airborne Division near Fallujah, watched Pentagon officials give congressional testimony with growing disbelief. Rumsfeld "testified that we followed . . . the letter of the Geneva Conventions in Iraq, and as soon as he said that I knew something was wrong," Fishback said later. In Iraq and in Afghanistan, where he had also served, he remembered bewilderment about how prisoners should be treated. "I am certain that this confusion contributed to a wide range of abuses including death threats, beatings, broken bones, murder, exposure to elements, extreme forced physical exertion, hostage-taking, stripping, sleep deprivation, and degrading treatment," he later wrote. "I and troops under my command witnessed some of these abuses in both Afghanistan and Iraq."

Fishback, who had been class president, football MVP, and "most likely to succeed" in high school in Newberry, Michigan, talked to West Point classmates about it over the following weekend, and to a chaplain he respected, and then decided to approach his chain of command. His company commander wasn't welcoming: "Don't expect me to go to bat for you on this issue if you take this up," he recalled being told. (It was an unfortunate phrase to use, given that one of the allegations was that a soldier in Fishback's unit had amused himself by beating a prisoner with a baseball bat.) Next Fishback talked to his battalion commander, who sent him to a military lawyer who reassured him that, while there were some gray areas, the law had been followed. Unsatisfied, and feeling that Army soldiers deserved better, Fishback continued to ask questions. Ultimately, after seventeen months of pushing the issue internally, he would contact Sen. John McCain, who had questioned Rumsfeld's handling of detention issues. "We owe our soldiers better than this," Fishback wrote.

Chalabi bolts

At the same time, the U.S. relationship with Ahmed Chalabi soured. The politician had been a longtime ally of the Pentagon, and a major source of its intelligence information; as late as January 2004, he had remained in the good graces of at least part of the Bush administration, and had been given a place of honor behind Mrs. Bush at that year's State of the Union address. But just five months later, early on the morning of May 20, 2004, Chalabi's home in Baghdad was raided. Officially the operation was conducted by Iraqi police, and was a matter for Iraqi police and the Iraqi judge who had issued a warrant. Chalabi called the raid "an act of political intimidation" and said that he believed that Bremer had been behind it. In fact, while the raid officially was an operation of Iraqi forces, it was actually conducted by the CIA and SEAL Team 6, said a senior U.S. intelligence official with direct access to that information. "We hit his place hard because he had the records of Sunni generals that were directing the insurgency" but wouldn't turn them over, this official said.

Other U.S. officials hinted darkly that there was more to the matter, and it only took a few phone calls by reporters to be told by another U.S. intelligence official that Chalabi's organization had conveyed information to the Iranian government that was considered very damaging to U.S. intelligence gathering. An American intelligence official in Baghdad had gotten drunk and told Chalabi that the Americans were routinely listening in on all his conversations and reading his e-mails, the first senior intelligence official said. He said that the American eavesdroppers then caught Chalabi telling an Iranian intelligence contact, "You have to understand, the Americans are reading your traffic."

Chalabi denied that allegation. "The whole thing is ridiculous," he told the *Middle East Quarterly* in an interview later that year. "I did not give any such information to the Iranians, and no U.S. official told me classified information." But he conceded that he had met with Iranian intelligence officials, adding that he had met with such officials from every country bordering Iraq.

Chalabi also seemed nonchalant about the possibility that his organization had helped mislead the U.S. government into war. Told by another interviewer that some people who had once supported the war now felt they had been suckered, he said, "Okay." Asked if he felt any discomfort with the fact that many of the arguments for justifying the invasion had crumbled, Chalabi indicated that the ends justified the means. "No," he said. "We are in Baghdad now."

In his new incarnation, Chalabi began to sound like one of the Bush administration's harsher critics. "What did fourteen months of occupation achieve?" he asked rhetorically in the interview with the *Middle East Quarterly.* "The electricity still doesn't work, thousands are dead, the United States has lost the moral high ground in the Middle East, and the UN, which opposed the liberation of Iraq, has been allowed to impose Baathists back on the Iraqi people."

In June, President Bush was asked at a Rose Garden press conference about the Iraqi exile leader. "Chalabi? My meetings with him were very brief," the president said. "I mean, I think I met with him at the State of the Union and just kind of working through the rope line, and he might have come with a group of leaders. But I haven't had any extensive conversations with him." Asked then whether Chalabi had misled the U.S. government, Bush said, "I don't remember anyone walking into my office saying, 'Chalabi says this is the way it's going to be in Iraq.'" Then the president chuckled.

18.

TURNOVER

SUMMER TO WINTER 2004

On June 28, 2004, Ambassador Bremer quietly handed over official control of Iraq to Iraqi Prime Minister Ayad Allawi, head of the new interim government, in a small, almost secret ceremony that lasted just five minutes and was shrouded from the public by the multiple layers of security still necessary to bring safety to the Green Zone. It was conducted two days ahead of schedule in order to keep terrorists from trying to disrupt it. A few minutes later, Bremer sent his 779th and last "cable" from Baghdad. Addressed "To SecDef/To SecState/To White House NSC," it stated, "This is the final message to be transmitted by the Coalition Provisional Authority headquarters in Baghdad, Iraq, Baghdad 779."

At a NATO summit meeting in Turkey, Condoleezza Rice passed a note to President Bush: "Mr. President," she wrote, "Iraq is sovereign. Letter was passed from Bremer at 10:26 AM Iraq time. Condi."

Across the lower left-hand corner of the note Bush scrawled, "Let freedom reign!"

Bremer boarded a helicopter to the Baghdad airport and departed the country almost stealthily, with no public ceremony at the airport and only a previously taped farewell address aired on Iraqi television. He climbed aboard an Air Force C-130 transport aircraft, and then, for security reasons, after his small farewell party left, transferred by helicopter to another plane. Contrary to official expectations when he landed thirteen months earlier, there were still few commercial flights at the Baghdad airport, and none operated by U.S. carriers.

"I knew there were big security concerns, but I figured that at the very least we'd have a ceremony with a few hundred Iraqis—something that would be televised for the country to see," one American working for the CPA said. "This was embarrassing."

"He left Iraq in such an appropriate way, running out of town," sneered one former Special Forces officer who worked in the Green Zone.

"Put bluntly, CPA never got on top of it, and they did not do their job to a passing grade level," said Charles Costello, who at the CPA was trying to establish an Iraqi government. "I thought highly of Bremer and hesitate to criticize him, and yet he took bad advice and acted on it on a couple of big issues, and failed to see, I think, that he needed to really clean out his staff about halfway through. . . . Even though he had the right instincts and was a very hardworking, good manager and all, in the end you've got to hold him accountable and say, 'Guess what: You guys did not get the job done.'"

Casey takes command

The occupation was hardly over—there would be more U.S. troops in Iraq at the end of 2005 than there were on the day Bremer left the country. But his departure, and that of Sanchez soon afterward, were the most positive events in a long time. The biggest shift in the U.S. effort in mid-2004 wasn't in policy but in people. Bremer was replaced by John Negroponte, a career diplomat who had been the U.S. ambassador to the United Nations. The change was felt immediately, both in Washington and Baghdad. The U.S. effort suddenly felt less hapless. "As soon as we got Negroponte out there, and got State involved, everything changed," said Richard Armitage, who was deputy secretary of state at the time. "We had reporting, it was orderly, things started to run." Under the new team, "we started getting reams of reporting, so we got the texture of society, we got the debate of society, we got all of it." Also, Armitage said, Negroponte's aides set out to clean up the Green Zone. "They weren't screwing in the chapel anymore. I don't know about the Blue Goose or whatever that place was"—a reference to a supposed brothel in the zone, said to have been named after a Panamanian establishment notorious among U.S. Navy sailors.

In a parallel improvement, Army Gen. George Casey, Jr., was tapped to replace Sanchez. Abizaid had been expected by some to play a bigger role in Iraq but had concluded that doing so would distract him from paying sufficient attention to the rest of the region for which he was responsible. The two immediate tactical problems he faced were Iraq and Afghanistan, he told reporters, but "the two broadest strategic problems that we have to deal with, that must be dealt with in a broad range, happen to be Pakistan and Saudi Arabia. So it was never an issue of getting the Centcom headquarters into the tactical fight—you do that at great peril to the broader mission." This is a credible argument, but it also begs the question of why Abizaid let Sanchez remain the top commander in Iraq for so long.

"Historians will remember Sanchez as the William Westmoreland of the Iraq War—the general who misunderstood the nature of the conflict he faced and thereby played into the enemy's hands," commented retired Army Col. Andrew Bacevich. When Sanchez took command, the insurgency had hardly begun, while a year later, when he left, "Iraq was all but coming apart at the seams." This is a harsh judgment but a fair one.

Like Sanchez, Casey had commanded the 1st Armored Division. He had no combat time but more political experience. Also, while Sanchez was a junior three-star general, Casey was a four-star officer, a former director of the Joint Staff, and vice chief of staff of the Army and so knowledgeable in political-military affairs, all of which gave him more heft both in dealing with the Pentagon and with his civilian counterparts. He soon formed a close working relationship with Negroponte, a welcome contrast to the debilitating strains subordinates had seen between Bremer and Sanchez.

The United States launches a counterinsurgency campaign

In the wake of the personnel changes, U.S. policy also began to shift. Most notably, the summer of 2004 saw the beginning of fundamental changes in U.S. military presence and posture. On August 5, 2004, Casey issued a campaign plan, a classified document of about twenty-five pages, plus a series of appendices detailing aspects of the campaign. Remarkably, this was the first time that the U.S. effort in Iraq had a road map for attacking the insurgency. ("We did not have a campaign plan the whole time Sanchez was out there," recalled a senior military intelligence officer. Until Casey's arrival there had been only a kill and capture mission statement and "an endlessly debated draft of a campaign plan.") It was no accident that the British military, which had been unhappy with Sanchez and the performance of the U.S. Army, played a major role in shaping Casey's statement, remembered an officer who was involved. Casey's campaign plan essentially called for containing the insurgent violence, building up Iraqi security forces, rebuilding economically, and reaching out to the Sunni community through both coercion and cooptation, in an effort to persuade them of the inevitability of success for the U.S.-led side.

Casey's office assembled a strategy shop that reported to Maj. Gen. Stephen Sargeant, a veteran A-10 close attack jet pilot who worked the military personnel system to pull in nine of the smartest, best-educated officers in the U.S. military establishments, men who had commanded in the field and had also earned doctoral degrees at Stanford, Harvard, and MIT. Running the office was Col. William Hix, a veteran of special operations who was also the son of a CIA operative. These nine officers with Ph.D.s jokingly called themselves Doctors Without Orders, a play on the name of the French charitable organization Doctors Without Borders. But in fact they had a very clear mandate to think innovatively about how to improve U.S. strategy in Iraq.

Typical of this office was Kalev Sepp, the retired Special Forces officer. Lanky and mild-mannered, Sepp had fought in El Salvador, and gotten a Ph.D. in history at Harvard, and then he became a professor at the Naval Postgraduate School, where he specialized in counterinsurgency issues. One day in the fall of 2004, Hix took Sepp aside and asked him to write down the best practices of counterinsurgency campaigns for Casey. What works? What doesn't? What are the commonalities of successful campaigns, and what are the pitfalls seen in past failures? It was the ideal assignment for Sepp, who had advised two brigades of the Salvadoran army and had read widely in the history of other counterinsurgencies. In a thirty-six-hour binge, writing mainly off the top of his head and occasionally checking facts on the Internet, Sepp drafted a short paper that distilled the lessons of fifty-three counterinsurgency campaigns in the twentieth century, with an eye to identifying the characteristics of those that had won and those that hadn't. The study amounted to an indictment of the Army's approach to Iraq in 2003–4. Sepp listed twelve best practices of winners, and concluded that the U.S. effort in Iraq had followed only one: emphasis on intelligence. It hadn't established and expanded secure areas. The insurgents weren't isolated from the population. There was no program of amnesty and rehabilitation for them. There was no single authority, and there was no dynamic or charismatic figure leading that authority. The police were not in the lead of the fight, supported by the military. And so on.

Sepp's chart of the nine unsuccessful characteristics reads like a summary of the U.S. occupation in 2003–4. These were his hallmarks of failure:

- primacy of military direction of counter-insurgency
- priority to kill-capture enemy, not on engaging population
- battalion-size operations as the norm
- military units concentrated on large bases for protection
- Special Forces focused on raiding
- adviser effort a low priority in personnel assignment
- building, training indigenous army in image of U.S. Army
- peacetime government processes
- open borders, airspace, coastlines

The U.S. occupation hit each of these bad targets squarely, except the last; the military controlled the small coastline but still faced a stream of trouble coming over the Syrian border, and had lost its total dominance of the air as insurgents demonstrated their ability to down helicopters, forcing the restriction of some flights. Hix took the study to Casey and walked him through it. Over the next year, Casey would remake his campaign in part to address the points made by Sepp and others.

Casey at first didn't entirely get it, but officers subordinate to him did, as did some of his British advisers. And he was willing to learn. In the summer of 2004, his greatest contribution appears to have been mostly one of tone—especially his work to ensure that henceforth the U.S. civilian and military efforts would cooperate rather than clash.

Training Iraqis begins again

After nearly a year of indirection and collapse in the program to train Iraqi security forces, Lt. Gen. Petraeus was put in charge of it in mid-2004. Essentially, the U.S. plan was to keep a lid on Iraq until such time as newly created Iraqi forces could take over the fight. "When Dave came on there was a palpable feel of dynamism, increased pressure on us to train," recalled one Army officer, a veteran of 2003 in Iraq. Most notably, Petraeus reoriented the training of the Iraqi army. The initial thought had been to create a mechanized force at least able to deter Iran, Iraq's traditional foe. Petraeus, observing that there was an enemy already present—that is, the insurgency—focused instead on creating a lighter force able to fight it.

Even so, training Iraqis was a fragile foundation on which to base U.S. operations, because they were nowhere near ready to take the lead role in putting down the insurgency. When Rand Corporation researchers visited Baghdad in the fall of 2004, they found there was a gap of sixty thousand between the number of trained police claimed by the top Iraqi police officer and the number cited by U.S. officials.

U.S. public attention wanes, Iraqi violence increases

By the early fall of 2004, the bloom was off the new rose of the interim Iraqi government. In a September survey conducted by Iraqis and funded by the U.S. government, Iraqis blamed the U.S.-led occupation force and foreign terrorists equally. "Thinking about the difficult situation in Iraq currently, whether in terms of security, the economy or living conditions, who—in your view—is most to blame?" the pollsters asked. The occupation force was blamed by 33 percent of the two thousand respondents, and "foreign terrorists" by 32 percent. Some 45 percent of those polled said the country was heading in the wrong direction, an increase from 31 percent earlier in the summer, just after the handover of official control, though the U.S. military remained the most powerful entity in the country. Most of those who thought it was going wrong cited the security situation.

The attention of the U.S. public seemed to be drifting elsewhere, but the violence intensified in the summer and fall of 2004. Battles were being fought in cities for a second and third time. A fierce fight in August to take back the city of Najaf from Moqtadr al-Sadr's militia attracted only passing notice in the United States. A total of 148 U.S. troops were lost during the summer, 10 more than had died invading the country in the spring of 2003. One division alone, the 1st Cavalry, lost seventy tanks during its one-year tour in Baghdad, according to Army Brig. Gen. David Fastabend. (One of the 1st Cav soldiers hit hard was the son of Maj. Gen. Odierno, who lost most of his left arm to an RPG shot in Baghdad in August 2004.) By September, recalled Sattler, the Marine commander, every U.S. vehicle that moved near Fallujah was shot at. In an official Army survey conducted in the late summer, 76 percent of soldiers questioned said they had been on the receiving end of rocket or mortar attacks during their time in Iraq. A year earlier only 57 percent of soldiers had said this.

More than a year into the occupation, U.S. forces were no longer surprised to be engaged in high-intensity combat. Iraq had become a real war, one that would occupy space in future history textbooks far more than, say, the 1991 Gulf War, which was celebrated as a great victory at the time but now appears to have been the opening skirmish of a very long war. By May 2004, the new conflict had produced more U.S. military casualties than the Spanish-American War, and about as many wounded as the War of 1812 and the Mexican War.

On June 24, 2004, a platoon of National Guard soldiers from North Carolina was ambushed while patrolling in Baqubah. Insurgents then overran several government buildings in the central part of the city, killing a score of Iraqi policemen. A young tank commander from the 1st Infantry Division named Lt. Neil Prakash led the rescue mission. "Captain Fowler came sprinting over, all out of wind, and says, 'All right, the whole company is going to Baqubah, I've just been given the order,'" he recalled. "'Baqubah is under siege—the police station, the CMOC [Civil Military Operations Center]—all have been attacked, so we're going in.'" Prakash, in the lead tank, ran straight into a kilometer-long ambush in which his tank was struck seven times by rocket-propelled grenades, and by roadside bombs and machine-gun fire. One hit blew the navigation system off the vehicle. Another one, to the tank's rear deck, twisted a metal plate upward and blocked the turret from rotating, forcing Prakash to maneuver his tank in order to fire his guns at the enemy fighters.

"There's a shockingly loud explosion ahead, and a plume of smoke comes off Lieutenant Prakash's tank in the lead," Steve Mumford, a New York artist embedded with the unit, wrote in an account of the battle. He was in an M-113 armored troop carrier following Prakash. "The column stops. His tank has been hit with an RPG from over a wall on the left, and his gunner blasts a round through the wall."

Insurgents were also trying to toss hand grenades into the open hatches and fire into them from rooftops, so Prakash ordered his men to close all their hatches. "We just kept rolling, getting shot at from everywhere," the lieutenant later said in a statement.

Prakash was very much a product of the twenty-first-century United States. Born in Bangalore, India, he grew up in Syracuse, New York, and graduated from Johns Hopkins University in 2002, having majored in neuroscience. While in Iraq he also maintained a blog, in which he noted that he was "currently enrolled in the School of Hard Knocks."

When Prakash's platoon was ordered to establish a defensive perimeter, he took advantage of the pause to roll back to the edge of town for emergency repairs on his tank. "The mechanics beat the twisted metal plate down with sledgehammers until the turret can move," Mumford wrote. His M-113 also had been hit by an RPG. "It looked like a baseball coming straight at us," Mumford recalled one soldier saying. The hasty repairs completed, Prakash headed back into the fight and saw a truck that he thought was resupplying the insurgents. "We blasted it with a main round from about one hundred meters away," Prakash later told the Army. It apparently was loaded with RPGs and other weaponry. "The thing just blew to shreds. You could see the tubes from the launchers go flying in the air."

Prakash's platoon was told to establish a blocking position, which it held until the following morning. All told, the Army credited him and his crew with killing numerous enemy fighters and destroying eight enemy strongpoints or bunkers, plus the truck. For his actions that day he would be awarded the Silver Star, the Army's third highest decoration, after the Medal of Honor and the Distinguished Service Cross. "Lt. Prakash turned the momentum against the enemy in Baqubah on 24 June," Maj. Gen. Batiste, the commander of the 1st Infantry Division, wrote later in recommending Prakash for the medal. Looking back almost two years later, Batiste said that the action involving Prakash was typical of the division's time in Iraq from February 2004 to February 2005. "Something like that would go on for three days, then we'd get it quiet, and it would stay that way for weeks."

That fall would find Prakash heading into the second big battle of Fallujah, where his unit was sent to augment the Marines. After that fight, another soldier told him that Hollywood was going to make a movie about it, and asked who would play him. Probably, Prakash responded, Apu—the hangdog Indian immigrant who in *The Simpsons* television cartoon show manages a Kwik-E-Mart convenience store.

Air Force Senior Airman Brian Kolfage's war was different but ended with similar intensity. At about two o'clock on the afternoon of September 11, 2004, the twenty-three-year-old military police officer who worked the night shift as a customs inspector at Balad air base, north of Baghdad, woke up and decided to go exercise. He walked out of his tent to pick up a bottle of water to help stave off the intense heat and was blasted sideways by the impact of an incoming 107 millimeter mortar round. He regained consciousness and tried to stand up. He couldn't. Both his legs were pretty much gone. His right arm also was destroyed. One of his friends applied tourniquets, but doctors later told him that what probably saved him from dying was that the heat of the blast had melted shut some of his severed arteries.

"The pain was really bad," he later told the *Washington Post*'s Clarence Williams. "I was like, 'Give me some fucking pain killers or put me to sleep.'" He woke up two days later in a bed in Walter Reed Army Medical Center. "I was charred so bad, one of the doctors didn't even know I was white."

Despite the increase in violence, the abuse of detainees by troops appears to have declined in 2004, compared to the previous year, if the number of cases brought by the Army against soldiers is any indication. Cynics might say that this was because the Army was less inclined to bring cases, but in reality it likely occurred because U.S. tactics and training had improved as the Army adjusted to fighting an insurgency—and certainly because U.S. soldiers and their commanders had been sensitized to the issue.

Still, cases did occur. On October 24, 2004, Sgt. 1st Class Jorge Diaz, a senior sergeant in a company of the 1st Infantry Division, held a 9 millimeter pistol to the head of a teenager who he had been told was guarding an insurgent weapons cache, and then Diaz hit and choked him. He then forced the youth to hold a smoke grenade from which the pin had been removed. He later released the boy. The next day, Sgt. Diaz was in the courtyard of a house in the village of Albu Shakur, north of Baghdad, watching over three prisoners whose hands were cuffed behind their backs. He had been told that one of them was the leader of an insurgent group. Frustrated that the men wouldn't talk, he had his men stand one of them up, told them to step back, and then shot the Iraqi in the face with his M-4 rifle, killing him. "I'm going to go to hell for this," Diaz said later, according to subsequent testimony. Eight months later he was found guilty of unpremeditated murder, maltreatment of a prisoner, and impeding an investigation, and he was sentenced to eight years in prison. "He just lost it," said Batiste, the division commander.

Second Fallujah: November 2004

The key element in Gen. Casey's campaign plan was to eliminate safe havens for insurgents before the first round of parliamentary elections in January 2005. The biggest of those was in Fallujah. The battle to retake that city started just after the U.S. presidential election in November 2004. It was a once-and-for-all attack to send a message to the rest of the cities in the Sunni Triangle: You don't have to like the Americans, but if you tolerate the presence of the insurgents, this will be your fate.

Second Fallujah, as some in the U.S. government called it, was a fierce battle, but careful preparation prevented it from becoming a civilian bloodbath. While covered adequately by journalists, it probably received less attention than it should have. If a battle of this intensity had occurred during the spring 2003 invasion, reporters would have treated it like another D-Day. But by the fall of 2004, after eighteen months of roadside bombings, kidnappings, suicide attacks, and lengthy battles in Samarra, Baqubah, Fallujah, Najaf, and then again in Najaf and Samarra, journalists were fatigued and probably numbed somewhat to the violence.

The new battle followed months of military planning and political measures. The force assembled for the assault was more than three times the size of that in April, and included two Iraqi units. Another lesson learned from April was that the insurgents responded by attacking supply lines, so the Marines conducted a huge logistical buildup, stocking a mountain of food, ammunition, fuel, and other provisions that would enable the severed bases near the city to operate at full bore for fifteen days without being resupplied. In addition to using stocks on hand, some eleven million rounds of ammunition were brought in. Also, U.S. units were dispatched to the Iraqi-Syrian border to close ports of entry to all military-age males who might seek to reinforce the insurgents. Meanwhile, a concerted effort was made to encourage civilians to leave the city—the U.S. count was that by the time the offensive was launched, only 400 civilians remained, out of a city of perhaps 250,000. "It almost looked like the town was abandoned," remembered Col. Michael Shupp, commander of the 1st Marine Regiment, which would play a major role in the assault. Also, the interim Iraqi government was prepared to support the attack in its public statements.

"This was a truly epic fight," said Capt. Winslow, the Marine historian who was there. It featured, he said, "two groups willing to die for what they believed in: U.S. Marines and extremist insurgents." On the insurgent side, "we had people coming in from all over the world—franchise players and free agents." On the Marine side, there were determined young men, "educated, trained, comfortable with technology, and wanting to show these guys what we're made of."

On the cold, rainy day of November 8, several big 2,000-pound bombs were dropped on the railroad tracks on the northern edge of the city, signaling the beginning of the attack. Soon afterward some 6,500 Marines, 1,500 Army soldiers, and 2,000 Iraqi troops launched an assault on Fallujah that lasted about ten days. On top of that there were 2,500 Navy personnel in support roles—medics, doctors, Seabees, and air liaison officers. "It was huge," more than three times the size of the force used in April, said Toolan, who in August drafted the battle plan for Second Fallujah. It was probably the toughest battle the U.S. military had seen since the end of the Vietnam War more than three decades earlier. It certainly was the hardest combat seen by U.S. troops during thirteen years of military operations in and around Iraq. "The fighting was intense, close and personal, the likes of which has been experienced on just a few occasions since the battle of Hue City in the Vietnam War," Sattler and Lt. Col. Daniel Wilson, one of his planners, later wrote in the *Marine Corps Gazette*.

Marine units moved into the city from an unexpected direction—not from the east, where they had a big base and where many of the hundreds of insurgent bunkers had been built to face them, but from the northwest. The 3rd Battalion of the 5th Marines "advanced south, with three companies and tanks abreast, in a systematic, block-by-block clearing movement called 'the squeegee,' preceded by rolling mortar and artillery fires, with airstrikes employed whenever a hard point was encountered," West, the former Pentagon official and expert on urban warfare, who was embedded with the Marines, wrote in the *Marine Corps Gazette*. An Army artillery unit fired what it called shake-and-bake missions—using incendiary white phosphorous smoke rounds to flush out entrenched insurgents, and then high-explosive rounds to kill them.

The Marines compared the fighting to the Vietnam War, but in some ways the battle of Second Fallujah better evoked the island combat in the Pacific in World War II, in which the Japanese defenders knew they had no escape and so fought suicidally, from holes and fighting positions with no exit routes. Like the Pacific war, the fighting in Fallujah also had an episodic feel, going quickly from relative quiet into a blaze of violence, followed by weeks of mopping-up operations, and then the return of relative quiet.

Eighteen elite Special Operations snipers hid inside the city, picking targets and reporting back on enemy movements. Polish snipers working alongside U.S. forces had been given less restrictive rules of engagement by their government, said a senior U.S. intelligence official with direct access to information about them. "The Poles could kill people we couldn't," he said. For example, he said, American snipers couldn't shoot unless they saw a weapon in the target's hands, while the Poles were allowed to fire at anyone on the streets of Fallujah holding a cell phone after 8:00 P.M. "They had an eighty percent kill rate at six hundred yards," the intelligence official said. "That's an incredible range."

For the first several days the Marines and the Army moved southward across the city. After ten days of fighting, U.S. forces captured the city, killing at least 1,000 insurgent fighters, and by some estimates perhaps twice that. But most of the fighters had left the city before the fighting began, with some launching attacks elsewhere. U.S. casualties were 54 dead and 425 seriously wounded, with 8 Iraqi allied soldiers lost and 43 wounded.

Then, said Capt. Winslow, "the heavy lifting begins—going from room to room, clearing the city, pulling the weapons caches out." All told, that clearing phase—checking every one of 20,000 to 30,000 structures in the city at least two or three times—took about six weeks. During this phase, U.S. troops uncovered 2 car-bomb factories, 24 bomb factories, and 455 weapons caches. They also found 3 hellish buildings where hostages had been kept and tortured. One Iraqi prisoner was discovered alive, chained and stuffed into a crawl space, presumably left to starve and die. In another building corpses were found in cells with their legs chopped off, their wounds apparently inflicted while they were still alive. "It was mind-numbingly manual labor, under terrifically difficult conditions, under fire in many cases," Winslow said, showing a photograph of a group of Marines crouching in combat postures while the one in front of them swung a big sledge-hammer at a padlocked metal gate.

This mop-up phase was in many ways more taxing than the initial assault. West noted that one platoon's log showed that it had searched seventy buildings every day for more than a week, engaging in an average of three firefights a day, resulting in the killing of sixty insurgents, usually inside buildings. The standing order was, he wrote: "Enter every room with a boom." He continued:

> It was exhausting, dangerous work . . . walking down narrow, dust-clogged alleys
> behind growling tanks, barely able to hear the shouts of the fire team and squad
> leaders, hurling grenades in windows, slapping C-4 to door fronts, ducking from
> the blast, waiting for the dust to clear a bit, then bursting in, a stack of four or six
> Marines with rifles and pistols, firing and blasting from room to room.

Some of the fighting was literally eye-to-eye: West described one encounter in which a Marine, 1st Sgt. Brad Kasal, burst into a room and found an AK-47 barrel pointed at his nose. He jumped back a foot and so avoided the insurgent's fire as he pulled his own trigger and sent a volley of bullets into the man's chest.

The firepower expended in Second Fallujah was extraordinary, especially for a battle that came long after victory had been declared and the military was supposed to be engaged in peacekeeping. "The amount of ammo we have fired since the operation has kicked off is staggering and continues to climb," one Marine tank commander recorded. "My company has fired close to 1,600 main gun rounds, over 121,000 7.62 mm [rifle ammunition rounds], and over 49,000 [heavy machine gun] caliber .50 rounds." Underscoring what a close fight it was, he said that nearly all targets fired on were within 200 meters. Overall, the Marines fired four thousand artillery rounds and ten thousand mortar shells into the city, while warplanes dropped ten tons of bombs. At least two thousand buildings were destroyed and another ten thousand were badly damaged, the historian West estimated after reviewing unit logs. This amount was expended by a force that had entered Iraq eight months earlier hoping not to use air strikes or artillery fire against the insurgents.

An incident that underscored the tenacity of the fight came on November 13, when an embedded television cameraman filmed an incident in which a Marine corporal apparently shot and killed a severely wounded and unarmed Iraqi in a Fallujah mosque. The videotape, by Kevin Sites, a freelance correspondent working for NBC News, showed a squad of Marines from the 3rd Battalion of the 1st Marine Regiment entering the building and seeing several insurgents lying against a wall, either dead or gravely wounded. A Marine looked at one and shouted, according to the account posted by Sites on his blog, "He's fucking faking he's dead — he's faking he's fucking dead." The Marine then shot the man in the head.

"Well, he's dead now," another Marine said, according to Sites.

Sites said the wounded men were insurgents who had battled a different group of Marines the day before. In that firefight, ten Iraqi fighters were killed and five were wounded. Those five were treated with field bandages and left in the mosque because the conditions of combat had not allowed the Marines to bring them out. Other Marines were supposed to collect the injured Iraqis and take them for treatment, but for some reason that had not happened.

The next day, the Marines had received a report that the area, which they thought had been cleared, had been reinfiltrated by insurgents—a condition that proved typical during this battle. ("There were no real front lines, because they'd get behind you constantly," Lt. Gen. Sattler later said.) A squad of Marines that had not been involved in the previous day's encounter was sent to investigate. They entered the mosque and saw the men lying on the floor. It was then that the shooting occurred.

In a striking open letter to the Marines with whom he had been embedded, Sites at the time explained his decision to send his videotape for broadcast. "When the Iraqi man in the mosque posed a threat, he was your enemy," he wrote. "When he was subdued he was your responsibility; when he was killed in front of my eyes and my camera—the story of his death became my responsibility. The burdens of war, as you so well know, are unforgiving for all of us. I pray for your soon and safe return."

The incident was most noteworthy not because it occurred but rather because, when it was disclosed, it caused such a small, short-lived stir. Articles about it ran deep inside newspapers, if at all. There was no sense of scandal, no congressional calls for investigation, no alarmed discussions on Sunday talk shows. Rather there was a sense of resignation: Everyone knew this had become a tough, bare-knuckled war. Indeed, seven months later, the Marine Corps would announce that it had determined that under military law the corporal had acted in self-defense.

A document that captured the fierceness of Second Fallujah was a lessons learned summary written by a group of scouts/snipers in the 3rd Battalion of the 5th Marines. Among their findings about house-to-house combat in the close confines of the city were that the interior walls of most houses were sufficiently thick to permit the use of fragmentation grenades without hurting Marines waiting on the other side of each wall. "Each room can be fragged individually," they reported. They also had learned that it is better if possible to attack from the ground floor up rather than move onto a roof from an adjacent house and attack downward. That's because it is nearly impossible to haul up stairs a limp, wounded Marine in body armor, helmet, and other battle gear. Also, it is more difficult to maintain control of a downward attack, because "top down is always in high gear."

They came to believe in shooting first. "There is no reason to place Marines into the building until it is thoroughly prepped" with heavy fire, preferably from 120 millimeter cannon rounds from a tank. Likewise, if forced by enemy contact to withdraw from a house, they recommended blowing it up or burning it down—preferably the latter, because, they noted, humans fear death by flames more than death by explosion, and other members of the enemy force will see what happens. The best way to bring down a house, they had found, was with a device the Marines in Fallujah came to call house guest—two propane tanks filled with gas and ignited by a block of C-4 plastic explosive. "Creates a fuel air explosive," the snipers reported, that not only sucks the oxygen out of the house and suffocates its occupants, but also destroys the house.

Their experiences were hardly unique. Another young officer, 2nd Lt. Elliot

Ackerman of the 1st Battalion of the 8th Marines, battle hardened after less than two years in the Corps, concluded in his platoon's after-action report, "To send Marines in to clear an enemy-occupied structure without heavy preparatory fires was tantamount to suicide. . . . Whenever we located an enemy position that needed to be cleared, we used a combination of rockets, tanks and bulldozers to destroy the structure." Even with that caution, 40 percent of Ackerman's platoon was wounded or killed in the fighting.

Lt. Carin Calvin, a weapons platoon commander in Lima Company, 3rd Battalion of the 1st Marines, reported that each of his assault teams on an average day used six explosive satchel charges, three cases of mine-clearing Bangalore torpedoes, and ten shoulder-launched bazookalike assault weapons. Overall, about one-third of the rounds fired by Marines using this last weapon were in the form of the new thermobaric novel explosive. This fuel-rich warhead, which is built around a newly developed aluminum-based, long-burning explosive called PBXIH-135, was designed for urban warfare, especially multiroom buildings and sewers. Its high-temperature detonation reaches through several rooms, consuming the oxygen in them and, in addition to suffocation and burns, causes extensive injuries to anyone caught in it, including, according to *Inside the Navy*, a trade publication, "concussions, collapsed lungs, internal hemorrhaging and eardrum ruptures."

This extraordinary round of fighting in Fallujah tended to overshadow the smaller battles that broke out elsewhere around the same time. In Mosul, insurgents launched a swift and effective uprising in support of the fighters in Fallujah, causing some thirty-two hundred of the four thousand members of the city's police force to desert. Those who remained came under heavy attack. An adviser to an Iraqi police commando unit, Army Col. James Coffman, Jr., was in the middle of a four-hour-long firefight in which twelve of the Iraqi commandos were killed and another forty-two wounded. At one point, according to an Army document, his shooting hand was shattered and his M-4 rifle damaged, forcing him to pick up AK-47s from casualties and fire with his other hand. At another, an RPG exploded against the wall behind him. The battle only ended four hours later when U.S. Stryker armored vehicles and attack helicopters finally arrived on the scene. Of his attackers, Col. Coffman, who later received the Distinguished Service Cross, the second-highest award for valor, told the *Berkshire Eagle*, his hometown paper. "They were organized, they were disciplined, and they had well-placed firing plans." (It isn't clear why it took so long for the Army to come to the rescue. Coffman said by e-mail that he was in communication with the U.S. military through a Thuraya satellite phone, and that he had provided his grid coordinates—that is, his precise location on a military map. "I really have no good answer why there was a delay on the Strykers responding to reinforce the [Iraqi police] commandos," he said.)

Conclusions on second Fallujah

Marines tended to portray the second Fallujah battle of the year as a great victory. "We feel right now that we have . . . broken the back of the insurgency and we have taken away this safe haven," Lt. Gen. Sattler said in Fallujah on November 18. He later wrote that it had "produced a turning of the tide in the fight against the insurgency in the al Anbar Province. . . . The insurgents are on the run."

Added Winslow, "These Marines have reversed the perception in the Islamic world that you can thump Americans and go home" without a response.

The Marines also thought that what they had seen in Fallujah was the sort of challenge the U.S. military would face repeatedly in the coming years. "In my opinion, Fallujah is an example of what we're going to fight in the future—and not a bad example of how to fight it," the Marine commandant, Gen. Michael Hagee, would say in a talk at the big Marine base at Quantico, Virginia, in 2005. "It is about individual Marines with small arms going from house to house, killing. We may not want to say that, but that's what it is about."

Privately, some Marines feared that the victory ultimately could prove Pyrrhic. "In the recesses of my mind, it bothered me," said Col. John Toolan. He found himself wondering, "What's the impact on a ten-year-old kid when he goes back in and sees his neighborhood destroyed? And what is he going to do when he is eighteen years old?"

Proceedings, the Navy's professional magazine, came to a similarly sober conclusion. "The Battle of Fallujah was not a defeat," wrote Jonathan Keiler, a former Marine officer. "But we cannot afford many more victories like it."

Probably the best assessment was that of Army Col. William Hix. The two key battles of 2004, he said, were shutting down Sadr in Najaf in August and then removing Fallujah as an insurgent sanctuary in November. "Given that containing insurgency and political progress are key elements of counterinsurgency, these 'actions' were essential to the campaign," especially for the political benefit of undercutting the ability of the insurgents to launch attacks to block the January 2005 election. "The coalition fought its way to the elections." That is likely accurate, but if major military operations were necessary preambles to political movement, it likely meant that the U.S. was in for a very long war.

Some advice from advisers

In an official review of the performance of Iraqi forces in and around Fallu-jah, two Marine officers made it clear that it would be a long time before many Iraqi forces would be able to operate against insurgents on their own. "Iraqi army units are not ready for independent operations at any level," they reported. Marines sent to advise the Iraqi units found that they instead had to command them. "These companies were, by necessity, led, not merely advised, by U.S. per-sonnel. These advisors had to run the company and conduct all external coordi-nation such as requests for fire support, casevac [casualty evacuation] and logistic support. . . . The 5th Battalion advisors were taxed to the limit of their mental and physical limits [sic] by the fact that none of them had within their companies a functioning chain of command."

The one bright note emerging from the experience was that properly led and advised Iraqi units actually were more effective than Marines at some tasks, most notably in getting the population to help them find weapons caches and in interrogating detainees. Even so, the report repeatedly underscored how difficult the advisory task was—and how lengthy the job of producing effective Iraqi forces was promising to be. In addition, advisers needed to be proficient in a wide range of military skills that extended well beyond the usual infantry training. Company-level advisers needed, among other things, sound knowledge of how to use and fix military radios, training in urban warfare, the ability to operate and troubleshoot a variety of heavy machine guns, and basic training in demolitions.

Reading the document, Zinni was reminded of one of his two tours in Vietnam, the one in 1967 in which he advised the Vietnamese Marines. "I attended the Spe-cial Forces advisory course at Fort Bragg at the time," he wrote in an e-mail. But he was dismayed to see that nowadays the training was of necessity occurring on the job. In 1966, "We received language, culture, survival, insurgency, weapons, tactics, etc. The Marine Advisory Unit had among their ranks the very best junior officers. It was created by a remarkable officer who was with the French in Indochina. We forgot all those lessons after the war, and this one caught us by surprise, thanks to the Pentagon idiots who didn't understand what they were getting into."

Colin Powell's regrets

Another old Vietnam adviser, Secretary of State Powell, privately agreed with many commanders that there weren't enough forces to get the job done. On No-

vember 12, 2004, just ten days after the presidential election, and as Second Fallujah was still under way, he saw Bush and British Prime Minister Tony Blair at the
White House and told them that there weren't sufficient forces on the ground—
whether American, British, or Iraqi—to provide security. "We don't have enough
troops," Powell said, according to a U.S. official who reviewed the top-secret transcript of the meeting. "We don't control the terrain." (Oddly, Bremer surfaced at
about the same time, saying in speeches in the fall of 2004 that a lack of adequate
troops had hampered the occupation. "We paid a big price for not stopping it, because it established an atmosphere of lawlessness," he said about the looting of
Baghdad. "We never had enough troops on the ground.")

Powell also submitted his resignation to Bush that day, although it wasn't
made public until the following week. After leaving office Powell would spin his
record, talking about how he had won victories within the Bush administration
and with allies. Yet, sadly, he also would seem to recognize that his term as secretary of state is likely to be remembered mainly for making the false case at the
United Nations in February 2003 that Iraq possessed a threatening arsenal of
weaponry. At the time it was seen as a moment that cemented a statesman's reputation, but by the time he left office it had come to be seen as rather the opposite, a speech that left a sour taste at the end of decades of public service. "I'm the
one who made the television moment," he told the London *Daily Telegraph* in his
first post–State Department interview. "I was mightily disappointed when the
sourcing of it all became very suspect and everything started to fall apart. The
problem was stockpiles. None have been found. I don't think any will be
found. . . . I will forever be known as the one who made the case."

By contrast, Mohamed ElBaradei, the director of the International Atomic
Energy Agency, whose findings were brushed aside by Powell in 2003, and who
called the day the United States invaded Iraq "the saddest in my life" because he
was so sure the Bush administration's assertions about Iraq's weapons stockpiles
were wrong, would receive the Nobel Peace Prize in the fall of 2005.

Bush vs. the realities of Iraq

President Bush talked frequently to Rumsfeld and his top commanders, and
he generally insisted that steady progress was being made. But in the fall of
2004 he began to hear some unusually pessimistic assessments of the situation. "I
told the president in November [2004] . . . that we weren't winning, and he was
shocked," a former senior administration official recalled in an interview. "And

John Negroponte backed me up. I called John and said, 'I told the president this and I want you to know it, so if you've got a different view' . . . and he said, no."

One reason the administration could drift along in its own world, this official added, was because it simply refused to admit mistakes or to act to correct or remove those who made them. "What I object to is, [and] what you see throughout this administration, [is that] there is no accountability." As an example he cited the Abu Ghraib prison scandal, for which only a handful of soldiers were punished. "The biggest stain on our soul I can imagine," he said, "and there's just no accountability."

In December 2004, two unvarnished official reports hit the White House. The first was a somber assessment by the CIA station chief in Baghdad, at that point the agency's largest station. Called an aardwolf in agency jargon, the assessment enjoys special status under CIA regulations. It cannot be edited by the ambassador, and it is delivered directly to the agency's director. Just a few other copies are distributed, and only to people at the top of the government, with recipients including the president, the secretaries of state and defense, and the national security adviser. "We face a vicious insurgency, we are going to have 2,000" dead, the CIA station chief's report stated, according to a senior U.S. intelligence official with direct access to the document.

A few days later, on December 17, 2004, according to a former senior administration official, President Bush received an extensive briefing on the situation from Army Col. Derek Harvey, a senior U.S. military intelligence expert on Iraq. Unlike most U.S. military intelligence officials involved in the region, Harvey understood Arabic, and also had a Ph.D. in Islamic studies. He had a far less rosy view than what the president had been hearing. CIA and NSC officials who already had received the longer, four-hour version of his briefing sat in. The insurgency was tougher than the American officials understood, Harvey told the president, according to three people present at the meeting. "It's robust, it's well led, it's diverse. Absent some sort of reconciliation it's going to go on, and that risks a civil war. They have the means to fight this for a long time, and they have a different sense of time than we do, and are willing to fight. They have better intelligence than we do." The insurgents had managed to mount about twenty-six thousand attacks against U.S. forces and Iraqis during 2004, and the trends weren't good.

The president wanted to know where Harvey was coming from. Who was he? And why should his minority view, so contrary to the official optimism, be believed? Harvey explained that he had spent a good amount of time in Iraq, that he had conversed repeatedly with insurgents, and had developed the belief that the U.S. intelligence effort there was deeply flawed.

The other officials present weren't entirely at ease with Col. Harvey and his perspective. "There was always a view that Harvey was a little over the top," especially in his certainty that he was right and everyone else was wrong, said a former senior administration official.

Okay, what about the Syrian role? the president asked.

One of the CIA officials spoke up to say that his agency didn't see clear financing coming from Syria. The CIA long had thought that Harvey and other military intelligence officials were overemphasizing the role of Syria and foreign fighters in Iraq.

No, Harvey bluntly responded with striking specificity, in fact, we do. "We see four different tracks of financing from Damascus. All go to Ramadi, to the tune of $1.2 million a month. And it is based, in a very Arab way, on relationships and shared experiences. And all the sigint [signals intercept intelligence] isn't going to tell you that." But don't focus on the foreign fighters, Harvey told the president, breaking a bit with the orthodox view in military intelligence. We've zeroed in on them too much because our intelligence apparatus can intercept their communications. But they aren't at the core of the Iraqi insurgency, which is "the old Sunni oligarchy using religious nationalism as a motivating force. That's it in a nutshell."

In the wake of the briefing, a study group led by retired Army Gen. Gary Luck was sent to Iraq to review operations there. Among its conclusions, reported back to the president in February 2005, was that the security situation was worse than was being depicted, the insurgency was gathering steam, the training of Iraqi security forces was slower than officials had said, and the U.S. intelligence operation continued to be deeply flawed. In his peculiar way, Bush would take many months before his public comments began to reflect this more sober assessment. Even then, in a series of speeches on Iraq late in 2005 and early in 2006, he would refer to setbacks only in vague terms.

The commanders move on

The Marines' Gen. Mattis left Iraq in the summer of 2004, having seen seventeen of the twenty-nine men in his headquarters company killed or wounded in the previous five months. "It's fun to shoot some people," Mattis said a few months later to a meeting of military officers, retirees, and contractors in San Diego. "Actually, it's a lot of fun to fight. You know, it's a hell of a hoot. I like brawling." Such sentiments weren't all that unusual for Mattis—it was how he talked to his Marines. But in this case he did it with a TV news camera rolling. "You go into Afghanistan, you got guys who slap women around for five years because they didn't wear a veil," he said, thinking back to his time on the ground in that country in 2001. "You know, guys like that ain't got no manhood left anyway. So it's a hell of a lot of fun to shoot them."

When his remarks were posted on the Web site of the NBC affiliate in San Diego, it caused a minor fuss. Hagee, the Marine commandant, issued a statement that said, "I have counseled him concerning his remarks, and he agrees he should have chosen his words more carefully." Mattis's many supporters in the Marines came away worried that he had damaged his chances of succeeding Gen. Hagee as commandant.

The television station's Web site did not report Mattis's far more serious point that day, about the fighting in Iraq. It is "almost embarrassing intellectually," he said, that U.S. military thinkers were looking at unlikely war scenarios to help them plan the future structure of the U.S. military, instead of closely studying the real war under way in Iraq. "Don't patronize this enemy," he warned. "They mean business. They mean every word they say. Don't imagine an enemy somewhere in the future, and you're going to transform so you can fight him. They're killing us now. Their will is not broken. They mean it."

After two sterling tours in Iraq—first as the only American division commander to leave behind an area in which the insurgency wasn't active, and then in turning around much of the training effort—David Petraeus came back to a senior job at Fort Leavenworth, Kansas, in the Army's training command, overseeing the education of officers and the writing of doctrine. These were not insubstantial jobs, and they fit with his academic background—he has a Ph.D. from Princeton. But despite carrying a promotion to lieutenant general, the post was a relative backwater compared to the jobs that the Army's most successful general in Iraq might have expected to be sent to, such as head of planning for the Joint Staff, or perhaps director of the Joint Staff. After all, two generals who arguably had failed in Iraq had received promotions and higher ranks—Lt. Gen. Sanchez was tapped for a four-star command, but was held up by congressional skepticism of his handling of Abu Ghraib, and the 4th ID's Maj. Gen. Odierno received a third star and an important job as military assistant to the chairman of the Joint Chiefs, a position that effectively has become the liaison between the military and the State Department.

Meanwhile, unusually, two other division commanders retired upon finishing assignments in Iraq: the 82nd Airborne's Gen. Swannack and the 1st Infantry Division's Gen. Batiste, who told friends he was disgusted with Defense Secretary Rumsfeld. Likewise, Col. Teddy Spain retired from the Army not long after getting back, and quickly found a good job in civilian life overseeing a major corporate security operation. He still checked the news on Iraq every day before going to work, and then again when he came through the door in the evening. "It does break my heart," he said. "My old sergeant major tells me all the police stations we renovated have been burned."

Despite such outcomes, Tommy Franks held on to the notion that he had won a famous victory. "Let's not be too hard on our own country," he said in Washington in 2004. "The plan was just fine. The plan was OK. . . . It was not the one-hundredth-percentile plan because we didn't know everything."

Franks sometimes was contradictory in his discussions of Iraq. In his memoir he said, "Phase IV was actually going about as I had expected—not as I had hoped, but as I had expected." Yet in promoting that book he told reporters, "I don't know that I expected an insurgency."

Pressed again on this subject a few months later, he responded by pushing back. "We spend a lot of time in this country trying to find fault," he said. "I am not a fault seeker. My personal frustration, my personal bias, is a lot of times, we spend a lot of time trying to pick the flyspecks out of the pepper," instead of trying to move forward. This was, of course, a way of belittling his critics and of minimizing the problems that he had helped create.

Like him, the Bush administration followed one of its basic patterns and hung tough. A few weeks later, Bush awarded the Presidential Medal of Freedom to Franks, Bremer, and Tenet—three of the figures most responsible for the mishandling of Iraq in 2003 and 2004. Among other things, Bush said the three men had "made our country more secure."

Rumsfeld bulled on as defense secretary. Aides said he was focused on transforming the military, seemingly unaware that history almost certainly will judge him largely on his mishandling of the Iraq war. In December 2004 his blustery facade cracked a bit at a town hall meeting with National Guard troops in Kuwait, where they were preparing to deploy northward into Iraq. Rumsfeld faced a series of skeptical questions from the soldiers, mainly about problems in receiving adequate equipment. "Our vehicles are not armored," said Spec. Thomas Wilson, an airplane mechanic with the Tennessee Army National Guard. "We're digging pieces of rusted scrap metal and compromised ballistic glass that's already been shot up . . . picking the best out of this scrap to put on our vehicles to take into combat. We do not have proper . . . vehicles to carry with us north."

Rumsfeld's reply struck many as callous or dismissive. "As you know, you go to war with the Army you have," the defense secretary said. "They're not the Army you might want or wish to have at a later time."

When another soldier asked an additional pointed question about inadequate gear, there was some chatter in the crowd. Rumsfeld responded in a manner unusual for him, pleading the weakness of age. "Settle down," he told the soldiers. "Hell, I'm an old man and it's early in the morning. I didn't take—just gathering my thoughts here."

If Rumsfeld is widely blamed for the botched occupation, Wolfowitz is even more closely associated with the decision to invade. His repudiation of Gen. Shinseki's estimate of the necessary size of the U.S.-led invasion force likely will go down as the most memorable moment of his time as deputy defense secretary. In the wake of the January 2005 election in Iraq, Wolfowitz appeared before the Senate Armed Services Committee and essentially argued that his view of the situation in Iraq had been vindicated. He returned to one of his favorite themes: He had confronted the modern version of the Nazis, and they now were hooked up with the terrorists of 9/11. "The secret security forces of the former regime—best analogized, I think, to the Gestapo and the SS of the Nazi regime—are now allied with new terrorists drawn from across the region," he said. "Like their Baathist allies, these new terrorists are ideologically opposed to democracy and fearful of what the success of freedom in this important Arab country will mean for them."

Wolfowitz left the Pentagon for the presidency of the World Bank a few months later, in April 2005. In a subsequent interview he said he really had no regrets. "Three years is a very short time into this," he said. "War is a tough business. This has been a tough war. The early stages were much easier than we feared they would be, and the subsequent stages were much tougher than people anticipated."

Several months later Gen. Myers stepped down as chairman of the Joint Chiefs. In September 2005, on his final day of congressional testimony in that position, Sen. John McCain questioned Myers's record of rosy assessments. "Things have not gone as we had planned or expected, nor as we were told by you, General Myers," the Arizona Republican said.

Myers responded that he had never been all that positive about the situation. "I don't think this committee or the American public has ever heard me say that things are going very well in Iraq," he said, inexplicably.

19.

TOO LITTLE, TOO LATE?

2005

In 2005, the U.S. military fought a rolling series of battles across central Iraq in an attempt to tamp down the insurgency and permit Iraqis to move forward politically: Parliamentary elections were held in January, a constitutional referendum was held in October, and a national assembly was elected in December. Following Casey's campaign plan, U.S. forces focused first on Baghdad, then in the summer of 2005 turned to Tall Afar in northwestern Iraq to try to seal the Syrian border, and then in the fall fought in the small towns along the Euphrates Valley between the capital and that border. The idea of this incremental approach was to clear and hold territory, rather than simply to fight and withdraw. Once again, troop numbers proved the limiting factor: U.S. troops did the clearing, and there were only so many of them, and Iraqi forces were supposed to do the holding, and there were even fewer of them that were effective.

Yet despite a solid year of fighting and those three major elections, by the end of 2005, the insurgency had intensified. The number of bomb attacks had increased steadily, eventually hitting eighteen hundred a month in the fall of 2005. In addition, the bombs became more powerful, capable of utterly destroying an armored Humvee. Another twist was that some bombers figured out how to attach propane or jellied gasoline, effectively creating napalm bombs. "We got better armor, they started getting better ordnance," Col. Bob Chase, the operations chief for the 2nd Marine Division, said after fourteen Marines and an Iraqi civilian were killed in a single blast under an amphibious assault vehicle near Haditha in August 2005.

There would be a total of 34,131 insurgent attacks in 2005, compared to 26,496 in the previous year. "The insurgents are getting a lot better," said Sgt. 1st Class Charles Ilaoa, an American Samoan platoon sergeant operating at an outpost southwest of Baghdad called San Juan. In his first tour, he said, it was easier to spot homemade bombs. Now "the IEDs are a lot more complicated. . . . They have more sophisticated, deeply buried ones." Likewise, said a Humvee gunner, Sgt. James Russell, in 2003 it was common to come across insurgents in the open, carrying AK-47 assault rifles and rocket-propelled grenade launchers. "Now you don't see them," he said. Overall, during the year the insurgency remained as robust and lethal as ever, noted Jeffrey White, a former analyst of Middle Eastern affairs at the Defense Intelligence Agency.

The U.S. military also was changing. Pushed by his two counterinsurgency advisers, Sepp and Hix, Gen. Casey endorsed the concepts of counterinsurgency and began to indoctrinate incoming unit commanders in that way of thinking. Late in 2005 he established a COIN Academy—the military's acronym for counterinsurgency—at the big U.S. military base at Taji, just north of Baghdad, and made attending its course there a prerequisite to commanding a unit in Iraq. Back in the United States, Petraeus, now at Fort Leavenworth, the Army's central educational establishment, made the thousands of Army officers who were students there also begin to study this peculiar way of war, so unlike what the U.S. Army had studied for the previous three decades.

A different war

In 2005, American soldiers began to think about the war in ways that would have been unrecognizable two years earlier. The major Army units deployed to Iraq in 2005 and 2006—the 3rd Armored Cavalry Regiment, the 4th Infantry Division, the 101st Airborne—were full of veterans on their second tours who had been trained to take a new approach. During his first tour two years earlier, recalled Army Sgt. James Eyler, "the mind-set of the whole unit was, if they pose a threat at all, shoot to kill." Back then, "we didn't trust any Iraqis," he added, as he manned a machine gun atop a Humvee and prepared to go out on a raid one humid night in Baghdad in February 2006. Eyler said he was forcing himself to be more patient with Iraqis. "Now we understand that to get out of here, we're going to have to." Added Russell, the Humvee gunner, "It's a lot less brute force and a lot more hearts and minds now."

There was also a quiet and uncomfortable awareness that the U.S. military committed several major errors in 2003–4. "The first time we were here, there was a lot of overreacting," said Staff Sgt. Jesse Sample. "Now, with experience, we react a lot more calmly." Preparing for a convoy on a particularly bomb-infested stretch of highway south of the capital, Sample added, "This tour is 180 degrees different from the last time." Now, he said, "we don't roll out into the city intimidating anyone we see."

On his first tour, Sgt. Kris Vanmarren saw his mission as being to "bust up the insurgency." The second time, he said, it was geared more toward supporting Iraqi security forces—outfitting their checkpoints, helping with their training, and providing perimeter security for their operations. "The focus has definitely shifted," agreed Capt. Klaudius Robinson, the Polish-born commander of a cavalry troop based south of Baghdad. On his second tour, he estimated, he spent half his time on engagement with the population, perhaps a quarter working with Iraqi forces, and "maybe twenty percent going after the bad guys." Robinson noted that every patrol he sent out included an interpreter, in contrast to the first year of the U.S. military presence. "It's a huge difference" being able to communicate clearly instead of using "hand signals and broken English."

The changes were particularly noticeable in the 4th ID, which had had such a checkered first tour. For its second tour, the division had its own cultural adviser, who wrote a kind of advice column on Islamic and Iraqi mores in the *Ivy Leaf,* the division newspaper. Even shooting had changed. The rules of engagement that govern the use of force had grown much tighter, and most soldiers interviewed said they thought the new restrictions were for the good. "It's a little bit harder. You're kind of tied down," said Ilaoa. Even so, he said, "we treat locals a lot better and have a lot better relations with them." In 2003, if two men were seen walking on a road in the middle of the night and carrying shovels, they would be assumed to be planting bombs and be shot, said Capt. John Moris. But "what was allowed during the first tour in Iraq, isn't," he said. Now the order likely would be to detain and question the men, if possible.

Overall, the U.S. effort was characterized by a more careful, purposeful style that extended even to how Humvees were driven in the streets. For most of the occupation, "the standard was to haul ass," noted Lt. Col. Gian Gentile, commander of the 8th Squadron of the 10th Cavalry Regiment, which was based in the sewage-drenched southern suburbs of Baghdad. He now ordered his convoy drivers to travel at 15 miles per hour. "I'm a firm believer in slow, deliberate movement," he said. "You can observe better, if there's IEDs on the road." It also was less disruptive to Iraqis and sends a message of calm control, he noted.

Gentile and other U.S. commanders also spent their time differently. Where they once devoted much of their efforts to Iraqi politics and infrastructure, they had shifted their focus more to training and supporting the Iraqi police and army. "I spent the last month talking to ISF commanders," noted Gentile. "Two years ago I would have spent all my time talking to sheikhs." Real progress was being made in training Iraqi forces, especially its army. U.S. commanders had been surprised to find that an Iraqi soldier—even one who was overweight and undertrained— was more effective standing on an Iraqi street corner than the most disciplined U.S. Army Ranger. "They get intelligence we would never get," said Gen. Abizaid. "They sense the environment in a way that we never could." An afternoon spent with one Iraqi army brigade in western Baghdad showed that while it occasionally was poor at keeping its American advisers informed, it was capable of competently carrying out basic military functions. When it set up an impromptu checkpoint on a busy thoroughfare in a neighborhood known for its hostility to U.S. forces, it maintained consistent security, with soldiers on the perimeter vigilantly facing outward, and it also was able to control civilian movements. Underscoring Abizaid's point, the soldiers checking each automobile engaged in friendly conversation with drivers in a way that Americans simply could not.

The growing availability of Iraqi troops began freeing up U.S. forces. When Capt. Robinson came across a bomb planted in a southern Baghdad intersection, he stopped to make sure that an Iraqi army unit already at the scene had the situation under control, then moved on. "Two years ago, we would have had to handle this," and spent most of the day at the intersection waiting for the Army's bomb disposal experts to show up, he noted as his Humvee pulled away. "Now, they've got the road blocked off."

The quality of life of most soldiers also improved remarkably. Almost all troops, except those out at patrol bases and other outposts, slept in air-conditioned rooms and had ready access to the Internet. Forward Operating Base Falcon was in a rough area southwest of Baghdad called the Triangle of Death, but inside its high blast walls it was a different world, with a café, a mess hall serving abundant food, and even a pseudo nightclub, the Velvet Camel, that served alcohol-free beer and advertised that "every Friday night is Hip-Hop Night," featuring "the Desert Pimps."

At Mosul, where one mess hall featured a particularly artful pastry chef, a cynical Air Force sergeant watched a convoy of heavily armored military trucks roll into the base, and then commented, "This place is a cross of *Road Warrior* and Las Vegas—it's catered, well lighted, and with good movies, and then there is this barren desert and a fight over oil. Also like Las Vegas, most people lose."

In contrast to 2003–4, when some troops ate mainly prepackaged rations, food was plentiful, and tailored to the palates of young men happy to dine on unlimited cheeseburgers, soft drinks, and ice cream. Dinner one night in January 2006 in one of the four big mess halls at the U.S. base at Balad offered entrées of baked salmon, roast turkey, grilled pork chops, fried crab bites, breaded scallops, and fried rice. The smiling servers standing behind those dishes were from Sri Lanka, Bangladesh, India, and Nepal. Soldiers who were still hungry could hit the two salad bars, the sandwich line, or a short-order stand. There were also two soup offerings and a dessert stand near the exit with chocolate mint and vanilla ice cream, banana pudding, pumpkin pie, cherry pie, and yellow cake. For those bored with the mess halls, there were a Subway, a Pizza Hut, and a Popeye's, an ersatz Starbucks called Green Beans that served up triple lattes, and a twenty-four-hour Burger King. The abundance was such that military nutritionists were beginning to worry. In 2003, the average U.S. soldier had lost about ten pounds while stationed in Iraq for a year. "Now they gain that much," reported Maj. Polly Graham, an Army dietitian at Balad, the biggest U.S. base in Iraq.

Other amenities also were being laid on. Balad boasted two shiny PXs, where fifteen soldiers a day on average bought a television. The biggest change in buying preferences over the previous two years, said one PX manager, John Burk, was that T-shirts advertising service in Iraq were no longer selling quickly. "A lot of people don't want shirts with OIF on it," he said. "They want clothes they can wear when they get home, and OIF has kind of lost its pizzazz."

Yet these two major changes in the U.S. military—a better understanding of counterinsurgency and a better quality of life—may have been fundamentally at odds. In order to keep a volunteer force relatively happy and willing to come back for third and perhaps fourth tours, the Pentagon had to provide a high quality of life for its people. But classic counterinsurgency doctrine says that the only way to win such a campaign is to live among the people. One of the nine hallmarks of failure identified by Kalev Sepp was "military units concentrated on large bases"—and that was precisely the new force posture of the U.S. military. In this way the military, for all the changes it was making, was still a square peg in the round hole of Iraq.

Brother, can you spare a COIN?

Gen. Casey's way of rounding that peg was to create the COIN Academy and to make attendance mandatory for new commanders, starting in late 2005. "When the insurgency started, we came in very conventional," said Army Col. Chris Short, the Special Forces officer who was the new school's commandant. Its curriculum taught that the U.S. military needed to fight differently. As a sign on the wall in an office near Short's put it, "INSANITY IS DOING THE SAME THING THE SAME WAY AND EXPECTING A DIFFERENT OUTCOME."

Some commanders balked at the idea of parting with their troops for the five-day course, which covered subjects from counterinsurgency theory and interrogations to detainee operations and how to dine with a sheikh. When told that he had to leave his battalion of Marines in Fallujah to come here, recalled Lt. Col. Patrick Looney, his reaction was disbelief: "You're shittin' me!"

"I didn't want to come," concurred another student, Lt. Col. David Furness, commander of the 1st Battalion of the 1st Marine Regiment, which was operating between Baghdad and Fallujah, "but I'm glad I came."

Again and again the immersion course, which thirty to fifty officers attended at a time, emphasized that the right answer was probably the counterintuitive one, rather than something that the Army had taught the officers in their ten or twenty years of service. The school's textbook, a huge binder, offered the example of a squad that busted into a house and captured someone who had mortared a U.S. base. "On the surface, a raid that captures a known insurgent or terrorist may seem like a sure victory for the coalition," it observed in red block letters. "The potential second- and third-order effects, however, can turn it into a long-term defeat if our actions humiliate the family, needlessly destroy property, or alienate the local population from our goals."

But even at the school there were doubts about how much the U.S. military really could change. Speaking inside his sandbagged office in Taji, Short said he was disturbed by "this big-base mentality" that kept tens of thousands of troops inside the FOBs, or forwarding operating bases, which they would leave for patrols and raids. He knew that classic counterinsurgency theory held that troops must live among the people as much as possible, developing a sixth sense of how the society works.

The major criticism of the school offered by students was that it would have been better to have had the education six months earlier, when they were training their troops to deploy to Iraq, rather than after the units had arrived. Col. Short's tart response was that that wasn't a bad idea, but the Army back home hadn't stepped up to the job. "They didn't do it for three years"—the length of the war at the point he was talking. "That's why the boss said, 'Screw it, I'm doing it here.'"

The Army back home was also trying to change, especially as more senior officers returned with the message that change was urgently needed. At Leavenworth, Gen. Petraeus made studying counterinsurgency a requirement at the Army's Command and General Staff College, where midcareer officers are trained. In an adjacent institution, the School of Advanced Military Studies, where the Army educates the planning specialists colloquially known as its Jedi knights, thirty-one of seventy-eight student monographs in the 2005–6 academic year were devoted to counterinsurgency or stability operations, compared with only a couple two years earlier. David Galula's monograph, "Counterinsurgency Warfare: Theory and Practice," only recently unknown at Leavenworth, became one of its bookstore's best sellers. "It's a survival thing for us," said one student, Maj. Scott Sonsalla.

The Army and Marine Corps also engaged in a joint rewriting of the U.S. military manual on counterinsurgency. "What we're trying to do is change the culture, to modify that culture, that solving the problem isn't just a tactical problem of guns and bombs and maneuver," said retired Army Col. Clinton J. Ancker III, director of the doctrine-writing office at Leavenworth, and one of the leaders of the revision effort. Conscious that it largely had walked away from counterinsurgency after the Vietnam War—the subject was not mentioned in the mid-1970s' version of the Army's key fighting manual—the Army was trying to ensure that the mistake was not repeated. "This is about institutional change, and the whole Army is included. It is kind of a generational change," said Petraeus.

The 3rd ACR leads the way

But the most striking place to see how the Army was changing was in Tall Afar, a town of about 250,000 in far northwestern Iraq, near the Syrian border. As the U.S. military had reduced its presence in northern Iraq in 2004, insurgents had taken over the medieval-feeling town, which is dominated by an old castle on a hill in its center. Just as Fallujah in central Iraq was used as a base to launch attacks on Baghdad, the biggest city in the country, they made Tall Afar a base from which to send suicide bombers and other attackers 40 miles east into Mosul, the major city in the north.

The unit given the job of fixing the situation was the 3rd Armored Cavalry Regiment. In sharp contrast to its mediocre first tour in Iraq, the unit did an extraordinary job in recapturing Tall Afar. The 3rd ACR's campaign in 2005 "will serve as a case study in classic counterinsurgency, the way it is supposed to be done," said Terry Daly, a retired intelligence officer who specializes in the subject. The Army agreed: When U.S. military experts conducted an internal review of the three dozen major U.S. brigades, battalions, and similar units operating in Iraq in 2005, they concluded that of all those units the 3rd ACR had done the best at counterinsurgency.

The 3rd ACR's campaign really began back at its home base at Fort Carson, Colorado, in June 2004, when Col. H. R. McMaster took command of the unit and began to train it for going back to Iraq. His approach was that of a football coach who knew that he had a bunch of able and dedicated athletes, but that he needed to retrain them to play soccer. McMaster was an unusual officer. Like many of the most successful U.S. commanders in Iraq, he was well educated, and had earned a Ph.D., in his case in military history at the University of North Carolina, where his subject had been the failures of the Joint Chiefs during the U.S. decision to intervene in the Vietnam War. But like the Marines' Gen. Mattis, he also was a dynamic leader, constantly moving among his troops and talking to them. He taught them from the outset that the key to counterinsurgency is focusing on the people, not on the enemy. He changed the standing orders of the regiment: Henceforth, all soldiers would "treat detainees professionally"—which hadn't happened with the 3rd ACR during its time in Iraq in 2003–4. McMaster visited every component unit in the regiment to reinforce that message, telling every soldier in his command, "Every time you treat an Iraqi disrespectfully, you are working for the enemy." Recognizing that dignity is a core value for Iraqis, he also banned his soldiers from using the term *"haji"* as a slang to describe them, because he saw it as inaccurate and disrespectful of their religion. (It actually means someone who has made the Muslim pilgrimage to Mecca.) Cultural understanding became a major part of the regiment's training. One out of every ten soldiers received a three-week course in conversational Arabic, so that each small unit would have someone capable of basic exchanges. McMaster distributed a lengthy reading list for his officers that included studies of Arabian and Iraqi history and most of the classic texts on counterinsurgency. He also quietly relieved one battalion commander who just didn't seem to understand that such changes were necessary.

McMaster also challenged U.S. military culture, all but banning the use of PowerPoint briefings by his officers. The Army loves these bulleted briefings, but McMaster had come to believe that the ubiquitous software inhibits clarity in thinking, expression, and planning.

When the 3rd Armored Cavalry Regiment moved into northwest Iraq in May 2005 it faced a mess. In 2003, a U.S. commander faced with an insurgent stronghold in a city likely would have immediately set about staging a major raid. He would sweep up suspects and move back to his base somewhere else. In 2005, McMaster took a sharply different tack, spending months preparing before attacking the entrenched insurgents in Tall Afar. That indirect approach demonstrated the key counterinsurgent quality of tactical patience, something that didn't come easily to the U.S. military.

McMaster began his preparations by dismantling the insurgents' support infrastructure outside the city. He had the 3rd ACR bolster the security operation along the Syrian border, in an effort to cut off support and reinforcements from coming in. He then eliminated safe havens out in the desert, beginning in June with a move against the remote town of Biaj, which had become a way station and training and outfitting post for those fighters coming in from Syria. Immediately after the 3rd ACR took Biaj, Iraqi forces set up a small patrol base there. "This was the first 'clear and hold,'" McMaster recalled in his plywood-walled office on a base just southwest of Tall Afar. State Department officials heard about this move and briefed their boss, Condoleezza Rice, on it. A month later she mentioned it in congressional testimony.

One of the keys to winning a counterinsurgency is to treat prisoners well, because today's captive, if persuaded to enter politics, may become tomorrow's mayor or city council member. As more remote small towns surrounding Tall Afar were "rolled up," recalled Maj. Chris Kennedy, the 3rd ACR's executive officer, Iraqi police immediately moved into each—and were reminded to treat the locals well, a departure for some heavily Shiite police units operating in the Sunni-dominated region.

The 3rd ACR also set up a system to poll all its detainees on how well they were treated, and also to interview some about their political views. "The best way to find out about your own detainee facility is to ask the 'customer,'" said Maj. Jay Gallivan, the regiment's operations officer. This system of checking with detainees was unique to the 3rd ACR, and it apparently worked: In sharp contrast to the unit's first tour in Iraq, not one 3rd ACR soldier was charged with acting abusively during the regiment's second tour, McMaster said.

In late summer, McMaster started receiving more cooperation from local Sunni leaders who had been sympathetic to the insurgency. One reason, according to U.S. military intelligence analysts, was that some insurgents were unhappy with their foreign allies, who seemed determined to start a civil war. Another was that McMaster did something few commanders had been willing to do in public: Admit the obvious and say that U.S. forces made mistakes in Iraq. "We understand why you fight," McMaster told Sunni leaders with ties to the insurgency. "When the Americans first came, we were in a dark room, stumbling around, breaking china. But now Iraqi leaders are turning on the lights." The conciliatory concession helped break down barriers of communication, he said, and made them willing to listen to his conclusion: The time for legitimate resistance had ended. This in fact was a threat, stated as politely as possible.

McMaster strengthened his position in another innovative way: by taking his officers for an outing with Iraqi army officers during which he conducted a staff ride—the military term for a formal professional examination of a historic battlefield—of a spot near Mosul where Alexander the Great had routed the army of the Persian Empire. It was a subtle way of showing that the Americans recognized that they were representatives of one of the world's youngest cultures trying to work with a people from one of the world's oldest.

With the insurgency's support infrastructure weakened in outlying areas, McMaster moved on Tall Afar. But even then he didn't attack it. First, following the suggestion of his Iraqi allies, he ringed the city with a dirt berm nine feet high and twelve miles long, leaving just a few checkpoints where all movement could be observed. This was a nod to the counterinsurgency principle of being able to control and follow the movement of the population. Building on that, U.S. military intelligence had traced the kinship lines of different tribes, enabling the 3rd ACR to track departing fighters to likely destinations in the suburbs of the city. As they fled the impending attack, some 120 were then rounded up. Next, to minimize the killing of innocents, civilians were strongly encouraged to leave the city for a camp prepared for them just to the south. Some more insurgents were caught trying to sneak out with them.

Finally, in September 2005, after four months of preparatory moves, Mc-

Master launched his attack. By that point, there were remarkably few fighters left in the city. Those who remained seem to have expected a swift U.S. raid that they would counter with scores of IEDs—that is, roadside bombs. Instead, U.S. forces and their Iraqi allies moved slowly, clearing each block and calling in artillery strikes as they spotted enemy fighters or IEDs, using firepower precisely and quickly.

Next came Phase IV: Unlike the invading U.S. forces in the spring of 2003, Mc-Master had a clear plan in hand for his postcombat operations. He also knew how he wanted to measure his success: Would he asked, Iraqis—especially Sunnis—be willing to join the local police, to "participate in their own security"? The first step in Phase IV was to establish twenty-nine small bases across the city. That, along with steady patrolling, gave the American military and its Iraqi allies a view of every major stretch of road in the compact town, which measured only about 3 miles by 3 miles. This degree of observation made it extremely difficult to plant bombs. Also, said Lt. Col. Chris Hickey, who commanded the U.S. troop contingent inside the city, "It gives us great agility." Instead of predictably rolling out the front gate of his base, he was able to order an attack to come from two or three of the small bases that dotted the city. Unlike most commanders, who ate and worked on big forward operating bases and then ventured out into Iraqi society, Hickey lived in the city, sleeping back at the base only rarely. From his perch downtown, he said, "I hear every gunshot in the city." His conclusion: "Living among the people works, if you treat them with respect." When Iraqis' electricity went out, his did as well, except for military communications equipment that was hooked to a freestanding generator.

Ultimately, fourteen hundred police were recruited, of which about 60 percent were Sunni, many of them from elsewhere. In addition, by year's end the city was patrolled by about two thousand Iraqi troops, and it had a working city council and an activist mayor. Tips on insurgent activity began to pour into a new joint operations center. The Army officer running the center, Lt. Saythala Phonexayphoua, a Laotian-American West Point graduate, said it had been "a surprise, the actionable intelligence we get. We get cell phone calls—'there's an insurgent planting an IED.'"

But there were two nagging problems even in this most successful of U.S. operations. First, by midwinter the 3rd ACR was getting ready to go home, its one-year tour of duty coming to an end. The city's mayor, Najim Abdullah al-Jubouri, was extremely unhappy about that prospect. "A surgeon doesn't leave in the middle of the operation!" the mayor exclaimed to McMaster and Hickey over a lunch of lamb kabobs and bread. He waved his index finger under McMaster's nose. "The doctor should finish the job he started." They tried to calm him down. "There's another doctor coming," Hickey ventured. "He's very good." But the mayor had seen other American units in Tall Afar, and he believed they didn't know how to coordinate with Iraqi forces as well as the 3rd ACR. "When you leave, I will leave too," the mayor threatened. "What you are doing is an experiment, and it isn't right to experiment on people." In the spring of 2006, there were worrisome signs of increasing insurgent activity in the city. In mid-April, the 1st brigade of the 1st Armored Division, which had replaced the 3rd ACR, rounded up all military-age males, defined as from eighteen to sixty-five years old, in one part of Tall Afar. "This was the mother of all military-age roll-ups," commented Col. Sean MacFarland, the brigade commander.

Nor was it clear that McMaster's example could be followed elsewhere in the country by American commanders. The biggest problem the United States faced in Iraq was Baghdad, a city about thirty times the size of Tall Afar. With the current number of U.S. troops in all of Iraq, it would be impossible to copy the approach used in Tall Afar, with outposts every few blocks. "Baghdad is a much tougher nut to crack than this," said Maj. Jack McLaughlin, Hickey's plans officer. Standing in the castle overlooking the city, he said, "It's a matter of scale—you'd need a huge number of troops to replicate what we've done here."

Ultimately it appeared that McMaster's approach in Tall Afar would prove to be yet another road not taken. In 2006, much of the rest of the U.S. military in Iraq was pursuing a different course. Instead of living among the people, as classic counterinsurgency dictates, they were closing smaller outposts and withdrawing to a handful of big super FOBs.

Journalism at its limits

Baghdad was indeed much tougher. Almost all foreign reporters in the country were based there. With the passage of time during 2004–5, their ability to work became increasingly constrained. The conditions were some of the most dangerous any journalists have ever experienced. A spate of kidnappings of journalists continued, with a macabre pattern established in which someone would disappear, then surface on an Internet video, and then sometimes be released. In just three years, eighty-four journalists were killed in Iraq, more than the sixty-six killed during twenty years of fighting in Vietnam, from 1955 to 1975. For journalists working in Iraq, observed USA Today's Jim Michaels, "oftentimes the decisions are between bad and worse."

Thinking about dying became a daily part of the job. A *Washington Post* reporter, Jackie Spinner, said at the end of nine months in Iraq, "There were days, strings of days, when every morning I was prepared to die." One day near the Abu Ghraib prison, two men tried to shove the small, reserved Spinner into a car. Confusing her beginner's Arabic phrases, she tried to yell that she was a journalist, but instead shouted, "I'm a vegetarian"—which also was true, but irrelevant. She was rescued by two passing Marines. Spinner took to sleeping in the dark, dusty stairwell of her hotel, for fear of being slashed by flying glass if a mortar shell detonated outside her bedroom window.

Gina Cavallaro, a staff reporter for *Army Times*, an independent newspaper, wrote of becoming friendly with Spec. Francisco Martinez, a lively twenty-year-old artilleryman from Puerto Rico, where she had grown up. A few days later she cradled his head as he died after being shot in the back near Ramadi. *"No te me duermas,"* she said to him—"don't fall asleep." After he was gone, she wrote, she "cried like a baby."

Coming home proved to be one of the hardest aspects of the job. Reporters would get by on adrenaline, building up a cumulative debt of stress that began to be repaid when they landed back in a normal place. Realizing her newsroom was unprepared to help her, Cavallaro sought out counseling, but found it difficult to locate someone who understood what it means to be mortared every day. "You gotta help yourself when you get back" she said, "because right now there's no culture in the newsroom that says, Help reporters when they get back."

Hearing this, Sig Christenson, the *San Antonio Express-News*'s military reporter, commented at a meeting of military correspondents, "When you come back from Iraq, if you feel a little disconnected and crazy, you are." After one reporting tour he went camping for several weeks in the high desert of Texas and New Mexico to clear his head. During the day he would hike. At night he sipped Wild Turkey whiskey and read T. R. Fehrenbach's *Lone Star,* a history of the Texans, by the light of his campfire. "It was very cool reading about how the Comanche Indians, using a form of guerrilla warfare strikingly similar to our opponents in Iraq, drove the Spaniards out of New Mexico and much of the Texas plains," he said. "They'd ride their horses up to one thousand miles, raid a Spanish encampment, and then split up into dozens of smaller groups, making it impossible for the king's soldiers to wage effective punitive expeditions on the Indians." It made him wonder how the United States could prevail in Iraq.

The *Washington Post*'s Steve Fainaru finished a reporting tour in late 2004 in which he had been subjected to several mortar attacks, and once had a bomb detonate near him in Baghdad that killed several Iraqi soldiers. He traveled from Baghdad to Amman, Jordan, had a nice dinner, and the next day flew to New York to stay with a female friend. In the middle of the night, he awoke, rose to go to the bathroom, walked a few steps, and blacked out. He woke up on the bathroom floor. "The next day I felt okay," he said a few months later. "But ever since then, I've been a step slow."

Many military officers, meanwhile, grew deeply distrustful and resentful of the media, feeling that it focused on the negative—bombings and casualties— while neglecting the positive, such as political progress and reconstruction efforts. "I would speculate that the vast majority of American soldiers, . . . by the time they left Iraq, we pretty much hated them," said Maj. Jay Bachar, an Army Reserve civil affairs officer. "They are bald-faced liars. . . . I could just go on and on, but the media clearly, clearly as any soldier over there will tell you, have an anti-U.S. agenda and are willing to propagandize falsehoods in furtherance of their own agenda."

The battle of Baghdad

By late 2005, the war was settling into the area in and around Baghdad. Inside the capital it promised to be primarily a political fight over the makeup of the future government, and whether there would be one that worked, or a civil war, which appeared increasingly likely. But on Baghdad's outskirts, the effort remained very much a military campaign. The flat agricultural plain south and southwest of the capital "is what I would call the most lethal area in Baghdad," said Col. Todd Ebel, a brigade commander there.

This became the war of "the 'Iyahs," as American troops called the cluster of hard-bitten towns named Mahmudiyah, Yusufiyah, Latifiyah, and Iskandiriyah. They had become insurgent strongholds, with a rash of bombings, kidnappings, and shootings that intimidated locals into cooperating. Not coincidentally, these towns between Baghdad and Karbala also lay on the fault line between Sunni Iraq and Shiite Iraq, and likely would be a flash point for any civil war. It also became known to U.S. troops as the land of the big IEDs, because of the huge roadside bombs there, some consisting of two five-hundred-pound bombs buried under cement plates that concealed them from the Army's metal detectors. When troops of the 101st Airborne first pushed into the area to establish a patrol base, they ran a gauntlet of bombs, with one platoon encountering fourteen in a three-hour stretch. "My job, above all things, is to keep them out of Baghdad," said Capt. Andre Rivier, the Swiss American commander of Patrol Base Swamp, a half-ruined house bristling with dull black machine guns and surrounded by green sandbags, shin-deep mud holes, and shadowy palm groves. "The important thing is to keep them fighting here. That's really the crux of the fight."

By taking the battle to rural-based insurgents, the Army hoped to gain the initiative, pressuring the enemy at a time and place of its choosing, rather than simply trying to catch suicide bombers as they drove into the capital. Despite its proximity to the city, this area had been visited surprisingly infrequently by U.S. troops over the previous three years—one of the chronic side effects of the relative lack of forces. As late as early 2006, there would be pockets within an hour's drive of the capital where the U.S. military had never operated, and where there still were no-go areas for U.S. troops—the roads were heavily seeded with bombs. Col. Ebel said a defensive belt akin to a minefield protected the insurgents' safe havens and car bomb factories along the Euphrates Valley. Following classic counterinsurgency doctrine, he didn't want to take areas and then leave them. So he moved his forces slowly, first establishing a checkpoint, then conducting patrols to study the area and its people, and then after a spell he pushed his front line half a mile forward and put up another checkpoint.

That slow-motion tactic was probably the right approach, but it was a frustrating way for soldiers to wage war. On one typical day, there were twenty-four significant acts—small-arms attacks, bombings, and other noteworthy events—recorded in one relatively small part of Ebel's area of operations. At the medic's station in Patrol Base Swamp—which with its bare cots and hanging lightbulbs felt like a scene from World War II—three soldiers of the 101st said they loathed their time at the base, especially since the death of a beloved squad leader a week earlier. "It's like trying to track down a bunch of ghosts," said Sgt. Chad Wendel, sitting on an Army cot under a window frame shielded by an Army blanket.

"I think it's the way we're losing more soldiers" that is most bothersome, added Spec. Frank Moore, a medic from Lynchburg, Virginia. "It makes you wonder, what do you gain by sticking around?"

"I don't like anything about being here," agreed Spec. Matthew Ness. All three men had spent nearly half their time in the Army serving in Iraq. Now, well into their second tour of duty there, they were wondering whether to reenlist for a third and maybe a fourth rotation. "People are leaving [the Army] now," said Ness. "The guys who are good, who should stay in for the Army, are saying, 'I've had enough.'"

Pursuing this sort of measured campaign also raised the question of whether the political clock would run out on the effort, either in Iraq or in the United States, before the American military and its Iraqi allies could become effective in large parts of the country. "That's what I worry about," said Army Lt. Gen. Peter Chiarelli, the number-two U.S. commander in Iraq.

Despite the major changes in the U.S. approach, two huge questions hung over the U.S. effort at the end of 2005. Foremost was the question of whether the situation had spun out of U.S. control, as Iraq moved toward a civil war. That in turn raised the question of whether Iraqi forces believed they were training to put down an insurgency, or preparing to fight a conflict that would pit pro-Iranian Shiite Iraqis against largely Sunni anti-Iranian Iraqis. In an ominous sign of the growing rift within Iraqi security forces, the first thing an Iraqi army battalion staff officer did as he briefed a reporter was denounce the Iraqi police and its leaders at the Shiite-dominated interior ministry. "The army doesn't like the ministry of interior," he began, as other Iraqi officers listened approvingly. "The people don't like the police, either." Former Iraqi officers from Hussein's era began flocking to join the new army, fanning Shiite fears that parts of the army were becoming the anti-Iranian force that would square off against the pro-Iranian national police, who were armed nearly as heavily.

In some ways, the U.S. military was beginning to feel irrelevant. In the capital, the biggest difference from two or three years earlier was the near total absence of U.S. troops on its streets. In a major gamble, the city largely has been turned over to Iraqi police and army troops, but they appeared to be having little effect in bringing security to the city, where murder, kidnapping, rape, robbery, and bombing were rampant. As one U.S. major put it, Baghdad resembled a pure Hobbesian state, where all are at war against all others, and in which any security is self-provided. "There is a total lack of security in the streets, partly because of the insurgents, partly because of criminals, and partly because the security forces can be dangerous to Iraqi citizens, too," said Army Reserve Capt. A. Heather Coyne, an outspoken former White House counterterrorism official who served in Iraq for almost three years, first for a year in her military role and then as part of a nongovernmental effort to develop Iraqi civilian leaders. After three years she was going home despairing of the American effort in Iraq. "I'm heartbroken," she said. "I had great expectations for this. We never got to the hard stuff. We did the easy stuff so badly."

The promised land

One cloudy evening that winter, several hundred 101st Airborne troops gathered in a hangar on their base in Mahmudiyah for a memorial service for four dead soldiers—three killed by a massive bomb, the fourth shot dead while fighting insurgents. An Army chaplain, Capt. Primitivo Davis, chose as the theme of his homily the thought that Moses had served his God well, yet wasn't allowed to enter the Promised Land, and only saw it from afar before dying. So, too, he preached, did these four dead soldiers serve well and catch "a glimpse of promise" in Iraq. The mission of their assembled comrades was to achieve the completed victory of a free, stable, and peaceful Iraq, he said. "Like Joshua, who followed Moses, we must pick up where they left off." Then a soldier slowly sang "Amazing Grace," and from the distance came a haunting version of "Taps." The service concluded, soldiers filed out of the hangar, many with tears streaming down their faces, and some crusty old sergeants embraced. It was at once very public, with senior officers present and rank observed, and also searingly personal.

But some questioned whether the U.S. effort would ever reach the desired end state described by Chaplain Davis. "It seems to be getting better, but you really can't tell," said Cpl. Toby Gilbreath, as he stood outside Patrol Base San Juan, an imposing bunker west of Baghdad.

"I would like to think that there are still possibilities here," Army Reserve Lt. Col. Joe Rice said in the coffee shop of the al Rasheed Hotel downtown in the Green Zone. "We are finally getting around to doing the right things." Rice was working on an Army lessons learned project but was expressing his personal opinion. "I think we're getting better, I do." But, he continued, "is it too little, too late?"

AFTERWORD:
BETTING AGAINST HISTORY

MID-2006

History will determine if President Bush was correct in asserting that the invasion of Iraq "made our country more secure." But the indications at this point, during the war's fourth year, aren't good. Globally, fear and distrust of the U.S. government increased. Regionally, the war in Iraq distracted the U.S. military and intelligence establishments from maintaining a single-minded focus on the pursuit of bin Laden and al Qaeda. So while there is a small chance that the Bush administration's inflexible optimism will be rewarded, that the political process will undercut the insurgency, and that democracy will take hold in Iraq, there is a far greater chance of other, more troublesome outcomes: that Iraq will fall into civil war, or spark regional war, or eventually become home to an anti-American regime, or break up altogether. In any of these forms it would offer a new haven for terrorists.

In January 2005, the CIA's internal think tank, the National Intelligence Council, concluded that Iraq had replaced Afghanistan as the training ground for a new generation of jihadist terrorists. The country had become "a magnet for international terrorist activity," said the council's chairman, Robert Hutchings. There was no question that there were more terrorists in Iraq in 2005 than there were early in 2003, when President Bush had accused the country of harboring terrorists.

Juan Cole, an Iraq expert at the University of Michigan and an outspoken opponent of the war, said that under the care of the Bush administration, Iraq had become a failed state of the sort that produces terrorists. "Iraq was not a failed state in 2002," he noted.

The invasion of Iraq has proven unexpectedly costly, with the loss of several thousand American soldiers and of an untold number of Iraqis. During 2004 and 2005, the cost to the American taxpayer was running at about $5 billion a month, meaning that by mid-2006, the total cost of the adventure had surpassed $200 billion. It is staggering to think of how that amount of money could have been spent differently to achieve the Bush administration's stated goals of countering terrorism and curtailing the proliferation of weapons of mass destruction. Just $1 billion in aid, for example, might have changed the face of education in Pakistan and helped draw out the poison of anti-Western teachings there.

The policy costs to the United States

The costs go well beyond that initial bill of blood and treasure; Iraq is likely to dominate American foreign policy for years. As the "National Strategy for Victory in Iraq," the document released by the White House in November 2005, put it, "What happens in Iraq will influence the fate of the Middle East for generations to come, with a profound impact on our own national security."

In Iraq, the U.S. position also suffers from the strategic problem of the fruit of the poisoned tree—that is, when a nation goes to war for faulty reasons, it undercuts all the actions that follow, especially when it won't concede those errors. The administration stubbornly won't deal with being wrong on WMD, and its refusal to make amends appears to have intensified the reluctance of many other nations to participate in the pacification and rebuilding of Iraq. Likewise, the administration won't admit to propounding tenuous links between Iraq and anti-U.S. terrorism. This is an arguably greater error, because it may have contributed to the problem of some U.S. troops' conflating the war in Iraq with the 9/11 attacks, and so led some to treat Iraqis as despised terrorists rather than as the prize in the war.

Another policy cost, yet to be paid, is the damage done to the credibility of its policy of preemption. Admittedly, waging preventive war will always be controversial in the United States. But the threat of it may be precisely what is needed to deal with a belligerent, nuclear-armed North Korea when that regime is on the verge of collapse, or for dealing with the Pakistani nuclear arsenal after an Islamic extremist coup. "How many people are going to believe us when we say, 'It's a slam dunk'—to use George Tenet's phrase—'Iran has nuclear weapons'?" David Kay asked on CNN. "The answer is going to be, 'You said that before.'"

A third strategic error has been less noticed—the cost of being backed by a phony coalition. By pretending to have the West behind it, the Bush administration committed the *prestige* of the West to a military adventure in the Mideast without having the *resources* of the West behind it. This became increasingly evident as the U.S. presence was challenged and the coalition continued to dwindle. There is a possibility that the incompetence of the U.S. occupation and the unwillingness of other Western nations to become involved will lead Islamic extremists to underestimate the genuine strength of the West, which is extraordinary, and barely tapped yet. Of such miscalculations, wars are made.

There are two additional costs that grow out of the way the Bush administration handled the coalition it brought to Iraq. One general at the Pentagon worried—given what he called the shabby treatment of those nations that did participate, such as Poland and Spain, which were invited to a peacekeeping mission and then asked to participate in combat—about what will happen the next time the U.S. government seeks international participation in a military operation. And allies have a new distrust of the U.S. government's decision-making processes, which proved defective during the run-up to the war, and then again during the occupation. "The fact that our judgment was flawed has created an enormous legitimacy problem for us, one that will hurt our interests for a long time to come," commented Francis Fukuyama, a political theorist who first came to Washington as an intern for Paul Wolfowitz.

Then there are opportunity costs that may become painfully evident as events unfold. What if we wake up one morning and there has been an Islamic extremist coup in Saudi Arabia or Pakistan? The U.S. military is already stretched thin, so if a military response is deemed necessary—and it likely would be, given that one country dominates the world oil market and the other possesses nuclear weapons—we may be sending in tired troops or units that lack training.

One way to prevent war is by early engagement. In particular, the use of small numbers of highly skilled troops who can train local militaries in humane but effective methods of operation is a proven way of quenching possible insurgencies, and also of deterring terrorist organizations from finding new sanctuaries. (Individuals can hide but groups generally need safe locations in which to meet and plan, and to cache supplies.) In the U.S. military, the troops expert in that sort of foreign internal defense mission are Special Forces. Yet, said one Special Forces veteran, by mid-2005, the missions in Iraq and Afghanistan were consuming more than 80 percent of the Special Operations forces, meaning that smaller problems elsewhere may be growing through neglect.

Another cost of continuing heavy engagement in Iraq is that it could embolden adversaries to act. For example, former Defense Secretary William Perry warned in a January 2005 talk in Hong Kong that some senior Chinese generals were advising the Beijing government that it was the right time to deal militarily with Taiwan, while the "U.S. is pinned down in Iraq and will not be able to come to the defense of Taiwan." Likewise, the U.S. investment in Iraq may have given Iran a window of opportunity in which to develop nuclear weapons.

Yet inside all these problems there lay a major victory for President Bush and his plan to transform the Middle East. Like it or not, the U.S. government through his actions has been tethered to Iraq and to the region around it as never before. Under him, the U.S. military has carried out its first ever occupation of an Arab nation, and the United States has spent hundreds of billions of dollars in an attempt to change the nature of politics there. Whether or not his vision of transforming the Middle East occurs, it appears that the United States won't be detaching from the region anytime soon. "If the government falls, we'll have to go back in," in a third war, commented John Lehman, a Reagan-era Navy secretary. The stakes are simply too high to let Iraq become a sanctuary for anti-U.S. terrorists.

The best case scenario: The Philippines, 1899–1946

For the U.S. government, success really means staying in Iraq for years. The alternatives are failure in some form—either a unilateral withdrawal and abandonment of Iraq, or ejection by an anti-American government. "The average counterinsurgency in the twentieth century has lasted nine years," Gen. Casey said late in 2005. "Fighting insurgencies is a long-term proposition, and there's no reason that we should believe that the insurgency in Iraq will take any less time to deal with." So while it is likely that there will be a series of cuts in the U.S. military presence in Iraq in 2006 and 2007, it also remains likely that thousands of troops will be there for many years to come.

The analogy here is to the American war in the Philippines at the end of the nineteenth century. That episode began badly in 1899, with a combination of poor strategic planning and presidential inattentiveness, and a media that acted as cheerleaders for war. Also like Iraq in 2003, it began as a conventional conflict and was transformed into a guerrilla war. And when U.S. troops proved poorly prepared, and some reacted with brutality, the American public was dismayed.

But by late 1900, the U.S. Army had begun to adjust. Commanders spread their troops among the people, where they were able to learn the identities of their enemies and to seize many weapons. They trained local police units that, though troubled, eventually became an effective counterinsurgency force. Drawing on its experience in the American West, and resolved not to repeat the mistakes it had made there, the Army was "determined to preserve the Filipino by raising his standards and cultivating his friendship," said one officer quoted by Brian Linn in his history of the Philippines War. By 1902 the war was over, but U.S. forces remained in the country for decades. It was, wrote Linn, "the most successful counterinsurgency campaign in U.S. history."

Settling into such a posture of keeping a lid on the insurgents while whittling them down to irrelevancy would mean that the U.S. war in Iraq was returning to its pattern of containment—albeit this time on the ground. If that happens, it is likely that future historians will come to look at the U.S. effort from 1991 on as one long war, beginning with a short ground battle, followed by twelve years of containment done largely from the air, then another short ground fight in 2003, followed by another decade or so of containment—this time on the ground, and inside Iraq. No one expects the insurgency to disappear, but the hope would be to keep a lid on it, limiting its reach and intensity.

The doubt that hangs over even this most optimistic of scenarios is the duration of American popular support for maintaining a significant military presence for years to come. The question will become increasingly pointed with the passage of time, because as long as American soldiers are in Iraq, some are likely to die violently. The aim would be to reduce U.S. losses from two or three a day to that number a week, and eventually to that number a month, on the calculation that the American people would stand for such a rate of casualties.

The middling scenario: France in Algeria or Israel in Lebanon

It is equally possible that while the U.S. military makes improvements in its tactics and in the quality of Iraqi security forces, the political clock will run out on the effort there, either domestically or in Iraq itself, and that the U.S. will retreat before the job is done. Even if the U.S. military is able to turn most security functions over to Iraqi forces, that is unlikely to end the fighting. Because the Sunnis aren't reconciled to being a minority in a democracy, said Bing West, the

Shiite-dominated Iraqi security forces essentially are going to have to conduct their own occupation of the Sunni Triangle for years to come. Thus, any U.S. withdrawal would almost certainly lead to far more violence.

The closest analogy to the U.S. experience in Iraq may be the French in Algeria. There are of course many differences—France was a colonial power, it had a million citizens residing in Algeria, and its military was reeling from a stinging defeat in Vietnam. Also, the French had been in Algeria for over a century and had a much better feel for its Arab and Berber cultures. The biggest difference is that a sovereign Iraqi government able to stand on its own would represent a victory for the United States, while an independent Algeria was a defeat for France. Yet there also are some striking similarities; most notably, in both wars a Western power found itself enmeshed in an Arab land fighting a primarily urban battle against a murky mix of nationalists and Islamicists.

Algeria ended badly for the French. Their military became steadily more effective, but so notably brutal, with three thousand prisoners supposedly murdered, that the French public was repulsed. Ultimately, parts of the French army, feeling betrayed by the nation's politicians, rebelled, and even tried to assassinate President Charles de Gaulle. "They won tactically on the ground but brought down the French government by losing its moral authority—that's not a victory," noted Gen. Mattis, a Marine commander who has long studied the Algerian conflict in the belief that it was emblematic of the wars the United States was likely to fight. That said, France recovered smartly, and in the decades since the Algerian crisis has enjoyed more political stability than it had for most of the twentieth century.

The U.S. Army isn't going to launch a coup d'état, no matter what happens in Iraq, but a premature U.S. withdrawal likely would have severe consequences, especially for the Mideast. "To push Iraqi forces to the fore before they are ready is not 'leaving to win,' it is rushing to failure," said Sepp, the insurgency expert who advised Gen. Casey in 2005. If we leave too soon, he and his colleague Col. Hix argued, we might just be setting ourselves up for another war. "It is not beyond the realm of the possible that the United States would find itself in the position of leading another invasion of Iraq . . . to make right what was allowed to go wrong for the sake of expedience," they warned.

An Iraqi blogger writing under the title The Mesopotamian laid out a scenario of what might come after a precipitous U.S. pullout. On Day 2, he wrote, al Anbar province would fall, "even before the last American soldier leaves Baghdad." That would be followed by fighting between Shiite and Sunni groups along the murky ethnic dividing line running southwest from Baghdad. In the capital, "[a]ll shops and markets are closed and start to be looted." Next, the Kurds would move to capture the key oil city of Kirkuk, on the edge of their historical territory. "Turkey cannot allow that and invades from the north." The Kurds would turn to Iran for protection, as would the Shiites, who would feel abandoned by the West and betrayed once more by the United States. In response to the Iranian intervention, he predicted, a torrent of Arabs from Syria, Jordan, and Saudi Arabia would pour into Iraq to support their Sunni brothers. "All join an infernal orgy of death and destruction the likes of which have seldom been seen," he said, and oil prices would rocket past one hundred dollars a barrel as "fanaticism sweeps the region."

The prospect of such a catastrophe makes it more likely that the United States will remain in Iraq even if the country hovers for years on the edge of civil war. In that scenario, the U.S. strategy essentially would have to be to keep a lid on a low-level civil war for as long as possible, while also trying to keep U.S. casualties low enough that the American public doesn't demand an unconditional withdrawal. That sort of chronic occupation raises the possibility of another historical parallel. The U.S. experience in Iraq may come to resemble that of yet another Western-style military's attempt to pacify an Arab population: Israel's painful eighteen-year occupation of parts of southern Lebanon.

A worse scenario: civil war, partition, and regional war?

Even if the United States stays, there is no guarantee that Iraq won't slip into civil war. That threat hovers constantly, discussed quietly by American officers as a possibility and more openly by many Iraqis. Americans tend to remember the horrors of their own civil war and so assume that all parties would do their best to avoid it, a perspective that obscures the fact that there is a considerable pro–civil war lobby in Iraq. Essentially, there may be more people in the region who want to see the United States leave Iraq than want to see it stay, from Sunni Islamic extremists to their Shiite foes. The quickest way to achieve that ejection of the U.S. presence may be to start a civil war, on the calculation that the U.S. public wouldn't stand for seeing American troops die trying to keep apart the warring factions.

Some maintained that civil conflict already had begun in 2005. "This is one of the stages of civil war we are in right now," said Ayad Allawi, who served as Iraq's interim prime minister in late 2004 and early 2005. "What you have is killings, assassinations, militias, a stagnant economy, no services." Yet a genuine, full-blown civil war would be far worse. It likely would involve major massacres of civilians and a variety of foreign interventions, both covert and overt. A Shiite-dominated Iraqi government with its back to the wall might very well invite the Iranian military to join it in putting down the Sunnis, which likely would be done with such brutality that it would horrify the world.

Were Iraq to break up, it is possible that a Shiite south eventually would harness its oil money to build its military capacity, and then move southward to "liberate" its Shiite brethren who live on top of Saudi Arabia's oil fields, warned T. X. Hammes, the Marine counterinsurgency expert who served in Iraq. Meanwhile, he predicted, there would be a multination fight for the oil fields of the north, likely including Turkey, a member of NATO. "We have lit multiple fuses" in the region, he said. "There will be multiple explosions. I'm thinking our grandkids could easily be there," carrying on the fight decades from now.

Amin Saikal, director of the Australian National University's Center for Arab and Islamic Studies, worried that the United States, by turning over control of Iraq to its Shiites, had altered the balance of power in the region. "The traditional power equation in the Gulf is rapidly shifting in favor of Shiite Islam," he wrote. "If the present trend continues, the Iraq conflict could cause wider sectarian hostilities across the Muslim world, with a devastating impact on the region and beyond."

Indeed, in the fall of 2005 there already were small but worrisome signs of the regionalization of the Iraq war. Not only was there a steady trickle of foreign fighters into Iraq, there were indications that the insurgency might also be exporting violence. For example, the rockets fired at U.S. Navy ships anchored off Aqaba, Jordan, in August 2005 had been smuggled out of Iraq by three al Qaeda operatives. A month later, the Saudi foreign minister, Prince Saudi al-Faisal, traveled to Washington to warn, "All the dynamics are pulling the country apart." He could have said the same thing at home, but his choice of venue indicated that he would fault the U.S. government for this outcome. Two months later, "al Qaeda in Iraq," an insurgent group, detonated a series of bombs in three hotels in Amman, Jordan, killing fifty-seven people. "This is the first of a heavy rain," said a statement posted on the Internet, purportedly by these insurgents.

It was at this time that a thoughtful U.S. Army officer who had served in Iraq sketched out what he expected for the next ten years of his career. "In 2009, after we withdraw, and the south turns into Shiastan, and the Kurds declare independence, and Turkey invades, and Sunnistan leads to the fall of the house of Saud, and Arabia becomes the first step in the caliphate, and oil goes to two hundred dollars a barrel, then we have to invade Arabia with a broken Army, and then it's our Algeria," he said.

The nightmare scenario

But that dark vision is not the worst possible outcome. Even more worrisome would be that perhaps in the wake of those regional wars, a new Iraqi leader emerged to unify his country, and then perhaps the region. This was one variant hinted at in a U.S. government intelligence study, "Mapping the Global Future," in which the National Intelligence Council presented as one future scenario the rise of a new pan-Arab caliphate. "A caliphate would not have to be entirely successful for it to present a serious challenge to the international order," the report noted. Nor would its proclamation likely lessen the incidence of terrorism. Rather, it "could fuel a new generation of terrorists intent on attacking those opposed to the caliphate, whether inside or outside the Muslim world."

A poll taken in 2005 by Oxford Research International of 1,711 Iraqis reported that 74.8 percent felt that what their country needed was a single strong leader. At first the appearance of a new Iraqi strongman might also appear to be a relief to the U.S. government and the West, especially if he weren't a radical cleric. He might be a former Iraqi major or lieutenant colonel. He could be young, energetic, moral, modest, even austere, spurning luxury and driving an old Volkswagen. Admirers might speak of how he retreats into the desert for a week at a time to cleanse himself spiritually through solitary meditation. He might be of mixed ethnic origin, with a Kurdish father and a Sunni mother. There would be embellished tales of his spontaneous generosity, taking care of widows and children, and giving away personal goods without hesitation. But he likely also would have a harsh side, perhaps illustrated by his summary execution with his pistol of one of his soldiers caught in the act of raping a woman.

There is a precedent for the emergence of just such a figure: Salah ed-Din Yusuf, or Saladin, as he was known in the West, came out of the fractionalized chaos of the twelfth-century Mideast and rose to power in response to the invasion of the Crusaders. He was the son of a Kurd who had been the "governor" of Tikrit. "He was a man of great ambitions, but simple and modest in his private life, careless of protocol and so good-natured as to be almost weak," wrote Zoe Oldenbourg, the French historian of the Crusades. He also unified the Arab world in responding to the Crusader invasion.

The new Saladin would emerge first as a relief from the madness of chaos and terrorism. He would be a unifier, bringing together the disparate and weary parts of Iraq. He might even extend his influence beyond Iraq's borders, calling for the revival of the Arab world. Bolstered by Iraq's oil revenues, he might succeed in creating a wave of new pan-Arab feeling. Riding that wave, he might confront the West as it hasn't yet been—that is, as an Arab leader combining popular support with huge oil revenues. And he may seek also to harness that oil money to a new program to secure nuclear weapons. Such a program could threaten the existence of Israel or, by secret means of delivery, New York or Washington. Before that happened, the West would have to consider a war of preemption—but this time its soldiers might really face nuclear, biological, or chemical weapons.

POSTSCRIPT: APRIL 2007

When I started writing this book in January 2005, I was asked several times by colleagues and others if I really intended to call it *Fiasco*. Some warned that the word seemed extreme, or at least premature. But by the time the hardcover edition appeared in mid-2006, almost no one questioned the title.

I wish I could say that this book appeared just at the low point of the U.S. effort in Iraq, and then a rebound began shortly afterward. Unfortunately, the deterioration of the situation not only continued but accelerated in 2006, with an epidemic of death squads torturing and killing Iraqis even as roadside bomb attacks on Americans became more lethal. Overall, attacks recorded by U.S. military intelligence increased by 22 percent during the late summer and early fall, and that record almost certainly undercounted the total amount of violence. "Attack levels . . . were the highest on record," the Pentagon would somberly report.

In August, the chief of intelligence for the U.S. Marines in Iraq concluded in a secret assessment that the American effort was failing in al Anbar province, to the west of the capital. In Baghdad, U.S. commanders launched a new effort to improve security, moving thousands of troops into the city, only to prove unable to reverse the downward trend. By early fall they pronounced the operation at best a disappointment and at worst a failure. "Operation Together Forward has made a difference in the focus areas, but has not met our overall expectations of sustaining a reduction in the levels of violence," Army Maj. Gen. William Caldwell, the top U.S. military spokesman in Iraq, said on October 19, using the U.S. military name for the operation. In other words, the U.S. military had played its ace in the hole—it had asserted itself in Iraq's most important city—yet had not been able to improve security there."

Two weeks later, when there was yet another murky sectarian firefight at an Iraqi government building, Qasim Yahya, a spokesman for the Ministry of Health, commented with dry precision, "It is just the usual daily shooting at the ministry, but today it has increased quite a bit."

Meanwhile, in the town of Balad, north of the capital, attacks by Sunni and Shiite militias on civilians of the other sect provided a whiff of what might occur across the middle of the country if a full-blown civil war erupted. A battle between two towns—one Shiite, one Sunni—on opposite banks of the Tigris River epitomized the factors tearing the country apart. A killing of a Shiite blamed on Sunni Arab insurgents based in the farm hamlet of Duluiyah prompted a killing spree targeting Sunnis in Balad. The U.S. military and residents of both towns accused the police of taking part in those murders. Looking for protection, Shiites in Balad turned not to their elected government or to the U.S. military but to Shiite militias, summoning them from Baghdad. By the time the killing ebbed three days later, at least eighty people were dead. Balad was all but emptied of Sunni families, which had lived among Shiites for generations. There has been no reliable census in Iraq for decades, but it is home to at least 5 million Arab Sunnis and far more than twice that number of Shiias—and they are on the verge of massive attacks on each other, replicating the horrific cleansing of Duluiyah on a national scale.

It soon became painfully evident that what was happening in Iraq was not simply a civil war, but something worse—a chaotic combination of insurgency, sectarian violence, criminality, and factional fighting. Happiness, said one Army officer, was meeting an Iraqi you knew from your previous tour who was still alive.

"F—in' Iraqis"

When a senior commander was preparing to deploy to Iraq late in 2006, a transition briefing warned him that the United States and its allies were not winning the war in Iraq and that if current trends continued, defeat could come on his watch.

Official Washington did begin to recognize the grim realities of Iraq at about this time. "The acceptance in Washington of a clear-eyed, realistic and necessarily pessimistic assessment of Iraq is to be welcomed, even though it took nearly four years to become conventional wisdom," commented British political scientist Toby Dodge. But that was far from discerning a solution.

The turning point seems to have occurred in early October, when both Secretary of State Condoleezza Rice and Sen. John Warner went public with their frustrations, warning the Baghdad government that it must do much more much faster. "The situation is simply drifting sidewise," Warner warned. A courtly Virginia Republican and the chairman of the Senate Armed Services Committee, Warner suggested that the United States should explore a "change of course" if security had not improved within ninety days—that is, by the end of 2006. His judgment gave voice to Republican doubt that had been suppressed in a campaign season. During a surprise visit to Baghdad in October, Rice said with uncharacteristic bluntness that the security situation was not helped by "political inaction" in Iraq, with no progress made toward a national reconciliation that would help curtail the violence.

In the following weeks, Republican support for the president's stance on Iraq appeared to collapse. After the Democrats won control of both houses of Congress in the November midterm elections, Sen. Gordon Smith, a low-profile Republican from Oregon, took to the Senate floor to give voice to the frustration that many of his comrades were feeling. "I, for one, am at the end of my rope when it comes to supporting a policy that has our soldiers patrolling the same streets in the same way, being blown up by the same bombs day after day," he said when the Senate reconvened for a postelection rump session. "That is absurd. It may even be criminal. I cannot support that anymore." Smith said that he had "tried to be a good soldier. . . . I have tried to support our president." Bush, he added, "is not guilty of perfidy, but I do believe he is guilty of believing bad intelligence and giving us the same." He said he would not have voted in favor of invading Iraq had he known what he known then what he had come to know. The positive events in Iraq, such as its elections and the toppling of the statue of Saddam Hussein, "now . . . seem much like ashes to me."

The air continued to seep out of George W. Bush's presidency. By late fall, some 62 percent of Americans reported disapproving of the way he was handling his job. Yet at the same time, American politicians of both parties began blaming

Iraqis for the situation. There was a feeling that the U.S. government had given them a chance that they had failed to seize.

At one hearing of the Armed Services Committee in mid-November 2006, amid much wrangling, there was one point that everyone agreed on. "We cannot save the Iraqis from themselves," said Sen. Carl Levin (D., Michigan).

"We all want them to be able to stabilize their country with the assistance that we've provided them," said Sen. Evan Bayh (D., Indiana). But, he added, "too often they seem unable or unwilling to do that."

Later the same day, the House Armed Services Committee held a hearing of similar tone. "If the Iraqis are determined and decide to destroy themselves and their country, I don't know how in the world we're going to stop them," said Rep. Robin Hayes (R., North Carolina).

The new tone reminded retired Army Col. Andrew Bacevich, a veteran of the Vietnam War, of the sour last days of that conflict, when "there was a tendency to blame everything on the 'gooks'—meaning our South Vietnamese allies who had disappointed us."

Looking forward, Bruce Hoffman, a Georgetown University expert on terrorism who had advised the Coalition Provisional Authority during the early days of the American effort, said he detected in the finger-pointing at Iraqis a brewing argument. "It is the first manifestation of a 'Who lost Iraq?' argument that will likely rage for years to come."

What those who blamed Iraq first failed to recognize was the reality on the ground in Iraq: Iraqis didn't seize the chance the Americans had given them because they had their own agendas. The Shiites especially seemed to believe that they had won the battle to control post-Saddam Iraq, and only needed to keep on American troops to beat on Sunnis while Shiites sorted out their own differences and consolidated their hold.

Jaysh al-Daoud

One result of this sad trajectory of events is that I don't find much that I would change in this book, had I to write it again. My confidence in its conclusions was bolstered by the warm reception the book received from hundreds of members of the U.S. military, especially those who had served in Iraq. Almost every day for several months in the second half of 2006, I received e-mailed notes of thanks and congratulations from soldiers who had felt I had gotten it right. One lieutenant colonel who had commanded an infantry battalion in Iraq thanked me for "finally saying publicly what we've been saying privately." A Pentagon intelligence official said he found the book the most comprehensive study of the war he had seen, including those produced inside the government. Another Defense Department insider wrote to say that he felt as if I had listened to the conversations inside his office over the last three years.

One event that I do wish I had emphasized more was the ascendancy of the Shiite militias, especially those allied with Moqtadr al-Sadr, the radical cleric who dominates eastern Baghdad. The U.S. government had hopefully dubbed 2006 as "the year of the police" in Iraq. "It was a total failure," commented an Army colonel, reflecting on how the Shiite-dominated police units intensified sectarian violence. Instead, 2006 turned out to be the year of armed factions. Many in the U.S. government blamed this ugly trend on the February 2006 bombing of Samarra's Golden Dome Mosque, a shrine venerated by Shiites. Everything was going pretty well until that attack, the generals and Bush Administration officials would argue. But as James Miller, a former Pentagon official, put it, "The evidence on the record makes that not credible. The mosque bombing was just gasoline on a fire that already was burning pretty well." In other words, the attack didn't initiate a new direction, it simply confirmed and intensified an existing one.

It astonishes me that in early 2007 it appears that the two most likely outcomes of the current turmoil in Iraq are either that the country will break up, or that Sadr—an anti-American ally of Hezbollah—will become the country's ruler. However, neither of those events is likely to end the violence, but rather simply to open a new and even more dangerous phase, along the lines of the four scenarios outlined in the original afterword to this book.

If 2006 proved to be the year of shocking deterioration, then 2007 may be remembered as the year of the big gamble. The Bush Administration took two major steps early in the new year: It increased the U.S. combat troop presence in Baghdad by about 17,000 and at the same time sent out Gen. David Petraeus to replace Gen. George Casey as the top commander in Iraq. Casey was a hardworking and rather conventional commander who tried hard to adapt his forces to waging a counterinsurgency campaign. Petraeus, by contrast, had that knowledge in the marrow of his bones, as he demonstrated during his first tour in Iraq, when (as described in chapters 11 and 12 of this book) he commanded the 101st Airborne Division in Mosul and kept that area unexpectedly quiet by reaching out to Iraqi politicians, sheiks, and civic leaders.

"A decisive moment approaches," Petraeus wrote in a letter to his troops when he took command of all U.S. forces in Iraq on February 10, 2007. Petraeus was an exception among U.S. commanders. Understanding that the tools the Army had given him were not working, he was able to critically examine the situation and set another course. "I'd like to think that a modest knowledge of history, economics, and political philosophy stood me, and a number of other leaders, in good stead in those early days in Iraq," he said later.

In Mosul, Petraeus had laid down three rules for his subordinate commanders: We are in a race against time, give the locals you deal with a stake in the new Iraq, and don't do anything that creates more enemies than it stops.

In 2007, Petraeus would seek to replicate his success in Baghdad—though, he noted, he was "taken aback" when he saw how desolate some parts of the city had become, especially in mixed "fault line" neighborhoods. He planned to move more troops into the capital and establish about thirty-six outposts across it where American and Iraqi forces would live and operate. Iraqi troops and police were supposed to lead the way, with Americans backing them up and also monitoring them, to ensure that they treated both Sunnis and Shiites fairly, and also didn't defer to militias. In this way, it was hoped the mistake of the past would not be repeated: Instead of taking towns and neighborhoods again and again, the joint operation would "clear, hold and build" in areas. Rather than focus on killing the enemy, Petraeus would concentrate his efforts on protecting the population—something the U.S. military generally had failed to do in Iraq.

Essentially, early in 2007 the Bush Administration and the U.S. Army turned the war over to their dissidents, people like Petraeus who had criticized the way much of the U.S. effort in Iraq had been conducted for most of its duration. After more than three years of trying it the Army way, Washington was going to let them try it their way. "Their role is crucial if we are to reverse the effects of four years of conventional mind-set fighting an unconventional war," said a Special Forces colonel who knew many of the officers around Petraeus.

The group he brought with him to Iraq made up one of the world's more exclusive clubs: military officers with doctorates from top-flight universities and combat experience in Iraq. Many of them are familiar to readers of this book—among them were Col. H. R. McMaster, a University of North Carolina-trained military historian whose successful campaign in Tall Afar in 2006 is described in chapter 19, and Lt. Col. John Nagl, who is quoted in three different parts of the book. "I cannot think of another case of so many highly educated officers advising a general," said Carter Malkasian, who had advised Marine Corps commanders in Iraq on counterinsurgency and himself holds an Oxford doctorate in the history of war.

Counseling Petraeus on insurgent strategies was Ahmed Hashim, a professor of strategy at the U.S. Naval War College who had worked for McMaster in Tall Afar. Notably, he also was an advocate of partitioning Iraq along ethnic and sectarian lines. Petraeus's chief economic adviser was Col. Michael J. Meese, who was to coordinate the holding and "building" phases of economic reconstruction. Meese, who received a PhD from Princeton on Army budget issues, is the son of former attorney general Edwin Meese III.

As counterinsurgency consultant, Petraeus picked an outspoken Australian anthropologist, Lt. Col. David Kilcullen, who had studied Islamic extremism in Indonesia. In 2006 he also had written an essay about how to better operate in Iraq that found its way to Petraeus, who sent it rocketing around the Army by e-mail. Among Kilcullen's dictums was "Rank is nothing: talent is everything"—a subversive thought in an organization as hierarchical as the U.S. military.

Another aide was Lt. Col. Douglas Ollivant, who had caught Petraeus's eye by winning first prize in an Army "counterinsurgency writing" contest sponsored by the general. Ollivant scorned the U.S. military's reliance in Iraq on big "forward operating bases," writing that, "Having a fortress mentality simply isolated the counterinsurgent from the fight." Ollivant, a veteran of the 2004 battles in Najaf and Fallujah who earned a political science PhD studying Thomas Jefferson, argued that U.S. forces should instead operate from small patrol bases shared with Iraqi military and police units—which is exactly what Petraeus aimed to do in Baghdad.

The two most influential members of the brain trust were McMaster and Col. Peter R. Mansoor, whose influence already outstripped their rank. Both had served on a secret panel convened in the fall of 2006 by Gen. Peter Pace, the chairman of the Joint Chiefs of Staff, to review Iraq strategy. The panel's core conclusion, never released to the public but briefed to President Bush on December 13, was that the U.S. government should "go long" in Iraq by shifting from a combat stance to a long-term training-and-advisory effort. But to make that shift, their report also concluded, the U.S. military might first have to "spike" its presence by about 20,000 to 30,000 troops to curb sectarian violence and improve security in Baghdad. This afterthought came to be known as "the surge," attracting more attention from Congress and the news media than it deserved.

Strikingly, Petraeus's deputy was Lt. Gen. Raymond Odierno, who had commanded the 4th Infantry Division in Iraq in 2003–04 when its aggressive approach and incidents of abuse raised the eyebrows of other commanders, as is detailed in chapters 11 and 12. But people around Odierno reported that nowadays he "gets it," in terms of how to operate more intelligently in Iraq. (He wasn't the only old hand to resurface. Ahmed Chalabi, the exile politician and onetime Pentagon favorite, had seen both his American backing and public career in Iraq fizzle, with his party failing to win a single seat in the parliament elected in December 2005. But early in 2007 he reappeared, appointed as the intermediary on issues between the citizens of Baghdad and the security forces operating in it.)

With the coming of Petraeaus, what had been dissent four years earlier was fast becoming the conventional wisdom. "That's the key element of a counter-insurgency effort here, we have to reach out and protect the people," General Caldwell, the senior military spokesman, pointed out to reporters in a February 2007 news conference. "What we have realized, to protect the population, we can't . . . be living on some big operating base." In his concluding remarks he returned to the point: "If we are going to protect the population, we have to be down there with the population. We will in fact gain greater security by being embedded with and living with the population that we will back . . . on some large operating base."

The unspoken aspect of Petraeus's approach was that he seemed to be intending to operate not on behalf of the Shiites, but as an independent actor, pursuing the American interest. In this sense, the U.S. military was becoming the biggest militia on the ground in Iraq—"Jaysh al-Daoud," the Army of David. It could operate in such a manner as to push the current Iraqi government to collapse by forcing Iraqi leaders to address their internal contradictions: Were they really willing to see Shiite militias disarmed? Would they permit the U.S. military to confront the Jaysh al-Mahdi, the army of Moqtadr al-Sadr? And would the Americans really care if the government collapsed and were replaced by a general of the new Iraqi army?

As of this writing, it is too early to tell whether Petraeus will succeed. Initial indications were the most powerful militias and some insurgents were going to ground or actually moving out of the capital to focus their attacks elsewhere. Many American troops were skeptical of the plan, even in the hands of an accomplished commander such as Petraeus. "If anyone has a chance to pull this out, it is Petraeus," said one Army lieutenant colonel. But privately, many senior officers gave him only a 10 percent chance. "If anyone can, Petraeus can, and he'll do it or die trying," said one general who knows Petraeus well. "However, I don't think he can do it—it's all too little too late. I'm just waiting for the end now, and wondering how it will come."

Troops on the ground in Baghdad often were even more skeptical. "All the Shiites have to do is tell everyone to lay low, wait for the Americans to leave, then when they leave, you have a target list and within a day they'll kill every Sunni leader in the country," Army 1st Lt. Alain Etienne told Tom Lasseter of McClatchy News Service.

It likely will take many months to see whether genuine progress is being made, and whether parts of the capital actually are being "held." Barring some unforeseen departure, the real test is likely to come in September of this year, when Ramadan begins. In each of the four years of the American presence in Iraq, violence has spiked sharply during that holy month. If Petraeus is able to break that pattern, he may be on a slow road to success. If he fails to do so, then Americans almost certainly will begin talking about ending at least the combat mission there and letting Iraqis fight a full-blown civil war. The end could come fast: If Iraqi allies sense that the U.S. is edging toward the exit, they are likely to pull in their own troops to conserve them for the post-U.S. round of fighting. "Iraqis who believe that we are approaching the end game are unlikely to allow their security forces to get chewed up in advance of a U.S. withdrawal," predicted one U.S. defense expert working in the region.

There was little evidence that a nonsectarian Iraqi security force was developing that would be able to hold Iraq together. Indeed, the Iraqi army, dominated by Shiites, wasn't even the most powerful Shiite militia in Iraq—that was Sadr's Jaysh al-Mahdi. "As soon as we leave, the slaughter will start," said the general who knows Petraeus. "We are merely delaying the inevitable." As if to emphasize that sentiment, the coalition in Iraq continued to shrink, with Britain announcing that it planned to cut its presence in Iraq to 5,500 by the end of 2007, and Denmark saying it intended also to withdraw its small force. Lithuania said it was considering following suit.

There were two Iraq wars being waged, according to military officers on the ground there and defense experts back in the United States: the one fought in the streets of Baghdad, and the war as it was perceived in Washington. General Petraeus noted this disparity not longer after taking command. "The Washington clock is moving more rapidly than the Baghdad clock," he said. "So we're obviously trying to speed up the Baghdad clock a bit and to produce some progress on the ground that can, perhaps . . . put a little more time on the Washington clock."

Washington appeared in the spring of 2007 to be headed toward a political endgame on Iraq, with the White House and Congress sparring over benchmarks and pullout dates. Meanwhile, the war on the ground was at kind of an ebb tide, as all sides—from U.S. military strategists and Iraqi sectarian leaders and insurgents, as well as regional players such as Iran, Syria, Saudi Arabia, and Turkey—

were waiting to see whether the new U.S. approach to make the Iraqi capital safer would work. Soldiers on the ground tended to see the Washington debate as irrelevant, while the perspective of many politicians in Washington was that the military schedule is simply too slow. "The time scale to succeed is years," said John Hamre, a former deputy defense secretary, but "the time scale for tolerance here is 12 months for Democrats and 18 months for Republicans." In Washington, he said, the key political breakthrough happened when the November 2006 midterm elections turned into a referendum on the war. "The American people have been waiting to hear how we were going to win in Iraq, and they never heard that, so they turned against it. But the political evolution is moving much faster here than events there."

One result of this disparity was the emergence of radically different views of the impact of the new strategy being implemented by Petraeus, which was often called a "surge" because it sent more troops into Iraq but which was more noteworthy for moving U.S. troops off large, isolated bases and into smaller outposts across the capital. Hawks were eager to detect progress. Not long after Petraeus took command, President Bush said that "there's been good progress." Senator John McCain concluded a few weeks later on a trip to Iraq that "we have a new strategy that is making progress." But officers in Iraq tended to be far more wary, with Petraeus himself repeatedly cautioning it was too early to tell whether the new strategy was leading to sustained progress. He and others said that it would be late summer or early fall of 2007 before they would be able to whether they were succeeding or failing. That timetable made the congressional debate over a possible 2008 withdrawal seem to prove beside the point.

Officers in Baghdad also were worried that executing the new approach would take more time than Washington was willing to give. "Early signs are very encouraging—huge drop in sectarian killings in Baghdad, return of thousands of refugee families," said one U.S. official in the Iraqi capital, speaking on the condition of anonymity so that he could be candid. "But there is no way we can defeat this insurgency by summer. I believe we can begin to turn the tide by then, and have an idea if we are doing it. To defeat it completely is a five-to-ten-year project, minimum—and rushing it along to meet a D.C. timeline is rushing to failure."

In Baghdad, there indeed were a few signs of improvement, but they tended to be offset by worrisome indications elsewhere in Iraq. Sectarian killings were down about 50 percent since the new strategy began, according to U.S military spokesmen. Car bombings were up, but so were tips from Iraqis. It is impossible to know how much of the decrease in violence was attributable to the biggest Shi-ite militia, Sadr's Mahdi army, deciding to lie low. In addition, noted a U.S. Army officer preparing for his third Iraq tour, when one side in a war alters its tactics, the other side will usually take time to study the shift and assess vulnerabilities before renewing attacks. Also, in Anbar province, there were solid indications of tribal leaders turning against al-Qaeda extremists. But, reported one Special Forces veteran who had worked in Iraq both in the military and as a civilian, "the surge in Baghdad is pushing the sectarian violence to other parts of Iraq." That was one reason for the increased fighting in nearby Diyala province that led U.S. commanders to send in a Stryker battalion that was part of the troop buildup. Likewise, the Marine Corps's new success in Anbar appeared to have forced some al-Qaeda fighters to shift eastward to Mosul, Baqubah, and Tall Afar. A military intelligence officer warned of other troubling signs outside Baghdad: Kirkuk edg-ing closer to explosion, the Turks increasingly unhappy with Kurdish activity and threatening to do something about it, and an impending British drawdown in the south that could make U.S. supply lines from Kuwait more vulnerable.

Officers also said they were uncertain of the sustainability of any positive mo-mentum. More effective military operations built around protecting the popula-tion could buy time but couldn't solve the basic problem in Iraq: the growing threat of a full-blown civil war. The U.S. government kept pushing for reconcili-ation, but there were few signs of movement toward that goal, or even that Iraqi leaders shared that agenda. "Nothing is going to work until the parties are ready to compromise, and I don't see any indicators yet that they are," said A. Heather Coyne, who worked in Iraq both as a military reservist and as a civilian. "Until then, any effect of the surge will be temporary."

If Iraq does descend into a full-out civil war, U.S. government efforts may turn to shaping a new policy of containment that seeks to prevent the country's conflict from flaring into a regional one. The question then, perhaps to be debated later this year but certainly by the 2008 presidential election, will be whether the Amer-icans are taking on yet another open-ended and ultimately impossible mission.

General Anthony Zinni, a key figure in the first two chapters of this book, told me early in 2007 that during his meetings with American political leaders, he laid out three options: Commit enough forces to win in Iraq, leave altogether, or plan to contain the disaster. He concluded that he didn't see much stomach for either of the first two options and that Congress was "drifting toward containment." If so, we will be back essentially to where we were after the 1991 war—but now in a far weaker position, having lost tens of thousands of Iraqi and American lives, spent hundreds of billions of dollars, and squandered an extraordinary amount of good will.

As grave as the situation has become in Iraq, I see one sliver of reason for hope: I think that the United States is regaining the equilibrium it lost five years ago. The 9/11 attacks knocked us all off balance, but especially the U.S. Congress. I also believe that 9/11 gave the Iraq hawks an unexpected opening—they were able to argue that the intelligence had been wrong, and so had the conventional wisdom, and their minority view of the Middle East that would blossom after an unprecedented American intervention was the path to follow. In 2006 and 2007, I think, Congress shook off its post-attack stupor and began to reassert itself as a coequal branch of the federal government.

Reading it over now, this book strikes me as profoundly conservative, in that it calls for a return to American traditions—for the U.S. military to heed its values and history, for the American people to remember their roots, for the executive branch to be more inclusive in going to war, and especially for Congress to exercise the oversight function designed for it by our founding fathers. I think the American system is again beginning to work as they intended. That doesn't mean that we will be able to find an easy way out of the mess in Iraq, but it does mean that we may be able to deal better with its tragic consequences, which are likely to be with us for decades. Shakespeare's tragedies have five acts, and I fear we have not yet seen the beginning of Act IV.

NOTES

This volume is not an academic study written at long remove from its subject, but an attempt to write narrative history on the heels of the events it covers. I decided against using formal footnotes, yet I also think that the curious are entitled to know the sources of much of my information. So where the source is particularly significant or deserving of notice, I have tried in the text to say what it was. When sources aren't explained there, I have tried to list them here.

This book is based foremost on several hundred interviews and my own coverage of events in Washington, D.C., and in Iraq, and in several other places. I was surprised in reading my notes, for example, to realize that I had covered Defense Secretary Rumsfeld in Munich early in February 2003, then Deputy Defense Secretary Wolfowitz in Detroit later that month, then the Washington end of the invasion the following month, and then was embedded with the 1st Armored Division in Baghdad not long after that. It gave me a renewed appreciation of my wife's tolerance of my job. While writing I also relied on a steady stream of e-mails to and from soldiers in the field. It is a pleasant surprise of the modern world that I was able to send a just written paragraph from my desk near Washington, D.C., to a commander operating in al Anbar province and ask, "Does this accurately capture what happened, in your view?" I frequently would receive a response within the hour.

I also have relied extensively on a vast number of documents. The biggest surprise to me in writing a work of nonfiction now, compared to a decade ago, was the extraordinary increase in the amount of information available, in the form of memoranda, depositions, PowerPoint summaries of military briefings and plans, and transcripts of congressional hearings and press conferences. At the end of one interview, for example, one U.S. official handed me a CD-ROM with his entire work output related to Iraq, including most of his internal briefings and all the memos he had sent to the CPA. I estimate that in the course of writing this book I have read more than thirty-seven thousand pages of such official documents.

This book also draws frequently on the work of my colleagues in journalism. Because of my direct involvement I have used *Washington Post* stories most often to add to my own experience. But I also have referred to articles that appeared in dozens of other publications, most notably the *New York Times,* the *Los Angeles Times,* and *USA Today,* as well as the work of journalists in the Knight-Ridder chain.

EPIGRAPH

  vii "Know your enemy, know yourself": The quotation from Sun Tzu appears in Jeffrey Race, *War Comes to Long An: Revolutionary Conflict in a Vietnamese Province* (University of California, 1972).

CHAPTER 1: A BAD ENDING

In addition to interviews and e-mail exchanges, this chapter relies heavily on the published memoirs of American leaders of the 1991 Gulf War. These include George H. W. Bush and Brent Scowcroft, *A World Transformed* (Knopf, 1998); Colin Powell, *My American Journey* (Random House, 1995); and H. Norman Schwarzkopf, *It Doesn't Take a Hero* (Bantam, 1992). For this chapter and throughout the book I found very helpful the transcriptions of postwar interviews with Cheney and Schwarzkopf available on the Web site of *Frontline,* the Public Broadcasting System's extraordinary documentary series. In addition, the Pentagon's "Final Report to Congress: Conduct of the Persian Gulf War" (Defense Department, 1992) remains a useful reference document. For outside views of the end of the 1991 war I consulted Michael Gordon and Bernard Trainor, *The Generals' War* (Little, Brown, 1995) and Rick Atkinson, *Crusade* (Houghton Mifflin, 1993).

  6 "I was not an enthusiast": Cheney's comment is from a *Frontline* transcript.

  7 "With hindsight it does seem like a mistake": Wolfowitz's comment appeared in an essay in *National Interest* magazine (spring 1993). My discussion of the unhappiness of the Shiites with the end of the1991war was influenced by Yitzhak Nakash, *The Shi'is of Iraq* (Princeton, 2003). For the beginnings of the subsequent U.S. containment of Iraq I also have used Kenneth Pollack's *The Threatening Storm* (Random House, 2002).

  7 "More than any of the other dramatis personae": This is from Andrew Bacevich, "Trigger Man," *American Conservative* (June 6, 2005). For the account of Operation Provide Comfort I began with the official history by Gordon Rudd, *Humanitarian Intervention: Assisting the Iraqi Kurds in Operation Provide Comfort, 1991* (Department of the Army, 2004).

  9 "We moved our ground and air forces": This quotation from Abizaid about his approach is from the March 1993 issue of the Army's *Military Review.*

CHAPTER 2: CONTAINMENT AND ITS DISCONTENTS

In addition to Pollack's *Threatening Storm,* this chapter relies heavily on a variety of reports, summaries, and chronologies produced by analysts at Congressional Research Service, most notably Alfred Prados, "Iraq: Former and Recent Military Confrontations with the United States" (Library of Congress, 2002) and Christopher Blanchard, "Al Qaeda: Statements and Evolving Ideology" (Library of Congress, 2005). My discussion of al Qaeda's fatwas was influenced by Daniel Benjamin and Steven Simon, *The Age of Sacred Terror* (Random House, 2002).

15 **"Given that no-fly zones":** The quotation by Cmdr. Huber is from his essay, "Thou Shalt Not Fly," which appeared in the August 1999 issue of *Proceedings of the Naval Institute.*

17 **"demonstrating that your friends will be protected":** Wolfowitz's assertion is in his "Remembering the Future," *National Interest* (spring 2000).

22 **"a weakened, fragmented, chaotic Iraq":** This Zinni comment is from his meeting with the Defense Writers Group on October 21, 1998.

23 **"Toppling Saddam is the only outcome":** Wolfowitz's criticism of that comment appeared in the December 7, 1998 issue of the *New Republic.*

24 **"for the United States to try moving from containment":** The criticism of Wolfowitz appeared in Daniel Byman, Kenneth Pollack, and Gideon Rose, "The Rollback Fantasy," in the January–February 1999 issue of *Foreign Affairs.*

24 **"the Iraqi army surrendered the northern third":** His letter of response, cowritten with former Rep. Stephen Solarz, was carried in the March–April 1999 issue of that magazine. Former Treasury Secretary Paul O'Neill's views are represented in Ron Suskind's *The Price of Loyalty* (Simon & Schuster, 2004).

28 **"Powell's influence":** Keller's article, "The World According to Powell," appeared in the *New York Times Magazine,* November 25, 2001.

28 **"far from transforming containment":** The quote from Lawrence Kaplan and William Kristol is from their book, *The War Over Iraq* (Encounter, 2003).

CHAPTER 3: THIS CHANGES EVERYTHING

The account of Bush administration deliberations in the days after the 9/11 attacks relies on both *The 9/11 Commission Report: Final Report of the National Commission on Terrorist Attacks upon the United States* (W. W. Norton, 2004; no copyright) and on Bob Woodward's extremely useful *Plan of Attack* (Simon & Schuster, 2004).

CHAPTER 4: THE WAR OF WORDS

Here again the transcripts of interviews posted on *Frontline*'s Web site were very helpful—in this case, those with Greg Thielmann, Richard Perle, and Ahmed Chalabi.

46 **"the administration started speaking about Iraq":** This Thielmann quotation is from his *Frontline* interview. The biographical material on Zinni given here is based mainly on interviews with him, but also reflects the account in Dana Priest's *The Mission* (W. W. Norton, 2003).

53 **"Within a very short period of time":** Richard Perle, in *Frontline* interview.

56 **"As they embellished ":** The Beers quote is from a Cable News Network (CNN) documentary on Iraqi intelligence issues, *Dead Wrong,* that aired in August 2005.

56 **"He told us, we told Judy Miller":** Chalabi's quote is from a *Frontline* transcript, as are his other comments in this section.

57 **"It was true that Chalabi":** Wolfowitz's views on Chalabi are discussed at some length in the Downing Street Memos, internal British government documents from the spring and summer of 2002 that were leaked to the media in 2005. The British discussions also are reflected in Christopher Meyer, *DC Confidential* (Weidenfeld & Nicholson, 2005), the weak memoirs of a former British ambassador to the United States. The data on U.S. payments to Chalabi's organization is from a Congressional Research Service study by Kenneth Katzman, "Iraq: U.S. Regime Change Efforts and Post-Saddam Governance" (Library of Congress, 2004).

CHAPTER 5: THE RUN-UP

The quotes from Skelton are from a series of interviews with him.

60 **"Well, Congressman, we really don't need your vote":** A White House spokesman said that Keniry's recollection of the exchange was somewhat different, and that he recalled simply telling Skelton that the Iraq resolution would pass with a large bipartisan majority.

64 **"We have got to go in and win":** The exchange between Michael O'Hanlon and Richard Perle is from the American Enterprise Institute's transcript of its conference titled "The Day After: Planning for a Post-Saddam Iraq" that was held on October 3, 2002. The quotations from Patrick Clawson, Alina Romanowski, and Amatzia Baram are from the Washington Institute for Near East Policy's transcript of its conference, "Bush Administration Middle East Policy," held October 4–6, 2002. The Army War College's August 2002 seminar on Afghanistan was summarized in internal documents and also is reflected in part in a monograph by Conrad Crane and Andrew Terrill titled "Reconstructing Iraq: Insights, Challenges and Missions for Military Forces in a Post-Conflict Scenario," published by the U.S. Army War College's Strategic Studies Institute in February 2003. The account of the workshop meeting, "Iraq: Looking Beyond Saddam's Role," held by the Institute for National Strategic Studies at the National Defense University on November 20–21, 2002, is based largely on an internal report on the meeting.

75 **"a key point in the planning":** The material from Maj. Gen. James Thurman and Lt. Gen. David McKiernan is from interviews conducted by Army historians and held on file at the Army's Center of Military History, Ft. McNair, Washington, D.C.

78 **"the dumbest fucking guy on the planet":** Franks's description of Feith appears in both his autobiography, *American Soldier* (HarperCollins, 2004) and Woodward's *Plan of Attack.*

78 **"may be the most planned operation":** The quotation from Lt. Col. James Scudieri is from his paper titled "Iraq 2003–04 and Mesopotamia 1914–18: A Comparative Analysis in Ends and Means," published by the Army War College's Center for Strategic Leadership in August 2004.

78 **"Overall, this approach worked poorly":** The quotation from the Rand Corporation report is from a study that hasn't been released but was faxed by the office of James Thomson, Rand's president and chief executive officer, to the office of Defense

Secretary Rumsfeld on February 8, 2005. My discussion of Phase IV planning at Central Command and subordinate commands is based in part on my study of several classified U.S. military PowerPoint briefings, including "Phase IV Reconstruction," "CFLCC Stability Operations," and "Annex G to CFLCC OPLAN COBRA II."

CHAPTER 6: THE SILENCE OF THE LAMBS

The editorial reviews of Powell's UN speech were collected by *Editor & Publisher* magazine.

98 **"Given that the requisite additional troops":** This comment from Bacevich is from the same article quoted in Chapter 1. The attendees at the February 21–22, 2003, rock drill meeting at the National Defense University are listed in an internal ORHA document titled "Interagency Reconstruction Planning Conference." The account of that conference is based in part on a summary written by the political adviser to the commander of the Army's V Corps. Garner's briefings to Rumsfeld are contained in two February 2003 PowerPoint briefings, titled "Macroview of Issues: Funding, Stability Forces, Iraqi Security Forces, UN Resolutions" and "Reshaping the Iraqi Military," as well as a one-page Talking Points memo prepared by Garner's staff.

103 **"What the hell":** Powell's angry exchange with Rumsfeld over expelling State Department officials from Garner's staff is described in Woodward's *Plan of Attack*. The discussion in the March 7, 2003, secure video teleconference is reported in a formal internal ORHA summary titled "Notes from the Phase IV SVTC." The full title of the ORHA document quoted on the postwar challenge is "Initial Working Draft/A Unified Mission Plan for Post Hostilities Iraq," dated April 21, 2003. The paper by Maj. Isaiah Wilson presented to the Peace Studies Program at Cornell University on October 14, 2004, is titled "Thinking Beyond War: Civil-Military Operational Planning in Northern Iraq." The Marine Corps history is *Basrah, Baghdad, and Beyond: The U.S. Marine Corps in the Second Iraq War* (Naval Institute Press, 2005) by retired Marine Col. Nicholas Reynolds. The Army War College review of the assumptions of the war plan is summarized in a June 2003 PowerPoint briefing titled "The Stabilization and Reconstruction of Iraq: Initial Strategic Observations." The Rand Corporation report is the one cited in the previous chapter.

CHAPTER 7: WINNING A BATTLE

This chapter relies throughout on the Army's official history of the spring 2003 invasion, *On Point* (Combat Studies Institute Press, U.S. Army, Fort Leavenworth, Kansas, 2004) by retired Army Col. Gregory Fontenot, Lt. Col. E. J. Degen, and Lt. Col. David Tohn. This section also was informed by a briefing by the Army War College's Conrad Crane titled "Too Much Phase IV Planning: Coordinating Theater Plans for Iraq," delivered at a conference cosponsored by the War College and Johns Hopkins University's School of Advanced International Studies in November 2005. My discussion of the flaws of the war plan also was influenced by two very different early assessments of the war and the occupation: Thomas Donnelly, *Operation Iraqi Freedom: A Strategic Assessment* (AEI Press, 2004) and Jeffrey Record, *Dark Victory: America's Second War Against Iraq* (Naval Institute Press, 2004). In some ways this chapter is a dialogue with those two thoughtful analyses. The quotation from the war plan is from a document titled "Coalition Forces Land Component Command (CFLCC) OPLAN COBRA II," dated January 13, 2003.

116 **"If the intent of operations":** The quotations from retired British Maj. Gen. Bailey are from his monograph "'Over By Christmas': Campaigning, Delusions and Force Requirements," published by the Institute of Land Warfare at the Association of the United States Army in September 2005.

122 **"You know, there was probably a moment":** Col. Benson's comments are in a transcript contained in an Army study edited by Lt. Col. Brian De Toy, *Turning Victory into Success: Military Operations After the Campaign* (Combat Studies Institute Press, U.S. Army, Fort Leavenworth, Kansas, no date), which also contains a reproduction of "Phase IV—Troop to Task Analysis," the study done by the U.S. Army in Iraq in the late spring of 2003 that concluded that about 250,000 to 300,000 troops were needed to carry out the postwar mission.

122 **"It's turning out right now":** The Thurman and McKiernan comments are from the Army oral histories cited in Chapter 5.

124 **"These are Iraqi citizens who want to fight for a free Iraq":** Pace's comment was made on ABC's *This Week* (April 6, 2003). The history by the Special Operations Command was excerpted in an article by A. Dwayne Aaron and Cherilyn Walley titled "ODA 542: Working with the Free Iraqi Fighters" that was carried in the winter 2005 issue of their official publication, *Veritas: Journal of Special Operations History.*

124 **"a waste of time and energy for us":** This and subsequent comments by DeLong are from his memoir, *Inside Centcom: The Unvarnished Truth about the Wars in Afghanistan and Iraq* (Regnery, 2004).

125 **"They were hiding":** The series of quotations is from an article by the *Washington Post*'s William Branigin, "A Brief, Bitter War for Iraq's Military Officers" (April 27, 2003). The account of the captured Iraqi general who had no idea that U.S. troops were near the capital is in "Third Infantry Division (Mechanized) After Action Report," an extremely thorough document. The observation about Baghdad Bob believing what he said is from the official Army interview with Col. Boltz, which like the others is on file at the Army's Center of Military History.

131 **"an intense interest in the reform of tactics":** Romjue's discussion of the post-Vietnam changes in Army thinking is found in his *From Active Defense to AirLand Battle: The Development of Army Doctrine, 1973–1982* (U.S. Army Training and Doctrine Command, Fort Monroe, Virginia, 1984).

133 **"Its underlying concepts":** Echeverria's analysis is *Toward an American Way of War* (Strategic Studies Institute, Army War College, March 2004).

134 **"as good as it got":** The Atkinson comment about the high point is from his memoir, *In the Company of Soldiers* (Henry Holt, 2004).

136 **"A finite supply of goodwill":** Lt. Fick's observation is from his memoir, *One Bullet Away* (Houghton Mifflin, 2005).

136 **"Some senior officials":** Fred Ikle's criticisms of the Bush administration's handling of the early days of the occupation are contained in the preface to the second revised edition of *Every War Must End* (Columbia, 2005).

138 **"Continued armed opposition to coalition forces":** The Central Command assessment that there wouldn't be an insurgency is contained in a PowerPoint briefing titled "Phase IV 'Rule of Law'/Logical Line of Operation/Operational Planning Team" (March 2003).

138 **"a cruel, hard, desolate land":** The comment by Field Marshal Sir William Slim about the hardness of Iraq is from his memoir, *Unofficial History* (Corgi, 1970).

139 **"We came in to show presence":** Bray is quoted in the Human Rights Watch report on the events of April 2003 in Fallujah, titled "Violent Response: The U.S. Army in al-Falluja" (June 2003).

144 **"We slowly drove past 4th Infantry":** Williams's recollection is in her memoir *Love My Rifle More Than You* (W. W. Norton, 2005).

145 **"more than a million metric tons":** Christopher Hileman's estimate of the amount of munitions in Iraq was in a letter published in the May 2005 issue of *Proceedings* magazine.

146 **"In Iraq, there was not only a failure to plan":** The quotation from Schlesinger and Brown is from their "Final Report of the Independent Panel to Review DoD Detention Operations" (August 2004).

147 **"the minimalist force structure":** Some of Mines's comments about the thinness of the U.S. military on the ground are in "On Fighting a 16-Division War With a 10-Division Force," posted on the Web site of the Foreign Policy Research Institute on March 8, 2005.

CHAPTER 8: HOW TO CREATE AN INSURGENCY (I)

This chapter was influenced by retired Marine Col. Thomas X. Hammes, *The Sling and the Stone: On War in the 21st Century* (Zenith, 2004), and by several unpublished essays by Maj. Isaiah Wilson.

150 **"3RD ID transitioned into Phase IV SASO":** The 3rd ID report is the same one cited in Chapter 7. Brig. Gen. Fastabend's anecdote about the general who watched sofas go by in Baghdad is from the transcript of a conference held at the American Enterprise Institute, "The Future of the United States Army," April 11, 2005. Maj. Gavrilis's essay, "The Mayor of Ar Rutbah: A Special Forces Account of Post-Conflict Iraq," was provided directly to me by the author; a slightly different version was later published in the November–December 2005 issue of *Foreign Policy* magazine.

154 **"The problem with Garner":** Chalabi's comments are from the transcript of his interview with *Frontline*, as are Bremer's comments later in this chapter beginning, "I found a city that was on fire." The pamphlet on Gen. Shinseki's career is by Richard Halloran, "My Name Is Shinseki and I Am a Soldier" (Hawaii Army Museum Society, 2004). The comments by David Nummy and Lloyd Sammons in this chapter are from interviews conducted by the United States Institute of

Peace as part of its oral history project, and are available on the institute's Web site. MPRI's plan for the Iraqi military is described in an undated company document titled "MPRI Phase II Execution Plan: Iraqi Armed Forces Reconstruction Support Program."

161 **"it would have gone easier for us"**: Gen. Dempsey's assessment of de-Baathification was made at a seminar at the annual meeting of the Association of the U.S. Army in October 2004.

161 **"Cannot immediately demobilize"**: Garner's plans for the preservation of the Iraqi military are contained in a briefing slide titled "Iraqi Security Forces: Post-War Use of Regular Army," part of a PowerPoint briefing prepared by his office titled "Presentation for the National Security Advisor," and dated February 19, 2003. Those plans also are discussed in a memorandum for record, which was written the same day after that meeting, that summarizes the views of meeting participants.

163 **"We expected to be able to recall"**: Col. Benson's discussion of the impact of the dissolution of the Iraqi military is in *Turning Victory into Success,* cited in the previous chapter, as is the comment from Maj. Madison later in this chapter, "This is going to be a problem." The joint report by the inspectors general of the Defense and State Departments on the training of Iraqi police apparently has no formal title, and was released in July 2005.

166 **"Taking revenge is a Neanderthal strategy"**: Ikle's criticism is in his book, *Every War Must End,* that is cited in Chapter 7.

166 **If America was a liberator:** Maj. Varhola's account of the stormy meeting between sheikhs and Amb. Horan is, in part, in his essay "American Challenges in Post-Conflict Iraq," which was posted by the Foreign Policy Research Institute on its Web site on May 27, 2004.

168 **"There is absolutely no doubt"**: Pace's assertion was made at a special briefing for the Arab and Muslim press corps at the State Department's Foreign Press Center, April 11, 2003.

169 **"The fact that pre-war planning assumptions"**: Rathmell's discussion of the inability of the CPA and its overseers in Washington to adjust when assumptions were proven wrong is in his article "Planning Post-Conflict Reconstruction in Iraq: What Can We Learn?" which appeared in 2005 in *International Affairs* magazine (vol. 81, no. 5).

175 **"pretty introverted"**: Lt. Gen. Metz's description of Lt. Gen. Sanchez is in a legal interview related to the Abu Ghraib case given by video teleconference to military lawyers in Mannheim, Germany, on August 25, 2004.

177 **"despicable"**: This comment and others made by Iraqis in this section were made to my *Washington Post* colleague Anthony Shadid, with whom I collaborated on an article headlined A TALE OF TWO BAGHDADS that appeared in the *Post* on June 1, 2003.

179 **"No explicit, unambiguous and authoritative statement"**: The Congressional Research Service study of the legal status of the CPA by Elaine Halchin is called *The Coalition Provisional Authority (CPA): Origin, Characteristics and Institutional Authorities* (2005).

180 **"It was quite a spat":** The account of the stormy meeting of generals with senior CPA officials on November 4, 2003, is based on extensive notes taken by one CPA participant, as well as on interviews with some of the officers and other CPA officials who attended.

181 **"bowing out of the political process":** Rumsfeld's comment is in L. Paul Bremer III, *My Year in Iraq* (Simon & Schuster, 2006).

185 **"The dog got louder":** The material on the death of Lt. Nott is from a series of internal 4th Infantry Division documents titled "Informal Investigation of Incident on 22 Jul 03."

CHAPTER 9: HOW TO CREATE AN INSURGENCY (II)

189 **"From the beginning of July":** This and subsequent quotations from British Lt. Gen. Haldane are from his memoir, *The Insurrection in Mesopotamia, 1920* (William Blackwood, 1922).

192 **"then the presence of troops ... becomes counterproductive":** The quotation from Holshek is from his essay, "Integrated Civil-Military and Information Operations," as prepared for delivery at George Mason University, August 25, 2004.

193 **"did not understand the targeting process":** This and subsequent quotations are from the report by the Center for Army Lessons Learned titled "Operation Outreach" that was posted on its Web site in October 2003, but unfortunately that Web site is no longer available to the public.

194 **"Actionable intelligence is the key":** Gen. Abizaid's recollection of recognizing the need for intelligence is from a legal interview conducted by Army lawyers in Mannheim, Germany, via video teleconference on August 26, 2004.

194 **"Everybody likes to fight the war":** The comment by Bernard Fall was made in a lecture, "The Theory and Practice of Insurgency and Counterinsurgency," delivered at the Naval War College on December 10, 1964.

195 **"very few men occupy themselves":** The quotation from Saxe is as carried in Lucien Poirier, ed., *The Art of War in World History* (University of California, 1994).

195 **"grabbing whole villages":** The official finding that large sweep operations clogged the U.S. military interrogation system in Iraq is in an undated 2004 memorandum for the chief of the Army inspector general's inspections division titled "4th Infantry Division Detainee Operations Assessment Trip Report (CONUS Team)," which summarizes interviews and discussions with sixty-seven members of the 4th ID conducted between April 5 and April 8, 2004.

197 **"In three towns that summer":** Shadid's memory of the summer of 2003 is in *Night Draws Near* (Henry Holt, 2005), his marvelous account of the occupation as seen by Iraqis.

197 **"The gloves are coming off":** Capt. Ponce's e-mail and the responses to it were attached to a reply to the formal reprimand of another soldier issued by Lt. Col. Conrad Christman, the commander of the 104th Military Intelligence Battalion, on November 6, 2003. Col. Boltz didn't respond to e-mails seeking his views on the "gloves" e-mail exchange.

198 **"They're prisoners, Janis":** The quotations from Karpinski in this chapter are mainly from my interview with her, but also from a sworn statement given by her to Maj. Gen. Antonio Taguba in Kuwait on February 15, 2004, and from her interview with *Frontline*, as transcribed on its Web site.

199 **"to rapidly exploit internees":** Gen. Miller's comment is in his once-classified report titled "Assessment of DoD Counterterrorism and Detention Operations in Iraq," which is undated but which discusses his work in Iraq from August 31 to September 9, 2003. Miller's credibility on how he recommended that detainees be handled was called into question later by an official Army investigation of FBI allegations of detainee abuse at Guantánamo, which pointedly reported that Miller's testimony was inconsistent with an earlier letter he had sent to his commander. The FBI's criticism is mentioned in the Schmidt-Furlow report, formally titled "Army Regulation 15-6: Final Report/Investigation into FBI Allegations of Detainee Abuse at Guantanamo Bay, Cuba, Detention Facility," as amended June 9, 2005.

200 **"It was 120 degrees out":** Lt. O'Hern discussed his depression after his platoon suffered casualties in a posting on www.companycommand.com on September 1, 2003.

202 **"When I got to Washington":** The Bremer statement is from the interview posted on *Frontline*'s Web site.

CHAPTER 10: THE CPA: "CAN'T PRODUCE ANYTHING"
In writing this chapter I relied heavily on more than thirty oral histories posted on the Web site of the U.S. Institute of Peace. The quotations in this chapter from Kraham, Raphel, Sammons, Coyne, Bachar, Dehgan, and Crandall are from that valuable collection.

203 **"my time as an ice cream truck driver":** This quotation appeared in Naomi Klein, "Baghdad Year Zero," *Harper's* (September 2004).

204 **"The tour length for most civilians":** This comment by Synnott is in his article "State-Building in Southern Iraq," *Survival* (summer 2005).

207 **"Time off for me":** Diamond's recollection is from his *Squandered Victory: The American Occupation and the Bungled Effort to Bring Democracy to Iraq* (Times Books, 2005).

209 **"What this means is that for the first nine months":** Krohn's memory of his time with the CPA was in his article "The Role of Propaganda in Fighting Terrorism," *Army* (December 2004). The finding of a problematic relationship between the CPA and the Army is also discussed in "Operation Iraqi Freedom: Strategic Assessment," a briefing by the War College's Strategic Studies Institute (November 2004).

210 **"The military was there to win the conflict":** This and subsequent quotations are from Rear Adm. Oliver's unpublished memoir titled "Restarting the Economy in Iraq" (November 2003).

210 **"The 101st and 4th ID are beginning to get frustrated":** This is from the "ORHA Daily Situation Report, 18 June 03."

212 **"The common perception throughout the theater":** The analysis by the Center for Army Lessons Learned of the troubled relationship between the CPA and the military, and of the lack of adequate planning, is in the center's report titled "Operation

Iraqi Freedom: Information Operations, Civil Military Operations, Engineer, Combat Service Support" (Center for Army Lessons Learned, Fort Leavenworth, Kansas, May 2004). The polling data is from a CPA document titled "Opinion in Selected Iraqi Cities, November–December 2003."

CHAPTER 11: GETTING TOUGH

This chapter was influenced by Bruce Hoffman's study "Insurgency and Counterinsurgency in Iraq" (Rand, June 2004).

215 **"As time went on, it became very":** The Sanchez and Abizaid quotations are mainly from their unreleased legal interviews, with Army lawyers, relating to Abu Ghraib. The discussion in this chapter of the roadside bombs, or IEDs, relies heavily on several official studies: "Improvised Explosive Devices in Iraq," an undated briefing by the Army's National Ground Intelligence Center; "Improvised Explosive Devices in Operation Iraqi Freedom" (November 1, 2003) by William Schneck of the Army's Research, Development and Engineering Command; and an untitled briefing by the CPA's Force Protection Working Group, dated January 16, 2004. Additional data came from Robert Bunker and John Sullivan, "Suicide Bombings in Operation Iraqi Freedom," *Military Review,* January–February 2005, and from Ian F. W. Beckett, *Insurgency in Iraq: A Historical Perspective* (Strategic Studies Institute, Army War College, January 2005).

218 **The typical IED cell:** This discussion of IED cells relies on an account, by Greg Grant, of the Army's findings that appeared in the *Army Times* edition of August 15, 2005, under the headline ANATOMY OF AN IED.

219 **"IEDs are my number one threat":** Abizaid's statement in a memo to the Joint Staff was quoted in Col. Eric Litaker, "Efforts to Counter the IED Threat," *Marine Corps Gazette* (January 2005).

220 **"A guy is lying on the seat":** Spec. James King's moving essay on being bombed appeared in the January 3, 2005, edition of *Army Times.*

220 **"When I got there I was taken aback":** Maj. Robinson was quoted in an article by Tom Philpott that appeared in the December 4, 2005, edition of *Stars & Stripes.*

221 **"Coalition forces are forced to interact":** The article by Chiarelli and Maj. Patrick Michaelis, "The Requirement for Full-Spectrum Operations," appeared in *Military Review* (July–August 2005). The Center for Army Lessons Learned study quoted twice in this chapter is the same one cited in the previous chapter.

223 **"As commanders at all levels sought operational intelligence":** The report by Lt. Gen. Jones is titled "AR 15-6 Investigation of the Abu Ghraib Prison and 205th Military Intelligence Brigade,"an internal Army investigation conducted in 2004.

226 **"The military leadership . . . did not do a good job":** The Rathmell observation about this failure is from the article cited in Chapter 8.

226 **"Currently, the U.S. military does not have a viable counterinsurgency doctrine":** Maj. Peterson's monograph, done at the Army's School of Advanced Military Studies, was titled "The French Experience in Algeria, 1954–1962: Blueprint for U.S. Operations in Iraq" (May 2004).

227 **"The struggle against the guerrilla":** This Trinquier quotation is from his *Modern Warfare: A French View of Counterinsurgency,* first published in France in 1961, published in Great Britain in 1964 by Pall Mall, and reprinted by the Combat Studies Institute at Fort Leavenworth, Kansas, in 1985.

228 **"The eerie silence and absence":** The quotations from Maj. Wilson are mainly from the study quoted in Chapter 6. Also, the discussion of the 101st Airborne's operations in this chapter was especially influenced by Wilson's unpublished 2004 essay titled "What Kind of War?" while the discussion of the Iraqi sense of honor in this chapter reflects the conclusions of his unpublished essay "Tribal Engagement in Northern Iraq." Data on the 101st also came from a PowerPoint briefing titled "101st Abn Div (AASLT) AO NORTH (As of: 25 January 2004)."

229 **"a combination of being the president and the pope":** This Petraeus comment was quoted by the *Washington Post*'s Scott Wilson in "A Mix of 'President . . . and Pope'; Army General Given Reins to Remake Mosul" (May 16, 2003). Odierno's comments in this chapter are mainly from an interview, but as noted some are from a seminar at the October 2004 annual meeting of the Association of the U.S. Army. Also, as noted, two quotations are from the interview with him in the March–June 2004 issue of the Army's official *Field Artillery* magazine.

235 **"This is the way an administration caught":** Alistair Horne's observation is from his classic *A Savage War of Peace* (History Book Club edition, 2002).

235 **"Arresting authorities entered houses":** The Red Cross criticism of U.S. raids is in "Report of the International Committee of the Red Cross (ICRC) on the Treatment by the Coalition Forces of Prisoners of War and Other Protected Persons by the Geneva Conventions in Iraq During Arrest, Internment and Interrogation" (February 2004).

236 **"This does two things":** The Hicks & Associates conclusion that indiscriminate raids demonstrated to Iraqis the ignorance of U.S. forces is in a briefing titled "Micro-Foundations of Insurgent Violence: Implications for Iraq," by Mark Smith, Janine Davidson, and Peter Brooks (October 5, 2005). The Schlesinger report is the one cited in Chapter 7. The quotations from Bremer and Chalabi are from the interview transcripts posted on *Frontline*'s Web site. Odierno's reluctance to have detainees released is discussed in the report by Army Maj. Gen. George Fay, "AR 15-6 Investigation of the Abu Ghraib Detention Facility and 205th Military Intelligence Brigade" (undated), as are the quotations later in this chapter about Fay's conclusion that detainees swamped the intelligence system. Fast's statement about the 4th ID not wanting detainees to be released also is in this report. The estimate of ten thousand detainees being taken by the 4th ID is mentioned, among other places, in a semiofficial history of the division's operations during its first tour in Iraq by Robert Babcock, *Operation Iraqi Freedom I: A Year in the Sunni Triangle, the History of the 4th Infantry Division and Task Force Ironhorse in Iraq, April 2003 to April 2004* (St. John's Press, 2005).

240 **other countries:** The two Sanchez memoranda on permissible interrogation techniques are "CJTF-7 Interrogation and Counter-Resistance Policy," dated September 14, 2003, and the superceding document with the same title dated October 12, 2003.

240 **"They shot at us for about an hour":** The *Stars & Stripes* article quoting Iraqi police about being shot by U.S. troops near Fallujah was by Terry Boyd, and was published on September 13, 2003.

240 **"It was the deadliest friendly-fire incident":** Bing West's book *No True Glory: A Frontline Account of the Battle for Fallujah* (Bantam, 2005).

244 **"Then all hell broke loose":** Wallen was quoted in an article by the *Washington Post's* Vernon Loeb, "Combat Heroine: Teresa Broadwell Found Herself in the Army—Under Fire, in Iraq," that ran on November 23, 2003.

249 **"We think the insurgency is waning":** Hertling was quoted by Ron Jensen in "Iraqi Insurgency Is Waning, General Says," *Stars & Stripes* (November 9, 2003).

253 **"the means toward the strategic goal":** This T. E. Lawrence quotation is from his essay "The Evolution of a Revolt," which appeared in the October 1920 edition of the British *Army Quarterly and Defence Journal.* This entire book was influenced by Lawrence's *Seven Pillars of Wisdom* (Dell, 1962). The David Brooks column on Bremer's surprising the White House appeared in the *New York Times* edition of July 3, 2004.

254 **"declared it unacceptable":** Greenstock's article appeared in the *Economist* issue of May 8, 2004.

255 **"The decision on 15 November":** This Synnott comment is from his article cited in the previous chapter. Costello's observation is from the transcript of his interview posted on the USIP Web site. The changes in convoys are summarized in "Initial Impressions Report: Operations in Mosul, Iraq" (Center for Army Lessons Learned, December 21, 2004). The data on the stress in transportation units is from "Operation Iraqi Freedom (OIF-II) Mental Health Advisory Team Report (MHAT-II), Chartered By: The U.S. Army Surgeon General" (January 20, 2005).

258 **"Seems like I pick up a lot of people's pieces":** The quotations from Lt. Col. Wood and Sgt. Maj. Coston appeared in an article by Anna Badkhen in the *San Francisco Chronicle* (October 14, 2005).

259 **"The problem of overpopulation at Abu Ghraib":** This and other quotations from Herrington are from his report to Brig. Gen. Fast titled "Report of CI/HUMINT Evaluation Visit" (December 12, 2003). Herrington's Vietnam memoir has appeared under two titles—originally as *Silence Was a Weapon: The Vietnam War in the Villages,* and more recently as *Stalking the Vietcong* (Ballantine, 1982). Krepinevich's classic book, *The Army and Vietnam,* was published by Johns Hopkins in 1986.

265 **"the best of them all":** The editions of Bernard Fall's *Street Without Joy* used here were published by Schocken Books in 1972 and by Stackpole Books in 1994. Gwynn's *Imperial Policing* was published by Macmillan in 1939.

265 **"Clearly, more than any other kind of warfare":** Galula's essential little book, *Counterinsurgency Warfare: Theory and Practice,* was published by Praeger in 1964, and is also available through Hailer Publishing, among other outlets.

267 **"Scholars are virtually unanimous":** This comment by Maj. Moten is from a memorandum titled "Suggested Historical Reading List for Commanders and Staffs Supporting OIF" (November 19, 2004).

CHAPTER 12: THE DESCENT INTO ABUSE

This chapter relies foremost on several thousand pages of Army investigatory documents obtained under the Freedom of Information Act by the American Civil Liberties Union (ACLU) and posted on its Web site. The part of this chapter about Abu Ghraib draws frequently from several Army reports, most notably Maj. Gen. Taguba's undated "Article 15-6 Investigation of the 800th Military Police Brigade."

270 **"the result of intentional acts":** This conclusion in the investigation of the broken jaw incident in the 101st is contained in a document titled "Report of Proceedings by Investigating Officer" dated December 19, 2003. Simon's view that military torture diminishes the honor of the nation is quoted in Alistair Horne's *Savage War of Peace*.

272 **"told my sergeant that he didn't want them":** The incident in the 2nd Armored Cavalry Regiment about an officer telling a sergeant to take detainees out back and beat them is related in a series of sworn statements taken by the Army in August 2003 and available on the ACLU Web site.

273 **"I was standing at the front":** The discussion of the two mock executions by soldiers in the 1st Armored Division are contained in a series of documents beginning with a memorandum titled "Allegations of 'Mock Executions'" that contains many sworn statements from June 2003, and ending with a memorandum titled "Recommendation on Resignation for the Good of the Service" dated October 1, 2003.

274 **"I have to be very careful":** The series of articles by Nir Rosen was titled "Every Time the Wind Blows," and appeared in *Asia Times Online*, October 24 through October 30, 2003.

275 **"I am devastated":** The responses to Rosen from Lt. Col. Reilly and Sgt. 1st Class Qualls were forwarded to me by Rosen.

276 **"the robberies occurred on nearly every TCP":** The report of an Army investigation of robberies by a platoon in the 3rd Armored Cavalry Regiment and statements made in the course of that investigation are in a document titled "CID Report of Investigation—Final C—0011-04-CID 679-83487-5N2E/5X2/5X4" and dated August 30, 2004.

276 **"He thought Ar Rutbah":** The initial investigation report on the 3rd ACR's Capt. Martin was summarized in a memorandum titled "Investigations of the Allegations of Misconduct" (July 21, 2003), with sworn statements attached.

277 **"He had what's referred to as 'facial suffusion'":** The testimony of Maj. Smith, the military forensic pathologist, is from the same transcript cited above.

278 **"The year that we were there":** The quotations from Col. Teeples are from the transcript of the Article 32 investigation—a military judicial procedure similar to a grand jury—conducted on December 2, 2004, at Fort Carson, Colorado, in the case of *United States v. CW2 Williams, SFC Sommer and SFC Loper*. Teeples at first agreed to be interviewed for this book, but then changed his mind. "I've decided not to interview with you," he wrote in an e-mail. "My concern is that the historical context of the actions of the 3d Armored Cavalry Regiment may be turned into your personal commentary."

278 **"Shit started to go bad":** The Human Rights Watch report on the torture of Iraqi detainees by members of the 82nd Airborne Division is titled "Leadership Failure" (September 2005).

279 **"Few of the raids and detentions":** The July 2003 complaint by a member of the 4th Infantry Division and related statements and documents are contained in "Commander's Report of Commander's Inquiry," dated September 12, 2003.

280 **"We're here for one reason":** The case of Lt. Col. West is summarized in a document titled "CID Report of Investigation—Final—0152-03-CID469-60212-5C1A/5C2/5T1" (February 6, 2004), to which exhibits and sworn statements are attached.

282 **"These acts could . . . bring extreme discredit":** The discussion of the overall command climate in the 4th Infantry Division and how that affected its interrogation procedures is in the documents attached to the response to the reprimand issued by Lt. Col. Christman and cited in Chapter 9. The name of the staff sergeant overseeing the interrogation section at the 4th ID's main detainee holding pen in Tikrit who was responding to the reprimand was blacked out from documents obtained by the ACLU under the Freedom of Information Act.

284 **"detainees arriving at the cage badly beaten":** The report of attacks on handcuffed detainees by soldiers in the 4th ID is from the investigatory report of the office of the Army inspector general of detainee operations in the 4th ID that was cited in Chapter 9. Facts on the disposition of cases stemming from the alleged drowning are in an Army document titled "Samarra Bridge Incident—4th Inf. Div. (Mech)" (July 15, 2004).

284 **"When Captain Paliwoda died":** This and subsequent quotations from Sassaman are from the court-martial transcript titled *United States v. Jack M. Saville, Lieutenant, U.S. Army* (Fort Carson, Colorado, October and December 2004).

287 **"I fired a controlled pair":** The Perkins case is summarized in the untitled findings of an Army investigation, and in attached sworn statements and exhibits, dated March 9, 2004.

291 **"I took it to another level":** Frederick recounted his version of events to Army investigators as a sworn statement during debriefing sessions from October 22 through November 3, 2004.

292 **"they handcuffed their hands together":** Statements by Adel Nakhla and by detainees are in the Taguba report, which also assesses the credibility of some of them.

295 **"I don't care if we're holding fifteen thousand innocent Iraqis":** Karpinski's account is mainly from an interview with her but also draws on her sworn statement to Maj. Gen. Taguba. Additional details about the situation at Abu Ghraib and the conduct of the Army investigation are in the sworn statement of Col. Thomas Pappas given on February 11, 2004, and in the sworn statement of Capt. Donald Reese given on January 18, 2004.

297 **"She felt herself a victim":** Col. Nelson's assessment of Karpinski is in an undated annex to the Taguba report titled "AR 15-6 Investigation: Allegations of Detainee Abuse at Abu Ghraib/Psychological Assessment."

297 **"often reminded his men that they were an army of liberty":** David Hackett Fischer's quotation from George Washington is in *Washington's Crossing* (Oxford, 2004).

CHAPTER 13: "THE ARMY OF THE EUPHRATES" TAKES STOCK

302 **"It would be better if our working assumption":** The quotation from Bailey is from the essay cited in Chapter 7.

302 **a world-class sprinter:** This paraphrases a comment by Krepinevich in his essay "The Thin Green Line," which was posted on the Web site of the Center for Strategic and Budgetary Assessments on August 14, 2004.

302 **"We had to learn the hard way":** Morgan's comments are both from there and from an essay he wrote titled "Going to Fight in Iraq? Here's How!" which circulated by e-mail and was later printed in somewhat different form in *Army* magazine (April 2004).

303 **"There was too much crap":** The observations by Wrann, Braeger, Titus, Murphy, Mason, McCormick, Evangelista, Williams, and Smith are from the Web site of www.companycommand.com, which unfortunately is no longer available to the public.

304 **"The enemy is clever":** The Marine Corps study is titled "Fort Irwin National Training Center Trip Report, 7–9 Nov 03."

304 **"When possible, travel in large convoys":** Estep's undated briefing was titled "Enemy Tactics, Techniques and Procedures (TTP) and Recommendations." This section also reflects the conclusions offered in "Tactical Convoy Handbook" (U.S. Army Transportation School, undated) and "Convoy Leader Training Handbook, Revision III" (Military Professional Resources Inc., Kuwait Observer Controller Team, Camp Doha, Kuwait, October 2003). Also influencing my discussion of the changes in the Army was a study by retired Army Lt. Col. Leonard Wong titled "Developing Adaptive Leaders: The Crucible Experience of Operation Iraqi Freedom" (Strategic Studies Institute, Army War College, July 2004).

306 **One survey by a professor at West Point:** This survey of e-mail usage by soldiers in Iraq was mentioned in an article by Irene Wielawski that appeared in the *New York Times* on March 15, 2005.

308 **"Of particular concern has been the conflation":** Record's monograph, "Bounding the Global War on Terrorism," was published by the Strategic Studies Institute at the Army War College in December 2003.

309 **"the majority of soldiers":** The survey of the Illinois National Guard troops was summarized in a memorandum by Brig. Gen. Fleming titled "Operations Order 05-01 (Operation Strength Readiness)" (January 29, 2005).

310 **"Mission/endstate uncertainty has seriously eroded morale":** PowerPoint briefing by Holshek, "In-Theater Mission Extension Transition Decision Briefing," September 8, 2003.

CHAPTER 14: THE MARINE CORPS FILES A DISSENT

The discussion of the Marine Corps perspective in this chapter is influenced by one of the classic U.S. military manuals, *Small Wars Manual: United States Marine Corps, 1940,* republished by Sunflower University Press in an undated edition.

312 **"will stand in contrast":** Mundy's op-ed appeared in the *New York Times* on December 30, 2003.

312 **"The insurgents should not be allowed":** Russell was quoted by Vernon Loeb in "U.S. Isolates Hussein's Birthplace; Razor-Wire Fence Helps Troops Keep Tabs on Residents in Pocket of Insurgency," *Washington Post* (November 17, 2003).

312 **"That will not be our method":** This comment by Conway appeared in an article by Michael Gordon that ran in the *New York Times* on December 12, 2003.

312 **"Our expectations were pretty high":** Toolan's comment is from *Frontline*'s transcript of its interview with him.

313 **"The first time you blow someone away":** This comment by Mattis appeared an article by veteran UPI military reporter Pamela Hess that ran on the UPI wire on August 4, 2004.

314 **"Religious leaders are normally going to be critical publicly":** This and subsequent quotations about the Marine plan on how to operate when returning to Iraq are from a document titled "Points from the SASO Conference, 1 MarDiv 19 Dec 03." (SASO stands for security and stability operations.)

CHAPTER 15: THE SURPRISE

321 **"It was also the low point":** The best source for U.S. troop levels is the Brookings Institution's "Iraq Index," which is on-line at www.brookings.edu/fp/saban/iraq/index.pdf and is updated regularly.

322 **"The insurgents grew more proficient":** This quotation from Hashim is from his article "Iraq's Chaos: Why the Insurgency Won't Go Away," *Boston Review* (October–November 2004).

322 **"American forces had killed":** Hashim, "Iraq: From Insurgency to Civil War?" *Current History* (January 2005).

323 **"I don't think we came in":** Chevallier is quoted in Dennis Steele, "Commanders in Iraq: Some Lessons Learned," *Army* magazine (June 2005).

323 **"The actionable intelligence improved":** The Sanchez quotation is from the legal interview cited in Chapters 8 and 11.

324 **As the troop contingent in Tall Afar:** This passage relies on an article titled "For U.S. Military, A Key Iraq Mission Is Averting Civil War," by Greg Jaffe, *Wall Street Journal* (October 14, 2005).

325 **"Over time Iraqis became disappointed":** The quotation from Dunford is from the interview posted on the USIP Web site, as are the later ones from Coyne, Sammons, and Bauer. The polling data cited in this chapter came from two surveys done for the CPA: "Public Opinion in Iraq," May 14–23, 2004, and "Public Opinion in Iraq/First Look at June 10–15 Poll."

326 **"Bremer and his most trusted CPA advisers":** Diamond's assessment of Bremer and his advisers is in his book, cited in Chapters 7 and 10. The memorandum by him quoted later in this chapter is also in his book, as is his comment on the outcome of the confrontation with Sadr.

329 **"almost wholly substandard":** Sepp's congressional testimony is from a statement submitted March 14, 2005, to the House Subcommittee on National Security, Emerging Threats and International Relations.

331 **That morning nearby shops were warned:** The Marine PowerPoint briefing on First Fallujah is titled "Operation Vigilant Resolve: The Battle for Fallujah" (undated).

333 **"without time to insert human intelligence":** Frank Hoffman's assessment of the two battles of Fallujah is in his "The Marines in Review," *Proceedings* (May 2005).

333 **"We felt like we had a method":** Conway made the comment to the *Washington Post*'s Chandrasekaran and other reporters.

334 **"The first enemy RPG":** Popaditch's recollections were gathered by a Marine public affairs representative.

335 **PFC Jeremy Church, a National Guardsman:** Spec. Church's account of the convoy ambush near the Baghdad airport on April 9, 2004, was given to Lisa Burgess of *Stars & Stripes* (June 14, 2005).

336 **Sadr's populist strain of Shiism:** The account here relies heavily on Shadid's *Night Draws Near.*

338 **"Back then, there was a fifty-fifty chance":** Steele's account of Sadr City in the spring of 2004 is from his "Back with the 3-15," *Army* (September 2005). The account of the Taji mutiny relies in part on information in Bing West's *No True Glory.*

338 **"The Mahdi army fought very courageously":** Capt. Moore's comments on the quality of insurgent fighters are in his article "Sadr City: The Armor Pure Assault in Urban Terrain," *Armor* (November–December 2004).

340 **"months behind schedule":** The GAO study is titled "Rebuilding Iraq: Resource, Security, Governance, Essential Services, and Oversight Issues" (June 2004).

341 **"No single mission":** The quotation from Cordesman is from his "Inexcusable Failure: Progress in Training the Iraqi Army and Security Forces as of Mid-July 2004" (Center for Strategic and International Studies, July 20, 2004).

341 **"Dual loyalty and HUMINT":** Cordesman, "Iraq's Evolving Insurgency" (CSIS, May 11, 2005). Bremer's comment about food rationing wasn't mentioned in his book but was made in his discussion of it and quoted in Richard Sisk, "Bremer Had Hunger Pain," New York *Daily News* (January 15, 2006). The list of nations belonging to the coalition is from the State Department's "Iraq Weekly Status" report of September 15, 2004. Michael Knight's observation is in the volume he edited, *Operation Iraqi Freedom and the New Iraq* (Washington Institute for Near East Policy, 2004).

350 **"By April 8, almost all stockpiles":** The quote from Maj. Granger is from her article "The 1st AD in Operation Iraqi Freedom," posted in the U.S. Army's online "Professional Writing Collection."

357 **"hunting down the triggerman":** This observation by Powledge appeared in his article "Beating the IED Threat," *Marine Corps Gazette* (May 2005).

357 **"We had a different understanding":** Dempsey was quoted in Richard Lowry, "What Went Right," *National Review* (May 9, 2005).

357 "During my initial screening": The complaints by DIA officials and DIA Director Jacoby's comments on them are in a series of documents beginning with Jacoby's "Alleged Detainee Abuse by TF 62-6" (June 25, 2004) that are posted on the ACLU's Web site.

361 "Boss, we're losing": This quote by an Army major appeared in "Army General Sees Brighter Days Ahead for Iraqi People," by Scott Huddleston, *San Antonio Express-News* (December 1, 2005).

CHAPTER 16: THE PRICE PAID

The CPA polling data is from the second survey cited in the previous chapter.

368 "We have become locked on kill or capture": The Special Forces officer was quoted in a paper on Special Forces by Armando Ramirez, "From Bosnia to Baghdad: The Evolution of US Army Special Forces from 1995–2004" (Naval Postgraduate School, September 2004).

368 "This move surrendered influence": This is from Kalev Sepp's congressional testimony, cited in the previous chapter.

369 "We are the hated occupier": Scholl's unpublished essay is "Path Forward in Iraq for the United States of America" (October 10, 2004).

370 "The Special Forces were the only soldiers": Robert Wright is quoted in John Nagl, *Eating Soup with a Knife: Counterinsurgency Lessons from Malaya and Vietnam* (revised edition, University of Chicago, 2005).

371 In 2003–4 alone some $750 million: The Government Accountability Office study is "Rebuilding Iraq: Actions Needed to Improve Use of Private Security Providers" (GAO, July 2005).

371 "more than any single U.S. Army division": Singer's article, "Outsourcing War," was in the March–April 2005 issue of *Foreign Affairs.* The discussion of contractors in this chapter additionally was influenced by Deborah Avant, "The Role of Contractors in the US Force" (paper prepared for the Center for Strategic and International Studies, undated) and Army Reserve Capt. Brian Hayes, "Breach of Contract," *Proceedings* (October 2004), as well as Herfried Muenkler, *The New Wars* (Polity Press, 2004.). Some of the information on Vinnell's contract and performance is in David Isenberg, "A Fistful of Contractors: The Case for a Pragmatic Assessment of Private Military Companies in Iraq" (British American Security Information Council, September 2004).

CHAPTER 17: THE CORRECTIONS

377 "A year has passed": Riggs's article, "Where Are the Weapons of Mass Destruction?" appeared in the March 2004 issue of *Proceedings.* Hersh's article, "Torture at Abu Ghraib," was in the May 10, 2004, issue of the *New Yorker,* but was posted on the magazine's Web site on April 30.

378 "Between October and December 2003": The Taguba report was cited in Chapter 12.

379 "To stop abuses": Laird's criticism of Rumsfeld was in his article "Iraq: Learning the Lessons of Vietnam?" in *Foreign Affairs* (November–December 2005).

380 "This administration needs": Friedman's call for an overhaul of Iraq policy ran in the *New York Times* on May 6, 2004. Related to this, an explanation of his prewar views appeared in an online discussion, "On Iraq: What Was I Thinking? Here's What" (October 14, 2005), in which he stated somewhat obscurely that his prewar position hadn't been so much in favor of the war as it was not being against it. "It was my view that the Bush team was going to invade Iraq no matter who was against it," he wrote.

380 "Bush has such an incredibly strong case": Brooks made this comment on the *NewsHour with Jim Lehrer* on August 2, 2002.

380 "This has been a crushingly": Brooks's column appeared in the *Times* on May 11, 2004, and Ajami's ("A year or so ago") in the same newspaper on May 26.

381 "All but the most blindly": Kagan's column in the *Washington Post* ran on May 2, 2004.

381 "We believe that there has been": The *Post* editorial that discerned both progress and mistakes in Iraq appeared on October 12, 2003.

381 "The *Post*'s continued editorializing": Di Rita's letter ran in the *Post* on May 15, 2004.

382 "I intend to write about this decision": Kurtz's articles on Miller's work in Iraq and her disputes with other *Times* reporters ran on May 26 and June 25, 2003.

382 "She didn't bring MET Alpha anywhere": Rosenthal was quoted in the latter Kurtz story.

383 "In my reporting experience": The article by Quinn quoting Miller on her Chalabi coverage appeared in the *Washington Post* (November 24, 2003).

383 "we found an enormous amount": The *New York Times*'s review of its Iraq coverage ran on May 26, 2004.

384 "dysfunctional system": Okrent's account appeared on May 30, 2004.

384 "Compared to other major papers": Massing's reviews of the coverage of Iraq by the *New York Times* and other news outlets appeared as "Unfit to Print?" in the *New York Review of Books* (June 24, 2004), and "Iraq, the Press and the Election," *Mother Jones* (November 22, 2004).

384 "really very bad journalism": Okrent's comment was made on PBS's *NewsHour* (June 8, 2005).

384 "wrote the best assessment": Accounts of Miller's appearance at the University of California at Berkeley appeared in an article by Justin Berton the in *East Bay Express,* March 23, 2005, and in an online news release by the university posted on March 18, 2005. Michael Rubin's interview with Chalabi was carried in the summer 2004 issue of *Middle East Quarterly.*

389 Then the president chuckled: This is according to the Federal News Service's transcript of President Bush's remarks in the White House's Rose Garden (June 1, 2004).

CHAPTER 18: TURNOVER

391 "Put bluntly, CPA never got": The comments by Costello and Wheelock are from their USIP interviews.

392 **"the two broadest strategic problems":** Abizaid's remark about his strategic problems being Pakistan and Saudi Arabia was made at a meeting with the Defense Writers Group (January 29, 2004).

394 **"primacy of military direction":** An edited version of Sepp's study, "Successful and Unsuccessful Counterinsurgency Practices," appeared as "Best Practices in Counterinsurgency" in the May–June 2005 issue of *Military Review.* The polling data here is from "Survey of Iraqi Public Opinion," International Republican Institute (September 24–October 4, 2004).

396 **"Captain Fowler came sprinting over":** Prakash's accounts of fighting in Baqubah and Fallujah were posted on his Armor Geddon blog. Mumford's accounts appeared as Baghdad Journal on www.artnet.com. The message about not becoming "the next Fallujah" is in a briefing by Maj. Rob Watwood, 4th Psychological Operations Group, "US Centcom JPTOF Operational Overview, 19 April 05/IEDs: Reducing the Threat in Iraq," and also is discussed in another briefing, "MNF-I Commander Guidance," January 11, 2005.

399 **"The fighting was intense":** The article by Sattler and Wilson is "Operation Al Fajr: The Battle of Fallujah, Part II," *Marine Corps Gazette* (July 2005).

400 **"advanced south, with three companies":** West's article, "The Fall of Fallujah," ran in the same issue.

402 **"When the Iraqi man in the mosque":** Sites's "Open Letter to Devil Dogs of the 3.1" (November 21, 2004) appeared on his Web site, www.kevinsites.net.

403 **"Each room can be fragged":** Two different versions of lessons learned by the scout/snipers platoon of the 3rd Battalion of the 5th Marines are quoted here—one is a document that circulated by e-mail, and the second is a slightly different version by Sgts. Earl Catagnus, Jr., and Brad Edison and Lance Cpls. James Keeling and David Moon, that appeared as "Infantry Squad Tactics," *Marine Corps Gazette* (September 2005).

404 **"concussions, collapsed lungs":** The article by Malina Brown in *Inside the Navy* appeared in its edition of August 26, 2002.

405 **"The Battle of Fallujah was not":** Jonathan Keiler's article "Who Won the Battle of Fallujah?" appeared in the January 2005 issue of *Proceedings.*

406 **"Iraqi army units are not ready":** The study by the Marine Corps advisers is Majs. Andrew Milburn and Mark Lombard, "After Action Report: The Iraqi Security Forces (ISF) in Operation Al Fajr" (November 28, 2004). My discussion of Second Fallujah was influenced also by "TF 2-2 in FSE AAR," an article by Capt. James Cobb, Lt. Christopher LaCour, and Sgt. 1st Class William Hight in *Field Artillery* (March–April 2005). Powell's interview with the London *Daily Telegraph* appeared on February 26, 2005.

CHAPTER 19: TOO LITTLE, TOO LATE?

425 **"No te me duermas":** Cavallaro's account of having a soldier die in her arms appeared in *Army Times* (April 4, 2005).

426 **"I would speculate":** Bachar's comment is from his interview with the U.S. Institute of Peace.

AFTERWORD: BETTING AGAINST HISTORY

This discussion was influenced by an essay by Michael Eisenstadt and Jeffrey White, "Assessing Iraq's Sunni Arab Insurgency: Problems and Approaches," that was circulated by e-mail in draft form (November 2005).

431 **"What happens in Iraq":** This is from "National Strategy for Victory in Iraq," which was posted on the White House Web site in November 2005 and attributed to the National Security Council.

434 **"determined to preserve the Filipino":** Brian Linn's history is *The Philippine War, 1899–1902* (Kansas, 2000).

436 **"This is one of the stages":** Allawi was quoted in Toby Harnden, "We Have Civil War, Says Ex-PM," London *Sunday Telegraph* (October 16, 2005).

437 **"The traditional power equation":** Saikal's article, "Iraq's Conflict Is Fueling a Bitter Mideast Split," ran in the *International Herald Tribune* (October 9, 2005). The episode of al Qaeda firing rockets in Jordan was first reported in an article by Jay Solomon, Yasmine El-Rashidi, and Glenn R. Simpson, "Radicals in Iraq Begin Exporting Violence, Mideast Neighbors Say," in the *Wall Street Journal* (October 7, 2005).

438 **"A caliphate would not":** The National Intelligence Council report, "Mapping the Global Future," was published in December 2004.

438 **"He was a man of great ambitions":** Oldenbourg's assessment of Saladin is in *The Crusades* (Random House, 1966).

ACKNOWLEDGMENTS

Thanks, first and last, to my wife, Mary Catherine. It has been a long journey, and I am thankful to her for sticking with it and me. I also am indebted to my children, Chris and Molly.

Nor would this book have been possible without its editor, Scott Moyers. In some ways this book was a collaborative effort, discussed over several years with him, most memorably by satellite linkup from a windowless, broken hut in the flat desert northwest of Najaf, Iraq.

Likewise, it has been a pleasure to work with my agent, Alice Martell, on our second book together. I look forward to the next.

I also am grateful to the Center for Strategic and International Studies for giving me a home in which to write. Not only did Kurt Campbell, the head of the center's international security program, invite me to join the institution, he also years earlier suggested that the scope of my next book be broad—a helpful thought I have tried to follow here. I also owe thanks to John Hamre, the president and CEO of CSIS, whose insight and decency are known across Washington. Julianne Smith of CSIS also helped make my time there productive.

Equally important to the making of this book have been my colleagues at the *Washington Post*. I have relied heavily on their work and their thoughts, especially in covering the increasingly dangerous situation in 2003–6. Rajiv Chandrasekaran and Anthony Shadid for years were the twin pillars of the *Post*'s Baghdad bureau, the Maris and Mantle of the first year of covering the occupation. Karl Vick is my idea of a model foreign correspondent, someone I was thankful to learn from in Iraq. Steve Fainaru repeatedly wrote memorable and moving accounts of the life of the U.S. soldier in this war that would have made Ernie Pyle proud. I also am grateful to the intrepid Josh White for obtaining and sharing documents growing out of the investigation of the abuse of prisoners at the Abu Ghraib prison and other facilities. Other *Post* reporters who have shared their thoughts or filed memorable stories that I have relied on here include Vernon Loeb, Brad Graham, Ann Tyson, Ed Cody, Theola Labbe, Jackie Spinner, Scott Wilson, Pam Constable, Kevin Sullivan, Doug Struck, Peter Slevin, Ariana Cha, Dana Priest, Bart Gellman, Walter Pincus, Jon Finer, Nelson Hernandez, and Ellen Knickmeyer. The Iraqi journalists in the *Post*'s Baghdad bureau—Naseer Nouri, Omar Fekeiki, Bassam Sebti, and K. I. Ibrahim—also made an essential and especially courageous contribution in recent years. To my mind they are heroes, as is the *Post*'s security chief in Baghdad.

I also am grateful to my current and former editors at the *Post*, including Scott Vance, Matt Vita, Andy Mosher, Alan Cooperman, Mike Abramowitz, Liz Spayd, Bob Woodward, David Hoffman, Steve Coll, Phil Bennett, and Len Downie. The *Post* is a wonderful place to work; thanks to all of them and to the publisher, Boisfeuillet Jones, Jr., and the chairman, Donald Graham. The Graham family's stewardship of the *Post* is, in my opinion, an important act of patriotism in a troubled time for our country.

Thanks also to Shadid and Nora Boustany for instruction in some of the finer points of Arabic slang.

I also must recognize other colleagues in journalism, having relied on both their published work and their private insights. In addition to the very good reporting that has appeared in major newspapers—the *New York Times*, the *Los Angeles Times*, *USA Today*, the *Philadelphia Inquirer*, and other Knight-Ridder newspapers—I also am indebted to the solid work that has consistently appeared in two journals written for military audiences, the *Army Times* and *Stars & Stripes*.

I also was influenced in my writing by the background on Paul Wolfowitz provided in James Mann's impressive work of intellectual history, *Rise of the Vulcans*.

In addition, I have turned back at several points to reread passages from Alistair Horne's compelling history of the Algerian war, *A Savage War of Peace*. Readers also will note that I was particularly influenced by the insights offered by David Galula, a French veteran of Algeria, in his classic little book, *Counterinsurgency Warfare: Theory and Practice*.

Not one page of this book could have been written without the help of researchers. Adam Comis did a marvelous job at the Center for Strategic and International Studies, double-checking obscure facts, reading vast amounts of material, obtaining forgotten documents and obscure books, and poring through them for more facts. He deserves special credit for his work in two areas: assembling the portfolio of photographs and other artwork, and reviewing hundreds of pages of transcripts of congressional hearings on the Bush administration's handling of Iraq.

Also, thanks to Army Capt. Lesley Kipling not only for her enthusiastic and dogged research aid as this book project got off the ground, which reflected upon the best traditions of the U.S. Army, but also for her candor in sharing her letters home to her boyfriend. I am sorry it didn't work out between them.

I also am grateful to a group of academics, think tankers, and other defense experts who have helped educate me on military affairs. They are a diverse group of strategic thinkers whose common traits are intellectual curiosity, good humor, and uncommon tolerance of differing views: Eliot Cohen, Andrew Bacevich, Tom Donnelly, Peter Feaver, Tom Keaney, Bob Killebrew, Richard Kohn, and Michael Vickers. I think of them as the intellectual godfathers of this book. I also am thankful to Donnelly for coining the evocative phrase "the Army of the Euphrates."

In addition, I owe an intellectual debt to the continuing education given me on a daily basis by John Collins and his Warlord Loop, a floating electronic seminar on military history, strategy, and practice, with a faculty that most notably includes Terry Daly (who introduced me to the works of Galula, the Clausewitz of counterinsurgency), John Crerar, Caleb Carr, and more than one hundred others, some of whom must remain unnamed here.

Thanks also to John Pike and his encyclopedic Web site, www.globalsecurity.org, which saved me countless hours of research, especially on weapons systems and specific U.S. military operations in Iraq.

I also owe thanks to the military officers who gave their time to be interviewed, and frequently followed up with documents ranging from diaries to official records of their command time. Some are named in the text, while others wish to remain anonymous. I am especially grateful to those senior officers who, despite the current atmosphere of intimidation in the Pentagon, trekked to my office or met me in other places to convey views and facts that didn't always conform to the official version of events.

Finally, I wish to thank the many friends and colleagues who gave the manuscript of this book a critical reading.

The errors are my own.

INDEX